B R Y G H T   L A N T E R N I S

**Essays on the Language and Literature
of Medieval and Renaissance Scotland**

AUP Titles of Related interest

THE NUTTIS SCHELL
essays on the Scots language
edited by Caroline Macafee and Iseabail Macleod

SCOTLAND AND THE LOWLAND TONGUE
editor J Derrick McClure

LITERATURE OF THE NORTH
edited by David Hewitt and Michael Spiller

NORTHERN VISION
edited by David Hewitt and Michael Spiller

ANE RESONYNG
of ane Scottis and Inglis Merchand betuix
Rowand and Lionis
William Lamb
edited and introduced by Roderick Lyall

A HISTORY OF THE SCOTS BIBLE
with Selected Texts
Graham Tulloch

THE PSALMS IN SCOTS
reprint of The Psalms Frae Hebrew intil Scottis
by P Hately Waddell, first published 1871
Introduction by Graham Tulloch

SCOTTISH HANDWRITING 1150-1650
an introduction to the reading of documents
G G Simpson

Dictionaries from AUP

THE CONCISE SCOTS DICTIONARY
editor-in-chief Mairi Robinson

THE POCKET SCOTS DICTIONARY
editors Iseabail Macleod, Ruth Martin and Pauline Cairns

THE COMPACT SCOTTISH NATIONAL DICTIONARY
From the seventeenth century to the present day
editors William Grant and David D Murison

A DICTIONARY OF THE OLDER SCOTTISH TONGUE
From the twelfth century to the end of the seventeenth
editors Sir William Craigie, A J Aitken, James A C
Stevenson, H D Watson

GAELIC DICTIONARY
Malcolm MacLennan

B R Y G H T   L A N T E R N I S

Essays on the Language and Literature
of Medieval and Renaissance Scotland

edited by
J Derrick McClure and Michael R G Spiller

ABERDEEN UNIVERSITY PRESS
Member of the Maxwell Macmillan Pergamon Publishing Corporation

First published 1989
Aberdeen University Press

British Library Cataloguing in Publication Data

Bryght lanternis: language and literature of
medieval and Renaissance Scotland
1. English language. Scottish dialect, History
I. McClure, J Derrick   II. Spiller, Michael R G
427'.9411'09

ISBN 0 08 036593 0

Printed in Great Britain
The University Press
Aberdeen

At my begynnyng first I clepe and call
To ȝow Cleo, and to ȝow Polyme,
With Thesiphone, goddis and sistris all,
In nowmer nyne as bokis specifye;
In this processe my wilsum wittis gye   ,
And with ȝour bryght lanternis wele connuoye
My pen to write my turment and my joye.

James I, <u>The Kingis Quair</u>, Stanza 19

CONTENTS

Preface   ix
List of Participants   xi
List of other papers presented but not included   xii

 1   Folk Tradition and Literature till 1603 David Buchan   1
 2   The Scottish Makars and the Ballad Tradition
     Matthew P McDiarmid   14
 3   Views of King and People in Sixteenth- and Seventeenth-
     Century Ballads A Gardner-Medwin   24
 4   The Lost Literature of Medieval Scotland R J Lyall   33
 5   Scotland's Greatest Composer: An Introduction to
     Robert Carver (1487-1566) Richard Turbet   48
 6   Stories and Storytelling in Barbour's Brus
     W F H Nicolaisen   56
 7   Aspects of the Snake in the Legends of the Saints
     Regina Scheibe   68
 8   Golagros and Gawane: a Word for Peace Elizabeth Walsh   90
 9   On Some Literary Traditions of 'Colkelbie's Sow'
     Klaus Bitterling   104
10   Beginning and Ending The Kingis Quair Alan MacColl   118
11   The Austrian Connection c.1450-1483: Eleonora and the
     Intertextuality of Pontus und Sidonia A M Stewart   129
12   Robert Henryson and the Ars Dictaminis
     Robert L Kindrick   150
13   Elrich Fantasyis in Dunbar and Other Poets
     Priscilla Bawcutt   162
14   William Dunbar: Grand Rhetoriqueur Joanne S Norman   179
15   William Dunbar: The Elusive Subject Antony J Hasler   194
16   Dunbar and the Nature of Bawdy Edwina Burness   209
17   William Dunbar and the Morris Dancers Annette Jung   221
18   Gavin Douglas on Love: the Prologue to Eneados IV
     Elizabeth Archibald   244
19   'Thus Euery Man Said For Hym Self': the Voices of
     Sir David Lyndsay's Poems Janet H Williams   258
20   The Scottish Kirk in Medieval and Renaissance
     Literature J Schwend   273
21   Dismantling a Straw Man: the Religious Personality of
     John Knox David W Atkinson   285
22   The Rhetorical Application of Syntax in Knox's Familiar
     Epistles to Mrs Bowes Kenneth D Farrow   298
23   A Mirror for a Divine Prince: John Ireland and the
     Four Daughters of God Sally Mapstone   308

24   John Ireland's Literary Sensibility: The Meroure of
     Wyssdome, Book 7   J C McDonald   324
25   Rutherford as Enthusiast   David Reid   337
26   Montgomerie's Language   David J Parkinson   352
27   Dungeons and Larders: the Romances of Patrick Gordon
     Michael R G Spiller   364
28   The Crathes Ceiling Inscriptions   Henry Hargreaves   373
29   The Scots-Gaelic Scribes of Late Medieval Perthshire:
     An Overview of the Orthography and Contents of the Book
     of the Dean of Lismore   Donald E Meek   387
30   From Saga to Folktale: 'The Deirdre Story' in Gaelic
     Tradition   Caoimhín Mac Giolla Léith   405
31   The Other Scottish Language - Orkneyinga Saga
     O D Macrae-Gibson   420
32   Middle Scots Dialects - Extrapolating Backwards
     C I Macafee   429
33   The Sources of the ⟨I⟩ Digraphs: the Place-Name
     Evidence   Veronika Kniezsa   442
34   The Helsinki Corpus of Older Scots   Anneli Meurman-Solin   451
35   'The Weasel Scot': Some Characteristics of Shakespearian
     Depiction in Henry V and 1 Henry IV   A C Calder   459
36   The Scotching of Shakespeare   David Angus   473

PREFACE

The papers collected for the present volume were originally presented at the Fifth International Conference on Scottish Language
and Literature, Mediaeval and Renaissance, held at Aberdeen
University from 6-13 August 1987.

It is one of the regrets of native Scottish literary scholars
that the Medieval and Renaissance period, arguably the greatest in
the history of our national literature, often seems to be studied
with more enthusiasm furth of Scotland than in its own homeland.
But it is always a pleasure to think how many colleagues and
friends we have abroad, and it was a source of delight that so many
of them came to Aberdeen for the latest in what is now an established series of triennial conferences.

The enormous range and variety in the field of Medieval and
Renaissance Scottish literature is amply demonstrated by the papers
published here. The mainstream literature in the Scots tongue is
well represented, almost every major writer from Barbour to Montgomerie being the subject of at least one article. The Gaelic
contribution to Scottish letters received some attention; though
the most memorable and delightful Gaelic episode in the Conference,
a lecture with numerous musical illustrations on the history of
Gaelic song, presented by Anne Lorne Gillies at the Conference
banquet, could not be included in the present volume. Folk literature, like Gaelic, was the subject of a plenary paper; and the
seldom-appreciated fact that Scottish literature includes works in
other languages than Gaelic, Scots and English was demonstrated by
a paper on the Orkneyinga Saga. Other arts besides literature
featured in the programme: the great tradition of Scottish medieval
music inspired not only a lecture on the composer Robert Carver but
an excellent concert presented by an Aberdeen medieval music group
known as the Goliards; and the visual arts were treated in a paper
by Helena Shire, unfortunately not included here, and in a detailed
account of one of Aberdeenshire's many historical treasures, the
painted ceilings of Crathes Castle. An unexpected irruption into
the gathering of Scottish scholars was made by Shakespeare, whose
Scottish connection was argued in two papers. All this bears
witness not only to the enduring fascination of Scottish Medieval
and Renaissance studies but to the devotion and thoroughness with
which our culture is taught, from Venice to Helsinki and from
Ottawa to Canberra.

To place this work on record by publishing the fifth volume of
Proceedings of these conferences will, we hope, give a well-
deserved sense of achievement to all our contributors, and also

allow those colleagues and friends who were unable to come the opportunity to study the most recent work in the Medieval Scottish field.

Socially as well as academically, this conference maintained the high standards set by its predecessors. Besides the banquet and concert already mentioned, the social programme included an excursion to Crathes and Kildrummy Castles, and a reception in the unique surroundings of Provost Skene's House, at which one of the conference's most distinguished participants, Professor A J Aitken, was presented with his Festschrift. The organised social events, however, were of no greater importance than the general atmosphere of camaraderie always engendered by these conferences, which becomes ever stronger as the series progresses and each new conference becomes an occasion for renewing old contacts and friendships as well as forming new ones.

The successive conferences in the series have been alternately in and outwith Scotland: Edinburgh 1975, Strasbourg 1978, Stirling 1981, Germersheim 1984, Aberdeen 1987. This tradition, as it now is, will be maintained when the Sixth International Conference on Scottish Language and Literature, Medieval and Renaissance, convenes in South Carolina in 1990. Awaiting this event, the editors of the present volume offer their thanks to all who contributed, whether in performance, publication or participation, to the success of the meeting in Aberdeen, and record their particular gratitude to Marjorie Leith of Aberdeen University Press and to Anne McIntosh for their help at every stage in the editing and preparation of this collection.

J Derrick McClure
Michael R G Spiller

LIST OF PARTICIPANTS

Aitken, Professor Adam J (Edinburgh)
Aitken, Mrs A J
Alexander, Mrs Flora (Aberdeen)
Angus, David (Stirling)
Archibald, Dr Elizabeth (Cambridge)
Ashmeade, Professor John (Pennsylvania)
Assbeck, Dr Johann (Regensburg)
Atkinson, Professor David (Lethbridge)
Atkinson, Mrs D
Bailey, Professor Richard (Michigan)
Bawcutt, Dr Nigel (Liverpool)
Bawcutt, Mrs Priscilla (Liverpool)
Bitterling, Dr Klaus (Berlin)
Brownlee, Colin (Stirling)
Bruford, Alan (Edinburgh)
Buchan, Professor David (Newfoundland)
Burness, Dr Edwina (London)
Caird, James B (Inverness)
Caird, Mrs J B
Calder, Charles (Aberdeen)
Courter, Jean M (Buffalo)
Coventry, Charles S (Edinburgh)
Cartwright, Dr John (Cape Town)
Crawford, Thomas (Aberdeen)
Farrow, Kenneth D (Glasgow)
Gardner-Medwin, Dr Alisoun (Newcastle)
Garden, Ronald J B (Aberdeen)
Garden, Mrs D B (Aberdeen)
Gillies, Miss Anne L (Glasgow)
Gillies, Professor W (Edinburgh)
Goldstein, Dr James (Aichi, Japan)
Hargreaves, Henry (Aberdeen)
Hasler, Antony (Cambridge)
Houwen, Luuk (Sheffield)
Jung, Annette (Copenhagen)
Kindrick, Professor Richard L (Illinois E)
Kinghorn, Professor Alexander M (Kent)
Kirkpatrick, Professor Hugh (Texas)
Kirkpatrick, Mrs H
Kirk, John M (Belfast)
Kniesza, Dr Veronica (Budapest)
Leith, Mrs Margaret J (Aberdeen)

xi

Lorenzoni, Professor Maria (Venice)
Lyall, Dr Roderick J (Glasgow)
Macafee, Caroline (Glasgow)
MacColl, Alan (Aberdeen)
MacDiarmid, Matthew P (Aberdeen)
McClure, J Derrick (Aberdeen)
MacDonald, Professor Alasdair A (Groningen)
McDonald, Dr Craig (Tennessee)
MacGiolla Leith, Caoimhin (Edinburgh)
MacKay, Dr Margaret M (Edinburgh)
Macleod, Iseabail (Edinburgh)
Macrae-Gibson, Dr O Duncan (Aberdeen)
Mapstone, Dr Sally (Oxford)
Meek, Dr Donald (Edinburgh)
Meurman-Solin, Anneli (Helsinki)
Milton, Dr Colin (Aberdeen)
Nicolaisen, Professor Wilhelm F H (New York)
Norman, Dr Joanne (Ottawa)
O'Sullivan, Mrs Helen (Sevenoaks)
Paetzold, Dr Kurt-Michael (Bielefeld)
Parkinson, Dr David J (Saskatchewan)
Pollner, Dr Claus (Vienna)
Purser, John W (Glasgow)
Reid, Dr David (Stirling)
Ross Roy, Professor G (S Carolina)
Scheibe, Regina (Berlin)
Schwend, Dr Joachim (Mainz)
Shire, Mrs Helena (Cambridge)
Spiller, Michael R G (Aberdeen)
Spiller, Liesa M (Edinburgh)
Spiller, Juliet A (Aberdeen)
Stewart, Dr Alasdair (Aberdeen)
Strauss, Dr Dietrich (Mainz)
Swales, G A (Ontario)
Swales, Mrs G A
Swann, Isla (Aberdeen)
Turbet, Richard (Aberdeen)
Upton, Dr Christopher (Birmingham)
van Buuren-Veenenbos, Dr Catherine (Leiden)
Walsh, Professor Betsy (San Diego)
Wilkie, Professor John R (Aberdeen)
Williams, Ian (Canberra)
Williams, Dr Janet (Canberra)
Wiseley, Miss J T (Aberdeen)
Wood, Dr Juliette (Bangor)
Zenzinger, Dr Peter (Berlin)

The following papers presented at the Conference were not
submitted for the Proceedings volume

The Language of Highland Dress:
Alan Bruford, University of Edinburgh

Sir Gilbert Hay as Translator:
John Cartwright, University of Cape Town

Elizabeth St Clair - her Songs and Ballads:
Thomas Crawford, University of Aberdeen

Gaelic Song before the Enlightenment:
Anne Lorne Gillies, Glasgow

Blind Hary's Myth of Blood: the Ideological Closure of The Wallace:
James Goldstein, Aichi University, Japan

The Sex Werkdayis and Agis: Text and Context:
Luuk Houwen, University of Sheffield

The Sense of Place in Middle Scots Verse:
Alastair MacDonald, Rijksuniversiteit, Groningen

Scottish Language and Literature and the Teaching of
Scottish Ethnology:
Margaret MacKay, University of Edinburgh

Back to Dunbar: Medieval Poets and Modern Makars:
Colin Milton, University of Aberdeen

Images of Monarchy: Three Royal Stewarts:
Helena Shire, University of Cambridge

A Structural Comparison of Henryson's Orpheus and the Testament:
Dietrich Strauss, Johannes Gutenberg Universitat, Mainz

Patronage and the Renaissance Poet: the Role of Local Government:
Chris Upton, University of Birmingham

Official and Folk Models of Scottish Witchcraft:
Juliette Wood, Welsh Folk Museum, Cardiff

Chapter 1

FOLK TRADITION AND LITERATURE TILL 1603

David Buchan

The title of the lecture suggests a comprehensiveness that will be belied by its content. Properly, the title should be preceded by a nineteenth-century saving phrase like 'Prolegomena to a Study of' or 'Some Animadversions upon', for the subject is both too complicated and too lacking in groundwork research to warrant any commentary claiming comprehensiveness. What follows will, rather, attempt to establish some perspectives on the subject, a subject which has been habitually misregarded, largely because basic assumptions about its simpleness have masked its inherent complexities. In specific, the lecture has three parts: the first two deal with the literature in folk tradition, namely folk literature, and the third deals with folk tradition in 'literature', or, to be precise, in high literature.

The need for that terminological clarification underscores the somewhat unfortunate arrogation of the unqualified term 'literature' for one kind of literature. From the viewpoint of cultural history, which constitutes our governing context, there exist three kinds of literature, the literatures of high culture, of popular culture, and of folk culture, interacting but broadly distinguishable by their different means of transmission, and sometimes composition, and consequently by different though overlapping audiences. The literature of popular culture will not figure in this paper but the other two obviously do, differentiated by terms corresponding to the German-language model of <u>Volksliteratur</u> and <u>Hochliteratur,</u> concepts discussed most illuminatingly by Professor Max Lüthi of the University of Zürich in his book entitled <u>Volksliteratur und Hochliteratur.</u>[1]

How, then, do we define folk literature? First, let us consider how it has been viewed. Although most of the surveys of Scottish literature have a chapter on the ballads, only one actually contains a chapter entitled 'Folk Literature' (Mackenzie, 1933).[2] In that chapter she discusses ballads, songs, and <u>The Gude and Godlie Ballatis</u> because some of these are remodellings of secular song, but beyond that she finds herself in a quandary, because her criteria for what constitutes folk literature are somewhat vague. The nearest to an explicit statement is the comment that poems like '"The Freiris of Berwyk" may be folk literature, and they may not, at all events in the sense of literature made by "the people"'.[3] And who are the people? In practice, the people would seem to be those without names: if a piece is by Anon it is likely to be folk. This leads to the ludicrous problem presented by dubious attributions

whereby she does not know if <u>Peblis to the Play</u> is folk or — not
'made by "the people"' but — by a king. Of the poem itself she says
it 'looks ... "folk"', presumably on the premise that it deals with
romping peasants.[4] In short, her conception of what constitutes
folk literature is hazy and impressionistic; and this conception,
fifty years on, is still not entirely unknown. If folk literature
is not to be defined as couthy treatments of romping peasants by
Anon, what is it?

Folk culture is that area or, in Professor Nicolaisen's happy
term, register of culture maintained and transmitted primarily by
word of mouth and customary practice. It follows, then, that folk
literature, the literature of folk culture, is the literature
maintained and transmitted primarily by word of mouth, that is, by
verbal means rather than by manuscript or print. That of course is
not to say that it never reaches manuscript or print; naturally it
does, and fortunately, for otherwise we would have no record of the
material; the central point, however, is that the material is
primarily transmitted by word of mouth. For the material to achieve
one pinned-down permanency in print does not diminish its status as
folk literature; it is not suddenly transformed into high literature, for the material still continues being transmitted by the
traditional verbal processes. A result of these processes is that
the written-down records of this verbally-transmitted literature
are likely to be in our period both scanty and accidental.

To differentiate folk literature by the means of transmission
leads also to differentiation by social context, by audience, and
to differentiation by the nature of the material, by its generic
and textural features. The social context will alter with the
centuries, the central, though not the only factor, being for long
whether or not the verbal means of transmission is rendered imperative for a given group by that group's nonliteracy. Mass literacy
came to Scotland along with the Industrial, Agrarian, and other
Revolutions approximately in the period 1770 to 1830, a time which
marks an important divide in the evolution of folk tradition
between pre-industrial tradition and post-industrial tradition. In
the latter, changes occurred in the methods of transmission, the
audience, and the nature of the material. In the former stage, one
must take account of such factors as the gradual extension of
literacy over the centuries, from a presumably very small base,
until the arrival of mass literacy in the later eighteenth century,
and the higher literacy rate throughout Western Europe for urban or
burghal centres than for rural areas. For the pre-1603 period, and
with those provisos in mind, the audience of folk literature was
predominantly nonliterate, or in the limited, ethnological sense,
'oral'. (The appearance of this term here in this acceptation will
explain why it was not used earlier instead of the more cumbersome
'by word of mouth'.) To describe the audience in this fashion and
leave it at that would be to create too stark a picture, however,
and one that requires some shadings. Nonliterate people could
conceivably participate in certain performance contexts of high
literature though practically the social likelihoods for many would
have been slim, and the solitary practice of visual reading would
have been impossible. Literate people could participate in the
performance contexts, and some probably in the processes of folk

literature. And material from folk literature was taken into and adapted to high literature just as material from high literature was taken into and adapted to folk literature. With these shadings, the picture now presents a continuum with the two poles of folk literature and high literature at either end and, midway between, an area of interaction. But that is the static model; a more dynamic model would be to conceive of a folk register and a high register of literary culture, where not all the participants in one could be participants in the other.

I said earlier that differentiation by means of transmission leads also to differentiation by audience and by the nature of the material: its cultural concerns and artistic features. The features were delineated in essentials eighty years ago by the Danish scholar, Professor Axel Olrik,[5] and the cultural concerns surveyed most succinctly by William Bascom of Berkeley.[6] It would seem a reasonable assertion that the distinctive concerns and character- istics of the literature are closely related to the means of transmission and the nature of the audience. It is a small, but crucial, step further to state that these distinctive concerns and characteristics derive from a means of transmission, one involving conscious creativity, rendered functionally necessary by the cultural exigencies of the nonliterate audience. Any attempt to deny that statement must address effectively three problems. How does one explain the pervasive evidence in folk literature of creative adaptation? How does one explain precisely the pronounced differences in concerns and characteristics between folk and high literatures? How does one explain why the distinctive concerns and characteristics of the folk literature of one culture area, such as Scotland, are those which inform the folk literatures of, mutatis mutandis, all Western Europe; or, to put it another way, why Scot- tish folk literature has more in common with other European folk literatures than with Scottish high literature?

If ethnocentricism is the sin of being bound by the precon- ceptions of one's own culture then literacentricism is the sin of being bound by the preconceptions of one's own literacy. The two major literacentric responses which have precluded a clear under- standing of the nature and processes of folk literature, responses which implicitly deny the earlier statement, are the theory of gesunkenes Kulturgut and the theory of memorial transmission. The first theory holds that nonliterate people had no creative litera- ture of their own but depended solely on crumbs from the high literature tables. The second holds essentially that transmission involves rote memorisation of a fixed text; that is, the process is conceived of in terms of the known practices of a literate society. Neither of these literacentric theories manages to address any of the three central questions just posed.

Folk literature, then – the literature maintained and transmit- ted primarily by word of mouth – is differentiable by its means of transmission, its audience, and its concerns and characteristics: factors all closely bound up with one another. Folk literature has its own medium, genres, performance contexts, and aesthetic canons; hence it has its own critical methodology: our next topic. This methodology, it is worth stressing, has evolved internationally and multilingually; it consists of cross-cultural methods for the study of literature that crosses cultures.

At the most basic level, this methodology involves the consideration of five essential factors: medium, genre, type, version, and context and function. The medium, as we have seen, is word of mouth transmission, which varies somewhat in kind within the pre-industrial and the post-industrial cultural contexts. Varying slightly also in those periods are the genres of folk literature, conventionally grouped in the four large divisions of folk poetry and song, folk narrative, folksay, and folk drama. The constituent genres of these divisions possess their own concerns and even, on occasion, their own inbuilt meanings. Perhaps I can exemplify in short compass by referring to the most artistically complex genres of folk narrative and folk poetry and song respectively: the Zaubermärchen or wonder tale and the classical ballad. The wonder tale is concerned essentially with the maturation of the individual while the classical ballad, in most of its subgenres, is concerned essentially with close human relationships in small-group interaction. The wonder tale genre, as Vladimir Propp[7] and his followers have shown, can be seen at a certain level of abstraction to have a metanarrative, one which informs all individual generic manifestations and which consequently supplies an element of inbuilt generic meaning to all types and all versions. Which takes us to type and version.

'Version' refers to any one specific recording of a piece of folk literature (for example, story, song, proverb, play); one refers, then, to the version of The Twa Sisters recorded in 1783 from Anna Brown. A 'type' constitutes, on the theoretical level, the aggregate of all the versions of a single story, song, play, etc, and, on the practical level of classification, the constants which inform the versions and identify their genetic relationship. The type The Twa Sisters, which manifests itself in its narrative constants in Anna Brown's version, comprehends not just the one version but all the versions ever recorded of that particular sung story (numbering over one hundred in the anglophone world alone). For the wonder tale, and indeed the other fictional genres of folk narrative, there exists an indispensable international catalogue of types, listing their narrative constants and references to the known versions (Antti Aarne and Stith Thompson The Types of the Folktale).[8] If, then, the student of folk literature wishes to make useful generalisations about, say, The Twa Sisters, he can not simply deal with one text, with one abstracted version, but must deal with the type, comprehending all the versions, their constants and their variabilities. I have heard that recently these critical concepts from folk literature, type and version, have been utilised in biblio-textual thinking on Shakespeare's plays, to stimulating effect. The fifth essential factor in the methodology is that of context and function. Here the analyst takes into account at least the social context, the cultural context, and the performance context of any given version, since performers of folk literature habitually vary their material to serve different functions in accordance with differing social, cultural, and performance contexts.

Beyond these are two more, governing, factors: the dimensions of time and space. Folk literature has existed over many centuries. So of course has high literature, but in the case of folk literature not only genres but also individual types have existed for as long as two and a half to three millenia. One of the earliest laments, that of David for Saul and Jonathan in II Samuel (I:19-27), has been dated to the eleventh century BC. The earliest Halslösungs-rätsel, neck riddle, that involving Samson (in Judges, XIV:8-18) has been dated to the same period. Narrative material found in The Odyssey, of c.700 BC, has been recorded in recent decades from the field. One of the results of this spread in time is that tradition - which is paradoxically always in a state of self-renewing evolution - contains within itself both old and new elements. To exemplify briefly from one genre: Linda Degh, the Hungarian folk-lorist now in America, has shown how the wonder tale genre involves three 'layers' of material - early pan-animism, medieval feudalism, and elements from the contemporary life of the tale-tellers.[9] This co-existence of ancient and contemporary elements, while textually fascinating, calls for considerable care in analysis. One cannot of course assume that all elements are old, as some earlier scholars of an antiquarian bent tended to do, any more than one can assume that all elements are contemporary. Here, as elsewhere, one must exercise scholarly and critical discrimination. The spread in time parallels the spread in space, for much of the material of folk literature exists in many cultures. This fact dominated the think-ing of early scholars who in a post-Darwinian climate concentrated on origin and diffusion studies. The corollary for critical method of the spatial spread is that one approaches the material mono-culturally only at one's peril. David Fowler, for example, in A Literary History of the Popular Ballad attempts to explain the origin of the ballad in specifically English, not even British, terms, ignoring the European existence of the genre. The same author states as a basic premise, 'I ... assume that a given ballad took the particular shape it has about the time it was written down', which neatly bypasses the problems of the temporal spread by assuming they don't exist.[10] Here in short is an example of a critic regressing to the norm: when faced with the problems specific to folk literature he evades them and treats the folk literature like - rather awkward - high literature anyway. (I use David Fowler's book as a convenient example, but in fairness and for balance, it should be said that this work at the detailed descriptive level contains much that is very useful). For a different kind of balance I should point out, along with the perils of ethnocentricism, that some genres and types do not occur inter-nationally but are limited to specific culture areas.

The material of folk literature possesses certain features which have pronounced implications for the critical methodology. Its internationality and timelessness mean that much cannot be pinned down to one culture or one period, like most high literature ('A Burns epistle composed in 1785'). Versions can, but to understand the version fully one has to know about the type and the genre, which may well take one outside both the culture and the period of a given version. In discussing type and version we came across folk literature's multiformity, whereby a typic essence achieves a multitude of textual realisations, and the analyst must operate at the same time with the constants of the type and the changeables of the versions. This duality is paralleled in other methodological proceedings when the analyst must work on both macro and micro levels simultaneously, as when dealing with motifeme and allomotif (at the level of narrative episode), with tale role and character (at the level of dramatic agent), and with formulaic system and formula (at the level of language). Finally, among the stressed features there is adaptation. Performers may adapt material from one medium to another, from one genre to another, and from one type to another; performers may adapt material to suit differing social, cultural, and performance contexts, and to accord with the performer's own values. Clearly, the performer stands at the centre of the adaptive activity. Early scholars tended to treat the material superorganically, as if it diffused by mystic laws without much in the way of human intervention; but the Swedish scholar, Carl von Sydow,[11] rectified perspective by placing the 'traditor' at the heart of the traditional processes, and now in modern studies a large emphasis is placed on the performer, performance, and the communicative activity. International textual evidence of adaptation shows that, especially for pre-industrial tradition, one cannot assume as a basic premise the existence of 'a fixed text' followed by largely ineffectual attempts at memorial reproduction. Rather, one has to bear in mind as a pervasive feature of folk literature the conscious and necessarily creative adaptation of the material on the part of many, though not all, traditors to serve particular functions in particular contexts.

It will have become clear that in dealing with folk literature one is dealing with a range of constants and inconstants, of stabilities and changeabilities. As with the material, so with the methodology: it involves a constellation of variables. Let me give a very brief exemplification. Anna Brown produced a splendid version of Gil Brenton (type no. 5 in Child[12]). That version was recorded in 1783, and the earliest Scottish versions probably date from about 1730. The type, however, goes back further, for it was recorded in Denmark in the sixteenth century (type no. 274 in Grundtvig's Danmarks Gamle Folkeviser[13]); the genre even further back, for it was in existence in Scotland at least by the fifteenth century and the medium may go back some millennia (with the type existing in some other generic form, like Child 45, King John and the Bishop, which was recorded in prose novella form in the ninth century[14]). That example may serve to show: first, how the researcher has to be aware concurrently of version, type, genre, and medium, in relation to time and space; second, how material that apparently does not belong to our period may in fact prove to have some connection with it; and third, how very difficult it is to compress the protean shape of folk literature into even the generous scope of the Middle Ages and the Renaissance.

That was a lengthy but necessary exordium; it provides the background and rationale for the premises underlying the next two sections, the first of which addresses the question of what folk literature Scotland possessed before 1603. For 'Scotland' read in fact 'half of Scotland', since the discussion treats only the culture area of Lowland Scotland and not Highland Scotland with its own distinct and rich Celtic culture. For the question there exist three varieties of evidence. First, there is evidence from pre-1603 sources. By the nature of things, this does not amount to much: folk literature was not normally written down. What, then, do we have? There is the manuscript which contains actual textual material, such as the rhymed proverbs found in the Bannatyne and Maitland MSS.[15] There is the scholarly compilation of scattered material, like B J Whiting's 'Proverbs and Proverbial Sayings from Scottish Writings before 1600'.[16] There is the valuable but tantalising listing of material that one comes across in The Complaynt of Scotland[17] and Colkelbie Sow.[18] There is the utilisation within high literature of folk literature genre and type, as in Henryson's Fables, and there is the appearance within high literature of analogues of folk literature types, as in the romances King Orphius and Sir Colling ye Knyt found and edited in the last fifteen years by Marion Stewart.[19] History provides another source. If Archibald Bell-the-Cat was so called because of the fable, then the type (Aarne-Thompson 110) and the genre must have existed in the fifteenth century. Stray bits of information contribute their fragments to the overall mosaic. Sir David Lindsay, we discover from The Dreme, used to tell the young James V the tale of The Red Etin (Aarne-Thompson 303), a wonder tale with an extensive European spread. Versions of The Red Etin were recorded here in Aberdeenshire by Peter Buchan in the early nineteenth century[20] and by Gavin Greig early this century;[21] the first was somewhat Englished and the second, like the other wonder tales recorded by Greig, has disappeared. From these versions and the density of its European recording one could, however, have hazarded the likelihood - no more - of the type's earlier existence in Scotland. Which leads to the second variety of evidence.

It consists of evidence from post-1603 sources within the same culture. As the case of The Red Etin demonstrates in minuscule, some at least of what was recorded in later centuries - once people began consciously to collect - may have existed in earlier centuries. With certain kinds of material the possibility becomes a near-certainty, as with the historical legends about James V recorded in the last two hundred years. With others, one returns to the realm of probabilities or possibilities. Here is John Leyden writing at the turn of the nineteenth century:

> It is a curious fact, that the subjects of some of the popular stories which I have heard repeated in Scotland, do not differ essentially from those of some of the ancient Norman fabliaux presented to the public in an elegant form by Le Grand. Thus when I first perused the fabliaux of the Poor Scholar, the Three Thieves, and the Sexton of Cluni, I was surprized to recognise the popular stories which I had often heard repeated in infancy, and which I had often repeated myself, when the song or the tale recited by turns, amused the tedious evenings of Winter.[22]

That account, which incidentally furnishes a small glimpse of an eighteenth century performance context, establishes the later existence in Scottish tradition of a particular kind of story which appeared in writing in the Middle Ages and which therefore probably existed in earlier Scottish tradition. To help establish perspective

on the possible relationships of relatively modern and early
material I shall move over the Border and utilise the work of A E
Green, who has constructed 'a prima facie case ... for classifying
as oral texts certain poems extant in medieval manuscripts'. Green
points out, inter alia, that three pieces from R H Robbins's
Secular Lyrics of the XIVth and XVth centuries have been recorded
from the field over a wide area in the nineteenth and twentieth
centuries (nos 45, 48, 49: I have a yong suster; It fell ageyns
the next night; The Fals fox came vnto our croft).[23] Here, then,
versions of the same type, current over five centuries, are
classified both as medieval lyric and as modern folksong. This
example may serve to underline the timelessness of the material
and to indicate the flexible usefulness of the type and version
distinction for categorising material related by type but separated by centuries and classed as both high and folk literature.
The third variety of evidence is that derived from the international body of knowledge about folk literature, especially that
pertaining to neighbouring culture areas and pre-1603 periods.
Clearly, considerable care is required in the using of this
comparative evidence.

Given these three varieties of evidence, how best can one
address the question of what folk literature Scotland possessed
before 1603? For precision of response one has to ask that
question not at the general level of folk literature but at the
four subordinate levels of medium, genre, type, and version.
Immediately one can state that the medium certainly existed, and
that, from pre-1603 sources at any rate, we have only little and
scattered evidence on the types and the versions. I could enumer-
ate the known types and versions of the four generic divisions but
I doubt if any great benefit would ensue. What I propose to do,
rather, is to present on the basis of the three varieties of
evidence a putative picture of the genres that comprised folk
literature in Scotland before 1603.

In folk narrative there would have been the wonder tale, the
novella, the religious tale, a number of kinds of jocular tale
(Schwanke, jests, tales of lying), the fable, and the formula
non-fiction, the genre of legend with its six subcategories. In
folk poetry and song there would have been the classical ballad
with its five subcategories, and folksong also in a number of
subcategories. In folksay, among the language genres, there would
have been the proverb proper, and the proverb-related genres
(proverbial phrases, proverbial comparisons, conventional phrases,
dites), and the rhyme, in possibly two or three dozen subcategories, and the riddle. In folk drama the picture is too blurred to
warrant any firm generalisation.[24] Time precludes any detailed
substantiation of the evidence piece by piece for all the genres,
but for an exemplification of the processes involved in the
consideration of one genre, the classical ballad, I would refer
those interested to a paper entitled 'British Balladry: Mediaeval
Chronology and Relations'.[25] It is, then, by a holistic picture of
the genres, rather than by an atomistic catalogue of a meagre
number of types and versions, that one obtains the most complete
sketch of the likely nature and range of folk literature in this
period.

In this final section the concern will be folk tradition in high literature. In one way or another, through material or, more vaguely, influence, it has quite a large presence. The nature of that presence I shall try to convey selectively, by indicating some relationships, offering some methodological models and one or two areas of exploration, and providing a brief case-study.

In order to indicate a cross-section of possible relationships I took The Oxford Book of Scottish Verse and looked at its earlier entries.[26] The first poem excerpted is the thirteenth-century Sir Tristrem, attributed, with a query, to Thomas of Erceldoune. The author here constitutes a prominent figure in Scots tradition: he has many legends told about him, he has many - perhaps most - local prophecies throughout Scotland, including the Northeast, attributed to him, and of course he is the hero of the classical ballad (Child 37) most recently recorded in a version from the traveller Duncan Williamson, in 1977.[27] Barbour's Brus - which also has a local link via its author - is itself founded on fourteenth century tradition, but there have been local legends about Bruce noted this century which might make for an interesting correlation.[28] Holland's Buke of the Howlat, in the light of Dr Flora Alexander's perceptive account of it in Literature of the North,[29] would seem to be worth investigating from the standpoint of orality and oral composition: this is not to suggest that the work itself was orally composed, but rather that it may embody in transformed fashion some oral practices and aesthetic as the early written literature of a culture often does, whether in medieval Europe or modern Africa. Of the anonymous fifteenth-century poems, Rauf Coilyear contains a frequent narrative pattern of traditional literature, the 'King in disguise' theme, and King Berdok contains among its motley elements motifs that may derive from, or may parody, traditional material. So: in just the first ten entries in The Oxford Book of Scottish Verse one encounters a work based largely on legendary tradition, one based on a traditional narrative pattern, one with traditional motifs, one which might repay analysis in the light of tradition's patterns of orality, and one whose author himself bulks large in subsequent tradition. These examples, then, suggest the extent of the presence and portray some of the basic relationships between folk tradition and high literature.

Just two months ago there was published a work which provides an excellent methodological model for the study of these relationships: the author is Carl Lindahl and the title is Earnest Games: Folkloric Patterns in the Canterbury Tales.[30] In this book Lindahl - trained conjointly in folkloristics and medieval literature - brings to bear on The Canterbury Tales the knowledge and techniques of modern folkloristic scholarship to produce a strikingly fresh understanding of the poem. Within Scottish criticism, Priscilla Bawcutt's article in the Proceedings of the last conference, 'Dunbar's Christmas Carol', utilises very sensibly material from later tradition to shed light on the meaning of the Dunbar poem.[31] It, like the former though on a considerably smaller scale, furnishes a useful model for critical method.

Recent scholarship also provides some potentially valuable areas of exploration for researchers in the medieval and Renaissance periods. I shall highlight just two. The first is language. The Danish scholar Flemming Andersen, and the American Barre Toelken, have demonstrated convincingly through work on the classical ballad how the language of traditional genres may carry a rich connotative meaning not immediately observable to the modern hearer or reader;[32] it could be that this work carries a useful relevance, at general or specific level, for studies of high literature as well. The other area is that of performers and performance. A few years ago Joyce Coleman gave a paper (as yet unpublished, as far as I know) to the American Folklore Society in which she assembled the various terms for medieval performers and performance and analysed their functions and processes.[33] Comparable research on the Scottish material would furnish valuable information on the social and cultural contexts of both high literature and folk literature, and would provide concrete knowledge about the practicalities of possible interrelations.

Now, the case-study, which turns out to be more of a case-synopsis. Scotland possesses one version of The Corpus Christi Carol, recorded in the early nineteenth century from James Hogg's mother. R L Greene in The Early English Carols gives five versions, the A version being from sixteenth-century England.[34] The type has attracted considerable speculative attention; Greene himself con-structs an ingenious theory based on the presence of the 'fawcon' in the A version burden and the presence of a falcon in the heraldic badge of Anne Boleyn. In the classical ballads, however, there is a small group of types which share basic structural similarities, including the distinctive presence of marvellous birds or beasts, and a common concern with faith, fidelity and faithlessness. In these the knight is a secular figure where in the carol the knight is Christ, but otherwise there exists between this group and the carol a strong correspondence, both structural and thematic, which provides a cogent illumination of the carol.[35] One conclusion to be drawn is that on occasion an awareness of the patterns within folk literature may serve the researcher better than ingenious speculation about heraldic badges.

Enough, I hope, has been said to indicate that folk literature does not consist of the simplicities of the simple minded, and to show that the critical methodology of folk literature, with its daunting constellation of variables, spurns the merely simplistic approach and demands quite complex respondings. Unfortunately folk literature is largely untaught within the anglophone academies on this side of the Atlantic. The reasons are various, but one can highlight the widespread tacit assumption that literature consists solely of the literature of high culture. Folk literature, there-fore, is taught only where there exists the discipline devoted to the study of traditional culture, when folk literature is taught along with the history, music, religion, law, arts, etc, of traditional cultures. This is a pity, because a basic knowledge of folk literature is, to put it no higher, very useful for all students of literature, and essential for students of particular periods and areas. Lack of knowledge can of course lead people into unfortunate blunders, like that perpetrated by a recent SLJ reviewer of a collection of essays on Scott, who quoted from Professor Nicolaisen's article on 'Scott and the Folk Tradition' –

'students of folk narrative well know [that] the journeys to and through an alien land are really outward projections of an inner process of development, the road is the highway to selfhood', - only to dismiss it scornfully with the magisterial comment, 'Nobody knows any such thing at all ...'[36] To which the rejoinder is that everyone knows, everyone, that is, who possesses the most rudimentary acquaintance with folk literature, a category that should include SLJ reviewers given to magisterial pronouncements.

After that magisterial pronouncement I shall end by turning to the Im Thurn Lecture for 1983 given by Derek Brewer. In the lecture, entitled 'The Concept of Literary Culture', he advocates that

> If we are concerned with serious, intellectually responsible study, we might well set up an anthropological model for the understanding of literature. ... We would then investigate major works of literature within their contexts to see how they work and in order to find the implications of their presence. ... Besides the premises of sentiment, of manners and attitudes which need to be explored, we must also follow out the actual structures of the work, which operate both on the immediate verbal level, and at a deeper implicit level of pattern, such as the patterns of relationship. ... As we follow through structures so we shall naturally begin to discover what the anthropologists describe as the rules of a society. ... If we ask what the rules are, we can begin to understand what the work of art is saying both about itself and to us. ... The consequence of these series of investigations ... is that we shall come to a sense of the work of art's intrinsic original meaning in its original context.[37]

This scenario in fact describes the mode of operation of the best of contemporary scholarship in folk literature. Which prompts the fantasy picture of folk literature shedding her status as the Rashiecoat of literatures and receiving the silver slipper from the princely avant-garde. Well, 'There's nae ill in a merry mind as said the wifie fan she gaed ben the kirk fustlin.'

Notes

1   Max Lüthi, <u>Volksliteratur und Hochliteratur</u> (Bern and Munich, 1970).
2   Agnes Mure Mackenzie, <u>An Historical Survey of Scottish Liter-ature to 1714</u> (London, 1933), pp 158-68.
3   Ibid., p 159.
4   Ibid., p 159.
5   'Epische Gesetze der Volksdichtung', <u>Zeitschrift für Deutsches Altertum</u>, 51 (1909), 1-12; translated as 'Epic Laws of Folk Narrative' in <u>The Study of Folklore</u>, Alan Dundes (ed) (Engle-wood Cliffs, NJ, 1965), pp 131-41.

6   'Four Functions of Folklore', in Study Dundes (ed), pp 279-98; originally published in Journal of American Folklore, 67 (1954), 333-49.

7   Morphology of the Folktale (Austin and London, 1968); originally published in Russian (Leningrad, 1928).

8   2nd rev edn (Helsinki, 1961).

9   'Folk Narrative', in Folklore and Folklife: An Introduction, Richard M Dorson (ed) (Chicago, 1972), pp 63-5.

10   David Fowler, A Literary History of the Popular Ballad (Durham, NC, 1968), pp 18, 5.

11   Selected Papers on Folklore, Laurits Bødker (ed) (Copenhagen, 1948).

12   The English and Scottish Popular Ballads, Francis James Child (ed), 5 vols (Boston, 1882-98).

13   Danmarks Gamle Folkeviser, Svend Grundtvig et al. (eds), 12 vols (Copenhagen, 1853-1976).

14   English and Scottish Popular Ballads, H C Sargent and G L Kittredge (eds) (Cambridge, Mass, 1904), p 78.

15   The Bannatyne Manuscript, W Tod Ritchie (ed), III (Edinburgh, 1928), 8-10; The Maitland Folio Manuscript, W A Craigie (ed), I (Edinburgh, 1919), 159-61.

16   Mediaeval Studies, 11 (1949), 123-205 and 13 (1951), 87-164.

17   The Complaynt of Scotland, Alasdair M Stewart (ed) (Edinburgh, 1979), pp 50-2.

18   The Bannatyne Manuscript, III, 290-1.

19   'A Recently-Discovered Manuscript: "ane taill of Sir colling ye knyt"', Scottish Studies, 16 (1972), 23-39; 'King Orphius', Scottish Studies, 17 (1973), 1-16.

20   'Ancient Scottish Tales - An Unpublished Collection Made by Peter Buchan', J A Fairley (ed), Trans. of the Buchan Field Club, 9 (1908), 143-7.

21   J F Tocher, 'Editorial introduction', Ibid, xv. The tale was also current in Lindsay's natal Fife, according to J E Simpkins, County Folklore VII ... Fife ... Clackmannan and Kinross-Shires (London 1914), p 222.

22   'Preliminary Dissertation', The Complaynt of Scotland (Edinburgh, 1801), p 222.

23   'Folk-song and Dialect', Trans. Yorkshire Dialect Society, part 72, vol 13 (1971), 27-35 (32).

24   For an overview of the genres throughout the centuries see David Buchan, Scottish Tradition: A Collection of Scottish Folk Literature (London and Boston, 1984).

25   In The European Mediaeval Ballad, Otto Holzapfel (ed) (Odense, 1978), pp 98-106.

26   Chosen by John MacQueen and Tom Scott (Oxford, 1966).

27   Tocher, no. 27 (1977), 175-8; also in Buchan, Scottish Tradition, pp 143-6.

28   See, e.g. James Kennedy, Folklore and Reminiscences of Strathtay and Grandtully (Perth, 1928), pp 26, 105.

29   Literature of the North, David Hewitt and Michael Spiller (eds) (Aberdeen, 1983), pp 14-25.

30   Carl Lindahl, Earnest Games: Folkloric Patterns in the Canterbury Tales (Bloomington, Ind, 1987).

31   Scottish Language and Literature, Mediaeval and Renaissance, Dietrich Strauss and Horst Drescher (eds) (Germersheim, 1986), pp 381-92.

32   Flemming G Andersen, Commonplace and Creativity (Odense, 1985). Barre Toelken, 'Figurative Language and Cultural Contexts in the Traditional Ballads', Western Folklore, 45 (1986), 128-39.

33   'The Performance of Mediaeval Romance: Reports from the Field', delivered at Minneapolis, October 1982.

34   R L Greene, The Early English Carols, 2nd rev edn (Oxford, 1977), pp 195-7, 423-7.

35   Discussed in an unpublished paper delivered to the American Folklore Society in Baltimore, October 1986.

36   Scottish Literary Journal, Supplement No. 20 (Autumn 1984), 17.

37   Scottish Studies, 27 (1983), 17-30 (25-7).

Chapter 2

THE SCOTS MAKARS AND THE BALLAD TRADITION

Matthew P McDiarmid

No one seems to have thought of reviewing the evidence for the makars' knowledge, and use, of their country's ballads, the peculiar traditions transmitted by them concerning witches, the king and queen of Fairy, their characteristic matter and symbolism of scene and dress. Lowry Wymberly in his folkloristic study of the ballad asserts that it 'stands nearer to the people than do the romances or other literary types', yet a few pages later thinks 'it is altogether probable that the ballads mirror ideas which were entertained by people in both high and low stations of life'.[1] If we accept the obviously required view, that in the great days of Scots ballad-making, the fifteenth and sixteenth centuries, the form was quite classless, following a prescription that forbade personal, original or fashionable treatments, we should go on to note that its best specimens were enjoyed and admired by men of letters, in England by Sir Philip Sidney and William Shakespeare,[2] and in Scotland not only enjoyed and admired but used for their special purposes by the makars.

The earliest recorded mention of ballads in Scotland occurs in a royal context. In 1491 minstrels 'sang Graystiel' before James IV,[3] presumably just after the appearance of the Scots romance Sir Eger and Sir Gryme about 1485. In his Palice of Honour 1501, dedicated to the same king, Gavin Douglas cites the ballad of Glasgerion. In The Dreme, c.1528, Sir David Lindsay recalls reciting tales (?ballads)to the boy-king James V 'Of the Reid Etin and the Gyre Carlying' (The Red Giant and the Ogress), and in the Papyngo, c.1530, his mention of 'the Queene of Fairy' probably refers, as we shall see, not to Henryson's Orpheus but to such ballads as Thomas the Rhymer and Tam Lane. The author of The Complaynt of Scotlande 1549, addressing himself to the Queen Regent, lists these titles, some certainly ballads: 'the reyde eyttin vitht the thre heydis', 'quhou the kyng of est mure land mareit the kyngis dochtir of vest mure land', 'Skaill gillenderson the kyngis son of skellye', 'the yong tamlene', 'Opheus kyng of portingal', 'the thre veird systirs', 'the battel of hayrlau', 'the huntis of cheuet', 'the persee and the mongumrye met'.[4] Only four ballad texts from this very selective list have come down to us, most notably Sidney's admired Chevy Chace, Tam Lane the greatest of all ballads, and The Ballad of Otterbourne, which celebrates the engagement of 1388, and details of which make the author seem to have been reading his Froissart; but the four are enough to tell us that the ballad was enjoyed in ranks above that

of the peasant or ordinary townsman, and perhaps composed by
persons from such superior ranks. Thus I have wondered if the
inspired author of The Queen's Maries, writing after the murderous
execution of his queen, derived his fiction from her known French
residence, her death, the court scandal of Darnley's profligacy,
and the gossip about an abortion and the misconduct of Marie that
he found in Knox's History.[5] Certainly the speculation comes
naturally that the best ballads were composed by men with the
literary equipment and inventive genius of the makars.

Wymberly as a folklorist advances the concept of a 'ballad
mind', a very primitive, uncivilised, credulous, but still very
active mind. The concept, however, is more relevant to the matter
of the story than to the ballad as poem, or to its author, and has
the same merely generic relation to these as the heroic mind in
poetry has to any given heroic poem and its composer. Once established, convention in the ballad as in other 'kinds' directs the
content and general effect. Wymberly's notion that the balladist
believed or half-believed in his wonders, so that he could give a
sort of credence to the idea of bones and hair singing the crime
and identity of the criminal as in The Milldams of Binnorie, must
be ingested with a deal of salt. Coleridge's idea of a 'willing
suspension of disbelief' seems more applicable. Of course, that
there were storytellers then as now glad to exploit actions and
scenes with strange circumstance and aura is quite believable.

For the ensuing argument an important aspect of certain ballads
is the special significance given to scene, colour, number. Seas
and rivers are always ominous, as in Sir Patrick Spens, Annan
Water and Clyde Water. It is not simply in the nature of things
that so much fateful action or talk, such sinister encounters, so
many events having to do with love, happy or unhappy, are set in
the green countryside or greenwood. In the ballad green is powerfully associated with love and lust – topics that, oddly enough,
are entirely unnoticed by Wymberly – and also with death, ill-
luck, and whatever is otherwordly, witches or fairies. The first
of these associations, though the others may accompany it, is the
most obvious. When Thomas makes love to the Fairy Queen on Huntly
bank, under the Eildon tree, both the scene and her green dress
are appropriate to their love making and the consequent seven year
capture of his soul. When Janet casts her green mantle over the
'mother-naked' Tam Lane both action and colour have their simple
sexual symbolism; she makes him her man in just the way the Queen
had previously done. In the incestuous Bonny Hynd – stanzas of
which Scott 'decently' omitted – when the brother unknowingly
meets his sister and at once says to her, 'Give me your green
manteel/Or else your maidenhead', the first gift symbolises the
second. In folk-song the idiom 'lost her grass-green skirt' has
the same meaning. And everyone must know Burns's use of one folk-
song: 'Green grow the rashes O,/Green grow the rashes O,/The
sweetest hours that e'er I spent/Were spent amang the lasses O.'
Perhaps it is not too surprising that so many female ghosts, like
the one at Crathes Castle beside Aberdeen, are known as 'The Green
Lady', and for the same reason. I have never myself heard of a
green bride. Other appropriate applications of green we will come
to later.

As for numbers, three and seven are ominous. There are three dead babes and three hell-hounds in the grave of the not so sweet Sweet William, and it is three dead sons that return to the Wife of Usher's Well. The seven year capture of Thomas the Rhymer has been noticed. Why the seven brothers should appear so suddenly and mysteriously in the bedroom where the doomed Clerk Saunders sleeps with his love long puzzled me, till a Cypriot student translated for me a related ballad in which they are May Margaret's guardians come from the world of death. It is always worth remembering that ballad ghosts are corporeal, so torches and swords are quite in keeping. It is the special business of this paper, however, to notice instances of the influence of ballad matter, its fantasy, its symbolism, in quite different verse.

The ballad's predecessor, if not indeed its translated form, in early Scotland was the lay or 'geste'. Lays of Malcolm Canmore in his battle with Macbeth, and of Wallace, probably of the twelth and fourteenth centuries respectively, have been preserved in Andrew Wyntoun's Original Chronicle of about 1407-20. Poets had to favour the victor, so we learn that one bright morning Macbeth's mother walked in the greenwood and met a 'fayr man', a devil of course, who fathered Macbeth on her. As a young man the latter dreamed that he sat in his hunting seat and saw passing 'Thre werd sisteris',[6] witches, who looked at him and uttered the famous prophecies; so duly he murdered his uncle King Duncan and married the king's queen, in those days an act of incest.[7] From the 1535-39 Scots version of Hector Boece's Historia we get the significant detail that the witches' dress was 'of elritche hew', that is, was green.[8] John Barbour too was interested in demons: Edward I had a demon familiar, and the mother of the count of Flanders, a witch, had a demon lover.[9]

The Wallace 'geste' in Wyntoun, re-written in Hary's epic, is a tragic love-story. He goes in June, dressed in the gay yet ominous green, to visit his 'leman' or mistress. Pursued by English soldiers who mock his colourful garb he escapes through her house, but she is put to death. Midnight sees the hero take his revenge in the sheriff's lodging and truly begin his own tragic career.[10]

Our next poem for mention is Richard Holland's Buke of the Houlat 1449,[11] notable here only for the setting that the young author gives to his ideal of a beneficent Nature at work in a harmonious society of nations, the Community of Europe. He sees the Community as a forest of birds, each of its citizens performing its natural function of service, except the one too significant dissident, the discontented bird of night, the owl, eaten with 'Lucifers pride'. Dame Nature mockingly exalts him, only to reduce him to his natural condition, unfortunately the human condition. He has at least learned that 'We cum pure, we gang pure, baith kind and comoun'. The tale begins with the usual symbols, the 'grene meid', the 'riche Revir', and then we are with Lucifer's owl. It ends delightfully with the poet's patrons, the Douglas earl and countess of Moray pictured as familial doves flying together 'in the forest frely parfit'. One thinks of the bowers and lovers of balladry, as in Brown Adam and Rose the Red and White Lilly.

In Hary's Life of Sir William Wallace 1476-78 the hero as a guerrilla freedom fighter is more than once vividly dramatised in

greenwood settings, and there is one that smacks very much of
ballad fantasy. In his desperate flight from the Perth area to the
Gask Hall Wallace is angered by the delaying pace of the suspect
Fawdon, and with the famous sword strikes off his head. At once,
as Wallace later guesses must have happened, a demon possesses the
dead body. Arrived in the Hall Wallace hears a horn blow outside, and one by one sends his few remaining comrades to investi-
gate. They do not return, but the decapitated Fawdon appears in
the doorway and throws his head at Wallace who fearfully throws it
back, and taking to a wooden stair that breaks under him makes a
great leap to the ground and flees up the river. Looking back he
sees the Hall as one huge flame of fire, Fawdon standing in it and
holding a great rafter in his hand. G L Kittredge suggested that
this was a peculiar version of the legend of 'The Returning Head'[12]
but Hary shared Dante's knowledge that the body of a dead traitor
was reanimated by a demon,[13] and to Fawdon's character and appearance gave traits from the Satanic god Saturn. In brief, the tale
is Hary's invention, but the horn and fiery spirit he got from
balladry. Everyone knows about the alluring horns of Elfland and
devilry as they are combined in Lady Isabel and the Elfin Knight,
where the lover is a devil; and in The Demon Lover, the demon
becomes a flame of fire that engulfs all the ship. The Fawdon
story has ballad sources.

When we come to the great Scots romance Sir Eger and Sir Gryme,
of about 1485,[14] several ballad themes or symbols are recognisable. They show first in the wooded wilderness and rivers that the
two heroes successively cross to enter the Land of Doubt (Dread)
and challenge the mysterious Sir Graystiel. The heroine, Lillias,
is shown always in a bright outdoors bower; her proud opposite,
Wynliane, in a dark castle. In the bower Lillias cures the vanquished Sir Eger's wounds with a green drink, seemingly sharing
the medical lore of witches, and warns him that the drink must
lose its virtue as he approaches the woman who does not love him.
The two barriers to an otherworld, wilderness and river, are of
course also mentioned in Thomas the Rhymer; and the green bower of
love, as it will be for the successful Sir Gryme, has already been
remarked on here. By contrast with its healthful light and peace
the peculiarly violent ending of Sir Graystiel, tearing up herbs
and roots in his death throes, is felt as a scene of daemonic
possession, as is that of the horses savagely fighting on when
their riders have been thrown. The irresistable sword of a dead
king sought by Sir Gryme is certainly an idea from balladry, and
probably from the Danish ballads then influential in Scotland.[15] I
would like to learn of a ballad precedent for Graystiel's practice
of cutting off one finger from vanquished foes. But only the
reader of this dark and sad tale – as it is, since even Graystiel
has friends that grieve for him, Sir Gryme is killed in a tournament, Sir Eger abandoned by the wife who then learns his secret,
that it was not he who killed Graystiel, Lillias widowed till she
is able to marry Sir Eger – can appreciate how much of ballad
feeling and drama is in the romance.

Statements about a ballad reference in Robert Henryson's Orpheus
and Euridice have to be made carefully in view of a probable memory
of the romance Sir Orfeo,[16] and the poem's use of Nicholas Trivet's

commentary on the few lines of Boethius, which coincides with ballad symbolism in two points. If there is indeed a memory of the romance,[17] one must still observe that before her capture Henryson's Euridice walks in a wooded, bushy 'medowe grene', but the Heurodis of Sir Orfeo sleeps in an orchard; in Orpheus the heroine, stung by a serpent, is fallen into 'a dedly swoun' when her maid sees her borne out of sight by the Queen of Fairy and her court, but in Sir Orfeo, warned and with an armed guard, Heurodis is carried off by the King of Fairy, seen by no one; in Orpheus much is made of the hero's journey over a thorny wilderness and bridge above a dreadfully deep river, where wait the vengeful goddesses, here called 'sisteris thre', past other dangers and so into hell, but in Sir Orfeo there is nothing of all this, only an easy finding of hell and happy winning of Heurodis. Henryson's hell is Christianised in part, but his pale Erudices is 'lyke an elf'. On their way out he talks of 'play', the common word for sex, and so looks and loses.

As for Trivet, his serpent just happens to be a common creature of balladry, but his prata, fields, representing the sensual world as often in the ballads, are translated in ballad style as a 'medowe grene'. There is nothing on elves, wilderness, river, bridge.

Reviewing the significant details or images, one recognises in the 'swoun', deadly as it may be, and in the maid's tale of seeing Erudices made invisible, the strange sleep and mist that amid his hunting makes Tam Lane a captive of the Queen of Elfland, the same sleep that in some versions may have fallen on the idling Thomas as he 'lay on Huntly bank' and had his vision of the Queen of Elfland. In Hind Etin the elfin lover takes a maiden by casting a similar mist about her. The natural, yet here ominous, green of the meadow need only be noted. And the phrase for the vengeful goddesses, the 'thre sisteris', if only a phrase, is worth a mention for 'the thre veird systeris' of the Complaynt and the tradition followed in the Macbeth fable and children's rhymes that witches go in threes. No one at least will dispute the ballad origin of the spellbinding Queen as used by Henryson, but the underground wilderness and rivers that Orpheus crosses should also recall these features in Thomas's underground journey. And the thorny face of the wilderness that Orpheus walks, with the dreadful bridge, should remind us of The Lykewake Dirge, its 'Whinny Muir' and 'Brig o' Dread', on the same way to hell.

Concerning Henryson's acquaintance with, and use of, the situations and symbols of balladry I rest my case, and turn to the brilliantly various William Dunbar. The influence of ballad symbolism on his two most impressive poems, The Goldyn Targe and The Tretis of the Tua Mariit Wemen and The Wedo, has gone unremarked. Even a poet so rich in artifice, so individual and personal as Dunbar, could not fail to be touched by his countryman's love and understanding of the ballad and its traditions, especially in poems that are fantasies of love and sex. It is indeed surprising that scholars who notice so many verse traditions in his work, who make so much of one avowed debt to Chaucer that is not reflected in his style, and only by remote cousinship to the Wife of Bath in his Widow, say nothing of an influence felt nearer home.

The Goldyn Targe has a deal of allegoric dressing better called symbolic dressing - I have suggested elsewhere that it is a fairly early poem[18] - and of fine phrasing that is neatly described by Lindsay as 'language at large' (where 'at large' means 'given its freedom'). It treats of the old, ever new theme of reason, of the golden shield vainly trying to ward off the arrows of desire; but the treatment seems to me to be the reverse of impersonal, as so often assumed, and rather to show the hurt of an unhappy love affair. So read, it becomes easy to recognise and interpret the obvious ballad symbolism, especially its colour symbolism.

The time chosen for this lover's fantasy is May. Like the ballad's greenwood lovers the birds are 'Within thair courtyns grene into thair bouris', the same wild rosebuds flourish that Janet plucked to make appear her elfin lover Tam Lane: not by a 'well', that is, little stream, it is true, but by a broad and clear river with green banks and green overhanging boughs. The poet sleeps on such a bank, as did 'true Thomas', and like him has his vision. Rivers, as I said, are ominous, and now a ship 'Als fal- coune swift desyrouse of hir pray',[19] makes to the bank and lands a hundred ladies. Of course, as enemies of chastity they wear 'kirtillis grene'.

I have said enough about the symbolism of green in ballad and folk song, but something more is in place here. Anything or anyone desirous, having to do with growth or love or lust, or with the freedom, mystery, menace of the wildwood, is naturally given its green wear or green setting - always that setting. As in the balladists so also in the makars. We remember Macbeth's three witches in 'elritche' green, Wallace's green livery as an unlucky lover and later the green setting of his flight and visitation by the daemoniac Fawdon, the green bower of Lillias and her miraculous green drink, not to mention the green scene of Graystiel's death. In the Testament Henryson prays to Venus that 'my faidit hert of lufe sche wald mak grene'. Before he is espied by the ladies Dunbar lies under green leaves, showing that he is in fact prepared for love; elsewhere he speaks of his love poems as made 'undir the leiffis grene'. In King Hart, attributed to Douglas, the phrases 'grene lufe', 'grene lust', 'grene appetit', are repeated and repeated. But to return to our poem, gods land with goddesses, 'And eviry one of thir in grene arrayit', among them naturally the king of Fairy, 'Pluto the elriche incubus/In cloke of grene, his court usit no sable'. Kinsley's edition absurdly only cites St Augustine, for sylvan fauns and incubi who molest women.

And so we come to the heart of the fantasy, Dunbar's painful love affair, 'All throuch a luke quhilk I have boucht full dere'. The ladies 'lete fall thair mantillis grene', a gesture whose significance we know. Reason cannot defend against love's arrows, being blinded by 'Presence' and 'Hamelynes', that is, sexual intimacy.[20] So the poet-lover is banished, exiled from the ways of Reason, 'amang the bewis grene', like so many ballad lovers, for example Brown Adam and the captives of the fairy queen. But he is a happy lover only 'quhill men mycht go a myle', for his sweetheart 'syne tuke hir leve, I saw hir nevir mare'. When she left she 'gert ane hell my paradise appere'. A great wind, presumably from the devilish north, blows through his dream, and 'All was hyne went, thare was bot wildernes'. The wilderness symbol we know from Thomas the Rhymer, The Lyke-Wake Dirge and Henryson's Orpheus; but unlike Orpheus Thomas leaves it for a bright, pleasant land, as does the poet here when he wakes. The concluding praise of other poets is an inartistic intrusion, though keeping to the idea of a land 'bare and desolate' till transformed by their colours of rhetoric; it has diverted readers from the theme to the style, and critics from his use of the ballad symbolism to his respect for a few end-of-fourteenth-century English poets, by his time stylistically outmoded.

The Tretis introduces us to three women, a traditionally other-world number as we have seen, the two married women having as their devilish mentor and priestess the widow - like the devil she can quote scripture - who hears their confessions concerning the 'blist band that bindis so fast', and then gives her own instructive confession. Their tongues loosened by wine, the 'thre gay ladeis' 'sparit no matiris' of marital and extra-marital sex. The time chosen for such licence is suitable, Midsummer Eve, a festive time that has left us the phrase 'midsummer madness'. It suits also a fact of which we are aware: however realistic the issues of talk may be, this is very much a poet's fantasy, as much a fantasy as many a scene in the ballad or folk tradition that he obviously knows.

Action begins with his passing 'ane gudlie grein garth' and hearing high-raised, arrogant voices. The garden is hedged round with the green hawthorn that is holy to elves or fairies. The stress on the garden's colour and its being a secret enclosure recalls indeed the enchanted taboo groves in Tam Lane, Jellon Grame, Hind Etin, Lady Isabel and the Elf Knight. As in Tam Lane such groves seem hostile to sexual continence, certainly to virginity. The listening poet stands under 'ane holyn hevinlie grein hewit', and so according to balladry is protected from the spells and deceits of witches. We still bring the holly into our homes at the winter festivals. Through the hedge the daring poet looks into 'ane grein arbeir', where sit the three women whose 'mantillis grein war as the gress'. The green mantles need no further comment, nor does the implicit suggestion that the three women are, in their own kind, a coven of witches. Green is, of course, the colour appropriate to the dress and setting of such women, who make a mock of marriage, who would change their mates with the same free- dom that the birds enjoy, who use the institution as a convenient disguise for their licence. It is proper too that the colour should recur in the ending of this sexual fantasy, when the three 'maid game amang the grene leiffis', and as they took a parting drink 'maid a glorious gle amang the grene bewis'. Green, after all, was the right colour for pagan Nature. A farcical, licentious fantasy with serious overtones, it leaves a bemused poet asking with which of these liberated women a man would enter what the widow ironically calls 'the blist band'. There may be no ballad-style witches, or indeed lovers, in Dunbar's poem, but the women who are witches and lovers after their own fashion, seeking and enjoying freedom from their chains, certainly get their suitable setting and dress from the symbolism of balladry.

A brief word will do for the few other makars who display knowledge and use of the ballad world. There is Dunbar's friend Roull
who, in his comic Cursing 1492–1503 directed against the stealers
of his hens,[21] consigns them to the malice of witches, to be
transformed into wolves or werewolves, a transformation exempli-
fied in Tam Lane, Kemp Owyne, and in a Danish ballad,[22] or else to
be captured for the court of the Queen of Fairy. King Hart,
attributed to Gavin Douglas, has been noticed. In Part I of his
Palice of Honour 1500–1501 not only is the ballad harper Glasgerion set alongside Orpheus, but the poem opens with the prescribed
swoon and immediate transference of the author to the most impressive of his scenes, a wilderness with blood-red river: features,
we remember, of Thomas the Rhymer's famous journey to Elfland.
Douglas's river, however, has one feature even more disconcerting
than its colour to any angler; its fish are 'yelland lyke elves'.
And the poet dreads the coming of the mischievous fairies Skrym-
morie and Chippynutie. Similarly one must think that the most significant scene of Lindsay's Papyngo, which mentions the Queen of
Fairy, the one that shows the three birds of prey waiting to dine
on the dead parrot, has been suggested by a ballad like The Three
Ravens or The Twa Corbies. Finally, Alexander Montgomerie's Flyting
1582 describes the Halloween riding of the fairy court just as we
know it in the greatest of ballads Tam Lane; and in his comedy
Philotus 1583–86 he has a lover conjure a supposed fiend 'be
Alrisch king and Queen of Faerie'.[23]
    That the makars knew, understood and used the ballads is quite
clear.

Notes

In these notes STS signifies Scottish Text Society.

1   Lowry Charles Wymberly, Folklore in the English & Scottish
     Ballads, (New York, 1965), pp 15–20. For texts see Sir Walter
     Scott's Minstrelsy of the Scottish Border, 4 vols, T F
     Henderson (ed) (London 1902); F J Child, English & Scottish
     Popular Ballads, (Boston, Mass, 1957); The Greig-Duncan Folk
     Song Collection, Patrick Shuldham and Emily B Lyle (eds)
     (Aberdeen, 1980–   ).
2   See Sidney's Apologie for Poetrie, though he assumes that the
     ballad was the work of a blind harper. That Shakespeare cites
     many ballads is well known.
3   The Scottish Accounts under 1491.
4   J A H Murray (ed) (London, 1872), pp 63–5; Alasdair Stewart
     (ed), STS, 1979. The red giant may have three heads, the
     giant in the ballad of Sir Cawline has five. In his Intro-
     duction Murray asks if 'the kyng of est mure land' is the
     'King Estmere' that Percy tore from his Reliques. In 'Skaill
     Gillenderson' the first word should be Danish for 'harper';
     Glasgerion is another ballad about a king's son who was a
     harper. The description 'yong tamlene' is phonetically the

same as 'young Tam Lane' in Burns's and Scott's versions of
the ballad. Murray improbably suggests that 'Opheus' and
'portingal' are ignorant substitutions for Henryson's
'Orpheus' and 'Thrace'; and it seems unlikely that the
goddesses of vengeance should be meant by 'the thre veird
systeris', a phrase that suggests witches. Harlaw was fought
in 1411. Chevy Chase is a largely fictional account of the
battle near Otterbourne 1388; in The Battle of Otterbourne
the author gives times, even time of day, and circumstances,
except for the 'bracken bush' burial, as given in Froissart;
even Douglas's wish to be secretly buried there need not mean
burial but derive from his reported wish to be hidden.

5   See Scott's notes to the ballad. Darnley's licentiousness,
which made him hated by his wife the queen, was well known.

6   The Original Chronicle, F J Amours (ed), STS, vol 4, 1906,
pp 272–80. The title in the Complaynt will be remembered.

7   Ibid, p 274.

8   William Stewart, The Buick of the Croniklis of Scotland, W B
Turnbull (ed) (London, 1858), vol 2, p 636.

9   Barbour's Bruce, M P McDiarmid and J A C Stevenson (eds), STS
vol 2, 1980, pp 82–5.

10 The Original Chronicle, vol 5, pp 298–306; M P McDiarmid in
Hary's Wallace, STS, vol 1, 1968, pp 114–16.

11 Scottish Alliterative Poems in Rhyming Stanzas, F J Amours
(ed), STS, vol 1, 1882, pp 47–81; vol 2, 1897, pp. xx–xxxiv
M P McDiarmid, 'Richard Holland's Buke of The Howlat: An
Interpretation', Medium Aevum, vol 38, 1969, no. 3 pp 277–90.

12 See notes on the Fawdon tale in Hary's Wallace, vol 1, 1968,
cxxix, n.1; vol 2, 1969, pp 168–70. I had not then considered
the use of ballad ideas.

13 Hary's Wallace, V 222; Dante's Inferno, canto xxxiii 124–32.

14 Editions are these: David Laing, Early Popular Poetry in
Scotland, vol 2 (London, 1885), pp 119–210; J R Caldwell,
Harvard Studies in Comparative Literature, vol 9, (Cambridge,
Mass, 1933). The date is given by reference to the Turkish
attack on Cyprus 1479 and mention of 'Graystiel' in the
Scottish Accounts 1491. Gryme was a used form of Graeme, a
Scots Border family that won Garrieston and Alston, Cumber-
land place names in the romance. 'Eger' probably comes from
the now ruined castle of Eger, here down as Egerness, on the
Scots side of the Solway.

15 Wymberly, op.cit., pp 94, 105.

16 Sir Orfeo, A J Bliss (ed) (Oxford, 1966).

17 Carol Mills, 'Romance Convention and Robert Henryson's Orpheus
and Eurydice', in Bards and Makars, A J Aitken, M P
McDiarmid, D A Thomson (eds) (Glasgow, 1977). She argues
plausibly for at least a 'memory' of Sir Orfeo.

18 For the period of the Targe see M P McDiarmid, 'The Early
William Dunbar and his Poems', Scottish Historical Review,
vol 59, Part 2, 1980, pp 126–39.

19 On the sport of hunting with falcons by a river see The
Poetical Works of Gavin Douglas, John Small (ed), vol 1,
(Edinburgh, 1874), p 140.

20 This is what the character 'Hamelynes' signifies in Lindsay's
Satire.

21   The Cursing is in The Maitland Folio Manuscript, W A Craigie
      (ed), STS, vol 1, 1919, p 161.
22   Wymberly, op.cit., pp 58-9.
23   Philotus, st. 122, Miscellany volume, STS, 1933. For author-
      ship and date see M P McDiarmid, 'Philotus: A Play of the
      Scottish Renaissance', Forum For Modern Language Studies, vol
      3, No. 3, July 1967.

Chapter 3

VIEWS OF KING AND PEOPLE IN SIXTEENTH AND SEVENTEENTH
CENTURY BALLADS

A Gardner-Medwin

What a king is and how he behaves must always have been of vital
interest to his people. In various ways the people made this known
to the monarch; a mirror was held up to the king in which he could
see his ideal self reflected. The manner of presentation varied
from the theoretical, allegorical manner of Ireland's Meroure of
Wyssdome, to the direct way in which Lindsay advises the young King
James V in The Dreme. Another way of making clear to all what was
expected of the king was to show a king in action, in drama. From
Lindsay's Satire of the Three Estates, through Shakespeare's history plays to Calderon de la Barca's play of 1630, Life is a Dream,
kings good and bad were shown performing to court and people and to
the monarchs themselves. Abstract qualities might be brought into
the plays, as when Calderon de la Barca discussed magnanimity or
when in Macbeth Malcolm speaks of

> the king-becoming graces
> As justice, verity, temperance, stableness
> Bounty, perseverance, mercy, lowliness,
> Devotion, patience, courage, fortitude.

These few examples are but a reminder of the widespread interest in
and varied ways of writing about the king and how he should behave
which are known from the late Middle Ages and Renaissance.

Since there was this widespread interest, it is perhaps worth
looking at how kings are treated in a different form, ballads,
which may reflect a different viewpoint. Ballads are defined as
narrative songs transmitted through oral tradition. They are known
to us from written records often of a much later date than that of
the event to which they appear to refer, and therefore ballads are
tricky to use as historical evidence. It is however possible, as
Professor David Buchan wrote, that

> They can contain emotional truths, the attitudes and
> reactions of ballad singing folk to the world around
> them.[1]

It is the attitudes and reactions to kings as preserved in ballads
that is the subject of this paper.

Scotland possesses a magnificent collection of ballads, but most
of them are known to us only through the versions written down in

the eighteenth century or later. What remains from the sixteenth century are occasional brief references, hints, no more, that might refer to a ballad known in a fuller variant from a later source. However, in Scotland's neighbour across the North Sea, Denmark, there existed already by 1591 many written collections of ballads. These MSS were made for the nobility and the fashion culminated by 1591 with the publication of <u>A Hundred Selected Danish Ballads</u> by Vedel.[2]

This collection was a celebration of national identity. Vedel started with legends, then had a section of Danish history and finished with ballads about the exploits of great men. He said in his introduction that the ballads of history were the ones which were 'most concerned with the truth'. Yet Vedel also said they were

> Songs for enjoyment and moral profit. (They concern) valiant and noteworthy people in virtuous deeds and also in faulty and unworthy act, as a warning and as an example to others ... to love and follow the good and hate and flee evil ... Faith serves his Lord well; Faithlessness and Falsehood stab their own lord in the back.[3]

There is an echo in the final sentence here of the allegorical method of depicting qualities.

The historical events retold in the Danish ballads are coloured by a code of heroism, of courage and honour. The Danish ballad of <u>Neils Ebbesen</u> (DgF 156),[4] who successfully fought against the German aggressor, is a splendid monument to Danish heroism and apparently accurate as an historical document. In these Danish ballads it is not the kings who are the heroes; indeed the kings come out rather badly. One king, from a ballad thought to have been composed about 1600 and inaccurate historically, himself entered enemy territory as a spy, but had to leave in a hurry because the inhabitants recognised the initialled silver knife and fork he insisted on eating with.[5] A group of Danish ballads is about strife between the king and one of his nobles, Marsk Stig (fl 13c). Another well-known ballad, from a source later than Vedel, is the account of King Valdemar I, his mistress and the queen. Suspect as historical evidence, this ballad shows a pleasure in scandal quite at odds with Vedel's moral viewpoint. More attractive, and included by Vedel, is the ballad of <u>The Death of Queen Dagmar</u> (DgF 135). She lies in Ribe, dying in childbed, and the king has to ride from the far east of his kingdom to be at her side. Queen Dagmar dies in her waiting woman's arms as the king rides into Ribe. This ballad is still popular and seems to reflect truthfully the affection in which Dagmar was held.

Among the Danish ballads recorded in a MS of 1616 is an allegory, <u>King Christian II and the Nobleman</u> (DgF 173). This relates to how King Christian (ruled 1513-23, died in exile 1559) was forced out of his kingdom. The eagle was chosen as king by the little birds, but the hawk objected, and together with other hawks drove out the eagle, leaving the little birds defenceless against the depredations of the hawks. The author of this political piece seems to have known of the allegorical intepretations of hierarchy elsewhere in Europe, and from this ballad it would seem that the common people saw the king as their protector against the nobles.

In these ballads the king is a central figure, but sometimes his role lies outside the main action. In <u>King Hans's Wedding</u> (DgF 166) the king sits in Copenhagen. He orders a confidential letter, a <u>lønbreffue</u>, to be written and sent to Jutland to Sir Erick Ottesson. Sir Erick is sent to a foreign land, to seek the king's bride. He is eager to undertake the task, and does so successfully. (There is a Norwegian parallel, <u>Asmundr Fraegdjaeva</u>,[6] in which the messenger is reluctant to go to the land of the trolls, but does so successfully). Later in Vedel's book, among the ballads of the deeds of great men, there is <u>The Death at Sea of Jon Remorssøn</u>.[7]

> The Danish king he sits in Ribe
> and he writes out far and wide:
> He bids all his good courtiers
> ride out from Styreshavn.
>
> And it was Sir Jon Rimaardssøn
> threw his armour upon his white neck:
> He who will not sail today
> serves his lord falsely.
>
> And it was Sir Jon Rimaardssøn
> he girt himself with his sword:
> He who will not sail today
> he serves his lord with deceit.
>
> This even we would drink,
> if we could get the beer:
> Tomorrow we would sail
> if but the wind would cease.
>
> To that replied Sir Jon Rimaardssøn,
> our lord does not have to ask about that:
> He sent us a message and a letter as well,
> we must hear and obey it.
>
> It was the skipper Hogen the good,
> he lifted his eyes to the clouds:
> He who will sail the sea today
> will never come alive to port.
>
> To that replied Sir Jon Rimaardssøn
> and he who turned round again:
> He who will not take ship today
> is unfaithful to his king.

This last stanza was apparently added by Vendel, for it is not in the MS he used as a source. Even without it the moral is clear: the king's orders must be obeyed, at whatever cost, especially if they come in the form of a written command. (Sir Jon's task was not that of fetching a princess, and he died at sea, but not from a storm).

It is easy to pick out the motifs which one of the most famous Scottish ballads, Sir Patrick Spens (Child 58), shares with one or both of these Danish ballads. The king is sitting in state in Copenhagen, Ribe or Dunfermline; he sends a written command to fetch a princess, and the letter must be obeyed even if the weather is threatening. In spite of warning from a seaman, the chosen nobleman sets sail. In the second of these Danish ballads Vedel makes it clear that unflinching obedience is required; in the Scottish one this is implied by Sir Patrick Spens's reaction to the letter, laughter, then tears.

Much effort has been expended in trying to find an event in history upon which Sir Patrick Spens might have been been based. The details were set out by F J Child, and he was not convinced by them. He wrote

For one, I do not feel compelled to regard the ballad as historical.[8]

None of the suggested historical occasions fit the ballad as we have it, and since the Scottish ballad is known only from Scottish tradition of the late eighteenth and early nineteenth century there is an even longer gap than usual between possible event and recorded ballad. I suggest that instead of looking for Sir Patrick Spens in the thirteenth or fourteenth centuries we ask instead whether his ancestor might not be Sir Jon Rimaardssøn, nobly obeying his king's order, combined with the plot from King Hans's wedding and turned into a greater story than either by the tragic ending. Both Danish ballads were published by Vedel in 1591 and derive from MSS of the late sixteenth century; this implies that they were current in Denmark then.

It is a coincidence that there were contacts between Denmark and Scotland in the last decade of the sixteenth century. King James VI of Scotland set out late in 1589, spent several months at the Danish court, married there the Danish princess Anne, and was delayed by storms from his return the following spring. The courtiers he met in Denmark, some of whom accompanied him and his queen back to Scotland, included men of the Bille and Brahe families. These names, although not the individuals, are associated with Danish ballad MSS of the sixteenth and early seventeenth centuries.

Although these coincidences cannot be taken further, and there is no record of the Scottish ballad before its first appearance in Percy's Reliques[9] in 1765, they are intriguing. The starts of the ballads are remarkably similar, as are the emphases on the written command. It is interesting to speculate on the type of letter sent. A 'braid letter', which comes in many of the Scottish variants, suggests that it might have been a formal letter patent, a paper which was open, patent, to inspection and which when opened was noticeably broad, as were the litterae patentes of the Scottish kings from medieval times.[10] The Danish word lønbreffue appears to mean a confidential letter,[11] so in that respect it is the opposite of the 'braid letter'. Of course it is possible that 'braid letter' was inserted in the ballad in the eighteenth century, since other variants have simple terms such as 'long' or 'loving' for the letter, but I suggest that the ballad was created in the late sixteenth century, using, as so often when ballad variants arise, a local term for a detail, while maintaining its importance in the plot. Certainly the fundamental aspect, the relationship expected between king and nobleman emphasised by Vedel in his introduction, is strikingly similar in Sir Jon Rimaardssøn and Sir Patrick Spens.

The relationship between king and nobleman is a theme found elsewhere in Scottish ballads, and it is not an easy one. One might see in this a reflection of the difficulty kings had in maintaining royal power over the powerful nobles, or perhaps it is that strife and tragedy make for a better story than does peaceful co-operation. Two ballads are connected with King James VI and the strife of the early 1590s between him and his cousin Francis Stewart, Earl of Bothwell. The Bonnie Earl of Murray (Child 181) is a lament for the death of the Earl. The king had ordered his capture, but Huntly had killed Murray. In the ballad the king reprimands Huntly

> I bade you bring him wi you,
> But forbade you him to slay.[12]

Variant A is full of slanderous hints - 'He might have been a King!', 'Oh he was the Queen's love!' - unsupported by historical evidence, but the ballad clearly suggests that the king had difficulty in keeping control over his lords. In the second ballad, The Laird of Logie (Child 182), Logie, a gentleman at court, has been arrested. (The ballad gives no reason, but it was for aiding Bothwell). He escaped with the help of a Danish lady in waiting and her mistress the queen. In both ballad and historical account Logie married the Danish lady, and was in the end reinstated. A less gripping subject than the death of the Earl of Murray, this ballad shows here the king coping with the problem of controlling his nobles.

> But since it is my gracious queen
> A hearty pardon we will gie
> And for her sake we'll free the loon
> The rantin young Laird of Logie.[13]

King James VI is here showing magnanimity, one of the qualities expected of a king.

An earlier James, the young King James V, did not show such grace. On gaining control of his kingdom in 1528, he set out to bring to heel the powerful noble families, especially those along the border with England, who had grown too strong during his boyhood. In 1530 James captured and executed John Armstrong, whose family controlled the western end of the Border, known as 'The Debateable Land' because it was so often fought over. This tactic of the King's seems to have worked, for the Borders were peaceful for most of James V's reign, although the final battle at Solway Moss took place in 'The Debateable Land'. The ballad, Johnie Armstrong (Child 169), tells the story from the point of view of the Armstrongs. As soon as Armstrong came into his presence, the

King called him a traitor, refusing to be mollified by Armstrong's gifts. Indeed, the more magnificent the gifts become, the more they reveal the extent of Armstrong's power, and the less the King is pleased. In the end, Armstrong realised there was no escape.

> To seik hot water beneath cold ice
> Surely it is a great follie;
> I have asked grace at a graceless face,
> And there is nane for my men and me.[14]

The ballad is powerful propaganda for Armstrong, but it is not entirely to be believed; Armstrong's claims to power might well be exaggerated, and there is considerable doubt over his claim never to have hurt any poor Scots. It perhaps reveals, from a different viewpoint, the need for a strong central power, the king, to shield the ordinary people from the powers of the great lords, a need put more plainly by the Danish allegorical ballad, King Christian II and the Nobleman which probably refers to events of a similar date. King James V himself gained popularity with the common people by his stern treatment of the great lords, by laws passed in 1535 and 1541 to protect the common people from exploitation and also perhaps because of his habit of travelling incognito as the Goodman of Ballangeich.

The Scottish ballads discussed so far have been concerned in one way or another with the relationship between the king and his nobles. I suggest that they also share an approximate date of creation, the sixteenth century. Johnie Armstrong appears to have been created as an angry response to the execution of Armstrong by James V in 1530. Although the earliest extant record, Child's A, is from a London print of 1658, the Scottish variant C, 'copied from a gentleman's mouth of the name of Armstrang, who is 6th generation from this John', rings true in the emotion recorded, although published in 1724.[15]

The Bonnie Earl of Murray and The Laird o Logie refer to known episodes in the 1590s, and it is my contention that Sir Patrick Spens derives from two Danish ballads published and known at the Danish court in the 1590s. These four ballads must thus be seen as a group which support in their fashion the ongoing debate about the behaviour expected of a king, as do very many of the ballads published by Vedel.

There are other Scottish ballads in which the king has a role, but they are of a very different type. The Death of Queen Jane (Child 170) is known from tradition of the late eighteenth and early nineteenth centuries, mostly from Scotland, and yet it refers to the death of the English Queen Jane Seymour at the birth of Prince Edward. There is a poem on this subject in an English Garland of 1612,[16] but it is not a ballad. It is a dynastic poem which starts with Edward's birth and of his mother's death, gives the whole of his reign and of his sister Mary's, and ends with a celebration of Queen Elizabeth. In contrast, the ballad is a lament for the death of the queen. She is in labour, asks for the king to be fetched and begs that the baby be cut from her side.

King Henry was sent for, and sat by her bedside:

'Why weep you, Queen Jeany? your eyes are so red.'
'O Henry, O Henry, do this one thing for me,
    Let my side straight be opend, and save my babie![17]

In a couple of details, not in the English poem of 1612, this
ballad resembles the Danish Death of Queen Dagmar: the king has to
be sent for, and the queen's eyes are red. However, there was a
Lamentation of Quene Jane registered in 1560,[18] but not extant, so
one cannot easily speculate about the source of the ballad version
of this event. It may be said, however, that this is a ballad
celebrating in a lament a tragedy that might happen in any family,
which has been given place, time and an aura of romance by being
attached to a royal person.

Similarly, the well-known Scottish ballad Mary Hamilton (Child
173) tells of a girl who killed her illegitimate baby and connects
this event with the king.

        Word's gane to the kitchen,
        And word's gane to the ha
        That Mary Hamilton gangs wi bairn
        To the hichest Stewart of a'.[19]

Any Stewart would do, apparently, from these words. As with Sir
Patrick Spens many efforts have been made to find the historical
event about which this ballad might have been made. Child traced a
scandal at the court of the Tsar about a Mary Hamilton who was
executed in 1719 for murdering her illegitimate baby. Child also
suggests that the mention of the Netherbow Port in some variants
points to the composition of the ballad between 1719 and 1764,
since between these dates there was such an edifice in Edinburgh.[20] I think one might add to these pointers the suggestion
that at that time the Stewarts were romantically but hopelessly in
the news. We may have here a ballad on a common theme, which has
become localised, in the manner of oral tradition, by being placed
in Edinburgh, given a heroine whose name, a well-known Scottish
one, happened to be in the news and which has been given extra
romantic appeal by being attached by a hint only to the Scottish
royal line.

A couple of ballads, The Jolly Beggar and The Gaberlunzie
Man,[21] have also been attached by tradition to the Scottish King
James V, presumably because of his habit of going in disguise
among his people. Indeed, it is said that James himself wrote one
of them. On examination, this seems unlikely. Why should a king
write a ballad about a rich man who disguises himself as a beggar,
seduces the daughter of the house in which he has been made
welcome, and then leaves, either giving her money for the nurse's
fee or cruelly saying she might have been a great lady if only she
had been honest. Certainly, this ballad is about a great man in
disguise, and certainly James's wanderings were not all innocent,
but the ballad feels like a comment by ordinary people about the
strange and sometimes dangerous ways of the great, not like a song
written by a king. It might be argued that it shows perception by
the king of how ordinary people were oppressed by the lords, but
this seems farfetched. It is surely more likely that a ballad

about a greatman in disguise should have become, at some date long after the king lived, associated with a king who went round in disguise. Although there is a variant which states that the disguised man is a king, this is surely an attribution with no foundation in historical fact.

In conclusion, there seem to be two separate comments that may be made. There is a group of four Scottish ballads, Johnie Armstrong, The Bonnie Earl of Murray, The Laird of Logie and Sir Patrick Spens, which contribute to widespread discussion about the king and how he should behave and which continued from the late Middle Ages through the Renaissance. The other group contains ballads on themes which might occur in any time and place, but which have become attached to the king because that makes them more romantic and thus more appealing. Mary Hamilton, The Jolly Beggar and The Gaberlunzie Man, I suggest, are comments on the king only in this limited sense. The Death of Queen Jane seems to belong to both groups; certainly it has a universal theme. It is firmly connected with a specific historical occasion in the six- teenth century, and also, like Sir Patrick Spens, it may be com- pared with a similar ballad found in Vedel's printed collection of 1591. As in The Death of Queen Dagmar the historical occasion is used to make a lament on a theme of universal import. Mourning may indeed represent an 'emotional truth" recreated in ballad form, and The Death of Queen Jane could be called 'a song for enjoyment and moral profit' as Vedel required his ballads to be. What emerges finally from this overview of a selection of ballads is that the well-known similarity between Danish and Scottish ballads is even more marked when specific reference is made to the sixteenth century.

Notes

1 David Buchan, 'History and Harlaw', in Ballad Studies, E B Lyle (ed), The Folklore Society, 1976, p 39.
2 A S Vedel, It Hundrede vduaalde Danske Viser (A Hundred selected Danish Ballads) (Ribe 1591). References are to the edition by Paul V Rubow, Anders Sørensøn Vedels Folkevisebog (Copenhagen, 1926).
3 Vedel, in Rubow, Vedels Folkevisebog, p 15. Translations from the Danish in this paper are by A Gardner-Medwin.
4 Svend Grundtvig, Axel Olrik, H Gruner-Nielsen, Karl-Ivar Hildeman, Erik Dal and Iorn Pio (eds), Danmarks gamle Folke- viser, 10 volumes (Copenhagen, 1853-1965). This, the standard collection of Danish ballads, was reprinted in photocopy with additional editorial material, including prefaces in English, in 1966. References are to the 1966 edition.
5 Frederick II in the Ditmarsh (Frederick den anden i Ditmarsken) DgF 175.
6 Knut Liestol and Oltke Moe (eds) re-edited by Olav Bo and Svale Solheim, Norske Folkedikting: Folkeviser (Oslo, 1958- 59), I, pp 126-7. Liestol comments on this ballad and on Sir

Patrick Spens in 'Scottish and Norwegian Ballads', in <u>Studia Norvegica</u> I (Oslo, 1946), pp 12-14.

7   <u>Jon Remorsøns Dod paa Havet</u>, DgF 375.

8   F J Child, <u>The English and Scottish Popular Ballads</u>, 5 vols (Boston 1882-98). Photographic report (New York, 1956), II, 19.

9   Thomas Percy, <u>Reliques of Ancient English Poetry</u>, 3 vols (1765) I, 71.

10 'braid letter': 'a letter on a broadsheet or long letter' (SND).

11 'lønbreffue': 'secret letter' as defined in Verner Dahlerup <u>Ordbog over det danske Sprog</u> (Copenhagen, 1932).

12 Child III, 448.

13 Child III, 455 Variant D Stanza 13.

14 Child III, 371 Variant C Stanza 22.

15 Child III, 370.

16 A <u>Crowne-Garland of Goulden Roses</u> 1612 (by Richard Johnson) edited by W Chappell, Percy Society VI (London, 1842).

17 Child III 374, Variant C, Stanza 2.

18 Child 372.

19 Child III 384, Variant A, Stanza 1.

20 Child III 381-3.

21 Gavin Greig, <u>Folk-Song of the North-East</u> XXX and XXXI, The reference is to the edition by Kenneth S Goldstein and Arthur Argo (Folklore Associates, Pennsylvania, 1963). See also Child V 115, 116 and 305.

Chapter 4

THE LOST LITERATURE OF MEDIEVAL SCOTLAND

R J Lyall

In his pioneering and neglected essay on the poetry of Dunbar, published in the collection Dreamthorp in 1863, Alexander Smith writes movingly - if a little complacently - of the huge gulf which separated the medieval poet from his modern reader. He ends:

> He is the Pompeii of British poetry. We have his works, but they are like the circumvallations of a Roman camp on the Scottish hillside. We see lines striking hither and thither, but we cannot make out the plain, or divine what purposes were served. We only know that every crumbled rampart was once a defence; that every half-obliterated fosse once swarmed with men; that it was once a station and abiding-place of human life, although for centuries now remitted to silence and blank summer sunshine. [1]

Modern textual and critical scholarship has done much since Smith's time to bridge that gulf of incomprehension, although it has been left to a more recent school of criticism to assert on more theoretical grounds - and, in my view, mistakenly - the essential alterity, or otherness, of medieval literature.[2] Over the past hundred years, the world of the Makars has been carefully, if a little erratically excavated; perhaps, indeed, we have moved beyond excavation and into reconstruction, so that the site is less like Pompeii and more like Jorvik. We have, whatever the continuing gaps in our knowledge and understanding, recovered something of the sounds and feeling of Older Scots poetry. Yet one of the most striking aspects of Scottish criticism has remained its particularist tendency: we now have excellent critical studies of Henryson and Dunbar, and to a lesser extent of Lindsay and others, but there have been few attempts to develop a more holistic view of the lie of the literary land. Corners of the site have been studied exhaustively; the relation of these parts to the whole hillside remains in many respects obscure.

Where the evidence itself is so fragmentary, we do of course constantly run into the problem of knowing how representative the materials available to us actually are. One certainty is that much of the literary culture of medieval Scotland has been irretrievably lost. Perhaps few of the books which we know to have been in the cathedral libraries of Aberdeen and Glasgow in the fifteenth century were Scottish in origin; but the almost total disappearance of those fine collections, and of others such as those of

St Andrews priory, the abbeys of Dunfermline, Kelso, Arbroath and the rest, which must surely have rivalled or surpassed them, attests to the vast scale of the loss.[3] Were it not for the unscrupulousness of a sixteenth-century agent of the Duke of Braunschweig, indeed, we would have nothing of the St Andrews or Arbroath libraries at all.[4] The line between survival and total obliteration is frighteningly small: with the exception of the Aberdeen _Breviary_, the productions of Chepman and Myllar's South Gait press are all found in single copies, all of which might well have disappeared without trace even in the course of the nineteenth century.[5] And how many other Older Scots texts survive in a unique copy?

Of all the historian's problems, the interpretation of negative evidence is among the most intractable. Consider, for example, the virtual absence of pre-Reformation sermon literature in Scotland, and compare it with the wealth of such material found in England, both in Latin and in the vernacular. The Reformers, of course, made much of the negligence of the clergy in this and other respects: appropriations, pluralism and absenteeism undoubtedly all had their effect on the life of the later medieval Church, and the lack of surviving homiletic literature before 1560 has been taken as evidence of the justification for contemporary attacks on the level of pastoral care.[6] Questions do, however, remain. Should we infer that the neglect of preaching had been a feature of the Scottish Church throughout its history? If not, why are there no sermon texts from, say, the fourteenth century, when such materials begin to occur in some numbers in England? Might we not equally infer that sermon manuscripts, both because of their content and because of their physical characteristics, might have been particularly subject to the vicissitudes of the sixteenth century? After all, not a single manuscript of a medieval Scottish play survives before the Bannatyne version of Lindsay's _Thrie Estaitis_, and yet we know from documentary sources that such plays existed in many Scottish burghs, and there is a little evidence that copies were in fact made.[7] Of burgh drama alone, we can be reasonably sure that there were at least two and probably three plays performed at certain dates in Aberdeen, a play of ly Haliblude at Corpus Christi, a Purification play at Candlemas, and perhaps a play of Belial on some other occasion, in addition to the annual festival of the Abbot of Bon-Accord. There were fifteenth-century Corpus Christi plays at Perth and Edinburgh, and in the sixteenth century there are similar references at Lanark, Dundee, Arbroath and elsewhere. There were Robin Hood plays in many places; student plays at St Andrews and Glasgow; regular plays at Court in Linlithgow and Edinburgh. Not a word survives.[8]

Although much has certainly been lost, not all of it has disappeared without trace, and R M Wilson's classic study of _The Lost Literature of Medieval England_[9] demonstrates the value of sifting through the literary and documentary debris of our archaeological site for a few shards of information. In a variety of ways, we can at least establish the size and shape of some lacunae; and it is perhaps too soon to abandon hope that more evidence will be turned up if we have a clearer idea of what we are looking for. My purpose in reviewing the evidence is therefore twofold: to map the whole area a little more thoroughly, concentrating upon the pre-Reformation period; and to begin to establish as complete a finding-list of missing pieces as is currently possible. I should add that I propose not to tackle the material generically, as Wilson did, but by the nature of the surviving record; and I am reserving for the latter part of the paper some brief discussion of the difficult question of the evidence provided by sixteenth- and seventeenth-century bibliographers.

The most unequivocal materials are those which exist in the form of surviving fragments. Technically, perhaps, we should include under this heading an acephalous text like The Talis of the Fyve Bestes, where only a small proportion of the whole has been lost. A more interesting case, from many points of view, is the substantial fragment — the first 500 lines — of the octosyllabic romance Florimound of Albanie, discovered by Marion Stewart in a manuscript in the Scottish Record Office and published by J D McClure in 1979.[10] That such a work had existed could be inferred from a reference in The Complaynt of Scotland, in a very important list to which we shall have to return; but only with the publication of the SRO fragment have we been able to begin to assess the poem's relationship to the Older Scots romance tradition. In a less strictly literary vein, we should also note the single leaf of a Scots version of Donatus' Ars minor, possibly printed by Myllar in France and recorded by Duff at the end of last century.[11]

I stated above that such pieces are unequivocal, but that is only very broadly true. The difficulties which frequently arise can be illustrated by two types of example. On the one hand, we have two fragments to which Professor A J Aitken recently drew my attention, one a pair of single leaves in the Laing collection in Edinburgh University Library (MS Laing II.318), the other a bifolium found in MS Rawlinson Q.b.4 in the Bodleian. The exciting thing about these fragments, which seem fairly probably to come from different manuscripts — the hands are different, and the Laing MS is on paper while the Rawlinson piece is on parchment[12] — is that both give texts, in Scots four-stress couplets, of works of spiritual guidance of a kind common in England but relatively rare in Scotland: the various poems in Cambridge University Library MS Kk.1.5, Ratis Raving and so on, providing the principal Scottish instances. Rawlinson, quite clearly, gives two passages from an exposition on the Pater Noster; Laing has a passage on the power of prayer and another, in some ways the most distinctive of the lot, on sin in marriage:

> The secund case *that men syn may
> Dedly in wedlaik is thus to say:
> Is quhen a man has no dreid
> With his wif to do that deid
> Throu delite and lust, that may fal sone,
> In tyme quhen it suld nocht be done;
> That is, quhen sche has maledy

---

*Please note that þ has been replaced by th throughout this collection of essays.

That sum women has commonly.
He that his wif nocht that tyme sparis,
Gif sche knew first how that sche faris
And quhat state sche is of body,
Forsuth he synnis than dedly,
For quhy, Our Lord God forbedis
That ony man that perell dredis
With his wif dele quhen that sche wate
That sche is propirly in sic state,
For perell that ar than to dreid
That mycht fal to be froyt of the deid;
For, as Sant Ierome schawis and tellis,
That in sic tyme ar gottin messellis
And sum that has no schap of man,
And fulis that neuer mair wit can,
Baith halt and lame, crukit and blind,
And dum and defe, sic may men fynd.
Quharfor, ye wemen that weddit is ...(f. 2ᵛ)

The notion that children conceived during a menstrual period are likely to be handicapped was a prevalent one in the Middle Ages, but this particular version of it, referring to Jerome and associating such circumstances with leprosy, is distinctively found in Frere Laurent's Somme des Vices et des Vertus (the Somme le Roi), and both Laing and Rawlinson fragments prove on investigation to provide parts of a version of this influential compendium. A Scots translation of the Somme le Roi would be wonderful to have, but it is unfortunately possible to go further still, for the version which these manuscripts preserve, albeit in Scottish transcriptions, is actually from northern England, the much-copied Speculum Vitae attributed to William of Nassyngton.[13] Thus, the passages on the Lord's Prayer in Rawlinson Q.b.4 correspond to ff. 62ᵛ-64ᵛ in BL MS Royal 17.C.viii, while those occurring in the Laing text are found on ff. 225ᵛ, 227ᵛ, 232ᵛ and 233ᵛ. These apparently Scots fragments are, in truth, not Scots at all.

While this means that they will have to be expunged from the DOST corpus — the Laing fragment is, for example, cited as evidence for the currency of messellis in Scots — in other respects the original provenance of the text may not make too much difference. For I doubt whether any contemporary reader of these Scottish copies would have spotted their underlying alien character: the original (and perhaps the exemplars) being Northern, a conversion to Scots orthographic practice leads to a virtually complete assimilation of the text so that, without clear cues in a title or colophon, which may of course have existed, the scribes would in effect have created a Scots version of the Speculum Vitae in a way which is not true of a less transparent text such as the Troilus and Criseyde copied for Lord Sinclair around 1488. If we are interested in the total cultural environment of Older Scots literature, rather than in the authorship or provenance of particular works, the discovery that there were almost certainly at least two manuscripts of the Speculum Vitae in Scots dress is nearly as important as the existence of an independent Scots version of the Somme le Roi would have been.

We can, I think, have more confidence in the Scottishness of the
fragmentary quotations in Scots included in Walter Bower's Scotichronicon, but here another problem arises. When, for example, the
chronicler cites the twelfth chapter of I Kings on the desirability
of choosing wise counsel and gives point to his allusion, which is
directed against David II, with a pair of Scots couplets:

> Kyngis state giff ꝡou will lede,
> Till ald mennis consall tak gude hede:
> Roboam his kyngdam lesit
> ꝡonge mennis consall for he chesit,[14]

it is impossible to tell whether we are dealing with a popular tag,
a verse specifically written for the context, or a quotation from a
larger work of political advice. Our knowledge of the advice
tradition in Scotland is generally later than Bower's day – the
Scotichronicon was complete by 1449[15] – but there is nothing
inherently improbable about the existence of such works in the
first half of the fifteenth century.[16] More problematical is
another moral passage, provoked by Bower's account of Margaret
Logie, David II's queen, who resisted his attempts to divorce her
and who travelled to Avignon to fight her case in the Papal Court.
Taking the opportunity to moralise on the vanity of the things of
this world, Bower cites in Latin Isaiah 3:24, and then adds, ut
quidam vulgariter dicet:

> And for swet smel at thi nose, stink sall thou fynd;
> And for thi gay gylt girdyll, a hard strop sal the bynd;
> And for thi crisp kell and fair hair, all beldit sall thou be;
> And as for wild and wanton luk, nothing sall thou se;
> And for thi semat semand cote, the hair sall be unset;
> For thi pantit face and proud heart, in Hell sall be thy fet.[17]

It is, in my view, not absolutely certain from the context that
Bower intends us to infer that these lines by the mysterious
'quidam' were contemporary with the events to which they are
applied; if they were, they would presumably date from between
1368, when Margaret Logie fell from favour, and her death in 1375.
Still less certain is the question of their literary context: was
only this one verse of Isaiah translated into this rather rough
ballad-measure, or is Bower quoting part of a larger work? The
inclusion of the 'pantit face and proud heart' here, which are not
found in the Vulgate text and are presumably intended to make the
reference to Queen Margaret more specific, may suggest that this
was a variation on a Biblical theme rather than part of a larger-
scale translation; the fact that the passage begins with 'And', on
the other hand, implies that something went before. Whether or not
such passages are attributable to the later fourteenth century,
these and other references in Book XIV of the Scotichronicon,
including two to a mysterious Babio and his 'comediis',[18] suggests
that Bower was familiar with a good deal of vernacular material
which no longer survives.
  Fragmentary survivals then, whether as leaves of broken-up
manuscripts or as quotations in other works, bring with them their

own difficulties. Where we have no text at all things are naturally less certain still, though sometimes simpler. An author's own references to his other works, for example, can be fairly straight-forward and presumably reliable, especially where he favours us with a plot summary:

> Thar-for, sene I ma nocht wirk
> As mynistere of Haly Kirke
> For gret eld and febilnes,
> Yet, for til eschew ydilnes,
> I hafe translatit symply
> Sume part, as I fand in story,
> Of Mary and hir sone Ihesu,
> That, as I trew, is notyt now
> In syndry placis in wryt,
> To gere deuot men think on it:
> Hou Oure Lady consawit wes,
> And of hir birth the blissitnes,
> And of dedis of hir barned,
> And hou scho can hir-selwyn led
> Demaynand hir in althing ewine
> Til scho consawit Godis Sone of Hewyne
> Thru steryng of the Haly Gest,
> Scho beand altyme vergine chaste ... [19]

This is the anonymous translator of the Saints' Lives, and he gives us a further fifty lines of precis, leaving us in no doubt of the comprehensiveness of his coverage of the lives of the Virgin and Christ, culminating in an account of the miracles of the former. This work, earlier in date than the Saints' Lives themselves, would have been among that vital first group of Older Scots texts had it not vanished without any other trace than its author's testimony: a testimony, it will be noted, which appears to include an assertion that his translation has been copied several times.[20] Such examples of self-advertisement are, however, rare, and generally less elaborate. John Ireland does refer from time to time to his other works in the course of the Meroure of Wysdome, but he seldom gives more than the barest details; the most interesting is the work De auxilio speciali,

> ... a buk writtin at the request of the noble and wourthi king thi fader, Jacobus Tertius ... [21]

This doctrine of special help is a central feature of Ireland's thought, derived directly from Gregory of Rimini and frequently alluded to in the Meroure and elsewhere. It would be good to have Ireland's treatise, not only because we are told that James III commissioned it but also because there seem to be tantalising traces of the doctrine in the works of Henryson.[22]

A much more problematical example is the mysterious translation claimed by Gavin Douglas in the 'Mensioun of thre of his pryncypall warkis' which he prefixes to the thirteenth book of the Eneados:

> ʒoir ago in myne ondantit ʒouth
> Onfructuus idlynes fleand, as I couth,
> Of Lundeys Lufe the Remeid dyd translait ... [23]

The manuscripts are unanimous about the reading 'Lundeys', while there is a 4:1 majority that it was 'Lundeys lufe' rather than 'lyfe' of which Douglas translated the remedy. It is natural to suspect an allusion to Ovid's Remedium amoris here, but Priscilla Bawcutt is in my view correct in suggesting that a scribal corruption of 'Ovidis' to 'Lundeys' is 'paleographically not very convincing'.[24] I am less convinced about the interpretation of this difficult word proposed by David Coldwell and Mrs Bawcutt, namely that 'Lundeys' is an unusual form of loun, meaning 'a whore'.[25] The DOST evidence for an intrusive final /d/ depends entirely upon the Englishman Patten's Expedition of the Duke of Somerset into Scotland (1548) and therefore seems somewhat insecure, though it is not, perhaps, altogether incredible linguistically. It does seem to me, however, to be a little forced as a reading of Douglas's line, and no Latin or French work has so far been identified which might have been the source. All I would add, by way of casting another stone into the pool, is that Lundie, derived from the parish of that name between Dundee and Coupar Angus, is a not uncommon surname in fifteenth-century Scotland, and that it is not impossible that 'Lunde' refers to an individual; although why a work of the character we would then have to infer, a forerunner perhaps of Lindsay's Squyer Meldrum, would have been composed initially in a language other than Scots I am at a loss to explain.

Somewhat less reliable than authors' statements about their own work are ascriptions by their contemporaries, but these too can yield valuable information. Thus we have the allusions in Wyntoun and in manuscripts of the Scotichronicon to Barbour's genealogy of the Stewarts, a work written in 'faire metyre'.[26] Barbour's royal service seems to have begun after the accession of Robert II in 1371, and the Stewartis Originall may have been either a celebration of the new dynasty or a vindication of John Stewart's aspirations during the difficult last years of the reign of David II. Its broad character is clear enough: it traced the Stewart line from 'Schir Dardane lord of Frigia' through the British kings and 'Fleanc de Waran'. Matthew McDiarmid is surely correct in asserting that Wyntoun's references to 'Brute' in association with the name of Barbour in these passages does not imply that the latter had produced a comprehensive British chronicle, merely that the eponymous progenitor of the Britons was a key figure in this mythological genealogy.[27] I am, however, less certain that Barbour was such a scrupulous historian that he could not have filled the gap between the ancient kings of Britain and the Stewarts' allegedly Welsh ancestors with a few intervening generations: such accounts were, after all, commonplace in late mediaeval genealogy. At any event, Barbour clearly did write a verse narrative of the Stewart descent, a work known to the learned Augustinian chroniclers Wyntoun and Bower in the first half of the fifteenth century.

This lost text is a model of certainty by comparison with the problems Wyntoun has created through his allusion to the writings of an otherwise-unknown 'Huchoun of the Aule Reale':

> He maid the gret Gest of Arthure,
> And the Anteris of Gawane,
> The Epistill als of Suete Susane.[28]

Of these three works, only the last can now be identified with
reasonable certainty: The Epistill of Susane does, of course,
survive, and the best of recent scholarly opinion agrees that it is
of English provenance, probably from the north-west.[29] Whoever this
Hugh was, therefore, he may well have been English, and the two
parts of his Arthurian writings, that large 'Gest Historiall' which
Wyntoun discusses and which clearly contained a good deal about
Arthur's Continental exploits, and the Anteris of Gawane, could
then be removed from our list of missing Scottish works. Nothing
that Wyntoun says about Hucheoun, certainly, need be taken as
implying that he was Scottish, and the identification with the
'Hugh of Eglinton' mentioned by Dunbar is purely conjectural.

Another category of evidence is the lists of texts which can
occasionally be found. Among the most reliable of these is the
original contents-list of the Asloan manuscript, including the
several quires which are now lost. Many of the missing works exist
in other copies, such as the six of Henryson's Morall Fabillis
which were once items 42-47 and the Flyting of Dunbar and Kennedy;
but others survive only in Asloan's titles. One of the more tantalising is The Buke of the Otter and the Ele, which followed The
Buke of Colkelby: it looks like a lost fable, one without any
Aesopic precedents as far as I can establish and perhaps a genuinely native contribution to the tradition. Equally suggestive is
'Master Robert Hendersonnis Dreme On fut by Forth', which is
apparently also mentioned in The Complaynt of Scotland as 'On fut
by Forth as I culd found'. The specificity of Henryson's locale is
interesting: the Forth may have been suitable for its alliterative
quality, but given the unspecific settings of most late medieval
dream-poems (Skelton's Bowge of Courte being a notable exception),
we might wonder why Henryson chose to root this one so firmly in
Scotland. Then we have a damaged and perplexing entry referring to
a work

> of the angell/Deid/ quhyte dragoun Devill wysman blak dragoun
> зoung man and of the sawlis in hell.

This is quite unlike anything else I know of, in Scotland or elsewhere: was it a dialogue or a short play, presumably on the themes
of sin and damnation? It might seem to be a more elaborate version
of the 'Ressoning betuix Deth and Man' pieces which survive in
other manuscripts, but the presence of the two dragons, white and
black, is puzzling. Another interesting group, puzzling for
different reasons, immediately follows: 'the buke of curtasy and
nortur', 'the document of schir gilbert hay', and 'the Regiment of
kingis with the buke of phisnomy'. All three were evidently works
of instruction and advice: the last-named is presumably a version
of the Secreta Secretorum, and it is interesting to find it juxta-
posed with 'the document of schir gilbert hay'. But Hay's Buke of
the Governaunce of Princis, preserved in the Abbotsford manuscript
of his prose works, does not include the physiognomical sections,
while the verse version incorporated in his Buke of King Alexander
the Conquerour does.[30] Whichever way we try to make these pieces
fit known texts, therefore, we seem to have a bit missing, while I
am unwilling even to speculate as to whether 'the document' - which

Hay himself regularly uses with the sense of 'teaching' — is a disguise for one of his known works or another, lost work. It might, for example, just fit the instructional framework of The Buke of Knychthede.

Enough has been said, I think, to demonstrate that the missing section of the Asloan manuscript contained several unique and valuable items, knowledge of which would substantially augment our understanding of the totality of Older Scots culture. How much more true that is of the lists which were so happily added to the Complaynt of Scotland as its originally straightforward propagandist purpose was diffused during the process of publication! The catalogue of forty-eight or forty-nine stories is a curious mixture, as the Complayner himself seems to realise: 'sum vas in prose', he says, 'and sum vas in verse; sum var storeis and sum var flet taylis'.[31]

Twenty of them are works which we have, in whole or in part; of these, about half are Scottish, including Golagros and Gawain, Rauf Coilȝear, Lancelot du Lac (assuming this refers to the fifteenth-century Scots version preserved in CUL MS Kk.1.5), Clariodus, Eger and Gryme, The Goldyn Targe, The Palice of Honoure, The Bruce and the Wallace, The Ryng of the Roy Robert, and now Floremond of Albanye. Of the rest, few can with absolute certainty be regarded as Scottish. We have noted 'On fut by Forth as I culd found', which must be Henryson's Dreme; there is 'the tail of syr valtir the bald leslye', which looks very like an account of the exploits of Sir Walter Leslie, a fourteenth-century Crusader and subsequently Earl of Ross; and 'the taiyl of the reyde eyttyn vitht the thre heydis', presumably bearing some relation to the story of 'the reid Etin' which Sir David Lindsay claims to have told, along with one of 'the Gyir Carling', to the young James V.[32] Several lost romances might also have been in Scots: Ferrand erl of Flandris was certainly known in Scotland in Barbour's day; The Tail of Syr Euan Arthours knycht is too vague to be helpful; and The Tail of the Brig of the Mantribil, an episode in the career of Charlemagne, is mentioned in passing by Barbour.[33] Then there is 'the tayl of the volfe of the varldis end', which the editors J A H Murray and A M Stewart wanted to emend to 'the well at the world's end', relating this title to a folk tale summarised by Murray as follows:

> ... a nasty queen, with a nastier daughter, sends the nice daughter of a king to fill a bottle with water. The nice daughter comes back ten times nicer, and marries a bonnie young prince; but the nastier daughter, when sent, comes back ten times nastier, and marries a cobbler, who licks her every day with a leather strap.[34]

The loss of a written version of this, if such ever existed, would not perhaps be a great loss, but I am not sure that this emendation is necessary. The printed title is surely intelligible: we do have beast narrators, in The Talis of the Fyve Bestes for example, and one could imagine a lupine account of the Apocalypse which would be no stranger than some of the other framed fictions of Older Scots literature. The emendation may be right, but I would suggest that we should pause before leaping at it.

Two other groups of stories can be identified in the Complayner's

list, those which seem clearly to belong in folk tradition, and
those of Classical, principally Ovidian, provenance. The first
probably incorporates 'the tail quhou the King of Estmureland
mareit the Kyngis dochtir of Vestmureland' (which may be related to
the ballad King Estmere), as well as 'The tayl of the ong Tamlene
and of the bald Brabane' - but the Complaynt does not make clear
whether this was one work or (more likely) two. There is also an
evocative but unexplained couplet:

> Arthour knycht he raid on nycht
> Witht gyltin spur and candill lycht.

The dozen Classical stories listed by the Complayner may well have
been among the 'flet talis', for it would be a bold literary archae-
ologist who attempted to construct from these scraps an Older Scots
tradition of Classical narrative. Perhaps the most interesting is
'the tayl of the thre veird systirs' which may well refer to the
Fates but which has an uncanny echo of the phrase used by both
Wyntoun and Bellenden of Macbeth's witches.[35] Even more miscellan-
eous are the thirty-eight songs supplied in a further list, several
of which apparently correspond to lyrics by Alexander Scott or to
songs 'godlified' (to use Murray's wonderful term) in the Gude and
Godlie Ballatis, itself a valuable source of information about
secular songs now lost.[36] Some of the others, like 'Sal I go vitht
ʒou to Rumbelo Fayr?', manifestly belong in a folk tradition, but
it is more difficult to place

> God sen the Duc hes byddin in France,
> And Delaubaute hed neuyr cum hame.

This must have been an anti-Albany piece, presumably dating from
the internecine feuding of 1515-17; its author was evidently
sympathetic to the cause of the Angus-Margaret Tudor faction and/
or the Homes, who were responsible for the assassination of the
Seigneur de la Bastie, Albany's agent, in September 1517.[37] Like
many such political songs, 'God sen the Duc hed byddin in France'
may have been intended for popular circulation, but it was probably the product of a more clerkly milieu. It is different in tone
from the recognisable ballad references among the Complayner's
list: 'The perssee and Mongumrye met', for example, appears to
belong within the Battle of Otterburn tradition, while in a totally
different vein we have a first line, 'The frog cam to the myl dur',
which suggests the Scottish end of a widely-distributed range,
still current, of popular frog songs.

All in all, the lists in the Complaynt of Scotland give clear
indications of a diverse cultural tradition, one in which Scots and
English works are still intermixed without differentiation but
which was even richer and more varied than our surviving texts lead
us to believe. This impression is, of course, confirmed by the
catalogues of famous authors given by Dunbar in 'Timor mortis
conturbat me' and by Lindsay in The Testament of the Papyngo. These
are too vague to be much help, since the names are in general not
associated with any texts: the principal exception is actually more
confusing, for Dunbar gives us an alternative candidate to Wyntoun's

'Hucheoun' for the authorship of The Anteris of Gawane, Clerk of
Tranent. Nine or ten of Dunbar's makars cannot be linked with any
extant work: Sir Hugh of Eglinton, Heryot, James Afflek, Sir Mungo
Lockhart of the Lee, Alexander Traill, at least one of the Roules
of Aberdeen and Corstorphine, John the Ross, and 'gud gentill
Stobo', and quite probably Mr John Clerk as well, although any of
these might of course have been responsible for one or more of the
anonymous works which survive.[38] To these we can add a further
handful of names from the Papyngo: Galbraith, Kinloch, Stewart of
Lorne, Alexander Kyd (the latter two quite probably the authors of
pieces in the Bannatyne and Maitland Folio manuscripts respectively, but presumably more prolific than these occasional survivals
admit), and Sir James Inglis, singled out by Lindsay for his
'ballatts, farses and ... plesand playis'. There is poignancy
indeed in these catalogues of famous authors, whose very existence
is in many cases now attested only by the praise of their contemporaries.
    Most of the materials which we have been surveying must origin-
ally have circulated in manuscript, but there is no reason to
suppose that the survival of early Scottish printed texts, despite
the much larger number of copies involved, have fared much better.
These, too, often survive only in a single exemplar or, as in the
case of the AUL Donatus, in a fragment, and there are occasional
traces of works now lost. John Durkan, for instance, has recently
published a note on a lost Trumpet of Honour from the reign of
James V; [39] and we must consider carefully how much weight should
be given to assertions such as that of the 1552 Parliament that

> ...thair is diuers Prentaris in this Realme that daylie and
> continuallie prentis bukis concerning the faith, ballattis,
> sangis, blasphematious rymes, alsweill of Kirkmen as temporall,
> and uthers Tragedeis alsweill in Latine as in Inglis toung ...[40]

'Daylie and continuallie' need not be interpreted too literally: it
was regularly used at this period as a formulaic expression of
widespread abuse, and is employed four times in the acts of this
same Parliament. But this allegation clearly implies a considerable volume of printing by several workshops, and all we now have
is a few editions printed by John Scot, the first of which, the
Catechism published with the authority of Archbishop Hamilton and a
Provincial Council of the Scottish Church, was actually completed
six months after the act in question.[41] We can be reasonably sure
that early editions of the Gude and Godlie Ballatis were among the
works complained of; how much more there was can only be a subject
of speculation.
    Space does not permit more than a cursory glance at the final
category of evidence, one which really deserves a paper to itself:
the testimony of the first bibliographers. This is treacherous
territory, and the witness of such writers as Thomas Dempster has
long been regarded as so unreliable that it is territory which
remains largely unexplored. The information offered by Dempster,
with great circumstantiality, about huge numbers of early writers
has coloured the data which he provided about more recent personalities, and the result has been the rejection of virtually all his

testimony. But he was only one of several collectors of bibliographical materials at this period, and by no means the most
important. What we know about the methods of the Englishman John
Bale, for example, indicates that he is a source of great significance. From his notebook Index Britannie Scriptorum we can
observe him gathering information from antiquaries, printers,
monastic libraries and a host of other sources, all of which found
its way into his two published lists, the Summarium (1548) and the
much larger Catalogus (1557).[42] The data he compiled became the
basis of virtually all later bibliographies, including those
published by Francis Thynne (1587) and by Dempster himself. In the
Catalogus, for instance, he gives four works by Sir David Lindsay:
Psittacum loquacem, Acta sui temporis, De mundi miseriis, and
Testamentum Cardinalis Betoni. The first and the last are immediately identifiable, while De mundi miseriis might conceivably
refer to the Complaynt; Acta sui temporis is harder to place. But
from the Index we know that he derived this list from two London
booksellers, John Day and John Allen, and there is no reason to
doubt that Bale had actually seen these books. Thynne follows him,
but adds Dialogi aulici et experientie, Somnium and Deploratio
mortis Reginae Magdalenae, all of which were of course available
in print by 1587 (and, for that matter, by 1557). Dempster unfortunately, if understandably, ignores the Reformer Lindsay, but his
contemporary David Buchanan gives substantially the same list as
Thynne, omitting only the Dialogue of Experience and the Courtier
and adding the Justing betuix Watson and Barbour. Another early
seventeenth-century bibliographer, Gilbert Gray, writing in 1623,
also makes his own adjustments, leaving out the Dreme but including both the Dialog and De quattuor Monarchiis, which are clearly
the same work. Presumably Gray had seen a copy of the Dialog/
Monarche and did not realise that it was the same work listed as
the Dialogus by Thynne and his successors.

These revisions to the Lindsay canon prove that the early
bibliographers operated to some degree independently, despite
their tendency to adopt fairly uncritically the statements of
their sources. In the case of the Lindsay list, each successive
writer makes his own additions and subtractions, revealing his
capacity for independent, if sometimes mistaken, judgement. I
suggest that we should look carefully at such attributions,
especially where they come from Bale, and that some credence
should be given to the former existence of works like Gavin
Douglas's Narrationes aureae and James I's Cantilenae scoticae,
both of which are listed by the English bibliographer. And as the
Lindsay listings show, works described by Latin titles might
easily be in the vernacular. The claims of the bibliographers must
always be treated sceptically, I admit; but Bale and Thynne had no
reason to invent Scots works. A greater risk, as we have just
seen, is that a work may appear under two titles, and sometimes
parts of a text are given separate existences; a clear case of
this is the way in which Bale (and everyone after him) lists the
prefatory materials of Bellenden's translation of Boece as
separate treatises.[43] But if in general the lists of works of
known authors are more reliable than they have often been thought
to be, greater weight should perhaps also be given to the evidence

about less well-known names (at least in a literary context), such
as that of William Scheves, archbishop of St Andrews, stated by
David Buchanan to have written treatises De conjunctione siderum
et planetarum and De futuris prenoscendis.[44] Which reader of
Henryson's Testament of Cresseid and 'Confessioun of the Fox'
would not want to catch a glimpse of one or other of these lost
works? The full variety and richness of later medieval Scottish
culture is only apparent when we begin to identify the extent of
what has gone, and to reject uncritically the help available from
these admittedly difficult quarters is merely to reverse the error
which has made us so mistrustful in the first place. The archaeo-
logist who refuses to attend to the earliest descriptions of the
landscape will never fully understand the evidence uncovered by
his trowel.

Notes

1   Alexander Smith, Dreamthorp (London/Edinburgh 1863; 2nd edn
    London 1874), p 92.
2   See, in particular, Hans Robert Jauss, Alterität und Moderni-
    tät der Mittelalterlichen Literatur (Munich, 1977), pp 9-47.
    Jauss traces the idea to Paul Zumthor's Essai de poétique
    médiévale (Paris, 1972).
3   For inventories of Aberdeen cathedral library in 1436 and
    1464, see Abdn Reg., II, 127-38, 154-9; there is an inventory
    of Glasgow cathedral library in Glas. Reg., II, 334-9.
4   For an account of the visit of Marcus Wagner to Scotland in
    1553, see Copiale Prioratus Sanctiandree, J H Baxter (ed) (St
    Andrews, 1930), pp. xx-xxxi.
5   The vicissitudes of the Chepman and Myllar prints are de-
    scribed in William Beattie's introduction to the facsimile
    edition (Edinburgh, 1950), pp. xx-xxiv.
6   The claim that preaching was neglected does not only come
    from the Reforming side: the General Council of 1549 declared
    that bishops and rectors should preach 'at least four times a
    year'. Statuta, J Robertson (ed) (Edinburgh, 1866), II
    95-100).
7   Thus, Walter Balcancole was paid five shillings in 1449 by
    the Aberdeen council pro scriptura ludi in festo Corporis
    Christi; see A J Mill, Mediaeval Plays in Scotland (Edinburgh
    and London, 1927), p 117. This presumably refers to copying
    rather than to composition, as does a reference to a payment
    for writing a play (probably the Candlemas play) in an unpub-
    lished set of Dean of Guild's accounts for 1471-72, also from
    Aberdeen, now in the Beinecke Library, Yale University.
8   Most of the surviving evidence is collected by Mill, op.cit.
9   R M Wilson, The Lost Literature of Medieval England (London,
    1952).
10 J D McClure, 'The Florimond Fragment', SLJ, Suppl. 10 (Summer
    1979), 1-10.

11   E Gordon Duff, 'Notes on a Leaf of an Early Scottish Donatus
      printed in Black Letter', Publications of the Edinburgh Bib-
      liographical Society, I, 11 (1892-93).
12   This is not, of course, absolutely conclusive evidence: it is
      not unknown for the outer (and, occasionally, the central)
      leaves of the quires of paper manuscripts to be of parchment,
      presumably to strengthen the whole. But the gap between the
      two Rawlinson passages is insufficient for these leaves to be
      the outermost ones of any reasonably-sized gathering.
13   See Robert Raymo's summary in A Manual of the Writings in
      Middle English 1050-1500, VII (New York 1986), pp 2261-2.
14   Walter Bower, Scotichronicon, J Goodall (ed) (Edinburgh,
      1747-9), II, 344.
15   D E R Watt, 'Editing Walter Bower's Scotichronicon', in
      Proceedings of the Third International Conference on Scottish
      Language and Literature (Medieval and Renaissance), Roderick
      J Lyall and Felicity Riddy (eds) (Stirling/Glasgow, 1981), pp
      161-76, at 164.
16   There is, clearly, an element of political advice in Barbour's
      Brus, and the European tradition of advice to princes flour-
      ished throughout the Middle Ages. It is also reflected in
      Holland's Buke of the Howlat, which was written about the
      time of the completion of Barbour's chronicle.
17   Bower, Goodall (ed), II, 374-5.
18   Ibid, II, 376-7.
19   Legends of the Saints, W M Metcalfe (ed), 3 vols, STS
      (Edinburgh, 1896), I, 2.
20   There is, I would concede, an ambiguity here: is 'That ... is
      notyt now/In syndry placis in wryt' referring to copies of
      the Scots translation, or does the compiler mean that the
      legend of the Virgin exists in many versions?
21   John Ireland, The Meroure of Wysdome, II, F Quinn (ed), STS
      (Edinburgh, 1965), p 131.
22   Morall Fabillis, 2434-47, Poems, Denton Fox (ed) (Oxford,
      1981), p 91; and 'The Praise of Age' (Bannatyne version),
      17-24, ibid, p 166. Professor Fox suggests that these
      references to 'special grace' reflect Protestant revision,
      but there is a clear possibility, particularly in the former
      case, that Henryson was aware of the doctrine of special
      help, introduced into Scotland by John Ireland.
23   Gavin Douglas, Virgil's Aeneid, David F C Coldwell (ed), 4
      vols, STS (Edinburgh, 1957-64), IV, 139.
24   Priscilla Bawcutt, Gavin Douglas (Edinburgh, 1976), p 49.
25   Coldwell, op.cit., I, 256; Bawcutt, op.cit., p 215.
26   Wyntoun, Original Chronicle, VIII, 1411-16, F J Amours (ed),
      7 vols, STS (Edinburgh, 1902-14), V, 256.
27   Barbour, Bruce, Matthew P McDiarmid and James A C Stevenson
      (eds), 3 vols, STS (Edinburgh, 1980-85), I, 18.
28   Wyntoun, V, 4232-4, Amours (ed), IV, 22.
29   See, for example, E J Dobson's review of the edition by Alice
      Miskimin, N & Q n.s. 216 (1971), 110-16.
30   Cf. John Cartwright, 'Sir Gilbert Hay and the Alexander
      Tradition' in Scottish Language and Literature, Medieval and

Renaissance, Dietrich Strauss and Horst W Drescher (eds) (Frankfurt am Main 1986), pp 229–38, at 234.

31 Complaynt of Scotlande, A M Stewart (ed), STS (Edinburgh, 1979), p 50.

32 Sir David Lindsay, The Dreme, 45, Works, Douglas Hamer (ed), 4 vols, STS (Edinburgh, 1931–36), I, 5.

33 See Barbour's Bruce, McDiarmid and Stevenson (eds), I, 74.

34 The Complaynt of Scotland, J A H Murray (ed), EETS (London, 1872), p. lxxiii.

35 Wyntoun, VI, 1902, Amours (ed), IV, 274; Bellenden, The Chronicles of Scotland, R W Chambers, Edith C Batho and G Winifred Husbands (eds), 2 vols, STS (Edinburgh, 1938–41), II, 149–50.

36 See H M Shire, Dance, Song and Poetry of the Court of Scotland under King James VI (Cambridge, 1969), pp 25–33.

37 For a brief summary of the complex politics of this period, see Gordon Donaldson, Scotland: James V–James VII (Edinburgh, 1965), pp 31–8.

38 The little that is known about these shadowy figures is briefly summarised by James Kinsley in his edition of Dunbar's Poems (Oxford, 1979), pp 354–6.

39 John Durkan, 'The Trumpet of Honour (Edinburgh?, 1537)', The Bibliothek 11 (1982–83), 1–2.

40 APS, II, 488–9.

41 The colophon is dated 29 August 1552; see The Catechism of John Hamilton, T G Law (ed) (Oxford, 1884), p 292.

42 John Bale, Illustrium Maioris Britannie scriptorum summarium (Ipswich: John Overton 1548); and Scriptorum illustrium maioris Brytannie catalogus (Basel: J Oporinus 1557). Cf Index Britannie scriptorum, R L Poole (ed) (Oxford, 1902).

43 Bellenden, Chronicles, Chambers, Batho and Husbands, (eds), II, 453–5. This valuable biographical and bibliographical note was contributed by E A Sheppard.

44 David Buchanan, De scriptoribus Scotis (Bannatyne Club, Edinburgh, 1837), pp 88–9.

Chapter 5

SCOTLAND'S GREATEST COMPOSER: AN INTRODUCTION TO ROBERT CARVER
(1487-1566)

Richard Turbet

Robert Carver was born exactly five hundred years ago. A combination of his own excellence and, it has to be admitted, the paucity
of what has come after, leaves him unchallenged as Scotland's
greatest composer. The reasons for this abject and criminal neglect
of such music in Scotland have been documented elsewhere[1] and in
any case my purpose is to concentrate on Carver. First I shall
provide a brief biography; then an account of his music, its manuscript source and printed editions; an annotated bibliography of
criticism; a critical discography; and finally a brief summary of
his position in the musical history of Europe.

Biography

The most comprehensive account of Carver's life occurs in Isobel
Woods's doctoral thesis 'The Carvor Choirbook' (see below). On
pages 13-25 she provides evidence that Carver (whose name she
spells Carvor throughout - as irritating as the recent book on John
Dunstable whose publisher allowed the author to affect the spelling
Dunstaple)[2] was born in 1487 and that he used the alias Arnot,
either because he was the natural son of one of that powerful
family (such as David, archdeacon of Lothian) or was related to it
and wished to emphasise the connection. There was a David Kervour
employed at the Chapel Royal in Stirling, where the composer
subsequently spent much of his career, who could have been Robert's
father. Robert himself seems to have become a monk in 1503 and may
have entered the University of Louvain in 1504. Musically he seems
to have been active at the Abbey of Scone near Perth where, in
1511, he became a canon, and in Stirling, at the parish church and
the Chapel Royal. He is not mentioned after 1566.

Music

Only seven of Carver's pieces survive, all in the Carver choirbook, sometimes known as the Scone antiphonary, MS 5.1.15 in the
Advocates' Library now part of the National Library of Scotland in
Edinburgh. Other pieces may exist elsewhere and possibly within the
same manuscript, unattributed. Those surviving consist of five
masses and two motets. The masses are in ten parts (Dum sacrum

mysterium) possibly composed in 1508 and sung at the coronation of
James V in 1513, in six parts, in five parts (Fera pessima) and two
in four parts: Pater creator omnium dated 1546, and the only
British mass based on the popular song L'homme arme. Of the two
motets, Gaude flore virginali is in five parts, O bone Iesu in no
fewer than nineteen.

A complete edition of the works of Robert Carver is scheduled to
begin publication in 1988. The publishers are Bardic Edition
(Aylesbury, England) and the works have been edited by Muriel
Brown. The first work scheduled to be published is the mass in ten
parts Dum sacrum mysterium, and included in the edition of this
mass will be a full discussion of the biographical evidence
concerning Carver. (The same house has also published a motet in
twelve parts, In memoriam Robert Carver by Ronald Stevenson). Of
the masses, only L'homme arme exists in another modern published
edition, by Kenneth Elliott, Music of Scotland, 1500-1700, Musica
Britannica, vol 15 (London, 1975). The motets form the as yet sole
contents of Robert Carver: opera omnia, edited by Denis Stevens,
Corpus mensurabilis musicae, no. 16 (Rome, 1959). O bone Iesu is
also in the volume of Musica Britannica mentioned above, but was
first published nearly forty years earlier in an edition by J A
Fuller Maitland, Yearbook Press series of anthems and church music,
no. 43 (London: Deane, 1926). All of Carver's then unpublished
masses were edited by Isobel Woods for her thesis. D James Ross
(Nairn Academy, Nairn, Scotland) has edited the mass in four parts
Pater creator omnium according to contemporary rules of faburden,[3]
and copies of his manuscript are available to scholars and choirs.

Bibliography

Fuller-Maitland, J A, 'A Scottish composer of the 16th century'.
   Gedenkboek aangeboden aan Dr D F Scheurleer op zijn 70sten
   verjaardag, bijdragen van vrienden en vereerders op het gebied
   der muziek. 's-Gravenhage (Nijhoff, 1925), pp 119-22. Consists
   of a brief biographical sketch and an introduction to O bone
   Iesu. The correct form of the author's surname is Fuller
   Maitland.
Steven, Denis, 'Robert Carver and his motets'. Monthly musical
   record 89 (1959), pp 170-5. After a brief biographical sketch,
   provides an introduction to the texts and music of Carver's two
   surviving motets.
Elliott, Kenneth. 'The Carver choirbook'. Music and letters 45
   (1960), pp 349-57. Reviews contents of entire manuscript
   including items not attributed to Carver himself. Some
   additional information, such as the identity of the cantus
   firmus of the mass for five voices, is included in Elliott's
   article about Carver in The new Grove Dictionary of Music and
   Musicians (London, 1980). An enlargement of Elliott's plan forms
   the basis of Dr Woods's dissertation (see below), which
   nevertheless contains some disagreements concerning, for
   instance, interpretation of biographical material and the title
   of the mass mentioned above.
Woods, Isobel Paterson, 'The Carvor choirbook', Dissertation,

Princeton University, 1984. So far the outstanding study of Carver and his music. The biographical evidence is carefully weighed and tentative conclusions offered. The book itself is studied palaeographically and its contents analysed individually. The transcriptions of hitherto unpublished items by Carver were valuable until superseded by Muriel Brown's complete edition, mentioned above.

Marshall, John, 'When music was musyck', The Scotsman Magazine 6 part vii (1985), pp 22-3. Brief but informative introduction to Carver's music with account of the revival of performances of his music in the years leading up to his quincentenary.

Ross, D James, 'Robert Carver: a quincentenary celebration', Brio 24 (1987), pp 14-25. A revision of the author's paper to the 1987 annual study weekend of the United Kingdom branch of the International Association of Music Libraries held appropriately that year in Scotland, at St Andrews. The author weighs conflicting biographical evidence, analyses all the music with special attention to the question of performance, and suggests some additions to the Carver canon.

Ross, D James, 'Robert Carver (1487-1566): a sixteenth century Scottish master of polyphony', The Consort 43 (1987), pp 1-12. Based on the previous article. In both, the author is keen to draw attention not only to Carver's uniqueness but to his affinities with composers as varied as Dufay, Josquin, those of the Eton Choirbook, and his younger contemporary the Englishman John Sheppard. Both articles are well illustrated.

Ross, D James, 'Robert Carver: quincentenary of a neglected genius', Musical Opinion 110 (1987), pp 358-60. Condensed and unillustrated version of IAML:UK paper, above. James Ross is also contributing an essay on Carver and Byrd to a volume of essays scheduled to be published in 1992 to celebrate the 450th anniversary of the birth of Byrd, and is the author of Music Fyne: the Art of Music in 16th-century Scotland (London, forthcoming).

Discography

The efforts of the scholars mentioned above have ensured some performances of Carver's music this century. The number of such performances has risen in recent years through the efforts of James Reid Baxter (Luxembourg). Since 1982 he has organised a reconstruction of a mass in Aberdeen, either in St Machar's Cathedral or King's College Chapel, using music by Carver for the ordinary. In 1985 he founded the Carver Choir which is based in Aberdeen and performs mainly Carver's music throughout the northeast of Scotland from Inverness to Fife. The choir is also dedicated to recording works by Carver hitherto unrecorded, as will be seen from the following discography.

At the time of writing (February 1988) three of Carver's masses have been commercially recorded. They can be purchased in the normal way, or heard in such sound archives as the Scottish Music Information Centre in Glasgow or the National Sound Archive in London. The first to be recorded was L'homme armé by the Renais-

sance Group of the University of St Andrews, on Alpha, ACA 518.
This is a large choir of over thirty, with contraltos rather than
counter-tenors, and their recording was in the vanguard of the
Carver revival. Solo voices sing the sections of reduced scoring
and, although Carver's relentless creativity occasionally affects
the choir's intonation, this is a performance of considerable
impact. If the final Agnus does not quite come to terms with
Carver's mysticism, the exuberant Gloria is a credit to the choir
and indeed to Carver's music, especially from 'nostram' to the
close.

The next mass to be recorded was Fera pessima by the Carver
Choir on Tape to Disc Service TD 8720, a cassette, distributed by
Donselco Ltd, Centre 11, 11 Thistle Place, Aberdeen, Scotland.
Using counter-tenors rather than contraltos, this choir is less
than half the size of the Renaissance Group and is more 'authentic', or less 'Romantic', in its interpretations. Again Carver's
unrelenting inventiveness places some strain on the soloists in
the passages of reduced scoring, and occasional insecurities of
intonation obtrude, but there is an electrifying sense of commitment throughout the performance and an excellent awareness of
idiom. These are best conveyed in the huge final Agnus, of which
more later.

The mass for six voices has also been recorded by the Carver
Choir, cassette TD 8801. After again making allowance for the
demands placed by the restless and unflagging Carver on what is an
admirable amateur choir, there is some thrilling singing in the
Gloria and in the alarmingly martial 'Dona nobis pacem', and some
sensitive and well-balanced solo trios in the Creed. Both masses
were recorded in the superb acoustic of St Andrew's Cathedral,
Aberdeen. Between movements of the mass for six voices, Mark
Duthie plays three hitherto unrecorded organ pieces by Byrd. The
Sanctus of this mass has been recorded by the King's Singers on
volume 1 of the History of Scottish music, Scottish Records SRCM
111, but this is one of that fine ensemble's least idiomatic
renditions and, now that the entire mass has been recorded by the
Carver Choir, is not a recommendation.

By the time this article is published it is intended that the
Carver Choir will have recorded Carver's other mass for four
voices, Pater creator omnium, on the same label as the previous
two masses. There also exists a good recording of the anonymous
Scottish mass for six voices Cantate Domino by the Choir of
Paisley Abbey, on Alpha ACA 532. In the articles cited above James
Ross gives his reasons for relating this work to Carver and for
possibly introducing it into the Carver corpus. It remains to
mention the motet Gaude flore virginali which has been robustly
recorded by the Edinburgh University Renaissance Singers, on EURS
Records, EURS 001. Conspicuously absent from this discography are
the nineteen-part motet O bone Iesu and the ten-part mass Dum
sacrum mysterium, potentially a stunning pairing.

The Historical Context

Although it is quite easy to place Carver in an historical context,

what is most obvious and tangible in his music is its burning
individualism. Indeed, much that has been written to describe the
music of Byrd, England's greatest composer, in the monographs by
Fellowes, Neighbour and Kerman, can well be applied to Carver.[4]
There is the same exploitation of scoring and melodic line to
produce extreme intensity in their respective five-part masses.
Carver seems to have owed some of his technique to the composers
in the Eton Choirbook, if one compares a work such as Wylkynson's
nine-part Salve Regina with the mighty O bone Iesu, but the most
tantalising relationships with Englishmen are with Sheppard and
Tallis. Although it has been suggested that the much younger
Sheppard influenced Carver's late mass Fera pessima, it cannot be
outwith the bounds of possibility that Carver's attitude to
scoring, spacing and dissonance in fact influenced Sheppard and
helped him to evolve his unique sound-world. Perhaps too Carver's
nineteen-part O bone Iesu was known to Tallis before he composed
his forty-part Spem in alium. Certainly there was north-south
musical traffic between the two countries, in the person of Robert
Johnson. More certain is the influence on Carver of Dufay, whose
own mass L'homme arme is in the Carver choirbook, and Josquin,
whose use of the beguiling harmonic sequence $\frac{5}{3\flat}\ \frac{4}{2}\ \frac{4}{2}\ ^{76}$ in, for
instance, the Agnus of his mass La sol fa re mi, is echoed in
Carver's six-part Credo at the word 'factus'. Particularly
exciting is to trace the continuity of the development of Scottish
music from the 'Pleni sunt coeli' section of the mass Fera pessima
with its apparent debt to improvisatory piping, to a modern work
such as Francis George Scott's haunting song St Brendan's
graveyard with its debt to pibroch.[5]
    Most exciting of all remains Carver's music itself, for its
inherent quality and for its emotional and structural range. Most
immediately impressive is the overwhelming but carefully constructed O bone Iesu in nineteen parts. Yet within a musical
corpus of only seven known works are also pieces as different as
the exuberant mass Dum sacrum mysterium and the austere Pater
creator omnium; and what are we to make of the creativity of a
composer who can write two such varied settings of 'Dona nobis
pacem' as those which conclude his masses for five and six voices?
Indeed Carver's control and exploitation of melody and sonority in
the former, Fera pessima, marks it out as one of the very greatest
of all settings of the mass ordinary. A passage such as 'lumen de
lumine' from the Creed seems timeless in that it is hard to
realise today that the technical, intellectual and conceptual
equipment existed at that time to create such music. But it is in
the final Agnus that Carver's inspiration reaches its height.
Here, over a steady pulse like the tread of a funeral march,
Carver winds up the tension, exploiting extremity of vocal range,
variety of scoring and of note-value, towards a sustained climax
during the final repetition of 'pacem'; whereafter a melismatic
phrase in the bass, itself an inversion of a carillon figure heard
earlier at the first appearance of the words 'dona nobis pacem',
releases the tension, and the mass concludes with a mystical
resignation, born of purgation from an ecstatic spiritual experience: the most sublime music ever to have flowed from a Scottish
pen.

Appendix

Not long after this paper was delivered, there was a performance of Carver's mass <u>Fera pessima</u> in Manchester, England. This occasioned a short but scholarly programme note by David Fallows, which appears below with his permission. The biographical information in the first paragraph can be adjusted by reference to Dr Woods's dissertation. The works by Machaut and Compère to which he refers are respectively the motets <u>Fons tocius / O livoris feritas</u> with the melody <u>Fera pessima</u> in the tenor, or lowest of the three parts, and <u>Sola caret monstris</u> (SATTB) with the melody <u>Fera pessima</u> in the two tenor parts in canon at the fifth.

Robert Carver counts as the most prolific known Renaissance composer in Scotland. Born in about 1490, he was evidently connected with the Royal Chapel by the time of James V's coronation in 1513, for which he composed a Mass in ten voices. He is last heard of in 1546, the date on the last of his five surviving Mass cycles.

Scotland at this stage looked primarily to France for its cultural model; so it is perhaps surprising that Carver's work is so florid, very much in the style of the English composers in the first years of the 16th century. But in the court of the handsome and music-loving James V (1513-42) Carver would have had access to a wide range of culture. Even so, his style remains highly individual, particularly in its use of irregular dissonance patterns that would scarcely have been used in either England or France.

This five-voice Mass is loosely based on the chant 'Fera pessima' which appears occasionally in the baritone voice – particularly in the 'motto' opening that begins each movement – and otherwise permeates the texture. This chant had already been used by Machaut in the 14th century and Loyset Compere in the 15th, both times in contexts concerned with severe strife between church and state. It is not too much to suppose that Carver composed his Mass in similar circumstances. Perhaps, for example, it was associated with the fight between King and Pope for control of the Scottish churches in 1539-40, which gave rise also to George Buchanan's satirical poems <u>Palinodia</u> and <u>Franciscanus</u> as well as Sir David Lindsay's play <u>The Satire of the Three Estates</u>.

Characteristically for its date, each movement is in two main sections: the first in triple time and the second in duple. The cycle has four long and elaborate movements: Gloria and Credo will be performed in the first half of the concert; we shall omit the Sanctus; the enormous Agnus Dei with its extended final melisma will open the second half of the concert.

Notes

1   For instance Cedric Thorpe Davie, Scotland's music (Edinburgh, 1980), pp 35-6.

2   Margaret Bent, Dunstaple, Oxford studies of composers (London, 1981).

3   See 'An anonymous Scottish treatise on music from the sixteenth century: British Museum, Additional Manuscript 4911: edition and commentary', by Judson Dana Maynard. (Dissertation, Indiana University, 1961).

4   Edmund H Fellowes, William Byrd, 2nd edn (London, 1948). Oliver Neighbour, The consort and keyboard music of William Byrd, The music of William Byrd, vol 3 (London, 1978). Joseph Kerman, The masses and motets of William Byrd, The music of William Byrd, vol 1 (London, 1981). See also the introduction to chapter II of Richard Turbet, William Byrd: a guide to research, Garland composer resource manuals, vol 7 (New York, 1987).

5   See also John Purser, 'The celebrated trumpet tune', Stretto 7, part iv (1988), p 10, for a reference to the probability that Carver is echoing contemporary trumpet tunes at the beginning of his mass for six voices.

Since this paper was written up for publication there have been two developments. First, Donselco Ltd has moved to 27 Rose Street, Aberdeen, Scotland. Second, in October 1988 the Renaissance Group of the University of St Andrews released a recording on black disc and cassette of Carver's Missa Dum sacrum mysterium for ten voices with his motet Gaude flore virginali on Alpha ACA 582.

Chapter 6

STORIES AND STORYTELLING IN BARBOUR'S BRUS

W F H Nicolaisen

Predictions have a habit of misfiring, but surely even the most
surly and sceptical of academic sour-pusses must agree that a
lengthy tale written in 1375 in octosyllabic couplets by an Aberdeen archdeacon in his mid-fifties about one of Scotland's great
national heroes, the victor of Bannockburn, eminently qualifies
under the label of appropriateness in the present context and
therefore deserves our attention. As to the special focus of our
discussion, the nature and function of stories and storytelling in
Barbour's 'carefully planned and purposeful narrative',[1] composed
before Chaucer's great works, its degree of suitability is a more
personal matter. For practically all my life, I have been fascin-
ated by the ubiquitous phenomenon of story, especially in the
folk-cultural register, and in recent years I have made several
attempts to come to grips with it by observing, describing and
analysing it in as many environments and applications as possible.[2] This is another one of those attempts, for I find the
temptation irresistible to explore some of the ways in which a
fourteenth century Sir Walter (not a Geoffrey Barrow, mind you, or
a Nigel Tranter, but a medieval 'Author of Waverley') harnesses
the storying potential available to him for his own narrative
purposes.
    I am, in this respect, less concerned with the character of the
poem as a whole, although something will have to be said about
this too, than with its structuring features and narrative ingredients. A writer who is as self-conscious and adamant about his
role and credentials as a storyteller as John Barbour can be
expected not only to have a good nose for what might be suitable
grist for his narrative mill, but also to be sensitive to the
techniques and accomplishments of other tellers of tales; particularly in his quest for retellable narrative items that can be
incorporated in a larger, adulatory biographical storying framework. What is there in the narrative substance of the Brus, the
question seems to be, that has been filtered into the poem via
Barbour's own craftiness as a romancer, in pursuit of those un-
identical twins suthfastnes and carpyng, uneasy bedfellows in the
aftermath of the uncomfortable semantic divorce of story and
history?
    Before I try to answer this and related questions, it is only
fair that I should say a little about my own perception of story
and our need for it. To put it in the proverbial nutshell, for me
story creates the past; by which I mean that story not merely

recreates it, not merely opens a window on it, not merely makes the past accessible, but truly <u>creates</u> it, <u>makes</u> it. In other words, I have become convinced that the past does not exist until it has been narrated. This is a conviction that has not come as a flash of inspiration but as a hard-earned piece of experience which, because I have acquired it so gradually and so effortfully, I would find very difficult to let go again; in fact, I find it difficult to imagine that there was a time when I did not know it and therefore did not have that conviction.

Closely linked with it is the realisation that only the past is narratable, and by that I mean the past as both time and place,[3] whereas the present is the time in which the past is narrated and the future provides both new pasts and new presents in which these pasts can be narrated. In fact, the present narrating of the past can become part of the past! The experience of narrated pasts enables us to cope with the present and to face what would otherwise be an overwhelming future. The wonderful thing about these interwoven and very necessary processes is that they have built into them pleasurable entertaining qualities, so that the creation of the past through narration becomes, beyond necessity, a delight. Perhaps that explains the ubiquity of the cultural phenomenon 'story'. Apart from naming, storytelling must be the most essential, socialising human preoccupation.

Naturally, this perspective has several important implications, only two of which are applicable to our topic. One is that, as the Latin verb <u>narrare</u> is cognate with both the Latin adjective <u>gnarus</u> 'knowing, acquainted with, expert, skilful' and Greek <u>gnosis</u>, the idea of narrative can be said to refer to 'a mode of knowledge emerging from action' - one knows by doing, or, equally plausibly to knowledge motivated through the word in time, one converts knowing into telling. Consequently, the narrator, the storyteller in this sense, finds his place close to the gnome, the teacher, the wise man: he is one who narrates because he has <u>gnosis</u> and is <u>gnarus</u> - 'the skilful sage'.[4] The other unavoidable complication is that <u>story</u>, which paradoxically is both process and product of the creative act of narration, despite the fateful etymological bifurcation which I referred to earlier, straddles the apparently irreconcilable opposition of fact and fiction, blurs the boundary between subjective fabulation and objective reporting, thus approximating 'fictitious reality', the time and place of the mind, to what is often called 'truth'. As a result, all narrated chunks of the past are potentially 'true', even when on the surface they contradict each other. There are as many true pasts as there are tellings of them, unless deliberate deception is intended. The question is not whether something actually happened in one way or another - that we will never know - but whether it has been convincingly and deliciously narrated. The storyteller who gives us the past gives us something that is believable; and the contract between teller and listener contains a clause which demands that the teller, the purveyor of story, be credible and the listener, the consumer of story, be credulous. Otherwise the credibility of the whole transaction is in danger.

For the exercise in hand this general view of story has some very specific practical consequences. Above, all, it permits me to

display a good deal of tolerance when it comes to defining
precisely what The Brus[5] is in terms of conventionally accepted
genres. As one critic rightly says, it 'is without parallel in the
Middle Ages',[6] which could be particularly puzzling as it is the
first major surviving literary work in Scots. Without any known
antecedents, influences and models are difficult to pinpoint and
there is room for plenty of speculation. When perceiving The Brus
fundamentally as a story – which is why I like Lois Ebin's description of it as a 'carefully planned and purposeful narrative',
quoted above (p 55) – or narrative deliberately and validly creating a biographical, as well as a political, national, ideological
and martial past, it is not terribly important to be able to
pigeon-hole it incontrovertibly, to the satisfaction of everybody
in the literary trade. What in other types of enquiry are legitimate concerns, become secondary considerations under the set of
traffic rules by which I propose to operate in this essay. It may
well be true that The Brus is 'in form and style a metrical
romance'[7] with strong affiliations to the chanson de geste; it may
well be regarded as an 'exemplum';[8] one might with justification
call it 'a verse chronicle written in the spirit of a noble
romance',[9] a 'narrative of heroic action'[10] which is both historical document and literary artifact'[11] or, in the words of
another writer, observe that 'beneath the garnishings of poetry
... is a record of recent violent historical events';[12] or one can
try to combine a number of concepts in order to come to terms with
its remarkable multifacetedness, by summing it up as bridging 'a
gap between history and literature, using the techniques of both
chronicle and romance to tell [an] essentially true story.[13]

When all is said and done it remains, above all, 'a rousing
story,'[14] demanding to be treated as such, even if this means
sacrificing some of our puzzlement as well as most of our genre-
mongering definitions. Although these are, as I have said, by no
means irrelevant in certain scholarly climates, they are not going
to be very helpful in our current undertaking because there is no
room in them for what Wittig has so felicitously referred to as
'the gusto of the story-teller' in connection with 'the Scots
approach to Roxburgh Castle in the dusk of Shrove Tuesday, on all
fours'[15] (X, 384-385).

Obviously some much more basic considerations and perhaps even
concepts concerning the art of storytelling and the nature of
story are needed to assist us at this point; some of these may
well be derived from kinds of ways in which students of folk-
narrative have over the years studied the marchen or folktale
proper. As has been noted before, there is plenty of evidence to
suggest that most of the accounts, anecdotes, gossip, rumours, etc
which have gone into the making of The Brus have understandably
come from oral rather than written tradition.[16] Phrases like 'as
ik hard say' (IX, 120), 'as ik hard tell' (IX, 660), 'and ʒeyt
haiff ik hard som men say' (XIII, 244), 'As ik heff hard syndry
men say' (XVIII, 322), 'ik hard oft-sys tell' (XV, 553), are too
numerous and too strategic in their position to be regarded as
mere line and rhyme fillers. Their genuineness is underlined
further by their negative counterparts like 'I wate nocht' (XII,
435), or, with reference to those who died at Bannockburn, '& oyer

ma/Yat yar namys nocht tell can I' (XIII, 472-473), or, on a later
occasion, 'to surnam Maundwell had he/His awn name I can nocht
say' (XV, 208). Even stronger support for the oral origins of his
evidence comes from the admission, after a long and detailed
account of the King's escape from John of Lorne's sleuth-hound,
that there is another story in circulation which explains his
survival differently:

> Bot sum men sayis yis eschaping
> Apon ane oyer maner fell
> Yan throw ye wading ...' (VII, 54-6)

which is such a central part of the first version. In fact, after
a somewhat uncomfortable indecisiveness concerning these two conflicting versions which both seem to be true creations of this
chunk of the past,

> Bot quheyir yis eschaping fell
> As I tauld fyrst or I now tell   (VII, 75-6)

there is an almost audible sigh of relief from the honest storying
broker

> I wate weill without lesing
> Yat at ye burn eschapyt ye king   (VII, 77-8)

Stronger yet is Barbour's naming of two of his informants who participated in the events the stories of which he is retelling as
part of The Brus. With regard to Sir Edward Bruce's exploits in
Galloway,

> Schyr Alane off Catkert be name
> Tauld me yis taile as I sall tell:
> Gret myst in-to ye mornyng fell ... (IX, 580-2)

launching immediately into a retelling of it; and when he relates
the grisly and somewhat unlikely story of Gil Harper's head being
mistaken for the King's brother's because the former was wearing
the latter's armour, he cites as his source

> As Jhone Thomas-sone said suthly
> Yat saw his deid all halily (XVIII, 147-8)

whom he has earlier introduced as

> ... leder
> Off yaim of Carrick yat yar wer (XVIII, 117-18).

His evidence therefore sometimes comes from anonymous sources,
partly a kind of common knowledge perhaps, from conflicting
accounts put forward by several people on either side, or from
named individuals. One has the impression that Barbour acknowledges such sources most frequently in the Irish and English
campaigns and that sometimes he is without personal contacts, as

in the extremely brief description of the King's taking of the
Isles which Barbour follows with the summary transition to the
story of Edmound de Cailow:

> Quhill ye king upon yis maner
> Dawntyt ye Illis as I tell her (XV, 319-20)

While it is not impossible that Barbour had available to him
shorter literary versions – I am reluctant to use the term ballads
in this context – of some of the exploits and events he depicts,
his most likely sources appear to have been differently structured
oral narratives displaying many of the features characteristic of
storytelling in the folk-cultural register, including personal
experience stories told in both the first and third persons. These
are most likely to have reached him in various ways from single or
several individuals, and one must regard as somewhat speculative
R L C Lorimer's assertion that Barbour combined 'two groups of
stories from oral tradition, those relating to the Bruce-Stewart
family and those relating to the Douglases,'[17] if the term 'group'
here implies more than the loosest affiliation of disparate
accounts, perhaps even an organised corpus or 'cycle' of traditions. Nor am I suggesting that Barbour was writing an extended
folk tale or deliberately employing narrative strategies derived
from oral tradition, despite the fact that his buk and his carpyng
were obviously as much intended for listeners as for readers. The
point which I am trying to make is that his narrative style, in
addition to features shared by all good stories, includes so many
characteristics usually associated with folk rather than artful
narrative that these may well have found their way into The Brus
as frequent, perhaps even dominant, ingredients in the stories
which he collected from some of those who had been there or had
heard such accounts from that most elusive of all sources, the
'friend of a friend'. Here are some of these features:[18]

a) The triad as a structuring element; examples would be, among
others,
   James Douglas lives in Paris close to three years (I, 345)
   Bruce defeats three felons who ambush him (III, 93-146)
   Bruce and his companions reach Loch Lomond on the third day
   (III, 407)
   The King stays three nights at Dunaverty (III, 677)
   There are three traitors in Carrick (V, 490)
   Three more traitors are in the empty farmhouse (VII, 111)
   Another three opponents appear during the hunt (VII, 416)
   There is three days' skirmishing in the Sliach (IX, 137)
   Edward Bruce attacks three times in Galloway (IX, 622)
   (this from Alan of Cathcart)
   Bruce, in his speech to his men before the battle of
   Bannockburn lists three advantages that the Scots have
   over the English (XII, 234) – (1) Being in the right,
   (2) Riches to be had, (3) Fighting for family, country
   and freedom
   D'Argenton makes three assaults on the Saracens (XIII, 324)
   Edward Bruce stays in Dundalk for three days (XIV, 239)

He also beats Richard of Clare three times (XVI, 4)
He wins nineteen battles in fewer than three years (XVI, 182)
There are three battles in these campaigns which deserve to be admired for ever (XVI, 551)
The English army remains in Edinburgh for three days (XVIII, 263)

Naturally, other numbers also occur sporadically but the incidence of triads of all sorts (opponents, military undertakings of various kinds, time spent in a place or spent to reach it, encouraging advantages over the enemy in a decisive battle) is too great to dismiss the lengthy list of them as accidental or to accept all of them as historical triplings. Repetition, especially in threes, is a well-known structural device in all aspects of the folk-cultural register, particularly in its belief system, and seems to have infiltrated Barbour's narrative from oral tradition, in addition to being part of his own culture-specific way of organising the world. Many of these threes, by the way, serve to structure shorter stories within the longer story.

b)   The principle of 'Two to a Scene'

This rule applies throughout The Brus. It limits the active participants in any one scene to two and is responsible for the use of dialogue as the prevalent form of direct or indirect speech. From the numerous instances of the application of this principle may I simply cite the scenes involving Bishop William of Lamberton and King Edward (I, 416-36), Bruce and Comyn (I, 485-510) and Bruce and King Edward (I, 604-25) in Book I; the Bishop of St Andrews and James of Douglas (II, 93-129), as well as Sir Aylmer of Valence and Sir Ingram of Umphraville (II, 260-300) in Book II; McNaughton and the Lord of Lorne (III, 153-81) in Book III, and James Douglas and Robert Boyd (IV, 342-63) in Book IV. An intriguing combination of the principles of the triad and of 'Two to a Scene' occurs in Book XVIII, 31-48, when Sir Edward Bruce asks Sir John Stewart, Sir William de Soulis and Sir Philip de Mowbray in turn to advise him on his decision to fight Richard of Clare under adverse circumstances: advice, by the way, that is ill received and not heeded, indirectly leading to his defeat and death.

c)   Rehearsing the Future[19]

In view of the fact that only the past can be narrated, the unknown future frequently becomes a debilitating threat to folktale protagonists. When on a quest, they are often found to be 'at their wits' end what to do', and it is only when the future is anticipated for them through narrated rehearsal by some helpful creature or person and they obey the injunctions embedded in the narrative, that they can successfully complete the task which they have set out to accomplish. Such narrative rehearsals are also quite common devices in the The

Brus, although some of them differ from their folktale counterparts insofar as they are performed by the protagonists
themselves. Before the Battle of Methven, Sir John of Umphraville is the rehearser (II, 260-300); during the escape to
Rathlin the Earl of Lennox takes on that role (III, 611-22);
Sir Robert Boyd briefly rehearses the Scots' moves before the
raid on Brodick (IV, 352-63); Tom Dickson's rehearsal is referred to in indirect speech before the attack on St Bride's
Chapel (V, 315-29); the king himself rehearses his troops
before the battle of Loudoun Hill (VIII, 235-57); and William
Francis, through narrative rehearsal, makes the sack of Edinburgh Castle possible (X, 543-53). There are several other
instances. Granted that the rehearsing helpers are never
supernatural, although one or two not mentioned here are
miracle workers or have the second sight, the narrative
rehearsal of the future nevertheless serves the same function
in The Brus as in folk-narratives - to deal successfully with
an unknown and threatening future when one's own resources
are likely to be inadequate. The frequent need for such
rehearsals, as well as the repeated use of secret stratagems,
ruses and deceptions, is directly related to an important
folktale feature central to the telling of The Brus.

d)   The Unpromising Hero[20]

This kind of protagonist is well known to all acquainted with
the märchen and is usually epitomised in the figure of Cinderella. Often deprived by some evil antagonists of their inheritance or rightful place in society, the unpromising heroes or
heroines win back what is theirs against heavy odds, often
aided by supernatural helpers. This is a protagonist with
whom audiences can identify whole-heartedly, as many human
beings are aware of considerable 'unpromise' in their lives
and feel that the odds are stacked against them. If therefore
'unpromise' is overcome on the listeners' behalf by folktale
protagonists, these have acted out vicariously the desires
and aspirations of those who will never be able to achieve
such feats themselves. Bruce himself is such a prototypical
protagonist; and Barbour, from the very beginning of his
account of the Cinderella king's adventure, goes out of his
way to stress, possibly even to exaggerate, the potentially
overwhelming strength of the opposition to be overcome. Such
royal 'unpromise' is particularly expressed in the number of
opponents he has to fight single-handedly, and if it were not
for the fact that Barbour's unpromising hero of The Brus is
also conveniently an all-conquering one[21] who takes on all
comers and through his own personal strength and valour and a
careful choice of terrain overcomes them, he would be in a
sorry plight. King Robert is indeed fortunate if his opponents number only three, as the traditional triad demands; on
several occasions he has to face even larger numbers.
     The same is true of the other two heroes of the poem, Sir
James Douglas and Sir Edward Bruce; although their all-
conquering status is compromised in the end, for the one in

the Holy Land, for the other in Ireland. More importantly,
however, the quality of extreme unpromise also applies to the
bands of men they lead and, in a more extended, almost
metaphorical, sense, to the country whose crowned king Robert
is - Scotland. There is not a battle before 1314 in which the
Scots are not heavily outnumbered in victory, and the martial
events at Bannockburn to which Barbour devotes such a large
portion of his work are the most prominent and most
far-reaching culmination of all the rehearsals that have gone
before, for the very fate of 'unpromising' Scotland is at stake
or, one might claim at a further remove, the 'unpromise' of
freedom per se.

There are several other folk-narrative features of The Brus
which can only be alluded to here, among them the apparent overuse
of 'coincidence' (help coming at the very moment when all seems
lost, Bruce blinking his eye when the three traitors are about to
slay him in his sleep, and so on) and the employment of well-known
folk-motifs at strategic points in the narrative, again especially
in the aim of deception against a numerically stronger foe:
Bruce's escape from the sleuth-hounds by wading along the bed of a
stream to make them lose his scent (X, 1-53: significantly,
Barbour also retells another version that does not contain this
folk-motif, and is perhaps from eye-witness reports rather than
from folk stories of the event); the use of haywagons to block the
gate at Linlith- gow (X, 149-260) - between the 'cheeks' of the
gate as Barbour says so memorably (X, 231); similarly the disguise
of heavily-armed soldiers as sack-carrying farm-labourers at
Douglas Castle (VIII, 437-72); the somewhat ludicrous and cumbersome but ultimately effective cattle-like movement of soldiers on
all fours in uncertain Roxburgh twilight (X, 384-5); the priest as
spy at Melrose (XVIII, 300-32); or the knowledge of a secret,
though perilous, path to the top of Edinburgh Castle rock because
of a previous amour in town, and the subsequent punning fulfilment
of St Margaret's prophecy through the equation of William
Francis's (or Francois's) name with the epithet Francais 'French',
or perhaps even the encounter with the Irish washerwoman in child-
birth (XVI, 277-96).
It is worth noting that quite frequently when a folk-motif from
oral tradition like the foregoing is employed, the folk themselves, or their individual representatives, sometimes even
named,[22] play an active part in the proceedings. One cannot help
wondering whether these might indeed be genuine folk stories,
based either on actual personal experience or on fabulation, and
the impression is given that the Aberdeen archdeacon, in the
course of and in the cause of his presentation of the larger
story, is at his storying best in the octosyllabic retelling of
them. Whether retold from memory or with the aid of notes, fuller
summaries or even verbatim transcripts (if that is not too modern
a method for the fourteenth century), they smack of the delighted
reminiscences of veterans present on these occasions, and the
named commoners, whether real or fictitious, add a persuasive note
of authenticity to the narrative vignettes. Truth is always so
much more believable when one can name its practitioners, and the
created past takes on personal dimensions.

This brings me to the final major point which I want to make in this examination of the narrative facets of Barbour's Brus - its episodic nature. This is, of course, also a well-known characteristic of all folktales, but this obvious structural parallelism should not be interpreted as implying the conscious imitation of folktale structures by Barbour. Rather I would like to regard it, on the one hand, as representing one of the essential elements of most good story-telling, i.e. the judicious selection of narratable and therefore narrated portions coupled with the rejection of non-narrated segments out of the total recounted time in a story.[23] Linked with this general, almost abstract, principle are, however, two more practical considerations. Many of the episodes, i.e. the often self-contained narrated units introduced typically by quhen and structured sequentially through several thens, were probably collected by Barbour in that very status and form, on their own and unconnected with other episodes; and to all intents and purposes continued to be treated by him as such, without any strenuous attempt at producing a continuous narrative, or even lengthy connective transitions. Secondly, they lent themselves easily to oral retelling, whether in a reading from his manuscripts, perhaps during the composition of his longer work, or in an independent oral prose version like, let us say, Bruce's single-handed combats, the siege of Perth, the Pass of Brander, the sleuthhound, the crossing of Loch Lomond, and so on. Several of them may delight an audience in an hour's entertainment whereas the whole of the poem would be difficult to accommodate even in several sittings. Sometimes The Brus's episodic structure has been linked to the leaping and lingering so common in the narrative, often incremental, progression of ballads,[24] but it is, in my view, dangerous to think of The Brus as one of their forerunners - the scales involved are far too different.

We cannot leave The Brus and our theme without making mention of what are regarded by some critics as digressions. I am referring to the stories, mostly from ancient mythology and classical history, inserted in the text to illumine through illustrious parallel a particular feat or event in the primary narrative itself. Most of them, like the four classical examples of betrayal (Troy, Alexander, Caesar, and Arthur) preparing the audience for Comyn's treachery concerning the covenant Bruce has signed (I, 521 - II, 24) or the classical parallel to the survival of the queen and other fair ladies in Aberdeen to share their men's troubles (II, 531-52) - also VI, 181-270, and X, 710 - are told by Barbour himself who, as a narrator, is ever present and ready to comment on, mediate, interpolate, intervene, disclaim, compare, verify, deny, as well as to tell his tale (again a peculiar feature of the storyteller who presents his story orally rather than in writing). But at least two of them are said to have been told by the two major protagonists themselves, King Robert and James Douglas. Whether the Bruce did indeed tell the story of Rome and Hannibal (III, 207-66) as an example of how a few can overthrow a mighty king, and, if he did, whether he told it in this particular way, is of only secondary importance compared with the delightful notion of the King as accomplished storyteller who knew the effects of a good story well told. Similarly, James Douglas's

telling of the fable of the Fox and the Fisherman as an instance
of how one might escape out of a perilous situation, exemplifies a
valiant aristocratic attempt at positively influencing a distraught audience through story (XIX, 651-97). A third aristocratic
storyteller is Sir William Keith who, in a panegyric on loyalty,
compares the slain Douglas to loyal Patricias who was sent to make
war on Pyrrhus (XX, 531-568). Such storytelling opens the narration of purely Scottish events to the wider world of classical
model and experience, thus depriving it of its regional isolation
and unique Scottishness. Far from being digressions, such storying
insertions - perhaps incorporations is a better term to show their
work-specific integrity - deepen one's consciousness of being
involved as a listener or reader, in the narrative unfolding of a
heroic life.

In conclusion, allow me to do two things. First, let me offer
once again the reassurance that it has not been my intention to
turn John Barbour, the educated archdeacon of our host city, into
something like a folk poet or somebody who wrote in a popular
vein. My purpose has rather been to inject into the mainly literary
discussion of his Brus some of the terminology and concepts of the
folklorist. I consider this potentially helpful because so much of
Barbour's material must have come from oral tradition and either
already contained or begged for the appropriation of motifs,
structural strategies, and perceptions of his chief hero, current
in the folk-'literature' of the time. Although the comparison may
carry with it inapplicable reverberations of a much later age, I
see John Barbour's relationship to popular narrative and folk-
culture as not dissimilar to that of Sir Walter Scott more than
400 years later, and therefore deserving of similar scrutiny.[25]
Second, let me by cunning sleight of hand play my trump card, or
perhaps rather call my most important witness, Perry Mason style,
at the very last moment. If readers have found it difficult to
share my sincere vision of The Brus as story par excellence and my
enthusiasm for its episodic structure, let me refer them to the
archdeacon himself. Would anybody whose very first word in a poem
thousands of lines long is storys have in mind the writing of
something different, of history perhaps or of biography or of
romance in the French or Arthurian fashion? And would someone who,
in a rare reference to chronology and to dynastic circumstances,
states that he is engaged in the compiling of this buk (XIII,
709-14) be doing anything other than just that - a shaping,
moulding, arranging, sequencing compilation of episodes diligently
garnered from a variety of sources? It is thus John Barbour himself who tells us that he is writing an episodic story (or, as I
would put it, a suthfast creation of a chunk of Scottish past);
and who are we to gainsay him? John Barbour is, I submit, not just
a teller of a tale but a teller of tales.

Notes

1   Lois A Ebin, 'John Barbour's Bruce: Poetry, History and Propaganda', Studies in Scottish Literature 9 (1972–3) p 220.

2   W F H Nicolaisen, 'Space in Folk Narrative', in Folklore on Two Continents: Essays in Honor of Linda Degh, (Bloomington, In., 1980), pp 14–18. 'Time in Folk-Narrative', in Venetia J Newall (ed), Folklore Studies in the Twentieth Century, (Woodbridge, Suffolk, 1980), pp 314–19. 'Concepts of Time and Space in Irish Folktales', in Patrick K Ford (ed), Celtic Folklore and Christianity, Studies in Memory of William W Heist (Santa Barbara, Ca., 1983), pp 150–8. 'The Structure of Narrated Time in the Folktale', Le conte pourquoi? comment? Editions du Centre National de la Recherche Scientifique (Paris, 1984), pp 417–36. 'Names and Narratives', Journal of American Folklore 97 (1984) pp 259–72. 'Legends as Narrative Response', in Paul Smith (ed) Perspectives on Contemporary Legend (Sheffield, 1984), pp 167–78. 'Rehearsing the Future in the Folktale', New York Folklore 11 (1985) pp 231–8. 'Perspectives on Contemporary Legend', Fabula 26, 3–4 (1985) pp 213–18.

3   W F H Nicolaisen, 'Once upon a place, or where is the world of the folktale?' Festschrift Gerhard Lutz (Berlin, forthcoming).

4   Nicolaisen, 'Legends as Narrative Response' pp 174–5, following Hayden White, 'The Value of Narrativity in the Representation of Reality', Critical Inquiry 7.1 (Autumn, 1980) pp 5–6.

5   The edition used for this paper is Barbour's Bruce, Matthew P McDiarmid and James A C Stevenson (eds), STS, 2 vols (Edinburgh, 1985). All textual references are to this edition.

6   Kurt Wittig, The Scottish Tradition in Literature, (Edinburgh, 1958), p 11.

7   The Bruce by John Barbour, trans and ed by A A H Douglas (Glasgow, 1964), p 2.

8   Ebin, p 220.

9   A M Kinghorn, 'Scottish Historiography in the fourteenth century: A New Introduction to Barbour's Bruce', Studies in Scottish Literature 6 (1968–9), p 131.

10 Ibid, p 134.

11 Ibid, p 135.

12 James Kinsley, 'The Mediaeval Makars', in: James Kinsley (ed) Scottish Poetry : A Critical Survey (London, 1955), p 2.

13 Bernice Kliman, 'The Significance of Barbour's Naming of Commoners', Studies in Scottish Literature 11 (1973–74) p 108.

14 Loc.cit.

15 Wittig, p 19.

16 For example, Bernice W Kliman, 'John Barbour and Rhetorical Tradition', Annuale Medieavale (1977) p 163.

17 Quoted in Ebin, p 218.

18 For (a) and (b) see Axel Olrik, 'Epic Laws of Folk Narrative', in Alan Dundes (ed), The Study of Folklore (Englewood Cliffs, NJ, 1965), pp 129–41 (Originally published as 'Epische Gesetze der Volksdichtung', Zeitschrift Fur Deutsches Altertum 51 (1909) pp 1–12.

19   Nicolaisen, 'Rehearsing the Future in the Folktale' (see note 2).

20   For the motif of the 'Unpromising Hero (Heroine)' see Stith, Thompson, _Motif-Index of Folk-Literature_, vol 5 (Bloomington, In., 1964) pp 8-16 (Motifs L 100 - L 199).

21   _Ibid_, vol 1, pp 116-25 (Motifs A 500 - A 599 'Demigods and Culture Heroes') etc.

22   See Kliman, 'The Significance of Barbour's Naming of Commoners' (see note 13).

23   Nicolaisen, 'The Structure of Narrated Time in the Folktale' (see note 2).

24   Wittig, p 20.

25   W F H Nicolaisen, 'Scott and the Folk Tradition', in Alan Bold (ed), _Sir Walter Scott: The Long-Forgotten Melody_, (London, 1983) pp 127-42. 'Sir Walter Scott: The Folklorist as Novelist', in J H Alexander and David Hewitt (eds), _Scott and His Influence_, ASLS (Aberdeen, 1983), pp 169-79.

Chapter 7

ASPECTS OF THE SNAKE IN THE LEGENDS OF THE SAINTS

Regina Scheibe

I

The snake is one of the most important animals drawn upon in
Middle Scots literature, and some of the earliest evidence for its
imagery is provided by the late fourteenth century collection of
the Legends of the Saints. A discussion on the traditional elements of the snake figures used in the Scottish legendary and on
their contribution to the whole concept of the work seems therefore to be most worthwhile.

II

Apart from the general term 'serpent', the Scottish collection of
saints' lives differentiates between adder, asp, colubre, viper,
and dragon.[1] The word colubre, deriving from Latin coluber m. or
colubra f. 'a serpent', represents a certain kind of venomous
snake, probably unidentifiable for us.[2]
    The legend of St Christina refers to three of the different
kinds of snakes just named. Asps, colubres and vipers are applied
to the martyr as a punishment for her persistence in keeping to
the Christian faith:

> Thane twa serpentis he gert bryng on ane,
> That haspidis has to name,
> & als fellone vthyre twa,
> That to nam has vypera,
> & twa colubris rycht fellone
> before hire he gert lay done.
> The serpentis hire fete can lyke,
> & hurt hire nocht, tho thai var wyk.
> aspidis til hir papis socht,
> & sukyt thame, & noyt nocht.
> Colubres a-bout hyr nek lay
> vnhurtand, lykyt suet away.[3]

    The asp is not mentioned in any of the other saints' lives of
the Scottish legendary. But on turning to John Trevisa's translation of Bartholomaeus Anglicus' natural encyclopedia De Proprietatibus Rerum we learn that

> Aspis is an addre worst and most wikke in venyme and in
> bytynge ... [4]

Descriptions of the viper's and colubre's outstanding dangerousness are supplied by the Scottish collection of saints' lives
itself. St Paul is bitten by

> a serpent ... callit wipera,
> That of venim fillit is sa
> That quham it bittis, it mon be ded
> Thar agane is no remed ... [5]

That the viper's bite is fatal and that there is no remedy against
it is already implied in Acts 28:6:

> at illi existimabant eum in tumorem convertendum
> et subito casurum et mori
> diu autem illis exspectantibus et videntibus nihil
>   mali in eo fieri
> convertentes se dicebant eum esse deum [6]

In his Collectanea rerum memorabilium Solinus shares the view that
the viper's bite is lethal.[7] Bartholomaeus considers the viper as
an extremely venomous snake, and we further learn from the translation of his encyclopedia:

> ... tirus is a manere serpent that hatte vipera also ... to
> his bytynge is no medicyne yfounde. Ambros in Exameron seith
> that among alle serpentes the kynde of vipera is worst.[8]

And in the legend of St Eugenia we read about the colubre:

> ... wrytine is in the haly wryt,
> & we mone treu that suth is It,
> That na serpent has a hed sa fel,
> sa venamuse, na sa cruel,
> as the hed of the colubre is ... [9]

The reference here is to the non-canonical Book of Sirach 25: 22f:

> Non est caput nequius super caput colubri
> et non est ira super iram inimici
> commorari leoni et draconi placebit
> quam habitare cum muliere nequam

The activities of licking or sucking as well as of drinking milk
are named as some of the traits of the colubre in On the Properties of Things.[10]
    The source of the serpent scene in the legend of St Christina
is a passage from the thirteenth-century Legenda aurea by Jacobus
de Voragine, which was one of the most popular collections of
saints' lives in the Middle Ages:

> ...duas aspides, duas viperas, duos colubros ad eam mitti
> fecit, sed serpentes ejus pedes lingunt, aspides nil nocentes
> ad ubera pendent, colubri collo se volventes sudorem lingunt
> ... [11]

The text of the Scottish legend conveys a vividness and density of scene contrasting with the matter-of-fact account provided in the Legenda aurea. This liveliness is achieved by an extended introduction of the snake pairs which serves the carefully worked-out contrast between their ferocious character and their caressing behaviour towards the saint. Whereas the snakes' fierceness is only hinted at in the Latin version by providing the words 'nil nocentes', the Scottish version supplies '(rycht) fellone', 'hurt hire nocht, tho thai var wyk', 'noyt nocht' and 'vnhurtand'.

None of the published Middle English versions of the serpent scene in the legend of St Christina equals the Scottish one in its emotional impact on the listener or reader.[12] The most obvious example can be found in the South English Legendary (SEL), here quoted from Charlotte D'Evelyn and Anna Mill's edition of the early fourteenth century MS Corpus Christi Cambridge 145:

The Iustice him het anon . the neddren forth bringe
And caste hom to this holy maide . that hi ssolde hure to
    dethe stinge
This neddren were forth ibro3t . grislokest of alle thinge
Hi crope & mad ioie inou . tho hi were to hure ido
Hi biclupte hure holy limes . & lickede hure wonden also
Hi pleide with hure bresten bothe . hure children as it were
Hi custe hure & likked ek ... [13]

The three pairs of extremely dangerous snakes are reduced to simply 'neddren', a word frequently used as a synonym for snakes in Middle English.[14] What the snakes are expected to do is directly stated at the beginning of the scene, instead of being implied by constant remarks on the beasts' usual fierceness. The emphasis is on joy over the peaceful behaviour of the reptiles and not on the horror as created in the Scottish legendary.

In William Paris's fifteenth-century version of the legend and in the version of the Northern Homily Cycle (NHC) as preserved in the fifteenth-century MS Harley 4196 as well as in Caxton's Golden Legend (1483), St Christina is exposed to six snakes.[15] As we have already seen, the text in the SEL does not specify the number of the snakes, and Osbern Bokenham's 'Vita S. Christianae' (1443-47) mentions just four beasts.[16] However, the number six is not without importance to the underlying religious concept of the passage. Based on the Platonic idea of perfect numbers, of which six is the first, it came to represent 'perfection of work'[17] in Biblical numerology.[18] God created the world in six days and the sixth day of creation

corespondis the vj age in the quhilk god become man for our
saluacoun ... [19]

On the allegorical level, the saint represents Christ in a vita and events in the life of a saint are 'reflections' of the events of the life of Christ.[20] The snakes as symbols of sin and of the devil's power over man, as well as their association with wilderness both in the Bible[21] and in the legend of St Christina, suggest the devil's temptation of Christ in the desert as described in Luke

4:1f.[22] Jesus overcoming the devil in the wilderness is celebrated
as one of his major victories over Satan in the Scottish rendering
of the legend of St Bartholomew.[23] St Christina, who named herself
after Christ,[24] commands the snakes to retreat into the wilderness
after having overcome their ferocity by the purity of her soul
modelled on the moral perfection of Mankind's Saviour.

> Thane cristine, that wes nocht rad
> for thai bestis, but bad thaim bad
> that thai suld pase til wildirnes ...[25]

Since Christ was brought to death on the sixth day of the week at
the sixth hour of the day, the number six also recalls his Crucifixion and Redemption of Mankind.[26] After his Resurrection he says
about those who believe in him:

> in nomine meo daemonia eiecient
> linguis loquentur novis
> serpentes tollent
> et si mortiferum quid biberint non
>   eis nocebit   (Mc. 16:17f)

None of the published Middle English versions of the scene
draws on the three kinds of snakes used in the Scottish passage.
With the exception of the NHC, all these versions use snakes,
whether specified or not.[27] The NHC mentions two scorpions apart
from the four snakes applied to St Christina. This choice is not
surprising in view of Deut. 8:15, Luke 10:19 and Rev. 9:3-5, since
these Bible passages connect the scorpions with snakes, with
wilderness, with the devil and with torment for those opposing
God's commandments. But neither do the passages reveal any association with enchantment; nor do they emphasise the role of the
beasts as divine instruments of punishment, two important points
in our snake scene. Throughout the legend St Christina refuses to
sacrifice to pagan deities and the snakes applied to her belong to
an enchanter. When they fail to harm her and the enchanter tries
to entice them into action, the reptiles turn against him and kill
him instead of the saint:[28]

> Thane he profit his craft to do;
> & al thai bestis socht hyme to
> in mykil brath in-to that sted,
> & gert hyme fal done stane ded.[29]

The most common characteristic of the snakes in the Legends of the
Saints is their ability to inflict poison on humans.[30] Num. 21:6,
8f (which should be viewed with 2 Kings 18:4), Eccles. 10:11 and
Jer. 8:17 name this characteristic in conjunction with snakes and
enchantment or paganism. They also stress the use of snakes as
divine instruments.

In summary, the impact of the passage largely depends on the
choice of the snakes and on the knowledge of their extreme dangerousness, on additions stressing the snakes' unusual behaviour, and
on the spiritual implications of the number six.

III

A short representative scene regarding the use of dragon imagery in the Scottish collection of saints' lives is to be found in the legend of St Margaret:

> Thane rase scho fra hyr oracion ...
> and saw a dragon nere hyr by,
> sa mykil, sa gret, and sa vygly
> that of wit scho wes wel nere,
> of that best for the fellon bere;
> tha scayland schalis set vp rath,
> with vryss ful lang & ful herd bath,
> & tung & tetht brynnand as fyre,
> & schot on hyre in gret Ire,
> & tuk hyr in his mouth hale,
> to suely hyr in mekil bale.
> bot, as scho enterand was to pas
> the throt of that ful sathanas,
> the takine of the croice scho mad
> on hyre, & the best but bad
> brast in twa, & scho but hurt
> eschapit wele or ony sturt.[31]

How lively appears to be the description of St Margaret's encounter with the dragon when compared with the meagre and unemotional description of the event in Jacobus de Voragine's Legenda aurea:

> ...ecce draco immanissimus ibidem apparuit, qui dum eam devoraturus impeteret, signum crucis edidit et ille evanuit, vel, ut alibi legitur, os super caput ejus ponens et linguam super calcaneum porrigens eam protinus deglutivit, sed dum eam absorbere vellet, signo crucis se munivit et ideo draco virtute crucis crepuit et virgo illaesa exivit. Istud autem, quod dicitur de draconis devoratione et ipsius crepatione, apocryphum et frivolum reputatur.[32]

The force of the Scottish scene depends on the fright felt by the saint when turning around from her prayer, on the detailed description of the dragon and on the author's choice of using the second version which Jacobus de Voragine calls 'apocryphum et frivolum'.

Of the ten Middle English versions preserving the legend of St Margaret,[33] only four explicitly state the saint's fear, the early-thirteenth-century Seinte Marherete of the Meidenhad (or Katherine) Group, the thirteenth-century MS Trin. Cambr. 323, the fourteenth-century MS Bodl. Libr. 6922 and Osbern Bokenham.[34] The ballad-like rendering of the legend in the thirteenth-century MS Nat.Libr.Scotl. 19.2.1 remarks on the plight of St Margaret being locked up with the dragon in the prison cell.[35]

In his Historia naturalis Pliny refers to huge snakes attacking elephants in India as 'dracones', the word deriving from L draco, -onis m., from Gk. δράκων, 'a sort of serpent, a dragon'.[36] And Isidore of Seville tells us about the size of the dragon in his Etymologiae:

Draco maior cunctorum serpentium, siue omnium animatium super terram.[37]

Isidore's statement makes its reappearance in such works as De bestiis et aliis rebus, MS Cambridge Univ. Libr. II.4.26, MS Ashmole 1511, Thomas of Cantimpré's Liber de natura rerum, Vincent of Beauvais's Speculum naturale and John Trevisa's translation of Bartholomaeus Anglicus' De Proprietatibus Rerum.[38] The author of the Scottish legendary himself calls the dragon in the legend of St George 'a serpent fel'.[39] The view of the dragon being the largest of all snakes on earth corresponds to the view of the devil being the greatest of all evils. Thus we read about the devil's expulsion from heaven in Rev 12:9:

> et proiectus est draco ille magnus
> serpens antiquus qui vocatur Diabolus et Satanas
> qui seducit universum orbem ... [40]

One of the most obvious characteristics of snakes mentioned in the natural encyclopedias and bestiaries just referred to is the fact that they have scales.[41] Avicenna, drawn upon by Vincent of Beauvais in his Speculum naturale, tells us that scales are also one of the dragon's characteristics.[42] They frequently seem to be a feature of the beast in the visual arts.[43]

None of the natural encyclopedias, bestiaries or catalogues on animal figures in medieval literature I consulted[44] names bristles as one of the dragon's physical attributes. However, early medieval illustrations depicting St Michael spearing the dragon show part of the beast covered with what could be either bundles of hair or bristles.[45] And it is again Avicenna who mentions a dragon with sturdy hair:

> Vidi ego quendam huius generis, super cuius collum in
> latitudine descendente erant pili crassi.[46]

Scales and bristles recall the snake's and boar's dangerousness and the beasts' association with sin. Together with the dragon's behaviour of rushing towards its victim in wrath, a traditional trait often used in serpent and boar imagery,[47] they direct our attention towards the tropological level of the scene. In De bestiis et aliis rebus, MSS Cambridge Univ. Libr. II.4.26 and Ashmole 1511, the dragon symbolises the most damnable of all deadly sins, pride.[48] In medieval animal lore the beast also represents anger, gluttony and envy.[49] The boar too is frequently associated with the seven deadly sins;[50] and anger, gluttony, avarice, envy and lechery are often symbolised by snakes.[51]

The choice of the dragon representing Satan is not only in accordance with Rev 12:9, but again recalls the devil's temptation of Christ as described in Luke 4:1-3.[52] Only someone free from the seven deadly sins is able to defeat the progenitor of all evil, Satan. Thus we are told about St Margaret:

> ... the feynd scho ourcom wel
> & his werkis Ilke dele.

> for pride in hyre, na auarise
> herbryt in hyre mycht be na vise,
> na slawnes, na lychery,
> na wreth, na gnedschepe, na gluto[ny] ... [53]

On the basis of Psalm 79:13f the medieval boar was frequently identified with the Antichrist, too.[54] Compare, for example, Richard Rolle of Hampole's translation of the Psalm and his comment on it:

> The bare of the wod outtermyd it: and the syngulere wildbest has etyn it. The bare is the deuel, prynce of ill men. that has kastyn out of the termys of goed life. and he is the wild best that is of syngulere cruelte. in all that seruys him. that has etyn thaim. that is, all the goednes of thaire saule he wastis when thai assent till dedly sin.[55]

In The Avowing of King Arthur the boar is thrice called Satan and before finally killing the beast Arthur calls on St Margaret:[56]

> 'Send me the victoré,
> This Satanas me sekes'.[57]

The dragon's traditional connection with fire[58] is well illustrated by a passage in On the Properties of Things:

> ...somtyme he setteth the ayer afuyre by hete of his venyme so that it semeth that he bloweth and casteth fuyre out of his mouth.[59]

The well-known association of fire and hell need not be commented upon.[60]

The dragon's poisonous and wrathful character and its habit of swallowing up its victims are referred to in Deut. 32:33, Jer. 51:34 and Rev. 12:4, 17. These Bible passages prove to be in accordance with the tropological and allegorical implications of the dragon figure in the Scottish legendary. Taken together, they imply that those opposing God's commandments have to face Satan's poisonous and overall consuming power over their souls and that Christians keeping to God's laws will be exposed to the devil's wrath, but they will finally defeat him by taking Christ as their example.

That the dragon has to be ugly can be deduced from Satan's character. Like the Secreta Secretorum, ancient and medieval treatises on physiognomy establish a link between evil character and outward appearance:

> ... the Sowle ... sueth the kynde and the complexcion and the propyrteys of the body.[61]

All the Middle English versions of the dragon scene in the St Margaret legend can be divided into those influenced by the thirteenth-century Legenda aurea and those affected by the much earlier Mombritius type of the legend whose earliest English manuscript dates back to c.1000 AD.[62] The first group includes the SEL, John Mirk's (a.1415) and John Lydgate's version (a.1450), the Gilte Legende and William Caxton's rendering of the scene.[63] The version of the Meidenhad collection, of the MSS Nat. Libr. Scot. 19.2.1, Trin. Cambr. 323, Bodl. Libr. 6922, and of Osbern Bokenham's 'Vita S Margaretae' make up the second group. Being restricted in space, I would like to direct the reader's attention to some of the more striking features in the dragon scenes of the two groups as they compare themselves with the concept of the Scottish St Margaret legend.

There is no description of the dragon in the SEL. And though its author decides in favour of the beast swallowing the saint, he expresses excessive doubts over the episodes:

> Ac this netelle ich no3t to sothe . for it nis no3t to sothe iwrite
> Ac wether it is soth other it nis . inot noman that wite
> Ac a3en kunde it were . that the deuel were to dethe ibro3t
> For he nemai tholie nanne deth . i nemai it leue no3t
> And also i neleoue no3t . that is mi3ten were so stronge
> A so holy creature . inis wombe auonge.[64]

John Lydgate, John Mirk and William Caxton hardly make any explicit statements on the dragon's outward appearance in their renderings of the episode. John Lydgate's text might serve as an example:

> And sodeynly appered in hir sight,
>   Where as she lay bounden in prisoun,
>   In the lykenesse of a felle dragoun
> The olde serpent, whiche called is Sathan,
> And hastyly to assayle her he began;
>
> With open mouthe, the virgyne to deuour,
>   First of alle, he swolwed in hir hede,
> And she deuoutly, hirself to socoure,
>   Gan crosse hirself, in hir mortal drede;
>   And by grace, anoone or she toke hede,
> The horrible beste, in relees of hir peyne,
> Brast assondre, and partyd was on tweyne.[65]

Since William Caxton's dragon scene is closely modelled on the version given in the Legenda aurea, he, too, remarks that the beast's swallowing of St Margaret and its final bursting is said to be apocryphal.[66] The remaining Middle English versions of the dragon scene provided the swallowing of the saint without attaching a critical note to it.[67] The lack of a detailed description of the dragon and of comments on the likelihood of the dragon devouring the saint are in accordance with the character of each individual work. John Lydgate puts his emphasis on the panegyric description of the saint while John Mirk hopes to favour the devotion of St Margaret within the limits of a short sermon.[68] The Gilte Legende and William Caxton stress factual report and credibility.[69]

According to T Wolpers, the Mombritius version is the most

popular of all renderings of the St Margaret legend in the Middle
Ages. Yet our Scottish author does not draw on it for his dragon
scene.[70] This seems striking since the Mombritius type of the vita
S. Margaretae provides an extensive description of the dragon as
well as the undisputed devouring of the saint:

> Et ecce subito de angulo carceris exivit draco horribilis
> totus variis coloribus, deauratis capillis, et barbae eius
> aureae videbantur, dentes eius ferrei. Oculi eius velut
> margaritae splendebant. De naribus eius ignis et fumus
> exibant. Lingua eius anhelabat, super collum eius erat
> serpens, et gladius candens in manu eius videbatur et foe-
> torem faciebat in carcere et erexit se in medio carceris et
> sibilavit fortiter et factum est lumen in carcere ab igne,
> qui exibat de ore draconis. ... draco ore aperto posuit os
> suum super caput beatissimae Margaretae et linguam suam
> porrexit super calcaneum eius et suspirans deglutivit eam in
> ventrem suum.[71]

An examination of some of the dragon's characteristics adopted and
stressed in the Middle English versions influenced by the Mombritius type of the legend might give us an indication to why the
Scottish author refused to draw on it.

In their description of the dragon the Mombritius type of the
legend and all the Middle English versions probably influenced by
it draw to a varying degree on an imagery of colour and light. MS
Trin. Cambr. 323 and MS Bodl. Libr. 6922, both works with a distinct popular character,[72] describe the dragon as being green.[73]
This colour is traditionally connected with the underworld in
folklore. The devil in Chaucer's 'Friar's Tale' appears to the
summoner in the green garments of a hunter.[74] But on the spiritual
level green could also signify faith in God, hope, Christ and
eternal life. In the medieval lore on the virtues of stones the
spiritual significance of green jewels hints at Christ's Incarnation. And in connection with the qualities of transparency and
purity, precious green stones could indicate the virtue of chastity
and even human perfection achieved by the grace of God.[75] In the
Mombritius version the dragon's hair and beard are of a golden
colour. In the St Margaret legend of the Meidenhad collection, the
oldest of the Middle English versions, the beast is 'glistinde as
thah he al ouerguld were'.[76] Osbern Bokenham also refers to the
dragon's golden hair.[77] On account of its brightness and purity
the golden colour is superior to all other colours.[78] In heraldry
it signifies obedience and gentility and is a colour only to be
worn by a prince.[79] On a spiritual level it can imply faith,
Christ's supremacy in heaven and on earth as well as the reward
awaiting the soul in heaven.[80] In the Mombritius version the sword
held by the dragon is said to be of a white glittering colour, a
colour which indicates divine messages and refers to the glory
achieved by having faith in Christ.[81] Since the images of the
serpent in the Scottish legendary are frequently in accordance
with Bible passages, why did its author not choose the red colour
for the monster?[82] In medieval stone lore the colour red in
association with fire often refers to someone being filled with

the Holy Spirit or to someone devoted to the Christian lore.[83]
In heraldry red is, like gold, a colour only suitable for princes.
It indicates cruelty towards enemies.[84] As Satan is the prince of
all evil and the dragon's cruelty is well-known,[85] the colour red
might seem a suitable attribute of the beast. And yet, there are
good reasons for excluding such an image from the Scottish legendary. For the Scottish author colours generally seem to provide the
scene with a much too cheerful character, a scene which should
rather aim at deterring from sin by creating a frightful picture
of the dragon. This finds its support in two facts. Firstly,
bright colours are occasionally used elsewhere in the Scottish
legendary.[86] Secondly, when the devil reappears in a man-like
shape he is 'blakar thane ony sut',[87] the colour denoting deform-
itas of the soul and thus the antichrist.[88] The only versions of
the St Margaret legend providing a man-like black creature are the
Mombritius version,[89] the Meidenhad version[90] and the Scottish
legendary. Bokenham, who uses the colour and light imagery most
intensively, does not refer to the black colour of the creature.[91]
The Scottish author might further have refrained from using bright
colours in his dragon description because of their positive spiritual connotations and because he is generally at pains to avoid
using traditional mythical traits of beasts in his legendary. Just
two more examples to illustrate my points. Firstly, the colour
white is repeatedly used in the imagery concerning the saint.[92]
Secondly, though the dragon is clearly associated with the seven
deadly sins in the Scottish collection of saints' lives, the
author never refers to the beast's seven heads or crowns, two
important features of the apocalyptical dragon.[93]

Closely connected with medieval colour symbolism is the imagery
of light.[94] In De bestiis et aliis rebus the devil, disguised as a
dragon, is said to use light in order to make people believe he
has got divine authority:

> Saepe in aerem a spelunca sua [draco] concitatur, et lucet
> per eum aer, quia diabolus ab initio se erigens transfigurat
> se in angelum lucis, et decipit stultos spe falsae gloriae,
> laetitiaeque humanae.[95]

In the Mombritius version one of Satan's devices for deceiving man
into believing that he has got divine authority is that his eyes
sparkle like pearls. The extensive prologue to the legend in which
the Scottish author compares St Margaret's character to the virtues
of the pearl testifies that he knew of the spiritual implications
of the margarita:

> Qwa wil the vertu wyt of stanis,
> in the lapidar ma fynd ane is
> of tham that callyt is 'margaret',
> vertuyse, clere, lytil, and quhyt.
>   ...
> ȝet of this margarit the name
> of margaret ma wele be tane,
> that lytil was & mylk quhit clere
> & vertuyse, be causis sere.[96]

According to the natural encyclopedias and medieval lapidaries, the pearl was regarded as the most previous of all white stones. It was believed to be engendered either by a drop of dew falling from heaven into an open oyster or by lightning striking the open mollusc. Thus its creation without sin came to represent moral perfection and the Virgin Birth, the pearl being identified with Christ.[97] The anagogical meaning of the pearl is especially implied in the twelve gates of New Jerusalem, the heavenly city. Each of the gates consists of a pearl.[98] The image of glittering glass, one of the illusions created by the devil in Osbern Bokenham's dragon scene,[99] provides the same spiritual implications. The Annunciation is frequently compared to the sun shining through glass,[100] and in Rev. 21:18 & 21 the golden city of New Jerusalem is, in its brightness, paralleled to just that material. By holding a glittering sword in its claws the beast misuses the sword as an image of divine judgement.[101] That the Scottish author knew of the sword as a portent of God's impending judgement can be proved by a passage in his legend of St James the Less. When the people of Jerusalem do not repent their murders of the apostle and of Jesus Christ:

> a sterne brycht and clere,
> a-beoufe the citte can appere,
> of a fyery swerd in the lyknes,
> till fal one thame al redy wes,
> & in sik wyis as brynand clere,
> as to fal al redy were.[102]

I have already commented on the whiteness of the sword's glittering mentioned in the Mombritius version.

By excluding an imagery of colour and light from his dragon description, the Scottish author puts an emphasis on the tropological rather than on the allegorical level of the scene. Colourful illusions only betray the devil's ability to deceive. They do not stress the individual's responsibility for his soul's welfare after death. In contrast to the grim and colourless description of the devil in the Scottish legend, the Mombritius version, the Meidenhad text and Bokenham's rendering seem, like those versions deriving from the Legenda aurea, to be directed rather towards the listener's or reader's intellect than towards his emotions.

In the Scottish legendary Satan assumes the shapes of a dragon and of a black misshapen man in order to lead St Margaret astray from her Christian faith.[103] In the Mombritius type of the legend and in all Middle English versions drawing on it, the shapes are adopted by two of his subjects instead, by the fiends Ruffin and Beelzebub.[104] But for the author of the Scottish legendary the dragon is the personification of all evil and not just of an individual sin for whose representation he would have drawn on a different kind of serpent.[105]

To sum up, the author chooses those characteristics for the dragon's description which help to stress the moral implications of the legend and which imply the allegorical level of the vita. The dragon's features and his undisputed devouring of St Margaret ensure a frightening effect not only on the saint but rather more

on the people the legend was written for. Only someone leading a
life free from all the seven deadly sins will defeat the monster
as St Margaret and Jesus did. Thus the figure of the dragon representing Satan, king to Ruffin and Beelzebub,[106] is in accordance
with the whole concept of the Legends of the Saints, the deter-
rence from sin to enable the soul to reach the New Jerusalem.

                                IV

The use of the snake imagery in the remaining legends confirms the
author's interest in intensifying the moral impact of the legend
on the reader or listener. Since I am not able to discuss all the
serpent figures provided in the Scottish legendary, I will re-
strict myself to naming three further examples. Like the previous
specimens, they will illustrate how the author achieves his afore-
mentioned aim by excluding, adding to and changing the traditional
material available to him.
    The legend of St Paul provides us with an example for the
exclusion of material unimportant to the moral instruction offered
by the actual vita, even though the material presented in the
Legenda aurea would be extremely suitable for showing God's grace
on those who do good:

> Dicitur quoque, quod omnes, qui de progenie illius hominis,
> qui Paulum hospitio excepit, nascuntur, a venenosis ullatenus
> non laeduntur, unde cum pueri nati sunt, in cunis eorum
> patres serpentes ponunt, ut probent, si veri eorum filii
> sint.[107]

The story was well-known in medieval exempla tradition.[108]
    In the legend of St Eugenia we find an extensive discourse on
lecherous women for which there is no example in Jacobus de
Voragine's Legenda aurea.[109] It is introduced by the characterisation of the colubre already discussed above:

> ... na serpent has a hed sa fel,
> sa venamuse, na sa cruel,
> as the hed of the colubre is,
> na is na wikitnes I-wyse
> as is the ewil of the woman,
> quhare scho wald wengeans be tan.[110]

The introduction is followed by three examples of lecherous and
revengeful women: the story of Potiphar, the story of the alleged
wife of the German emperor Otto III and a reference to St Theodora
who, disguised as a monk, was falsely accused of being the father
of an illegitimate child.[111] According to F C Tubach's Index
Exemplorum, these stories were frequently used as exempla in the
Middle Ages.[112] The discourse concludes with the author's discussion about the negative results of female will-power.[113] The
Scottish legendary provides the earliest version of the legend of
St Eugenia in medieval Britain,[114] and none of the later renderings offers such an excursus. The version in the fifteenth-century

Alphabet of Tales is, however, preceded by the Latin note 'Fallacia mulieris. Infra muliere'[115] and Caxton's Eugenia makes a short speech of six lines on the lecherous woman who provoked the Scottish discourse.[116]

In the Legenda aurea we learn about the genealogy of the dragon defeated by St Martha:

> Venerat autem per mare de Galatia Asiae, generatus a Leviathan, qui est serpens aquosus et ferocissimus, et ab Onacho animali, quod Galatiae regio gignit, quod in sectatores suos per spatium jugeris stercus suum velut spiculum dirigit et quidquid tetigerit, velut ignis exurit.[117]

In the Scottish legendary this passage is changed into:

> a fel beste of the kynd of thai
> that ar generyt in asya;
> ...
> & quha to fle mad hyme faste,
> his foylȝe eftir hyme cane he caste,
> the quhilk, quhat thinge It ourtuke,
> a[s] fyr gregois brynt at a luke.
> & that swith he wald ger ga
> eftyre ony, that he wald sla,
> of ane oxgange hale the space ... [118]

In accordance with the Legenda aurea, W M Metcalfe suggests identifying the Onacho with the onager or wild ass.[119] The casting of ordure towards its pursuers is, however, no characteristic of the onager.[120] Onacho should be glossed with 'bonasus (or bison)',[121] a beast first mentioned by Pliny:

> tradunt in Paeonis feram, quae bonasus vocetur, equina iuba, cetera tauro similem, cornibus ita in se flexis, ut non sint utilia pugnae; quapropter fuga sibi auxiliari reddentem in ea fimum, interdum et trium iugerum longitudine, cuius contactus sequentes ut ignis aliquis amburat.[122]

The monster is also included in Solinus' Collectanea rerum memorabilium, in De bestiis et aliis rebus, in Thomas of Chantimpre's Liber de natura rerum, in MS Cambridge Univ. Libr. II.4.26 and in MS Ashmole 1511.[123]

The version of the SEL does not refer to the dragon's parentage.[124] And though William Caxton provides information on the dragon's origin, he, like the Scottish author, transfers the bonasus' characteristic to the dragon.[125] An explanation might be that the mythical beast was not commonly known among the laity, a fact which made it possible to apply the bonasus' characteristic to the dragon.[126] Instead of forgetting about the frightening habit of the bonasus, a device preferred by the author of the SEL, the Scottish author adopts it in order to create a more terrifying picture of the dragon.

V

An examination of the serpent imagery in the Legends of the Saints
suggests that it should not be judged as the tedious and simplistic work it was frequently thought to be.[127] Such views easily
arise when we are not taking the trouble of carefully retracing
the knowledge available to medieval man and when we disregard the
fact that he greatly enjoyed recognising his knowledge in a series
of new combinations offered to him in a piece of literary art.[128]
By studying the traditional traits of snakes in conjunction with
the narratives they appear in, we are able to discover a complex
system of associations which direct our attention mainly to the
moral but also to the allegorical implication of each legend. The
author's achievement lies in his great skill in adapting the
traditional material to suit his overall intention, the moral
instruction of his readers or listeners. Thus any claim that he
was not interested in the people he wrote for would be clearly
wrong.[129] The narrative quality of his snake scenes leads to an
increase in their emotional impact on those who read or listen to
them, an aim which also takes the anagogical implication of the
saints' lives into consideration:

> ...
> thai suld dresse thare deuocione,
> in prayere & in oracione,
> or thingis that thare hart mycht stere
> tyl wyne hewine, tyl thai are here.[130]

When using serpent imagery our author does not apply new
methods. By favouring material from the natural encyclopedias and
bestiaries for his serpent figures, he is in line with the preachers of the fourteenth and fifteenth century who rather draw on an
animal's natural characteristics than on one of its mythical
traits.[131] Unlike their predecessors, they put a greater emphasis
on the narrational qualities of sermons.[132] Moral instruction was
of prime importance, allegorical interpretation of animal figures
of secondary importance.[133] The anagogical level was only used in
so far as it hinted at the reward of proper moral conduct. As an
old minister,[134] our author must have known these practices well.
Animal lore and saints' lives were recurrent elements in medieval
sermons.[135]

Notes

1   All references to the Scottish legendary will be to W M
    Metcalfe's edition, Legends of the Saints in the Scottish
    Dialect of the Fourteenth Century, 3 vols, STS, 1st Series,
    13/18, 23/25, 35/37 (Edinburgh, 1888, 1891, 1896).
        The following numbers refer to the individual legends and
    lines in which the name of a snake is given:

SNAKE: i. 237; ii. 35, 39; x. 67, 87, 89; xi. 299; xxxi.
    395; xxxiii. 50; xxxix. 240, 249, 259; xlv. 255, 261.
ADDER: xi. 305, 310f, 316, 321, 325; xvi. 302; xviii. 427.
ASP: xlv. 256, 263.
COLUBRE: xxxi. 397; xlv. 259, 265.
VIPER: ii. 35; xlv. 258.
DRAGON: iv. 340; viii. 16, 39, 49; x. 153, 169; xvii. 25;
    xxviii. 409; xxxiii. 105, 158, 180, 194, 254, 260,
    262, 266, 282, 294, 299, 305.

2 See C T Lewis and C Short, <u>A Latin Dictionary</u> (Oxford 1879,
repr 1980), s.v. <u>coluber, -bri</u> m. and <u>colubra, -ae f</u>.; DOST,
s.v. <u>colubre</u> n.; MED, s.v. <u>coluber</u> n.; OED, s.v. <u>colubre</u> n.
 Isidore of Seville as well as the compilers of <u>De bestiis
et aliis rebus</u> and the Latin bestiary of MS Cambr. Univ.
Libr. II.4.26 (the latter two apparently obtained their
information about the reptile from Isidore of Seville's
<u>Etymologiae</u>) seem to have regarded the word <u>colubre</u> as a
synonym for 'snake; (see Isidore de Seville, <u>Etymologies,
Livre XII: Des Animaux</u>, ed and trans J Andre (Paris, 1986),
iv 2; <u>De bestiis et aliis rebus</u>, in <u>Patrologiae</u>, ed J-P
Migne, vol CLXXVII (Paris, 1879), III. xl; and <u>The Book of
Beasts</u>, trans T H White (London, 1955), p 165). In John
Trevisa's translation of Bartholomaeus Anglicus' natural
encyclopedia <u>De Proprietatibus Rerum</u> the word is obviously
used as a equivalent for 'snake' as well as for indicating a
specific kind of venomous serpent (see Bartholomaeus Anglicus, <u>On The Properties of Things</u>, trans John Trevisa, ed M C
Seymour <u>et al</u>, 2 vols, vol II (Oxford, 1975), pp 1125, 1182).
Vincent of Beauvais adopts the latter view (see <u>Speculum
Maius</u>, 4 vols, vol I: <u>Speculum Naturale</u>, facsimile edition of
the Douai 1624 print (Graz, 1964), XX. xxviii, col 1476). In
his annotations to his edition of Isidore of Seville's
<u>Etymologiae</u>, J Andre identifies the colubre with a kind of
water snake (see <u>Etymologies</u>, XII, p 133, note 133). But it
is apparently only Pliny who associates the colubre with
water (see <u>Natural History</u>, ed and trans W H S Jones, Loeb
Classical Library, 10 vols, vol VIII (London, 1963), XXXII
xix §53; <u>On the Properities of Things</u> II. 1182; and Vincent
of Beauvais, op.cit.).
3 <u>Leg. S.</u> xlv 255-66.
4 <u>On the Properties of Things</u> II. 1134f.
5 <u>Leg. S.</u> ii. 35-8.
6 All Bible quotations are taken from R Weber's edition <u>Biblia
Sacra Iuxta Vulgatam Versionem</u>, 2 vols (Stuttgart, revd edn
1975).
7 See C Iulius Solinus, <u>Collectanea rerum memorabilium</u>, ed T
Mommsen (Berlin, revd edn 1958), 2/32.
8 <u>On the Properties of Things</u> II, 1267, see also p 1266, 11.21f.
 The reference is probably to St Ambrose, <u>Exameron,</u> V 18 (in
<u>Sancti Ambrosii Opera</u>, pars prima, ed C Schenkl, Corpus Eccle-
siasticorum Latinorum, XXXII (Vienna, 1897). For St Ambrose
retelling and discussing the incident of St Paul and the
viper see <u>Exameron</u> VI. 38.
 Vincent of Beauvais, MS Ashmole 1511 and MS Cambr. Univ.

Libr. II.4.26 also refer to St Ambrose when writing on the viper (see Vincent of Beauvais, Naturale, XX. xlviii, col 1485, Bestiarium, Die Texte der Handschrift MS Ashmole 1511 der Bodleian Library Oxford, ed and trans F Unterkircher, Interpretationes ad codices, 3 (Graz, 1986), pp 174ff; Book of Beasts, p 170).

9   Leg.S. xxxi 393-97.

10 See On the Properties of Things II 1182. With the saints' legends having been read on the appropriate saints' days during the ecclesiastical year, an audience could have learned about the viper's and colubre's dangerousness by the time it was St Christina's day. From the fatal property of these two snakes the one of the asp, which was a well-known beast due to its alleged ability of closing up its ears, could have been easily deduced.

11 Jacobus a Voragine, Legenda Aurea vulgo Historia Lombardica dicta, ed T Graesse (Dresden, 1846, 3rd edn 1890, repr in Osnabruck, 1965), ch xcviii, p 421.

12 The Middle English versions of the St Christina legend are to be found in (1) The South English Legendary, ed C D'Evelyn and A Mill, 3 vols, vol I, EETS, O S, 235 (London, 1956), pp 315-27; (2) the Northern Homily Cycle, in Altenglische Legenden, N F, ed C Horstmann (Heilbronn, 1881, repr in Hildesheim, 1969), pp 93- 6; (3) William Paris, Cristine, in Sammlung altenglischer Legenden, ed C Horstmann (Heilbronn, 1878), repr in Hildesheim, 1969), pp 183-90; (4) Osbern Bokenham, Legendys of Hooly Wummen, ed M S Serjeantson, EETS, O S, 206 (London, 1938), pp 58-86; (5) the unpublished St Christina legend in the Gilte Legende of 1438; and (6) William Caxton, The Golden Legend or Lives of the Saints, ed F S Ellis, Temple Classics, 7 vols, vol IV (London, 1900), pp 93-7. (Cf. C D'Evelyn, 'Bibliography: Individual Saints', in A Manual of the Writings in Middle English, 1050-1500, gen ed J Burke Severs, vol II (Hamden, 1970), pp 575f).

13 SEL, vol I, p 325.

14 See MED, s.v. naddre n., and OED, s.v. adder[2].

15 See William Paris, Cristine, 1.498; NHC, 11.259-63; and Caxton, Golden Legend, IV 96.

16 See Bokenham, Hooly Wummen, p 80, 11.2935f.

17 J MacQueen, Numerology, Theory and Outline History of a Literary Mode (Edinburgh, 1985), p 17.

18 See MacQueen, Numerology, pp 17, 55, 59, 61, and H Meyer, Die Zahlenallegorese im Mittelalter, Methode und Gebrauch, Münstersche Mittelalter-Schriften, 25 (Munich, 1975), pp 129-32.

19 The Sex Werkdayis and Agis, in The Asloan Manuscript, A Miscellany in Prose and Verse, Written by John Asloan, ed W A Craigie, 2 vols, vol I, STS, 2nd Series, 14 (Edinburgh, 1923), p 326, 11.12f. See also MacQueen, Numerology, p 51, and Meyer, Zahlenallegorese, pp 131f.

20 Dr T J A Heffernan kindly granted me permission to quote from his unpublished PhD thesis Studies in the Lives of the Saints with Special Attention to the 'Northern Homily Cycle', University of Cambridge, 1977, p 5, cf. also p 21.

21 See, for instance, Num.21:5-7, Deut. 8:15 and John 3:14.

22   Iesus autem plenus Spiritu Sancto
                      regressus est ab Iordane
                   et agebatur in Spiritu in desertum
                      diebus quadraginta
                   et temptabatur a diabolo

23   See Leg.S. ix. 153-62.
24   See Metcalfe, Leg.S. vol. III, p 444.
25   Leg.S. xlv. 277-79. For St Philip sending a dragon into
     wilderness see Leg.S. viii. 44.
26   See Meyer, Zahlenallegorese, p 132. That the Scottish author
     has a knowledge of medieval numerology can be well illus-
     trated by a passage on the election of St Matthew as one of
     the Twelve Apostles:

                   thane petyre saw thare wantyt ane,
                   that for apostil suld be tane
                   yn-sted of Iudas, that tynt had
                   sik dingnite, fore he cause mad.
                   bot sa to be in nowmyre ode,
                   It wes nocht til thai dwelte with god;
                   for-thy he wald thai vare twelfe ewyn,
                   & nocht to be in nowmyre lewyne,
                   for twelfe foure tymis partyt in thre
                   betaknis the treutht of the trinyte
                   that tha foure thryse to purchas suld fond
                   In foure partis of this warld rond.
                                   (xii. 304-15)

27   The beasts named are as follows: SEL, 'neddren', vol I p 325,
     11.300ff; NHC 'Two scorpions ... And two nedders ... And a
     wilde wurme on ai ther pap', p 95, 11.259-61; William Paris,
     Cristine, 'sexte serpens', p 188, 11.408; Bokenham, Hooly
     Wummen, 'Two hornyd serpentys ... And two snakys', p 80,
     11.2935f; and Caxton, Golden Legend, 'two adders, two
     serpents and two asps', IV 96.
28   On the devil and his association with idolatry see R Woolf,
     'Saints' Lives', in Continuations and Beginnings: Studies in
     Old English Literature, ed E G Stanley (London, 1966), pp 41f.
29   Leg.S. xlv. 273-6.
30   See ii. 35-8; x. 65-70, 87f; xi. 320-3; xviii. 423-7; xxxiii.
     50; xlv. 255-76.
31   Leg.S. xxviii. 407-24.
32   Jacobus a Voragine, Legenda Aurea, ch xciii, p 401.
33   The ten Middle English versions and their editions, if avail-
     able, are: (1) Seinte Marherete pe Meiden ant Martyr, ed F M
     Mack, EETS, O S, 193 (London, 1934, repr 1958). pp 2-55; (2)
     'St Margaret', in SEL, vol I, pp 291-302; (3) Seynt Mergrete
     (MS Nat. Libr. Scotl. 19.2.1), in Altenglische Legenden, pp
     266-35; (4) Meidan Maregrete (MS Trin. Cambr. 323), in Alten-
     glische Legenden, pp 489-98; (5) Mergarete (MS Bodl. Libr.
     6922), in Altenglische Legenden, pp 236-41; (6) 'De Solemp-
     nitate Sancte Margarete Virginis', in John Mirk, Mirk's
     Festial: A Collection of Homilies, ed T Erbe, EETS, E S, 96

(London, 1905), pp 199-202; (7) John Lydgate's 'The Legend of Seynt Margarete', in Minor Poems of John Lydgate, ed H N MacCracken, part I, EETS, E S, 107 (London, 1911), pp 173-92, (8) the St Margaret legend in the yet unpublished Gilte Legende; (9) 'Vita S Margaretae', in Bokenham, Hooly Wummen, pp 7-38; (10) 'The Life of S. Margaret', in Caxton, Golden Legend, IV. 66-72. (Cf. D'Evelyn, 'Bibliography: Individual Saints', pp 606ff).

34   See Seinte Marherete the Meiden ant Martyr, pp 22f, 11.4ff; Altenglische Legenden, p 238, 11.307-9, p 494, 1.174; and Bokenham, Hooly Wummen, p 19, 11.701ff.

35   See Altenglische Legenden, p 230, 11.204f.

36   See C Plinius Secundus, Naturalis Historiae, liber VIII ed and trans R Konig in co-operation with G Winkler, Tusculum Bucherei (Munich, 1976), xi, 32.

37   Isidore de Seville, Etymologies, XII, iv. 4.

38   See De bestiis II xxiv; Book of Beasts, pp 165; MS Ashmole 1511, pp 172f; Thomas Cantimpratensis, Liber de natura rerum, ed H Boese, 2 parts, part I (Berlin & New York, 1973), VIII xvi. 1f; Vincent of Beauvais, Naturale, XX xxix, col 1476; and On the Properties of Things II. 1184.

39   Leg.S. xxxiii. 50.

40   See also Book of Beasts, p 167 and MS Ashmole 1511, p 174f.

41   See, for example, Isidore de Seville, Etymologies, XII, iv. 45; De bestiis III xl; Book of Beasts, p 165; Thomas Cantimpratensis, Liber de natura rerum, VIII i. 51; and On the Properties of Things II 1245.

42   See Vincent of Beauvais, Naturale, XX xxix, col 1476.

43   See, for example, F Klingender, Animals in Art and Thought to the End of the Middle Ages (London, 1971), figs 104, 192; and M D Anderson, Misericord, Medieval Life in English Woodcarving (Harmondsworth, 1954, repr 1956), fig 20.

44   For the latter group see F McCulloch, Medieval Latin and French Bestiaries, University of North Carolina Studies in the Romance Languages and Literatures, 33 (Chapel Hill, 1960, repr with addenda and corrigenda in 1962), pp 112f; N Fischer, 'Handlist of Animal References in Middle English Religious Prose', Leeds Studies in English, N S, 4 (1970), pp 73f; and B Rowland, Animals with Human Faces, A Guide to Animal Symbolism (Knoxville, Tennessee, 1973, London, 1974), pp 66-70.

45   See A Survey of Manuscripts Illuminated in the British Isles, gen ed J J G Alexander, vol II: E Temple, Anglo-Saxon Manuscripts 900-1066 (London, 1976), ill. 310 (dated 1050); and vol III: N Morgan, Early Gothic Manuscripts [I] 1190-1250 (London, 1982), ill. 276 (dated c.1240-50). Illustrations of hairy dragons are also to be found in R S Loomis, Arthurian Legends in Medieval Art (London, 1938), figs 66, 180, 283, 349, 387.

46   Vincent of Beauvais, op.cit. See also Albertus Magnus, De Animalibus Libri XXVI nach der Cölner Urschrift (ed H Stadler, vol II, Beitrage zur Geschichte der Philosphie des Mittelalters, 16 (Munster, 1920)), XXV. §25:

Et visus est unus ab Avicenna in cuius collo secundum latitudinem colli erant pili descendentes longi et grossi ad modum iubarum equi.

47   See, for example, Fischer, 'Animal References', pp 64, 95; M W
      Bloomfield, 'Appendix I. Association of Animals and Sins', The
      Seven Deadly Sins (Michigan State University Press, 1952), pp
      246f; and Rowland, Animals, pp 40f.
48   See De bestiis II xxiv; Book of Beasts, p 167; and MS Ashmole
      1511, pp 174f. In his attempt to illuminate Rev.12:9, Nicholas
      de Lyre tells us that the dragon's size indicates the beast's
      great pride and power (see Nicolas de Lyre, Biblia sacra cum
      glossa ordinaria primum guidem a Strabo Fuldensis collecta, 7
      vols, vol VI (Paris, 1590), 1578ff). I owe this reference to
      L C Kordecki, Traditions and Development of the Medieval
      Dragon, unpublished PhD thesis, University of Toronto, 1980,
      p 155.
49   See Fischer, 'Animal References', p 73, and Bloomfield,
      'Animals and Sins', pp 246-8.
50   See, for example, On the Properties of Things II. 1118f;
      Fischer, 'Animal References', p 64; Bloomfield, 'Animals and
      Sins', p 246; Rowland, Animals, pp 37-41; and M Thiebaux, 'The
      Mouth of the Boar as a Symbol in Medieval Literature', Romance
      Philology 22 (1968-69), pp 281-4, 292, 296-8.
51   See Fischer, 'Animal References', pp 94f, Bloomfield, 'Animals
      and Sins', pp 246-9; and Rowland, Animals, pp 143, 146.
          According to B Rowland, a boar, two serpents and a dragon
      are found together on a misericord in the Henry VII Chapel of
      Westminster Abbey (op.cit., p 42).
52   See note 22. For the dragon's association with wilderness or
      desert see, for example, Mal.1:3, Isa. 13:21, 34:13, 35:7,
      43:20, Jer. 9:11, 49:33, 51:37; Thomas Cantimpratensis, Liber
      de natura rerum, VIII xvi. 12; Vincent of Beauvais, Naturale,
      XX xxix, col 1476.
53   Leg.S. xxviii. 47-52.
54   See Thiébaux, 'Mouth of the Boar', pp 283ff, 297. (The boar is
      only mentioned once in the Legends of the Saints; see the
      legend of St Thecla xlix. 207-16. It is one of the beasts
      attempting to assail the saint).
55   Richard Rolle of Hampole, The Psalter, or Psalm of David and
      Certain Canticles, ed H R Bramley (Oxford, 1884), p 296.
56   Cf. Thiébaux, 'Mouth of the Boar', pp 290f, and see The
      Avowing of King Arthur, ed R Dahood, Garland Medieval Texts,
      10 (New York & London, 1984), 11.67, 120, 211, 228.
57   Avowing, 11.227f.
58   See, for example, Fischer, 'Animal References', p 73.
59   On the Properties of Things II. 1185.
60   See, for example, Mark 9:47 and Jas. 3:6.
61   Secreta Secretorum, ed R Steele, EETS, E S, 74 (London, 1898),
      p 218.
62   See T Wolpers, Die englische Heiligenlegende des Mittelalters
      (Buchreihe der Anglia Zeitschrift, 10 (Tubingen, 1964), p 170.
63   Manfred Görlach, too, sees a clear influence of the Legenda
      aurea on the SEL and Mirk's Festial. Due to the subject of his
      study, he does not comment on Lydgate's version of the St
      Margaret legend (See The 'South English Legendary', 'Gilte
      Legende' and 'Golden Legend', Braunschweiger Anglistische
      Arbeiten, 3 (Brunswick, 1972), pp 7ff). But Theodor Wolpers

regards the _Legenda aurea_ as Lydgate's source for the St
Margaret legend (see _Heiligenlegende_, p 309).

Since I had no access to any of the MSS of the _Gilte
Legende_, I had to rely on T Wolfers' discussion of the St
Margaret legend (See _Heiligenlegende_, pp 376ff).

64   SEL, p 297, 11.165-70; see also 1.158 where the author
expresses the same doubt.

65   Lydgate, _Minor Poems_, p 183f, 11.283-94; see also _Mirk's
Festial_, p 200, 1.30, and Caxton, _Golden Legend_, IV. 68.

66   See Caxton, _Golden Legend_, IV. 68f.

67   See _Seinte Marherete the Meiden ant Martyr_, pp 24f, 11.9ff;
Altenglische Legende, p 231, 1.207, p 238, 11.310f, p 494,
1.175; _Mirk's Festial_, p 200, 11.31f; Lydgate, _Minor Poems_,
p 184, 11.288f; Wolpers, _Heiligenlegende_, p 376; and Bokenham, _Hooly Wummen_, p 20, 11.708-12.

68   See Wolpers, _Heiligenlegende_, pp 309, 371f.

69   See Wolpers, _Heiligenlegende_, pp 376, 391.

70   See Wolpers, _Heiligenlegende_, p 170.

71   _Angelsachsische Homilien und Heiligenleben_, ed B Assmann,
(Kassel, 1889, repr in Darmstadt, 1964), pp 213f, 11.179-86,
199-202. The text is taken from the eleventh or twelfth
century MS Harley 5327, one of the earliest manuscripts
preserving the Mombritius version of the St Margaret legend;
see Wolpers _Heiligenlegende_, p 170, and Assmann, op.cit.,
p 268.

72   See Wolpers, _Heiligenlegende_, pp 188, 295.

73   See _Altenglische Legenden_, p 238, 1.304, p 494, 1.172.

74   See D W Robertson, 'Why the Devil wears green', _Modern
Language Notes_ 69 (1954), pp 470-72, and 'The Friar's Tale',
in The Complete Works of Geoffrey Chaucer, ed F N Robinson
(Oxford, 1957, 2nd edn 1978), pp 90f, 11.1379-83, 1447.

75   See F Ohly, 'Probleme der mittelalterlichen Bedeutungsforschung und das Taubenbild des Hugo de Folieto', in _Schriften
zur mittelalterlichen Bedeutungsforschung_ (Darmstadt, 1977,
2nd edn 1983), p 38; and C Meier, 'Die Bedeutung der Farben im
Werk Hildegards von Bingen', _Fruhmittelalterliche Studien_ 6
(1972), pp 285, 287, 289, and _Gemma Spiritalis_, part I,
Munstersche Mittelalter-Schriften, 34 (Munich, 1977), pp 153,
156.

76   _Seinte Marherete the Meiden ant Martyr_, p 20, 11. 22f; see
also 23f.

77   See Bokenham, _Hooly Wummen_, p 19, 1.692.

78   See Ohly, 'Probleme', p 65, and Meier, _Gemma_, p 180.

79   See _Medieval Heraldry, Some Fourteenth Century Heraldic Works_,
ed E J Jones (Cardiff, 1943), pp 15, 97f, 152, 216.

80   See Ohly, op.cit.; Meier 'Bedeutung der Farben', pp 278f, and
Gemma, pp 181f.

81   See Meier, _Gemma,_ p 165, and 'Bedeutung der Farben', p 263.
The St Margaret legend of the _Meidenhad Group_ and Osbern
Bokenham's version are the only Middle English texts mention-
ing the image of the sword. In the former version the dragon's
tongue is compared to a sword gleaming with fire (see _Seinte
Marherete the Meiden ant Martyr_, p 20, 1.31f). In the latter

text the beast holds the glittering weapon in its claws (see Bokenham, Hooly Wummen, p 19, 1.697).

82 ...

et ecce draco magnus rufus habens
capita septem et cornua decem
et in capitibus euis diademata septem
(Apc. 12:3)

83 See Meier, Gemma, pp 148, 150
84 See Medieval Heraldry, pp 19, 99, 148.
85 See, for instance, Leg.S. iv. 340, viii. 16, x. 169, xvii. 25, xxxiii. 50, 254; and Fischer, 'Animal References', p 73.
86 See, for example, i. 563; ii. 273; xix. 550; xxxiv. 19; xxxvi. 883; xl. 396ff; xli. 165, 327, 331; xliii. 108, 111.
87 Leg.S. xxviii. 428.
88 See Meier, 'Bedeutung der Farben', pp 256f, and Gemma, p 164. Alexander Neckam establishes a close connection between Ethiopians, vices and dragons (see Alexander Neckam, De naturis rerum, libri duo, ed T Wright, Rolls Series, 34 (London, 1863), II. cxlvii).
89 See Angelsachsische Homilien, p 214, 1.206.
90 See Seinte Marherete the Meiden ant Martyr, p 24, 1.22.
91 See Bokenham, Hooly Wummen, p 20, 11.718ff.
92 See Leg.S. xxviii. 4, 23, 29, 31, 708.
93 See note 82. Cf. also fig 20 of Anderson, Misericords, as an example of a dragon with seven heads symbolising the seven deadly sins.
94 See, for instance, Meier, Gemma, pp 236f.
95 De bestiis II. xxiv. See also Book of Beasts, p 167, and MS Ashmole 1511, p 174f. For the image of the devil as an angel of light see Luke 10:18f.
96 Leg.S. xxviii. 1-4, 21-4.
97 See F Ohly, 'Tau und Perle. Ein Vortrag' as well as 'Die Geburt der Perle aus dem Blitz', in Schriften zur mittel-alterlichen Bedeutungsforschung, pp 275, 293-311; A Salzer, Die Sinnbilder und Beiworte Mariens in der deutschen Liter-atur und lateinischen Hymnenpoesie des Mittelalters (Seit-enstetten, 1886-94, repr in Darmstadt, 1967), pp 76, 224, 243-8; McCulloch, Bestiaries, pp 154f; On the Properties of Things II. 856f; English Medieval Lapidaries, ed J Evans and M S Serjeantson, EETS, O S, 190 (London, 1933), pp 108ff.
98 See Apc. 21:21.
99 See Bokenham, Hooly Wummen, p 19, 1.689; and cf also Alexander Neckam, De naturis rerum, II. cxlvii.
100 See Salzer, Sinnbilder, pp 71f.
101 See, for instance, Deut. 32-41f, Ps. 17:13 and Rom. 13:4. Deut. 32:41 mentions the aspects of light with the sword.
102 Leg. S. vii 271-6.
103 See Leg.S. xxviii 425-32.
104 See Angelsachsische Homilien, pp 213ff, 11.179-249; Seinte Marherete the Meiden ant Martyr, p 20, 11.20f, p 24, 11.20f; Altenglische Legenden, p 230f, 11.201f, p 239, 1.323-52, p 494f, 11.170-205; Bokenham, Hooly Wummen, pp 19ff, 11.689-757. The Meidenhad legend provides no names for the two devils.

105   Cf., for example, xvi. 302, xviii. 427 and xxxi. 397.

106   See Bokenham, Hooly Wummen, p 21, 1.758.

107   Jacobus a Voragine, Legenda Aurea, ch. xc, p 381.

108   See F C Tubach, Index Exemplorum, A Handbook of Religious Tales, FF Communications, 204 (Helsinki, 1969), nos 49, 370.

109   See Leg.S. xxxi. 393–514, and Jacobus a Voragine, Legenda Aurea, ch. cxxxvi, pp 603f.

110   Leg.S. xxxi. 395–400.

111   See Leg.S. xxxi 401–86. Emperor Otto III was unmarried in real life (see Lexikon der deutschen Geschichte, ed G Taddey (Stuttgart, 2nd rev edn, 1983), p 929). The author of the Scottish legendary dates the incident with 984 AD, the year after the death of Otto II when Otto III was just four years of age) see Leg.S. xxxi. 479–81, and Taddey, op.cit.).

112   See Tubach, Index Exemplorum, nos. 1284, 2840, 3380 (cf. p 502).

113   See Leg.S. xxxi. 487–514.

114   See D'Evelyn, 'Bibliography: Individual Saints', p 585.

115   An Alphabet of Tales, An English 15th century translation of the 'Alphabetum Narrationem', ed M MacLeod Banks, 2 parts, part I, EETS, O S, 126 (London, 1904), p 218f.

116   See Caxton, Golden Legend, V. 122f. The unpublished Gilte Legende and Wynkyn de Worde's print (1495) of William Caxton's translation of a French rendering of the Vitas patrum also each contain a version of the legend (see D'Evelyn, 'Bibliography: Individual Saints', p 584). Unfortunately, I was not able to consult these versions.

117   Jacobus a Voragine, Legenda Aurea, ch. cv, p 444.

118   Leg.S. xvii, 29f, 43–9.

119   See Metcalfe, Leg.S., III. 200.

120   See, for example, McCulloch, Bestiaries, pp 144f; On the Properties of Things II. 1230; and Fischer, 'Animal References', p 56.

121   The OED, D Schmidtke and T H White identify the bonasus with the bison (see OED, s.v. bonasus; D Schmidtke, Geistliche Tierinterpretation in der deutschsprachigen Literatur des Mittelalters (1100–1500), 2 parts, part II, PhD Thesis, Freie Universitat Berlin, 1968, p 580, note 806; and Book of Beasts, p 33). On the basis of Pliny's Natural History and Solinus's Collectanea (see notes 124f), C T Lewis and C Short gloss the word with 'a species of bull in Paeonia, with the hair of a horse, and with horns unfit for fighting' (Latin Dictionary, s.v. bonasus).
      I prefer the name bonasus in this context since it implies the beast's mythical way of self-defence which the zoological name bison does not.

122   Pliny, Historia Naturalis, VIII. xvi. 40.

123   See Solinus, Collectanea, 40/10; De bestiis III. v; Thomas Cantimpratensis, Liber de natura rerum IV. xi; Book of Beasts, p 33; and MS Ashmole 1511, pp 38f.

124   See SEL, p 348, 11.15–24.

125   See Caxton, Golden Legend, IV. 136.

126   The bonasus is not found in any other Middle Scots literary work. The earliest evidence for the word given in the OED is the year 1592 (s.v. bonasus).

127 See Wolpers, <u>Heiligenlegende</u>, p 278; M P McDiarmid, 'The Northern Initiative: John of Fordun, John Barbour and the author of the <u>Saints' Legends</u>', in <u>Literature of the North,</u> eds D Hewitt and M Spiller (Aberdeen, 1983), p 9; Heffernan, <u>Lives of Saints</u>, p 2, and 'An Analysis of the Narrative Motifs in the Legend of St Eustace', <u>Medieval Hagiography and Romance</u>, Medievalia et Humanistica, N S, 6 (Cambridge, 1975), p 63.

128 Cf. Heffernan, <u>Lives of Saints</u>, pp 2f, 8, and 'Narrative Motifs', pp 85f.

129 See Wolpers, <u>Heiligenlegende</u>, p 278.

130 Leg.S., Prol., 11.17-20; see also 11.28-32.

131 Cf. D J McFarland, <u>Animal Lore and Medieval English Sermon Style,</u> PhD thesis, Florida State University, 1980, pp 253-77.

132 See McFarland, op.cit., and S C Aston, 'The Saint in Medieval Literature', <u>Modern Language Review</u> 65 (1970), p xxxvi.

133 See McFarland, op.cit.

134 See <u>Leg.S.</u>, Prol., 1 35f.

135 On checking the motifs of the Scottish legendary passages discussed above with the <u>Index Exemplorum,</u> one perceives a considerable resemblance between some of the medieval <u>exempla</u> and some of the motifs of the snake episodes in the <u>Legends of the Saints</u>. Thus, we read, for instance, of <u>exempla</u> deal-ing with snakes suckling at breasts (no. 4281), of a dragon vision (no. 1780), of dragons swallowing people (nos. 1778f), of a devil appearing to persons of great moral purity (nos. 1520, 1528, 1537, etc), and of Satan assuming the shape of a snake or of another animal (nos. 529, 1530ff, 1557). I would also like to recall the three <u>exempla</u> of lecherous women told in conjunction with the figure of the colubre in the legend of St Eugenia.

Chapter 8

GOLAGROS AND GAWANE: A WORD FOR PEACE

Elizabeth Walsh, RSCJ

Sir Philip Sidney spoke of the power of story: to hold children
from play and old men from the chimney corner. Certainly it is
true that storytelling is one of the deepest instincts of the
human heart.

N Scott Momaday invests story with an even greater significance.[1] In his essay 'The Man Made of Words', he relates an experience he had one night when he had nearly completed The Way to
Rainy Mountain. As he looked down at the page he began to focus on
the name of an old Indian woman with whom he had once spoken. As
he focused on her name, Ko-Sahn, he began to experience 'the sense
of the magic of words and of names'. Suddenly the old woman was in
the room with him, and they began to converse. She explained that
her existence in his imagination was a very real kind of existence. She herself, through her imagination, was present when her
people, the Kiowas, 'came into the world through a hollow log'.
She took part in their great migration; she saw the stars fall.
One of the earliest episodes in the Kiowa tradition was the falling of the meteors in North America on 13 November 1833. She became
for the author the locus of the tribal memory, the repository of
the imagination of the race. Then she disappeared.

Momaday goes on to discuss the subject of storytelling. 'We are
what we imagine. Our very existence consists in our imagination of
ourselves'.[2] The work of the imagination is embodied first in the
myths, legends, and tales of the oral tradition, and then in
literature. Storytelling is an imaginative and creative act 'by
which man strives to realise his capacity for wonder, meaning and
delight. It is also a process in which man invests and preserves
himself in the context of ideas. Man tells stories in order to
understand his experience'.[3] We are defined through words. Only
through language can we take possession of ourselves. The year of
the falling stars marked the beginning of decline and deterior-
ation for the Kiowa. The storyteller took that fact and wove a
story, investing the historical fact, and the years of subsequent
decline, with meaning.

The imagination of the people found in the falling stars a symbol,
an omen of their destiny. A meaningful story was born, a story
which enabled the people to endure defeat and suffering because it
placed their defeat in a wider context, gave it a cosmic dimension, gave it meaning: '... it was all meant to be ... The order
of the world was broken. ...'[4]

The early myths of a people are precious, for they are emblem-

atic of the perceived destiny of that people. Myths can be viewed
in a variety of ways. For Roland Barthes 'myth is a means of
portraying historically contingent phenomena as if they were
natural and universal, a conservative force "whose very end ... is
to immobilize the world." The purpose of myth is to make the
values of a culture vivid and immediate and to justify the power
relationships it embodies and perpetuates.'[5] In his study of the
mythology of the American frontier, Richard Slotkin writes:

> The mythology of a nation is the intelligible mask of that
> enigma called 'the national character'. Through myths the
> psychology and world view of our cultural ancestors are
> transmitted to modern descendants, in such a way and with
> such power that our perception of contemporary reality and
> our ability to function in the world are directly, often
> tragically, affected.[6]

Myths are constructs of the human mind, drawn almost subconscious-
ly from historical reality, expressed through images which have a
cosmic dimension. The myth structures reality in a certain way and
induces a pattern of behaviour in its believers. Thus Slotkin
defines a mythology as 'a complex of narratives that dramatizes
the world vision and historical sense of a people or culture,
reducing centuries of experience into a constellation of compelling metaphors'.[7] The power of myths to organise and explain
experience is very real. The danger is that people may continue to
live by them when the historical and cultural circumstances which
contributed to the formation of the myths have changed. Myths do
express universal realities. Yet there is an element of historical
and social contingency as well.

The obscure Battle of Mount Badon was the fact out of which
grew the cycle of legends concerning Arthur and his knights. The
efforts of the Welshmen to repel the invasions of the Saxons
became the compelling symbol of the desire to preserve civilis-
ation from destruction, to defend the ordering of society against
the forces which threaten to disturb our way of life. Winston
Churchill spoke eloquently of the enduring meaning of that early
struggle:

> And wherever men are fighting against barbarism, tyranny, and
> massacre, for freedom, law, and honour, let them remember
> that the fame of their deeds, even though they themselves be
> exterminated, may perhaps be celebrated as long as the world
> rolls round. Let us then declare that King Arthur and his
> noble knights, guarding the Sacred Flame of Christianity and
> the theme of a world order, sustained by valour, physical
> strength, and good horses and armour, slaughtered innumerable
> hosts of foul barbarians and set decent folk an example for
> all time.[8]

The work of the poet is the same: to discern some order in the
chaos of experience, to provide some bulwark against the forces of
destruction. The early poets seized upon the singular facts of
their existence, projected meaning into these facts, and created

stories to embody and communicate their ideals. The imagination, however, perhaps necessarily, is flexible. As one image of society replaces another, the myth is altered to correspond to the new reality. The Arthurian legends spread through France, Germany, England; they formed a powerful influence on the medieval imagination and in turn that imagination continually altered and revised the stories to express new modes of thought, new patterns of behaviour, new ideals, new dreams.

The early stories of Scotland were also rooted in history. The legends of Robert Bruce, James Douglas and William Wallace also became 'a constellation of compelling metaphors' for the struggle for freedom and national identity which marked the early history of that country. The stories of Wallace and Bruce were more central to the Scottish imagination than were the stories of Arthur. One Scottish romance, however, which relates a tale of Arthur and his knights is The Tale of Golagros and Gawane. This fifteenth-century story challenges many of the assumptions of medieval society and culture. It also reflects some of the preoccupations of the Scottish people. In a world that took warfare for granted, the poem speaks for peace; in a world which glorified the bonds between vassal and lord, the poem speaks for freedom. It is worth exploring as a myth in transition.

In 1508 Walter Chepman and Andrew Millar published the first book to be printed in Scotland. This 1508 volume contains eleven pieces, originally published separately. One of the eleven is 'The Knightly Tale of Golagros and Gawane'. This romance is one of the few appearances of Arthur in Scotland.[9] The Chepman and Millar print is the only extant copy of the poem. The Asloan Manuscript, compiled seven years later, in 1515, would seem to have once contained a copy of the poem as it is referred to in the index, but this manuscript version may have been nothing more than a copy of the printed version. So, of the origin and genesis of the poem we know very little. In his 1897 edition of the poem, F J Amours assigned a date of about 1470 to the poem, and that seems to be a fairly accurate supposition.

Golagros and Gawane is interesting in its literary relationships. By form and metre it is associated with a small group of alliterative poems written in the north of England or Scotland. By content it is French, or at least based upon a French original. The Golagros is written in the same stanzaic form as The Buke of the Howlat, The Tale of Rauf Coilyear, and The Awntyrs off Arthure at the Terne Wathelyne.[10] The stanza, combining alliteration and rhyme, consists of nine long alliterative lines rhyming ababababc and a wheel of four shorter lines rhyming dddc. The Pistill of Susan differs only in having a 'bob' of two syllables for the ninth line. Sir Gawane and the Green Knight also has a bob and wheel to punctuate the narrative flow, but the alliterative lines are unrhymed and the stanzas formed by the bob and wheel are of varying lengths. The content of the story is French in that the romance is a Scottish rendering of one section of the First Continuation of Chrétien's Perceval.[11] The changes wrought by the Scottish poet focus the particular concern of this paper.

One section of the First Continuation recounts the story of the rescue of Arthur's knight Girflet from the Chastel Orguellous.[12]

William Roach divides the section into sixteen episodes. The Scottish poem includes the story of Kay and the Spit (Episode 3, pp 249-58, 11. 9149-495) and the story of the assault on the castle (Episodes 8-15, pp 304-9, 11.11206-12490). The Scottish poet who composed the _Golagros_ created a frame which holds these tales together. A brief outline of the Scottish poem follows. We will then move on to the French poem to note the major differences.

As Arthur and his knights proceed on their journey to the Holy Land they come upon a walled city and decide to ask to be allowed to purchase food there. Sir Kay is sent to request the lord's permission for Arthur's knights to enter the city. This is the first episode. The story illustrates Kay's rudeness and the courtesy of Sir Gawane. It has no direct connection to the second episode of the poem, but both illustrate the courtesy of Sir Gawane and so might be said to form a kind of diptych, two images representing a similar theme. The second episode is of considerable interest, for the Scottish poet has so altered it that it becomes, in many ways, an independent creation.

After feasting with the lord of the walled city the expedition passes on through many distant lands until they come upon a marvellous dwelling, the grandeur of which intrigues Arthur. He wants to know who is lord of such a great castle. When he learns that the lord is an independent chieftain, owing allegiance to no one, he vows that he will return after the pilgrimage to exact homage of this man. Even though one of his own knights, Sir Spinagros, rebukes him for his pride and arrogance, Arthur holds to his purpose and besieges the castle upon his return from Jerusalem. Many knights lose their lives in the contest which follows, a contest which culminates in the encounter between the lord of the castle, Golagros, and Arthur's greatest champion, Gawane. Golagros is defeated but begs Gawane to save his (Golagros's) honour by pretending to be vanquished. Magnanimously Gawane concurs and feigns defeat. Golagros then takes Gawane to his castle and before his assembled followers declares the truth to them. He then asks them whether they prefer to have him as lord, although vanquished in the field, or to transfer their allegiance to another who will be their defense in the future. His people declare their loyalty to Golagros, and he submits to Gawane. The final twist of the story occurs at the end after Golagros has yielded his lands to Arthur and the two companies have feasted for nine days. Upon turning to leave, Arthur releases Golagros from his promise of fealty and restores his autonomy.

The alterations made by the Scottish poet are very significant. In the French version, at the beginning of the section Arthur is found lamenting that one of his knights, Girflet, has been imprisoned in the Chastel Orguellous for four years and no one has made any attempt to rescue him. Arthur's followers all agree that they should journey to the castle to free Girflet. This justification for the attack on the castle is omitted by the northern poet. Instead, Arthur is soundly rebuked for his warfaring propensity by one of his own followers. This knight, Sir Spinagros, is a creation of the Scottish poet.

The French version contains an incident wherein Gawane meets a knight in a trance-like state in the forest. He then meets a beautiful damsel riding to see the knight whose trance has been caused by her delay. The knight turns out to be the Riche Soudoier, lord of the castle, and the lady his 'amie'. Finally, the Riche Soudoier (Golagros in the Scottish version) and Gawane joust against each other. Gawane is the victor in both versions. In the French, however, the Riche Soudoier begs to be granted a seeming victory so that he would not be disgraced in the eyes of his 'amie'. He fears that news of his defeat will kill his lady. Gawane goes along with his plan; they proceed to the castle where Gawane hands his sword over to the lady. She is then sent away. Girflet and another of Arthur's knights are released from prison and all proceed to Arthur's camp where the Soudoier pledges his fealty to the king. Great feasting takes place in the castle and after a fortnight Arthur and his knights take their departure. The ending of the Scottish poem has already been related. It is clear that the northern poet made some radical changes in his text.

Chrétien wrote his _Perceval_ near the end of the twelfth century. The _Continuation_ was written at the very end of the twelfth or at the beginning of the thirteenth century. The courtly love motif is very evident in the episode of the Chastel Orguellous. It is totally suppressed in the Scottish poem. Instead, the Scottish poet turns the poem into a questioning of the warlike way of life which dominated medieval society, and beyond that, of the very feudal system which justified and perpetuated continual war.

In a recent article Barbara Nolan writes:

> Multiple voicing as a mode of argument was essential to later medieval narrative, whether in allegorical debate or exemplary private conversation or interior monologue framed by first- or third-person narration. Indeed, romance and allegory, the two dominant narrative forms of the later Middle Ages, positively required multiple voicing. These essentially dialectical forms typically pose challenging social or moral or spiritual questions to be solved by means of the narrative process.[13]

In his challenge to Arthur, Spinagros poses the dialectic of peace. He challenges the authority of the feudal lord to appropriate lands and kingdoms not his own. Moreover, Spinagros asserts the power and dignity of the knight Arthur is threatening:

> A! lord, be sparing of such speech until you inquire further
> For abandoned will he not be to warrior that is born.
> Before he be constrained by strength, yon brave man to
>   threaten
> Many people shall be lost, and lives destroyed.
> Speak no presumption, for Christ's son (sic) dear,
> If you scare this knight with harm, you will not escape
>   without scorn.
> It is honourable enough to be fellow and friend
> To the best man that has ever been celebrated before your
>   time.

> The mighty king of Macedonia, worthiest without doubt
> There he received no homage

For all his noble lineage
Nor has any since.

stanza XXII

The man who goes to war whenever he likes best,
All his power in this world, as well as his wealth,
Shall yet be as light as the smallest leaf of the lime-tree
That tosses about with the wind, so shaky it is.
Exercise your might and majesty with moderation and without
    offence.

Arthur's answer, however, is the intransigent response of the
stubborn tyrant:

In faith, believe firmly,
My promise shall be held to, for grief or for bliss;
My body shall never be laid unlaced to sleep
Until I have forced yon knight to bow
As I have made my vow;
Or else many a widow
Full angrily shall weep

stanza XXIII 14

Spinagros speaks in a different voice. He counters the assumptions
of pride and arrogance with the reminder of the transience of
earthly glory:

The wy that wendis for to were quhen he wenys best,
All his will in this warld, with welthis I wys,
Yit shall be licht as leif of the lynd lest,
That welteris doun with the wynd, sa waverand it is.

The image of falling leaves, tossed by the wind, has been used as
a symbol of death as far back as Virgil and Dante. Here it
suggests all that is weak, wavering, fragile, vulnerable, mortal
in the human enterprise. Arthur, of course, is heedless. He refuses to listen to Spinagros, and 'Thair wes no man that durst mel
to the king,/Quhen thai saw that mighty sa mouit in his mude' (11.
299-300). The same stanza tells of their journey to the city of
Christ where the king made his offering with great honour, then
hastened home along the same route. If the poet saw the irony in
this, he does not seem to emphasise the point. I suppose the irony
is obvious.
    Stanzas 26-35 are concerned with sending an embassy to Golagros
to ask for his allegiance. A worthy and wise unnamed warrior recommends this action to Arthur. Lancelot, Gawane and Ywain are
chosen for the mission. Spinagros speaks again, pleading to be
heard. His description of Golagros is the description of a noble
and pre-eminent man. He is a warrior of great strength, yet he is
also 'meik as ane child, / Blith and bousum ... as byrd in hir
bour' (11. 350-1). He is a royal lord, a seemly sovereign. The
courteous reception which the knights receive in Golagros's court
proves the validity of Spinagros's words. Golagros's response to
their re- quest is also a model of diplomacy and courtesy:

> I thank your gracious grete lord and his gude wil;
> Had euer leid of this land, that had bene leuand,
> Maid ony feute before, freik, to fulfil,
> I suld sickirly myself be consentand,
> And seik to your souerane, seymly on syll.
>
> 11.429-433

But none of his forbears has ever been thrall, and should he bind himself in bondage, he would deserve to be hanged high on a tree. He is willing to offer Arthur any honour saving the subjection of his own person. Integrity, and loyalty to his own ancestors, demand that he preserve his own freedom:

> Quhill I may my wit wald,
> I think my fredome to hald,
> As my eldaris of ald
> Has done me beforne.
>
> 11.450-4

Both sides begin to prepare for the inevitable battle which, including the description of military preparations, is recounted in stanzas 37 through 59. At this point Golagros decides to take the field himself. The encounter between Golagros and Gawane begins in stanza 71. Their fight continues until stanza 87 when the two knights retire to Golagros's castle, making it appear that Gawane has been defeated. The battle scenes, then, occupy fifty stanzas, or 650 lines, of the poem: nearly half.

If the voice of Spinagros represents a philosophical attitude toward human life, the voice of Golagros represents grace and wisdom. This may be seen in two scenes in particular. The first takes place in the great hall of his own castle after Gawane's seeming capitulation. In a gesture which is just the opposite of Arthur's obstinacy, Golagros asks his own subjects to decide his destiny: 'Whether you like me to remain your lord after being defeated in the field, or whether I should give up my life at last and deliver you to some man that would defend you'.[15] Who can wonder that their choice is himself? Golagros then yields obeisaunce to Gawane, surrendering not only his lands and himself, but his mind and heart as well. In defeat he shows himself not only magnanimous but wise: a true man recognises the moment of grace.

> As fortune has been directing the course of events through
>   her cunning,
> What I did was not due to fear of death,
> Nor to failing of courage, nor to faint-heartedness;
> Where Christ directs the course of events, it runs freely.
> No power or strength can strive against him.
> Who may his danger endure or destiny despise
> That makes men ever faint at heart
> Cannot endure that fate longer than the Lord decrees.
> Every man, be he knight, king, or emperor may prove
> [What I say] from his own concern [his own case],
> And muse in his mirror, [look on me as a mirror],
> As this matter is mostly mine.
>
> stanza XCV 16

Not even the Nine Worthies, the greatest heroes of history – Hector, Alexander and Julius Caesar, David, Joshua and Judas Macchabeus, Samson and Solomon – have withstood time, fate and fortune.[17] It is the part of wisdom to accept one's destiny.

The second scene occurs in Arthur's camp when Golagros pays homage to the king without rancour or resentment, and promises to follow and serve him faithfully. The final gesture of the poem is Arthur's:

> I mak releisching of thin allegiance;
> But dreid I sall the warrand,
> Baith be sey and be land,
> Fre as I the first fand,
> With outin distance. [strife]
> ll. 1358-62

Thus, the dialectic of the poem is resolved through the narrative process as Arthur comes to understand and respect the lord whom he had sought to subjugate.

The questioning of Arthur and his society was not a new theme in Middle English romance. The Green Knight, who appeared in the court for a Christmas game and whose proposal was met with a stunned silence, taunted the fearful knights:

> Where now are your pride and your conquests,
> Your ferocity and your wrath and your great words?
> (311-12)

The courtiers themselves blamed the king for accepting such a challenge 'for angardez pryde' (681). After his encounter at the Green Chapel Gawain blames himself for 'cowarddyse and couetyse bothe'.(2374) In The Awntyrs off Arthure at the Terne Wathelyne, another late fourteenth century romance, the terrifying ghost of Guenevere's mother appeals to her daugher warning her of the perils of a proud and pleasureful life. When Sir Gawain asks her: 'How shall we fare that venture out fighting and oppress people in many kings' lands and ride over realms without any right?' (ll. 261-3), she responds: 'Your king is too covetous ...' (265).[18]

The ghostly mother is one of several 'outlandish' figures who challenge the pretensions of Arthur's court in English romance. Raymond Thomson's study of this motif is quite thought-provoking.[19] He asserts that of the roughly thirty extant Arthurian romances in Middle English or Scots 'scarcely one-third can claim much in the way of independence of plot structure',[20] and even those which are not based upon some continental source depend upon traditional motifs for the basic structures of plot. Nearly all of the one third which are comparatively independent poems contain 'the presence of an outlandish figure who challenges the sophisticated attitudes of Arthur's court ...'[21] Although Golagros is neither an outlandish figure nor a shape-shifter, he is an outsider and his conduct clearly expresses the shallowness of Arthur and his knights. The thrust of the poem, moreover, is to present Golagros as an independent lord who is sovereign in his own right and by reason of his own excellence.

Consideration of the history of Scotland and England in the thirteenth, fourteenth, and fifteenth centuries might lead one to expect that the image of Arthur in Scottish literature would be unfavourable. In her reassessment of Scottish attitudes to the figure of Arthur in the chronicles and romances Flora Alexander has demonstrated that this is not necessarily the case:

> During the 14th and 15th centuries there are as many voices raised in Arthur's favour as against him. It is not until the 16th century that the majority of the accounts of him become antagonistic. These attacks on Arthur are in Hector Boece's Scotorum Historiae (1527), in the works of Boece's translators John Bellenden (1531) and William Stewart (1535), and in George Buchanan's Rerum Scoticarum Historia.[22]

Arthur is criticised extensively in the two extant Scottish Arthurian romances, Lancelot of the Laik and Golagros and Gawane, both directly based upon French romances. Mrs Alexander contends that the clerk's rebuke of Arthur in the Scottish Lancelot reflects his subjects' dissatisfaction with the administration of James III rather than hostility toward their southern neighbour. However, 'the view of King Arthur in The Knightly Tale of Golagros and Gawane is much more likely to have been influenced by defensive attitudes to the English'.[23] Even so, it is her belief that the presentation of Arthur in the Golagros is more positive than the figure presented in the English alliterative Morte Arthur. In this she disagrees with William Matthews's view that the image of Arthur reaches a nadir in the Golagros:

> Such an Arthur, guilty of willful war, covetousness, envy, cruelty, and tyranny, tearful and scared despite his unbridled anger, hypocritical and deaf to advice, is a debased version of the stern conqueror whose imperial war is the cause of tragedy in Morte Arthure, the vain trifler who puts Gawain's life in jeopardy in Sir Gawane and the Green Knight, and the penitent conqueror of Awntyrs of Arthure.[24]

Matthews also conjectures that the hostility toward Arthur expressed in the Scottish poem is generated by 'Scottish political feeling toward England that had arisen from Plantagenet claims to Scottish sovereignty and the bitter wars that had ensued'.[25]

The fifteenth century was a turbulent and violent one for both England and Scotland. This was the century which saw the eventual triumph of monarchy and the virtual end of the feudal age.[26] But feudalism did not die easily. Lancaster opposed York in England; in Scotland the struggle of the crown for power was symbolised and effected in the conflict between James II and the Black Douglases. In 1451 while William Earl of Douglas was on a pilgrimage to Rome the king moved against his castles. A short time later, because the Earl would not break the bonds of confederation he had made with the Earls of Crawford and Ross, alliances which the king perceived as a threat to his own position, he himself murdered Earl William in Stirling Castle. This occurred on 22 February 1452. The king succeeded in gaining the support of parliament and made it seem that Douglas had deserved to die. Following the death of Earl William the Douglases, led by James Douglas, rose up in rebellion against the crown.[27] A short period of peace ensued during which one of the most interesting of fifteenth-century Scottish poems, The Buke of the Howlat, was composed to honour the Douglas clan.[28] It was composed by Richard Holland for his patrons, Archibald Douglas, Earl of Moray, and his wife, Elizabeth Dunbar. By May of 1455, however, Archibald Douglas would be dead. In March of that year James II again moved against the Douglases. Earl James, failing to save his castle of Abercorn, fled to England. On 1 May his three brothers were defeated at Arkinholm on the Esk near Langholm. The Earl of Ormond was captured and later executed. Archibald, Earl of Moray, was killed in the battle; Lord Balvenie escaped to England. The ruin of the Black Douglas was completed by an Act of Parliament passed in August 1455. The act 'ordained that anyone who gave any aid or comfort to the survivors of the family would ipso facto incur the penalty of treason, and forfeiture of life, lands and goods'.[29] It is difficult to say whether any of this is reflected in the Golagros, written fifteen years later.[30] If so, the predatory Arthur would represent James II. It is more likely, however, that the world of the poem represents an evolving national consciousness, Golagros being ultimately respected as a power, a sovereign equal to Arthur.

In 1470, the supposed date of the Golagros, James III ruled Scotland. The country was temporarily at peace with England, the truce initiated by Edward IV being still in effect. Even so, Blind Hary, also writing at this time, struck a bitter tone in his poem about William Wallace. Friendly relations between France and Scotland continued. The 'Auld Alliance' was renewed six times in the fifteenth century.[31] The alliance was not only military. Particularly in the realms of education and culture the Scots were open and receptive to French influence. Both the Golagros and Rauf Coilyear reveal this influence, the other two Scottish poems having The Howlat's stanzaic form. Rauf Coilyear was written in the same decade as Golagros and has the same two-part structure. Verbal similarities also abound in the two poems.

What is even more striking, however, is their thematic similarity. The Taill of Rauf Coilyear is also a plea for peace. Here it is the voice of Sir Roland which calls for an end to fighting, and the Saracen who embodies pride, self-will, cruelty, violence: 'ȝe Saraȝeins ar succuderus and self willit ay' (909);[32] This is reminiscent of Spinagros's words to King Arthur: 'Spekis na succeudry, for Cristis sone deir!' (278). Like Spinagros also Roland rejects worldly vanity: 'This wickit warld is bot ane start', (892). Urging the pagan knight to become a Christian, Roland promises him wealth in this life and joy which will never end. The Sacracen is convinced, however, not by the promise of earthly goods but by the goodness of God: 'Thy Gold nor thy Grassum set I bot light./Bot gif thy God be sa gude as I heir the say' (936-7), he will abandon Mahoun and turn to the Christian God.[33] The poem ends with perfect peace and reconciliation: the Saracen is made a Christian knight and given Dame Jane of Anjou to be his wife; Rauf is made Marshal of France. Both of these poems, then, speak of peace.[34] In both poems, moreover, the stranger is brought into a relationship with the controlling power: Golagros becomes an ally of Arthur; Rauf is promoted to a higher rank of society; Magog becomes a peer. This, of course, is an indispensable condition of peace. It is the person who is perceived to be a stranger who becomes the enemy, the target in war. Both poems also reveal a more genial attitude toward sovereignty. Rauf Coilyear's unconventional relationship to the Emperor is humorous. Not realising whom he is inviting to his humble home, Rauf treats Charlemagne as an equal and makes it clear that he, Rauf, is lord of his own. Invited to return the visit and seek his new acquaintance at court, Rauf accepts with confidence and gusto.[35] Golagros, in his relationship to his own people, exhibits the same sense of collegiality. He places himself at their disposal. Spinagros, in challenging Arthur, reveals a similar spirit.

Perhaps the poets who composed these poems were reflecting the spirit of the new age. 'It was an age in which, for complex reasons, the people of Western Europe began to put trust in monarchy rather than in aristocracy'.[36] The sense of weariness with war which both poems also manifest may indeed have been inspired by the realisation that the perpetual feuds of the feudal age were futile. Let us now return to the idea of myth with which this paper began. What is the mythic element in these early stories of Scotland?

'Myth is the hidden part of every story, the buried part, the region that is still unexplored because there are as yet no words to enable us to get there'.[37] What are the myths underlying the fabrication of the stories of William Wallace and Robert Bruce, of Rauf Coilyear and Charlemagne, of Golagros and Gawane? These stories embody the spirit of freedom and independence, a recognition of the dignity and nobility of the common man, respect for the principle of collegiality, a desire for territorial integrity and peace. The hero, the leader, becomes a 'compelling metaphor' for a human society which embodies such ideals. When one thinks of the early history of England a parade of powerful rulers passes through the imagination: Alfred the Great, William the Conqueror, Henry II, Edward I, Edward III, Henry V, Henry VIII, Elizabeth I. When one thinks of the history of Scotland a host of powerful clans comes to mind: MacDonald, Ramsay, Lindsay, Stewart, Bruce, Douglas, Campbell. Our sense of Scotland is that of a nation composed of great people. Sadly enough, these great families often divided into warring factions but the spirit of brotherhood, at least in song and story, transcends the historical facts of civil strife and bloodshed. Indeed this may be one of the paradoxes of history: the story is sometimes lost in the details which fill the historical page. Perhaps this is why the legends, the stories, the imaginative inheritance of a people, is so terribly important, for it is the storyteller who tells us who we are. 'We are what we imagine. Our very existence consists in our imagination of ourselves.'

Notes

1   Momaday is an American Indian writer. His essay 'The Man Made of Words' is a prelude to his collection of old Kiowa tales, The Way to Rainy Mountain. The essay has been reprinted in The Essay, Stephen H Goldman and Bernard A Hirsch (eds) (Boston, 1986), pp 437-49.

2   Momaday, p 442.

3   Ibid, p 443.

4   Ibid, p 444.

5   Roland Barthes, Mythologies, 1957, trans Annette Lavers (New York, 1975), p 155. This has been quoted from an article by William W Stowe, 'Popular Fiction as Liberal Art', College English, 48, No. 7 (1986), 646-61.

6   Richard Slotkin, Regeneration through Violence: The Mythology of the American Frontier, 1600-1860 (Middletown, CT, 1973), p 1.

7   Ibid, p 6.

8   Winston S Churchill, 'The Birth of Britain', from A History of the English-Speaking Peoples, I, (New York, 1956), p 60.

9   Flora Alexander has discussed the image of Arthur as depicted in the Scottish chronicles of the fourteenth, fifteenth, and sixteenth centuries, and in the two surviving Arthurian romances in Scots: Lancelot of the Laik and Golagros. Anglia, 93 (1975), 17-34.

10 F J Amours included these four poems and The Pistill of Susan in his edition of Scottish Alliterative Poems published by the Scottish Text Society in 1897. Since that time further linguistic study has led to the conclusion that The Awntyrs and The Pistill are of a different provenance.

11 Paul J Ketrick has compared the twelve manuscripts containing the relevant episodes of the Perceval continuation. His conclusion is that the author of Golagros knew of a written French souce: 'Thirty passages distributed throughout the poem indicated one hundred and forty verbal agreements, sufficient surely to establish a definite and immediate relationship between the Scottish text and the French versions ...' The Relation of 'Golagros and Gawane' to the Old French 'Perceval', (Washington, DC, 1931).

12 This outline of the poem has been taken from The Continuations of the Old French 'Perceval' of Chretien de Troyes, William Roach (ed), I (Philadelphia, 1949).

13 '"A Poet Ther Was": Chaucer's Voices in the General Prologue to The Canterbury Tales', PMLA, 101 (1986), 154-69, 155.

14 All quotations from the poems have been taken from F J Amours edition: Scottish Alliterative Poems, STS (1897; repr New York, 1966). The translations are my own with the help of Amours's notes.

15 Amours: note on lines 1182-84, p 282.

16 Amours: note on lines 1226-32, pp 283-4.

17 Golagros here mentions six of the traditional 'Nine Worthies'. He substitutes Samson and Solomon for Arthur and Charlemagne, and omits Godfrey of Boulogne entirely. For an excellent study of this motif see Horst Schroeder, Der Topos der Nine

Worthies in Literatur und bildender Kunst (Gottingen, 1971).

18   The Awntyrs off Arthure at the Terne Wathelyne, Robert J Gates
      (ed) (Philadelphia, 1969).

19   Raymond J Thompson, 'Muse on thi mirrour ...: the Challenge
      of the Outlandish Stranger in the Arthurian Verse Romances',
      Folklore, 87 (1976), 201–8.

20   Thompson, p 201.

21   Ibid. Among the romances included in his study are Sir Gawane
      and the Green Knight, The Green Knight (a ballad), Gawane and
      the Carl of Carlisle, The Turk and Gowin, The Weddynge of Sir
      Gawane and Dame Ragnell, The Marriage of Sir Gawane, The Wife
      of Bath's Tale, The Awntyrs off Arthure, Sir Perceval of
      Gales, and Golagros and Gawane.

22   'Late Medieval Scottish Attitudes to the Figure of King
      Arthur: A Reassessment', Anglia, 93 (1975), 17–34, 19.

23   Ibid, p 28.

24   The Tragedy of Arthur, (Berkeley, 1960), pp 169–70.

25   Ibid, p 170.

26   The fifteenth century also witnessed a widespread interest in
      prose romance. This is seen in works such as Malory's Morte
      Darthur (1469) and in Caxton's commitment to promote the
      spirit and ideals of chivalry. See Larry D Benson, Malory's
      'Morte Darthur' (Cambridge, MA, 1976) and the Book of the
      Order of Chivalry, trans William Caxton, 1483–85, Alfred T P
      Byles (ed), EETS (London, 1926).

27   The history of this conflict has been taken from Ranald
      Nicholson, Scotland: The Later Middle Ages, The Edinburgh
      History of Scotland, II (New York, 1974), ch 13, pp 353–96.

28   Amours gives the date as 1450; Nicholson dates the poems
      somewhat later, 1453–54.

29   Nicholson, p 373.

30   It is not within the scope of this paper to take up the
      question of the dating of the poem. That is an important
      study, but one for another day. Hence, these reflections on
      the historical background of the poem are only conjectural
      and are included here because some of the shifting conscious-
      ness of the late fifteenth century seems to be reflected in
      the poem.

31   J D Mackie, A History of Scotland (Middlesex, England, 1964,
      revd 1969), p 99.

32   Quotations from The Taill of Rauf Coilyear have been taken
      from my own unpublished dissertation, Harvard, 1973.

33   William Hand Browne is the only editor (Baltimore, 1903) who
      emends 'God' to 'Gold' in line 936. Yet this reading makes
      far better sense than that of Lekpreuik whose early printed
      edition is the only extant copy of the poem. 'Gold' is
      parallel with 'Grassum' and it seems strange for the Saracen
      to contradict himself in the next line if the reading 'God'
      is retained.

34   It is interesting to note that in Golagros the English King
      Arthur is made the aggressor while in Rauf the French Emperor
      Charlemagne appears as a gracious and generous lord.

35   This, of course, was not uniquely Scottish. The king-in-
      disguise motif was universally popular in the early and later

Middle Ages. It was the central theme in a number of English ballads and romances of the fourteenth and fifteenth centuries. Four which are quite similar to <u>Rauf</u> are 'King Edward and the Shepherd', 'The Kyng and the Hermit', 'John the Reeve', and 'The King and the Miller'. See my article in <u>Folklore</u>, 86 (1975), 3-24.

36   Nicholson, p 374.
37   Italo Calvino, 'Readers, Writers and Literary Machines', <u>The New York Times Book Review</u>, 7 September 1986, p 31.

Chapter 9

ON SOME LITERARY TRADITIONS OF <u>COLKELBIE'S SOW</u>

Klaus Bitterling

The unique text of the curious poem commonly called <u>Colkelbie's Sow</u>[1] has been preserved in the last section of the main part of the Bannatyne Manuscript which is introduced by its compiler with the words: 'Heir followis the fyift pairt of this buik contenyng fabillis of Esop with diuers vthir fabillis and poeticall workis ...'[2] In the manuscript the nearly one thousand lines of the poem are divided into a prologue and three rather uneven parts, all of which have received very little or only passing comment in the histories of Scots literature.

It will be helpful here to give a very brief outline of the contents of the poem. In the prologue the poet – if I am allowed to give him this designation – apologises in advance for what is to follow, namely 'the fulich face of this mad metir' (50) of which 'the sentence to feill is fantastike' (51). He promises to build 'caisis upoun caisis' (54)[3] and leaves it to his audience to decide 'quhat cais ye think most nyce' (55), that is, most foolish. In the first fit he tells the story of a man named Colkelbie, who after selling his 'simple blak sow' (70) for three pennies spends the first for a girl, loses the second, and hides the third in a secret place. The lost penny is found by someone who buys with it a little pig of Colkelbie's sow. This pig is stolen by a 'harlot' (113) living in the neighbourhood who wants to roast it for a one-course dinner she intends to serve during a feast for a large host of rascals and villains of various professions. But when the piglet is about to be killed, its screaming calls for the porcine help of all swine living nearby. Boars, sows, and barrows come dashing along in order to rescue their companion. The ensuing tumult stirs up the owners of the swine and groups of other peasants, such as cowherds and shepherds, but out of fear of one another they flee in panic and assemble for a long series of curious Scottish, European, and exotic dances led by the swineherd Swanky and his cousin Copyn 'fowll of bellis fulfull' (364). At last they are reminded of the real purpose of their coming, and in a burlesque struggle the peasants rescue the pig, which afterwards grows into a strong boar of outstanding strength and valour so that it is able to come off victorious in a series of memorable single combats, not only against wild animals, such as elephants, tigers, and even unicorns, but also against some of the most famous heroes of ancient and medieval times.

In the second part we hear of Colkelbie meeting an old blind

man led by a young girl, the daughter of a pilgrim and his wife,
who both died at the blind man's house. Colkelbie makes up his
mind to spend his second penny for the girl and takes her home. He
and his wife Bellamourus bring up this girl Adria and eventually
give her in marriage to their son Flannislie. Later, the French
king awards the title of an earl to Flannislie and Adria becomes a
court lady. Finally they receive the earldom of Flandria which is
situated in a remote part of the country then still awaiting discovery. The sole witness for all this turns out to be our author's
great-grandmother Gurgunnald, an irritable, toothless old woman,
whose words are incomprehensible save to the ears of her great-
grandson to whom she now addresses a series of five moralising
counsels concerning the correct use of the three pennies.

In the last part Colkelbie stands godfather to the son of his
rich neighbours and offers a humble christening present of twenty-
four eggs bought with the third penny. These are indignantly refused by his neighbour's wife, and Colkelbie is forced to take the
eggs home again where his hen hatches them all, and the twenty-
four chickens – among them Chaucer's cock Chauntecleir – form the
basis of the enormous wealth Colkelbie is able to acquire for his
godson during the next fifteen years. But it goes without saying
that this last story equally rests on the sole authority of Gurgunnald and thus proves to be only an old wife's tale.[4]

It has been said – not without some degree of justification –
that <u>Colkelbie's Sow</u> 'defies the literary historian's attempt to
categorise it in terms of genre'.[5] It differs signifi- cantly from
other framed tales, such as <u>The Talis of the Fyve Bestis</u> or <u>The
Thre Prestis of Peblis</u>.[6] The work is not simply a patch-work of
incoherent elements of mock-poetry, which might be interesting
enough for their own sake; most of these elements can be related
to a substructure underlying the whole composition.

The beginning of the poem is really far more indebted to the
traditions of theory and practice of the prologue than has been
realised before. According to ancient and medieval doctrine, the
aim of a prologue is to render the hearer or reader benevolent,
attentive, and docile.[7] This aim can be reached by proceeding from
what is called <u>principium</u>, that is, a straightforward way to what
the poet has to narrate, or, when matters seem more complicated,
by <u>insinuatio</u>, involving secret means and often by-passes in order
to be successful. Our beginning appears to belong to the second
category.

The prologue is usually divided into the <u>prohemium</u> or <u>prologus
praeter rem</u> and the <u>prologus ante rem</u>, that is, the prologue
proper. This division can also be seen in <u>Colkelbie's Sow</u>: the
prohemium covers the first sixty-six lines as marked by Bannatyne
with an 'explicit prohemium' and the <u>prologus</u> covering lines 67-
104, that is, the beginning of the <u>pars prima</u>. But as I do not
want to go into the details of medieval rhetoric, I shall only
draw your attention to the last line of the proem, where the poet
– consciously or unconsciously – presents us with the clue to an
adequate understanding of his work: 'Now I begin with titill est.
Amen' (66).

'Tittles' are those three dots or pricks at the end of a cross
line or at the end of a whole book. They have their origins in the

medieval ABC-books, the predecessors of Elizabethan horn-books.
What the poet is doing, therefore, is nothing else than that he
purports to begin with the end, thus employing a variant of the
theme of the world upside down, which had developed from the
ancient tradition of the principle of adynata or impossibilia
known to the Middle Ages from Virgil's Eighth Eclogue (lines 53
seqq.), where the wolf flees the sheep, oaks bear golden apples,
and owls sing even better than swans. The theme had been equally
prominent in many of the songs of the wandering scholars, such as
in the famous Florebat olim studium of the Carmina Burana, and in
the marginal illustrations of Gothic manuscripts; but also in late
medieval vernacular poetry, especially in the satirical poems on
the Evils of the Times.[9]

One further most important aspect of the poem which cannot be
dealt with in my paper is the role of money, and especially the
increase and correct use of it. This is seen not only in the main
plot of the three pennies and the mock discussions on the best use
of them, but in several recurrent images closely connected with
money, and in the frequent use of words like 'fruct', 'fructefy',
or 'multeply',[10] featuring mainly in Part III of the poem, but
already present near the very beginning, when the author refers to
the biblical simile of the tree that bears either no fruit or bad
fruit,[11] paralleled by the allusion to the Parable of the Talents
near the end of Part III.[12] This theme has to be set against the
background of the Christian interpretation of Aristotle's value
theory in the casuistic economic literature of the Middle Ages, as
shown by the studies of Schumpeter and Langholm.[13]

The theme of the world upside down frequently occurs in the
prologue, when the speaker advises people 'nocht to begin flureist
and syne decres' (29) or when he uses the inverted image of 'a
fair ymp (that) fell doun a widderit tre' (32). This seemingly
nonsensical attitude and lack of logic can be detected throughout
the poem, even in its often awkward syntax. Compare the very
beginning, where a list of high social classes is introduced by a
temporal clause which has its first finite verb only in the
seventh line with the verb of the main sentence following in line
eleven. Later on, when the terrified pig is about to be butchered,
its cry for help is expressed in the following two lines as:

> The pure pig gaif a rore
> Him to kill quhen thay pynit,(182-3)

which evokes the misleading impression that the little pig is
going to kill itself or perhaps somebody else, but not that the
party is on the point of roasting it.

Most critics seem to follow the anonymous author who - at the
beginning of Part II - humbly begs pardon for 'thir mokking
meteris and mad matere' (562), when they characterise Colkelbie's
Sow as a 'rude and grotesque production'[14] or as 'a sorry end to
the old romances',[15] though some, as for instance C S Lewis, show
a certain
limited degree of appreciation for Part I at least while they
regret 'the prologue in wretched shambling couplets' and the
following 'two moral tales of no value'.[16] I do not hesitate to

adopt most judgements on the aesthetic value of the poem; nevertheless, I believe that it has not been properly understood by its
commentators. Let me, therefore, choose two aspects stemming from
the general theme of the world upside down in order to illustrate
my point. The first is its relationship with the tradition of the
beast-epic, and the second is its connection with the vast amount
of literature on fools so prominent during the fifteenth and sixteenth centuries.

Let me begin with the second first. Near the end of the prologue
the poet declares that he will tell a story out of his 'fantesy'
(47) in order to entertain his audience. He apologises for the
'fuliche face of this mad metir' (50) and the appropriate language
which seems necessary since 'the sentence to feill is fantastike'
(51). He is thus referring to the relationship between outer form
and inner contents which has been discussed in numerous prologues
since classical antiquity. This is nothing else than what Robert
Henryson describes more pleasingly with the help of the image of the
nutshell and kernel in the preface to his <u>Fabillis</u>,[17] when he
refers to the polarity of poetic fiction and truth, of rhetorical
mask and real intent.

But our author's aim is to offer the absurd proof that 'the wys
nycest the wisest quhile is' (60) because 'wisdome umquhile holdis
the nycest wys' (56). Consequently he urges his audience to decide
which of the following adventures seems the most foolish.

This argumentation brings the poet into line with the paradox
expressed by St Paul in his first letter to the Corinthians that
'the foolishness of God is wiser than men; and the weakness of God
is stronger than men' alluding to similar sayings, such as 'we are
fools for Christ's sake'.[18] A look at the text of the poem confirms
our suspicion that the theme of the fool and the foolishness of the
world may be one of the main traditions not so far sufficiently
recognised. Words from the semantic field of 'foolish' or 'mad'
abound.[19] Twice the poet asks his listeners whether 'this is nocht
a nyce cais' he is telling.[20]

We all know about the importance of the Feast of Fools for the
emergence of that fashionable literature of fools which culminated
in Sebastian Brant's <u>Ship of Fools</u> and Erasmus's <u>Praise of Folly</u>.[21]
On the side of the official church, there have been never-ending
attempts to suppress the excesses of this popular amusement which
often had a blasphemous and 'near-obscene' character.[22] But however much the church reformers might disapprove of these pastimes,
the lower clergy had their occasions for jollity which provided an
outlet from the normal restraints of ecclesiastical discipline.
They continued their <u>festum stultorum</u>, generally centred on a
cathedral and held on one of the feasts following Christmas,
usually the Day of the Circumcision or the Epiphany. In a letter to
the Dean and Chapter, Bishop Robert Grosseteste condemned this
practice and prohibited it in his Statutes for the diocese of
Lincoln in about 1239.[23] Nevertheless, the same customs were met
with when William Courteney, Archbishop of Canterbury, made a
visitation in 1390.[24] A similar pastime was the appointment of boy
bishops on the Feast of the Innocents, where

children be strangelye decked and apparelid to counterfaite

priestes, bysshopps, and women; and so ledde with songes and
daunces from house to house, ... and boyes doo singe masse,
and preache in the pulpitt, with suche other unfittinge and
inconvenyent usages, rather to the derision than to any true
glory of God ... [25]

These customs were only abolished by royal decree in 1541.

In our poem the three groups of peasants are led in their
dances by persons that are clearly characterised as fools, because
their clothing is covered over and over with bells:

> A maister swynhird Swanky
> And his cousing Copyn Cull
> Fowl of bellis fulfull
> Led the dance...(362-5),

and later

> Thair pressit in Pery Pull
> Full of bellis fulfull (406-7)[26]

There is a good deal of estate satire in the list of fools coming
to the feast of the so-called 'harlot', a designation which here
still means 'buffoon' or 'jester'.[27] Among the participants are
all kinds of wandering entertainers, such as ministrels, jesters,
bear- and ape-leaders, who compete with all sorts of preachers for
the attention of the public. Likewise we find professional beggars
and certain ill-reputed groups of the society, such as hangmen,
torturers, usurers, and customs collectors. But the satire is also
directed against otherwise perfectly honest groups, such as
weavers, carters, and ferrymen, and especially against shepherds,
cowherds, and swineherds. Here the author can conveniently use the
conventions of peasant-satire,[28] when, for instance, Gilby is
depicted riding on a gray mare or Symy as being sunburnt. The
peasants' clothing and their rustic occupations are equally ridi-
culed: Fergy Flitsy has a tar-bucket on his back, the name Toby
Carior suggests hard work, many people are playing such uncourtly
instruments as bagpipes.

It is this rural aspect of the poem that has been given a
rather exaggerated attention, as when Henderson calls it 'a
remarkable picture of ancient rustic manners';[29] a tendency that
led to a detailed comparison of Colkelbie's Sow with Heinrich
Wittenwiler's Ring, a fifteenth-century German poem in the tradition of peasant-poetry initiated by Neidhart von Reuenthal.[30]

The passage of the poem which describes the arriving of the
guests for the killing-day shows one of the most characteristic
recurrent features of the text, namely the frequent use of long
catalogues of designations of social classes, professions, pigs,
peasants, dances, countries and their towns, animals in combat,
hens and cocks. These turbulent accumulations of words or of
rhymes seem to contribute to a stylistic effect which runs counter
to and even neutralises the result which would otherwise be
reached by the means of individualising peasants and animals by
their names, when, for instance, a long anaphora making use of the

established sum-formula amounts to thirty-seven occurrences of sum
within thirty-seven continuous lines.[31] This formula, highly
famous for its appearance in the Old English elegy of the Wander-
erer,[32] had been of a very wide currency during the fifteenth
century, when it was used as a means of dialectic discussion in
the controversy between Jack Upland and his opponent Friar Daw,[33]
or between the rich man and the poor in Dives and Pauper,[34] or as
a structural device of whole poems, as in a late-fifteenth-century
anti-feministic carol.[35] Cataloguing had become a traditional
pattern for expressing the contradictions of fools and folly. You
need only think of the series of sixty-three fools forming The
Order of Fools[36] founded by Marcolf, the notorious opponent of the
wise Solomon, in Lydgate's poem, or of the seventy lines employing
one single rhetorical pattern - 'so manye ... so litill' - in
Skelton's Speke, Parrot.[37]

The second aspect of a world upside down and the changing of
roles is evident in the poet's use of the animal fable and the
beast epic as a means of masking the polarity of fiction and
truth. Elements of these traditions are to be found in the first
and the third parts dealing with pigs and chickens respectively.
These two sections are bound together by the figure of Gurgunnald,
who seems to be herself of porcine descent, as is shown by her
name.[38]

The genre of beast epic[39] is a medieval literary creation
developing mainly from the Aesopic fable. As an antitype of
courtly poetry, it usually serves a moral or political purpose.
Its repre- sentatives become more and more anti-idealistic. There
have been sporadic examples of the beast epic on the Continent
since the middle of the ninth century, when Sedulus Scottus wrote
his verses On a certain wether killed by a dog, telling of the
life and martyrdom of the wether Tityrus, who lives the life of a
holy ascetic and valiant fighter for God. The tradition of the
beast epic proper starts with The Escape of the Prisoner (Ecbasis
captivi), dating perhaps from the tenth century, the Roman de
Renart, and the Ysengrimus by the Flemish Magister Nivardus (about
1148).[40] Within the thirteen fables relating the adventures of
Ysengrimus the Wolf, it is the final and fatal experience of the
hero that is most interesting with regard to Colkelbie's Sow.[41]

In this episode Ysengrimus tries to dupe the old sow Salaura,
who is depicted as by far the most voracious sow in the world,
eating fifteen times as many acorns as others. She is more
experienced and shrewd than nine abbots and bishops and presides
over three hundred nuns of the Order of Pigs. Her age is six ages
of man. When Ysengrimus eventually tries to bite her, she begins
celebrating what the poet calls a sylvan mass by squeaking at a
higher pitch than even the devil can do, and sixty-six pigs come
rushing along making the earth quake. Her relatives coming to
rescue Salaura from the teeth of the wolf are the young boar Kono
with twenty-one brothers, both aunts of Kono, called Sonoche and
Becca, the last accompanied by fifteen sons, the sow Burgisa and
seven children, and the English bastard Baltero together with six
sons-in-law, four brothers, and eight daughters-in-law. This pack
of swine not only rescue Salaura but, in the end, kill and devour
the unfortunate wolf.

This episode from the twelfth-century beast epic not only
provides us with a striking literary demonstration of one of the
pig's traditional characteristics, its excellent sense of hearing,
but also of its musical qualities for the sow Salaura is accompanied in this mock divine service in the woods by Becca singing
in the fifth and Sonoche singing one fourth deeper, while Baltero,
the fattened pig, sounds the deep fifth. These precentors thus
give the intervals and the choir responds with the antiphony. The
pig's good sense of hearing has so far been documented only from
Bartholomew's Encyclopedia, where the relevant passage in
Trevisa's translation runs:

> Swyne louen euerich other and knowen euerich othere voice,
> and therfore if eny cryeth they crien alle and fonden to
> helpe him with al here might.[42]

But the sensitive hearing of the pig can also be paralleled from
Vincent of Beauvais[43] or Thomas of Cantimpre, where it is mentioned in a list of animals surpassing man's five senses:

> Nos aper auditu, linx visu, simia gustu,
> Vultur odoratu precedit, aranea tactu. (44)

The author's 'grit graundame' (694) — assuming the educational
role of wives in didactic literature, such as The Good Wife Taught
Her Daughter or The Thewis of Gud Women — is introduced as a
physically infirm, toothless, and extremely irritable person,
whose speech is incomprehensible except to her great-grandson. She
seems to have two literary antecedents, La Vieille in the Roman de
la Rose and the old sow in the medieval beast epic.[45] The Old
Woman in the Roman de la Rose shows the same features of physical
decay, for Guillaume de Lorris depicts her with no teeth left in
her mouth and later adds that she is not even able to walk the
short distance of four fathoms without the help of a stick, whereas Gurgunnald is not even able to rise.

But apart from these elements in her character which point to
an inversion of the medieval ideal of feminine beauty leading to
new conventions of a descriptio turpitudinis[46] still prevalent in
Shakespeare's Sonnet No 130 or Donne's The Anagram, there seem to
lie hidden certain parts which derive this portrait from the
medieval beast epic. This can significantly be seen in the name of
the old wife, Gurgunnald. The latest editor of the poem explains
it as meaning 'heavy-jowled' and assumes a possible association
with 'gurgulation' or 'rumbling in the bowels'.[47] Though this may
be correct, there is a connection within the text which should not
be overlooked. In the list of pigs coming to help their comrade,
there appears a sow Gunnald (227) suggesting that there must be a
porcine element in Gurgunnald's character. A similar use of animal
imagery in descriptions of ugliness is frequently met with. We
need only mention Skelton's Elynour Rummyng whose

> ... face (is) all bowsy,
> Comely crynklyd,
> Woundersly wrynklyd,

> Lyk a rost pygges eare
> Brystled with here.[48]

But the convention is of course older. Perhaps the most famous medieval example comes from Wolfram of Eschenbach's <u>Parzival</u>, where Cundrie, the messenger of the Grail, is depicted with a long plait of hair

> als eines swînes rückehâr (and)
> zwêne ebers zêne ir vür den munt
> giengen wol spannen lanc.[49]

His brother, appropriately called Malcreatüre, has a strikingly similar outward appearance:

> im stount och ietweder zân
> als einem eber wilde,
> ungelîch menschen bilde.[50]

But even more frequent is the stereotyped comparison of the warrior and hero with the wild boar, which is only very rarely extended beyond such formulas as 'brim as a bor'. One instance of an extension of this image occurs in the Middle English romance of <u>Sir Ferumbras</u> where Oliver and Ferumbras are so enraged that 'fom of hure mouth out sprenge so doth out of the bore'.[51] As is well known, the boar played an important part in many early cultures. You need only think of the drawings in the cave of Altamira in Spain. It has been known as a favourite royal hunting quarry and as a sign of imperial power from Indian, Greek, and Roman mythologies. Last but not least, it occupied a prominent place in Germanic and Celtic cultures where it was well-known as an animal accompanying gods. These Greek and Germanic associations are of special importance for the Middle Ages; and they are significantly different from the Jewish-Christian interpretation given in the commentaries on the boar devastating the vineyard in Psalm 79: 14.[52] Both the Greek and the Germanic evidently show a close connection with cults of fertility and death and reveal a sense of the demonic and the divine. In Germanic mythology – as Heinrich Beck[53] was able to prove in his monograph on the Sign of the Boar – the relationship between the boar and the heroic way of life plays the dominant role, a feature which is, by they way, not missing in ancient times and mythology as known to the Middle Ages from Virgil and Ovid.

This positive aspect of the animal is certainly ubiquitous in heroic poetry and the romances, where comparisons between the valiant knight and the fighting boar abound, where the boar is used as a heraldic sign, and where even King Arthur or Edward III is identified with this animal.[54]

Our text shows the reversal of this attitude. It is not man who is compared with certain aspects of an animal's traditional character, let alone the complete identification of man and animal, but it is the animal becoming man. The first stage of this anthropomorphic process is seen when the pigs hear their comrade cry,

> Thay come golfand full grim,
> Mony long tuthit bore
> and mony galt come befoir
> And mony grit gunnald, (224-7)

but also a company of individualised hogs which are not only classified according to zoological standards but are given individual
names. Their attack will guarantee their eternal fame, as the
author assures his public:

> So did thay this day
> That sowis sonis hard I nevir
> Win so grit wirschep for evir. (218-20)

This is a parodistic reflex of the attitude of a former heroic age
when people could be sure that 'fame was the best thing' they could
achieve or, as the Exeter Gnomes put it: 'Dom bith selast',[55] an
attitude which found its expression in Old English poetry such as
Beowulf and the elegy of the Seafarer, in the Old Norse Hávamál, or
in Virgil's Aeneid.[56]

The culmination of this process is reached when

> this pig ... a boir wes
> Off micht he grew maikles, (512-3)

and in a series of most adventurous meetings similar to those of
Alexander or Gawain in the medieval romances tests its knightly
prowess in single combats against

> ... antelop or oliphant,
> Tigir, pard, or pantere,
> Bull, wolf, or wyld bere,
> With the awful unicorne,
> Nor ony beist that wes borne. (515-9)

This reminds us of the 'wilde beste(s) ... lyones, beres, vny-
cornes, tygres, and pardez' of the Prose Life of Alexander,[57] or
the encounters of Gawain, on his way to the castle of Bercilak de
Hautdesert, where

> Sumwhyle wyth wormez he werrez, and with wolues als,
> Sumwhyle wyth wodwos, that woned in the knarrez,
> Bothe wyth bullez and berez, and bores otherwhyle
> And etaynez, ... [58]

Eventually our boar assumes the role of a timeless super-boar who
by a series of metamorphoses takes on the shapes of the best-known
mythical boars, such as the Calydonian boar fighting against
Meleager,[59] the Erymanthian boar fighting against Hercules,[60] and
the Sidonian boar fighting against Sir Eglamour of Artois.[61] It
does not even shrink back from a combat with the Germanic hero Wade
- known from the Old English Widsith and the Middle High German
Kudrun, etc[62] - though its role in connection with Wade remains a
little vague, since boar-hunting does not feature in his career.

But probably our author knew a variant of the legend told   by   Walter
Map   in   his   story of Gado, where the hero appears as the son of the
king of the Vandals who comes to the court of the   Old   English   King
Offa,   the   builder of the Welsh dyke, and is there known as a famous
huntsman.[63]

Be that as it may, contrary to all historical   evidence   our   boar
is not killed but comes out victorious time and again.

This   complete   misrepresentation   of heroic and knightly life had
already been prepared for in the late forms of medieval   romance.   It
seems   likely   that   stories like that of Sir Eglamour in its romance
or ballad versions were regarded   as   grotesque   old-fashioned   stuff
which   bore   in   it   certain   ridiculous   elements,   as   when   in the
romance Sir Eglamour

> ...fy3tes with the wylde swyne
> Thre dayes and mare.
> Tyll on the fowrth day abowte none
> (Eglamour) thow3t hys lyfe was nere done
> For fy3tyng with the bore.
> They kny3te can no bettur rede:
> He stroke at the swynes hede;
> Hys tuskes then brake he thore.[64]

Grotesque handling of knightly elements   had   become   fashionable in
Middle   English   romances, such as <u>Octavian</u> (Northern Version), where
the narrator revels in comic descriptions   of   the   emperor   and   his
wife's efforts to draw an old sword out of its scabbard:

> Clement the swyrde drawe owt wolde,
> Gladwyn, hys wyfe, schoulde the scabard holde,
> And bothe faste they drowe;
> When the swyrde owt glente,
> Bothe to the erthe they wente:
> There was game y-nowe!
> Clement fell to a benche so faste,
> That mowth and nose alle tobraste,
> And Florent stode and loghe.
> Hyt ys gode bowrde to telle,
> How they to the erthe felle,
> And Clement lay in swoghe![65]

That   is   not   a   very   far   cry from burlesque battle-poems like the
<u>Tournament of Tottenham</u> in which, in a   rustic   jousting   with   flails
used as weapons,

> The boyes were so wery for-fught
> Thay thay my3t not fy3t mare oloft,
> But creped then about in the croft
> As they were croked crepyls[66]

so that they have to be wheeled home in barrows by their own wives.

Similar   are   <u>The Battle of Brakonwet</u>, where the ancient heroes of
traditional chronicles   and   romances   are   transformed   into   house-
wives,   innkeepers,   jousting   bears,   and dancing pigs, or <u>The Hunting</u>

of the Hare, 'a jolly poem (in which) foolish villagers (get) into a terrible tangle over a hare-hunt'.[67]

The theme of the world upside down, as here depicted with the help of patterns taken from the literature on fools and the medieval beast epic, contributes to the resulting impression that Colkelbie's Sow cannot merely be looked upon as a piece of country merrymaking like Peblis to the Play or Christis Kirk on the Grene, which are 'full of rough country gaiety',[68] but that a more serious literary background is present, though admittedly treated in a mocking way and summed up in sham proverbs in the prologue, where the author announces that

> The wys nycest the wisest quhile is provit (60)

and

> Wisdome umquhile holdis the nycest wys. (56)

This must not only be understood at its surface meaning of an incompatible polarity but as indicative of a unity lying behind all worldly diversity, which the fifteenth-century philospher Nicholaus de Cusa succeeded in transcending in his De docta ignorantia (1440) by the speculative theory of the coincidentia oppositorum which was based 'on the mathematical hypothesis that the greatest cannot be greater nor less or it would not be the greatest; and the least could equally not be greater nor less or it would not be the least. Therefore, the greatest and the least are equal',[69] and - by extension - the fool and the wise, the animal and the hero are all the same.

Notes

1   'Colkelbie Sow' and 'The Talis of the Fyve Bestes', Gregory Kratzmann (ed) (New York and London, 1983). All citations are from this edition.

2   Fol. 298^r. See the facsimile of The Bannatyne Manuscript, National Library of Scotland Advocates' MS 1.1.6, with an introduction by Denton Fox and William A Ringler (London, 1980).

3   The word cais occurs in the following lines: 54 (twice), 55, 67, 105, 181, 261, 265, 504, 511, 538, 550, 554, 620, 656, 691, 749, 824, 837, 860, 958, 967.

4   That is, without any truth. See Boccaccio's 'diliratium vetularum inventio', cited by Hennig Brinkmann, Mittelalterliche Hermeneutik (Darmstadt, 1980), 105.

5   Kratzmann, p 10.

6   See Kratzmann, ibid.

7   See Hennig Brinkmann, 'Der Prolog im Mittelalter als literarische Erscheinung', Wirkendes Wort, 14 (1964), 1-24, repr in his Studien zur Geschichte der deutschen Sprache und Literatur. Band II: Literatur (Düsseldorf, 1966), 79-105.

8   OED, s.v. tittle sb., 1.c and Kratzmann, p 106.

9   See Ernst Robert Curtius, Europäische Literatur und latein-

isches Mittelalter (Bern and München, 3rd edn 1961), 104- 8, citing Virgil and the Carmina Burana.

10 Fruct 26, 732, 829, 832, 857, 877, 887, 911; fructefy 793, 823, 830, 846, 849, 851, 963; multeply 731, 792, 805, 854, 950; fructeous 942.

11 Matt. 3:8-10.

12 Matt. 25:14-30 and Luke 19:12-26.

13 Joseph A Schumpeter, History of Economic Analysis (New York, 1954); Odd Langholm, Price and Value in the Aristotelian Tradition (Bergen etc, 1979) and Wealth and Money in the Aristotelian Tradition (Bergen etc, 1983).

14 T F Henderson, Scottish Vernacular Literature: A Succinct History, 3rd revd edn (Edinburgh, 1910), p 84.

15 G Gregory Smith in The Cambridge History of English Literature, vol II (Cambridge, 1908; repr 1961), p 127.

16 C S Lewis, English Literature in the Sixteenth Century Excluding Drama (Oxford, 1954), p 72.

17 Lines 15-16 The Poems of Robert Henryson, Denton Fox (ed) (Oxford, 1981), p 3.

18 The Holy Bible (Cambridge, n.d.).

19 See fule n. 124, 251, 258, 268, 272, 483, 657, 725, 730, 735, 751; fule adj. 868, 871,; foly 492, 730, 743; fulich 50, 138, 743, ydiot 489; mad 50, 336, 452, 521, 562,; nyce 55, 56, 60, 261, 538; nycete 565.

20 Lines 261 and 538.

21 See Sandra Billington, A Social History of the Fool (Brighton and New York, 1984).

22 Glynne Wickham, Early English Stages, 1300 to 1660. Vol 1: 1300 to 1576 (London and New York, 1959; repr 1963), p 130.

23 See the Statutes of Bishop Grosseteste for the Diocese of Lincoln in Councils & Synods with Other Documents Relating to the English Church. II AD 1205-1313. Part I 1205-1265, F M Powicke and C R Cheney (eds) (Oxford, 1964), 265-78 (canon 35, p 273 and note 5).

24 E K Chambers, The Mediaeval Stage, Vol I (Oxford, 1903), 322.

25 For the text of the royal decree, see Chambers, Mediaeval Stage, pp 366-7, note 5 (citing Wilkins' Concilia).

26 See also Billington, Fool, 11-12.

27 See MED, s.v. harlot n., 2.a-b.

28 See Henrik Specht, Poetry and the Iconography of the Peasant. The Attitude to the Peasant in Late Medieval English Literature and in Contemporary Calendar Illustration. In Gower's Vox Clamantis the rebels of 1381 are transformed into asses, oxen, swine, and other animals.

29 Henderson, Scottish Literature, p 84.

30 By George Fenwick Jones in his translation of Wittenwiler's Ring and the Anonymous Scots Poem Colkelbie Sow. Two Comic-Didactic Works from the Fifteenth Century, University of North Carolina Studies in Germanic Languages and Literatures, 18 (Chapel Hill, 1956; repr New York, 1969). The standard edition of the Ring is still that by Edmund Wiessner, Heinrich Wittenwilers Ring, Deutsche Literatur in Entwicklungsreihen, Reihe Realistik des Spätmittelalters, 3 (Leipzig, 1931; repr Darmstadt, 1973). For a survey of scholarship see Bernward

Plate, <u>Heinrich Wittenwiler</u>, Ertage der Forschung, 76 (Darmstadt, 1977). Concerning Kratzmann's statement that the <u>Ring</u> is a 'contemporary German burlesque of peasant life' (p 10), we must remember that – in spite of the entry in the index to the Asloan Manuscript – we cannot say anything about a possible fifteenth-century poem of <u>Colkelbie's Sow</u> and that the <u>Ring</u> is to be dated before 1453.

31   Lines 367–404.

32   See J E Cross, 'On <u>The Wanderer</u>, 11.80–4: A Study of a Figure and a Theme', <u>Vetenskaps-Societetens i Lund Årsbok 1958–59</u>, 75–110.

33   See <u>Jack Upland, Friar Daw's Reply, and Upland's Rejoinder</u>, P L Heyworth (ed) (Oxford, 1968), <u>Friar Daw's Reply</u>, lines 42 and 200 and Heyworth's note, 140.

34   <u>Dives and Pauper</u>, Vol I Part I, Priscilla Barnum (ed), EETS, 275 (1976), 126/51–127/55 (14 occurrences of <u>sum</u>).

35   Mentioned by Heyworth, <u>Upland</u>, 140. See <u>The Early English Carols</u>, R L Greene (ed) (Oxford, 1977), no. 401A.

36   <u>The Minor Poems of John Lydgate</u>, Part II, H N MacCracken (ed), EETS, OS, 192 (1934 for 1933), no. 16.

37   Lines 449 seqq. See <u>John Skelton, Poems</u>, selected and edited Robert S Kinsman, Clarendon Medieval and Tudor Series (Oxford, 1969), pp 93–5.

38   The word <u>gunnald</u> is used as a designation for 'pig' in line 227.

39   See Max Wehrli, 'Vom Sinn des mittelalterlichen Tierepos', <u>German Life and Letters</u>, 10 (1957), 219–28; repr in his <u>Formen mittelalterlicher Erzählung: Aufsätze</u> (Zürich, 1969), pp 113–25.

40   <u>Ysengrimus</u>, E Voigt (ed) (Halle, 1884).

41   I have made use of the partial edition by Horst Kusch in his <u>Einführung in das lateinische Mittelalter. Band I: Dichtung</u> (Berlin, 1957), pp 392–415.

42   <u>On the Properties of Things. John Trevisa's Translation of Bartholomaeus Anglicus, De Rerum Proprietatibus. A Critical Text</u>, M C Seymour et al. (eds), vol II, 1237/31–3.

43   Vincent of Beauvais, col. 1328E, cited by Klaus Speckenbach, 'Der Eber in der deutschen Literatur des Mittelalters', in <u>Verbum et Signum. Erster Band: Beiträge zur mediävistischen Bedeutungsforschung</u>, Hans Fromm, Wolfgang Harms, Uwe Ruberg (eds) (München, 1975), pp 425–76, esp 438.

44   <u>Thomas Cantimpratensis, Liber de Natura Rerum</u>, H Boese (ed) (Berlin and New York, 1973), p 106. According to Speckenbach, 'Eber', 437, Thomas provides the earliest instances of this list. See also the use of these notions as a means of depicting the ideal man by Reinmar of Zweter (cited by Speckenback, 'Eber', 438).

45   <u>Le Roman de la Rose</u>, E Langlois (ed), II (Paris, 1920), 11.339 –60 (pp 18–19).

46   See Theo Stemmler, 'My Fair Lady. Parodien englischer Lyrik des 15 Jahrhunderts', <u>Mannheimer Berichte</u>, 24 (1984), 15–20.

47   Kratzmann, p 11.

48   <u>The Tunnyng of Elynour Rummyng</u>, R S Kinsman (ed), <u>John Skelton Poems</u>, 11.17–21, p 53.

49   Wolfram   von   Eschenbach,   Parzival,   Albert   Leitzmann   (ed),
     Altdeutsche Textbibliothek, 12 (Tübingen, 7th edn 1961), 313.
     17-23, p 245.
50   Ibid,   Altdeutsche   Textbibliothek,   13   (Tübingen,   5th   edn
     1959), 517.22-4, p 142.
51   Sir Ferumbras, 11.699 seq, cited by Heinrich Beck, Das Eber-
     signum   im   Germanischen: Ein   Beitrag   zur germanischen Tier-
     symbolik, Quellen und Forschungen zur Sprach- und Kulturge-
     schichte der germanischen Völker, NF, 16 (Berlin, 1965), 132.
     For German examples, see Speckenbach, 'Eber', 462.
52   See Wilfried Schouwink, Der Wilde Eber in Gottes Weinberg:
     Zur Darstellung des Schweins in Literatur und Kunst des
     Mittelalters (Sigmaringen, 1985).
53   Beck, Ebersignum, passim.
54   Beck, Ebersignum, 114-26.
55   Maxims I, line 80 in The Anglo-Saxon Poetic Records: A
     Collective Edition, III: The Exeter Book, G P Krapp and E V K
     Dobbie (eds) (London and New York, 1936), p 145.
56   Beowulf, 11.1386-9; Seafarer, 11.72-80; Hávamál, 11.76-7;
     Aeneid, X.467-9.
57   The Prose Life of Alexander, J S Westlake (ed), EETS; OS, 143
     (1913 for 1911), 69/25-7.
58   Sir Gawain and the Green Knight, J R R Tolkien and E V Gordon
     (eds), 2nd edn revd N Davis (Oxford, 1971), 11.720-23.
59   Ovid, Metamorphoses, VIII. 260-435.
60   Cf. Ovid, Metamorphoses, IX. 191-2.
61   Sir Eglamour of Artois, ed F E Richardson, EETS, 256 (1965),
     11.381-405.
62   Widsith, 1.99. See below.
63   On Wade, see R W Chambers, Widsith: A Study in Heroic Legend
     (Cambridge, 1912), pp 95-100.
64   Sir Eglamour, 11.381-405. For attitudes towards this romance,
     see Richardson, Sir Eglamour, xlii-xliii.
65   Octavian, Zwei mittelenglische Bearbeitungen der Sage, G
     Sarrazin (eds), Altenglishe Bibliothek, 3 (Heilbronn, 1885),
     11.889-90 (MS Cambridge Univ. Ff.2.38), p 116, cited by
     Dieter Mehl, The Middle English Romances of the Thirteenth
     and Fourteenth Centuries (London, 1968), p 114.
66   The Tournament of Tottenham in Middle English Metrical
     Romances, W H French and C B Hale (eds) (1930, repr New York,
     1964), II, 989-98, 11.168-71, p 996. For the use of the sum-
     formula in this poem, see 11.203-7 and 218-20.
67   See Thoralc Turville-Petre, 'Some Medieval English Manu-
     scripts in the North-East Midlands', in Manuscripts and
     Readers in Fifteenth-Century England ... Derek Pearsall (ed)
     (Cambridge etc, 1983), 124-41, esp 137-8.
68   A M Mackenzie, An Historical Survey of Scottish Literature to
     1714 (London, 1933), p 144.
69   Billington, Fool, p 24.

Chapter 10

BEGINNING AND ENDING THE KINGIS QUAIR

Alan MacColl

While this short paper is not the place for a long theoretical
preamble, it may be helpful if I preface what I have to say about
The Kingis Quair with a few remarks about models and perspectives.
I shall not be concerned, as many commentators have been, with the
poem as the expression and communication of its author's thoughts,
feelings and experience, nor with its structure in a formal and
static sense, but instead will be looking at it from the perspectives of composition and performance. My focus will be on the
poet's engagement with the problems of managing his narrative, and
I shall be thinking of his task primarily as that of composing an
effective production, one moreover designed not so much for silent
reading as to be delivered by a performer in order to move,
instruct and entertain a live audience. The poet's own reference
in his envoi to the role of his reader, like Chaucer's at the end
of Troilus and Criseyde, makes it clear that he himself thought of
his text in this way, as a script to be performed:

> Go, litill tretisse, nakit of eloquence,
> Causing simplesse and pouertee to wit,
> And pray the reder to haue pacience
> Of thy defaute, and to supporten it,
> Of his gudnesse thy brukilnesse to knytt,
> And his tong for to reulë and to stere
> That thy defautis helit may bene here.
>
> $\qquad\qquad\qquad$ (194)[1]

I hope my concentration on the opening and closing sections of the
poem will not seem capricious; it is simply that from the perspectives I have described these are the parts of the text where the
most interesting things seem to be happening.

I

No one would dispute that The Kingis Quair 'tells a story'. It is
far more concerned with the events of the narrator's waking life
than other dream poems, to the extent that the usual relation of
dream vision to waking experience is virtually reversed. Whereas
in other examples of the sub-genre the latter has a largely formal
function, providing a kind of prologue and epilogue to the dream,
framing it but very much subordinate to it, in the Quair, uniquely, the vision is seen to be significant as it relates to the

dreamer's life as a whole. In this as in other respects the poem is an ambitious and original composition. But the way the story element is managed seems to me more problematic than has commonly been supposed. James is an accomplished poet, and every reader must leave the poem having been engaged, moved and entertained, and with the sense of an action carried through to satisfactory completion.[2] Nevertheless, if we are reading attentively and not simply allowing our knowledge of the author's biography and our surmises about his private life to plug gaps in the text, there are times when the obliqueness of his method may leave us in some doubt as to just what is being related, and others where the narrative takes on an oddly halting quality, or where it turns in on itself and an element of self-reflexiveness enters whose effect is to impede or undermine the progress of the poem as story.

The opening of the poem arouses expectations of a good, conventional dream-poem. It is highly formal and literary, and conducted very much according to the book, James having employed three of the devices recommended by Geoffrey de Vinsauf for effective beginnings: the striking and significant images of stanza 1 (borrowed, though much improved in the process, from Lydgate's Temple of Glass); an exemplum (the stanzas on Boethius, which are after the manner of Chaucer's on the Dream of Scipio at the beginning of The Parliament of Fowls); and the sententiae of stanza 9.[3] These are far from being haphazard stabs at getting started. They complement one another and serve to introduce the poem's central themes of Providence and Fortune in three different modes: symbolic, exemplary, and philosophical. It is an assured beginning.

With the narrator's putting aside of his author and his robust promise to get on with his story - 'Therefore I lat him pas, and in my tong/Procede I will agayn to the sentence/Of my mater, and leve all incidence' - we are ready for the expected dream, a promise all but confirmed by the lines that follow:

> The long nyght beholding, as I saide,
> Myn eyen gan to smert for studying,
> My buke I schet and at my hede it laide
> And doune I lay but ony tarying.
>
> (8)

These expectations are suspended, though not quite defeated, by the reflections on Fortune of stanza 9. But by the time we get to stanzas 10 and 11, where the narrator tells us that he couldn't sleep after all and got up, we become aware that things are not going according to custom. A C Spearing perceptively remarks that the narrator's reflections on the message of the Matins bell form a small-scale parallel to those on the status of the later dream, though his point gets lost when he goes on, irrelevantly I think, to relate this to the narrator's 'character'.[4] What Spearing might have observed is that the speaking bell itself occupies the place that ought by rights to have been taken by the expected dream. It is a sideways nod towards the requirements of convention, and with it the poem ceases for the time being to be what it seemed and becomes instead a poem about writing a poem.

Stanza 10 introduces the first of the many compressed versions of the narrator's history that stud the text and contribute to the poem's pleonastic character, particularly, as we shall see, towards the end. At this point we also have a number of misleadingly definite gestures: '"Tell on, man, quhat the befel",' 'And so befell as I shall ʒou deuise', and most notably the measured, confident and purposeful lines,

> Determyt furth therewith in myn entent,
> Sen I thus haue ymagynit of this soune,
> And in my tyme more ink and paper spent
> To lyte effect, I tuke conclusioune
> Sum newë thing to write. I set me doune,
> And furth-withall my pen in hand I tuke
> And maid a croce, and thus begouth my buke.
>
> (13)

The apostrophe of the 'sely ʒouth' that follows, with its images of the unripe fruit and the nestling, also has the air of an opening. Apostrophe, however, is classed by Geoffrey as a device of delay, and that turns out to be its main function here.[5] Though the narrative has given the impression of getting under way, as yet it goes nowhere.

One of the things that work against the free development of a literal narrative in the earlier part of the poem is the management of the nautical references that (perhaps after Boethius) pervade this section. They make their first explicit appearance in stanza 15, in the form of a simile, as part of the apostrophe:

> Thus stant thy confort in vnsekirnesse,
> And wantis it that suld the reule and gye;
> Ryght as the schip that sailith sterëles
> Vpon the rokkis most to harmes hye,
> For lak of it that suld bene hir supplye,
> So standis thou here in this warldis rage
> And wantis that suld gyde all thy viage.

In the following stanza the narrator explains that by this generic youth he means himself, at least in part, and the figure is applied to his own situation as a young man lacking 'rypëness of resoune' and hence rudderless 'amang the wawis of this warld'. What happens next is disorientating. Stanza 16 has ended with a promise to go on at once to recount his early circumstances – 'how the case anone I will discriue'. Our expectation of a story, however, is frustrated by a continuation of the sailing metaphor, a move which becomes doubly unsettling as we realise that it is being given a literary application, to the author's present situation as he composes his poem. Even by the standards of narratorial self-consciousness usual in dream-poems, the degree of self-reflexiveness is extreme:

> With doutfull hert, amang the rokkis blake
> My feble bote full fast to stere and rowe,
> Helples, allone, the wynter nyght I wake
> To wayte the wynd that furthward suld me throwe.

O empti saile, quhare is the wynd suld blowe
Me to the port, quhare gynneth all my game?
Help, Calyope, and wynd, in Marye name!

(17)

For a moment, the distinctions of time that the poem has begun to
establish - the present in which the narrator is speaking, the
time when he read Boethius and reflected on his own history, and
the time of his early youth - are abolished. Detached from any
particular reference except to the activity of its own production,
the language all but floats free. It is a striking moment. For all
their close reminiscence of the first stanza of the proem to Book
II of Troilus and Criseyde, there is, if only briefly, a quality
of panic in these lines that goes beyond the merely literary:
'Helples, allone, the wynter nyght I wake'. The exclamation with
which the stanza ends is brilliantly expressive, though its art is
obscured by modern editorial punctuation, fussy over-pointing
disguising the bold zeugma 'Help Calyope and wynd' and the
confused-sounding but rhetorically tactful double invocation of
Muse and Virgin. It is an artful rendering of inarticulacy and
desperation. After all this, the unpacking of the marine trope
into a methodically expounded conceit has the effect of a re-
assertion of control:

The rokkis clepe I the prolixitee
Off doubilnesse that doith my wittis pall.
The lak of wynd is the deficultee,
Enditing of this lytill trety small.
The bote I clepe the mater hole of all,
My wit vnto the saile that now I wynd
To seke connyng, though I bot lytill fynd.

(18)

These lines open the way for the invocation of stanza 19, this
time a decorously sober and reverential one.
    The lack of direction evident in the earlier stanzas is gone
now, and authorial purposefulness and control become even more
apparent as we embark on what is, formally, a three-stanzas-long
sentence, its main clause suspended until the last line of this
impressively sustained period:

In Vere that full of vertu is and gude,
Quhen nature first begynneth hir enprise,
That quhilum was be cruell frost and flude
And schouris scharp opprest in mony wyse,
And Synthius begynneth to aryse
Heigh in the est, a morow soft and suete,
Vpward his course to driue in Ariete;

Passit mydday bot fourë greis evin,
Off lenth and brede his angel wingis bryght
He spred vpon the ground doune fro the hevin,
That for gladnesse and confort of the sight,
And with the tiklyng of his hete and light,

> The tender flouris opnyt thame and sprad
> And in thaire nature thankit him for glad.
>
> Nought ferre passit the state of innocence,
> Bot nere about the nowmer of ʒeris thre,
> Were it causit throu hevinly influence
> Off goddys will, or othir casualtee,
> Can I nought say, bot out of my contree,
> By thaire avise that had of me the cure,
> Be see to pas tuke I myn auenture.   (20-22)

Stanzas 20 and 21, with their putting behind of the rigours of
winter, their references to spring and morning, and their terms of
rising and forward movement, create a stronger sense of real
beginning than we have encountered so far. And in 22 we get down
for the first time to economically-presented narrative essentials
- the narrator's age and situation at the time of the action being
described, the causes of action, the role of other characters, and
the first event. The buoyant narrative impulse is maintained by
the syntax, which has the effect of carrying the sentence even
further on, into the next stanza, until a new syntactical centre
of gravity is established by the next main clause:

> Puruait of all that was vs necessarye,
> With wind at will, vp airly by the morowe,
> Streight vnto schip, no longer wald we tarye,
> The way we tuke.

The first interruption to this forward surge is the queasily
dangling participial clause that opens the next stanza: 'Vpon the
wawis weltering to and fro,/So infortunate was that fremyt day
...'   Control is quickly restored, however, in the succinct
account of the narrator's capture and imprisonment. Indeed the
story now proceeds with such despatch that it overshoots, as it
were, and in a few lines takes us through eighteen years to his
release. (Though it does not neglect opportunities for pathos and
suspense, The Kingis Quair is full of such reassurances of a happy
outcome.)
   This is where the narrative at last settles down. The line
'Vpon the wawis weltering to and fro' is the last of the swerves
towards metaphor and allegory that occur several times in the
first couple of dozen stanzas, where the language of sea, ship and
voyage is handled in such a way as to keep the door open to
multiple meanings. The interrupted sea journey is not just a
literal one, but a figure for a young life whose normal course is
painfully, almost tragically arrested. The additional application
of the sea metaphor to the mature narrator's state of mind as he
writes his poem further works against determinacy of meaning, and
the result is a metaphorical field of such potential that its
influence dominates the early part of the poem. (If I may back-
track a little, its pull can already be felt, with a strange kind
of pre-echoic effect, as early as stanzas 8, 10 and 11: 'This
matere new in my mynd rolling', 'Among thir thoughtis rolling to
and fro', 'Forwakit and forwalowit'.)

One of the reasons for the uncertain progress of this part of the poem seems to be the absence of any very clear literary precedent for what the author is doing. Perhaps the main thing that helps it settle down after stanza 25 is the stabilising influence of The Knight's Tale. For the time being we know where we are. We know, for instance, when the narrator tells us how he bewailed his loss of liberty and looked from his prison window on to a 'gardyn faire' with its 'herbere grene', that before very long he is bound to see and fall in love with a beautiful woman. To the thoughtful reader or listener, a large part of the pleasure is going to come not just from the suspense created by this expectation, and from its eventual fulfilment, but in seeing what the poet makes of a situation where there are not two imprisoned lovers but only one.

The subtlety and inventiveness of James's art in this section may be seen in a passage that has bothered some commentators, the stanzas (54-60) in which the narrator reproaches the nightingale for its silence and tries to get it to sing. If we look at this episode from the perspectives I have suggested, it becomes apparent that by this point the poet is approaching the limits of his chosen situation as material for literal fiction. His narrator has seen the lady in the garden, he has apostrophised her after the manner of Palamon and the ancient woman-or-goddess topos, he has described the tumult of his feelings and given an account of her appearance, as well as making, from his prison window, a comprehensive assessment of her moral character, and he has uttered a fervent prayer to Venus. There is not much left to do. Whereas in The Knight's Tale Arcite just has to get a glimpse of Emelye as well and the resulting conflict is good for another 2000 lines, the situation in The Kingis Quair offers no such possibilities for development. On the level of story, the only real shot left in the poet's locker is the narrator's reaction when the lady leaves the garden. The address to the nightingale is a way of suspensefully deferring that moment by prolonging the lady's presence in the poem ('O lytill wrecche, allace, maist thou nought se/Quho commyth ȝond?' (57)), a means of bringing in some more direct speech, and an opportunity for the introduction of further inner conflict. The comments of John Norton-Smith, for whom the passage exemplifies 'the individual, amateurish quality of the author's personality as author', and who comes near to making fun of 'James's ... indulgent concern about the nightingale's failure to sing, and ... his serious and irrelevant search for the reason', seem very strange.[6] The episode is both artful and fully functional, its tone ranging from the horror and the lyrical poignancy of the stanzas on Procne and Philomela to the sympathetically comic rendering of the agonies of the anxious lover with his distracted questions, imperatives and exclamations:

> Is it now tyme to wring?
> Quhat sory thought is fallin vpon the?
> Opyn thy throte. Hastow no lest to sing?
> Allace, sen thou of resoune had felyng!
> Now, suete bird, say ones to me 'pepe'.
> I dee for wo.
>   (57)

An obvious function of the passage is to reinforce the sense of immediacy. It is full of deictic or situational elements: 'this morowe tyde', 'Seis thou nought hir that sittis the besyde?', 'lo here thy goldin hour', 'Here is in fay the tyme and eke the space'. It is hard to imagine any member of an audience listening to the poem being delivered by a competent reader finding any of this irrelevant. One might, it is true, see evidence of carelessness in the change of sex undergone by the bird between stanzas 55 and 58. In 55 we are made sharply aware of the nightingale as Philomela and female by the references to breasts and maidenhead. But in 58 the bird has a female mate: 'Or is sche dede, or hath sche the forsake?' This ambiguity of gender, however, is a signal that we need to go beyond a naturalistic reading here. The Philomela stanzas are not a whimsically introduced piece of factitious ornament. They contribute to the wholeness of the poem's vision by reminding us, in this comic work, of the existence of extreme horror and suffering, providing while they do so an opportunity to moralise, altogether relevantly in a poem about the attainment of a happy marriage, on faithless husbands. On a rather less obvious level, Philomela also functions as a type of the poet: the woman ravished and cruelly tortured, dumb until blessed by the gods with the gift of song, becomes a figure for all poets singing out of the depths of their pain. What seems to happen is that in a poem of such strong self-reflexive tendencies this potential of the Philomela story brings about a merging of the identities of narrator and bird. By stanza 58 it is clearly not just the nightingale the former is exhorting, but himself as poet and lover: 'Sluggart, for schame, lo here thy goldin hour/That worth were hale all thy lyvis laboure!'; 'Gyf thou suld sing wele euer in thy lyve,/Here is in fay the tyme and eke the space'; 'And here, to wyn gree happily for euer,/Here is the tyme to syng, or ellis neuer!' As if in distant anticipation of Keats, the narrator imagines himself for a moment in stanza 61 as a bird ('Me thought I flawe for joy without arest'), and in 62 the nightingale's notes become the melody of the song to which his words are the 'ditee'.[7]

II

The Kingis Quair has even more false endings than it has illusory beginnings, the last seventeen stanzas containing a whole series of gestures towards closure. The first is in stanza 181, where after having described the dove's message as the 'first takyn' of all his 'help and blisse', the narrator sketches the subsequent favourable progress of his fortunes, paying particular attention to the passage of time:

> The quhich treuly efter, day by day,
> That all my wittis maistrit had tofore,
> From hennesferth the paynis did away;
> And schortly, so wele Fortune has hir bore
> To quikin treuly day by day my lore,
> To my larges that I am cumyn agayn,
> To blisse with hir that is my souirane.

The next two stanzas give us two further such 'conclusions'. Stanza 182, perhaps in recognition of the insufficiency, in a poem of such scope, of a purely personal ending, goes on to relate the private events to the world of public experience as expressed in the language of maxim and proverb: 'And euery wicht his awin suete or sore/Has maist in mynde, I can say ʒou no more'. This generalising is continued in stanza 183 with the much weightier reference to imprisonment and liberation – rhetorically more effective too because of its form as a question: 'Eke quho may in this lyfe haue more plesance/Than cum to largesse from thraldom and peyne?' Opening on this truly universal and atemporal level, the stanza proceeds to a satisfying close in the personal and present: 'Now sufficiance is my felicitee.'

What prevents these stanzas from working adequately as a full conclusion is an intrusive element of self-reflexiveness, especially evident in 182: 'Bot for als moche as sum micht think or seyne,/Quhat nedis me aponn so littil evyn/To writt all this?' Though less prominent in the following stanza, it persists as a weakening factor, the eloquent and impressive first five lines suddenly adopting a defensively self-conscious slant as the poet reverts to the subject of critical censure: 'Quho suld me wite to write thar-of, lat se?' At this stage in the poem, and in such terms, there is something distracting and a little indecorous about the expression of these authorial anxieties. As James himself finely demonstrates in his envoi, there is a right place and a right way to say such things.

There are half a dozen or more false conclusions of this kind. Stanza 187, for instance, in a review of the latter part of the narrator's history, has the effect of groping towards finality:

> To rekyn of euery thing the circumstance
> As hapint me, quhen lessen gan the sore
> Of my foos rancoure and my wofull chance,
> It war to long. I lat it be tharefor.
> And thus this floure, I can seye ʒou no more,
> So hertly has vnto my help attendit
> That from the deth hir man sche has defendit.

As well as making its own contribution to the poem's winding up, this stanza is a particularly clear example of the way the poet avoids giving us any more than the barest minimum of story. It is worth noticing the rhetorical skill with which he does so in a disarming show of consideration for the patience of his audience.

This is one part of the poem where James succeeds in his aim of writing 'sum newe thing'. The accomplishment of these closing stanzas may not be fully apparent if we are thinking of the text in terms of silent reading. But in the circumstances of a live performance, and in the care of the capable reader the poet prays for in his envoi, the multiple endings might, I think, take on something of the quality we find sometimes in surprise endings in classical music, when part of our pleasure lies in having our expectations of closure proved false, in realising that there is more to come, and in playing the game of trying to outguess the composer. A celebrated example is the end of Hadyn's Quartet Op.

33 no. 2 (popularly, if slightingly, known in Britain as the 'Joke' Quartet). These kinds of enjoyment would be available to the audience of a spoken performance in a way they are not to silent readers with the text laid out, static and predictable, before their eyes. This playful quality is not at odds with the poem's seriousness, but is in keeping with the general demeanour of a work which bears so gracefully its weight of literary reference and the intensity of the experiences it records.

An audience might also be better placed to appreciate the force of the stanzas of benediction and thanks (189-91) as intimations that the ending is near at hand. And their ears might be more keenly attuned to the lyricism of these and adjacent stanzas, the repetitions, the patterning, the musical redundancy of telling the same story over and over in different words. We have had the story several times already, in the as yet unconcluded poem itself, and in the various condensed versions of 181(4-7), 182(4), 183(1-2), 187, 188(1-3) (a version which briefly carries the story on into the future), 189 and 191. The versions of 192 and 193 are the most conclusive so far. These are also the stanzas where we are most conscious, in this part of the poem, of the manipulative presence of the narrator:

> Vnworthy, lo, bot onely of hir grace,
> In lufis ʒok that esy is and sure,
> In guerdoun dere of all my lufis space
> Sche hath me tak hir humble creature.
> And thus befell my blisful auenture
> In ʒouth, of lufe that now from day to day
> Flourith ay newe. And ʒit forthir I say:

In all it takes ten or so of these abbreviated versions of the story before the poet can formally take his leave of his work. The device of the envoi is a very powerful one for managing the difficult business of winding up a composition and letting it go, its effectiveness stemming from the combination, as here, of the assertion of 'authority' with its relinquishment: 'Go, litill tretise'. The earlier briefly heard note of authorial anxiety has disappeared, and the poet is able to make a decorous and eloquent profession of rhetorical inadequacy while at the same time committing his poem to the care of a performer and offering him tactful direction. Furthermore, he can voice the assurance that it will somehow remain under the beneficent guidance of the lady who has been its inspiration and to whom it is his petition.

Two particularly artful strokes in this finely managed ending deserve comment. One is the echo of the nautical metaphors of the beginning of the poem in the second-last line of each stanza of the envoi ('to reulë and to stere', 'thy gyd and stere'). The other is the unchanging rhymes of the envoi and the stanza that follows (a device used once earlier, in stanzas 189-91), whose effect is to make the splendid conclusion dovetail with the envoi proper by giving it the same tune. This ending could not be more conclusive, as it brings us back to the first line, and back to the causes of earthly action in divine providence, and to the ultimate original of texts like the one we have been reading, the master text written in the heavens by the Almighty.

But of course this is still not the end. One final rite needs to be performed, the acknowledgement demanded by convention of the poet's literary masters. Hence just as closure has apparently been effected, and the text shut up in a magic circle, the poem opens out once more in a coda, which itself ends in the only way possible in so thoroughly Christian a work. Having just looked back to the source of all things, the poem now looks forward in its last line to 'the blisse of hevin'.

More than most examples of its kind, The Kingis Quair remains an enigmatic poem, not least because of the lure of its unquestionable real-life element. In some ways it is a handicap that we know anything of its author. If we did not, we might find it easier to make out, and more fully appreciate, the modes in which it works. We might be less inclined to read it as anything like straightforward narrative, and might instead see it, as I believe we should, as more like an extended lyric. The Quair has many song-like features: a confessional narrator, passages which themselves could stand as lyric poems, references to song, general reflections on life and love, a pronounced element of self-reflexiveness, and a high degree of redundancy. As in many songs and lyric poems, the story we find in it is fragmentary, oblique and elusive, features enhanced in the sections I have been looking at by the tendency of the narrative to arrest, turn in on, repeat, and undermine itself. Attributes likely to commend the work to the modern critic, these are not flaws but make an important contribution to the poem's highly individual character and, particularly towards the end, to its lyrical quality. And like the best songs, the Quair has less to do with autobiography, spiritual or otherwise, than with moving and entertaining those in whose presence it was performed through its artful appeal to thoughts, emotions and experiences which they could perceive as universal.

Notes

1   Quotations are from The Kingis Quair of James Stewart, ed. Matthew P McDiarmid (London, 1973). Taking leave of Troilus, Chaucer prays,

> So prey I God that non myswrite the,
> Ne the mysmetre for defaute of tonge.
> And red wherso thow be, or elles songe,
> That thow be understonde, God I beseche!

(V, 1795-9; Works, F N Robinson (ed), 2nd edn (London, 1957)). Douglas concludes his Eneados with a similar appeal to 'writaris all, and gentil redaris eyk': 'Bot redis leill, and tak gud tent in tyme,/ʒhe nowder maggill nor mismetir my ryme.' ('The Tyme, Space, and Dait, of the Translatioun of this Buik', 23-4; Poetical Works, John Small (ed), 4 vols. (Edinburgh and London, 1874)). Romances frequently begin with a request to the audience to pay attention to what the reciter has to say, and sometimes even with an injunction to be quiet: 'And ther-fore pristly j ʒow praye,/That ʒe will of ʒoure talkyng blyne.' (<u>Thomas of Erceldoune</u>, James A H Murray (ed), EETS (London 1875), 7-8).

2 I mention James's authorship, the evidence for which seems to me convincing, not because it has any direct bearing on my approach but because I want to take the opportunity of demonstrating that it is possible to accept it without being led into a referential reading of the poem.

3 <u>The New Poetics</u>, trans Jane Baltzell Kopp, in <u>Three Medieval Rhetorical Arts</u>, James J Murphy (ed) (Berkeley, Los Angeles and London 1971), pp 37-40.

4 <u>Medieval Dream Poetry</u> (Cambridge 1976), p 183.

5 Ed.cit., p.43.

6 <u>James I of Scotland: The Kingis Quair</u> (Leiden 1981), pp. xiv-xv.

7 The MS 'he' of stanza 61, line 1, may not be simple scribal error, and should perhaps be retained by editors.

Chapter 11

THE AUSTRIAN CONNECTION c.1450-1483:
ELEONORA AND THE INTERTEXTUALITY OF PONTUS UND SIDONIA

A M Stewart

Pioneering studies of Scots-Continental links continue to be
supplemented by useful studies by historians.[1] However, there has
not yet been published any up-to-date full study in English of
Margaret, Isabella and Eleonora, three of the daughters of James I,
who are certainly worth including in any gallery of Scots abroad.

Even for the 'pauvre Dauphine' we are still mainly referred to
the almost unobtainable work of Gaston Du Fresne de Beaucourt, in
French, published in Paris in 1888;[2] or, with reservations, to
Francisque Michel's work, more readily available in Scots libraries
because the title is more obviously relevant to Scotland, but also
in French and published (in London) in 1862.[3]

For 'Ysabeau' we are still dependent on Barbé's account.[4] For
the third sister, Eleonora, however, we are in the fortunate position of having very useful sources available, albeit in German.[5]

It is in an attempt to outline the results of these German
language studies and put them in English in a 'nuttis schell', that
this excursion into the frontiers of history and literature highlights the intertextuality of Pontus and Sidonia, the popular
German translation from the French, undertaken apparently after
1450 and published in 1483, ascribed to Eleanora wife of Archduke
Sigmund of Austria-Tirol. This context is illuminating for an
assessment of the spread of humanism in the transitional phase
between the 'Middle Ages' and the early modern period.[6] Perhaps too
it may encourage a study linking the daughters of James I.

Translations of romances may indicate the sort of reading
popular with the educated aristocracy and the rising patrician
class in the second half of the fifteenth and the first half of the
sixteenth century. (The popularity of the romances was of course a
target for satirical comment from Chaucer through the Elizabethan
times down to later ages.) However, the popularity of the 'good
stories' for their entertainment value, should not obscure the fact
that the upsurge of translations is part of the enrichment of the
vernacular, an eminently 'Renaissance' activity, after the fall of
Constantinople, which in France lasted through the patriotic
'philological revolution' of the age of François I, in the years
c.1520-1540. Translations of romances, including prose versions of
earlier verse romances, appear to flood the market with the printing boom of the age of Caxton, Wynkyn de Worde and their successors.

It would be an interesting digression to consider the coexist-
ence in usage or the timing of the switch from Anglo-Norman French

Eleonora (Courtesy of Kunsthistorisches Museum, Vienna)

to English by the various types of audience for literary products.
(This point has been earlier discussed, for example, by John Orr
and M Dominica Legge.)[7] Translations may only be strictly necessary for people who are unable to read the originals; but on the
other hand translations are sometimes a response to a challenge
felt by the translator to show that his own vernacular is as rich
as the foreign tongue: a response to a request from a patron, or a
deliberate (didactic) manipulation of a popular theme.

The intertextuality of Pontus and Sidonia demonstrates the
migration of a good story. It is a 'rifacimento', a 'remaniement',
a 're-écriture', a retelling of the story of 'King Horn' from the
Matter of Britain; more precisely, an adaptation of the Anglo-
Norman version, Horn et Rimenhild.[8] By pillaging, the romancer
saves himself the responsibility and labour of invention by accepting as a whole the plot; by reshaping it slightly to suit the
changing taste of the time, expanding the descriptions of Pontus's
good looks, accomplishments and virtues and turning the tale into a
'book of Courtesy';[9] by amplifying and adding details from the
other examples of the 'genre', adding in the commonplaces, clichés,
'topoi', formulations his audience would expect from their expectations of the 'genre'; by adding 'energia' or 'enargia' by local-
ising the scenes in the geographical area most familiar to the
patron (one of the family De La Tour Landry);[10] and by inserting
names of the families which enhanced the fame of his patron by the
reflected glory of association.

The Celtic Arthur, the continental Charlemagne and other alien
figures tend to usurp the place of native English heroes in England
after the Norman Conquest. The earliest extant example of a Middle
English romance derived from an English story is King Horn, c.1225,
preceded by an Anglo-Norman version of the romance dated c.1170-80
(roughly contemporary with the activity of Chrétien de Troyes). The
story of Horn appears in a group of four versions: the Anglo-Norman
romance of Horn et Rimenhild, composed by a Mestre Thomas (c.1170-
1180);[11] the Middle English version King Horn (composed c.1225);[12]
the Ballad of Hind Horn[14] which may have been introduced into the
oral folk tradition early on (say in the fourteenth century).
Towards the end of the fourteenth century the Anglo-Norman Horn et
Rimenhild was transformed into its French guise of the prose
romance Ponthus et la belle Sidoine.[15] In the following half
century the French version was translated into the English prose
King Ponthus,[16] and some time after 1449 the French version was
translated into the German Pontus und Sidonia under the aegis of
Eleonora.[17]

Pontus und Sidonia thus is a disguised version of the King Horn
legend from the 'Matter of Britain'. As medievalists are well
aware, the classification of romances by themes is ultimately
derived from Jehan Bodel's categories:

'Ne sont que trois matieres, a nule home entendant
De France, et de Bretagne, et de Rome la grant' -

in other words, with a French or British or Classical background.
The category 'Matière de Bretagne' includes Celtic and Germanic
elements and matter transmitted via Brittany (little Britain).

The Anglo-Norman <u>Horn et Rimenhild</u>, when it is rewritten in Brittany as <u>Ponthus et la belle Sidoine,</u> is adapted to exemplify the rules of behaviour proper to a gentleman:[18]

> The plot follows that of <u>Horn et Rimenhild</u> closely, with a few additions borrowed by Chrétien de Troyes and other romancers; but the setting is entirely changed, the tone is sententious, and the primitive power of the original has disappeared. Ponthus (Horn) belongs to Galicia, and Sidoine (Rimenhild) to Brittany, and England is the scene of the hero's foreign exile.

The localisation of the tale in Brittany, with England as an exotic place for adventures and exile, is of interest. The references to Brittany, Galicia, Cornwall, Wales, Ireland, Scotland, are a sign of a perspective that we could describe as a focus of the western peripheral maritime regions of Europe. They reveal a coastal view of geography, a concentration on sea-routes, at a period of slow perilous overland travel.

Placenames, as Peter Rickard comments (p 120) have to be treated with caution, and he discusses the 'role of England in Romances of adventure' showing that the motives for going to England can be various: e.g. in <u>Galeran de Bretagne</u> the character goes to England because he is ordered to go as a feudal vassal to get a fief; in <u>Paris et Vienne</u> and <u>La Fille du comte de Pontieu</u> the motive is to attend a 'Tourney'; in <u>Palanus comte de Lyon</u> the motive is for adventure; in <u>Respon</u> the impoverished knight goes to England to see service as a professional soldier, a mercenary motive! Finally, in <u>Ponthus et la belle Sidoine</u> the motive is to see '<u>L'estat et la noblesse de la cour</u>'![19]

Why would the story of <u>Pontus und Sidonia</u> make an especial appeal to Eleonora, daughter of James I of Scotland and wife of Erzherzog Sigmund von Osterreich-Tirol? The historical background provides us with clues.

James I, son of Robert III of Scotland, was born in July 1394 and acceded on 4 April 1406. However, James was captured by English merchants at sea on 22 March 1406 and spent eighteen years in captivity in England until the end of March 1424. In his absence the two Dukes of Albany ruled successively as 'governors'. James married in England, in February 1424, the beautiful Joan Beaufort.[20] He returned to Scotland with his wife that same year.

They had eight children – Alexander, James, Margaret, Isabella, Joan, Eleanora, Mary and Annabella. Of these eight children, Alexander died in infancy and his twin brother was the future James II. The eldest daughter Margaret (born 1424, died 16 August 1445) married in 1436 the Dauphin (afterwards Louis XI, King of France). Isabella married in 1442 Francis I, duke of Brittany; Joan married c.1458 James, earl of Morton; Eleanora married in 1449 Archduke Sigmund; Mary married Wolfart count of Grandpré, lord of Campvere in Zealand; Annabella may have married firstly Louis, count of Geneva,[21] and secondly George Gordon, second earl of Huntly. In 1449, in the same year as Eleanora married, her brother King James II married Marie of Gueldres, a niece of the Duke of Burgundy.

James I only survived to see the marriage of his eldest daughter Margaret to the Dauphin Louis. In 1437 James was murdered in Perth by a group of his nobles who resented his energetic reforms. The regicide appalled commentators, such as Aeneas Sylvius Piccolomini, who had visited Scotland in 1435.[22] The Queen and the children escaped and the assassins were punished.

Eleonora was the sixth child, and German literary historians confidently state she was born in 1433, a conclusion based on the statement that she was married at the age of sixteen. After James I's death his widow acted as Regent for the six or seven-year-old James II. She was a virtual prisoner and in 1439 gave up her wardship of her children, married Sir James Stewart, 'the black Knight of Lorn', had by him two or three children, and died in Dunbar Castle in mid-July 1445. In the meantime in 1441 ambassadors came to Scotland from John, Duke of Brittany with an offer of marriage between the duke's eldest son and Isabella, James I's second daughter. The marriage took place in Brittany on 30 October 1442. In 1445 Eleonora and the other royal children were living at Linlithgow.

In a letter from Duchess Isabella to James II dated 20 April 1445, Eleonora and her sister Joan were invited to France. They reached Flanders between 16 and 19 August 1445, and there received the news of the death of their sister Margaret, 'la pauvre Dauphine', in Chalons. On 19 August the French king, Charles VII, sent a delegation to welcome Eleonora and Joan in Tournai and escort them to Tours. They reached the French court at Tours on 9 September 1445.[23]

Charles VII appointed Jeanne de Tucé, dame de Saint-Michel, who had previously served the Dauphine, as governess for the two princesses. (Account books of André Nonneau and Etienne Noyeu give details of household costs and include such items as ink and parchment rolls, suggesting some sort of literary activity perhaps.[24]) During the three years at the French court Eleonora would appear to have experienced a festive time. There were excursions from Tours to tournaments, for example, at Chinon, Saumur and Montils-les-Tours, in the years 1446 and 1447.[25] In June 1447 Eleonora went in the retinue of Queen Marie d'Anjou to Mont Saint-Michel. Her governess was at home there, so to speak; and Eleonora's sister, Ysabeau de Bretagne, was added reason to feel affinity for the impressive pilgrimage centre.

Charles VII would possibly have wished to see the Dauphin next marry Eleonora, but the Dauphin was apparently unwilling to do so, and he was helped in his resistance by the Pope, Eugenius IV, who refused to give his dispensation. Charles VII meantime had also been active in trying to arrange the marriage of Sigmund of Tirol and Radegunde, who unfortunately died, aged nineteen, in Tours in February 1445. Sigmund's proposed marriage is commemorated in the portrait of Sigmund and his three ladies in a sixteenth-century group portrayal in Schloss Tratzberg in the Lower Inn Valley.[26] Now that the way was open for a new marriage project for Sigmund, Charles VII, who regarded Sigmund as a protégé, 'très cher et très aimé fils et cousin', sent a delegation, including William Moneypenny who had earlier been involved in the negotiations for the marriage of Isabella and François I of Brittany, to discuss the marriage of Sigmund and Eleonora. Moneypenny informed Isabella en route.

The negotiations involving the agreement of James II, the Duke
of Brittany, the Duke of Savoy, and many details took the ambassadors Hans Pechl and Ludwig von Landsee some six months of 'shuttle
diplomacy' before the details were finalised and Eleonora was
engaged by Sigmund's proxy Ludwig von Landsee in February 1448. The
marriage was celebrated 'per procurationem' in the Augustinian
Church in Belmont near Chinon and was conducted by Bishop Thibault
of Maillezais in the presence of the French king and his queen, who
were both appropriately moved, on 8 September 1448.[27]

The arduous journey to Tirol took Eleonora till January 1449. In
the first few years there is no documentary evidence that she
engaged in any independent political activity.

Eleonora first emerges into political activity in connection
with the trouble after the controversial nomination of Nicolas
Cusanus as Bishop of Brixen in 1450 and his assumption of the
office in 1452.[28] Eleonora became involved in the long-running saga
of Cusanus's quarrel with the Benedictine nuns of Sonnenberg
convent. By June 1454 Cusanus threatened the nuns with excommunication and interdict, and was supported by the Pope. There was a
visitation on 4 March 1455. Also, Cardinal Nicolas of Cusa forced
through various unpopular reforms including a ban on the wearing of
armour and weapons and a ban on evening dances on the occasion of
the holidays connected with church anniversaries, which by custom
were also market days and days when the courts held sittings. This
was perceived as an intrusion into folklife customs. Eleonora was
left with the problems when Sigmund left for Austria for negotiations with Emperor Friedrich III.

Eleonora was given her own seals in the winter of 1445-46, when
Sigmund was called away again for negotiations in connection with
the perceived Turkish threat in 1456.[29]

From 1485 on, however, Eleonora seems to have ceased to have
anything to do with the trouble with Cusanus, which came to a head
in 1460. Her regency in 1457-58 reveals Eleonora's increasing
independence. In 1458 Eleonora had various lands transferred to her
as a legal device to prevent the loss of these territories if the
Pope, Calixtus III, should decide to impose an interdict on
Sigmund. This document bears her great seal and her signature.[30] At
the beginning of June 1460 Hans Pechl was sent on a mission to
Scotland, with a gift of armour and a crossbow, with a request for
diplomatic support in the strife with the Helvetic troublemakers
(Eidgenossen). James II had died in the meantime on 3 August 1460.
James III, son of James II and Mary of Gueldres, born in May 1452,
was, of course, 'too young'. Scotland was suffering from another of
the 'minorities' which gave deep meaningfulness to the biblical
complaint 'Woe to the kingdom that has too young a king'.[31]

In the military preparations Eleonora seems to have been very
active raising money and guns, gunpowder, copper, lead, horses,
waggons, mercenaries and provisions. However, the military operations took no notice of the legal niceties of the transfer of
property to Eleonora and the legal devices were allowed to lapse.[32]
During the years 1461-66 Eleonora seems to have been in the Tirol,
in Innsbruck or Imst or Sigmundsburg or Meran, but rarely in the
same place at the same time as Sigmund, who was often absent. In
1467 Eleonora went to Basle where she took part in the Fasnacht

pre-Lenten   celebrations,   along with Sigmund.[33] The pre-Lenten
tournaments and other chivalric exercises were entered into by
Sigmund with such gusto and enthusiasm that Eleonora was petrified.
On Ash Wednesday the Duke disguised himself and ran through the
streets of Basle with others in carnival disguise.[34]

   With Sigmund's return home in the summer of 1469 Eleonora seems
to have given up her political involvement but she would be only
too aware of the Turkish threat (1471-78).[35]

   In addition to Eleonora's political work we have clear evidence
of her administrative activities and can see from the archives her
itineraries in the years 1449 to 1480, which reveal, for example,
her visiting the health resort Wildbad Gastein to try the healing
warm springs, a two hundred kilometre trip taken in 1465 via Wörgl,
Kitzbühel and Zell am See, and taking about five days to get there.
As modern tourists find, spending money soon runs out, and Eleonora
had to send twice within ten days for extra money. And after less
than four weeks she left. On the way home she bought a fur coat in
Kitzbühel.[36]

   In 1474 she made another major excursion to Baden im Aargau.
This was to be her last trip 'abroad' outside Tirol.

   In the Innsbruck Landesregierungsarchiv für Tirol there are
preserved (at Sig IVa 8) nine letters to Eleonora in German dating
from the years 1458 to 1472; and (at Sig IVa 181), eighteen letters
to her in German, Latin, French and Scots, including letters from
James Lord Hamilton (in Scots), James earl of Buchan (2) and
William Tulloch, Bishop of Orkney.

   The letter from James Hamilton to Eleonora is of particular
interest. According to Dr Leslie J Macfarlane, who has transcribed
the letter, it dates from the period 1466-80, and reads as follows:

   Letter from James Lord Hamilton to Eleanor Archduchess of
   Austria, c.1466-80. MS. (Landesregierungsarchiv, Innsbruck).
   From a photostat in the possession of Leslie Macfarlane, Dept
   of History, King's College, Aberdeen.

   Rycht nobill ande worschepfull lady I commande me to ȝour
   gudlye ladischip als hartly as I can Ande plesit ȝou to wyt
   that a speciall man of myn callit Jhon Atkynson the beirar
   disponys to vesye the sege of rome this instant ȝher of grace
   Ande I haf ordande hym to vesye & ler the craft of fyning of
   lede & the maner bath of byrnyng & smeltyn of the samyn & to
   se in his passage quheder he may best furder therto in Ing-
   lande or in ȝour lande & quhilk plesis hym best to raman
   theron a ȝher or twa in his hamcummyn for the quhilk I besek
   ȝour ladischip gif he thynkis spedfull to raman in ȝour lande
   at ȝhe walde gar hym be enterit to men that ar best of that
   sciens that ȝhe cnaw in ȝour lande Ande walde ȝour ladischip
   gar the twa ȝoung men that war in the lande befor tym of
   ȝhouris cum agan in this lande & fyne the lede ther is eneuch
   to get & thai sulde be rycht weill cheryst And gif my ser-
   uande the beirar mystaris other lettiris or speciall takynnys
   of ȝouris thrucht the lande to conwoye hym I requer ȝour
   ladischip hartly therof Ande gif ther be other hors hawkis or
   hundis or ony other gudis that ȝhe desyr in this cuntre at ȝhe

walde send worde to my lady my wyf ʒour broder dochter my
souerane lorde was quham gode assolʒe & to me & the best that
can be gottyn ʒhe sall haf wyth all our hartly seruis betwyx
Ande gode kep ʒour ladischip in gude prosperyte at ʒour nobil
hartis desyr Vrityn in hammilton wythin scotlande vnder my
seill the fyrst fastyn day &c.

ʒouris at all tym redy

To my lady of hosterage &c.

James lorde hamilton &c.

James Lord Hamilton's letter reveals that the aristocracy is not
above indulging in commerce, in the metal craft: from extraction
through processing. James Hamilton is sending John Atkynson to
learn the craft of 'fyning of lede and the maner bath of byrnyng &
smeltyn of the samyn'. Hamilton also asks Eleonora to reverse the
'brain drain' and send back the two Scots who had previously gone
to learn these skills, assuring them of good employment prospects,
and assuring them that 'thai sulde be rycht weill cheryst'.

Changing the subject he reveals Eleonora's reputation as a keen
huntswoman when he offers her 'hors hawkis or hundis' or anything
else she requires. (This is a nice formulaic phrase, as David
Buchan has pointed out.) It is amusing to see Hamilton addressing
the letter 'To my lady of hosterage &c', an obvious corruption of
Österreich.

There are apparently only five letters in Eleonora's own hand-
writing. Two of these are in German to Sigmund, the others are in
French and are drafts of notes to relatives. Her letters to
Isabella of Brittany are in French. We do not have anything in
English or Latin in her hand.

The picture that emerges from the historical sketch we have
traced reveals Eleonora to be a determined and independent woman,
well able to run a separate household and to look after the administration of scattered properties in difficult terrain and difficult political circumstances.

Perhaps it was wise of the couple to agree to go their independent ways. Her sister Isabella's husband is reported (by Barbé) as
being the male chauvinist Duke who

> considered a wife to be quite clever if she could distinguish
> between her husband's shirt and his doublet.

These views, recorded by the sixteenth-century annalist Bouchet,
supplied Molière with an idea for one of the passages in 'Les
Femmes Savantes':

> Nos pères sur ce point étaient gens bien sensés
> Qui disaient qu'une femme en sait toujours assez
> Quand la capacité de son esprit se hausse
> A connaître un pourpoint d'avec un haut de chausse.[39]

Elisabeth von Nassau-Saarbrucken (1397-1456) was another strong
lady involved in literary activity and bracketed by literary
historians with Eleonora in the account of the beginnings of prose
novel writing in German literature.[40]

Eleonora emerges in a literary context in 1473 in the dedicatory preface of the translation by Heinrich Steinhöwel (1412-1478) of Boccaccio's De claris mulieribus.[41] The 1473 translation was entitled Von den synnrychen erluchten wyben (On wise and illustrious women). Steinhöwel, following Boccaccio, apologises for having to include the biographies of immoral women, justifying such inclusions with the argument that they might serve as deterrents, while their virtuous counterparts are to be regarded as shining examples. This echoes the (slightly left-handed) compliments in Boccaccio's dedication, but Steinhöwel promises to devote the hundredth chapter to Eleonora as the crowning representative of all women. Either he forgot this promise in course of time or he had meant it only symbolically; in any case the hundredth chapter is devoted, quite prosaically, to the rules of punctuation.

The work is dedicated to Boccaccio, in the belief that it will thus be safer 'from the insults of malicious people' (p. xxxv). Steinhöwel's translation was received well, and out of gratitude he dedicated his next undertaking, a translation of Speculum vitae humanae by the Spanish theologian, jurist and diplomat, Rodriguez Sanchez de Arevala (1404-1470), this time to Eleonora's husband Duke Sigmund.

This is an interesting dedication, a variation of the 'Tenth Worthy' topos, in that it demonstrates Eleonora's involvement in the early phase of humanism in the Northern Renaissance. In the early years after the Fall of Constantinople, parallel to the translations of the classics there were translations from French accompanied with reflections on the art of translation.

At the forefront of the efforts to enrich the vernacular in this early phase of prose writing in German were noble patronesses following the lead of Elisabeth von Nassau-Saarbrucken, as we have said. Oswald von Wolkenstein died in 1445 before Eleonora reached the Tirol. His son is mentioned in connection with administrative matters which suggest that Eleonora met him. It would be interesting to know whether Wolkenstein really went to Scotland and whether Eleonora was aware of the fact and knew his works. (A recent excruciating rendering of some of his works also made me wonder whether her judgement on such a performance would have been positive.)[42]

The ubiquitous peripatetic Aeneas Sylvius Piccolomini visited Scotland and met James I in 1435, and wrote about Scotland in what became a 'standard' account, printed in his De Europa and repeated in the Nuremberg Chronicle (1493) in Latin and German, repeated by Münster and Sleiden, and contradicted by Boece and Bellenden and John Major in the sixteenth century.[43] Aeneas Sylvius was also in touch with Sigmund. One of the key documents in the dissemination of the 'acquis' of the Renaissance was the famous plea for the studia humanitatis embodied in Aneas Sylvius's letter to Sigmund, translated by Niclas von Wyle as his tenth 'Translatze', which towards the end is expanded into a Furstenspiegel or Mirror for Princes.

Enea - and of course tacitly Wyle - voice sentiments that are considerably ahead of his time. Enea's statement for instance that a state should not exist for its sovereign but that the sovereign should be the first servant of the state, clearly

anticipates ideas expressed in the eighteenth century. Moreover, at a time when entire books were written about the
correct form of address, Enea's defense of the familiar Du as
opposed to the formally acceptable Sie, was likely to raise
the eyebrows of his blue-blooded recipient, in Wyle's case
Charles of Baden.[44]

Eleonora and Sigmund were politically so busy that it was only
after Eleonora's death that Sigmund had time to have more widely
known contacts with the German Humanists.

Eleanora's literary reputation is based on the romance Pontus
und Sidonia first printed after her death in 1483 by Hans Schön-
sperger in Augsburg.[45] In the 1485 edition, the subtitle shows the
aims and intentions of the 'Histori' which can be paraphrased as
follows:

> Here begins a fine Historia from which one may derive much in
> the way of good finer precepts, teaching, instruction; and
> also symbols, parables, allegory and examples; and especially
> the young if they hear and listen to the good doing and great
> honour, prestige, knightly skill and virtue, exercised by
> their elders and predecessors and ancestors, attributes
> inherently held by them. This 'Histori' the illustrious
> resplendent and highborn Lady, Lady Heleonora, born queen of
> Scotland, Archduchess of Austria (Erczhertzogin zu Öster-
> reich), praiseworthily transferred (getranszferiret) and made
> from the French tongue (von franczosiger Zungen in teütsch)
> into German, for the illustrious highborn prince and lord,
> Lord Sigmund, Archduke zu Österreich, etc, her spouse: as
> testimony of her love and well-pleased-ness.

Those who find the fifteenth-century German text laborious to
read, but who wish to follow the plot of Eleonora's version of
Pontus und Sidonia, have a reasonably close guide in the edition
of MS Digby 185 in the Bodleian Library, edited by Frank Jewett
Mather. A sentence-by-sentence comparison reveals only minor
differences, such as the inclusion or exclusion of lists of names,
perhaps a matter of taste where each scribe judges whether the
momentum of the narrative is overly retarded by a catalogue at a
particular juncture or whether a touch of 'copiousness' will
enhance the work. Both the German and English versions share the
evident enjoyment of tournaments and festivals.

The word 'gemacht' appears to suggest that the translation was
indeed 'made' by Eleonora personally. There exists only the MS
prepared by a scribe 'Per me Nicolaum Huber presbyter Brixin.
dyocen. Anno dni. 1465', which is considered to be of the same
group as the printed version.[46]

Parallel to this is another manuscript translation of the Pontus
und Sidonia, which naturally was eclipsed by the version linked
with the name of Eleonora.[47]

Perhaps we should regard Eleonora as a supervising patron rather
than as a translator in any modern sense. I find an interesting
parallel in the comments of Madame Danielle Buschinger[48] on the
'intentions' of the aristocratic patron of the Tristan of Eilhart

von Oberg, which mirror my own speculative interpretation of the
appeal of <u>Pontus und Sidonia</u> to Eleonora (Tome II, p 1043):

> Mathilde, venant d'un milieu courtois, hautement littéraire,
> celui de sa mère, Aliénor d'Aquitaine, introduit en 1168, date
> de son mariage avec Henri le Lion à la cour austère de Bruns-
> wick les moeurs courtoises et raffinées, les règles de la
> civilité et de l'urbanité courtoises, bref, le code de la
> courtoisie; en même temps elle y transporte une activité
> littéraire comme compensation à son exil forcé, comme réaction
> féminine aussi contre la rudesse guerrière de son époux et
> de son entourage; c'est elle qui donne à Eilhart commande
> d'écrire le <u>Tristrant</u> en lui procurant elle-même le manuscrit
> original.

Even if not herself undertaking the chore of translating,
Eleonora is also well able to assess the translator's version and
check its fidelity to the model original, and spot inconsistencies
requiring 'ironing out' (problems of 'conjointure'). The translation or adaptation, the 're-écriture' is aimed at a specific new
public, yet the 'public' held expectations that the version would
adhere to the accustomed 'matter' of the 'source' and the 'form of
the genre and to the overall message, the 'intention' (or 'sen'),
the didactic aim of the work, which is outlined in the Prologue or,
in the case of <u>Pontus und Sidonia</u>, on the title-page.

It would be a digression here, but a detailed analysis of the
structure of <u>Pontus und Sidonia</u>, comparing the scribal divisions,
editorial episodic segments (marked by Kindermann)[49] corresponding almost exactly to Mather's 'chapters'[50] and with sense 'blocs'
(Buschinger)[51] or 'substructure narremes' (Eugene Dorfman),[52] would
be illuminating, and possibly enhance the status of our <u>Prosaroman</u>,
which has been regarded as an inferior late derivative product, in
the light of the anachronistic Romantic requirement of 'originality'.

Similarly the application of subtler, more objective, or at
least less subjective techniques of translation evaluation, adum-
brated by modern language practitioners such as Koller,[53] could,
provided the analysis takes into account the contemporary fifteenth
century debates on compilation, translation, adaptation, originality, authority, etc, profitably replace anachronistic subjective
judgements, reflected for example in Mather's personal view of
<u>Pontus und Sidonia</u> as monotonous:

> Eleanor's rather dull version ... the edition of 1483 is a
> faithful rendering of a very early form of the French text,
> showing all the monotony of the French MS <u>R</u> of the British
> Museum.

Mather also speaks of 'the inevitable monotony of the genre' and
describes a romance as rising 'well above its class', and comments
that 'the fifteenth century took its instruction ... sturdily'.[54]

Eckhard Bernstein has made a useful move in the right direction
in his excellent discussion of Wyle and his translations. Even in
the mid-sixteenth-century writers were still tackling the problem

of 'defence and illustration' of the various vernaculars. Eleanora
is in the van of such efforts with her interest in translations
from the classics and from Italian and French. The didactic aims
are parallel to the primary entertainment value of such chivalric
courtly prose versions of earlier verse romances. Even a glance
through the headings of the various editions of Pontus as listed in
the British Library catalogue reveals the stress laid on the
didactic value of the book.

The 1498 edition calls the book a praiseworthy story (lobliche
histori); the 1539 Strasbourg edition is more effusive: Eyn rhum-
reich zierlich und fast fruchtbar Histori – a story celebrating in
an entertaining, rhetorically decorative way, usefully profitable
to the reader; another 1548 edition Von Adelischen Mannliche
Tugenten, Erbarkeyt, unnd Zucht, Ritter Pontus – of noble manly
virtues and chivalric skills, honourable court behaviour, observation of courtly chivalric codes inculcated by courtly education and
discipline the knight Pontus: the 1587 Buch der Liebe introduces
the story as Ritter Pontus, Von Adelichen Tugenden. Ein fürtref-
flich lustig und nützliche Histori, vom Edlen, Ehrenreichen, und
Mannhaftigen Ritter, dess Königes Sohn aus Gallicia, Und von der
schönen Sidonia, Königin in Britannia, darinnen viel nützlicher
Lehren und Underweisungen, wie man sich bey Fürsten und Herrn
Rittermessig, frömblich und höfliche sol verhalten – the last
phrase revealing that this is a book of etiquette almost, telling
the reader how to behave when meeting princes and noblemen,
repeating the 1547 title page, as in the Nationalbibliothek, Wien
copy.[55]

The appeal of Pontus und Sidonia to Eleanora must have been
overwhelming. Firstly, of course, its appeal is that of a good
story. It contains, chronologically, elements of the romances and
various folk-motifs: the 'unpromising hero'; children set adrift;
the dwarf (p 151); the setting of the 'Well of Mervelles': ('bey
dem wunderlichen Prunnen': p 162, 1.30); the guise of 'an ermyte &
wylde' ('Ir moechtent wild sein worden': the 'sylvestris' or 'wild
man', p 164, 1.3); the 'vera nobilitas' topos ('We be all comen of
oon fadre and modre', p 187, 11.10-11: 'Sey wir nit all von einem
Vater und von einer Muoter?' spoken by Pontus, in his guise of
'Surdyte', to the King of Scotland ('der kuenig von Schotenland');
treachery of the covetous Gendelet and the righting of his wrong-
doing and his punishment; disguise and anonymity: Pontus changes
his name and calls himself 'Surdyte de Droyte Voye', in German
'Sordit'[56] (p 187, 1.39); the 'pleasance' or 'garthyn' as a setting for entertainment, 'ein Garten, do spilten sy und viengen an
manigerley Kurczweil' (p 192, 1.7); the disguise as a pilgrim, with
a 'goune sved full of patches and a cappe full of broches' and the
'Burdone' (pilgrim's staff), 'het ein Kapen auff mitt Muscheln und
Ziechen daran gemacht' (p 194, 1.20-1); the dreams, e.g. 'I dremed
this nyght that I become a gret, blak wolfe, and that sett vpon me
a grete, whyte grehounde and a brachete, and the greyhounde slew
me' (p 208, 11.16-20), 'Es kam mir fuer, wye ich zuo einem schwar-
czen Wolff wer worden; vnnd das ein grosser weisser Winde nach mir
luff vnnd derselb streich vmb mich, pisz das er mich vom Leben zum
Tode prachte' (p 208, 11.16-20); Pontus dreams that a bear had
devoured his lady Sidonia (p 215, 1.19); the use of disguises

again, to get into the dance hall, 'Sume had stree hattes and sume
of grene bowes and sume had hoodes stuffed with hay, sume were
haltyng and sume were croke bakked, - euery man made aftre his awne
gyse': 'Und man liesz sy hinein in irem verkerten Gewand.   Sy hetten
gross Kappen angeleget, dye gefeult warn mit Heü. Der ander Teil
macht sich pucklet und yeglicher het ein besunder Geperd' (p 224,
11.26-9).

Firstly then it is a good entertaining story. Secondly it is
didactic, edifying, cortois, stressing the refining ideals of the
utopian golden age of the old verse romances. It is a reflection of
Eleonora's memories of the festivals and tournaments during her
time at the court of France, and a model for similar court events
in Innsbruck. It echoes Eleonora's own delight in hunting. It is in
accord with her taste for regal 'progress' trips from place to
place. The setting echoes evocative placenames meaningful to
Eleonora. The threat to Christianity presented by the Moors and
Saracens parallels the perceived threat to Austria from the Turks.
The cruelty of mercenaries would be a familiar theme to Eleonora.
The treachery at court was known to her from the assassination of
her father James. The treachery of a calumniator was familiar to
her from the fate of her sister Margaret, the Dauphine, maligned by
Jamet de Tillay. The detailed descriptions of the fine products of
silversmiths and other craftsmen would be attractive to Eleonora,
interested as she was in the metalwork crafts, from the mining of
the metals through to the finished products, as the accounts and
inventories reveal. As well as the arts and crafts, Eleonora was
interested in the humanist Renaissance activity of translation; she
exchanged books with the nearby court in Bavaria. She would be
exposed to literary activity in her childhood in Scotland, at the
court in France, and aware of the activity of the role of ladies in
the beginnings of the prose 'Roman' in Germany. Lastly the ending
of the story would commend itself to her. 'And aftre the quene and
the household went on pilgremage to Sainte Iames in Galice':
'ritten kyrchferten zuo sant Jacob in Galicia' (p 235, 1.14) before
ending their days in peace. St James (and St Andrew) would be
especially meaningful to Eleonora. We know of her donation to
Santiago and receipt of a present in return.[57]

This story is of the long-suffering heroine who is repaid for
her years of fidelity by finally settling down with the rich handsome hero whom she had loved while he was still an 'unpromising
hero', poor and in exile.

In Hartmann von Aue's versions of Chretien de Troyes' Erec and
his Iwein, the two tales can be seen as complementary, with Erec
exemplifying neglect of his chivalric knightly duty: 'er verliget
sich', he is overmuch involved with his wife, whereas Iwein exemplifies imbalance at the other extreme by neglecting ladies and
over-emphasising his knightly pursuits. Hartmann's didactic aim
would seem to be to encourage harmony, balance, and moderation,
observation of the golden mean, mesura, 'mâze', following the idea
(expounded e.g. in Aristotle's Nichomachean Ethics), that virtue is
the mean between extremes.[58]

Now in a dynastic marriage, love is not guaranteed. Sigmund is,
even today, notorious for the large retinue of illegitimate children claiming his parentage, and there is an anecdote of a courtier

who complained that he had to get out of Sigmund's court quickly before he suffered Erec's fate.[59]

What could be more ambivalent, perhaps ironic even, than the literary memorial to Eleonora; a formidable lady who reveals an appealing romantic side to her nature in her choice of this story.[60]

Notes

1   Francisque Michel, Les Ecossais en France: Les Français en Ecosse, 2 vols (London, 1862), especially I, ch VIII, pp 181-200. A Francis Steuart, Paper relating to the Scots in Poland 1576-1793, SHS, (Edinburgh, 1915). John Hill Burton, The Scot Abroad (Edinburgh, London, 1900). Th A Fischer, The Scots in Germany (Edinburgh, 1902). Th A Fischer, The Scots in Eastern and Western Prussia (Edinburgh, 1903). A I Dunlop, Scots Abroad in the Fifteenth Century (History Association Pamphlet, No. 124) (London, 1942). Mark Dilworth, The Scots in Franconia (Edinburgh, London, 1974). T C Smout (ed) Scotland and Europe 1200-1850 (essays by D E R Watt, John Durkan, J K Cameron and others) (Edinburgh, 1986).

2   Gaston Du Fresne de Beaucourt, Histoire de Charles VII (Paris, 1888). Dr Leslie J MacFarlane kindly drew my attention to Pierre-Roger Gaussin, Louis XI : roi méconnu: un roi entre deux mondes (Paris, 1976) and Paul M Kendall, Louis XI: the 'universal spider' (London, 1971). Kendall gives a very negative account of 'that fey little Scot, Margaret' (p 62), and her 'butterfly existence' (p 64), devoting most of his note on her (pp 393-5) to a denial that the scandalmonger Jamet de Tillay was connected with Louis the Dauphin (without sources). He suggests that her fatal inflammation of the lungs was self-inflicted by her carelessness, and in his main text only concedes in one sentence (p 66): 'In her last days she was tortured by the memory of scandalous insinuations noised against her by a courtier'. The note (p 393) explains in sympathetic detail, without identifying the sources, but following the account given in Francisque Michel, Les Ecossais en France (London, 1862, I, 181-90, based on Duclos, Histoire de Louis XI (1746), IV, 54-8. The experience with Jamet de Tillay is central to any understanding of Margaret, and is of interest for the 'intertextuality' of Pontus und Sidonia.

3   See n.1 above; n.2 Priscilla Bawcutt, 'A medieval Scottish Elegy and its French Original', in Scottish Literary Journal, 15, 1 (May 1988), pp 5-13.

4   Louis A Barbé, Sidelights on the History, Industries and Social Life of Scotland (London, 1919), especially pp 1-45, 'A Stuart Duchess of Brittany', but also for example, 'A Scottish Claim to a French Province', pp 69-75. (The following recondite gem was unearthed for me by David Ditchburn):

   'Iste vero relinquens post se filium suum Jacobum secundum, aetatis sex annorum, et sex filias, viz Margaretam

Dalphinellam Franciae, Isabellam ducissam Britaniae, Mariam comitissam Buchaniae in Selandia maritatam, ac Helienoram ducissam Austriae. Haeae vero quattuor filiae ultra mare nuptae sunt. Aliae vero duae in Scocia, viz Johanna comitissa de Mortoune et Maria comitissa de Huntly: quibus honor et gloria in saeculorum saecula'. Liber Pluscardensis, Liber undecimus, c.ix. ed F J H Skene (Edinburgh, 1877), Vol I, p 390. [Skene assumes the anonymous author to be Maurice Buchanan (Vol II, p xxv)].

5   The most convenient edition of Eleonora's Pontus und Sidonia is in Heinz Kindermann, Volksbücher vom sterbenden Rittertum (Weimar, 1928), pp 115-236. I am indebted to Dr Max Siller (Innsbruck) for pointing out that Dr Köfler's thesis on Eleonora is incorporated in Margarete Köfler und Silvia Caramelle, Die beiden Frauen des Erzherzogs Sigmund von Österreich-Tirol (Innsbruck, 1982), pp 15-114. Dr Köfler's work, pillaged for this paper, incorporates much interesting documentation of value to Scots historians, and collects illustrations well worth reproducing, including the homely portrait of Eleonora. Dr L J Macfarlane generously placed at my disposal his research results from Innsbruck Landesregierungsarchiv für Tirol (TLA), in particular his transcript of the letter in Scots from Lord James Hamilton to Eleonora, quoted above. See Leslie J Macfarlane, William Elphinstone and the Kingdom of Scotland 1431-1514: The Struggle for Order (Aberdeen, 1985), e.g. p 452.

   I am indebted to Professor Werner Arens (Regensburg) for his generous gift of a copy of Die anglonormannische und die englischen Fassungen des Hornstoffes: Ein historisch-genetischer Vergleich (Frankfurt, 1973), which magisterially covers the Middle English prose-romance, in which 'the strongly materialised notion of 'largesse' and other social virtues allows Ponthus to emerge as an active fidei defensor and a holy servant of God, adding new dimensions to the courtly world view of the Middle Ages' (pp 300, 301) (cf. p 216). Arens also characterises the work as 'a guide-book for young courtiers' (p 301).

6   Intertextualités médiévales (Texts of Colloquium, Columbia/ Princeton, 8 December, 1979), Littérature No. 41 (February, 1981) (Paris : Larousse, 1981). The literary context is admirably depicted by Eckhard Bernstein, German Humanism (Boston, 1983), and even more admirably in his Die Literatur des deutschen Fruhhumanismus (Stuttgart, 1978). Cf. A C Spearing, Readings in Medieval Poetry (Cambridge, 1987), p 250, n. 11: 'For the concept of intertextuality cf. Julia Kristeva Semiotike (Paris, 1969), p 146, cited by Jonathan Culler, Structuralist Poetics (London, 1978), p 139: 'every text takes shape as a mosaic of citations, every text is the absorption and transformation of other texts'. 'I use the term [intertextuality] here, however, in a simpler sense than is common among recent theorists; for them the 'citations' are of other cultural discourses rather than of specific sources and analogues. In this respect as in others, the concepts of

recent theory seem to have an application of a simpler and more obvious kind to medieval than to modern writing'.

7   John Orr, French the Third Classic, Inaugural Lecture, Edinburgh, 1933. H S Bennett, Chaucer and the Fifteenth Century (Oxford, 1947) suggests that 'macaronic prose written naturally and without self-consciousness, would be difficult to find before 1375 or after 1425' (pp 177-8). The period appears to be a transitional one in this respect as well. M Dominica Legge, Anglo-Norman Literature and Its Background (Oxford). It is now generally agreed that French never completely ousted English as the native tongue of England, and by the end of the fourteenth century English was again officially recognised as the primary language.

8   Francisque Michel, editor, Horn et Rimenhild (Bannatyne Club) (Paris, 1845); J R Lumby (ed) 1866 (EETS) revd G H McKnight 1901. J Burke Severs, A Manual of the Writings in Middle English 1050-1500 (New Haven, Connecticut, 1967) especially pp 17-23 of Charles W Dunn, pp 17-37, 'Romances derived from English Legends', also pp 206-11.

In King Horn various elements are found: Godmod; his disguise as a beggar; Rymenild's dream that a fish breaks her net; Horn's recall by a warning dream. There is an early discussion of the diffusion of French in England and the decline of Anglo-Norman, of course, in Johan Vising, Anglo-Norman Language and Literature (London, 1923); W H Schofield English Literature from the Norman Conquest to Chaucer (London, 1906) (summary of Horn and Rimenhild story pp 261-2, discussion of Ponthus et Sidoine, pp 265-6; W L Renwick, H Orton, The Beginnings of English Literature to Skelton 1509 3rd edn revd by M F Wakelyn (London, 1966), pp 385-7; G K Anderson, Old and Middle English Literature from the Beginning to 1485 (1950) (New York, 1962), pp 106-7; A C Baugh (ed) A Literary History of England (London, 1948), pp 141, 175-6. There is now an extensive bibliography of articles on Horn (including J Kieran Kealy, 'The Americanisation of Horn', Southern Folklore Quarterly 37 (1973), pp 355-84, as David Buchan pointed out to me, in connection with 'Child 17'). The Auchinleck version of 'Horne Childe' is MS Nat Lib of Scotland 19.2.1. See W Arens, op.cit. (n. 5 above).

9   John E Mason, Gentlefolk in the Making: Studies in the History of English Courtesy Literature (Univ Pennsylvania Press, 1935; repr New York Octagon Books, 1971) esp Ch I, pp 4-22.

10 J B Severs, A Manual of the Writings in Middle English 1050-1500 (Newhaven, Connecticut, 1967), p 22: 'probably Geoffrey IV de La Tour Landry' (not, as used to be assumed, Ponthus de La Tour Landry).

11 J B Severs, Manual, pp 17-22, and 207-11.

12 Ibid, pp 18-20.

13 Ibid, pp 20-21.

14 Ibid, pp 21-22. English and Scottish Popular Ballads, Helen Child Sargent and George Lyman Kittredge (eds) (Boston, New York, 1904), p 31: Child 17: Hind Horn: 'Certain points in the story of Horn - the long absence, the sudden return, the appearance under disguise at the wedding feast, and the

dropping of the ring into a cup of wine obtained from the
bride – repeat themselves in a great number of romantic tales.
(Examples of such stories are: the sixteenth-century chapbook
of Henry the Lion, Reinfrid von Braunschweig, Der edle
Moringer, Torello in Boccaccio's Decameron (x.9)). More
commonly it is the husband who leaves his wife for seven
years, is miraculously informed on the last day that she is to
be remarried on the morrow, and is restored to his home in the
nick of time, also by superhuman means.'

15 The French version is not readily available, but see n.16.
16 For the most convenient English version see: Frank Jewett
Mather, King Ponthus and the Fair Sidone: A Prose Romance
translated from the French about the year 1450 now first
edited from the unique MS Digby 185 of the Bodleian Library
(PMLA, XII) (Baltimore, 1897), Introduction, iv-lxvii: Text,
1-150. Another fifteenth-century German translation has been
edited by K Schneider, Pontus und Sidonia in der Verdeut-
schung eines Ungenannten aus dem 15. Jahrhundert (Munich,
1961); naturally it was eclipsed by Eleonora's version. Cf W
Arens op.cit. (n.5 above), passim.
17 Cf. n. 5 Kindermann. See also F J Mather (n.16), pp xli-xliv.
18 J B Severs, Manual, p 22.
19 Peter Rickard, Britain in Medieval French Literature 1100-
1500 (Cambridge, 1956), Ch V, The Role of England in Romances
of Adventure, pp 121-41. W Arens, op.cit. (n.5 above), 299;
also 57-65; 89-96.
20 E W M Balfour-Melville, James I, King of Scots (1406-1437)
(London, 1936): E B Fryde, D E Greenway, S Porter, I Roy,
Handbook of British Chronology 3rd edn, Royal Historical
Society (London, 1986).
21 This formulation is to reflect the caution (counselled by F
Michel and Dr G G Simpson) concerning Annabella's supposed
first marriage.
22 A M Stewart, 'Do They Mean Us?: The Nuremberg Chronicle (1493)
and Scotland' in Essays for Professor R E H Mellor, W Ritchie,
J C Stone, A S Mather (eds) (Aberdeen, 1986), pp 266-73; P
Hume Brown, Early Travellers in Scotland (1891), repr Edin-
burgh, 1978, pp 24-9; E W M Balfour-Melville, James I King of
Scots (1406-1437) (London, 1936), pp 235-7; Berthe Widmer,
Enea Silvio Piccolomini: Papst Pius II: Ausgewahlte Texte aus
seinen Schriften (Basle, 1960); C M Ady, Pius II Aeneas
Silvius Piccolomini, the Humanist Pope (London, 1913); R J
Mitchell, The Laurels and the Tiara: Pope Pius II, 1458-1464
(London, 1962); A Berg, Enea Silvio de Piccolomini als Geo-
graph (Halle, 1901); E Bernstein, German Humanism (Boston,
1983); E Bernstein, Die Literatur des deutschen Fruhhumanismus (Stuttgart, 1978), 9-13: ('Enea Silvio Piccolomini als
Vermittler').
23 Köfler, p 18 (see n. 5 above); Beaucourt, pp 4, 181 (see n. 2
above).
24 Köfler, 19: BN Ms Fr 10, 370.
25 Köfler, 19: Beaucourt, 4, 203; BN Ms Fr 10, 370, fol. 50, 51.
26 Illustration in Köfler (facing title page): Erzherzog Sigmund,
Eleonore von Schottland, Katharina von Sachsen, Prinzessin

Radegundis von Frankreich: in so-called Habsburg room, Schloss Tratzberg (Lower Inn Valley, 16th century).

27   Köfler, 27 (footnote 64): HHSA Fam Urk 608.

28   Köfler, 30.

29   Köfler, 32: Great Seal of Eleonora 1485: in Haus-Hof- and Staatsarchiv, Vienna.

Any reconstruction of a person's life from official records is bound to appear chronologically rather uneven and apparently abruptly changing, as historic events give way to unreported routine. Köfler overcomes this problem well, but the staccato-change of scene reappears in a summary account such as we are attempting. The fact that Eleonora was given her own seals is a clear indication of her political powers. Documents were subscribed 'Elionor geboren von Schotten, Hertzogin zu Österreich etc' and signed by her 'Elionor', but always with the addition 'Datum in consilio'. Eleonora's Great Seal bears the legend in Gothic script - +S(IGILLUM) ELIONORIS EX STIRPE REGIE SCOTORUM NATE DEI GRATIA DUCISSE AUSTRIE. The shield shows on the right the Austrian 'Bindenschild' and on the left the Scottish lion. The twin coats of arms are flanked by column-like architectural features. Eleonora's Private Seal has three coats of arms: in the right upper part the Austrian 'Bindenschild', on the left the Scottish lion, in the middle a shield with the Tyrolean eagle.

30   Köfler, 56 and footnote 243, HHSA Fam Urk 691.

31   'Woe to the kingdom' ... topos. Ecclesiastes X, 16-17: 'Vae tibi terra, cujus rex puer est': Cf. A M Stewart (ed), The Complaynt of Scotland, STS (Edinburgh, 1979), pp 23, 24 (fol. 23v-24v): 'Salomon hes said, cursit be the eird that hes ane ȝong prince ...'

32   Köfler, 52-62.

33   Köfler, 65.

34   Köfler, 65: TLA Raitbuch, 4, fol 135v: and Basler Chronik, Vol 4, p 430, quoted Köfler, 65 (footnote 324).

35   Turkish threat: Köfler, 76, 77, and footnote 396 ref to article by Huter Franz.

36   Köfler, 87-89.

37   Köfler, 89-92 (Eleanora's personal correspondence): (TLA Autogramme A/5, A/6, Sigm. IVa/181 and HHSA Family Correspondence A/38).

38   Köfler, 90, footnote 474 quotes TLA Autogramme A/6: Letter from Eleanora to Sigmund:

Mein herzen liewer her, ich pefilch mich mit aler diemitigkait eur liew und freuntschaft und due euch ze bissen, das ich ain winczig plot pin an der huest, sonst gefelt mir das pat gar wol und man hat uns ueberall, wor wir wein gebessen, gar wol empfangen und erpotten was wir sein gebessen pisher und haben kain ander abgang, dan das ir uns zu fer seit. Ich wolt gern, mocht es mit fueg gesein, das ir kemt und uns das pat gesegen, ben mich pedinkt fil leit sachesn es gern und pegirlich waren, euch zu sechen hie. Mein her nit mer wais ich euch jecz zu schreiben dan last mich euch pefolchen sein, damit pebar euch got.

This letter is useful evidence that Eleonora did not herself write the manuscript of Pontus und Sidonia although she may have dictated it or checked the version. On Sigmund's illegitimate children, cf Köfler, 10, 11 (footnote 3).

39   Barbe - see footnote 4.

40   Bernhard Burchert, Die Anfänge des Prosaromans in Deutschland (Frankfurt, 1987). Elisabeth von Nassau-Saarbrücken (1397–1456), daughter of a duke of Lorraine, married the Count of Nassau-Saarbrücken, who died in 1429. Thereafter she translated four French chansons de geste into German prose, completing the last in 1437. These narratives are the earliest German prose romances since Lanzelet (c.1225): 1. Loher und Maller, written in French by Elisabeth's mother, Margaret of Lorraine, is the story of an illegitimate son of Charlemagne; 2. Huge Scheppel (Hugo Capet) tells of the butcher's son who becomes the king of France; 3. Herpin has as its hero Herpin's son Löw; 4. Sibille is the story of an unjustly slandered queen. 1, 2, 3 were later chapbooks; 2 was printed as Hug Schapler in 1500; 1 was printed in 1513; 3 was printed in 1514.

41   Giovanni Boccaccio Concerning Famous Women, translated, with an Introduction and Notes, by Guido A Guarino (London, 1964): Dedication to the most gracious Lady Andrea Acciaiuoli of Altavilla, pp xxxiii–xxxix. Guarino makes a useful comparison, pp ix–xxxi, between De Claris Mulieribus and Decameron in his introduction. Cf. Bernstein, German Humanism (Boston, 1983); E Bernstein, Die Literatur (footnote 22 above). On the topic of outdoing, E R Curtius, European Literature and the Latin Middle Ages (New York, 1953): 'Neuf preux', Nine Worthies, 372; 'outdoing', 162; nobility, 179.

42   Oswald von Wolkenstein. Köfler, 64; Anton Schwob, Oswald von Wolkenstein, (Bozen, 1977); Dieter Kuhn, Ich Wolkenstein (Frankfurt, 1977); on Eleonora's literary activity, Köfler 93–8. I am indebted to Mrs Priscilla Bawcutt for drawing my attention to Alastair Cherry, Princes Poets and Patrons: The Stuarts and Scotland (Edinburgh, 1987), pp 17, 18, referring firstly to Eleonora's presentation of an early Italian incunable, an edition of St Jerome's Epistolae printed in Rome about 1467, to the Neustift religious foundation; and secondly, to the Vergil manuscript in Edinburgh University Library written in Paris by an Italian scribe in the middle of the fifteenth century, with the initials 'P' and 'L' beside the Scottish royal arms in this volume thought to stand for 'Principissa Leonora'.

43   See n. 22 above.

44   Bernstein.

45   Köfler, 93–8.

46   Köfler, 94 (Gotha Manuscript prepared by 'Nicolaum Huber presbyter Brixin. dyocesis Anno dni. 1465').

47   Karin Schneider, Pontus und Sidonia (n. 16 above), p 8 (=MS Heidelberg UB cod. palm. germ. 142).

48   Danielle Buschinger, Le Tristrant d'Eilhart von Oberg 2 vols (Lille, Paris, 1975), vol II, p 1043.

49   Kindermann, see n.5.

50   Mather, see n.16. Cf. Arens, (footnote 5).

51   Buschinger, see n.48.
52   See Arens (n.5), passim. Eugene Dorfman, The Narreme in the
      Medieval Romance Epic (Manchester, 1969); John Stevens,
      Medieval Romance: Themes and Approaches (London, 1973);
      Johanna Maria van Winter, Rittertum: Ideal und Wirklichkeit
      (Munich, 1969); Richard Barber, The Knight and Chivalry
      (London, 1970, repr 1974); Rudiger Schnell, Zum Verhältnis von
      hoch- und spätmittelalterlicher Literatur: Versuch einer
      Kritik (Berlin, 1978); Josef Fleckenstein (editor), Das
      ritterliche Turnier im Mittelalter (Göttingen, 1985). This
      volume includes (Illustration 17) a photograph of Sigmund's
      armour of 1484 for his next marriage celebrations: see article
      by Ortwin Gamber, 'Ritterspiel und turnierrüstung im Spät-
      mittelalter', ibid, pp 513-31. (Gamber also, p 527, tells us
      that Scottish 'targe' is from Arabic 'daraqa' via Spanish
      'adarga'. (Sigmund's armour is described in Thomas-Gamber, Die
      Innsbrucker Plattnerkunst, Ausstellungskatalog (Innsbruck,
      1954), p 53 ff). Another article, by Philippe Contamine,
      points out that the years 1445 to 1447 were high points in the
      French court indulgence in tournaments (ibid, p 445): once
      again we are referred to G Du Fresne de Beaucourt (index to
      vol VI 'joutes'); Eleonora could have attended the tourna-
      ments at Nancy, Chalons-sur-Marne, Razilly, Tours, Saumur,
      Bourges, enough to become an expert. (Cf. n. 25 above).
53   Gilbert Highet, 'The Renaissance: Translation' chapter six in
      The Classical Tradition (Oxford, 1949): Werner Koller, Ein-
      führung in die Übersetzungswissenschaft, 2nd edn (Heidelberg,
      1983), 192-216, 'Übersetzungsbewertung': E Bernstein, Früh-
      humanismus (n. 22 above), pp 41-98, especially on Wyle, pp
      43-62, and on Steinhöwel, pp 75-90, including reference to
      Boccaccio's De claris mulieribus translated by Steinhöwel as
      'Von den synnrychen erluchten wyben' by 1473, dedicated to
      Eleonora and printed by Johannes Zainer, Ulm (p 82). On the
      problem of translation into the vernacular in Scotland, even a
      century later, see John Durkan, 'The Cultural Background in
      Sixteenth Century Scotland', Innes Review, X, 382-439, and
      'Early Humanism and King's College (Aberdeen)', Aberdeen
      University Review, No 163 (Spring, 1980), 259-79; John
      MacQueen, 'Some Aspects of the Early Renaissance in Scotland',
      Forum for Modern Language Studies, vol III, No. 3, (July,
      1967), 201-22; A M Stewart, Complaynt (n. 1 above), pp xxiv,
      xxx-xxxii.
54   Mather, see n.16.
55   Illustration in Köfler (Ill. No. 4, Nationalbibliothek,
      Vienna).
56   Mather (n.16 above), page xi, explains 'Le Surdit de Droite
      Voie: the accused one who sought in vain the straight path of
      vindication by combat'. The Royal MS states, 'Le seurnom, pour
      ce quil lui auoit refuse droicte voye, pour ce qui se voulloit
      combatre contre deux ou trois'.
57   Santiago, Köfler, 100: Eleonora gave a Heinrich Claviger a
      golden statue of St James and relics to take with him to
      Santiago de Compostella. He did not return with the customary
      return present, so Santiago sent another pilgrim with a second

set of gifts the following year: a mussel and a gilt staff. Eleonora expressed her thanks by giving the pilgrim, a priest from Munich, a gift of '14 lb Perner' (Raitbuch 4, fol. 146v). St James was meaningful for the Scottish kings: see the well-known picture of James IV reproduced in L J Macfarlane, William Elphinstone and the Kingdom of Scotland, facing p 420, with his patrons St James and St Andrew (Vienna, National-bibliothek, Codex. Lat 1897, fo 24v). The Book of Hours of James IV and Margaret Tudor picture is also reproduced in A Cherry, Princes Poets and Patrons between pages 28, 29. Cf. L J Macfarlane, 'The Books of hours of James IV and Margaret Tudor', Innes Review, XI, 3-21. Klaus Herbers, Der Jakobsweg (Tübingen, 1986).

58   On Hartmann's central concept of 'maze', moderation in its context, see The World of Medieval Learning by Anders Piltz (Oxford, 1981), 179-182: the 'middle way', avoiding extremes; the 'golden mean', aurea mediocritas, virtues, temperantia, harmony, balance, mesura indicate some of the terms in the discussion. Cf. Aristotle, Nichomachean Ethics, M Oswald (ed) (Indianapolis, 1962) on the 'doctrine of the mean'. The Ethics of Aristotle, revd edn (Harmondsworth, 1976) includes a 'table of virtues and vices' (p 104) and very useful notes on the topic.

Hartmann's Erec and Iwein have been viewed, as stated, oversimply of course, as tales emphasising the didactic desirability of the restoration of harmony and balance between the habit of 'uxoriousness' and its opposite extreme vice of male chauvinist military chivalric uncourtliness. Eileen Power, Medieval Women (Cambridge, 1975), provides a context against which to see Eleonora in comparison and contrast with Elisabeth von Nassau-Saarbrucken (n. 40 above) or Christine de Pisan for example.

59   See Hannes Kästner, 'Pontus und Sidonia' in Innsbruck. Appell und Apologie im Hofroman des 15. Jahrhunderts', in Jahrbuch der Oswald von Wolkenstein Gesellschaft, Bd. 2 (1982-3), 99-128.

Xenia von Ertzdorff, 'Ritterliche Idealität im 15. Jahr-hundert', 245-52 in Festschrift Hugo Moser (Berlin, 1974). I am indebted to Dr J L Flood (Germanic Institute, London) for indicating these two articles.

60   The portrait of Eleonora, probably painted by Anton Waiss or Boys between 1578 and 1595, may have been based on a near-contemporary Habsburg genealogical-tree portrait. For per-mission to reproduce this item from the more than one thousand items of the Amraser or Ambraser collection I am indebted to HR Dr G Kugler of the Kunsthistorisches Museum, Vienna. Cf. S Caramelle, Köfler, p 218f. I am also indebted to Professor Dr C Rauchbauer, Vienna. Last but not least, I am indebted to colleagues in Eichstatt and Regensburg for their assistance.

Chapter 12

ROBERT HENRYSON AND THE ARS DICTAMINIS

Robert L Kindrick

The rhetoric of Robert Henryson combines the most interesting and traditional elements of medieval and Renaissance approaches to the subject. His use of the ars grammatica, for instance, demonstrates his transitional nature. While he anticipates many of the elements of Renaissance poetics, he clearly incorporates the best elements of medieval learning. I have elsewhere discussed his use of the ars praedicandi.[1] There is no doubt that he clearly owes a debt to medieval preaching, including its emphasis on multiple levels of interpretation. Yet, perhaps some of his most interesting rhetorical techniques are to be found in his use of the ars dictaminis. Given the extent to which Henryson is truly a political satirist, the role of the ars dictaminis in his work is clearly vital.

The phrase ars dictaminis is often translated as 'the art of letter writing'. Such translation is misleading. Indeed, the ars dictaminis was concerned with proper rhetorical approaches for correspondence.[2] Yet such correspondence was very often political in nature, having apparently developed from the traditional nuntius as a means of communication among spiritual or temporal leaders. The earliest uses of the ars dictaminis were confined to major political occasions by important dignitaries, either of church or state. While the 'so-called' art of letter writing broadened as literacy expanded, its political importance can hardly be underestimated. As Cassiodorus Senator points out in his discussion of the relationship between the Quaestor and the king:

> ... the Quaestor has to learn our inmost thoughts, that he may utter them to our subjects ... he has to be always ready for a sudden call, and must exercise the wonderful powers which, as Cicero has pointed out, are inherent in the art of an orator ... He has to speak the king's words in the king's own presence ... with suitable embellishments.[3]

This assessment is reinforced by other early rhetorics that deal with the ars dictaminis. Perhaps foremost among them is the rhetoric of C Julius Victor, a fourth-century Roman rhetorician. In stating that epistles should not be structured like orations, Victor is clearly referring to a type of 'conversational or semi-conversational discourse'.[4] His emphasis on the lack of audience response and the impossibility of dialogue also reinforces the notion that he is dealing with a new type of rhetorical subject.

The idea that the ars dictaminis deals with written, as opposed to spoken, language is reinforced by Alberic of Monte Cassino and Guido Faba.[5] Yet the emphases on written discourse and lack of audience response are not the only key elements that distinguish the ars dictaminis. As noted above Cassidorus Senator clearly outlines the importance of political discourse as a part of the rhetorical arts, especially the ars dictaminis. During the period of Cassiodorus Senator's writing, monarchs had become increasingly illiterate. Such was the trend during the rest of the early Middle Ages. But, in his letters, Cassiodorus clearly outlined the need for literate scribes and messengers on the part of the state. From his point of view it was essential that a king rely on literate élites to compose, transcribe, and transmit whatever messages might relate to the affairs of state. Certainly this break from ancient social and political traditions resulted in a very different emphasis in the study of rhetoric.

Finally, the ars dictaminis developed its own highly systematised structure with borrowings from the ars poetica. Both Alberic of Monte Cassino and Hugh of Bologna sought to bring more systematic organisation to the art of letter writing and political discourse in general. While Hugh took particular note of the fact that political speech was developed 'without accountability to metrical law',[6] it is clear that he shared Alberic's point of view with regard to the need for refinement of dictaminal discourse and the movement to include metrical discourse in its purview. While not all aspects of the ars poetica were applied to this type of writing, clearly the later Middle Ages witnessed a movement toward refinement of rhetorical principles and a more structured description of skills in this area. In addition to these elements, there was an emphasis on including forms and formats for models of official correspondence. The latter aspect of the ars dictaminis could be of only limited use to a person of literary interests in the late fifteenth century.

There are, then, three salient elements associated with the ars dictaminis: its emphasis on written discourse, its political nature, and its refined rhetorical skills; at least by the time Henryson would have studied the subject. Certainly these elements became blended with the ars praedicandi. As such works as the Summa praedicantium will clearly illustrate, the art of preaching had become blended with the political aspects of the ars dictaminis. Indeed, the political interests of the rhetorical art of preaching and the strategies used to deal with those interests occupy a major place in fourteenth- and fifteenth-century rhetorical study. Nonetheless, there are certain ways to separate and evaluate Henryson's debt to the ars dictaminis which clearly illustrate the political nature of his poetry.

Although the elements are hard to separate from other rhetorical traditions, Henryson's rhetoric is markedly literary as well as oral. His use of oral elements, nonetheless, has long been acknowledged. Phrases such as the following from 'The Scheip and the Doig' illustrate Henryson's debt to the oral tradition:

> O Lord, quhy sleipis thow sa lang?
> Walk, and discerne my cause groundit on richt;
> Se how I am be fraud, maistrie, and slicht

> Peillit full bair, and so is mony one
> Now in this warld richt wonder wo begone.[7]

There can be no doubt that Henryson depended upon his own speech rhythms and the Scots tradition of oral transmission. Yet it appears that his poetry was generally intended for a literate reading audience, perhaps suggesting courtly connections.

Henryson's use of such literary traditions was not new. First, Henryson followed the basic admonition to dictators – to be brief. Any comparison of his work with that of his predecessors will reveal how important brevity is in his artistic accomplishment. Yet, Henryson also informed himself about traditional literary genres and formulae. Chaucer, Gower, the Pearl-Poet and even earlier artists had such written transmission as a goal long after the end of literate Rome. Thus, Henryson's emphasis on the literary and literate tradition follows a long line of precursors. Perhaps one of the most important literary influences on Henryson was what J A Burrow has described as 'Ricardian Tradition'. Burrow lists a number of characteristics which define the Ricardian writers. He lists Langland, Gower, and the Pearl-Poet in that particular tradition. Their attention to style and rhetorical formulae demonstrates a commitment to both the literary nature of their writing and the highly structured system of ars poetica. One of the most salient characteristics of these writers, however, is their emphasis on the use of literate diction. While it may well be argued that the diction of Dunbar reflects auricular appeal as much as visual appeal, it is nonetheless true that he is often contrasted with Henryson as being a more 'literate' poet. The same kind of emphasis on the aureate, however, appears in Henryson's works. Steven Hawes points out that aureate diction is the use of 'Termes eloquent ... Electynge wordes whiche are expedyent In Latyn or in Englysshe after the intent'.[9] While aureate diction also developed through a separate line in the Scottish tradition, it is clear that this aspect of the Ricardian approach to poetry had a decided influence on Henryson. Perhaps most often cited with regard to his debt to this particular use of literary language is 'Ane Prayer for the Pest':

> Superne lucerne, guberne this pestilens,
> Preserue and serue that we nocht sterf thairin,
> Declyne that pyne by thy devyne prudens,
> For trewth, haif rewth, lat nocht our slewth ws twyn;
> Our syte, full tyte, wer we contryt, wald blin;
> Dissiuir did nevir, quha euir the besocht
> But grace, with space, for to arrace fra sin;
> Lat nocht be tint that thow sa deir hes bocht!
>
> (ll.65-72)

The attention to rhyme, assonance, alliteration, and the use of Latin derivatives demonstrates that Henryson, when he chose to, could compete with the best of the aureate poets. It might be suggested that 'Ane Prayer for the Pest' is too easy a case. Yet even Orpheus and Eurydice contains language of the same sort:

> The nobilnes and grete magnificence
> Off prince or lord, quha list to magnify,
> His grete ancester and linyall descense
> Suld first extoll, and his genology,
> So that his hert he mycht enclyne thare by
> The more to vertu and to worthynes,
> Herand reherse his eldirs gentilnes.
>
> (11.1-5)

Other examples could be adduced from The Testament of Cresseid and the Moral Fables. Henryson's use of these aureate techniques, involving the most literary and complicated diction of the rhetoric of his day, definitely places him in the Ricardian rhetorical tradition and also shows his debt to the ars dictaminis.

Yet another debt appears in his literary use of organisational structure, particularly the exordium in The Morall Fabillis. In discussing the importance of the introduction, Alberic explains that it should follow the basic Ciceronian objective of making the audience receptive and well-disposed, employing a proper mixture of delight and instruction.[10] Henryson conscientiously strives to fulfill these goals, as illustrated by the prologue to the Fables:

> The nuttis schell, thocht it be hard and teuch,
> Haldis the kirnell, sueit and delectabill;
> Sa lyis thair ane doctrine wyse aneuch
> And full of frute, vnder ane fenȝeit fabill;
> And clerkis sayis, it is richt profitabill
> Amangis ernist to ming ane merie sport,
> To blyth the spreit and gar the tyme be schort.
> For as we se, ane bow that ay is bent
> Worthis vnsmart and dullis on the string;
> Sa dois the mynd that is ay diligent
> In ernistfull thochtis and in studying.
> With sad materis sum merines to ming
> Accordis weill, thus Esope said, I wis,
> Dulcius arrident seria picta iocis.
>
> (11.15-28)

Henryson returns to the same theme in the prologue of 'The Lion and the Mouse', which has created speculation about both his sequence of composition of the fables and his own extended concern about the relationship between instruction and delight. Henryson could certainly have learned this principle, along with others regarding organisation, from a variety of sources. Yet, given his political interests in the fables, it is precisely in keeping with the formulae of the ars dictaminis.

I shall not belabour Henryson's use of irony, for that particular trope is found in virtually all forms of rhetoric. It is true that Henryson's particular gift for tragic irony, as in The Testament of Cresseid, would appear to be more in keeping with the literary modes of communication. Nonetheless, while Henryson is clearly Ricardian in this respect, I feel that it is impossible to show that his debt here is specifically owed to the ars dictaminis.[11] However, I believe that his techniques of literary

realism, another Ricardian element, show a distinct debt to the art
of letter writing. It has been argued that Henryson owes this debt
not directly to the _ars dictaminis_ or to the Ricardian tradition
but instead to the more specifically Chaucerian tradition.[12] The
lifelike character portraits of Henryson's animals are often
compared with those of Chaucer in The Canterbury Tales. Yet whatever the immediate source for Henryson, the main point is that
realistic description was a vital part of the _ars dictaminis_ and
that Henryson mastered this technique.[13] Because of the lack of
opportunity for audience response, realistic portrayal of character
and depiction of events were considered to be essential in the _ars
dictaminis_. Among the 'suitable embellishments' discussed by
Cassiodorus Senator was the virtue of realistic narration and
description to enhance the role of the _dictator_ as a 'verbal
minister' to handle political problems.[14]

Henryson's use of this technique has been widely recognised.[15]
Given the level of psychological understanding in his day, his use
of psychological realism is certainly emphasised in The Testament
of Cresseid during the final meeting between Troilus and Cresseid.
Stearns has shown that the subconscious recognition of Cresseid by
Troilus seems to be based upon principles in Aristotle's De anima
and De memoria.[16] The major Aristotelian principle used in this
scene is that of reproductive imagination:

> Than vpon him scho kest vp baith hir ene,
> And with ane blenk it come into his thocht
> That he sumtime hir face befoir had sene,
> Bot scho was in sic plye he knew hir nocht;
> ʒit than hir luik into his mynd it brocht
> The sweit visage and amorous blenking
> Of fair Cresseid, sumtyme his awin darling.
>
> Na wonder was, suppois in mynd that he
> Tuik hir figure sa sone, and lo, now quhy:
> The idole of ane thing in cace may be
> Sa deip imprentit in the fantasy
> That it deludis the wittis outwardly,
> And sa appeiris in forme and lyke estait
> Within the mynd as it was figurait.
>   (11.498–511)

For Henryson's day, his use of psychology was remarkably realistic.
Reliance on Aristotle is to be found in Orpheus and Eurydice[17] and
The Moral Fables. The latter work also shows his realism in the
depiction of social classes and grievances. Henryson's animal world
includes all categories of society, from the most noble to the most
poverty-stricken. He depicts nobility, with all of its magnificence
and grandeur, in the 'Tale of the Lion and the Mouse':

> 'A, mercie, lord, at thy gentrice I ase,
> As thow art king off beistis coronate,
> Sober thy wraith, and let thi yre ouerpas,
> And mak thy mynd to mercy inclynate.
> I grant offence is done to thyne estate,

Quhairfoir I worthie am to suffer deid,
Bot gif thy kinglie mercie reik remeid.'
(11.1461-7)

Yet he was not blind to the obverse side of the noble classes. In
'The Tale of the Wolf and the Lamb' and 'The Trial of the Fox'
Henryson is able to depict the stupidity and malice which sometimes inform the action of the upper classes. In the former tale,
for instance, he portrays the wolf (the representative of the
upper classes) as 'mychty men' and 'men of heretege' who are,
through their actions, 'fals pervertaris of the lawis' (1.100).
While Henryson has idealistic attitudes towards the role of king
and the possibilities of his providing for a just society, he also
understands that nobility itself is no guarantee of just and fair
action. In other class representations, he apparently portrays the
urban upper-middle class in the burgess mouse in 'The Two Mice'.
He is able to portray lower-level clergy in the depiction of the
sheep in 'The Sheep and the Dog', and even extends his portrayals
to rustics in 'The Fox, the Wolf, and the Husbandman'. Furthermore, he is able to emphasise not only human ills but human
ideals, as in his depiction of the swallow in 'The Preaching of
the Swallow'.[18]

Perhaps, however, his masterpiece of realistic description
occurs in The Testament of Cresseid. In describing Cresseid's
disease, a result of self-indulgence and venereal excess, Henryson
shows his observance of one real illness of the day. He describes
the curse on Cresseid in the following terms:

'Thy cristall ene mingit with blude I mak,
Thy voice sa cleir vnplesand hoir and hace,
Thy lustie lyre ouirspred with spottis blak,
And lumpis haw appeirand in thy face:
(11.337-40)

This description contains such detail that, in 1841, J A Y Simpson
was able to diagnose Cresseid's disease as elephantiasis leprosy.[19]
While syphilis might appear to be a more common venereal disease
to moderns, leprosy in the late Middle Ages was associated with
sexual excess. Given that perception in the Middle Ages and Henryson's detailed description, the disease which Cresseid must endure
seems particularly appropriate.

I should also touch on the trope of allegory. It is quite
possible that Henryson could have become acquainted with allegory
through his own educational background or even more specifically
through works such as Bede's De schematibus et tropis.[20] Very
early, C Julius Victor had noted the value of using figurative
language in official letters.[21] The basic emphasis on the importance of allegory is found in Alberic of Monte Cassino.[22] It becomes even more evident in the Rationes dictandi when it is noted
that securing the good will of a listener or reader requires 'a
certain fit ordering of words effectively influencing the mind of
the recipient'.[23] Whether Henryson's use of allegory is directly
related to this tradition or to the allegorical tradition of the
ars praedicandi can never be completely determined.

In all of these respects, Henryson's writing evidences two of
the three points associated with the ars dictaminis. He is, first,
clearly concerned about written discourse, having mastered written
forms that relate specifically to the ars dictaminis. Yet he has
also shown evidence of the third characteristic mentioned with
regard to this form of rhetoric – the highly stylised merger with
the ars poetica. In his use of the tropes listed above, Henryson
was following, whether fully aware of his actions or not, some of
the central principles of the ars dictaminis. Even, possibly, in
his use of irony and allegory, he was very much in harmony with
the Bologna school of thought.[24] In all of these regards it is
clear that, whatever the route, the ars dictaminis had a strong
hold on his writing. The strength of that connection is reinforced
by Henryson's political interests. Since 1949, when Marshall
Stearns outlined Henryson's sympathy for the 'pure peple',[25] it
has been debated whether Henryson was dealing with specific
political situations or working in the more general tradition of
advice to princes. Virtually no matter which way the issues are
considered, it is clear that Henryson did have political interests.

The argument that Henryson is working from the tradition of
advice to princes has been best summarised by Roderick Lyall.[26]
This tradition, he contends, exercised a powerful influence over
fifteenth-century Scottish poetry. Its emphasis is on accumulated
wisdom, political philosophy, and general principles of political
guidance. Examples which may appear to be specific are more likely
to have been drawn from the conventions and 'conventional wisdom'
of the literary tradition than from close observation of contemporaneous political events. Thus, while 'The Lion and the Mouse'
might appear to some to have reference to James III, Preston,
Cochrane and other individuals involved in the Lauder rebellion,
Lyall contends that it is more likely best read in a more general
literary and political context. He believes that it would be a
mistake to evaluate Henryson's poetry in terms of his reference to
the political events of his day. In many respects Lyall's arguments are the most persuasive of all about Henryson's use of the
ars dictaminis. It seems quite likely that the 'advice to princes'
tradition was very directly associated with the development of
this rhetorical tradition. If additional proof of Henryson's
political interests is needed, however, others have been even more
specific.

Stearns, MacQueen, Nicholson, and Kindrick[27] have all contended
that Henryson had more immediate political examples in mind. One
of the most marked is 'The Tale of the Lion and the Mouse'. In
his portrayal of the lion, Henryson has created a royal portrait
closely paralleling that of James III. As noted above, the lion
is clearly noble. The lion's regal elements show that he is a
creature of great promise, yet he is lazy:

> Ane lyoun, at his pray wery foirrun,
> To recreat his limmis and to rest,
> Beikand his breist and belly at the sun
> Vnder ane tre lay in the fair forest;
> Swa come ane trip off myis out off thair nest,
> Richt tait and trig, all dansand in ane gyis,
> And ouer the lyoun lansit twyis or thryis.

> He lay so still, the myis wes not effeird,
> Bot to and fro out ouer him tuke thair trace;
> Sum tirlit at the campis off his beird,
> Sum spairit not to claw him on the face;
> Merie and glaid, thus dansit thay ane space,
> Till at the last the nobill lyoun woke,
> And with his pow the maister mous he tuke.
>
> (11.1405-15)

He is also hunted by 'rural men', and he is capable of great cruelty:

> Quhen scho wes gone, the lyoun held to hunt,
> For he had nocht, bot leuit on his pray,
> And slew baith tayme and wyld, as he wes wont,
> And in the cuntrie maid ane grit deray;
>
> (11.1510-13)

Were any doubt left about the political implications of this tale, Henryson notes in his <u>Moralitas</u> that the lion may be 'a prince or emprior/A potestat or yet a king with crown' (11.254-5). The parallels between this portrait and that of James III have been well documented. Nicholson argues that the mice who free the lion, once he is seized by the hunters, represent the burgesses of Edinburgh who freed James III after his imprisonment.[28]

There appear to be other political overtones to Henryson's work. The 'Tale of the Two Mice' seems to Stearns to illustrate Henryson's sensitivity to the class struggle going on in fifteenth-century Scottish society. The upland mouse, visiting her city sister, is accustomed to a sense of security, appropriate to the country but not to the city. The meal that the two sisters enjoy is first disturbed by the spenser. More unsettling, perhaps, is the intrusion of the cat, a more disruptive force, possibly representing the king himself:[29]

> The burges vp with that,
> And till hir hole scho fled as fyre of flint;
> Bawdronis the vther be the bak hes hint.
>
> Fra fute to fute he kest hir to and fra,
> Quhylis vp, quhylis doun, als cant as ony kid.
> Quhylis wald he lat hir rin vnder the stra;
> Quhylis wald he wink, and play with hir buk heid;
> Thus to the selie mous grit pane he did;
> Quhill at the last throw fair fortune and hap,
> Betwix ane dosor and the wall scho crap.
>
> (11.327-36)

While the upland mouse's city sister seems undisturbed by these kinds of unusual activities, the upland mouse herself is frightened. She is unaccustomed to such rough treatment. She does indeed believe:

> Thy mangerie is mingit all with cair;
> Thy guse is gude, they gansell sour as gall;

> The subcharge off thy seruice is bot sair;
> Sa sall thow find heir-eftewart may fall.
> I thank ʒone courtyne and ʒone perpall wall
> Off my defence now fra ʒone crewell beist.
> Almichtie God keip me fra sic ane feist.
>   (11.344-50)

Whether the cat represents invasions, royal tariffs, or even com-
pulsory royal loans, it is clear that there were intrusions upon
the lives of all countrymen, especially the burgesses. Fifteenth-
century Scottish history would seem to confirm the political
intent of this tale.

   Perhaps one of the most controversial tales in terms of political implications is 'The Tale of the Wolf and the Wether'. The
basic argument of political critics is that the tale itself
represents James' unwise use of his counsellors. First, it should
be pointed out that criticism of the king's counsellors assumed
almost legendary proportions in later accounts. Buchanan and
Major, among other earlier Scottish historians, indicated that
James's judgement with regard to his counsellors was notoriously
bad.[30] This tale clearly reflects such a situation. The shepherd,
whose obligation is to guard his flock, loses his faithful sheep
dog. He is in depair, when a wether offers the advice that the dog
be skinned and that he substitute for the dog in protecting the
flock against wolves. The shepherd agrees, despite the proverbial
observation that 'Quha sayis ane scheip is daft, thay lieit of it'
(1.2492). Once the hound is skinned, the wether takes up his
watch. His first challenge is from a hungry wolf, who steals a
lamb. In pursuing the wolf, the wether loses all sight of reason.
He says to himself and perhaps to the wolf:

> To mak him mycht, he kest the lamb him fra,
> Syne lap ouer leis and draif throw dub and myre.
> 'Na,'quod the wedder, 'in faith we part not swa:
> It is not the lamb, bot the, that I desyre;
> I sall cum neir, for now I se the tyre'.
>   (11. 2532-6)

Finally, when the hound's skin is torn off in pursuit, the wether's
trick is discovered and the wolf turns upon him. Now that both are
properly attired in the state of nature, the wolf boldly questions
the sheep's effrontery:

> 'Is this ʒour bourding in ernist than?' quod he,
> For I am verray effeirit, and on flocht:
> Cum bak agane, and I sall let ʒow se'.
> Than quhar the gait wes grimmit he him brocht:
> Quhether call ʒe this fair play or nocht:
> To set ʒour maister in sa fell effray,
> Quhill he for feiritnes hes fylit vp the way?
>   (11.2560-6)

The appropriateness of the wolf's stance is echoed by the wether
in his reply:

'Schir,' quod the wedder, 'suppois I ran in hy,
My mynd was neuer to do ȝour persoun ill.
Ane flear gettis ane follower commounly,
In play or ernist, preif quha sa euer will.
Sen I bot playit, be gracious me till,
And I sall gar my freindis blis ȝour banis:
Ane full gude seruand will crab his maister anis'.
(11.2574-80)

His humble tone and the acknowledgement that the wolf is his
'maister' both show that the sheep realises his transgression. The
wolf, however, understandably angered by the act, breaks the
sheep's neck in a form of execution particularly appropriate to
political allegory.

It is possible that there are references in this work to the
Lauder rebellion of 1482.[31] During that rebellion, James was
seized by nobles dissatisfied with his reign. Some of his favourites were summarily executed. James himself was imprisoned, and
the chief conspirator, the Earl of Angus, subsequently became
known as 'Archibald Bell-the-Cat'. In his Moralitas Henryson
emphasises the importance of having advisors who are noble in the
most conservative sense. Since James's advisors had been lower-
born men, the general impression in the countryside was that their
opinions were also 'low'. And Henryson, very conservatively,
emphasises the importance of blood in the role of noble deeds:

Heir may thow se that riches of array
Will cause pure men presumpteous for to be;
Thay think thay hald of nane, be thay als gay,
Bot counterfute ane lord in all degre.
Out of thair cais in pryde thay clym sa hie
That thay forbeir thair better in na steid,
Quhill sum man tit thair heillis ouer thair heid.

Richt swa in seruice vther sum exceidis,
And thay haif withgang, welth, and cherising,
That thay will lychtlie lordis in thair deidis,
And lukis not to thair blude nor thair ofspring.
(11.2595-600)

He further warns:

Thairfoir I counsell men of euerilk stait
To knaw thame self, and quhome thay suld forbeir,
And fall not with their better in debait,
Suppois thay be als galland in thair geir:
It settis ne seruand for to vphald weir,
Nor clym sa hie quhill he fall of the ledder:
Bot think vpon the wolf and on the wedder.
(11.2609-15)

Such specific warnings seemed to indicate that Henrson has particular individuals in mind. These individuals, whom major Scottish
historians believe are primarily responsible for the limitations

on the government of James III, fit the descriptions in this fable.[32]

Yet, in one sense, it does not matter whether one accepts the position espoused by Roderick Lyall or that espoused by the other critics. In either case, there is no doubt that Henryson's rhetoric was oriented towards political events and political advice. It is quite true that, by this date, the ars praedicandi has developed its own guidelines for the treatment of political issues - a stock subject of medieval preachers. Nonetheless, that tradition also owes a great debt to the ars dictaminis in its treatment of political activities. Whatever the source of Henryson's learning of this rhetorical tradition, he was clearly sensitive to political events and activities, and wished to include them in his writings.

By the date of Henryson's education and the composition of his major works, the three major rhetorical traditions of the Middle Ages had clearly lost a great deal of their discrete identities. In some educational settings all of rhetoric was taught under the general framework of the ars praedicandi. In others, rhetoric was treated as one amorphous body of knowledge without regard to a specific purpose or audience. We therefore cannot be sure precisely how Henryson learned the arts of rhetoric. It is entirely possible that he never heard the phrase 'ars dictaminis' or studied the functions of the dictator. Yet, the ars dictaminis clearly appears in his work. Just as Henryson was influenced by the ars praedicandi and as his work shows a splendid knowledge of the ars poetica, there can be no doubt that the ars dictaminis was a powerful influence on his writing.

Notes

1   Robert L Kindrick, 'Henryson and the Rhetoricians: The ars praedicandi', Scottish Studies 4, Dietrich Strauss and Horst W Drescher (eds) (Frankfurt am Main, 1986), 255-70.
2   James J Murphy, Rhetoric in the Middle Ages (Berkeley, 1974), pp 195-7; see also Paul O Kristeller, 'Philosophy and Rhetoric from Antiquity to the Renaissance', Renaissance Thought and Its Sources, Michael Mooney (ed) (New York, 1979), pp 211-60.
3   Ibid, p 197.
4   Ibid, p 195.
5   Charles Sears Baldwin, Medieval Rhetoric to 1400 (Gloucester, Mass, repr 1959), pp 219, 223. See also Murphy, pp 203-4.
6   Murphy, p 215; Charles B Faulhaber, 'The Summa dictaminis of Guido Faba', Medieval Eloquence (Berkley, 1978), pp 92-3.
7   Denton Fox (ed), The Poems of Robert Henryson, (Oxford, 1981), p 53, 11.1295-9. All citations will be made from this edition; hereafter, only line numbers will be provided.
8   J A Burrow, Ricardian Poetry (New Haven, 1971), esp pp 1-10.
9   Stephen Hawes, The Pastime of Pleasure (London, 1865), p 38, chap. 11, 11.18-19.
10 Alberic of Monte Cassino, 'Flowers of Rhetoric', Readings in Medieval Rhetoric, Joseph M Miller, Michael H Prosser, Thomas W Benson (eds) (Bloomington, 1973), pp 135-6.

11 See Robert L Kindrick, Robert Henryson (Boston, 1979), pp 31-2.
12 C W Jentoft, 'Henryson as Authentic "Chaucerian": Narrator, Character, and Courtly Love in The Testament of Cresseid', Studies in Scottish Literature 10 (1972), 94-102; see also Tartyana Moran, 'The Testament of Cresseid and the Book of Troylus', Litera 6 (1959), 18-24.
13 Baldwin, pp 214-15; Faulhaber, pp 94-5.
14 Murphy, Rhetoric in the Middle Ages, p 94.
15 John MacQueen, Robert Henryson (Oxford, 1967), p 191; Kindrick, Robert Henryson, pp 32-5; Douglas Gray, Robert Henryson (Leiden, 1979), p 135.
16 Marshall Stearns, Robert Henryson (New York, 1949), pp 97-105.
17 See Matthew P McDiarmid, Robert Henryson (Edinburgh, 1981), pp 53ff.
18 J A Burrow, 'Henryson: The Preaching of the Swallow', Essays in Criticism, 25 (1975), 25-37.
19 J A Y Simpson, 'Antiquarian Notices of Leprosy', Edinburgh Medical and Surgical Journal, 56 (1841), 301-30; 57 (1842), 121-56, 294-429.
20 See Kindrick, 'Henryson and the Rhetoricians', 255, and Michael C Leff, 'Boethius' De differentiis topicis, Book IV', in Murphy, Medieval Eloquence, pp 3-24.
21 Murphy, 'Rhetoric in the Middle Ages', p 196.
22 'Flowers of Rhetoric', 138-9.
23 Anonymous of Bologna, 'The Principles of Letter Writing', James J Murphy (ed) Three Medieval Rhetorical Arts (Berkeley, 1971), p 16.
24 See Murphy, Rhetoric in the Middle Ages, pp 214-26.
25 Stearns, pp 127-9.
26 Roderick S Lyall, 'Politics and Poetry in Fifteenth and Sixteenth Century Scotland', Scottish Literary Journal, 3 (1976) 5-29.
27 Stearns, see especially pp 14-32; MacQueen, pp 1-23, 94-188, Ranald Nicholson, Scotland: The Later Middle Ages, pp 500-30; Kindrick, 'Politics and Poetry at the Court of James III', Studies in Scottish Literature, 19 (1984), pp 40-55.
28 Nicholson, pp 508-9.
29 See Kindrick, Robert Henryson, pp 77-8.
30 For a summary of these perspectives, see Nicholson, pp 397-530, and W Croft Dickinson and Archibald A M Duncan, Scotland from the Earliest Times to 1603 (Oxford, 1977), pp 235-48. Yet, for an opposing point of view, see Norman A T Macdougall, 'The Sources: A Reappraisal of the Legend', Jennifer M Brown (ed) Scottish Society in the Fifteenth Century (London, 1977), pp 10-32.
31 Kindrick, Robert Henryson, pp 114-15.
32 Nicholson, pp 500-30.

Chapter 13

ELRICH FANTASYIS IN DUNBAR AND OTHER POETS

Priscilla Bawcutt

The term elrich (or eldritch) has been applied by several critics
to a type or tradition of comic poetry. Referring specifically to
medieval Scottish poetry, C S Lewis used phrases like 'eldritch
material' and 'eldritch humour', and spoke of 'the eldritch
audacity which likes to play with ideas that would ordinarily
excite fear or reverence'.[1] A few years later Muriel Bradbrook
tried to place Dr Faustus within an 'eldritch' tradition that she
defined, in part, as 'horrific jesting'.[2] What does elrich mean?
Etymology offers no help, since the word appears from nowhere in a
way that is appropriately mysterious; the first recorded occurrences are in Dunbar and Douglas. But a word's meaning consists in
its use: throughout the sixteenth century Scottish writers applied
elrich to 'browneis' and 'bogillis', to Pluto and to the Cyclops
and the 'weird sisteris', to angels and also to elves (with whom
some etymological link has been posited), to the fairy queen and
to the desolate places inhabited by ghosts and demons. In the
measured words of The Scottish National Dictionary it is used 'to
denote some connection with the supernatural'; modern glosses like
'uncanny', 'weird', or 'spooky' perhaps give an idea of its connotations. The word usually carries some implication of fear, as in
Douglas's splendid line on the owl: 'Vgsum to heir was hir wild
elrich screke' (VII Prologue, 108): the witches in Tam O'Shanter
utter a similarly 'eldritch screech'. Disapproving critics of
Virgil, according to Douglas, found Book VI of the Aeneid pervaded
by the elrich:

> 'All is bot gaistis and elrich fantasyis,
> Of browneis and of bogillis ful this buke:
> Owt on thir wandrand speritis, wow!' thou cryis;
> 'It semys a man war mangit, tharon list luke,
> Lyke dremys or dotage in the monys cruke,
> Vayn superstitionys aganyst our richt beleve'.
> (VI Prologue, 17-22)

It was far from easy, in the sixteenth century, to distinguish
true Christian belief from superstition or delusive fantasyis, the
figments of the imagination that sometimes resulted from dreams or
lunacy.
    I find the phrase 'elrich fantasyis' a useful label for a small
group of humorous poems, preserved chiefly in the Bannatyne Manu-

script, that have won praise from a few critics but are for the most part ignored. Two are attributed to poets of whom we know virtually nothing but their names - Lichtoun's Dreme and Rowll's Cursing. But most are anonymous - Fergus Gaist, The Crying of Ane Play, Kynd Kittok, The Gyre Carling, King Berdok, The First Heland-man, and Colkelbie Sow.[3] Little is known definitely about the composition or date of these poems. It is probable that they belong to the last decades of the fifteenth or the early decades of the sixteenth century. They are metrically and linguistically inventive, the work of educated poets, some perhaps, like Dunbar, clerics. They seem popular in appeal, but not in origin. They have some resemblance to another group in Bannatyne: the 'ballatis of unpossibiliteis', sometimes known as lying-poems. But they should be distinguished from better-known comic poems, such as The Freiris of Berwick and The Wife of Auchtermuchty, which belong to a basically realistic mode; despite such comic exaggeration these deal with everyday life in a factual, rational way. In the fanta-sies, however, although the setting is usually close to home - often in Fife or the Lothians - our sense of place is rapidly shattered. We are disorientated when familiar names, such as Cramond, Haddington, North Berwick, are strangely coupled with remote or imaginary ones. Kittok finds an ale-house just outside the gates of heaven. We are transported to a dreamworld, to an underworld (in The Cursing), always to an otherworld. In Lich-toun's Dreme the poet dreams that he is 'tane' by 'the king of farye' (6), and lost for seven years (56). Kittok's adventures start when she comes to 'ane elrich well' (8). Such magic wells are often found in folk tales, and, according to Juliette Wood, seem to function in Scottish and Irish tradition, 'as the extreme limit of the known world'.[4] These poems are peopled with strange creatures: dwarfs and giants, elves, fairies, etins and demons. In one poem God and St Peter come to earth and take a walk in Argyle; in another the gyre carling, an ogress, marries Mahomet; and in a third the offspring of Fergus's ghost and 'the Spenʒie fle' are Orpheus and queen 'Elpha'. Each of these poems narrates a series of bizarre events, or 'farleis' (Dreme, 46); Fergus Gaist is introduced as a 'verry grit marvell' (2). They bring together ingredients from many sources: Celtic, Germanic and classical mythology, Arthurian romance, preachers' tales, and a repertory of popular stories, which are mostly lost but to which there exist tantalising references in Colkelbie Sow and The Complaynt of Scotland. But these poets should not lose the credit for a vivid imagination. Enoch and Ely are discovered in paradise:

> Sittand on ʒule evin in ane fresch grene schaw
> Rostand straberries at ane fyre of snaw
> (Dreme, 41-2)

King Berdok lodges in summer in 'ane bowkaill stok', but in winter in 'a cokkill schell' (6-8). Kittok overtakes a newt riding on a snail:

> Scho cryd ourtane fallow haill haill
> And raid ane inch behind the taill
> (11-12)

Other poets give us not this miniature world, but a Scotland
created by giants' farts and pisses. Yet The Crying swings from
such gross Rabelaisian comedy to the romantic image of a giant
standing on tiptoe, in order to

> tak the starnis doun with his hand
> And sett thame in a gold garland
> Aboif his wyvis hair
> (38-40)

Most of these poems are included in Bannatyne's 'mirrie ballatis', and are undoubtedly humorous. Unlike some great ballads or Sir
Gawain and the Green Knight they do not draw us far into an enchanted world, and invite us to suspend our powers of disbelief.
The Dreme voices the common-sense view: this 'fantasie' may spring
from the consumption of too much ale. Although they are not
strictly 'ballatis of unpossibiliteis', a genre that seems to have
developed from the ancient topos of adynata or impossibilia, their
comic method is similar: to pile up impossibilities, absurd juxta-
positions, bizarre incongruities. In the adynaton, however, absurdity is purposeful, and in its late-medieval form anti-feminist:
only when Aberdeen and Ayr are both one town, or with historical
irony 'Inglische tungis translaitit ar in grew [Greek]', will women
in general or 'Scho quhome I luve' in particular ever be true and
constant.[5]   But these fantasies seem to delight in nonsense for its
own sake. One is reminded of nursery rhymes, or, fleetingly, of
Edward Lear. But we should not forget that there exist medieval
parallels: the marginal grotesques and 'droleries' in Gothic
manuscripts, for instance, or humorous English poems, such as The
Land of Cokaygne, a group of fantastic carols, and a tale of
'marvels' that includes a church service entirely conducted by
fish, in which the salmon sings the high mass, and the herring is
his clerk.[6] There is no doubt that some of these Scottish poems
contain elements of parody or burlesque. The Cursing is a spoof-
cursing of those who stole five fat geese, 'With caponis henis and
vthir fowlis' (14). Fergus is essentially a mock-conjuration of a
troublesome ghost, 'With paternoster patter patter'(20). The Gyre
Carling certainly makes comic use of romance themes: its hero, who
is strangely besotted with the monstrous ogress, bleeds not blood
but 'ane quart of milk pottage', and besieges her tower with an
army of moles - presumably they are good at tunnelling. The First
Helandman makes a blasphemous allusion to Genesis, obscenely
mimicking the creation of Adam the first man, from the dust of the
earth. But such burlesque is mostly intermittent. With the exception of Kittok and The First Helandman, which are short and neat,
these poems ramble and drift in an inconsequential way. Most of
their readers will recall vivid lines or images, but I suspect that
I am not alone in finding it difficult to remember which poem they
come from. In the words of Colkelbie Sow they pile 'caisis upon
caisis'(54), and we may well feel that their authors intended 'to
bourd' but 'left it in a blondir'(46). What is also striking is
their pervasive geniality; the humour is remarkably good-tempered.
This is true not only of Kittok but even of The First Helandman;
both play jocularly rather than caustically with stereotypes -

woman as a drunkard, the Highlander as an incorrigible thief.

In the past several of these pieces were attributed to Dunbar, and even included in editions of his poems. But there is no early evidence that he wrote any of them - suggestions to this effect are sheer wishful thinking. Occasional similarities of phrase and rhyme-scheme are susceptible of several explanations; and any discussion of influence is impeded by the difficulty of dating all these poems, Dunbar's included. Nonetheless I am sure that Dunbar was acquainted with some of these comic poems, or with others like them. A few were definitely circulating in his lifetime - Kittok, for instance, appeared in an early print (c.1509), along with The Tua Mariit Wemen and the Wedo. What is more, he seems to have known some version of Colkelbie Sow; he refers to the 'Golk of Maryland', heroine of King Berdok; and he mentions two poets by the name of 'Roull', one of whom is the presumed author of The Cursing.[7] Dunbar shared the same imaginative heritage as these poets, and wrote for a similar audience; he was equally at home in the comic mode of elrich fantasy.

But Dunbar differs from most of them in two important respects. He is a dynamic poet, and his poems do not drift but drive onward, vigorously and purposefully - towards some climax, some disaster, some epigrammatic 'point'. Whatever the absurdity, Dunbar is in control; the elrich is harnessed and put to some purpose, though this is not always or primarily a moral one. But there is an even more striking difference. Dunbar's characteristic tone is not genial, but dark and sinister; we are told that God laughed 'his hairt sair' at Kittok's exploits, as also at the Highlander, but in Dunbar's poems the only laughter (apart from the poet's) is that of devils (Fasternis Evin in Hell, 29, and Renunce thy God, 39). It is not faerie that predominates in his comic poems, but diablerie. (In this respect the closest parallels are found in Rowll's Cursing and Montgomerie's Flyting). C S Lewis noted how often in Dunbar 'the comic overlaps with the demoniac and the terrifying'.[8] There is a striking ambivalence in his response to the devil: the superficially flippant and irreverent tone of some poems co-exists with a sombre and more fearful response. At the opening of The Flyting Dunbar threatens Kennedy with appalling consequences, and vows to 'rais the Feynd with flytting':

> The erd sould trymbill, the firmament sould schaik,
> And all the air in vennaum suddane stink,
> And all the divillis of hel for redour quaik
> To heir quhat I suld wryt with pen and ink ...
>
> (9-12)

This is mock-apocalyptic, a vaunt far out of proportion to the ostensible subject. It is comic, yet has an intensity that derives from the very solemnity with which hell, damnation and the devil were normally spoken of - not only by others but by Dunbar himself. No reader is disposed to laugh at the menacing figure of the devil in Dunbar's poem on the Resurrection - dragon, cruel serpent, and 'auld kene tegir with his teith on char'.

Dunbar's ambivalence had deep and complex roots. He and his contemporaries combined an intense interest in the world of evil

spirits with great uncertainty about their nature and mode of
operation. At every level, learned and popular, they were supplied
with abundant but conflicting information. When Robert Burton
questioned 'how far the power of spirits and devils doth extend',
he drew much of his material from medieval philosophers and theologians.[9] At a more popular level the imagination was fed in a
variety of ways, visually and verbally: in wall-paintings, sculp-
tured capitals, or the woodcuts in prints of the Ars Moriendi,
that showed fiends waiting to seize the soul of a dying man; in
sermons, saints' lives, such as The Golden Legend, and dramatic
representations of the Fall of Lucifer or the Harrowing of Hell.
It is tantalising to read only the title of the 'ludum de Belly-
ale' that took place in Aberdeen in 1471.[10] Devils were incor-
poreal, yet could assume many forms. By the late medieval period a
demonic iconography had evolved that is still familiar. Dunbar was
not alone in speaking of 'devillis als blak as pik' (H 56, 81) –
in their true ugliness devils were characterised by blackness and
deformity. They were depicted with horns and hooves, and sometimes
with feathers and wings – we should recall this when reading of
the flying abbot of Tungland, and the birds' belief that he may be
'the hornit howle' (K 54, 74). Devils could swell in size to
giants, and shrink small enough to sit under a lettuce leaf.
Devils could assume the shape of animals: Henryson gives the name
'Bawsy Broun' to a dog (Fables, 546), but Dunbar gives it to a
fiend (K 52, 30). This produces a curiously double effect. It
might seem reductive, yet it also instills suspicion of everyday
creatures, as the special sense of 'familiar' indicates – devils
might lurk in the shape of family pets.

The multitudinousness of devils was stressed, along with their
ubiquity. Picturesque similes were sought in an effort to convey
this. One medieval preacher said that they 'flye above in the eyer
as thyke as motis in the sonne'; the analogy recurs in Chaucer and
Rowll. Burton quoted learned authors to the same effect: 'the air
is not so full of flies in summer as it is at all times of invisible devils'.[11] It is within this tradition that Dunbar writes of
devils 'Solistand ... as beis thik' (K56, 82). The world of devils
bordered closely on that of ghosts and fairies, and also oddly
paralleled that of the angelic hierarchies. Some believed that
there existed nine orders of bad spirits, the first of which
comprised the false gods of the Gentiles.[12] Douglas thus equated
Pluto with Satan, 'Prynce in that in that dolourous den of wo and
pane' (VI Prologue, 151). Dunbar, however, in The Goldin Targe
(125-6) calls Pluto an 'elrich incubus'. This seems to fuse god,
demon and fairy, recalling Pluto's rape of Proserpina as well as
his medieval indentification with the king of faerie. Although
most devils were nameless, some acquired names and distinctive
personalities. Rowll speaks of 'Deventinus the devill that maidd
the dyce' (98); his Cursing provides a useful compedium of the
devil-lore likely to have been familiar to Dunbar. The 'Sanct
Girnega' of The Turnament thus appears as a devil in The Cursing
(95), and may have survived in the Scottish children's rhyme
concerning 'Girnigo Gibbie, the cat's guid minnie' (see Scottish
National Dictionary, Girnigo, n. and adj.). Perhaps the most
famous medieval devil was Tutivillus, who appears as a character

in the Towneley Judgement play and the morality <u>Mankind</u>. He is often depicted with a sack or in the act of writing, sometimes recording evil words, sometimes recording female gossip.[13] Kennedy includes Tutivillus among the clan of devilish relations he devises for Dunbar at the end of <u>The Flyting</u> (513); all is designed to lead to the taunt 'Tu es diabolus', and the final line that consigns Dunbar to hell.

Plenty of medieval jokes exist about the devils and hell. There is an excellent French tale of a minstrel who was carried to hell. One day he was left in charge of the lost souls, and gambled them away in a game of dice with St Peter. Lucifer was so enraged that he threw the minstrel out — and consequently to heaven – and commanded his subordinate devils to bring no more minstrels and gamblers to hell. The tale ends: 'Now cheer up, all you minstrels, rogues, lechers and gamblers, for the one who lost those souls at dice has set you all free!' This is a specimen of a recurrent folk-joke: why are there no members of a given group (e.g. job or nationality) in hell? Why no weavers? Because the devils find their noise intolerable. Welshmen are excluded from heaven, for a similar reason.[14] Dunbar alludes to stories of this kind, I think, at the end of <u>The Dance of the Sevin Deadly Sins</u>: he intends a double insult in keeping minstrels out of hell and in consigning highland entertainers to its deepest abyss. Some saints' lives show a reluctant admiration for the devil as a clever trickster, rather like the fox in beast fables. Devils are sometimes subtle and wily; at other times they dwindle into imps or the 'deblats' who attended upon the St Nicholas bishop; or they degenerate into the clowns and buffoons who bluster and make coarse jokes in medieval drama. Medieval devils were by turns sinister and ridiculous, figures of fear and figures of fun. Jean Frappier sought deep psychological explanations for this pervasive late-medieval mockery: it was an unavowed means of escape from a very real and otherwise almost unbearable fear, a defensive weapon against 'le terrorisme du Diable'. He drew a parallel with the behaviour of 'gens qui ont peur, la nuit, au coin d'un bois, et veulent se rassurer, cherchent a rendre leur crainte irréelle en plaisantant, en prenant un petit ton guilleret, en se racontant des histoires droles'.[15] Perhaps we should not seek one single explanation for such varied phenomena, nor even find them astonishing. Black comedy and a perverse delight in playing with fire are not confined to the Middle Ages. Nor is it only children who enjoy what the Opies call 'ghoulism' and 'spookies'. The latent horror is what contributes a comic 'frisson' to many a joke.

Some of Dunbar's most potent comic imagery involves ghosts and evil spirits. At the end of <u>The Dance</u> the Highlanders are summoned:

> Thae tarmegantis with tag and tatter
> Full lowd in Ersche begowth to clatter
> And rowp lyk revin and ruke.
>
> (115-17)

To gloss <u>tarmegantis</u> as 'blustering bullies' is not wholly adequate. The Scots may not have been aware that <u>Termagant</u> was originally a name given to a god of the Saracens in the romances, but they clearly knew its diabolic associations – both Henryson and Kennedy use the word as a name for devils. I would also like to revive an old discarded suggestion that Dunbar is making a punning reference to the ptarmigan, whose earliest recorded spellings (at the end of the sixteenth century) coincide with those of termagant. The habitat of this bird is confined, appropriately, to the highlands; and Dunbar's phrase, 'clatter/And rowp lyk revin and ruke', is not dissimilar to a modern naturalist's account of the ptarmigan's cry as a 'hoarse croak, with a crackling note'.[16] Dunbar wickedly depicts Highlanders as half-devils, half-birds. Even more effective is a passage in The Flyting (161-72), which portrays Kennedy as a Lazarus, returned from the grave as a grisly memento mori. Dunbar pretends to exorcise him – 'I conjure the, thow hungert heland gaist' – and ends by comparing Kennedy to 'the spreit of Gy', the central figure in a popular ghost story, known all over Western Europe. The tale was highly didactic, purporting to give information about purgatory and the afterlife. Normally the ghost is invisible, manifesting itself only by speech and an uncanny sound, like that of a broom sweeping the pavement. But Dunbar alludes to the ghost's appearance, which suggests that he may have seen some acted version. Lindsay, after all, amused the young James V by dressing up as 'the greislie gaist of gye' (Dreme, 16).[17]

In The Tua Mariit Wemen and the Wedo the Widow calls her last husband an 'evill spreit' (397), but earlier in the poem is an even more striking passage, in which the First Wife recalls her husband's love-making:

> Bot quhen that glowrand gaist grippis me about
> Than think I hiddowus Mahowne hes me in armes.
> Thair ma na sanyne me save fra that auld sathane,
> For thocht I croce me all cleine fra the croun doun
> He wil my corse all beclip and clap me to his breist
>
> ...   .
> The luf blenkis of that bogill fra his blerde ene
> As Bel$_3$ebub had one me blent abasit my spreit
>   (100ff.)

This husband is a shape-shifter: first a ghost, then different manifestations of the devil, lastly a 'bogill' who resembles Beelzebub. Dunbar suggests both the husband's ugliness and the wife's fear and repulsion. She speaks as if she were trying to ward off the embraces of an incubus. The 'ugsome' and the comic are deftly combined in this elrich passage.

Five of Dunbar's poems are pervaded by diablerie: Renunce thy God and Cum to Me (K 56), How Dunbar wes Desyrd to be ane Freir (K 55), The Ballat of the Abbot of Tungland (K 54), The Antechrist (K 53) and Fasternis Evin in Hell (K 52). All are bad dreams, or nightmares. A dream is an excellent frame for comic fantasy: the constraints of the waking world are absent, yet not totally abolished – they lurk on the margins of the dream. At the same time a dream's status is ambiguous; dreams provoke questions about their source, significance and truth, voiced by many medieval poets including Dunbar:

Thane thocht I thus, This is ane felloun phary,
Or ellis my witt rycht woundrouslie dois varie;
This seimes to me ane guidlie companie,
And gif it be ane feindlie fantasie
Defend me, Jhesu and his moder Marie!
(Ane Dreme, 11-15)

Many dreams had religious significance (such as Dunbar's concerning Christ's Passion), but others might indeed be 'feindlie fantasie', or diabolic illusion. Innocent III warned that dreams
caused many to go astray, and Aquinas said that although a demon
could not directly sway a man's reason he could incline the inferior faculties, such as imagination or the corporeal senses.[18]
But other dreams might be sheer nonsense: this commonsense attitude
is voiced by Douglas, somewhat ironically, at the end of Prologue
VIII: 'Thys was bot faynt [feigned] fantasy ... Nevir word of
verite' (175-6). Despite sharing a similar framework, these poems
have Dunbar's characteristic variety. The prominence of the dreamer
differs considerably: in How Dunbar wes Desyrd to be ane Freir he
is at the centre of the poem; in Renunce thy God he is marginal,
simply the ironic recorder of what he sees and hears. Our awareness
of the poem as a dream also varies. It is strongly felt in Fasternis Evin, to which the solemn word trance is twice applied, at
beginning and end. In The Antechrist phrases like 'ane dremyng and
a fantasy' and 'my dreme it wes so nyce' direct us more explicitly
than do some other poems to ponder how reliable and trustworthy
this dream may be. But in Renunce thy God, al- though the opening
lines of both versions imply that it is a dream, the dreamer almost
fades from our consciousness, and when the poem ends he is still
apparently asleep. This is unusual since most of Dunbar's dream
poems have abrupt, even explosive, endings. But there are so many
problems about this poem's text, that we should perhaps beware of
seeking deep significance in this failure to wake up.

Criticism of Renunce thy God has been scanty, and usually
depreciative. It tends to be regarded as a piece of social satire,
criticising the corrupt practices of the crafts, and the false
claims they make for the quality of their wares. This is linked
with an even more important and unifying theme: the misuse of oaths
and asseverations. Blasphemous refererences to God and the devil
had long been of concern to medieval moralists, and devotional
writers were particularly appalled by casual references to parts
of God's body, regarding them as a kind of second Crucifixion.
Preachers long before Dunbar singled out the market place as the
special haunt of swearers. They also, in an effort to frighten
swearers, told stories of terrible divine or diabolic retribution.
One, quoted by G R Owst, concerns a man whose favourite oath was
'the devel me adrenche' - it is no surprise to learn that he later
fell in a ditch and was drowned.[19]

The figure of the devil is at the heart of Dunbar's poem. He is
shown moving from one person to another, tempting and winning them
to himself. The very refrain consists of his words, which shock-
ingly invert the baptismal renunciation of the devil and all his
works: 'Renunce thy God, and cum to me". The theme is very ancient.
In the book of Job (1:7) Satan goes to and fro in the earth; and

in the New Testament Christians are warned that 'the devil, as a roaring lion, walketh about, seeking whom he may devour' (I Peter: 5, 8). In this poem the devil does indeed walk about among men, seeking his prey; but he is no roaring lion, nor a heroic figure like Milton's Satan preparing for his onslaught on mankind. This is an intimate and familiar devil, passing 'throw the mercat' (4) and 'Rownand to Robene and to Dik' (84). The devil is said to be tempting men, but he appears rather to be listening gleefully as one after another damns himself: 'The Feind ressaif me gif I le' or 'I gif me to the Feynd all fre'. The poem touches on the long-persisting fear that a moment's thoughtless oath might damn one forever. So in Webster's White Devil (V.i.72-3) Lodovico envisages poisoning his victim's tennis racket - 'That while he had been bandying at tennis/He might have sworn himself to hell'. Almost every stanza divides into two sections, containing the words first of some human, then of the devil. But although two voices are heard it is not strictly a dialogue; the devil comments in mocking asides on what has just been said:

> Ane tail3our said, In all this toun
> Be thair ane better weilmaid goun
> I gif me to the Feynd all fre;
> Gramercy tel3our, said Mahoun,
> Renunce thy God and cum to me.
>
> (26-30)

Much of the pleasure of reading this poem derives from its execution of small variations upon a fixed pattern. We wonder what craft will be next, which oath will be uttered, and what will be the devil's riposte.

Renunce thy God exists in two very different versions, one containing thirteen stanzas, the other seventeen. There has been much controversy about the relationship between these two texts, which I have no space to summarise here. What I would suggest, however, is that the two texts are so different that they should be given the status of independent poems, as is usual with carols and ballads; attempting to prove the superiority or priority of one to the other seems a fruitless task. Both poems are attributed to Dunbar, but it is likely that neither is wholly as he wrote it. His poem was perhaps so popular that it passed rapidly into the public domain, and was then reshaped in a way common with popular poetry. It would be particularly easy to add or omit stanzas in a work of this catalogue-structure. The poem combines two folk-tale motifs: the rash or heedless oath - 'The Feind ressaif me gif I le' - and the devil's visit to earth. (Chaucer's Friar's Tale also combines them, though in a more complex manner). Long after Dunbar's time the second motif was treated in vulgar ballads in a manner which recalls this poem.

A common seventeenth-century broadside, one which also made its way into the droleries, was a satirical tale of the devil's ascent to earth and his encounter with a series of persons, usually the representatives of various occupations.[20]

Four of the Romantic poets, like Dunbar, seized on the satirical possibilities of the theme. Coleridge and Southey collaborated fairly light-heartedly on a doggerel ballad - 'In ding-dong chime of sing-song rhyme' - which, like Dunbar's poem, exists in two versions. The first, The Devil's Thoughts, is included in Coleridge's Works; the second is usually attributed to Southey, as The Devil's Walk. Shelley gave the latter title to one of his juvenilia, printed in a broadside in 1812; and Byron too treated the theme in an 'unfinished rhapsody', which he called The Devil's Drive (1814). In an excursion through contemporary England the devil found that they had better manners in hell than in the House of Lords.

How Dunbar wes Desyrd to be ane Freir also treats of an encounter between man and devil. This amusing poem owes much to the traditions of anti-mendicant satire, though I do not see such satire as its primary object. I wish here to comment only on the poem's ending. The dreamer confesses

> Als lang as I did beir the freiris style
> In me, God wait, wes mony wrink and wyle;
> In me wes falset with every wicht to flatter
> Quhilk mycht be flemit with na haly watter -
> I wes ay reddy all men to begyle.
> This freir that did Sanct Francis thair appeir,
> Ane fieind he wes in liknes of ane freir;
> He vaneist away with stynk and fyrie smowk;
> With him me thocht all the hous end he towk,
> And I awoik as wy that wes in weir.
>
> (41-50)

Discomfited devils traditionally left ruin in their wake; one very similarly 'bare awey an ende of the house' in a sermon discussed by Owst. Still closer to Dunbar in time and place are Hector Boece's stories of defeated demons, circumstantially dated (in 1486) and located in Aberdeenshire or Mar: one flew off, accompanied with venomous odour and 'crak of fyre and reyk'; another flew away, 'berand the bed and ruf of the house'.[21] But why does Dunbar's devil vanish? Was it the dreamer's mention of God's name - a motif of many a folk-tale? Was it his reference to holy water, ritually used to exorcise evil spirits? Neither is sufficient. It seems that the dreamer's self-incriminating confession forces the devil to show himself in his true form. This passage is the culmination of a wit-combat, and the poem as a whole has a pattern similar to that of the medieval riddle-poem, Diabolus et Virgo, or the much later The Fause Knight upon the Road. What is effective against the devil in all such pieces are bold argument and getting the last word.[22]

Two of these poems concern a picturesque figure at James IV's court, John Damian. One has an unusually long title in Bannatyne, whose doggerel clumsiness would seem to rule out Dunbar's authorship: 'Ane ballat of the fenʒeit freir of tungland/how he fell in the myre fleand to turkiland'. Damian was not a friar, but in 1504 became abbot of Tongland, a house of Premonstratensian Canons. I have therefore adopted the title for the poem in Asloan's original

contents-list.: 'A ballat of the abbot of tungland'. Yet within
the poem itself there is no such precise identification; the
protagonist remains nameless throughout. This lack of a name does
not seem accidental, but corresponds to his lack of a fixed identity: the unnamed 'he' slips through roles, or rather disguises,
as easily as he passes through different countries. He is successively an outlaw, 'a religious man', a 'leiche', a 'prelat', 'a new
maid channoun' and an alchemist. This shape-shifting, like his
vagrancy, is in keeping with his mysterious and diabolic origin:
he is 'of Sathanis seid' and comes from Tartary, the land of the
Tartars, erroneously believed to be linked with Tartarus, hell.
But there is an interesting correlation also with the varying
references to Damian in The Treasurer's Accounts, as 'the Franch
leich', or 'Maister John' or 'new maid abbot of tungland'. Dunbar
had no need to name names; he dropped hints, which (to judge from
the titles given the poem) his audience picked up readily. Yet the
very absence of a name and of a location for that abbot's adventure more specific than 'Scotland' increase the potential for
comic invention. We shall never know the precise relation of this
tale to reality – far too much trust has been laid on John
Leslie's late and suspiciously varied accounts of the incident.
What seems certain is that Dunbar here, as so often, is blending
fact with fantasy.

I have space to comment only on one striking aspect of the
poem, its affinity with myth and folk-tale. Stories from many
countries testify to the significance of flight as something
superhuman, practised only by birds, spirits and demons. Men who
try to fly almost invariably come to disaster. Geoffrey of Monmouth tells how Bladud, father of King Lear, broke his neck in
such an attempt. Ranulph Higden tells a similar story of a monk of
Malmesbury, who attached feathers to his hands and feet, but fell
after a short flight and was lame for ever afterwards.[23] In Stith
Thomson's classification of folk-tale motifs the attempt to fly
is placed under the heading, 'Overweening ambition is punished'
(L 421). Occasionally an unsuccessful flight is treated tragically, as in Virgil's handling of the legend of Daedalus and
Icarus, a story alluded to by both Dunbar and Higden. But mockery
and derision are more common. There are several jests and facetiae
about tricksters who announce to gullible crowds that they are
going to fly. One is associated with the name of Scoggin:

> On a time Scoggin made the Frenchman believe that he would
> fly into England, and did get him many goose-wings and tied
> them about his arms and legs, and went upon a high tower, and
> spread his arms abroad as though he would fly, and came down
> again and said that all his feathers were not fit about him
> and that he would fly on the morrow ... On the morrow Scoggin
> got upon the tower and did shake his feathers, saying 'Go
> home, fools, go home. Trow you that I will break my neck for
> your pleasure?' ...
> There was a Frenchman had indignation at Scoggin, and he
> said, 'Tomorrow you shall see me fly to Paris'. And he got
> him wings, and went upon the tower, and spread his wings
> abroad, and would have flown, and fell down into the moat

under the tower ... Scoggin did take him by the hand, and
said, 'Sir, you be welcome from Paris, I think you have been
in a great rain'.[24]

This attempt to fly does not illustrate human daring and inventiveness, but folly and stupidity. Dunbar's poem is far funnier
(and his protagonist more depraved), yet embedded in it is a
similarly sensible, literally 'down to earth' view of man's
capacities, which (with hindsight) we may find limited and lacking
imagination. Yet we should recall that Samuel Johnson displayed
equal scepticism in his handling of the theme. In chapter 6 of
Rasselas, 'A Dissertation on the Art of Flying', the Artist 'was
every day more certain that he should leave vultures and eagles
behind him', but he ended, like Dunbar's abbot, in a lake, and
'the prince drew him to land, half dead with terror and vexation'.
In Dunbar's poem there is one striking motif that is not present in these other versions; it is the birds who are responsible
for the flight's failure. They take revenge for the invasion of
their element, and expel the intruder. The abbot's attempt to
assume their powers is seen as his culminating attempt to go
beyond man's earthbound limits - 'The hevin he micht not bruke'
(72). Drawing attention to his lack of identity, the birds marvel
as to what he is - 'All fowill ferleit quhat he sowld be' (63).
The flying abbot is as much a hybrid as the Minotaur, neither man
nor bird; he assumes the plumage, or 'fedrem', of birds as earlier
he had adopted the habit of a 'religious man'. There is a poetic
justice, as critics have noted, in the way the punishment inflict-
ed by the birds fits the abbot's crimes. The surgeon who shed
blood is now struck 'with buffettis quhill he bled' (78); and the
man who 'full clenely carvit' his victims is himself horribly
mutilated. In this passage Dunbar also presents us with powerful
illustrations of impossibilia, or 'the World Upside Down' topos.
One disturbance of natural order is countered by another, or by a
reversal of what is assumed to be the normal relationship between
birds and men. Birds attacking men are shown in some representations of the 'World Upside Down', along with an ox cutting up a
butcher or a fish eating a fisherman.[25] The poem derives much
power from our response to such a reversal, the basic human fear
of the sharp beaks of birds.
The Antechrist seems to have been inspired by the same incident
as The Abbot of Tungland, and they are regularly treated as companion pieces, although the only manuscript to contain both poems
does not place them together. The Antechrist is dominated by Dame
Fortune's speech to the dreamer, which occupies the six central
stanzas. Her speech is a prediction, not a sermon, and contains
in miniature several characteristic features of the medieval
prophecy. A future event is said to depend upon the fulfilment of
certain seemingly impossible 'taikinis', or signs. The dreamer's
troubles will be 'at ane end' (ominously ambiguous), only when an
abbot flies:

> He sall ascend as ane horreble grephoun;
> Him meit sall in the air ane scho dragoun;
> Thir terrible monsteris sall togidder thrist
> And in the cludis gett the Antechrist ... (26 ff)

Such bizarre events and such mysteriously symbolic creatures were
the stuff of medieval prophecy, particularly of that type associated with Merlin and Thomas of Ercildoun, and first given currency
by Geoffrey of Monmouth.[26] Shakespeare's Glendower was likewise
reported to speak

> Of the dreamer Merlin and his prophecies,
> And of a dragon and a finless fish,
> A clip-winged griffin and a moulten raven ...
> (<u>1 Henry IV</u>, III.i.143-5)

Although Hotspur termed it 'skimble-skamble stuff', such prophecy
was taken very seriously, not just by ignorant peasants but by
kings and their counsellors, throughout England and Scotland, well
into the seventeenth century. Fortune's words are characteristic
of the genre in their riddling and cryptic tone. What is more, her
prophecy is apocalyptic, ending with a vision of Doomsday:

> And syne thay sall discend with reik and fyre
> And preiche in erth the Antechrystis impyre;
> Be than it salbe neir this warldis end.
> (36-8)

In his flight the abbot meets an elrich company of witches,
magicians and evil spirits. They include Merlin, reputed son of a
devil; 'Mahoun', regarded as pagan god and devil, and thought to
have flown on a winged horse to Jerusalem; and Simon Magus, who in
the New Testament was condemned for his traffic in holy things,
and according to later legend made an attempt to fly to heaven,
aided by devils, but was dashed to the ground at the prayer of St
Peter. Dunbar clearly hints at parallels between the abbot and all
these nefarious beings.

But it is the Antichrist who is the key figure in this poem.
John Jewel, a sixteenth-century Protestant, provides some idea of
the enormous popular interest in Antichrist, and the amazing prophecies and 'fond tales' that circulated about what one Scottish
writer called his 'curst procreacon, werst lyf and most dampnable
end':

> Some say he should be a Jew of the tribe of Dan; some that he
> should be born in Babylon ... some that Mahomet is Antichrist
> ... some that he should be born of a friar and a nun; some
> that he should continue but three years and a half ... and
> then should flee up into heaven, and fall down and break his
> neck.[27]

This attempt at flight was a central part of the Antichrist
legend, and regarded as a blasphemous imitation of Christ:
climbing the Mount of Olives he tries to ascend into heaven, and
is killed, as was Simon Magus. Such beliefs were partly founded
upon Christ's own words concerning the false Christs who would
appear before His second coming and the end of the world (Matthew,
24). Antichrist was a pseudo-Christ, who would appear in human
form at a climactic point in history, leading the forces of evil:

he 'heads a body made up of pagans, unbelievers, false Christians, and all evil ecclesiastics'. Writing of the Last Judgement, a Scottish contemporary of Dunbar says:

> Gret taikin is the antechrist drawis neir,
> Fast flokis his furiouris, graithand his luging;
> His pursiphantis, propheitis, and precheouris can appeir.[28]

The abbot of this dream is clearly one of these 'evil ecclesiastics', and a harbinger of Antichrist, ready to preach his **impyre**, or reign; and in his own attempt to fly he joins Simon Magus as a diabolic type, or pre-figuration, of Antichrist himself.

Yet despite the apocalyptic tone we do not take this prophecy seriously. What hangs upon its fulfilment is hardly momentous – neither the end of the world nor the fate of a great kingdom, merely the bestowal of a benefice. We should recall that serious prophecies were often intended to exert pressure upon a king and his counsellors. This poem is, in part, a circuitous petition. It is a spoof-prophecy, rendered comic by the trivial nature of the subject-matter. It might be compared to the Enigma, or 'prophetical riddle', at the end of Gargantua, on which the Monk commented: 'it is the style of the Prophet Merlin: make upon it as many grave allegories and glosses as you will ... for my part, I can conceive no other meaning in it, but a description of a set at tennis in dark and obscure termes'.[29] At the time of Rabelais, according to M A Screech, there was a taste for such 'amusing enigmas, which seem to be dealing with great matters but which turn out to be merely hidden ways of alluding to trivial, ordinary or obscene things'.[30] The mock-prophecy was closely akin to the mock-prognostication, for which there was also a vogue in the fifteenth and sixteenth centuries, especially in France. The most famous example of the kind was Rabelais' Pantagrueline Prognostication (1533), but it had many precursors. The genre became popular in England, although the earliest surviving example is dated 1544, and in Scotland also in the later sixteenth century there was a market for 'Merry Prognostications'.[31] At the end of the poem the dreamer awakes and rejoices when he learns that an abbot is indeed preparing to fly:

> Full weill I wist to me wald nevir cum thrift
> Quhill that twa monis wer sene up in the lift,
> Or quhill ane abbot flew aboif the mone.

But this ending is highly ambiguous. The presence of several moons in the sky is more commonly a portent of disaster than of 'thrift'. When five moons are reported to have been seen, in King John (IV. ii.182), 'Old men and beldames ... Do prophesy upon it dangerously'. Fortune is an unreliable goddess – in another of Dunbar's poems she is called a whore (K 63). This dream is delusive, and the prophecy cheating. Dunbar's audience would know that whatever the abbot achieved he did not fly above the moon. If the dreamer feels 'confort', he deludes himself and he is still without a benefice. This poem makes fun of the poet himself as well as the abbot.

I have had space to discuss only a few features of these elrich poems, and virtually omitted the most famous of all, <u>Fasternis Evin in Hell</u>. In recent years we have heard much of Dunbar the moralist and writer of 'serious comedy'. Although I would not deny that some of these poems have very serious implications, I think it important to re-assert the comic and popular aspects of Dunbar's genius. Several of the anonymous poems I mentioned earlier end in a convivial way that recalls minstrel poetry: 'Drynk with my guddame quhen ȝe gang by' (<u>Kittok</u>); or 'skink first to me the can' (<u>Crying of Ane Play</u>); or 'gar fill the cop' (<u>Dreme</u>). We know sadly little of how Dunbar's poems reached their first audience, but it is worth recalling Maitland's comment on one usually known as <u>The Amendis to the Telȝouris and Soutaris</u>: 'Quod Dunbar quhone he drank to the Dekynnis for amendis to the bodeis of thair craftis'. Several of the anonymous poems end flippantly, but none can match Dunbar's throw-away ending to <u>Fasternis Evin</u>:

Now trow this, gif ȝe list.

Notes

1   <u>English Literature in the Sixteenth Century</u> (Oxford, 1954), pp 71, 72-3.

2   'Marlowe's <u>Doctor Faustus</u> and the Eldritch Tradition', in <u>The Artist and Society in Shakespeare's England</u> (London, 1982), pp 79-86.

3   Some of these poems are also extant in prints and in the Maitland Folio. As a group they are most easily consulted in <u>The Bannatyne Manuscript</u>, ed W Tod Ritchie, STS (Edinburgh, 1928-34). For bibliographical information, see Denton Fox and William A Ringler, facsimile edition of <u>The Bannatyne Manuscript</u> (London, 1980), nos. 165, 168, 176, 182, 197, 199, 208, 230 and 401. See also <u>Colkelbie Sow and The Talis of the Fyve Bestes</u>, Gregory Kratzmann (ed) (New York, 1983); and Earl Guy, <u>Some Comic and Burlesque Poems in Two Sixteenth-Century Manuscript Anthologies</u> (PhD dissertation, Edinburgh, 1952).

4   'Lakes and Wells: Mediation between the Real World and the Otherworld in Scottish Folklore', in <u>Scottish Language and Literature, Medieval and Renaissance</u>, Dietrich Strauss and Horst Drescher (eds), <u>Scottish Studies</u>, 4 (Frankfurt, 1986), p 526.

5   See Ritchie, <u>Bannatyne Manuscript</u>, iv, 43. There has been copious discussion of the figure <u>adynaton</u> - see articles by H V Canter and G O Rowe in <u>American Journal of Philology</u>, 51 (1930), 32-41, and 86 (1965), 387-96.

6   See further Lilian M C Randall, <u>Images in the Margins of Gothic Manuscripts</u> (Berkeley, 1966); <u>The Land of Cokaygne in Early Middle English Verse and Prose</u>, J A W Bennett and G V Smithers (eds) (2nd edn Oxford, 1968); <u>The Early English Carols</u>, Richard L Greene (ed) (2nd edn Oxford, 1977), nos. 471-4; and the poem beginning 'Herkyn to my tale that I

schall to yow schew', in Reliquiae Antiquae, Thomas Wright and J O Halliwell (eds) (London, 1845), i, 81-6.

7 See The Poems of William Dunbar, James Kinsley (ed) (Oxford, 1979), nos. 42, 13 and 62.

8 English Literature, p 94.

9 The Anatomy of Melancholy (Everyman: London, 1932), I.2.1.2.= vol. i, pp 180ff.

10 Anna Jean Mill, Mediaeval Plays in Scotland (Edinburgh, 1927), p 117.

11 See G R Owst, Literature and Pulpit in Medieval England (2nd ed. Oxford, 1961), p 112; Wife of Bath's Tale (C.T., D 868), ironically applied to friars; Bannatyne Manuscript, ii, 280, Anatomy of Melancholy, i, 188 and 183.

12 Anatomy of Melancholy, i, 187. But see discussion in Aquinas, Summa Theologica, trans. by the Fathers of the English Dominican Province (London, 1922), I.cix. 'The Ordering of the Bad Angels'.

13 The fullest study is by Margaret Jennings, 'Tutivillus: the Literary Career of the Recording Demon', Studies in Philology, 74 (1977), 1-95.

14 See Medieval Comic Tales, trans. Peter Rickard and others (Cambridge 1972), p 19-25; Stith Thompson, Motif Index of Folk Literature, 6 vols (Helsinki, 1955), X. 251.1; Medieval Comic Tales (From a Jestbook of 1526), pp 55-6.

15 'Châtiments infernaux et peur du diable', in Histoire, Mythe et Symboles (Geneva, 1976), pp 129-36.

16 See the useful discussions of both words in OED, also R S R Fitter, Pocket Guide to British Birds (London, 1952), p 73.

17 There are at least three versions of the story in English, as well as in other languages; it was clearly well known in Scotland (see also Crying of ane Play, 14).

18 De Miseria Condicionis Humanae, Robert E Lewis (ed) (Chaucer Library: Athens, U S A, 1978), pp 132-3 (i,23); Summa Theologica, I.cxi.

19 For Scottish legislation against swearing, see J W Baxter, William Dunbar (Edinburgh, 1952), p 111; on medieval attitudes, see Rosemary Woolf, The English Religious Lyric in the Middle Ages (Oxford, 1968), pp 395-400; and Owst, Literature and Pulpit, pp 414ff. and 424-5.

20 Albert B Freidman, The Ballad Revival (Chicago, 1961), p 268.

21 Literature and Pulpit, p 112; The Chronicles of Scotland, trans John Bellenden, R W Chambers and E Batho (eds), STS (Edinburgh, 1938-41), i, 346-8.

22 For parallels, see Stith Thompson, Motif-Index, G 303.3.1.8; G 303.16.8; G 303.16.9; and G 303.17.2.5.

23 History of the Kings of Britain, trans Lewis Thorpe (London, 1966), i.10 Polychronicon, C Babington and J R Lumby (eds) (Rolls series: London, 1865-86), vi.28 = vol vii, 222.

24 See John Wardroper, Jest upon Jest : A Selection from the Jestbooks and Collections of Merry Tales Published from the Reign of Richard III to George III (London, 1970), p 93.

25 See further, David Kunzle, 'World Upside Down: the Iconography of a European Broadsheet Type', in The Reversible World, Barbara Babcock (ed) (Ithaca, 1978), pp 39-94.

26   See R Taylor, The Political Prophecy in England (New York, 1911); and M H Dodds, 'Political Prophecy in the Reign of Henry VIII', Modern Language Review, 11 (1916), 276-84.

27   I owe this quotation to the useful study by R K Emmerson, Antichrist in the Middle Ages (Seattle, 1981), p 8. See also The Sex Werkdayis and Agis in The Asloan Manuscript, ed W A Craigie, STS (Edinburgh, 1923-5), i, 330.

28   See Emmerson, Antichrist, p 20; and Contemplacioun of Synnaris, 713-15, in Devotional Pieces in Verse and Prose, J A W Bennett (ed), STS (Edinburgh, 1955), p 112.

29   Gargantua and Pantagruel, trans Sir Thomas Urquhart (London, 1921) i, 180.

30   Rabelais (London, 1979), p 195

31   Cf. Rabelais, pp 195-200; F P Wilson, 'Some English Mock-Prognostications' in his Shakespearian and Other Studies (London, 1969); an example is mentioned in Robert Gourlaw's will: The Bannatyne Miscellany II, David Laing (ed) (Edinburgh, 1836), p 214; see also M A Bald, 'Vernacular Books imported into Scotland', Scottish Historical Review, 23 (1926), 258.

WILLIAM DUNBAR: GRAND RHÉTORIQUEUR

Joanne S Norman

In the introduction to their book, <u>Poetry of the Stewart Court</u>, Joan Hughes and W S Ramson justify their edition by noting that the compilation and arrangement of poems in the Bannatyne Manuscript represents a more accurate view of Scottish poetry than can be found in the more traditional editions of the works of individual poets, because it demonstrates how Scots poems were created in response to a particular social and cultural context and out of a common understanding of the function of poetry (viii). Since the milieu that provides the social context for the Bannatyne Manu-script is the royal Scottish court, their edition necessarily includes many of William Dunbar's poems and their commentary includes some useful and appropriate insights into Dunbar's work as a court poet. Many of his poems fit very neatly into the categories designated for them by Bannatyne and, when individual poems are viewed as part of a particular genre of verse, they seem more ordinary and less problematic than when they are gathered together and isolated as part of a single author's entire work. In fact, it would seem that Dunbar's verse clearly fulfills the four functions of a court poet outlined by Hughes and Ramson: the craftsman and performer, the public orator, the spiritual advisor, and the social entertainer, each of which has its own style or decorum (119). Yet the Bannatyne collection also highlights two characteristics of Dunbar's work that distinguish him from all his contemporaries: the technical virtuosity displayed within the various genres and the range of his work that encompasses all aspects of the court poet's role.

It is this extreme versatility that has created major problems for the interpretation of Dunbar's work. So diverse is his poetry that almost every study or commentary on him remarks on the con-trasting elements, the 'two voices' of a poet who celebrates the life of the court in golden ceremonial terms and then turns around and describes the same setting with obscene scurrility. Even more difficulty is found in his habit of 'yoking dissimilarities of "hautand" manner with realistic matter' (Ridley 180). This range of tone and style has led to important questions about the intentions of Dunbar as a poet. Is he a serious moralist? Then how are we to understand the satires and comic poems that seem to contradict and even to attack conventional morality? If the comic poems are to be understood as the more normative for the poet, then his moral, philosophical poems may be viewed as platitudinous technical exer-cises in verse where the emphasis is on sound or 'music' at the expense of sense.[1] Even more significantly, Dunbar's skill as a poetic craftsman has led some readers either to distrust his sincerity altogether, to see him as interested only in formal matters at the expense of life or passion; or to look for an ambiguity and ambivalence in all his work that precludes a simple, straightforward response to the poet's fragmented and detached view of reality. Where is the real, the true William Dunbar?

I do not believe that the common experience of many intelligent and sophisticated readers is mistaken. There are difficulties in determining the tone and intention of much of Dunbar's work. But these complexities create part of the richness of his poetry. They arise naturally from the milieu in which he works, from the nature of his audience, and from a common understanding of the function of poetry in that time and place. Without underestimating Dunbar's originality, it is possible to view him in a broader European context that may illuminate some of the peculiarities of his situation and lead to a better understanding of the function and style of his poetry, including the dual nature of his work.

The key to understanding Dunbar as 'makar' lies in his role as a court poet. He was the only one of the important fifteenth-century Scots poets who was directly and solely dependent on the patronage of the court for his livelihood (Wormald 63). This simple fact glosses over a complicated and ambiguous situation that has often been misinterpreted. Ridley, for example, in her discussion of Dunbar as court poet states that Dunbar received a stipend as an eminent poet and officer of the royal household (174), while McCarthy in his description of Dunbar's audience seems to think Dunbar's position at court was similar to that of a juggler or minstrel (140). The deliberate assumption of different roles or personae within Dunbar's poems makes any use of his poetry as a direct reflection of his actual life extremely problematic, and the documentary evidence itself is sometimes quite vague and open to interpretation.[2] Ian Simpson Ross simply states that graduates in arts, like Dunbar, were recruited for general diplomatic and administrative service (32-33), while McDiarmid's review of the chronology of Dunbar's works also emphasises the general, unspecified nature of his 'service'. Green's study of court life in Poets and Princepleasers is probably the most relevant and enlightening examination of the role of the poet at court, particularly as most of his direct sources are from the fifteenth century. According to Green, a noble or royal court, even in the fifteenth century, still had much of the character of a household directly governed by the personality of its head, the lord or king. Green perceives beginning in the fourteenth century a gradual shift in the social status of the poet from professional minstrel to man of letters, one who is a retainer rather than simply an entertainer. This change in position seems marked in Dunbar's case by his rather contemptuous dismissal of minstrels in some of his poems and by Kennedy's taunting association of Dunbar with such a low status in the 'Flyting': 'Tak the a fidill or a floyte, and geste' (507). But while the new status might be more elevated, it was, if anything, more ambiguous. The personal favour of the king or lord determined the actual life of every individual within his circle. Success, even one's basic livelihood, depended on direct access to the king and his inner

circle. Although the promotion of the man of letters resulted from
an increased literacy and a more sophisticated taste on the part of
the court as a whole, the poet did not simply supply a literary
product for the consumption of the lord and his household. Rather,
his ambition was to become part of the court and his literary skill
enabled him to participate in its life. In practical terms, his
verbal skills enabled him to perform a number of general services
for his lord for which he was rewarded with certain privileges and
variable income. According to Green, 'If the old minstrel literature was a literature of performance, the new courtly verse might
be characterised as a literature of participation' (111). Seldom
was a poet actually paid directly for purely literary work. He
might carry out an occasional specific commission or make a formal
presentation copy of some work to his patron, but generally literature was a spare-time occupation that helped to create the ambience
of the court, and that reinforced the values of the courtly
audience. For the individual, it was simply one way of making
himself and his talents known to his patron and ensuring himself a
place in the sunshine of royal favour. Dunbar's many requests for
support, his so-called 'begging' poems, all stress his direct
personal dependency on the king, and his sense of frustration and
insecurity, but they refer only to his services in general, not
just or even predominantly to his poetry.

These particular conditions affected the kind of poetry written
by the new poets of the fifteenth century. One of its most striking
characteristics is the topicality of the verse, much of it written
within very specific circumstances and governed by a decorum that
is suitable to a particular context. As the princes became more
literate and more sophisticated in their tastes, so their demands
or commissions for poems might become more specific with the result
that the poet had perhaps less freedom of choice of topic and style
or certainly had more restrictions placed on his writing. At the
very least, the interest and tastes of the prince would have to be
given a prominent place in the poetry of a 'princepleaser'. The
ceremonial poems of Dunbar, 'The Thrissill and the Rois', 'To Aberdeen', 'The Goldyn Targe', 'The Ballade of Lord Bernard Stewart',
are all examples of poetry written for special occasions. Other
poems, like 'The Dance in the Quenis Chamber', refer to specific
court pastimes. All of Dunbar's secular poems demonstrate how
closely tied his writing was to the circumstances of the court and
the current interests of an intelligent, energetic and ambitious
king by including references to cannon, the king's mistresses, a
court tournament or dance, or to court personalities like John
Damian or even the king's messenger. These topical allusions, often
obscure to a modern audience, are one symptom of how closely Dunbar
wished to be identified with the court and its pastimes; how he
tried to reflect the camaraderie of the court without going beyond
the line of what was acceptable to his courtly audience.

However, Dunbar's work as a whole surely goes beyond simple
flattery and toadying to James IV and his court. What about the
satire, the grotesque portraits of that king and court? What about
his serious moral reflections? What about the irony implicit in
those ceremonial poems? Just as the real life of a court poet
entailed a much more complicated existence than merely singing for

his supper, so the poetry that he produced reflected various functions of poetry, all, however, conditioned or directed by the court
milieu in which the poet worked. Dunbar seems to stand alone as a
court poet in Scotland; but just as the court of James IV imitated
the style of the greater European courts, so Dunbar's experience
may be considered analogous to that of the poets who served these
other courts.

The hallmark of the most significant and influential group of
continental poets of the fifteenth century was a preoccupation with
style and form, a quality that is also characteristic of Dunbar.
These men were known as the 'grands rhétoriqueurs' because of their
specific views of the nature and role of poetry that dominated
poetic practice in the great courts of France and Burgundy. It was
in their work that Dunbar could find the continuation and extension
of the concept of poetry as rhetoric. Although the general influence of French culture on Scotland through the Auld Alliance is
easily recognised (Donaldson; Watson 29-30), specific instances of
literary imitation are more difficult to come by. Unlike Chaucer,
and other English and Scots poets, the French poets are not singled
out by Dunbar for special praise or recognition. Neverthless,
there are enough actual quotations or references to demonstrate
that specific poems of the 'grands rhétoriqueurs' were known in
Scotland,[3] and it seems highly unlikely that Dunbar in his various
travels on the continent would not have become quite familiar with
at least some of their works. Janet M Smith in her survey The
French Background of Middle Scots Literature states that the grands
rhétoriqueurs provided up-to-date models for Dunbar's court poetry,
that is, his ceremonial verse and begging poems, but then withdraws
from this position to say that Dunbar preferred simpler forms and
was not influenced by the grands rhétoriqueurs because his poetry
was more 'real' and less 'serious'(62-4; 164-5). She is the only
critic to consider the possibility of a direct influence of these
contemporary poets on Dunbar, but her conclusions are certainly
ambivalent.

Nevertheless, the general parallels to be found in the careers
and work of the rhétoriqueurs to that of Dunbar are pervasive and
convincing. As in the case of Dunbar's imitation of Chaucer, the
influence is to be found more in a general attitude of style rather
than in specific quotations from individual texts. It is even
possible that similar circumstances and a similar perception of
poetry produced a common style without direct borrowing. Let us
consider the circumstances first. The grands rhétoriqueurs were
the professional court poets who served in the courts of France
and Burgundy during the fifteenth century. Broadly speaking, they
may be divided into two main groups: an early generation that
worked primarily in the Burgundian courts, first under Duke Philip
the Good and Duke Charles the Bold and then under Marguerite of
Austria. The second group was attached chiefly to the royal court
of France under Charles VII, Anne of Brittany, Louis XII and
Francis I (Zumthor, Masque 11-12; 21; Guy 14-20). Their influence
and poetic practices continued throughout Europe, especially in
France, Burgundy and the Low Countries, over three generations,
from 1440 to 1530, until they were gradually replaced by the new
ideas of the Pléiade.

All these poets shared both a common historic situation and a common poetic. All were highly educated men, usually university trained, and many were clerics. The central fact in their lives was their position at a court. The career of Jean Molinet (1460-1505) may be taken as typical. After completing his studies at Paris, he searched years for a patron, first serving the Duke of Savoy and then moving to the court of Burgundy where he became the official chronicler in 1475. He was rewarded with various ecclesiastical appointments for his service, but continued to live at court, pursuing his work as historiographer (Zumthor,'Hi(story)' 241). The similarities to Dunbar's contemporary career, particularly the travelling and years in obscurity after taking his degree, are obvious. The rhétoriqueurs are defined by their position of subordination, economic and social, within a rigidly defined hierarchy. Although they, like Dunbar, perform a variety of functions at court, their livelihood depends directly upon the grace and favour of the prince or duke (Zumthor, Masque 43-4). Much of their poetry reflects the uncertainty and dependency of their position. They write for 'material gains, board and lodging, a set of clothes for the new season, a New Year's gift' (Zumthor, Masque 45), and they are constantly beset by rivals in their ongoing quest for preferment. Dunbar aptly describes their predicament as well as his own in this address to the king:

> Schir, ye have mony servitouris
> And officiaris of dyvers curis:
>   ...
> And thocht that I amang the laif
> Unworthy be ane place to have
> Or in thair nummer to be tald,
> Als lang in mynd my work sall hald,
> Als haill in everie circumstance,
> In forme, in mater and substance
> But wering or consumptioun,
> Roust, canker or corruptioun,
> As ony of their werkis all –
> Suppois that my rewarde be small.[4]
>   [To the King] 44. 1-2; 25-34

It is only to be expected that their poetry would reflect this position. Much of their verse develops a highly ornate, rhetorical idiom that can be used to accompany the increasingly elaborate public displays that had become an integral part of the social and political life of the fifteenth century.[5] The intensely self-conscious, decorative and official quality of the poetry of the grands rhétoriqueurs offended the more romantic sensibilities of the modern critics of their work, who demanded a more personal, more sincere, even more intellectually challenging content in a poem. The most comprehensive study of the rhétoriqueurs sums up their achievement in these words:

> La liberté et la sincerité font défaut aux pièces politiques
> des rhétoriqueurs; leurs prédications et leurs satires morales
> s'enferment sans profit dans le lieu commun; ils travestissen⁺

la réligion, ignorent ou dédaignent la nature, et enlèvent a
l'amour toute verité, toute émotion ... pour finir, que ce qui
a manqué, presque toujours à cette école, ce ne sont pas
seulement 'les idées poétiques' mais, poétiques ou non et sans
épithètes, 'les idées' (Guy 71).

No wonder Janet Smith hesitated to align one of Scotland's
greatest, most original poets with such company. Yet in Guy's
comprehensive indictment one can find echoes of evaluations that
have been passed on Dunbar: Fox's comment that he is a poet of
'surfaces', C S Lewis's dismissal of a serious intent in the
'Tretis of the Tua Mariit Wemen and the Wedo' by describing it as a
linguistic joke, a 'romp' that may not be to everyone's taste (94),
or Speirs's conclusion about 'The Golden Targe':

> ... it remains a monument to the fact that a poem cannot be
> made out of an interest purely in language and the manipu-
> lation and arrangement of it: and when the interest is in
> 'poetic' language artificially enriched by overlavish borrow-
> ing from alien sources, the resulting kind of richness may
> easily be fatal to life (194).

Denton Fox even extends this pervasive interest in language as
ornamentation to all Scots poets of the period, not just Dunbar,
although he must remain the major example of this tendency (169).
  But more recent re-evaluations of the work of the grands rhétoriqueurs by critics such as Zumthor, who are primarily interested
in the interaction between text and audience, have discovered new
insights into this apparently sterile poetry with its emphasis on
style rather than content. According to Zumthor, a poet's court
position determines his poetics by making him a player of the Court
Game. He must promote a surface harmony in his environment by using
traditional language and at the same time create an imaginary,
ideal reality out of historical/political events ('Hi(story)' 243).
Huizinga agrees with this perception, although he is less sympathetic to its results. According to him, the poets of the late
Middle Ages attempted to elevate the ordinary social and political
realities of life by transferring to them symbols appropriate to a
higher, sacred level. The audience responded by recognising themselves and their values transformed and validated by a brilliant
form (274-75). Hence the widespread use of allegory to conceal/
reveal a political or social situation, such as Dunbar exploits in
'The Thrissill and the Rois'. Identification with the court meant
for the rhétoriqueurs not only that the conditions of its life,
its ceremonies, recreation and rituals provided the occasions of
poetry, as both Reiss and Hughes-Ramson have indicated for Dunbar's
work (Reiss 47-58; Hughes-Ramson ix), but that they have to adopt
the point of view of the court, an 'official' view of reality that
stresses convention, traditional values and hierarchical structures. This involves the poet in a complicity with his audience, a
shared acceptance of external world and its outward show of order
and coherence. Similarly, Hay sees as a central theme in Dunbar's
work an appeal to a hierarchical source of order.
  However this outward compliance to an established 'norm' could

only be maintained by means of a delicate balancing act. For the truth of the matter was that this ideal world of truth, order, and beauty was largely imaginary. Zumthor outlines at length the actual historic conditions that precluded any idea of the court as 'hevin's glory' which may be summed up rather arbitrarily as a world that was pre-Reformation and post-feudal, rocked by economic and social upheavals such as war, famine, and pestilence. Perhaps the contradictions between what man desires and reality were never so marked as in this time of determined gilding over of social and political reality. Although Scotland had reached a time of comparative peace and stability, she was not immune to the outside pressures of the rest of the world and the fragility of her golden age was demonstrated only too well at Flodden. The crown continually attempted to consolidate the power in the monarchy with varying success, and it is significant that no king from James I to James V lived beyond middle age and all died violently (Watson 29). The reaction of the rhétoriqueurs to these pressures of court life and its essential artificiality was a progressive alienation that led them to subvert language and traditional modes of thought by pushing them to extremes, to expose ironically their inherent contradictions and absurdities by going beyond their natural limits:

> Ils n'innovaient guère. Ils allaient jusqu'au bout des tendances latentes depuis des siècles, sporadiquement manifestés chez quelques-uns de leurs lointain devanciers. Incapables de démonter le moteur, ni même, peut-être d'en comprendre le mécanisme, ils l'emballaient. (Zumthor, Masque 55)

Two positions became possible for the writer in a world of transitions and contradictions. He could accept the surface of his world and express his acceptance by glorifying it and and by using the traditional myths or symbols to invoke an ideal world of coherence and unity. This kind of poetry Zumthor calls 'la fete' (Masque 244). Or the poet could underline the contradictions of his existence by inverting traditional norms and values and emphasising the irrational and the ambiguity of court and even human life. Zumthor calls this 'le monde à l'envers' or 'le carnaval' (Masque 252-4). Some grands rhétoriqueurs opted for one or the other, but more, like Dunbar, seemed to move between the two poles of poetic expression. Here surely are his two 'voices', the one devoted to 'panegyric' and the other to 'pasquinade' (Leyerle 316). This is the experience that informs both the exalted description of the natural order:

> The purpour sone, with tendir bemys reid
> In orient bricht as angell did appeir
> Throw goldin skyis putting up his heid,
> Quhois gilt tressis schone so wondir cleir
> That all the world tuke confort, fer and neir,
> To luke upone his fresche and blisfull face
> Doing all sable fro the hevynnis chace.
>   ('Thrissill and Rose' 50. 50-56)

and the bitter resignation of this:

> This waverand warldis wretchidness,
> The failyeand and frutless bissines
> The mispent tyme, the service vane,
> For to considder is ane pane.
> ([To the King] 39. 1-4)

The increasingly elaborate and extravagant spectacles created within the courts of Europe are well known and amply documented. Their fundamental purpose was to affirm the power and glory of the ruling class, to justify the maintenance of existing hierarchies and values, and promote a collective unity among the participants in these festivals. Therefore, many of the spectacles included allegorical figures or representations of the prince, court, counsellors and adversaries. The rhétoriqueurs provided texts for these communal rituals that emphasised their universality in the face of a shifting political and economic universe.[6] The court acted out its view of itself as the centre of the universe in which the prince played his own role as the ground of its being. The court became a theatre and life became art. One of the most common forms of this theatre was that of the outmoded chivalry which had ceased to be a social reality but which retained its imaginative hold on the minds of the court. If we turn to the Scottish court for an example, we see the famous tournament of 1507, the 'Turnament of the Black Knight and the Black Lady,' in which James IV disguised as the Black Knight was, of course, able to win all the honours. The later 'magical' disappearance of the Black Lady was stagemanaged by Andrew Forman, Bishop of Moray, who apparently found time among his ecclesiastical duties and his role as one of the chief counsellors of the king to act as theatrical producer. No one seemed to find this at all incongruous. Dunbar, following in the footsteps of the grands rhétoriqueurs, provides a poem on the occasion, 'Ane Blak Moir', that both commemorates the ostensible purpose of the tournament and subverts the convention at the same time by using the language of praise to underline the grotesqueness of the 'lady' and to mock the conventions of chivalry and courtly love. As long as both poet and audience were aware of the 'game,' then all was well. The application of the chivalric code to 'real' life, as James IV seems to have done in his fatal invasion of England, could be disastrous. As if to draw attention to the ironic contrast between the ideal courtly world and its actuality, most of Dunbar's 'occasional' poems or his formal ceremonial verse tend to have a strong element of theatricality and deliberate artificiality about them. In this they are a faithful reflection of court life and manners and observe the decorum appropriate to the function of such poetry. Dunbar, like his brother poets of France and Burgundy, is not rejecting the social order as much as he is questioning the one-dimensional nature of its view of human life (Zumthor, 'Hi(story)' 262).

Despite the charges of superficiality that have been made by modern critics, the grands rhétoriqueurs did have a highly developed poetic theory that adapted the tradition of the moral, didactic purpose of art to different social circumstances. This new concept, which gave these poets their collective name, was the identification of poetry with rhetoric in which the poet as orator attempts to persuade his audience to follow virtue and eschew vice. Like the orator, the poet is constrained by a specific time and place and must give primary consideration to the needs of his audience, but he is also free to choose the appropriate topic and mode. Ultimately he moves from the specific to the universal (Gordon 33). This 'second rhetoric', as it was called in the handbooks of poetic theory, saw poetry as primarily a vehicle of persuasion that used structure and language to move the listener. The poet 'seeks to manipulate the passions of his listeners, their feelings and the possibility of directing them, may be of more interest to him than his own' (Gordon 378). The ethical direction of this persuasion, together with the set forms and the use of allegory to express reality, were all part of medieval poetic tradition inherited by the grands rhétoriqueurs.[7] The poet/orator does not seek the personal and spontaneous expression of his own thoughts and feelings, but strives to rediscover universal truths (Guy 9). As orator, the poet is chiefly concerned with praising that which is good and castigating that which is evil. Both praise and blame have their particular structures, styles and ornament-ation (Gordon, Ronsard 42-53). The ornamentation was the special concern of the poetic treatises that proliferated throughout the fourteenth and fifteenth centuries following Eustache Deschamps' L'Art de dictier (1392) and culminating in the definitive work by Pierre Fabri, Le Grand et Vray Art de pleine rhétorique (1521). All develop the idea of poetry as a second rhetoric in which the only real distinguishing mark of poetry from prose is versification. All the poetry manuals are basic, practical handbooks of form and metrics. From Deschamps through to Fabri the grands rhétoriqueurs define poetry as verbal music (Patterson 132-3), and their own practice suggests that sound is at least as important as sense. The ultimate goal is not to invent original ideas, but to elevate language in order to express unchanging truth: truths 'to advantage dressed; What oft was thought but ne'er so well expressed.' Nor are the poetic forms or modes original. Instead, the grands rhétori-queurs are content to reproduce inherited forms with a progressive elaboration that ultimately destroyed the convention or at least distorted it beyond recognition (Zumthor, 'Hi(story)' 251).

How much of this definition of the poetics typical of the grands rhétoriqueurs can be applied to their Scottish contemporary, William Dunbar? I would suggest almost the whole of it. Unfor-tunately, there are no treatises on poetics, like Fabri's, in fifteenth-century Scotland (Jamieson 28). One can only follow Jamieson's advice and infer theory from practice. First of all, Dunbar's university education would have made him knowledgeable about rhetoric as a matter of course (Ross 28). Robert Kindrick in his paper 'Henryson and the Rhetoricians: The Ars Praedicandi', gives a comprehensive review of the application of traditional rhetorical practices in the work of Dunbar's contemporary. It seems safe to assume a common understanding of traditional rhetorical theory and practice among the educated Scots. Dunbar himself clearly associates poetry with rhetoric; first, in his famous

reference to poets in 'The Golden Targe' and again in the 'Flyting': 'Thow callis the rethory with thy goldin lippis' (97). And,
finally, his role of court poet inevitably drew towards the praise/
blame poles of rhetorical practice as his panegyrics and satires
bear witness.

But there are even closer connections. The three chief subjects
of grand rhetoriqueur poetry are love, especially courtly love,
historical and political topics, and religious and moral topics. As
almost any compilation of Dunbar's work, from Bannatyne to Kinsley,
demonstrates, these categories apply to Dunbar. If one looks at a
list of works by George Chastellain, a founding member of the grand
rhétoriqueur school, the similarities of topic and genre are striking. We have a meditation on death, a lament, a debate on love, a
moral treatise directed to court life, a hymn of praise to the
Virgin, and an occasional poem celebrating the entrée of King
Louis. Jean Molinet in his treatise, L'Art de rhétorique vulgaire
(1493) lists a number of genres and fixed forms that Dunbar also
uses, including the complainte amoureuse, rondeau, and ballade. An
example of all the major genres used by the rhétoriqueurs can be
found in Dunbar's work: oratio or moral instruction, debate or
dialogue, pastoral, complaint or lament, blason, and testament. The
last genre may be considered as a more specific instance of how
Dunbar's poetry comes close to that of the grands rhétoriqueurs.
Although the testament form originated in the thirteenth century,
it flourished most strongly in the fifteenth. The earlier, more
personal testaments that preceded Villon have little in common with
'The Testament of Mr Andro Kennedy' beyond a general similarity of
form. Nor do Villon's poems have much more in common with Dunbar's
poem. However, the satiric testaments of the fifteenth century,
created by the grands rhétoriqueurs, and the literary puns, are far
closer in tone, purpose, and form to Dunbar's 'Testament'. They
include a fictional narrative, a literary persona who, speaking in
the first person and using parodies of legal formulas, invokes
death and designates comic benefices. One very famous analogy is
'Le Testament de Tastevin, Roi des Pions' (1488), but Jean
Molinet's Testament de la guerre is also very close to Dunbar's
poem with its attacks on various 'estates' or social groups.

Even more significant than common genres is the exploitation by
both the grands rhétoriqueurs and Dunbar of complex metrical forms
and elaborate, Latinate language. For the grands rhétoriqueurs this
emphasis on sound may stem from the association of poetry with
music. Northrop Frye in turn has identified Dunbar as one of the
most 'musical' of poets, by which he means, not that the poetry has
smooth, harmonious rhythm, but that words are arranged in such a
way as to create their own aural patterns (257 and 279). There is
not a single poem of Dunbar's that does not exhibit such a pattern,
created through alliteration, internal rhyme, repetition of sounds,
puns, and other forms of syllabic manipulation. Each reader probably has his own favourite in this area, but perhaps C S Lewis's
appreciation of the Nativity lyric, 'Rorate celi desuper', may
stand as representative (95-96). It is important to recognise,
however, that all these sound effects underline and reinforce the
meaning and tone of the poem: 'the sound is an echo of the sense'.
Wilhelm Nicolaisen's paper, 'Line and Sentence in Dunbar's Poetry',

provides detailed analyses to disprove the notion that Dunbar's metrical skill is mere exhibition; it is rather the deliberate matching of syntax, grammar and metre to convey the meaning of a poem with clarity and precision. Moving in one direction, the poet's language is used to heighten and elevate a particular experience in time into one of universal significance and permanence. This style has been defined by Lois Ebin as a 'transforming of event into artifact', a concept that she develops through an analogy of Dunbar's aureate style to the technique of enamelling ('Occasional Poet' 292-5). However, as she goes on to demonstrate, the stylistic experimentation can also lead to the subversion of accepted forms and genres by using language to set up and then deflate the expectations aroused by a particular genre. Thus we have the courtly pastourelle undermined by language, 'In Secreit Place this Hyndir Nycht', or the tour de force of collapsing genres in the 'Tretis of the Tua Mariit Wemen and the Wedo' where courtly and anti-courtly codes are set up in a dizzying dialectic. Such a duality of perspective can also be found in 'duplication' of discourse among the rhétoriqueurs in which multiple meanings are created through the dissociation of traditional forms through hyperbole and systematic redundance, the 'racing of the (poetic) engine' (Zumthor, Masque 54). The accumulation of specific detail paradoxically becomes more abstract and 'unreal', as in the descriptions of the women's husbands or the Wedo's suitors. The movement of poetic discourse then that has been termed 'aureation' turns out to be circular. The poet sets out to transform everyday reality into an ideal and ends by discovering both the Protean nature of language itself and the ambiguous relationship between life and art.

And where does this place the poet in his role as mediator between the two? Certainly he becomes more self-conscious as a 'makar' and his voice becomes more intrusive in his poems, drawing his audience's attention both to himself and to the way he is writing. The character of Dunbar as revealed/concealed in his poems is one of the most crucial and perennially challenging problems in interpreting his poetry. For this vivid personality is not, as Blanchot has indicated in a comparison to Villon, the extension of an individual but the representative voice of a function or culture. According to Kratzmann, the creation of the 'I' persona and authorial presence may be the most important technique that the Scots poets learned from Chaucer the court poet (27). Derek Brewer in analysing Chaucer's use of persona sees it as a means of unifying experience, of bridging the gap between objective and subjective worlds. Again, the court environment shared by Chaucer, the grands rhétoriqueurs, and Dunbar may be the primary influence in donning a mask for public performance. Yet neither the grands rhétoriqueurs nor Dunbar seems to speak with the same ease and authority as Chaucer. The distinction between mask and man is often blurred, and perhaps role-playing would be a more accurate term. In petitionary poems, for example, Dunbar and the rhétoriqueurs simultaneously flatter and mock the patron, biting the hand that feeds them. Dunbar's attack on the false courtiers ends with a tongue-in-cheek picture of himself as a scourge of God, but one that could be bought off with a sufficient reward ('Schir, ye have

mony servitouris' 69–88). He castigates the vice and folly of the
court only to reveal his own willing complicity with that same
corruption. It is as if the poet in playing various roles before
and within the court exposes the ambiguities inherent in that
experience.

The ambiguities have a moral dimension, as the begging poem
example implies. The poet as rhétoriqueur is committed to the
traditional idea of the moral purpose of poetry, but he carries out
his didactic intention not through reasoned analysis but through
eloquent persuasion (Zumthor, 'Hi(story)' 245–6) working through
vivid images that can be apprehended and experienced. His success
depends on his ability to affect his audience and this in turn
requires the persuader to identify with those he wishes to persuade. In accepting the basic ideology of the court, he proceeds to
create in words an illusory world of beauty and order, 'une fiction
de bonheur', that shows (Zumthor's 'demonstration') what ought to
be and which the prince and court are to enact. So the entry of the
Queen in Aberdeen is recreated by Dunbar in extravagant terms that
associate the royal presence with the Annunciation and the Ador-
ation of the Magi. But if Dunbar uses epideictic forms to express
'la fête' of court public life, he also employs the negative form
of praising that which does not deserve praise[8] in order to criti-
cise at least implicitly the failure of that same world to fulfil
its ideal. And so we have 'The Dregy', 'The Testament', and other
comic poems of court life that describe 'le monde à l'envers'. Both
worlds are delineated by language that constantly goes beyond the
limits of the fixed codes of a particular discourse. Sometimes it
is a question of introducing text into a context that contradicts
its original meaning, as in the parodies; sometimes it is a case of
the contrast and juxtaposition of dissimilar units of content or
stereotyped expression, such as in the 'Tretis' or, less obviously
comic, but still ironic, the conventions of 'The Golden Targe'. All
of these techniques are part of the grand rhétoriqueur poetic.

For, like the grands rhétoriqueurs, Dunbar existed in a fragmented world in which he must either invent at least the appearance
of order and coherence or recognise and express its fundamental
contradictions. Like them, he manipulated language and traditional
forms to express his double vision. It is this ironic perspective
cultivated by his role as court poet that marks Dunbar as one of
the company of the grands rhétoriqueurs. The modern reader who
responds so immediately and strongly to Dunbar's poetry may be
hearing in the voice of the medieval makar the note of irony that
resonates with an acceptance – even a celebration – of the ambiguities of human existence only too familiar to us hundreds of
years later.

Notes

1   See Fox's comment that meaning in Dunbar's poetry is 'musical', not 'philosphical or discursive' (186). McDiarmid describes 'Ane Ballat of Our Lady" as 'exhibitionistic' intended for an audience that admires verbal acrobatics (135), while McCarthy views the same poem almost as parody (Note 23).

2   See Matthew P McDiarmid and Ian Simpson Ross for the most recent review of the chronology of Dunbar's life and the documentary evidence. The standard biography is J W Baxter, William Dunbar: A Biographical Study.

3   Bawcutt (15) notes a parallel invective in Guillaume Crétin to one in 'The Flyting'; Smith (62) sees a model for 'The Golden Targe' in Georges Chastellain's Epistre au bon duc Philippe de Bourgogne and Kratzmann (196) sees features in Lindsay's Satyre of the thrie Estaitis that are borrowed from Gringore's Jeu du Prince des Sotz.

4   All quotations from Dunbar's poetry are taken from James Kinsley (ed), The Poems of William Dunbar.

5   One of the most detailed analyses of the political and social objectives behind such feasts is the study of the 'Banquet de Faisan (1454)' at the court of Burgundy by Agathe Lafortune-Martel. Green (178) and Zumthor, Masque 23-36 note the same phenomenon in more general terms.

6   Green notes a comparable development in the treatment of rhetoric and poetry in Stephen Hawes's Pastime of Pleasure that also develops the public, rhetorical function of court verse.

7   Yates 54-5. The Ad Herennium, ascribed to Cicero, emphasises the ethical role of the orator. Medieval interpretation of this authoritative text gave it a Christian moral dimension (Gordon, Ronsard 31-3).

8   See Reiss's comments on the 'Dregy' as an example of negative praise (67).

References

Baxter, John W, William Dunbar (Freeport, N.W., 1952) Books for Libraries, 1971

Blanchot, Jean-Jacques, 'William Dunbar and François Villon: The Literary Personae'. Bards and Makars, A J Aitken, M P McDiarmid, D S Thomson (eds) (Glasgow: Glasgow UP, 1977)

Brewer, Derek, 'Deconstruction of Chaucer'. Paper delivered at the New Chaucer Society Conference, York 1984

Donaldson, Gordon, The Auld Alliance: The Franco-Scottish Connection. Saltire Pamphlets 6. Edinburgh: Saltire Society and L'Institut Français d'Ecosse, 1985

Dunbar, William, Poems, James Kinsley (ed) (Oxford: Clarendon, 1979)

Ebin, Lois, 'Dunbar's Fresch Anamalit Termes Celicall' and the Art of the Occasional Poet', Chaucer Review 17 (1983), 292-9

Fox, Denton, 'The Scottish Chaucerians', Chaucer and Chaucerians,
D S Brewer (ed) (Alabama: U of Alabama, 1966)

Frye, Northrop, Anatomy of Criticism (Princeton, NJ: Princeton
UP, 1957)

Gordon, Alex L, 'The Ascendancy of Rhetoric and the Struggle
for Poetic in Sixteenth-century France.' Renaissance Eloquence:
Studies in the Theory and Practice of Renaissance Rhetoric
(Berkeley: U of California, 1983)

————, Alex L, Ronsard et la rhétorique (Geneva: Droz 1970)

Guy, Henri, Histoire de la poésie française au XVe siecle: L'ecole
des rhetoriqueurs, I (Paris: Champion, 1968)

Green, Richard Firth, Poets and Princepleasers (Toronto: U of
Toronto, 1980)

Hay, Brian S, 'William Dunbar's Flying Abbot: Apocalypse Made to
Measure', Studies in Scottish Literature 11 (1974), 217-25

Hughes, Joan and W S Ramson, Poetry of the Stewart Court (Canberra:
Australian National UP, 1982)

Huizinga, J, The Waning of the Middle Ages, trans F Hopman (New
York: Anchor, 1954)

Jamieson, Ian, 'Some Attitudes to Poetry in Late Fifteenth-Century
Scotland', Studies in Scottish Literature 15 (1980), 28-42

Kindrick, R L, 'Henryson and the Rhetoricians: The Ars Praedicandi'
Scottish Language and Literature, Mediaeval and Renaissance,
Dietrich Strauss and Horst W Drescher (eds) (Frankfurt am Main:
Peter Lang, 1986)

Kratzmann, Gregory, Anglo-Scottish Literary Relations 1430-1550
(Cambridge: Cambridge UP, 1980)

Lafortune-Martel, Agathe, Fête noble en Bourgogne au XVe siecle
(Montreal: Bellarmin, 1983)

Lewis, C S, English Literature in the Sixteenth Century excluding
Drama (Oxford: Clarendon, 1954)

Leyerle, John, 'The Two Voices of William Dunbar', University of
Toronto Quarterly 31 (1961-2), 316-38

McCarthy, Shaun, 'Syne maryit I a Marchand' Dunbar's Mariit Wemen
and their Audience', Studies in Scottish Literature 18 (1983)

McDiarmid, Matthew P, 'The Early William Dunbar and his Poems',
Scottish Historical Review 59 (1980), 126-39

Morgan, Edwin, 'Dunbar and the Language of Poetry', Essays in
Criticism 2 (1952), 138-58

Nicolaisen, Wilhelm F H 'Line and Sentence in Dunbar's Poetry',
Bards and Makars, A J Aitken, M P McDiarmid, D S Thomson (eds)
(Glasgow: Glasgow UP, 1977)

Patterson, Warner Forrest, Three Centuries of French Poetic Theory,
I (1935) (New York: Russell and Russell, 1966)

Reiss, Edmund, William Dunbar (Boston: Twayne, 1979)

Ridley, Florence H 'Scottish Transformations of Courtly Literature:
William Dunbar and the Court of James IV', The Expansion and
Transformations of Courtly Literature, Nathaniel B Smith and
Joseph T Snow (eds) (Athens, GA: U of Georgia, 1980)

Ross, Ian Simpson, William Dunbar (Leiden: Brill, 1981)

Shuffelton, Frank, 'An Imperial Flower: Dunbar's The Golden Targe
and The Court Life of James IV of Scotland', Studies in Philology
72 (1975), 193-207

Smith, Janet M, The French Background of Middle Scots Literature

(Edinburgh: Oliver & Boyd, 1934)

Speirs, John, The Scots Literary Tradition, 2nd edn (London: Faber & Faber, 1962)

Watson, Roderick, The Literature of Scotland (London: Macmillan, 1984)

Wormald, Jenny, Court, Kirk and Community: Scotland 1470-1625 (Toronto: U of Toronto, 1981)

Yates, Frances A, The Art of Memory (London: Routledge & Kegan Paul, 1966)

Zumthor, Paul, 'From Hi(story) to Poem, or the Paths of Pun: The Grands Rhétoriqueurs of Fifteenth-Century France', New Literary History 10 (1979), 231-63

----, Le masque et la lumière (Paris: Du Seuil, 1978)

Chapter 15

WILLIAM DUNBAR: THE ELUSIVE SUBJECT

Antony J Hasler

> ... he disturbs us by a startling indifference to theme
> in poetry; we are uneasy as we watch him turn from the
> Rabelaisian endearments of 'In secreit place' to a
> religious Nativitie or Resurrection ...[1]

The discomfort here voiced by Edwin Morgan has long been something
of a leitmotiv both in Dunbar criticism and in discussion of other
poetry of the later Middle Ages; indeed, it is already implied in
Arnold's claim that Chaucer's work was wanting in 'high and excellent seriousness'. In Dunbar's case, it would seem, suspicion and
distrust are aroused by the spectacle of an absolute technical
assurance applied to any and every genre and topic, whilst remaining obstinately impervious to critical demands for an accompanying
sense of commitment. At stake here are not solely ideas such as
'sincerity' and 'seriousness', but the broader conceptions of
poetic production, and indeed the human subject itself, which
provide the context for such a critical vocabulary. To attempts to
produce the Dunbar canon as a coherent and consistent authorial
project, to be authenticated by appeal to a transcendant ego
('Dunbar') outside the text, the poet's promiscuous dissipation of
identity in generic difference, his switches from aureate diction
celebrating the Virgin to a surprising range of synonyms for the
female or male genitals, present a scandal.[2] Given this state of
affairs, it is hardly surprising that much criticism of Dunbar has
at bottom been an endeavour to recuperate the contradictions and
discontinuities perceived in the poetry. At one extreme, his oeuvre
has been read as the self-consistent autobiography of a unitary
post-Romantic subject, 'a spiritual order which would not be materially affected by any merely historical evidence that may come to
hand'.[3] At the other, we find the mirror-image of such a view; in
accordance with the lead given in medieval studies by D W Robertson
Jnr, and Bernard Huppé, the poetry comes to centre, not on any form
of self-expression, but on the religious faith which is the basis
of a curiously homogeneous 'medieval culture'.[4]
  The critical approach of these latter-day exegetes is in any
case an extreme manifestation of a far larger grouping of attitudes to the problematics of personality in the literature of the
later Middle Ages, whose common ground serves as the starting point
for a number of theoretically different paths. This basis is usefully summed up in H R Jauss's assertion that the medieval poet
wrote 'in order to praise and extend his object, not to express

himself'.[5] Indeed, we are by now used to such depictions of a poetic focused on given themes or ideals, rather than on the projection of individual personality.[6] This emphasis on the priority of rhetorical demand can in fact lead to diametrically opposed views. On the one hand, to claim that the 'I' in a given poem achieves a purely typical status can have the effect of foreclosing on the issue of subjectivity in medieval poetry, and can clear the way for totalising theories of a distinctly authoritarian kind.[7] On the other, however, to perceive of the 'I' as above all a rhetorical figure, a troping pronoun mediating text to audience but retaining in the process an essential multiplicity and openness, has a very different effect; its functions then change from moment to moment to preserve freedom of access to a text which becomes a site of debate for audiences or readers.[8] It is in analyses of the latter kind that the value of 'play', that highly popular term for commentators on medieval culture, comes into its own as a means of describing both the intertextual and thematic mobility of the text and the social functions for which many courtly poems of the later Middle Ages seem to have been intended.[9]

The question of subjection to rhetorical demand, however, already evokes the semantic range of the term 'subject' in a way which takes it beyond the purely grammatical. It is ultimately impossible to disengage the grammatical subject from wider consideration of the human subject, who is not the source of meaning and action that such terms as 'person' or 'self' would imply, but 'a position in a larger structure, a site through which various forces pass',[10] whether linguistic, psychological, institutional or more generally ideological. The poetic 'I', in other words, cannot meaningfully be considered in isolation from the various discourses which at any given historical conjuncture constitute the human subject as such. It may here be noted that the later Middle Ages have for several commentators come to represent a significant historical moment, the backdrop to a 'discovery of the individual'.[11] For others, who approach this matter from the theoretical basis of cultural materialism, it is through an illusion of freedom and autonomy that the deep inner controls of bourgeois ideology are exercised; the drama of the individual's emergence from a sort of grey collectivism is thus given a decidedly negative twist, with Francis Baker assigning a relatively late date to the appearance of 'bourgeois consciousness', 'the price that continues to be exacted for what was done to us in the seventeenth century'.[12] Such work has in many respects proved highly suggestive, but its assumptions about the diachronic development of subjectivity through history entail, I would argue, a degree of naive periodisation, a reduction to a simple linear process of what is in reality a historical field of complex and constantly shifting formations. My intention in the limited space available here is merely to examine the function of the grammatical 'I' in several poems by Dunbar, and to consider some ways in which what normally count as self-images of the poet may point to larger concerns in the area of subjectivity. These problems I consider to be central to any serious study of later medieval poetics.

Many of Dunbar's poems can clearly be seen to participate in discourses of a manifestly public and impersonal kind. The speaking subject in a number of the poems grouped together by Kinsley under the heading 'Moralities'[13] is analogous to the 'didactic speaker' of Stephen Nichols's analysis of troubadour lyric, who 'articulates authoritatively such universals as philosophy, politics, religion or ethics' and can be described as a 'model being-in-the-text' or 'idealised _cogito_'.[14] However, I intend here to examine, not one of the more abstractly homiletic or didactic poems, but <u>The Passioun of Christ</u> (no. 3), whose movement according to accepted devotional and meditative patterns foregrounds a particular cultural construction of subjectivity.[15] It is as well to remember here that, to Dunbar's contemporaries, self-knowledge was frequently equivalent to the recognition of one's own sinful state; this, at least, is how the Delphic injunction to 'Know thyself' largely emerges in the sermons of later medieval preachers,[16] and it is to the producing of such a recognition that Dunbar's poem is dedicated.

In this dream-narrative, the dreamer's first role is that of witness to Christ's torments at the hands of the Jews. In this initial section, we note several instances (11.14-16, 23-24, 30-32) in which the syntax of the poem, describing the brutalities of the torturers, refuses to accommodate the refrain line, 'O mankynd, for the luif of the'. This at once becomes a paradoxical insistence that in sacral history even the actions of Christ's persecutors are an expression of the divine love that has ordered man's redemption, and offers the reader a subject position which necessarily locates him as unregenerate, the refrain serving as a detachable exhortation. The reading subject is thus caught up in contradiction and division. However, the buffeting of Christ then gives way to its structural parallel,[17] a personification allegory in which various moral abstractions assault the 'I' of the poem on all sides and eventually bring about repentance. The subject now becomes a space in which personifications struggle for possession, the reassessment implied in the act of meditation here dramatised as narrative action:

> Methocht Compassioun, vode of feiris,
>   Than straik at me with mony ane stound,
> And soir Contritioun, bathit in teiris,
>   My visage all in watter drownit,
> And Reuth in to my eir ay rounde,
>   For schame, allace! Behald, man, how
>   Beft is with mony ane bludy wound
> Thy blissit salvatour Jesu!
>
>   (11.97-104)

This, however, prepares the way for the final metaphoric shift of the poem, in which the subject is transformed through this conflict into a new kind of allegorical space, the 'hous' which is scripturally the body. Several new personifications appear in this passage, which represents a final integration, the conclusion of the meditative process instituted by the poem, in which the body is prepared for the entry of Christ in the Eucharist:

> Grace become gyd and governour
> To keip the hous in sicker stait
> Ay reddie till our salvatour,
> Quhill that he come, air or lait;
> Repentance ay with cheikis wait
> No pain nor pennence did eschew
> The hous within evir to debait
> Onlie for luif of sweit Jesu.
>   (11.129-36)

In the final stanza, the dreamer awakens, and in a customary topos is pictured writing his poem down 'Richt heir as I have schawin to yow'(1.142).

In this poem, in other words, the subject observing the Passion becomes a series of metamorphoses of allegorical space; the engaged witness is transformed into the stage for a <u>psychomachia</u>, to emerge finally as the house fit for Christ to enter. This is clearly descriptive of what the reader is expected to enact inwardly; and the concurrent addresses to 'mankynd' and Reuth's admonitory 'man', the clear connections between the sufferings of God as man and the spiritual purgation the poem's recipient is expected to undergo, serve to insert this Good Friday poem into the public discourse of religious observance. The 'I' of the poem is thus ultimately a point of intersubjective exchange between the poet, the text's immediate recipient and the community of believers inevitably generalised as 'mankind', articulated around the body of the Passion itself and the risen Christ in the Eucharist. The stability finally generated, of course, is far from absolute. As the recurrent passive constructions indicate, the subject represented in the poem is not unitary, and initiates nothing; it is the site of contending forces, unfixed, in constant process. Man can soon be dragged back to a state of sin, and the progress embodied in the poem must be repeated indefinitely until death.

My second example from Dunbar's work is a personification allegory of a rather different kind. <u>The Goldyn Targe</u> (no. 10) unites this mode with what is clearly a reflexive commentary on Dunbar's own poetic art, but in a way which has led to curiously divided responses. Its readers often seem uncertain whether the poem's chief concern is with its own verbal self-consciousness or with its central allegory of the overthrow of Reason by a feminine appeal to the senses.[18] What I hope to demonstrate here is that the poem establishes connections <u>between</u> language and desire which do not permit of such one-sided readings, and that these are in turn closely bound up with its representation of subjectivity.

A number of studies of the <u>Roman de la Rose</u>, to which Dunbar's poem clearly stands closely allied, have observed the subtle interplay created in that poem between the treatment of the 'I' and that of narrative time.[19] As Evelyn Birge Vitz has stressed, several distinct 'I's are presented: the poem's Narrator comments on the Dreamer who is his younger self, who is in turn distinct from the Lover at the centre of the actual dream.[20] Subjectivity and temporality are thus closely interwoven, their relationship nuanced by the subtle use of the system of tenses available to Old French; and the <u>Roman</u> is in this respect a crucial influence on the

on the representation of narratorial voice in Chaucer's dream
poems.[21] In Dunbar's highly compressed dream allegory, of course,
this complex narrative apparatus does not exist; but we should
note what appears in its place. In 1.3 ('I raise and by a rosere
did me rest') an 'I' rapidly narrates the action it takes
Guillaume de Lorris's dreamer 1610 lines to accomplish. Such
insouciant abbreviation of a major poem already seems to stress
that this 'I' is a poetic device, and in the dream itself it has a
largely typical status, which is very much gender-based – 'man' as
opposed to 'woman' – the allegorical mode emphasising the typi-
cality of the speaker's case. Its initial tone of pleasurable
complicity with its assailants' 'wonder lusty bikkir' (1.144)
clearly indicates perception <u>within</u> the dream, Guillaume's Lover
turned into a voyeur. The narrative voice, however, does look
beyond the immediate temporal environment of the dream on certain
occasions. One of these comes with the particularly self-reflexive
'indescribability'-topos which occurs early in the dream:

> Discrive I wald, bot quho coud wele endyte
> How all the feldis wyth thai lilies quhite
> Depaynt war brycht, quhilk to the hevyn did glete?
> Noucht thou, Omer, als fair as thou coud wryte,
> For all thine ornate stilis so perfyte;
> Nor yit thou, Tullius, quhois lippis suete
> Off rethorike did in to termes flete:
> Your aureate tongis both bene all to lyte
> For to compile that paradise complete.
>
> (11.64–72)

There are other interpolations which also seem to be imposed
from a later state of consciousness. The tense in the lines

> ... I was rycht sudaynly affrayit,
> All throu a luke quhilk I have boucht full dere
>
> (11.134–35)

suggests this, and such comments as

> Quhy was thou blyndit, Resoun? quhi, allace!
> And gert ane hell my paradise appere,
> And mercy seme quhare that I fand no grace
>
> (11.214–15)

also imply a retrospective level of narration. But there is no
developed outer layer of narrative activity – no Narrator, for
instance, looking back with whatever degree of involvement on
youthful folly – to which such lines could finally be referred.
The only narratorial plane which could fulfil such a function is
seen in the 'Discrive I wald' lines cited above, and in the concluding stanzas which explicitly return us to the voice of the
poet who has just finished illuminating his 'matere'. The poem's
treatment of time, in other words, actually renders its narrative
action temporally coterminous with its writing, thus producing a
gesture of spectacularly elaborate literary self-consciousness.

The possiblity that poetic art as much as moral allegory may be
at the poem's centre is underscored by its opening, which gives us
not so much a text uttered by a body as an embodied text, no voice
but rather writing reified. In the opening stanzas, indeed, the
narrator appears less substantial than the 'natural' locus amoenus
described in aureate diction so vivid as to advertise its own
excess, and through an almost systematic use of metaphor. (We may
here recall Hult's point that allegory is a mode which renders the
bounds of the body diffuse and unclear - in the Roman, for instance, the mistress's body pervades the dream landscape, without
being wholly reducible to any one symbol or personification.[22])
However, in Dunbar's dream garden - itself basically continuous
with the waking one - matters are reversed, with artificial objects
depicted through images of nature, including the ship from which
the goddesses disembark:

> I saw approch agayn the orient sky
> A saill als quhite as blossum upon spray
> With merse of gold brycht as the stern of day,
> Quhilk tendit to the land full lustily
> Als falcoune swift desyrous of hir pray...
>   (11.50-54)

A garden 'cultivated' by the flores rhetoricae[23] gives place to
one which reminds us of a (potentially threatening) nature underlying the artifice; the tended 'felde' cedes to the forces of
nature to inaugurate the conflict between reason and desire, and
the stable harmony of metaphor is undermined by the dissociating
impulse of simile. The final defeat of the narrator-figure is
immediately followed by the landscape's collapse into entropy as
Aeolus blows his 'bugill':

> And sudaynly in the space of a luke
> All was hyne went; thare was bot wildernes,
> Thare was no more bot birdis, bank and bruke.
>   (11.232-34)

As the presence of sexual desire in the dream becomes increasingly
disruptive, rhetorical figures drift away from their metaphoric
anchorage in the garden of the poem's beginning. A further ground
of disruption appears with the female personifications who attack
the lover. These embody the various stages of a woman's life as
perceived by the insecure male, and thus represent a departure
from the earlier events of the dream, in which a static masque of
gods and goddesses celebrate May and the coming of spring; the
cyclic and seasonal allegory of the dream is, in effect, thrown
into disarray precisely as the woman becomes a presence in it. To
complicate matters further, the narrator relates the disappointing
progress of his love affair just before Aeolus's interruption
brings us back to the dream landscape and unpeoples it; although
they ostensibly share the same time and space, there are really
two allegories in this dream, one within another. The cumulative
effect of this blurring of fictive planes in the form of narrative
time-scales at all levels, and the shifts between rhetorical

artifice in describing nature and natural simile in portraying human artefacts, is highly disorienting. The allegory's apparent project may be to elaborate on the relations between nature and culture, and their correlates in the human psyche (in this respect, it shares certain concerns with The Parliament of Fowls). Dunbar's poem, however, seems to deconstruct this binary opposition, showing that its two terms inhere in one another and are reversible. The exchanges that occur in frame and dream leave us uncertain as to the difference between inside and outside in The Goldyn Targe.

Why does Dunbar appear to frustrate the allegorical drift of his poem with this reflexive overlay, in a manner which we can, surely, only consider deliberate? On one level, this may, as A C Spearing suggests, be associated with the erotic aspect of the work: 'There is no escape from sex into poetry, when the predominant poetic tradition is one that assumes that sex is what poetry is about.'[24] The main theme which emerges at the poem's conclusion, however, is that of how the poetic subject can speak itself in relation to its powerful literary forefathers.[25] After stating that Chaucer 'beris of makaris the tryumph riall' (1.256), it continues

> O morall Gower and Ludgate laureate,
> Your sugurit lippis and tongis aureate
> Bene to oure eris cause of grete delyte
> Your angel mouthis most mellifluate
> Oure rude language has clere illumynate,
> And fair ourgilt oure spech that imperfyte
> Stude or your goldyn pennis schupe to wryte;
> This ile before was bare and desolate
> Off rethorike, or lusty fresch endyte.
>   (11.262-70)

This vision of literary 'Inglis' as a barbaric tongue, civilised into eloquence by means of the rhetoric of Chaucer, Gower and Lydgate, is of course a commonplace of the period, but one whose implications are worth pondering.[26] In the last two lines quoted, the poem's concern with nature as itself a metaphor for language and its operations is made explicit, and this inevitably urges a reconsideration of what has been read. Dunbar's main figure here presents a language 'illumynit ... full brycht' (1.258) and 'ourgilt' by the workings of rhetoric. Chaucer's comment in the Clerk's Tale on Petrarch's 'enlumyning' art[27] has here developed into a full-scale illustration of the effects of rhetorical trope and aureate diction. All the images of the poem's opening serve to body forth in visual terms a pristine world of pure presence; the mediate status of language disappears in a plenitude analogous to that of the sensory world – although paradoxically, the landscape thus produced in The Goldyn Targe, with all its dazzling brilliance, is quite consciously one of rhetorical artifice. However – and, south of the border, Skelton and Hawes respond to this predicament in different ways – this moment of immediacy, of the ultimate mimesis, has always just passed, and the poets of the turn of the sixteenth century are left to struggle with its aftermath, and their sense that it is irrecoverable. In the stanza cited above, Dunbar presents this whole situation in a ironic perspective. After his series of paradoxical games with reality and artifice, he closes with an envoi de quare commanding his own poem, with its glitteringly aureate vocabulary, to be 'aferit of the licht' (1.279). His own self-conscious reflections on these questions of poetic belatedness, and the poet's complex relationship to literary origins, can be seen in a terminology which slides, with calculated unease, between the categories of speech (perceived partly as the 'angel mouthis' of divine revelation) and writing. Speech may be the origin of words, and writing may possess a purely secondary status; but Dunbar's mention of the occasion when his authors' 'goldyn pennis schupe to write' instals writing at the moment of origin which has just been characterised as a purely vocal epiphany. We are reminded that this whole version of literary history is itself a literary construct; and Dunbar's discussion of nature and culture issues in a meditation on the problems of authority, imitation and tradition which so frequently beset the poets of this period.

I end with some consideration of those poems by Dunbar most directly related to the context of James IV's court, a topic which I approach by way of some recent comments by Sarah Kay on the poetry of the troubadours. Kay is concerned to emphasise the extent to which the troubadour 'defines himself, at least in part, in function of his audience ... we return to the importance of the troubadour as historical performer, or at least as known author of his text'. Here again, the subject is not unitary, consistent or self-contained, but defined intersubjectively; public, in some sense exchangeable, stretched between the troubadour, the way in which he is realised in the corpus of his known work, and his 'ideologically alert' audience.[28] Whilst the works of the troubadour poets and those of Dunbar are worlds apart, they present us in this respect with similar interpretative problems. Across the Dunbar canon we recognise a number of constants: the Dunbar who is paraded as being 'of nobill strynd',[29] the consciously marginal figure who stands 'fastand in a nuke' (no. 40, 1.7) whilst others grab the benefices; the poet who in the Targe and the Tretis of the Tua Mariit Wemen and the Wedo (no. 14) may be deliberately playing on his identity as celibate cleric, restricted to a solely voyeuristic participation in matters sexual; and the particularly striking instance of the 'Dunbar the mackar' who cuts so absurd a figure in the Dance in the Quenis Chalmer (no. 28). The difficulty arises when we attempt to use such references to an immediate environment, valuable in themselves in the pursuit of historical evidence, as fragments from which to construct a Romantic-style personal biography of Dunbar. We arguably do better to recognise in them elements in a series of transactions between author and audience, in constant circulation, from which the poet's 'identity' is compiled. (This is almost graphically apparent in the Flyting (no. 29), where 'Dunbar' and 'Kennedy' emerge from the contest of style and technique between the two poets). The poet is not somewhere behind, and separable from, the face he presents, as traditional studies of persona would imply; in fact, it could rather be asserted that the rhetoric is prior to the self presented, and it is at this performative level that the poems need to be considered.

It is in the petitionary poems that these problems surface with especial clarity, not least if we bear in mind claims that have recently been made for this particular mode. J A Burrow has suggested that individualism finds its way into English literature by way of the versified petition,[30] and this point is relevant to some of Dunbar's poems, in which a purportedly autonomous subjectivity emerges on a basis of dependence and limitation. The equivocation and apparent complexity of attitude in these poems are in part produced by the conditions of court patronage and the uncertainty as to the status of poetry which they engender. According to Richard Firth Green, literature at the later medieval court occupied 'some kind of ill-defined no-man's-land somewhere between a job and a hobby', and Green discussed in some detail the ambiguous position of the poet, placed within hailing distance of a social status he yet did not entirely possess.[31] In Dunbar's begging-poems, this alienation is _performed_ through a conspicuous using up of all the roles the petitioner could possibly adopt, which is the obverse of the conspicuous consumption which we see in the public display of late medieval monarchy. The endless shifts of position even within single poems, the pervasive tonal instabilities, all serve to glorify through contrast the monarch who is the fount of Being (and of benefices). Claus Uhlig may well be right to state that Dunbar's assaults on the other occupants of courtly ambition's ladder are motivated by 'aristokratischem Ressentiment ... und Bewusstsein seines Dichtertums';[32] what is beyond question is that in the poems themselves, injured aristocratic merit and the humanist ascription of an autonomous value to poetry serve chiefly as parts of a rhetorical performance. The images of a Dunbar who is frustrated by unending delay in obtaining a benefice and thus displays a desire for imminent satisfaction, who laments the unfulfilled ambitions of youth and thus reveals a body subject to time, all operate to evoke their opposite, the timeless body politic of the monarch who is the source of infinite expenditure.[33] Indeed, the appearance of what Burrow views as an early form of autobiography in the begging-poem, most notably in the cases of Chaucer's Envoy à Scogan and Hoccleve's Male Regle, can be seen to result from this strategy. In contrast to the donor who by virtue of his greater proximity to 'the stremes hed/Of grace'[34] is the source of plentitude and renewal — as witness Hoccleve's puns on the name of Sir Henry Somer — the petitioner's body is subject to time and decay. Thus, in 'Schir, yit remember as befoir' (no. 42), he begins by urging through a series of traditional comparisons his noble blood against the parvenus who snatch away the benefice he desires; 'the falcounis kynd' (1.11) and 'the gentill goishalk' (1.14) are forgotten where others succeed. However, before long he is laying ironic claim to rights of a more egalitarian kind; he, too, is 'cum of Adame and Eve/And fain wald leif as utheris dois (11.38–9). And when his poetry is mentioned it is in a context of further reflexive irony, the poem itself becoming an emblem of impotence:

> Allace, I can bot ballattis breif,
> Sic barnheid leidis my brydill reynye.
> (11.48-9)

The text slides into the begging-poem commonplace which casts the
patron as the physician whose gift will heal his client — a topos
which neatly epitomises the points made above about the petitionary body[35] — then continues to plead Dunbar's case as against
those of typical upstarts. A similar ambivalence runs through
'Schir, lat it never in toune be tald' (no. 43), whose beast-fable
overtones make it 'replete with verbal jokes, double meanings and
ambiguities'.[36] Such poems, as Burrow has argued, clearly exceed
their given practical function;[37] in so doing, however, they may
respond to political demands of a rather different nature.

A product of these strategies is that the aggrieved petitioner
usually ends in (ostensibly) unwitting identification with the
'other' against whom his own identity has been defined. The poems
sometimes suggest explicit reasons for this. The opening of no. 45
puts matters especially clearly:

> Complane I wald, wist I quhome till,
> Or unto quhome darett my bill ...
> (11.1-2)

There follows a triple question: should the poem be addressed to
God, the Virgin or the 'wardlie prince heir downe' (1.7) who is
dispenser of justice? The position of the subject within the
chaotic and amorphous body known as the court is uncertain; we are
led to ask whether it is possible for a speaker to take up a
coherent and definite position 'outside' a structure whose limits
are so unclear, or whether any statement about the court is bound
to be entangled in its own contradictions. This poem seems to
privilege the position of the 'lerit sone off erll or lord'
(1.41), angry that so many should be preferred before him, but
this merely begs the question of whether his own stance is not
compromised by such requests. (The only option for rhetorical
detachment from the court comes with the different discourse
embodied in a poem like 'To dwell in court, my freind, gife that
thow list' (no. 77); and even this is undone by the fact that its
admonitory, hortatory quality foregrounds precisely those forms of
social interaction and communication which its sentiments discour-
age).[38] All the features so far described come together in 'Schir,
ye have mony servitouris' (no. 44), which also attempts a defence
of the enduring value of poetry along humanist lines. The poem
opens with a catalogue of those who work legitimately at court for
rightful reward, the speaker concluding with a claim for himself
which emphasises, not innate worth, but the enduring value of what
he produces:

> And thocht that I amang the laif
> Unworthy be ane place to have
> Or in thair nummer to be tald
> Als lang in mynd my work sall hald,
> Als haill in everie circumstance,

> In forme, in mater and substance,
> Bout wering or consumptioun,
> Roust, canker or corruptioun,
> As ony of thair wekis all –
> Suppois that my rewarde be small.
>
> (11.25-34)

Whilst this is a clearer and less compromised apology for poetry than anything else in the Dunbar corpus, it is stll hedged about with unease. In the poem it is immediately followed by a long list of those parasitic on the court – a bravura display piece – and it is in this awkward interstice, between those who can justly claim a place at court and the hangers-on, that the poet is inserted. This catalogue begins in open sarcasm; it is the king himself whose 'grace' and 'meekness' – royal virtues both – call into being this crowd of sycophants, who are thus in some sense inseparable from the court structure. At the end of the poem, the expression of grievance degenerates into a threat:

> ... owther man my hart to breik,
> Or with my pen I man me wreik;
> And since the tane most nedis be –
> In to malancolie to de
> Or lat the vennim ische all out –
> Be war anone, for it will spout
> Gif that the tryackill cum nocht tyt
> To swage the swalme of my dispyt.
>
> (11.81-8)

Spearing finds in this final alignment of the speaker with the '"Thrimlaris and thristaris" who are at court for what they can get' a 'cynical reflexive humour';[39] in effect, it seems rather to fissure the entire poem. In spite of the incipiently humanist emphasis, poetry cannot quite be joined either to Dunbar's first group or to his second; its value is not yet self-evident, and he is finally reduced to 'flyting'. Claims are made here both for Dunbar the autonomous subject and for the autonomy of poetry; but they are constituted entirely by the contradictory field dictated by the institution of patronage. 'Schir, ye have mony servitouris' tries to bring this poetic subject, in circulation between poet and patron, to rest in an ideology valuing the autonomy of the poet's art. But this opposition proves to be defined by the very contradictions it seeks to transcend. The difficulties involved here in mapping out a space for authorship suggest a parallel at the other end of the sixteenth century. As Peter Stallybrass and Allon White have pointed out, authorship for Ben Jonson entailed both a commitment to neo-classical aesthetics and a repudiation of the society on which he was dependent; but the rejected 'low' discourse manages, in Bartholomew Fair, to effect a return of the political repressed:

> ... disgust bears the imprint of desire, and Jonson found in the huckster, the cony-catcher and the pick-pocket an image

of his own precarious and importuning craft. Proclaiming so loudly how all the other plays were mere cozenings, did not (he) pursue the perennial techniques of the mountebank who decried the deceptions and false wares of others the more easily to practise his own deceptions and pass off his own productions as 'the real thing'?[40]

In Dunbar's work, too, the speaking subject is left identifying with what it began by defining itself against. In the process, however, new meanings are generated. Earlier implications that regal virtues can themselves corrupt, like other comments of the 'I say not, Sir, yow to repreiff/Bot doutles I go rycht neir hand it' (no. 42, 11.78-9) variety, are not in themselves so significant; their effect in this kind of complaint is above all to recuperate any real possibility of criticism, and to call attention to the subject's distance from the king. But in occupying the traditional physician-patient petitionary topos in its new subject position, that of rejected Other, the poem's 'I' suddenly bursts out with a new vehemence, a rhetorical excess which threatens fearful disruption. The rhetoric which appropriates the petitioner as metaphorically 'sick', an enfeebled counterexample to the perfect monarchic body, can be reappropriated and turned against itself.

I have only been able to examine a few specific forms taken by subjectivity in Dunbar's work, giving particular attention to religious discourse and to the relations between the poet and the two institutions of poetic tradition and monarchic power. This matter clearly deserves a far fuller treatment than is possible here. However, I would argue that a genuinely flexible and productive approach is not to be achieved by assuming the existence of some single factor - whether it be Dunbar's 'personality', medieval theology or a court milieu - which will make Dunbar's poetry into a unity. The poems should rather be examined as a complex series of negotiations between the desire of the poet and the demands which structure it. It is amidst these, by various means - sometimes through what Sheila Delany has called 'a nascent awareness of the self-sufficiency of fiction',[41] sometimes through a rhetorical excess which runs athwart a decorum to which it should be subordinate - that a space for an emergent subjectivity of a more interiorised kind is very occasionally hollowed out.

Notes

1   Edwin Morgan, 'Dunbar and the Language of Poetry', Essays in Criticism, 2 (1952), 138-58 (156).

2   E.g. in Allan Rodway's strikingly phrased claim that 'Dunbar's Muse turns to any subject with whorish readiness': English Comedy: Its Role and Nature from Chaucer to the Present Day (London, 1975), p 75.

3   Dunbar: A Critical Exposition of the Poems (Edinburgh and London, 1966), pp 339-40. For other examples of the strand in

Dunbar criticism which places 'personal experience' at the centre of the poems, see A M Kinghorn, 'Dunbar and Villon: A Comparison and a Contrast', Modern Language Review 62 (1967), 195-208 (198); H Harvey Wood, Two Scots Chaucerians: Robert Henryson, William Dunbar, Writers and their Work, 201 (London, 1967) p 43.

4   For examples, see: R J Lyall, 'Moral Allegory in Dunbar's Goldyn Targe', Studies in Scottish Literature 11 (1973), 47-65; W S Ramson, 'William Dunbar: "Kirkman, Courtman and Craftsman Fyne"', Words: Wai-te-ata Studies in Literature 4 (1978), 59-66 (65); Edmund Reiss, William Dunbar, Twayne's English Authors Series 257 (Boston, 1979), p 68 and passim, and 'The Ironic Art of William Dunbar', in Fifteenth Century Studies: Recent Essays, Robert F Yeager (ed) (Hamden, Conn., 1984), pp 321-31; and Ian Simpson Ross, 'William Dunbar and the Four Last Things', in Bards and Makars: Scottish Language and Scottish Literature: Medieval and Renaissance, A J Aitken, M P McDiarmid and D S Thomson (eds) (Glasgow, 1977), pp 88-106, and William Dunbar (Leiden, 1981), p 261 and passim.

5   Hans Robert Jauss, 'The Alterity and Modernity of Medieval Literature', New Literary History 10 (1979), 181-230 (192).

6   For an important early discussion see Leo Spitzer, 'Notes on the Poetic and Empirical "I" in Medieval Authors', Traditio 4 (1946), 414-20; see also the essays collected under the title 'Le "Je" du Poète' in Paul Zumthor, Langue, Texte, Énigme (Paris, 1975), pp 161-213.

7   E.g. in Judson B Allen, 'Grammar, Poetic Form and the Lyric Ego: A Medieval A Priori', in Vernacular Poetics in the Later Middle Ages, Lois Ebin (ed) (Kalamazoo, 1984), pp 199-266 (217); see also his The Ethical Poetic of the Later Middle Ages (Toronto, 1982).

8   See David A Lawton, Chaucer's Narrators (Woodbridge, 1985), pp xiii-xiv, 1-16.

9   For some valuable recent perspectives see Richard Firth Green, Poets and Princepleasers: Literature and the English Court in the Later Middle Ages (Toronto, 1980), pp 114-27; Richard A Lanham, The Motives of Eloquence (New Haven and London, 1978), pp 1-35; Lawton, Chaucer's Narrators, pp 42-3; Glending Olson, Literature as Recreation in the Later Middle Ages (Ithaca, N Y, 1982), esp pp 90-163.

10 H Marshall Leicester Jnr, 'The Wife of Bath as Chaucerian Subject', Studies in the Age of Chaucer: Proceedings 1 (1984), pp 201-10 (201). Some suggestions on the relevance of theories of the subject to Chaucer, with references, are given in Stephen Knight, 'Chaucer and the Sociology of Literature', Studies in the Age of Chaucer 2 (1980), 15-51 (37-45). David Aers, Individual, Gender and Community (London Methuen, forthcoming) will also be concerned in part with some versions of subjectivity in Middle English texts.

11 See Colin Morris, The Discovery of the Individual 1050-1200 (London, 1972); for a similar proposition with regard to Old French Literature, Michel Zink, La Subjectivité Littéraire (Paris, 1985).

12   Francis Barker, The Tremulous Private Body: Essays in Sub-
     jection (London and New York, 1984), p 68.
13   All references to Dunbar's works are to The Poems, James
     Kinsley (ed) (Oxford, 1979), and individual poems are cited
     by their number in this edition 3 is replaced where necessary
     by y.
14   Stephen G Nichols, Jnr, 'The Promise of Performance: Dis-
     course and Desire in Early Troubadour Lyric' in The Dialectic
     of Discovery: Essays in the Teaching and Interpretation of
     Literature, John D Lyons and Nancy J Vickers (eds)(Lexington,
     Kentucky, 1984), pp 93-108 (96).
15   For the poem's theological context see J A W Bennett, The
     Poetry of the Passion (Oxford, 1982), pp 120-27; Rosemary
     Woolf, The English Religious Lyric in the Middle Ages,
     (Oxford, 1968), pp 183-235.
16   J A W Bennett, 'Nosce te ipsum: Some Medieval and Modern
     Interpretations', in The Humane Medievalist and Other Essays
     in English Literature and Learning, from Chaucer to Eliot,
     Piero Boitani (ed) (Rome, 1982), pp 135-72 (150).
17   Not in the Asloan MS.
18   Several of the works listed in n.4 above, most notably
     Lyall's 'Moral Allegory', take the latter view; see Denton
     Fox, 'Dunbar's Goldyn Targe', English Literary History 26
     (1959), 311-34, and Lois Ebin, 'The Theme of Poetry in
     Dunbar's Goldyn Targe', Chaucer Review 2 (1972), 147-59, for
     treatment of the poem as a largely self-referential comment-
     ary on the poet's craft.
19   See Evelyn B Vitz, 'The "I" of the Roman de la Rose', Genre 6
     (1973), 49-75; and, for a fine recent account, David F Hult,
     Self-Fulfilling Prophecies: Readership and Authority in the
     First Roman de la Rose (Cambridge, 1986), pp 105-85.
20   Vitz, 'The "I" of the Roman', 52-5.
21   A C Spearing, Medieval Dream Poetry (Cambridge, 1976), pp
     28-9 and passim.
22   Hult, Self-Fulfilling Prophecies p 252.
23   See e.g. Geoffroi de Vinsauf, Poetria Nova, in E Faral, Les
     arts poétiques du xiie et du xiiie Siècle (Paris, 1924), p
     238, 11.1225-9; 245, 11.1584-7.
24   A C Spearing, 'The Medieval Poet as Voyeur' (unpublished). I
     am grateful to Professor Spearing for his permission to read
     this essay.
25   Harold Bloom's The Anxiety of Influence (Oxford, 1972) has
     now come to exert an influence of its own on studies of
     Chancer's fifteenth-century successors; see Louise O Fraden-
     burg, 'The Scottish Chaucer', in Proceedings of the Third
     International Conference on Scottish Language and Literature:
     Medieval and Renaissance, R J Lyall and Felicity Riddy (eds)
     (Stirling and Glasgow, 1981), pp 177-90, and A C Spearing,
     Medieval to Renaissance in English Poetry (Cambridge, 1985),
     esp pp 59-120 on the Chaucer tradition, 164-223 on the Middle
     Scots poets.
26   See Green, Poets and Princepleasers, p 208; P M Kean, Chaucer
     and the Making of English Poetry, 2 vols (1972), II 210-34;
     and, for a recent view, David A Lawton, 'Dullness and the

Fifteenth Century', English Literary History 54 (1987), 761-99 (765-7).

27 The Riverside Chaucer, Larry D Benson et al. (eds) (Boston, 1987), p 157, 1.33.

28 Sarah Kay, Troubadours and Subjectivity (unpublished). I am grateful to Dr Kay for her permission to read portions of her work in progress.

29 See 'Schir, yit remember as befoir' (no. 42); 'Complane I wald, wist I quhome till' (no. 45); 'Quhome to sall I complene my wo' (no. 63); 'How sould I rewill me or in quhat wys' (no. 82).

30 J A Burrow, Medieval Writers and their Work: Middle English Literature and its Background, 1100-1500 (Oxford, 1982), pp 37-44; see also his 'The Poet as Petitioner', Studies in the Age of Chaucer 3 (1981), 61-75, and 'Autobiographical Poetry in the Middle Ages: The Case of Thomas Hoccleve', Proceedings of the British Academy 68 (1984), 389-417.

31 Green, Poets and Princepleasers, pp 12, 110-12; for more extensive commentary on the petitionary mode itself see pp 206-7.

32 Claus Uhlig, Hofkritik im England des Mittelalters und der Renaissance: Studien zu einem Gemeinplatz der europäischen Moralistik, (Berlin, 1973), p 289.

33 On the poetics of sovereignty and its 'subjection of the subject to a newly politicised temporality', see Louise O Fradenburg, 'Spectacular Fictions: The Body Politic in Chaucer and Dunbar', Poetics Today 5 (1984), 493-517 (498-99).

34 Riverside Chaucer, p 655, 11.43-4.

35 Like much else in the begging-poem, this motif probably derives from those penitential lyrics that describe one of the persons of the Trinity, the Virgin or a saint as 'oure soules leche'. As Burrow's argument in 'Poet as Petitioner' makes clear, however, it is in later petitions for money, rather than those to a divine figure, that 'autobiographical' material becomes more pervasive.

36 Priscilla Bawcutt, 'Dunbar's Christmas Carol', in Proceedings of the Fourth International Conference on Scottish Language and Literature (Medieval and Renaissance) Germersheim, 1984, Dietrich Strauss and Horst W Drescher (eds) (Frankfurt-am-Main, Bonn and New York, 1986), pp 381-92 (389).

37 Burrow, 'Poet as Petitioner', 67,71.

38 See Uhlig, p 282, n.15 for further comment on the traditional motif of 'höfische Diskretion'.

39 Spearing, Medieval to Renaissance, pp 205-6.

40 Peter Stallybrass and Allon White, The Politics and Poetics of Transgression (London and New York, 1986), p 77.

41 Sheila Delany, Chaucer's House of Fame: The Poetics of Skeptical Fideism (Chicago and London, 1972), p 43.

Chapter 16

DUNBAR AND THE NATURE OF BAWDY

Edwina Burness

In recent years, certain critics, with varying degree of seriousness and success, have set themselves the task of defining the
term 'bawdy'. Roger Thompson claims that bawdy is 'intended to
provoke amusement about sex; most dirty jokes ... belong to this
category'.[1] Alan Bold calls bawdy 'an attempt to portray sex in
purely physical terms, to eschew the metaphysical apparatus that
generations of poets have imposed on a basically simple event'.[2]
For Thompson, bawdy is the equivalent of a smutty joke; to Bold it
represents an unpoetical, anatomical description of the sex act.
Neither interpretation is particularly useful for analysis of
literary texts. E A M Colman, however, provides a fuller, more
considered appraisal of the role of bawdy in written and spoken
language.

> to be bawdy, a piece of talk or writing has to have behind it
> the intention to startle or shock. It also has to be at once
> more and less than sensual. Inasmuch as it labours the phys-
> ical, it is sensual; but its other aspect is the exercise of
> wit, and this requires that the speaker remain partly at a
> distance from what he contemplates. Bawdy is often indirect,
> metaphorical or allusive. Only at its least subtle does it
> use blunt, unequivocal terms of sexual description, the
> familiar four-letter words.[3]

Colman recognises, in addition to the gross or comic physicality
noted by Bold and Thompson, the presence of wit, the use of
suggestion, allusion and euphemism, which demand that the writer
maintain some distance from his material.

Colman's identification of the subtler elements of bawdy would
seem to have most relevance to the poetry of Dunbar. It is
surprising that this important aspect of Dunbar's work has
received little critical attention. The most extended discussion
is by Lois Ebin, who argues persuasively that Dunbar exploits
bawdy not only as a source of comedy and irony but as a device by
which he revaluates styles, forms, and traditions.[4] She sees the
juxtaposition of aureate and bawdy language, in The Tretis of the
Tua Mariit Wemen and the Wedo particularly, as showing an attempt
on the poet's part to indicate the incomplete nature of our
perception of reality and the limits of the artist's ability to
convey that reality.[5] In this paper I propose to follow on from
Ebin's findings to consider Dunbar's bawdy en masse, and to

demonstrate its remarkable diversity and variety. I shall also use Dunbar to support Colman's contention that the bawdy writer, in his desire to shock, is at once more direct and less direct.

In the first place, the linguistic range and complexity of Dunbar's bawdy should be stressed. The variety of terms to denote female and male sex organs, as will be shown, is in itself remarkable; and in each case, I would argue, the choice of synonym reflects in a direct or indirect way on the context. In In Secreit Place,[6] for example, the use of bawdy, as Ebin observed, provides a parody of the courtly pastourelle and questions the actual and assumed purpose behind the tradition and genre. One might also note that along with the recognisable bawdy term for the penis, stang (13.48) (literally 'sting' K), there are several words of obscure meaning or origin (in DOST) which may be variants for genitalia, either invented by Dunbar or drawn by him from dialect or country usage — as Larry Benson has remarked, 'Words, especially indelicate words, can exist long before someone writes them down'.[8] Kinsley, for one, has suggested the gloss 'pudendum muliebre' for brilȝeane' (13.44), towdy (mowdy) (13.46, 48) and tirly mirly (13.46), while Edmund Reiss calls hony soppis (13.30) and sweit possody (13.30) sexual euphemisms and michane (13.37) a phallus,[9] a word for which Kinsley offers the gloss 'stomach'. Whether these particular suggestions are tenable is open to question, the two which might appear to have the strongest case are those for tirly mirly and towdy (mowdy). CSD and Kinsley connect tirly mirly with the eighteenth-century tirly-whirly ('female pudendum' SND), and Kinsley links towdy (mowdy) with the words towdy ('buttocks') and towdy-fee ('fine for fornication') (both in SND). It might also be suggested that mowdy is both a familiar rhyming echo of towdy and a variant on the verb mow: 'to copulate' (DOST). There is much room — perhaps too much room — for speculation over these obscure terms; but nevertheless editors have left unexplained one of the most interesting, curledoddy (13.29). Kinsley follows DOST in glossing it 'ribwort plantain', and offers the possible derivation curly doddy 'round headed'. He fails to see a potential link between his offered derivation and the shape of the vulva, for which curledoddy may be a euphemism. Even when there is agreement among editors about the meaning of the sexual terminology in this poem, there still remains the problem of provenance, even with quhillylillie (13.34). Although DOST, CSD, and Kinsley all gloss it 'penis', DOST only cites In Secreit Place for that meaning, and gives Lyndsay's Ane Satyre of the Thrie Estaitis (4372)[10] with a different interpretation 'an attack of sickness, a spasm'.

The lexis used to denote female and male genitalia in The Tretis of the Tua Mariit Wemen and the Wedo presents fewer problems. Kinsley and DOST agree, for instance, on the metaphorical sense of pene (14.135) and lume (14.96, 175) for 'penis', and purse (14.136) for 'scrotum'. All of these were presumably accepted terms as DOST cites them in works of other Scottish writers of the period; lume (ME lome) and purse were also current in England, as MED has several examples of both. Kinsley argues persuasively for talis (14.262) to mean 'sexual parts', quoting similar passages from Langland and Cocke Lorelles Bote (K p 269). He advocates ʒerd for 'penis' and <u>geir</u> for 'sexual implements', justifiably, given the exclusively sexual contexts. 3<u>erd</u> is twice linked by the two wives to their husbands' impotence – 'I may ʒuke all this ʒer or his ʒerd help' (14.130) and 'with a ʒoldin ʒerd dois ʒolk me in armys' (14.220). <u>Geir</u> is related to a girl's hatred of men with 'hard geir for hurting of flesch' (14.232) and to dislike of male sexuality. <u>Thing</u> (14.389, 486) Kinsley glosses as euphemisms for the vulva and the phallus respectively, an attribution the passages amply support: 'he my <u>thing</u> persit' (14.389) and 'a stif standand <u>thing</u>' (14.486). (A similar meaning for <u>thing</u> can be found in Chaucer, as I have noted elsewhere.[11]) A final metaphor for the female genitals I might add is <u>(Venus) chalmer/chalmir</u> (14.183, 194, 370, 431) which Ross finds in Chaucer to signify the vagina.[12] The greater variety of terms for the sexual organs in <u>The Tretis</u> points to an increased complexity in Dunbar's writing; the inclusion of a poetical metaphor, albeit ironic, like <u>Venus Chalmer</u> with the more colloquial bawdy terminology underlines the general themes of the poem as a whole: the irreconcilability of language and action, ideal and real behaviour, body and mind.

In <u>The Wowing of the King quhen he wes in Dumfermeling</u> Dunbar employs fewer synonyms for sex organs, as both the form (the beast fable) and the satirical target (the King) are less ambitious than those in <u>The Tretis</u>. Nevertheless, he still chooses his bawdy language for maximum effect. The female genitals are designated by a homely metaphor like <u>prenecod</u> (37.39) ('pincushion trans. to women's genitalia': sole citation in DOST; Partridge [13] has it as slang for 'the female pudenda' from seventeenth century onwards). The more complex figure for the male organs, <u>tribill</u> (37.19) ('treble/triple instrument' K) serves to underline the contrast between the sophisticated fox and the simple lamb. The choice of metaphors also reinforces the combination of satire and homely morality in <u>Ane wirkis Sorrow to him sell</u>; Dunbar uses the common image <u>schute</u>, 'shoot/have sex', but enlivens it with two images for the female genitals, <u>prop</u> (70.13), (in DOST it appears as a current figure in Scots for sexual mark), and <u>schell</u> (70.13), 'shell', a folkloric and Latin sexual quibble (K p 362). The male member is termed <u>genʒie</u> (70.11), ('arrow, bolt' DOST and K) with the Gaelic derivation of the word making the satire at once more direct and familiar. In a lighter vein the pun on <u>purse</u> (19.5f), in its literal and sexual meaning of 'scrotum' (as in <u>The Tretis</u>, discussed above), links impotence with financial embarrassment in one of the addresses to the King; the petition, as a result, appears more attractive because it is thus wittily couched. By contrast, in poems where male physicality is degraded for the purposes of satire, the use of a blunt term for penis, like <u>terse</u> in the portrait of Lust in <u>Fasternis Evin in Hell</u> (52.88), mirrors the harsh thrust of the moralising; similarly, the common Scots (and ME) synonyms for testicles, <u>bawis</u> (23.104) and <u>bellokis</u> (23.119) in the <u>Flyting of Dunbar and Kennedie</u>, underline the brutally explicit nature of the personal invective. In <u>Thir Ladyis fair that in the Court ar kend</u> the very choice of word to denote the genitals, <u>geir</u> (71.48), 'property/sexual apparatus' (K), controls a reading of the poem, and by focusing and fusing the themes of selling sex and legality, neatly satirises both women and jurisprudence.

Dunbar's characterisation of the sex act per se demonstrates a comparable verbal richness and complexity. As with the terminology for genitalia, what is most striking initially is the number of lexical items, some appearing only once, employed to delineate essentially the same human activity. In In Secreit Place, for example, Dunbar has the narrator use two explicit and consciously unpoetic words, glaikkis (13.12) ('sensual desire', origin obscure DOST), and fukkit (13.13) (first recorded use OED); both the plangently courtly refrain and the narrator's critical detachment are thereby undercut – his view of love, or sex, is as partial and incomplete as that of the couple he is mocking. Indeed, all the explicit terms for sexual intercourse which appear once in Dunbar's work are closely related to the speaker's persona. In The Tretis, for one, the women provide an almost clinically precise account of the sex act, in keeping with their unemotional, pragmatic attitude to human relationships: they refer graphically to 'leit that larbar my leggis ga betueene' (14.133), to how 'he my thing persit' (14.389) or 'falȝeis at the up with' ('climax' K) (14.401) and to a 'peronall that myght na put (thrust in copulation' K) thole' (14.231). The First Wife even links a further monosyllabic word for sexual intercourse to a blasphemous prayer – 'God gif matrimony wer made to mell for ane yeir' (14.56) – thereby reaffirming the impression she has already made of unchristian assertiveness. In Renunce thy God and cum to me, another, still stronger Middle English word of the same meaning is uttered by the 'menstrall': 'The Feind me ryfe/Gif I do ocht bot drink and swyfe' (56.61-2). According to Benson, by Chaucer's time at least swyven 'had become once of the most offensive words in Middle English'.[14] One might assume that it retained some of this element as it is put into the mouth of a coarse speaker like the 'menstrall'; at any rate it sets up a contrast with the Devil's sophisticated Latinate imperative 'Exers that craft in all thy lyfe' (56.64). In a somewhat similar fashion, thrist (ME, 'collide, copulate' K) in The Antechrist – 'Thir terrible monsteris sall togidder thrist/And in the cludis gett the Antechrist' (53.28-9) – gives a realistic edge to the allegorical high style of the rest of the poem. Finally ȝock (Old English 'copulate' K) in the line 'Thai sall repent quhai with tham ȝockis'(32.32) in To the Quene reflects the tough yet humorous tone of the speaker's satire on the ideal and real nature of court marriage.

If Dunbar in these instances might seem to satisfy one of Coleman's criteria, to shock by directly emphasising the physical in his lexical selection, he can also be seen elsewhere to fulfil another, achieving a comparable effect by less obvious means, through suggestion and allusion. Again Dunbar displays considerable ingenuity and versatility. At times he will insert a double entendre, even into the narrative detail of a poem, as in The Wowing of the King: 'I wait nocht gif he gaif her grace,/Bot all the hollis wes stoppit hard' (37.47-8). Although Kinsley glosses grace 'sexual satisfaction', he fails to identify hollis completely, giving only the literal meaning 'apertures'; but if the extended sense 'the orifice of the female pudendum' (MED) is

included, the lines read like a bawdy reference to sexual intercourse. Dunbar is equally adroit at handling one of the most
common metaphors for copulation, riding, which he gives added
freshness and resonance by connecting it to the animal images of
the ram and the horse. The ram appears to be associated with
aggressive male sexual activity; it is said of the 'fox' in The
Wowing of the King that he 'wald haif riddin hir (the lamb) lyk
ane rame' (37.6); the line recalls the simile describing the
licentious courtiers, 'ryatous as rammis' (32.16), in To the
Quene, a poem which itself begins with the double entendre 'Madam,
ʒour men said thai wald ryd' (32.1).

  The horse/ride connection is expressed with greater frequency
and complexity. Although the horse appears in its traditional role
as a symbol of lust when 'Lichery' is compared to a 'bagit hors'
(52.80) and when loose women are likened to 'gillettis' that
'riddin ar baith with lord and lawd' (43.47-8), equine images are
most often related to unsatisfied male desire. In one of his
addresses to the king, Dunbar's court persona is said to resemble,
severally, a 'ʒald' (43.2 and passim), a 'forriddin muill' (43.
40), and a 'palfray' (43.46). The metaphor seems to indicate that
his poverty is like or will lead to sexual inadequacy – although
the repeated use of the image, with variations, would tend to
reveal more self-mockery than self-pity. Aver ('cart-horse, old
horse' DOST) is also allied to lechery and poor male sexual performance in Ane Dance in the Quenis Chalmer, where Robert Shaw
'stackeret lyk ane strummall aver'(28.11), and in The Tretis, when
the First Wife claims that her husband 'fepillis like a farcy aver
that flyrit one a gillot'(14.114) and the Widow declares that she
'wes laith to be loppin with sich a lob avoir' (14.387). The
horse/ride metaphor is afforded greater significance elsewhere in
The Tretis. All three women allude to the bawdy meaning of 'to
ride' when they talk of their respective husbands' 'rousty raid'
(14.141), 'radis and rageing in chalmer' (14.194), and 'myrthles
raid' (14.391). In addition, the Biblical and medieval image of
the yoke of marriage is evoked by the First Wife imagining her
ideal lover 'ʒaip and ʒing, in the ʒoke ane ʒeir for to draw'
(14.79), and is linked to the folkloric image of sex as ploughing,
'forsy in draucht' (14.85). The Widow takes the metaphor a stage
further when she says of her second husband 'I wald haif ridden
him to Rome with raip in his heid' (14.331), and of herself 'I
wald na langar beir on bridill, bot braid up my heid' (14.348);
and finally boasts to her cronies, 'Se how I cabeld ʒone cout with
a kene brydill -/The cappill that the crelis kest' (14.354-5).
This last image, according to Klaus Bitterling, may allude to a
Platonic and penitential symbol of the domination of the senses by
reason,[15] and according to Ian Ross, to medieval and Renaissance
iconographical motifs of Phyllis astride Aristotle, satirising
female power.[16] One might also note that Dunbar's lexical variety
lends added freshness and vigour to the passage; for the inclusion
of the Middle English (from Old English) cout and the Gaelic
derivative cappill means that the colloquial tone of the whole is
not obscured by the religious and philosphical overtones which
might be there.

  Another traditional animal metaphor representing male sexual behaviour in Dunbar's bawdy is the bull. It appears in the romance parody Schir Thomas Norny when Quintene calls the eponymous 'hero' 'ane licherus bull/that croynd baith day and nycht' (27.41-2). The context would suggest gross and somewhat ludicrous sexual performance. The young bullock or calf is more specifically associated with inexperienced and clumsy male lovers. The 'maister almaser' in Ane Dance in the Quenis Chalmer who is awkward and ungainly in his movements is compared to 'a stirk stackarand in the ry' (28. 17). The woman in In Secreit Place addresses her gauche admirer with the same image, 'My strummill stirk ʒit new to spane' (13. 54), and, with further suggestions of mammary stimulation, 'my cawf' (13.23) and 'my sucker' (13.53). Notwithstanding her verbal freedom, her recourse to such metaphors shows her adherence (and presumably that of the poet also) to the notion of the female body, whether lactating or copulating, as a source of nourishment for the male. The man in his turn sees his beloved in terms of comestibles, albeit comically uncourtly ones, 'my hony sopis, my sweit possoddy'(13.30). Even the animal and bird he invokes as terms of endearment, kid (13.43) and capircalʒeane (13.43), are both edible. A similar, but more elegantly expressed, version of the woman as sexual titbit is to be found in the Wowing of the King when the lamb is designated 'ane morsall of delyte' (37.23). The female in In Secreit Place compares her suitor to a fruit and a vegetable when she calls him her 'chirry' (18.52) and declares that he is 'sweit as ony unʒeoun' (13.53). In each case, I would offer, the choice may not be purely random or comic, since both foods have sexual associations. The cherry is accredited with later slang meanings: 'a young man's (physical) virginity' and 'a virgin boy or youth',[17] either of which may have its origin here; the onion is involved in two folkloric superstitions regarding the identity of one's future husband.[18] Another of the woman's references to her lover, 'my unspaynd jyane' (13.36), continues to stress his sexual inexperience (unspaynd, 'unweaned' K), but also introduces the notion of masculine physical superiority with jyane, the same image used to describe the would-be lusty courtiers in To the Quene: 'Sum thocht tham selffis stark lyk gyandis (32.21). In this latter work male impotence is implied by two animal images. The first, 'tame lyk ony lammis' (32.17), carries with it the suggestion of cuckoldry found in the punning refrain in a poem about the Keeper of the Queen's wardrobe James Dog, 'He is na dog; he is a lam' (30.4f), and also the overtones of feminine timidity and vulnerability inherent in the character of the lamb in The Wowing of the King. The second simile, 'settin down lyk sarye crockis' (32.18) contains similar associations and is one of the insults hurled by Dunbar at Kennedy in The Flyting, 'rottin crok' (23.248). The infected courtiers of the Queen are also seen in terms of another nature image, 'waek lyk willing wandis' (32.22), with the potentially phallic associations of wandis ('slender, pliant sticks' CSD) undercut by the qualifying adjective willing ('yielding, pliant' CSD), a feminine characteristic. The most triumphantly witty application of female and gastropodic traits to the male is voiced by the Second Wife, who declares that her husband's penis 'lyis in to swonne' and resembles a 'snaill tyrit' (13.175-6).

The rich variety of lexis for sexual equipment and practice and the confident and original use of traditional and nature imagery are only part of Dunbar's bawdy. Several of his poems, even some of his most explicitly sexual, contain allusive, euphemistic passages which act as an ironic counterpoint to the tone of the whole. In The Tretis, for example, the First Wife prefaces her grimly realistic picture of her old impotent husband with a lyrical account of what her ideal, young lover would be like: 'als fresche of his forme as flouris in May;/For all the fruit suld I fang thocht he the flour burgeoun'(14.87-8). The stock poetic simile for youthful beauty (which Dunbar applies unambiguously to ladies in The Golden Targe, 'Als fresch as flouris that in May up spredis' (10.58)) is here set against another flower image, but one with phallic overtones: the man thrusts forth his sexuality (his 'flour') while the woman achieves greater sensual satisfaction (the 'fruit'). The Widow too scatters her racy discourse with euphemistic phraseology. With two neatly executed antitheses, for instance, she alludes to her apparent celibacy by day and her actual licentiousness by night: 'Thoght I haif cair undir cloke the cleir day quhill nyght,/ʒit haif I solace undir serk quhill the sone ryse' (14.470-1). The precise location of the ironically courtly and coy 'solace', 'undir serk', makes the sexual implication at once unequivocally comic. Again parodying poetic terminology, Dunbar has the Widow make mention of a 'secrete servand' who 'me supportis of sic nedis' (14.466-7) — needs of an exclusively sexual nature, like the 'confort' desired by the lover in In Secreit Place (13.5) and denied to the defeated knight by the 'Blak Moir' (33.24).

The Widow also includes several allusions to Venus in her blueprint of the perfect lover; 'valʒeandnes in Venus play' (14.399) is an essential requirement along with a physique suited 'maist forcely to furnyse a bancat/In Venus chalmir valʒeandly' (14. 430-1). The Second Wife has already linked linguistically male strength with the poeticisation of love when she says her husband looks like a man who is 'mare valʒeand in Venus chalmer' (14.183), and both wives have employed 'Venus werkis' (14.127, 200) as a euphemism for sexual intercourse. Although Dunbar in these instances, as elsewhere, may be questioning the validity of courtly attitudes and genre and the inadequacy of language to convey reality,[19] he may also be parodying an aspect of his own style. This self-mockery can most clearly be understood if the Tretis passages are considered in conjunction with those from a poem of an equally sexual nature, To the Quene.

This second work has as its repeated refrain 'libbin of the pockis' (32.5f) which has been taken to refer to fornication and/ or cures of venereal disease.[20] Again Dunbar's virtuosity is in evidence, since the poem boasts no less than three synonyms for 'whore'. Arguably, the origin of each word represents a different order of society: pamphelet (32.14), deriving from Old French, Medieval Latin and initially Greek (DOST), suggests sophisticated court life, harlott (pl. 32.32) with its Middle English (from Old French) source (DOST) represents middle-class speech and attitudes, and coclink (32.36) with its obscure origins (K), possibly a low-life term. The names may vary, but the activity is still the

same. Given the explicitly sexual nature of the subject-matter and
lexis, the two references to Venus, 'Off <u>Venus</u> feest to fang ane
fill' (32.7) and '<u>Dame Venus fyre</u> sa hard tham sted' (32.12), are
intentionally incongrous. Dunbar is thereby underlining the
disparity between poetic genre and reality, language and action,
the ideal court and the real court. He could also be said to be
recalling ironically here, as in the Venus quotations from <u>The</u>
<u>Tretis</u>, his own decorous treatment of the traditional contrast
between spiritual and secular love, <u>Trew Luve</u>, a poem which
contains both <u>Dame Venus</u> and <u>Venus fyre</u>: 'Now culit is <u>dame Venus</u>
brand' (17.3) and 'Quhill <u>Venus fyre</u> be deid and cauld' (17.7).

Another less complex image for copulation in Dunbar's work is
the dance. It is mentioned briefly and salaciously by the narrator
in <u>In Secreit Place</u>: 'Syne tha twa till ane play began/Quhilk that
thay call the <u>dirrydan</u>' (13.59-60). The obscure (K) name may have
its origin in country usage and would therefore suit the earthy
quality of the bawdy in the rest of the poem. The dance is the
controlling metaphor in <u>Ane Dance in the Quenis Chalmer</u>; and its
traditional associations with fertility rites and the rhythms of
sex, and Chaucer's 'old dance',[21] in particular, would tend to
indicate that the way the courtiers perform on the dance-floor is
directly related to the way they perform in bed - that is, poorly,
with the exception of 'Maesteres Musgraeffe'. The foot may be a
metaphor for male sexual expertise, even for the penis;[22] for Sir
John Sinclair cannot get his feet to work in unison (28.4-5) and
Mr Robert Shaw has one foot which throws him off balance (28.
10-11). Even 'Dunbar the mackar', in spite of dancing the <u>dirrye</u>
<u>dantoun</u> (28.24) - the possibly country name indicating unaffected
sexuality - overdoes it and 'trippet quhill he tint his panton'
(28.28); panton ('a kind of soft shoe' DOST) may perhaps be
another phallic symbol.

The 'dancing' of two of the retinue, the 'maister almaser' and
Dame Dountboir, reveals a further aspect of Dunbar's bawdy: the
fusion of sexual with scatological language. (There are numerous
references to bodily evacuations of various and often spectacular
kinds elsewhere in his work, which space alone prevents me from
discussing here.[23]) Although Dunbar has the two courtiers break
wind while dancing, he once more displays his ingenuity and
inventiveness by varying the tone and expression of each report:
the man's farting is endowed with an almost mock-heroic intensity:
'His hippis gaff mony hoddous cry' (28.18), while the woman's is
conveyed in equally comic but less inflated terms: 'Ane blast of
wind son fra her slippis' (28.41). The 'maister almaser' is also
tersely said to be 'bedirtin' (28.20); James Dog is considered to
have a similar problem of bodily hygiene, as 'He stinckett lyk a
tyk' (28.48). The combination of animal and excretory imagery may
indeed, as Ross argues,[24] show that sexual frenzy can reduce
people to their baser selves, the culmination of such behaviour
being the dance of death where those dying in lust are doomed to
an eternity of perverted and frustrated desire (52.88-90). An
additional layer of meaning might be elicited if another passage,
which connects dogs, bodily waste, and impotence, is taken into
consideration. In <u>The Tretis</u> the Second Wife compares her spouse's
flirtations to those of a 'dotit dog that damys one all bussis/An

liftis his leg apone loft thoght he nought list pische' (14. 186-7). The First Wife has already associated poor sexual perform- ance in a male with excretion when she speaks of her husband as 'ane scutarde ('?person who defecates' CSD) behind' (14.92). The linking of the sexual with the scatological in this way may be intended to demonstrate that sex is merely another form of bodily release, necessary or degrading, or, if viewed in others, comic. The mind/body dichotomy is perhaps being raised as well; how far can - or should - a person control his or her bowels, wind or libido?

Another element of Dunbar's bawdy is a tendency to apply a sexual connotation to certain words. Curage, for one, more often would seem to have the meaning 'sexual energy, desire'[25] than that of 'strength, ability' (K). Unsurprisingly, it often has a bawdy sense in The Tretis (14.67, 188, 203, 215, 485, 522), and once each in To the Quene (32.11) and To the King (43.39), primarily with the comic or satiric emphasis being on its absence in a man. Curage in this sexual aspect figures on occasion in more decorous contexts. In The Golden Targe it is said of Youth and her attend- ant maidens, innocence, modesty, fear, and obedience, 'The goldyn targe harmyt thay no thing;/Curage in thame was noucht begonne to spring' (10.157-8) - curage being presented as a disruptive force in youth in particular and the moral universe in general. Curage also carries with it, in a few instances, the suggestion that there is a correlation between male sexual and literary perform- ance (in both activities, presumably, the man must wield his 'pen' to its greatest effect). In The Thrissill and the Rois May tells the dreamer: 'The lork hes done the mirry day proclame/To raise up luvaris with confort and delyt;/ʒit nocht incress thy curage to indyt' (50.24-6). In a similar context the speaker in The Magryme declares, 'Full oft at morrow I upryse/Quhen that my curage sleipeing lyis' (21.11-12) and in To the King, 'the court hes done my curage cuill' (43.39).

Other synonyms for sexual potency contained in words of an otherwise non-sexual meaning occur frequently in The Tretis, again with the stress being usually on its absence. Natur (14.174, 198, 392) thrice appears with the restricted meaning 'one's physical needs or desires with specific reference to the natural ... sexual functions' DOST), as do pitht (14.80),'sexual potency or virility' (DOST),[26] and, arguably, force (14.189), virtu (14.189) and valour (14.185). The women in this way ridicule their men by stressing the disparity between the original, often poetic associations (martial or moral) and the specifically sexual charge they give them. Their preference for the bawdy possibilities of a word strengthens the anti-feminist satire of the poem as a whole. Lust (14.188, 283, 499) or lack of it (14.491) is most often purely sexual pleasure. Equally, berne (14.74, 237, 429, 494), blis(e) (14, 205, 238), favoris (14,364), gest (14,233, 359), mercifull (14.501), serf (14.491) and servand (14.466) gain an ironic dimension through the juxtaposing of the courtly or religious connotations with the women's exclusively bawdy ones. Fresch(e) occurs six times, with, I would argue, implications of sexual power[27] (14.62, 66, 87, 172, 209, 400), like unfulʒeit (14.62), straik (14.234), and the punning 'kene ('fierce' and 'piercing') knyghtis' (14.216). A few other poems demonstrate a tendency to focus on the sexual associations of a word; there is the daring use of grace for 'sexual satisfaction' in The Wowing of the King (37.47) (mentioned above) or the profusion of bawdy puns identified by Ebin in Thir Ladyis Fair, which range from the simple kend (71.3), do (71.5) and spend (71.46) to the complex legalistic/ sexual quibbles on compositioun (71.55), remissioun (71.56) and conditioun (71.59).[28]

Given the importance, both social, moral and economic, of successful male sexual performance, it is not surprising that several terms of abuse in Dunbar's work should involve impotence, itself a preoccuption in a partriarchal system where the phallus denotes power. The women in The Tretis draw on a variety of lexical items for impotence; they include larbar (14.67 133, 175) drupe (14.192, 370), ful eit/ful eid (14.63, 86, 173) gane (14.129), tume (14.219), sakles (14.97) and myrthles (14.391).[29] The protagonists in The Flyting offer insults to each other's sexual nature (or that of their parents) as much to display their own verbal dexterity as to humiliate their opponent. Like the women in The Tretis, Dunbar uses larbar (23.121, 169), and also c(o)unt-bittin (23.50, 239),[30] for 'impotent'. On the whole the men use simple sexual terms of abuse: Dunbar calls Kennedy cukcald (23.76), and Kennedy attacks Dunbar's very conception with his wan fukkit (23.38) ('ill conceived' K). Both accuse the other of sexual deviance, Dunbar employing the (probably) more colloquial ʒadswyvar (23.246) ('mare-buggerer', ON + ME K) and Kennedy retaliating with the (slightly) more formal sodomyt(e) (23.253, 527) and bugrist (23.526) (the only citation of the word in DOST).

In conclusion, it can surely be agreed that Dunbar is alive to all the possibilities of bawdy; he is direct and indirect, explicit and suggestive. The complexity of a poem's content, theme or treatment is often reflected in the diversity of the bawdy language. The kind of bawdy used at times reveals more about a speaker's attitudes, or underlines a moral, or makes a satirical point; the juxtaposition of figurative and literal bawdy within a poem at times reinforces dichotomies in the piece itself. Dunbar reworks accepted sexual metaphors and creates new ones, giving added depth and resonance to his material through a skilful selection of lexical items drawn from differing traditions. By isolating the sexual element in a particular word he implicitly shows the verbal links in various orders of experience. The abundance of words and phrases descriptive of the sexual act and organs, sexual proficiency, inadequacy or deviance could indicate in the poet a fascination or disgust with the body and its effect on moral and spiritual well-being. Dunbar may, on the other hand, be merely intending to surprise or delight his audience with his linguistic virtuosity and daring. Perhaps, though, it would be truer to say that neither interpretation explains his stance entirely. Like the ideal bawdy writer Coleman describes he remains detached from his material; for him there is no one bawdy style, just as there is no one view of sex. Dunbar therefore fuses the language of the court and the byre to suggest that there is no single way - perhaps no real way - to convey in words the full significance of human sexual activity.

Notes

1 Roger Thompson, Unfit for Modest Ears (London, 1979), p ix.
2 Alan Bold, The Bawdy Beautiful (London, 1979), pp ii-iii.
3 E A M Colman, The Dramatic Use of Bawdy in Shakespeare (London, 1974), p 3.
4 Lois Ebin, 'Dunbar's Bawdy', Chaucer Review, 14 (1979-80) pp 278-86 (278).
5 Ebin, 'Dunbar's Bawdy', p 285.
6 All quotations in the text are from The Poems of William Dunbar, James Kinsley (ed) (Oxford, 1979). I am therefore for the purposes of this paper following Kinsley's readings and attributions (to be designated 'K').
7 Ebin, 'Dunbar's Bawdy', p 282.
8 Larry D Benson, 'The Queynte Punnings of Chaucer's Critics', Studies in the Age of Chaucer: Proceedings No. 1 (1984), pp 23-47, (40).
9 Edmund Reiss, William Dunbar (Boston, 1979), p 111.
10 Sir David Lyndsay, Ane Satyre of the Thrie Estaits, James Kinsley (ed) (London, 1954), 'And ay scho cryis a preist a preist,/With ilk a quhillie lillie' (4371-2).
11 Burness, 'Female Language in The Tretis of the Tua Mariit Wemen and the Wedo', in Scottish Language and Literature, Mediaeval and Renaissance, Fourth International Conference 1984 - Proceedings, Dietrich Strauss and Horst W Drescher (eds) (Frankfurt, 1986), pp 359-68, (367).
12 Thomas W Ross, Chaucer's Bawdy (New York, 1972), p 56. Cf. Chambre of Venus, Wife of Bath's Prologue and Tale, James Winny (ed) (Cambridge, 1965), 618 and MED citation Chaumbre of Venus, 'the vulva'.
13 A Dictionary of Slang (1937), Eric Partridge (ed), repr Paul Beale (ed) (London, 1984), p 885.
14 Benson, 'The Queynte Punnings', p 30.
15 Klaus Bitterling, 'The Tretis of the Tua Mariit Wemen and the Wedo: Some Comments on Words, Imagery, and Genre', in Scottish Language and Literature, ed Strauss and Drescher, pp 337-58 (349-50).
16 Ian Simpson Ross, William Dunbar (Leiden, 1981), p 229.
17 A Dictionary of Slang, p 205.
18 'In the British Isles young girls sometimes scratch the names of their various suitors on each of four onions and put them in the dark to sprout. The first one to sprout bears the name of the one she will marry. An onion under the pillow on St Thomas's Eve is said to bring dreams of one's future spouse.' Funk and Wagnall's Standard Dictionary of Folk Mythology and Legend, M Leach (ed) (New York, 1950), II 823.
19 Ebin, 'Dunbar's Bawdy', p 285.
20 The verb is glossed in DOST 'apparently to treat for venereal disease by cutting the chancres'; Ian Ross comments that it acknowledges the prevalence of venereal disease in Scotland, and may be a canting reference to a superstition that sexual intercourse was a cure for the disease: Ross, William Dunbar, p 60; Kinsley adds that the phrase may represent a metaphor for illicit sex (K 307).

21   Thomas Ross cites similar usage in General Prologue 476, Troilus and Criseyde III 695, Physician's Tale 79. Ross, Chaucer's Bawdy, p 67.

22   Eric Patridge, Shakespeare's Bawdy (1947) (repr London, 1968), p 108 has foot 'to copulate'.

23   There are instances of vomiting in The Flyting (23.462), and Fasternis Evin in Hell (52.172–80; 200–7), farting (23.56, 110–11; 52.155, 207), and excreting (23.194–5, 200, 239, 248, 395, 449–52, 459–60, 467–72, 499, 519–20; 52.191, 218) which is also featured in Ane Ballat of the Fenȝeit Freir (54.41–4, 101–2).

24   Ross, William Dunbar, p 208.

25   According to Thomas Ross, Chaucer uses corage with the same sexual charge in Clerk's Tale 907, Merchant's Tale 1759, 1808, Tale of Sir Topas 1970, Ross, Chaucer's Bawdy, p 64.

26   DOST quotes a comparable use of pith in Wife of Bath's Prologue 475.

27   Fressh in Thomas Ross's view is so often associated in Chaucer with sexual prowess 'that it can almost be taken as a synonym'. Ross, Chaucer's Bawdy, p 89. (His examples include Wife of Bath's Prologue 508, Shipman's Tale 1367).

28   Ebin, 'Dunbar's Bawdy', pp 278–9.

29   Cf. Shipman's Tale 1508, 1565 where myrthe is 'a kind of euphemism' for sexual intercourse, Ross Chaucer's Bawdy, p 150.

30   Priscilla Bawcutt, 'Dunbar: new light on some old words', in The Nuttis Schell, Caroline Macafee and Iseabail MacLeod (eds) (Aberdeen, 1987), pp 83–95 (85).

Chapter 17

WILLIAM DUNBAR AND THE MORRIS DANCERS

Annette Jung

A few years ago when I sat in the Royal Library in Copenhagen perusing Comte P Durrieu's book about La Miniature Flamande, I came across a lovely pen-and-ink drawing called 'Danse d'un ballet grotesque' in which a group of five men court an elegant and rather aloof lady while they circle around her in a lively dance to entertain a select audience of well-to-do middle class or upper class people. The whole situation is rendered with a touch of fine irony (Fig.1). It immediately struck me that this could have been a perfect illustration of William Dunbar's poem, 'Ane Dance in the Quenis Chalmer' (Fig.2).

The drawing is in an anthology of historical novels from the middle of the fifteenth century that belonged to Jean, bâtard de Wavring, Seigneur du Forestel, who seems to have had a predilection for illustrated books of this kind. I showed it to the Danish art historian, Mrs Ulla Haastrup, and her first remark was, 'Moriskentänzer'. It then turned out that the drawing belonged to a category of illustrations in the history of art called 'Moriskentänzer' because they all describe a morris dance. This genre flourished in the later Middle Ages and the years around 1500, spread over an area comprising Germany, Flanders, Austria, Northern Italy and England. It encompassed drawings, etchings, reliefs and sculpture, and objects could also be decorated with morris dancers.

The experience was exciting, so I decided to find out whether Dunbar's poem could be about a morris dance and whether there existed any literary genre like the art genre of the 'Moriskentänzer' in Scotland or abroad in which the poem could be included. To begin my search I looked up the Dictionary of the Older Scottish Tongue, but it had very few references under the entries Moris and Moris-dauns to literature old enough to be of interest for an interpretation of Dunbar's poem. It refers to Dunbar's Aganis the Solistaris in Court, to an addition to Mapheus Vegius's text made by Gavin Douglas in his translation of the thirteenth book of the Eneados, and finally to the early fifteenth-century poem Chrystis Kirk on the Grene. In the first two references, however, the texts only mention that a morris was danced; in Chrystis Kirk there is much more of a description of the dance itself.

Together with an earlier poem, Peblis to the Play, the poem Chrystis Kirk marks the beginning of a tradition of comic poems in Scottish verse which has made itself felt up to the present day, and to which Dunbar also contributed. Both poems contain scenes of wild dancing, and Dunbar has employed this dance motif in two of his poems, Fasternis Evin in Hell, also called the Dance of the Sevin Deidly Sinnis, and Ane Dance in the Quenis Chalmer.

Le us leave out of consideration Fasternis Evin in Hell, since this is a kind of morality parading the seven deadly sins in a wild, grotesque dance as an admonition to the reader or listener not to follow their examples, but to lead a flawless life in preparation for a blissful after-life. This motif is quite common in medieval didactic literature and has its parallels in the visual arts too. Ane Dance in the Quenis Chalmer, on the other hand, seems to be unique in describing an actual dance; but since, after all, it belongs to a Scottish tradition of dance poems, it might share some features with the poems just mentioned.

The description of the dancing is much firmer in Chrystis Kirk on the Grene (Fig.3) than in Peblis to the Play. The opening lines of the first stanza say directly that the poem is going to describe the dancing and courting of young people, but that all will end up in an enormous disturbance that surpasses even what happened in Falkland on the Grene and Peblis to the Play.

In the fifth stanza the invincible Stephen proudly enters the stage and begins a leaping dance - perhaps a kind of Highland Fling! - to charm the much desired girl Mald. He is, however, not successful for he falls on his back, and in his attempt to get up emits some deplorable noises from his body.

Tom Lutar, their minstrel, now takes over. He is unsurpassed in dancing, and his playing and singing is so wonderful that one woman, Towsie, swoons as if she had been an Elvis Presley fan. After a while Tom abandons the vernacular way of dancing and turns to imitating the French dancing style. His tactics are wise and have the result that at last Towsie joins him in the morris dance.

Actually, Dunbar's poem does share some of the features of this description. Most conspicuous is the French way of dancing. It is with this that Tom Lutar manages to get Towsie to join the dance, and it is in order to show off and to teach his little group to imitate the French style that Sir John Sinclair begins to dance.

Wooing is a motif in both poems. Stephen and Tom are on the look-out for a girl to charm with their dance, and Dunbar performs his grotesque dance for love of Mistress Musgrave. Dunbar loses his slipper but is not as unfortunate as Stephen who fell on his back; this fate is in store for Sir John himself.

To me Tom Lutar and Towsie seem to dance a morris dance to-gether, and Tom's leaps seem to be part of this morris dance. Two stanzas in a single poem are, however, not enough to make a liter-ary 'Moriskentänzer'-genre, and despite common features do not constitute enough evidence to conclude that Dunbar's poem is also about a morris. So to define Dunbar's poem as a morris dance it will be necessary to collect further information about the dance in the Middle Ages.

In the fifteenth and sixteenth centuries the morris dance was mainly performed by a group of dancers. Before that time it was either a solo dance or was danced by pairs of dancers fighting each other in a kind of sword-dance. Most authorities agree that the morris originated in Spain as a folk dance representing the

fights of the Spaniards against the Moors, and that the sword-
dance was the symbol of this. Cecil Sharp, however, rejects such a
theory and asserts an origin further back in time in dances of
religious content.

During the later Middle Ages the morris spread from Spain to
the rest of Europe, where it became the most popular dance among
all social classes in the fifteenth century. The choreography was
very demanding and presupposed great virility and masculine
strength. The steps consisted of leaps and springs only, and of
vigorous swinging of the arms and legs. The movements were difficult to combine and the dancer had to be able to control his limbs
completely in order to unite strength with grace. The German
engraver Israhel van Meckenem gives a perfect illustration of this
in his ornament with morris dancers from about 1490 (Fig.4), where
in the loops of intertwined acanthus leaves we see six men, a
fool, a flute player, and a dog courting a lady with an apple in
her hand.

Only professional dancers were able to dance the morris because
of the difficult movements, and it never became a dance in which
everybody in the party participated. Instead, it was performed by
companies whose performance normally marked the opening of the
evening's entertainments. This parallels what we saw in Fig.1, the
Flemish drawing, and Israhel van Meckenem shows us a similar scene
in 'The Morris Dancers' or 'La danse pour le prix' from about 1475
(Fig.5), where three men, a fool, and a flute player court a lady
who holds a ring between two fingers.

The audience in the Flemish drawing seem to be well-to-do
people at the beginning of an evening's entertainment, perhaps
reflecting the custom in Seigneur du Forestel's house itself. In
Israhel van Meckenem's picture a much less blasé audience of
passers-by in the street get a glimpse of the pleasures of the
sweet life.

The earliest known illustration of a morris dance in England is
a stained glass window from a house in Betley, Staffordshire
(Fig.6), the panels of which depict twelve figures from a May
festival and a morris dance. The window no longer exists, but we
can get an impression of what it was like from a description by
its owner in the late eighteenth century, George Tollet, supplemented by an etching by J Keyse Sherwin from the same period. Both
description and etching were first published in George Steeven's
edition of <u>The Plays of William Shakespeare</u> (1778), and then in a
later edition of Shakespeare with notes by Samuel Johnston and
Steevens (1793). In his etching Keyse Sherwin numbers each panel
of the window beginning with the bottom row. Tollet then explains
which characters the figures represent. Beginning from the bottom
left corner they are:

1   Bavian, the fool, who could bark like a dog.
2   The Maid Marion, the Queen of May, with a red carnation
    in her left hand.
3   Friar Tuck.
4   Marion's gentleman-usher or paramour.
5   The Hobbyhorse.
6   The peasant, villain or yeoman.

   7 A franklin, a gentleman of fortune, or a private
     gentleman.
   8 The Maypole.
   9 Tom the Piper.
  10 A Spaniard.
  11 A Morisco.
  12 The fool — the <u>joculator regis</u>.

All the dancers are wearing bells.
   Tollet does not know anything about the age of the window or
its provenance, but dates it to 1510 at the latest. Halm, however,
in his book about Erasmus Grasser from 1928, dates it to about
1480 on the basis of the style of the costumes, especially the
peaked shoes and the breeches. Tollet's information cannot be
verified from other sources, but later scholars have found it most
likely to be correct and have accepted it.
   Since we now know who the characters are, let us see whether
they are also represented in the other illustrations. The lady is
in all of them, and so is the fool and the peasant with his broad-
brimmed hat. In Fig.1 he is sitting in front of the lady, in Fig.4
he is in the bottom left corner, and in Fig.5 next to Tom the
Piper. Tom the Piper is implied, not shown, in Fig.1, but he is
present in the rest of the illustrations. All the other characters
are only represented in the Betley window, but the other illustrations add some characters the window does not have: Fig.1, a
warrior with a martial helmet in the centre behind the lady, and
Fig.4, a dog at her feet. So the lady, the flute player, the fool,
and the peasant seem to make up the core of the morris dance, and
the others seem to be additional characters varying in number and
type.
   The 'Moriskentänzer' tradition in art ends in 1542 with Erhard
Schön's illustration of a morris dance (Fig.7), very much like van
Meckenem's 'La danse pour le prix'. All the men are now wearing
cap and bells, and the fool to the right in the group of dancers
approaches the lady like the fool in the middle of van Meckenem's
ornament. Schön's illustration stresses the foolishness of courting and expresses the attitude of the Reformation towards the
morris dance.
   From the list of characters in the Betley window we may infer
that the morris dance had a plot; the window itself, however, does
not tell what it was about. There are no literary sources in
Britain which contain the information we need, but there exist a
few fifteenth-century Shrovetide plays from Nuremberg in Southern
Germany which are renderings of morris dances.
   It was the habit of the citizens at that time to entertain each
other at Shrovetide with plays mocking their surrounding world,
secular as well as ecclesiastical. The more riotous of these plays
were generally performed in public houses for a meal and a drink,
and among them was one simply called <u>Morischgentanz</u>.
   In this play a group of actors enter a public house, assuring
the landlord that they are decent people who just want to make his
guests laugh at a play they are going to perform. This will show
the guests the way in which every fool lets himself be deceived,
and what fools have suffered because of women. A lady with an

apple in her hand steps forward. She promises the apple as a prize for the fool who has behaved most foolishly of them all, and urges them to tell their stories so that she can decide who will be the winner. Ten persons then describe how they have been deceived by their women and in this way turned into fools, and the last of them gets the apple.

There exist two more plays of this kind from Nuremberg. In one of them well-defined characters instead of fools compete for the prize, namely a knight, a peasant, a clergyman, a monk, and some craftsmen. The peasant was normally the scapegoat in such plays. He was the one who knew all the obscenities and whose clumsy and awkward movements in the dance made him the laughing stock of everybody.

It is in drama, then, that we find a literary genre parallel to the 'Moriskentänzer'-genre in art, and it is through these plays that we learn about the plot in the morris dance: a group of men competing for a prize by their dancing. It is, however, obvious that Dunbar's poem does not belong to this category. It has no plot; there is no prize; there are two ladies, Mistress Musgrave and Dame Dounteboir; and it is not drama. The Shrovetide plays are therefore of no use for determining whether or not Ane Dance in the Quenis Chalmer is about a morris dance.

The morris was popular as entertainment in princely circles, as proved by several descriptions. The clearest visual evidence of this is 'Das Goldene Dachl' in Innsbruck in Austria (Fig.8) and a woodcut by the German engraver Hans Leinberger (Fig.9). In both cases a morris is performed for the entertainment of a prince and his wife.

'Das Goldene Dachl' was designed for the emperor Maximilian I (1486-1519) so that he could follow the public festivals and plays in the square in front of the house from the oriel window. This was decorated with reliefs of morris dancers on the facade and had a golden roof from which it got its name. The reliefs were executed about 1489 by Niklas Türing, who portrayed the imperial family attending the morris dance in two reliefs which he placed in the centre of the facade surrounded by four other reliefs with morris dancer (Figs. 10 and 11).

In Fig.10 the Emperor himself is seen in the relief to the left together with his fool, the joculator regis, and a courtier; and in the relief to the right he is seen together with his two wives. His first wife who had died at that time stands behind his second wife, who holds an apple in her right hand and approaches him with virtuously downcast eyes. Their joint attitude elegantly suggests the parallel between the lucky winner in the morris dance and the Emperor's situation of once again having a loving empress.

To the left of the central scene are two reliefs with morris dancers (Fig.11, upper row). At the extreme left two dancers are quarrelling or fighting. They both have flowing sleeves and one of them has short woolly hair, so they could be the Morisco and the Spaniard from the Betley window. In the next relief a dancer gets up from a stool but stumbles over a dog. He is wearing boots like the peasant in Fig.5, so obviously he is the peasant. The character of the next dancer is difficult to decide.

In the two reliefs to the right of the central scenes (Fig.11, lower row) we find the flute player nearest to the two empresses, then a young man in a desperate attitude with long, flowing hair and his hand on his heart as if he were erotically infatuated, like Maid Marion's paramour in the Betley window. Next to them come two ordinary dancers with their dogs which have also learned to dance. All the dancers have their eyes turned towards the imperial family, as if they all formed one big circle with the lady with the apple and the winner of the prize in the centre, and the whole atmosphere is that of a grotesque but nevertheless courteous morris.

Hans Leinberger's woodcut (Fig.9) shows how 'Das Goldene Dachl' functioned. It imitates the motif from the reliefs, but the rendering is not at all kind. The Emperor and his courtier have become dotards, the Emperor a lecherous one at that. The Empress looks as if she were drunk and behaving so badly that the Emperor's first wife has to cry. The fool now stands next to the two women, but he is no longer the <u>joculator regis</u>; to judge from his ape-like face he is rather Bavian the Fool. The whole scene seems to have unpleasant, political overtones.

A group of morris dancers are performing a morris in front of the imperial family. The lady with the apple, Tom the Piper, and the fool are in the centre of the dance. It is difficult to decide whether the peasant is represented, but there is a martial warrior with a shield and a sword, and Maid Marion's paramour with the flowing hair from the relief. The lady also has a mirror in her left hand, the symbol of vanity and licentiousness, and the dance is not only grotesque, its obscene features are stressed.

In Scotland there is plenty of evidence in the Lord High Treasurer's Accounts that the morris dance was a popular entertainment at the court of James IV in the period 1501-1512, that is from just before the king married until the catastrophe of Flodden. The accounts for the period May 1498 - February 1501 are lost, but from the information in the accounts for the following years we can gather that the morris dance was usually performed at the great festivals in winter and first part of the year: Yule-tide, i.e. Christmastime, Shrovetide before Lent, and the May festivals. On 8 February 1502 a fee was paid to 'the men that brocht in the morice dance, and to their menstrales, in Strive-lin, be the Kingis command', and on 5 December 1512 the French ambassador De la Motte let his servants perform a morris dance before the king, an entertainment which was repeated on 16 Decem-ber with both the king and the queen as audience, exactly as in the reliefs on 'Das Goldene Dachl'.

The dancers seem to have been professionals with leaders who were responsible for the performances. It is possible to recognise a few of these from the accounts: Thomas Boswell and Pate Sinclair got some money with which to buy equipment for dancing in January 1504, and on the last day of December 1506 Thomas Boswell alone got the amount of four pounds twelve shil- lings for thirty dozen bells for dancers, in both cases perhaps in connection with the Twelfth Night entertainments. Colin Campbell was another leader. On 6 January 1504, the day of Epiphany, he received a fee for himself '... and his marowis that brocht in the Moris dauns ...', and on 15 January 1507 he got a recompense for a dance he had performed.

John Damian, the French leech, Dunbar's 'Fenʒeit Freir of Tungland', a prominent figure at court because of his alchemy, probably also had some authority in connection with the morris dance. On 5 January 1504 he received a sum for belts for a morris dance, and two days later a rather larger sum for taffeta for dancing costumes. The dancers must have formed a morris group, for the material was to be used for six dancing coats and a gown for the woman. This well-known pattern of a morris dance, the lady and the group of male dancers wooing her in the shape of various characters, is also recognisable in two other items: in 1506, on the penultimate day of December, a sum was paid for a set of five dancing coats and a gown, and Thomas Boswell got a set of seven dancing coats and a gown but did not get his bells till the next day. The morris dance seems therefore to have followed the same tradition in Scotland as on the continent: a group of men varying in number in competition for a lady, just as we have seen it in the illustrations.

'Ane Dance in the Quenis Chalmer' is also documented in the Lord High Treasurer's Accounts – not exactly Dunbar's dance, but a corresponding event. On 26 August 1505 a sum was paid to 'Carnavale, clerk of the Quenis closet be the Kingis command', and to make up for forgetfulness the accounts add, 'I traist quhen he maid ane dans'.

Queen Margaret had only been a few years in Scotland at that time and she was very young. Perhaps the court did their best to make her feel comfortable in her new home. James Kinsley suggests that Dunbar's poem might have been written for her entertainment in this period and dates it to the middle of 1506, a year after the entry in the accounts, on the basis of an identification of the personalities in her retinue and their doings.

It has up till now been impossible to determine whether Dunbar described a morris dance in his poem. In the light of the information in the Treasurer's Accounts and the habits of the court it seems evident that the dance must have been familiar to him. A way to solve the problem could therefore be to compare the courtiers' dancing situation in the poem with the various characters in the morris and to see whether the structure of the morris will emerge from the analysis.

Without circumlocution Dunbar opens the poem in mediis rebus when Sir John Sinclair is taking up his French dance. The French steps are difficult and he cannot gain control over his feet, which makes his dance look rather grotesque. Perhaps he does not possess the virility necessary to endow it with grace, and the result is that he falls to the ground and must be helped by the others. Somebody calls him the Queen's knight, somewhat ironically considering his present situation, but the association lay near at hand for Dunbar, for actually he was in the queen's service and can be seen still to have been so in 1513. However, the knight is also one of the characters in the morris dance, as in the literary description in one of the Nuremberg Shrovetide plays mentioned above. In the Betley window there is a representation of Maid Marion's gentleman-usher or paramour. Maid Marion could be identified with the Queen of May, so the gentleman-usher would be her knight. The paramour is irrelevant in our connection. In the

Flemish drawing and Leinberger's woodcut the content of the figure
has changed slightly and he has become a warrior.

Next Robert Shaw, a court physician, takes over. His manners
are supercilious, but pride goes before a fall: his performance of
the dance is a miserable show, he staggers along like a gaunt jade
in an unsteady trot. Dunbar compares him to an old horse with its
forelegs bound together, hopschackelt. To hopschackel is the same
as to hobble, and the Oxford English Dictionary says that it is
apparently cognate with Dutch hobbeln, to toss, to rock from side
to side, to ride on a hobby-horse. The Treasurer's Accounts inform
us that the royal stables also made use of hopschackling: there is
an entry of 5 July 1501 saying 'Item, for ij hopschakilles to the
coursouris, vi s'. So, lo and behold, Master Robert Shaw with his
peculiar pace plays the part of the hobbyhorse in the morris dance.

Already at this point in the poem it is clear that the dance is
a competition like the morris. Shaw thought he could outdo Sir
John but failed, and after him comes Dr Babington trying to out-
rival Shaw. The doctor, however, has an unsteady walk like a young
bullock in the rye, and whenever he tries to imitate the elegant
French steps a lot of hideous noises are emitted from his
buttocks. This inspires John Bute the Fool to cry out that he is
fouled with excrement.

Behaviour of this kind goes perfectly well with the descriptions in the Nuremberg plays where the peasant was normally the
scapegoat. The doctor's movements were clumsy and awkward –
hommiltye jommeltye. Everybody laughed at him and he was the one
who knew all the obscenities. The rural image in Dunbar's poem
stresses the impression of a man without breeding, so Dr Babington
plays the peasant in the morris.

Now for the poet himself. He must be Maid Marion's paramour
from the Betley window. He could not be the knight, just as Sir
John could not be the paramour. Dunbar is provocative and daring,
and his dance is wild and erotically infatuated like the relief
from 'Das Goldene Dachl'. He is like a rutting colt, dancing to
win Mistress Musgrave. It all ends up in laughter, however, when
he loses his slipper.

It is beyond discussion that Mistress Musgrave is the lady with
the apple. The moment she enters the stage the tone of the poem
changes from the rude and burlesque to a courteous, more dignified
mode. Her dance is graceful and in marked contrast to that of the
others. She is alone and dignified in her own 'space' while the
others circle around her with their grotesque capers, just as in
the Flemish drawing and the two etchings of van Meckenem. Dunbar
has indicated her function by placing the episode in the middle of
the poem, surrounded by the descriptions of the other characters
in the dance. His admiration for her and his own wishes bring her
out as the prize for which they all compete, and he has managed to
create in the reader the feeling of a genuine falling in love on
his own part.

Dunbar creates a relation between Mistress Musgrave and himself
similar to the relation between Maximilian and his Empress in the
reliefs on 'Das Goldene Dachl' and the fool and the lady in
Leinberger's woodcut; and he also places himself in the same
situation as the fools in Figs. 4 and 8, who approach the lady as

if they had already won her. Attempts have been made to identify
Mistress Musgrave among the staff of the court, but she still
remains unidentified. The possibility exists, however, that Dunbar
invented her name because anonymity made her better suited to
function as a symbol of love in the shape of the woman of the
dance.

To make the contrast felt, Dunbar lets Dame Dounteboir follow
immediately after Mistress Musgrave. She is utterly unattractive
and performs her dance with a somewhat exaggerated swinging of her
hips. Her efforts are so demanding that a blast of wind slips from
her during the dancing. A second woman seems out of place in a
morris dance, but Cecil Sharp informs us that other characters
could be added to the stock set. It could be a King and Queen, or
a cake-and-sword-bearer, or a prostitute, 'The Moll', who was
often played by a man. The dancers could also have a 'ragman' to
take care of their ordinary clothes while they were dancing in
their costumes. Like Musgrave, Dounteboir has never been identified, or else has been falsely identified as the wife of James
Dog. Why she is called by the name Dounteboir is uncertain too.
Dounteboir seems to be a derogatory epithet for some of the ladies
at court. I do not think that her title of 'Dame' is meant as a
real title, but rather as a personification after the use of the
time of the concept of 'dounteboir' as in Dame Nature, Dame Fortune, Dame Flora, and Dame Venus. Dounteboir's exaggerated wriggle
and unseemly behaviour could very well be executed by a man cari-
caturing one of the dounteboirs in an anti-feministic way. So I
find it quite reasonable to say that Dame Dounteboir represents
'The Moll'.

James Dog, the queen's wardrober, has up to now been totally
uninterested in the dancing, but now he shows signs of joining the
others in the finale. Dunbar cannot resist the temptation to pun
on his name: their relations were not always the best, as we know
from other poems, so we get a good caricature of him as a big,
heavy mastiff with something of the nature of a cur or mongrel. He
had been asleep at the feet of his mistress the Queen, who
actually had a hound or brachet leaping up in her letter-seal; he
had slept like the dogs in van Meckenem's ornament and the reliefs
on 'Das Goldene Dachl'; now he tugs his lead to indicate that he
wants to dance with the others like the dancers' small dogs. There
could also be an aspect of his profession associated with the
morris dancers, in that he could be the dancers' ragman. It seems
most likely, however, that he is the dog of the group.

John Bute the Fool does not participate actively in the dancing. He seems to be of importance as an observing commentator, in
the same double role as on 'Das Goldene Dachl'. The flute player,
the taubronar in Scots, is missing from the poem, which was also
the case in the Flemish drawing.

The dog does not get up until five or six men have delivered
their dance, but 'five or six' is the same as a morris side, the
fixed group of morris dancers. In the Treasurer's Accounts the
expenditures are always for morris sides: money for six doublets,
for five doublets, or for seven doublets. The morris sides in the
illustrations vary a good deal in size from three in Schon's
drawing to eight in the Betley window, but there are five in the

Flemish pen-and-ink drawing which was our starting-point.

An analysis of Dunbar's poem accordingly discloses both the structure of the morris dance, the morris side, and the morris characters. Five or six men, viz. the knight, the hobbyhorse, the peasant, Maid Marion's paramour, the Moll, and the dog, all circle around the lady in a wild, grotesque dance, and all of them have their parallels in literature and art. Dunbar's poem has thus revealed itself as a unique, independent Scottish parallel to the 'Moriskentänzer'-genre in art, with features that were also found outside Britain.

Whether the queen was present at the dance is not clear from the text. John Bute the Fool behaves as if he were in attendance, like the fool on 'Das Goldene Dachl', and the dog tugs his lead as if a hand, perhaps the queen's, was at the other end of it; so possibly she was. Kinsley suggests that the poem was written in the middle of 1506, but since the morris dance was normally performed at the greater festivals of the year it would be more obvious to connect the poem with one of these. The safest point to choose, considering the death of Dr Babington before May 1507, would then be Christmas time 1506/7. At that time the queen was pregnant with her first child, which was born in February 1507. One may readily imagine her as indisposed to be present at the performance, which perhaps was one of the morris dances mentioned in the accounts as being held on the penultimate day of December 1506 or thereabouts. Dunbar could then have brought her his mini-morris as a compensation and a New Year's gift, like his poem to the king earlier in his career, in order to cheer her up.

However, to be realistic: though our starting point, the Flemish pen-and-ink drawing, perfectly covers the scene in Dunbar's poem, it will never be possible to say with certainty that the poem is a representation of a morris dance. For that we would need the poet's own direct information. It most likely is about a morris, but even without this aspect it is a cameo of a situation in court life that is still able to delight the modern reader – 'A mirrear dance mycht na man see'.

Bibliography

Balfour Paul, James and Thomas Dickson (eds) Compota thesaurariorum regum Scotorum: Accounts of the Lord High Treasurer of Scotland (Edinburgh, 1877-1916), Vol II, pp 135, 157, 413, 414. Vol III, pp 313, 359, 362. Vol IV, p 399

Baxter, John W, William Dunbar: A Biographical Study (1952, repr New York, 1971), pp 153, 160

Busch, Harald, Deutsche Gotik (Vienna, 1969)

Craigie, W A (ed) The Maitland Folio Manuscript, STS n.s. 7, 20 (1919-27, repr New York, 1972)

Dolmetsch, Mabel, Dances of Spain and Italy from 1400 to 1600 (London, 1954), p 108, note 1

Douce, Francis, Illustrations of Shakespeare and of Ancient Manners (London, 1839), p 577

Durrieu, Cte P, La Miniature Flamande (Brussels, 1921)

Froning, R, Das Drama des Mittelalters (Deutsche National-Literatur, 12-14), Stuttgart n.d.

Grove, Lilly, 'Dancing', in The Badminton Library of Sports and Pastimes by His Grace the Duke of Beaufort, K.G. (London, 1895), p 136

Halm. Philipp Maria, Erasmus Grasser (Studien zur süddeutschen Plastik, 3) Augsburg 1928

Kinghorn, A M (ed) The Middle Scots Poets (London, 1970)

Kinsley, James (ed) The Poems of William Dunbar (Oxford, 1979), pp 100-1, 302-4

Lossnitzer, Max, Hans Leinberger: Nachbildungen seiner Kupferstiche und Holzschnitte (Berlin, 1913)

Mill, Anna J, Medieval Plays in Scotland (Edinburgh/London, 1927) pp 11-13

Oberhammer, Vinzenz, Das Goldene Dachl zu Innsbruck (Innsbruck/Vienna/Munich, 1970)

Ritchie, W Tod (ed) The Bannatyne Manuscript, STS ser. III, 5 and n.s. 22-23, 26 (1928-34, repr New York, 1972)

Sachs, Curt, World History of the Dance (New York/London, 1963) p 333

Sharp, Cecil J and Herbert C Macilwaine, The Morris Book (London, 1912), pp 27, 29

Strauss, Walter L (gen.ed.) Early German Artists (The Illustrated Bartsch, 9. Formerly Vol 6, Part 2) (New York, 1981)

Warburg, Anni, Israhel van Meckenem: sein Leben, sein Werk und seine Bedeutung fur die Kunst des ausgehenden 15. Jahrhunderts (Bonn, 1929), pp 1-8, 19-20, 37, 126-7

Wiles, David, The Early Plays of Robin Hood (Cambridge, 1981)

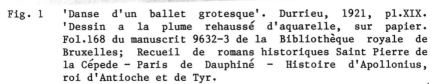

Fig. 1   'Danse d'un ballet grotesque'. Durrieu, 1921, pl.XIX.
'Dessin a la plume rehaussé d'aquarelle, sur papier.
Fol.168 du manuscrit 9632-3 de la Bibliothèque royale de
Bruxelles; Recueil de romans historiques Saint Pierre de
la Cépede - Paris de Dauphiné - Histoire d'Apollonius,
roi d'Antioche et de Tyr.
   Manuscrit sur papier, d'apparence vulgaire, et illustré
de dessins parfois presque enfantins. Porte les armoires
et la signature de Jean, bâtard de Wavring, Seigneur du
Forestel (1415-1471) qui a possedé plusieurs volumes du
même genre, tels, par example, qu'un Histoire d'Olivier
de Castile, conservé a la Bibliothèque de l'Université de
Gand, no.470. Petit in-folio (300 x 215 mm, ecrit a
longues lignes, justification 200 x 145 mm).'

28. [Ane Dance in the Quenis Chalmer]

Sir Jhon Sinclair begowthe to dance
For he was new cum owt of France;
For ony thing that he do mycht
The ane futt ʒeid ay onrycht
    And to the tother wald nocht gree.
Quod ane, Tak up the Quenis knycht!
    A mirrear dance mycht na man see.

Than cam in Maistir Robert Schau:
He leuket as he culd lern tham a,
Bot ay his ane futt did waver;
He stackeret lyk ane strummall aver
    That hopschackellt war aboin the kne;
To seik fra Sterling to Stranaver
    A mirrear daunce mycht na man see.

Than cam in the maister almaser,
Ane hommiltye jommeltye juffler
Lyk a stirk stackarand in the ry;
His hippis gaff mony hoddous cry.
    John Bute the fule said, Waes me,
He is bedirtin; fye, fy!
    A mirrear dance mycht na man se.

Than cam in Dunbar the mackar;
On all the flure thair was nane frackar,
And thair he dancet the dirrye dantoun;
He hoppet lyk a pillie wanton
    For luff of Musgraeffe, men tellis me;
He trippet quhill he tint his panton:
    A mirrear dance mycht na man see.

Than cam in Maesteres Musgraeffe;
Scho mycht heff lernit all the laeffe;
Quhen I schau hir sa trimlye dance,
Hir guid convoy and contenance,
    Than for hir saek I wissitt to be
The grytast erle or duk in France:
    A mirrear dance mycht na man see.

Than cam in Dame Dounteboir—
God waett gif that schou louket sowr;
Schou maid sic morgeownis with hir hippis,
For lachtter nain mycht hald thair lippis;
    Quhen schou was danceand bisselye,
Ane blast of wind son fra hir slippis:
    A mirrear dance mycht na man se.

Quhen thair was cum in fyve or sax
The Quenis Dog begowthe to rax,
And of his band he maid a bred
And to the danceing soin he him med;
    Quhou mastevlyk abowt ʒeid he!
He stinckett lyk a tyk, sum saed:
    A mirrear dance mycht na man see.

Fig. 2   Ane Dance in the Quenis Chalmer: 'Sir Jhon Sinclair begowthe to dance'. Kinsley, 1979, 100–01, no.28.

Stevin come steppand in with stendis,
No renk mycht him arrest;
Platfut he bobbit up with bendis,

For Mald he maid requeist;
He lap quhill he lay on his lendis,
Bot rysand he was prest
Quhill he hostit at bayth the endis
In honour of the feist
That day
At Chrystis Kirk on the grein.

Thome Lutar was thair menstrale meit;
O Lord, gif he culd lance!
He playit so schill and sang so sweit
Quhill Towsie tuik ane trance;
All auld lycht futtis he did forleyt
And counterfutit France;
He him avysit as man discreit
And up the moreis dance
Scho tuik
At Chrystis Kirk on the grein.

Fig. 3   Christ's Kirk on the Grene, st.5-6. Kinghorn, 1970, 59-60.

Fig. 4   Strauss, 1981, pl.201.

Fig. 5   Ibid., pl.186.

Fig. 6   Halm, 1928, pl.XCIII, fig.167.

Fig. 7   Halm, 1928, pl.XC, fig.161.

Fig. 8   Oberhammer, 1970, pp.11 and 154.

Fig. 9   Lossnitzer, 1913, pl.XVI, fig.30.

Fig. 10 Halm, 1928, pl.LXXXIX, fig.159-60.

Fig. 11   Busch, 1969, pl.143-46. (see also facing page)

Chapter 18

GAVIN DOUGLAS ON LOVE: THE PROLOGUE TO ENEADOS IV

Elizabeth Archibald

In the Prologue to the First Book of Eneados, Gavin Douglas criticises Chaucer for taking liberties with the Virgilian text, and
insists that he will make every effort not to incur the same
charge. His own first innovation – though hardly a culpable one –
is to add this initial prologue. It is not surprising that he
should wish to talk about Virgil and about the problems of translation (especially into Scots). The first-time reader may be surprised, however, to find that each subsequent book is prefaced by
a prologue, of varying length, metre, and subject.
   David Coldwell notes in the introduction to his edition of
Eneados:

> The most interesting part of Gavin Douglas's original poetry,
> however, is the thirteen prologues to the Aeneid. I am not
> sure that they are given a logical order, that there is a
> strategy in their relative position in the series, even
> though one could be invented.[1]

He proceeds to invent such a strategy, and to relate each prologue
to the book which it prefaces in a predictable and plausible manner; then he concludes:

> One can praise Douglas's intention in the prologues, then,
> but I am not sure that one should. I suspect that some of the
> prologues are poems 'too good to waste', draped on the Aeneid
> because no more suitable ones occurred. (p 88)

Denton Fox goes even further in regarding in prologues as entirely
independent and experimental poems: 'The prologues are above all
designed to demonstrate Douglas's competence at writing in various
styles on various subjects'.[2] Priscilla Bawcutt sees good in both
these views, but insists, quite rightly, that the prologues must
also be read in the context within which Douglas himself placed
them.[3] Discussing their strategy, she remarks that 'few would
question the relevance of the first six prologues' (p 172). She
continues:

> The moralizing of Prologue IV might seem remote from the
> dramatic sympathy with which Virgil portrays Dido and Aeneas.
> Nonetheless, the Prologue fits logically into its context; a
> reading of Book IV might well prompt such reflections in a
> pious reader.

None of these critics pays much attention to Prologue IV. Coldwell analyses its contents rather cursorily, and concludes that it is 'a competent exercise in late medieval rhetoric' (p 92). The subject, the perils of sex, is a highly conventional one, he points out, and he sums up the poem without enthusiasm:

> The best that can be said for the poem is that it is finely executed in comparison with most of the drab poetry of the next fifty years, and that Douglas is a poet of great skill compared with Lydgate and Hawes. I do not, however, mean this as warm praise.

Warm praise it is certainly is not — in fact it seems a perfect example of damning with faint praise!

Prologue IV was anthologised in the Bannatyne manuscript under the Ovidian title 'The prollog of the fourt buik of virgell Treting of the Incommoditie of luve and Remeid thairof compyld be bischop gawyne dowglas'.[4] It is the last work in section four, the part devoted to 'ballatis of luve'; this section is itself subdivided into love songs, 'contemptis of love and evill wemen', 'contemptis of evill fals vicius men', and 'ballatis detesting of luve and lichery'. Presumably Prologue IV was thought to be a significant and elegant statement on the subject of 'luve and lichery', and indeed a definitive one: it is followed by the rubric 'Heir endis the ballatis of luve/Remedy thairof and contempt of luve'. But can it be called 'a competent rhetorical exercise'? Does it offer a coherent view of both the 'Incommoditie' and the 'Remeid' of love? And does it really fit logically into its context in the Eneados? I shall be arguing in this paper that the argument is not coherent, that Douglas does not condemn love — or Dido — as harshly as the opening of the Prologue would suggest, and that his ambivalent view of love owes even more to Chaucer's Troilus and Criseyde than has been previously noticed.

It does not seem to strike critics as remarkable that this is the first prologue which Douglas develops at any length, apart from Prologue I which is really an introduction to the Eneados as a whole. Prologue II consists of a three-stanza invocation of Melpomene, the Muse of Tragedy; in its final stanza Douglas mentions rapidly the fatal beauty of women, the fury of Mars, the results of deceit, and ends with a pessimistic proverb: 'All erdly glaidness fynysith with wo' (1.21). Prologue III, which runs to five stanzas, begins with an invocation of Cynthia and culminates in a prayer to the Virgin to be the poet's lodestar and to save his bark from the improbable hazards of 'Harpyes fell and blynd Cyclopes handis' (11. 41-2). None of this prepares us for Prologue IV, which consists of 38 stanzas.

It begins, appropriately, with an invocation to Cytherea and Cupid: but Douglas does nòt praise their powers as he did Cynthia's in the previous prologue. In the fourth line of the first stanza, he establishes his position clearly by calling them 'fosteraris of byrnyng carnail, hait delyte'. Grudgingly he acknowledges their relevance to his story at this point:

> Wyth bemys scheyn thou bricht Cytherea,
> Quhilk only schaddowist amang starris lyte,
> And thi blyndyt weyngit son Cupyd, ye twa
> Fosteraris of byrnyng carnail, hait delyte,
> Your ioly wo neidlyngis most I endyte,
> Begynnyng with a fenyeit faynt plesance,
> Continewit in lust, and endyt with pennance.
>
> (1-7)

He spends the next 29 stanzas attacking love – or rather lust, for he borrows St Augustine's distinction between the two loves, 'perfyte and imperfyte,/That ane leful, the tother fowle delyt' (11.112-3; in a marginal note he refers the reader to <u>De Civitate Dei</u>, Book 15, c.22).

Douglas's views on love may be 'the conventional moralizing of a pious reader', but the strategy of his argument is hard to follow; I find it implausible that this prologue was originally composed as an independent poem, as Fox and Coldwell suggest. Stanzas 1-4 consist of a series of attacks on Cytherea and Cupid: their 'fykkil seyd' is said to flourish where sloth is present and shame absent, and the result is described in a string of oxymorons, such as 'Quhat is your drery gemme? a myrry pane' (1.23). Stanza 4 ends with the assertion that people must be mad to enjoy the distress caused by love.

At 1.29 Douglas launches into a list of men who have been injured or humiliated by love. The list is traditional, but also random: Old Testament heroes appear side by side with classical ones. There are two curious interruptions to this catalogue of woe. At 11.36 ff. Douglas introduces an entirely new and distracting argument: love is so powerful that even God was bound by it when He became Man, born of a virgin. Love is credited with the defeat of the Devil, the replenishment of Paradise, and the harrowing of Hell:

> Thou cheyn of luf, ha benedicite,
> Quhou hard strenys thi bandis every wyght!
> The God abuf, from his hie maieste,
> With the ybond, law in a maid dyd lycht:
> Thou venquyst the strang gyant of gret mycht;
> Thou art mair forcy than the ded sa fell;
> Thou plenyst paradyce and thou heryit hell
>
> (11.36-42)

This seems an incontrovertibly good effect of the power of <u>love</u>, but it is out of place in a catalogue of great men brought low by <u>lust</u>. In the next stanza Douglas returns to his traditional examples of amorous disaster, though in a slightly different mood: he notes that love is a great leveller – 'Thou makist febil wight and lawyst the hie:/Thou knyttis frendschyp quhar thar beyn na parage' – as in the case of David and Jonathan (11. 43-4). Again this seems a plus for love: but in the next stanza Douglas continues with traditional casualties such as Narcissus and Achilles, and laments the suicides and murders, the 'crimes passionelles'.

At 11.57ff there is another digression, this time to quote the

<u>Georgics</u> on the power of love over such non-human victims as
stallions, bulls, stags and rams. Again this might seem a strong
argument for love as a positive cosmic force: 'amor omnibus idem',
says Virgil, love is the same for all.[5] Once more Douglas does not
stop to draw conclusions, but returns hastily to his endless list
of victims of lust to tell the sad story of Hero and Leander,
which leads him to berate Venus for rewarding her servants by
driving them mad.

So far all the examples of casualties in love have been men,
except for Hero, who is included as Leander's other half. But at
11.100ff. Douglas begins to discuss love as a process in which men
deceive women, reproaching 'nyss lovaris' for their behaviour.

> Quhat, is this lufe, nyss luffaris, at ye meyn,
> Or fals dissait fair ladeys to begile?
> Thame to defowle, and schent your self betweyn,
> Is al your lykyng, wyth mony suttel wyle.
> Is that trew lufe, gude faith and fame to fyle?
> Gyf luf be vertu, than is it lefull thing;
> Gif it be vyce, it is your ondoyng.
>
> (11.100-6)

He goes on to make the Augustinian distinction between love and
lust, and recommends the compromise position of 'messure', comparing moderate love to a healthy body temperature (11.107-27). He
does not deny earthly love entirely: excessive love means loving
anything more than God; one should love first God, then oneself
('eschewing wykkytnes'), then one's neighbours (11.128-41). But
abruptly he abandons this biblical tack and turns to courtly love,
playing with the meanings of 'grace' in religious and courtly
terminology. He comments critically on the lover 'Grasless thow
askis grace' (11.144). A second pun applies to both lover and
lady: 'Or is it grace to fall fra grace?' (1.150). It is a mistake, he says, to spend one's youth 'in riot leif, in sport and
gam' (1.159), for this leads to 'byttir pane and wo' (1.163).

Lust and riotous living lead the young to ruin; but now Douglas
turns his attention to the old, and criticises them all, 'thou
auld hasard lichour, ... auld trat, agit wyfe, or dame' (11.164-
6). There can be no excuse for these old traffickers in flesh,
whom he calls 'Venus henwyffis' (1.188) and 'poyd makerellis'
(1.193); but he seems to sympathise sincerely with young women who
may be led astray, urging them to resist all immoral advances. He
concentrates on women, though his advice is extended to male
revellers too:

> Rew on your self, ladeys and madynnys yyng,
> Grant na syk reuth, for evir may causs yow rew:
> Yhe fresch gallandis, in hait desyre byrnyng,
> Refreyn your curage syk paramouris to persew;
>
> (11.201-4)

He sees love in courtly terms: men pursuing, ladies granting their
favours. The advice he gives them all is to 'Grund your amouris on
charite al new;/Found yow on resson' (11.205-6). Does this mean

that earthly love should be entirely abandoned in favour of heavenly love? The last line of the stanza runs 'God grant you grace in
luf, as I you tech' (1.207). The phrasing of this line might be
deliberately ambigous if it were by Chaucer, who plays on similar
language, simultaneously courtly and religious, in the address to
lovers at the beginning of the Troilus (I, 15-56).[6]

Douglas makes his meaning clear, however, by recommending the
reader to read 'moral Gower' (1.213).

> Bot al syk crymys in luffis causs I resyng
> To the confessioun of morale Ihonne Gower,
> For I mon follow the text of our mater.
> (11.212-4)

In the final episode of the Confessio Amantis, the Lover renounces
Venus's love in favour of 'thilke love which that is/Withinne a
mannes herte affermed,/And stant of charite confermed', that love
'which mai the soule amende'.[7] This is presumably what Douglas is
advising too: but instead of continuing the lesson himself, he
returns to 'the text of our mater', which means Dido. For although
Douglas is urging both men and women to renounce love, he is not
yet at the end of his text, but is merely introducing the tragedy
of Dido.

The increasing sympathy for betrayed women which is revealed
towards the end of his diatribe against lust helps to prepare us
for his treatment of Dido, which is much gentler than that given to
Cytherea at the beginning of the poem. Invoking Dido in terms of
her 'dowbill wound', Douglas recalls Augustine's confession that he
had wept over her tragic end.

> Thy dowbill wound, Dido, to specify,
> I meyn thyne amouris and thi funeral fait,
> Quha may endyte, but teris, with eyn dry?
> Augustyne confessis hym self wepit, God wait,
> Redyng thy lamentabill end mysfortunat.
> By the wil I repeyt this verss agane,
> 'Temporal ioy endis wyth wo and pane'.
> (11.215-21)

Douglas too seems to sympathise with Dido, although her story is
yet another excuse for stressing the disasters caused by love:

> Quhat is, bot turment, all hys langsum fayr,
> Begun with feir, and endyt in despayr?
> (11.234-5)

Douglas extends this criticism, culminating in a stanza packed with
sonorous rhyming Latinate adjectives characterising lust: 'devourar
of tyme onrecoverabill', 'inextingwybill', 'insaciabill', 'odibill'
(11.243-9). But then without further example or digression he
returns to the subject of Dido and her 'fraward destane'.

'Allace the quhile thou knew the strange Ene!', Douglas laments
(1.263). His final comment, expressed in the last stanza of the

Prologue, is not a condemnation of love, but a warning to women to beware of strangers:

> And sen I suld thy tragedy endyte,
> Heir nedis nane othir invocatioun:
> Be the command I lusty ladeis quhyte,
> Be war with strangeris of onkouth natioun
> Wyrk na syk woundris to thar dampnatioun;
> Bot till attayin wild amouris at the thai leir;
> Thy lusty pane begouth on this maneir.
>   (11.264-70)

The criticism that the story of Dido teaches women to achieve 'wild amouris' does not seem a logical sequel to the advice to ladies to beware of strangers.[8] Altogether this stanza makes a curious finale after such a lengthy diatribe against lust. In Prologue I, Douglas chides Chaucer for misrepresenting Aeneas as a deceiver, when he was only obeying the gods' commands in leaving Carthage for Italy (11.409-49). Yet here Dido's experience is used to argue that ladies are at risk when they fall in love with strangers: the emphasis seems to be on the unsuitability of the lover rather than the love.

An appeal to ladies at the end of a poem is of course not unusual in medieval or even Middle Scots literature: the Testament of Cresseid (which is largely written in rhyme royal, like Prologue IV and the Troilus, and is of course explicitly indebted to Chaucer's poem) ends with Henryson's advice to 'worthie wemen' to 'ming not your lufe with fals deceptioun'.[9] Earlier in the poem, Cresseid herself addresses the 'ladyis fair of Troy and Grece' in her complaint, urging them 'in your mynd ane mirrour mak of me' (11.452ff). At the end she advises both men and women: 'Lovers be war and tak gude heid about/Quhome that ye lufe, for quhome ye suffer paine' (11.561-2). But Henryson's poem is all about deception in love, first by Cresseid and then by Diomeid, so Cresseid's advice and the narrator's final comment do not seem at all out of place. Douglas insists in Prologue I that Aeneas was not a deceiver. Furthermore, Henryson's narrator describes himself at the beginning of the poem as one who has been obedient to Venus, and hopes that she will rejuvenate his heart (11.22ff). It is therefore natural for him to give sympathetic advice on love at the end, whereas Douglas does not present himself as a servant of Venus, and the tone of the beginning of Prologue IV makes the ending all the more surprising. Were there really ladies in his audience whom he wished to address, or is he slipping into a poetic convention without regard for the consistency of his argument?[10] Has the context of the Prologue, combined with the ubiquitous medieval sympathy for Dido, succeeded in obscuring the conventional moralising of the pious reader on the perils of sex?

Before considering in more detail the end of Prologue IV and the influence of the Troilus, I should like to look at Douglas's views on love as expressed in an earlier work, The Palice of Honour, which is based in large part on two of Chaucer's dream poems, The House of Fame and The Legend of Good Women.[11] Both Chaucer's poems are much concerned with love. In The House of

<u>Fame</u>, the narrator's dream begins with the story of Dido; although much space is devoted to fame in its various forms, it is 'tydynges of Loves folk' which the eagle promises Geoffrey (11.645, 675), and 'love-tydynges' which are being discussed in the corner where he is looking when the poem ends in mid-sentence (11.2141ff). In the Prologue to <u>The Legend of Good Women</u>, the narrator dreams that the God of Love accuses him of committing heresy in writing the <u>Troilus</u>. Like Chaucer's narrator, Douglas too is accused of heresy, in this case by Venus. But whereas the Chaucerian narrator incurs the god's wrath because of a real previous work, the <u>Troilus</u> (which as he says defensively is merely a translation of an existing story), Douglas deliberately brings the wrath of the goddess onto his head by singing a lay against love when he witnesses the arrival of Venus's court in his dream. In a marginal note he describes his song as 'a ballet of inconstant love', in which 'he curseth the worlds felycite, fortune and al his pleasure'. But he does more than that, for in the third and last stanza, he curses the very deities of love:

> Wo worth this dede that dayly dois me de.
> Wo worth Cupyd, and wo worth fals Venus
> Wo worth thaym bayth, ay waryit mot thay be,
> Wo worth thair court and cursyt destane.
>
> (11.633-6)

Douglas pretends to be frightened by his ensuing arrest, but one cannot help feeling that he does not take Venus's reprimand or her power very seriously, since he reminds her that 'ladyis may be Iugis in na place' (1.695), and furthermore that he is 'a spirituall man' (1.697), and therefore outside the jurisdiction of the civil courts. Venus' anger is further undercut by the arrival of Calliope, spokeswoman for the Muses, who plays the whole business down, calling Douglas's crime 'sa small' (1.957), and asking Venus 'Quhow may a fule your hie renoun chakmate' (1.960). Her reaction undermines the standing of both Venus and Douglas, but it also serves to save the poet from execution. Instead Venus orders him to write 'sum breif/Or schort ballat in contrare pane and wo/ Tuychand my laud and his plesand releif' (11.994-6). The three-stanza ballad which follows could hardly be called enthusiastic in its praise of Venus, who is only mentioned in the last stanza, in the context of ease rather than passion. But the goddess accepts it as 'sum recompence for my trespas' and as a sign of penitence (11.1049-50) – and the poem moves on to the more important themes of poetry and honour.

Little more is said of love. Ovid appears as Calliope's clerk: some of his martial characters are named – Hercules, Theseus, Perseus, Achilles – but no illustrations are given from his work on 'louys meditacionis,/The craft of loue, and the saluationis,/ Quhow that the furie lustis suld be flemyt' (11.1219-21). In the first entrance of the Palace of Honour Douglas sees tournaments and deeds of arms performed in Venus' service (11.1441-9), and then Venus herself with a mirror. But Venus's mirror turns out to reflect the whole history of the world: it shows not just lovers but 'All thinges gone lyk as they were present' (1.1497), including Old

Testament stories, Greek and Roman mythology, Roman history, and
heroes of Middle English and Middle Scots literature such as Piers
Plowman and Rauf Coilyear. The Theban widows described by Chaucer
at the beginning of The Knight's Tale are invoked by Douglas as
examples of constancy (11.1585-93); but most of the other characters mentioned are male, and are cited for their martial and
political feats. Venus's mirror is not designed to reflect love
stories. Furthermore, whereas Chaucer's penitential commission in
The Legend of Good Women was to write the stories of women who
were true in love, the book which Venus gives Douglas to put into
verse as penance for his crime is not named in The Palice of
Honour (11.1749-57). Douglas the narrator adds 'Twychand this buke
perauentur ye sall here/Sumtyme efter quhen I haue mare lasere'
(11.1756-7). A marginal note informs us 'By thys boke he menis
Virgil'; his translation may have seemed a penance at times, but
the Aeneid is not primarily a story of love.

The narrators of The House of Fame and The Legend of Good
Women, like other Chaucerian narrators, make much of their inexperience in love, their interest in it, and their willingness to
write about it. Douglas presents himself in The Palice of Honour
as much less interested in love, though he acknowledges that it is
an important theme for poetry. The characterisation of the narrator of the Eneados, as far as it can be judged by the beginning of
Prologue IV, suggests a man predominantly concerned with the art
of translation, so we would not expect him to make a strong
defence of love in his introduction to the story of Dido, though
we would also not expect such a diatribe against lust. Why is it,
then, that he apparently provides both? Many sources and parallels
have been suggested for the arguments presented in Prologue IV;
Douglas himself names two major influences, Gower and Augustine.
But even though this Prologue is not visibly modelled on any
Chaucerian narrative, I think that Chaucer is still a very
important influence. Mrs Bawcutt argues in her article on Chaucer
and Douglas that Chaucer's influence is most evident in the
Prologues, and that Prologue IV shows Douglas's familiarity with
the language and conventions that Chaucer had used in the Troilus
and The Knight's Tale.[12] She also remarks that towards the end of
this Prologue the tone increasingly recalls Chaucer's Parson and
the Palinode of the Troilus; I agree, particularly about the
Palinode, which I think deserves closer consideration as a source.

Among the numerous verbal echoes of Chaucer, Mrs Bawcutt and
others have noted that the phrase 'goddis apys', used by Douglas
of Venus's servants at 1.36, is aso used by Pandarus when he
recalls the unreformed Troilus jeering at lovers (I, 911-13). It
has also been remarked that the stanza beginning 'Thou cheyn of
luf, ha benedicte,/Quhou hard streynys thi bandis every wyght!'
(11. 36-7) recalls two speeches of Theseus in The Knight's Tale:
the speech beginning 'The god of love, a benedicitee' (11.1785ff),
and the speech on 'the faire cheyn of love' (11.2987ff). Another
echo has been noticed a few stanzas later, when Douglas inveighs
against Venus in commenting on the tragedy of Hero and Leander:

> Lo, quhou Venus kan hir seruandis acquyte!
> Lo, quhou hir passionys onbridillis al thar wyt!

> Lo, quhou thai tyne thame self for schort delyte!
> Lo, from all grace quhou to myscheif thai flyte ...
> (11.85-8)

Critics have compared the anaphora in this passage with lines from Lydgate's The Complaint of the Black Knight, 11.400-6; but it is also very reminiscent of the third-to-last stanza in the Troilus:

> Lo here, of payens corsed olde rites,
> Lo here, what alle hire goddes may availle,
> Lo here, thise wrecched worldes appetites,
> Lo here, the fyn and guerdoun for travaille
> Of Jove, Apollo, of Mars, of swich rascaille!
> (V, 1849-53)

Lydgate may well have been imitating this Chaucerian effect too.

But the first indication of Chaucer's influence seems to me to occur in the opening lines of Prologue IV:

> Wyth bemys scheyn thou bricht Cytherea,
> Quhilk only schaddowist amang starris lyte ...

They recall the first lines of the proem to Book III of the Troilus:

> O blisful light, of which the bemes clere
> Adorneth al the thridde heven faire!

Chaucer sings the praises of love, which dominates even the gods, and affects and unites everything in the cosmos; he begs Venus to teach him 'som joye of that is felt in thi servyse', before asking Calliope to inspire him to sing of Troilus's 'gladnesse' (11.39-49). The reader of the Eneados might well expect Douglas to go on to sing the praises of love in similar terms, since he begins in the same way by invoking the planet rather than the goddess; such praise would not be incompatible with the tragic story he has to tell, any more than it was with Chaucer's story of Troilus. But instead he writes of a different Venus: he does not appeal to her for help, but rather condemns her harshly. If Chaucer is celebrating the Venus whom George Economou has described as 'legitimate, sacramental, natural, and in harmony with cosmic law', Douglas is criticising the other Venus whom Economou characterises as 'illegitimate, perverted, selfish and sinful'.[13]

More parallels can easily be found. The digression on the power of love over animals is taken from the Georgics, Douglas tells us; but it also recalls the proem to Book III of Troilus, where Chaucer celebrates the cosmic power of love:

> In hevene and helle, in erthe and salte see
> Is felt thi myght, if that I wel descerne;
> As man, brid, best, fissh, herbe, and grene tree
> Thee fele in tymes with vapour eterne.
> God loveth, and to love wol nought werne;
> And in this world no lyves creature
> Withouten love is worth, or may endure.
> (III,8-14)

But as I noted before, Douglas does not develop this theme, returning instead to his catalogue of victims of lust. Again, Douglas's stanza attributing the Incarnation and the Harrowing of Hell to love's power even over God (11.36ff) might be compared with Troilus V, 1842ff, where the narrator reminds us that Christ died for love of us and that therefore we should love only Him. And when Douglas urges his readers to love God before all other (11.128ff), we may think of the insistent final stanzas of the Troilus (though Douglas's message is the less harsh, surprisingly, since he merely urges his readers to love nothing more than God, whereas Chaucer's narrator urges them to love nothing but God).

The heaviest Chaucerian echoes come at the end of the Prologue, as Mrs Bawcutt has said, but surprisingly she gives no examples. I mention here the parallels with the Troilus which seem to me most striking. The attack on 'brokkaris', 'Venus henwyffis', and 'poyd makerellis' may have been conventional in criticisms of love, but it is not particularly relevant to the story of Dido; the only intermediary in her love affair is her sister Anna. But the love affair of Troilus and Criseyde depends on Pandarus, the self-proclaimed 'meene' whose appeals to Criseyde to be kind to Troilus are very similar to the appeals cited by Douglas here as characteristic of bawds: 'Douchtir, for thy lufe this man hes gret dyseyss', and 'Rew on him, it is meryte hys pane to meyss' (11.190 and 192). The shift from addressing 'yyng virgynys and fair damycellis' at 1.194 to the inclusion of 'fresch gallandis' at 1.203 might be a reminiscence of the narrator's parting advice in the Troilus to 'yonge fresshe folkes, he or she' (V, 1835). As for the admonition to follow the teaching of 'morale Ihonne Gower' (1.213), the epithet is of course one used by Dunbar too (in The Goldyn Targe, 1.262); but here I think it is a deliberate reference to Chaucer's dedication in the penultimate stanza of the Troilus: 'O moral Gower, this book I directe/To the and to the, philosophical Strode' (V, 1856-7). In support of this argument I would cite Douglas's next stanza, in which he returns to Dido and her 'dowbill wound':

> Bot al syk crymys in luffis causs I resyng
> To the confessioun of morale Ihonne Gower,
> For I mon follow the text of our mater.

> Thy dowbill wound, Dido, to specify,
> I meyn theyne amouris and thi funeral fait,
> Quha may endyte, but teris, with eyn dry?
> (11.212-17)

Surely the phrase 'dowbill wound' encourages a comparison between Dido's story and 'the double sorwe of Troilus' (the very first words of Chaucer's poem).[14]

Both Troilus and Dido move from the pain of unrequited love to the joy of consummated passion, and back to the pain of loss. Douglas notes the degradation produced by 'blynd luffis inordinate desyre' (11.250-1), just as the dead Troilus laughs at 'the blynde lust, the which that may nat laste' (V, 1824). But instead of following the ending of Chaucer's Palinode, and insisting that his

readers, 'he or she', should put all their trust in the Trinity
and the Virgin, Douglas finishes with a surprisingly indulgent and
sympathetic piece of advice addressed specifically to women: 'Be
war with strangeris of unkouth natioun' (1.267). This recalls the
Troilus narrator's address to women late in Book V, when he apologises for telling the story of Criseyde's infidelity, and points
out defensively that men often betray women too: 'Beth war of men,
and herkneth what I seye!' (V, 1785). But it is an even closer
echo of the comments of the dreamer in The House of Fame on seeing
the story of Dido in the temple of glass:

> Loo, how a woman doth amys
> To love hym that unknowen ys!
> (11.269-70)

A few lines later the dreamer repeats this assessment of Dido's
tragedy:

> Al this seye I be Eneas
> And Dido, and hir nyce lest,
> That loved al to sone a gest;
> Therfore I wol seye a proverbe,
> That 'he that fully knoweth th'erbe
> May sauffly leye hyt to his yë';
> Withoute drede, this ys no lye.
> (11.286-92)

Douglas had criticised Chaucer for being too harsh to Aeneas and
too sympathetic to Dido, but here he seems to be borrowing from
this Chaucerian version of the story which he had previously
criticised. (It is worth noting that he seems to have changed his
mind about Dido and Aeneas at least twice: in The Palice of Honour
he includes in Venus's entourage 'The Quene Dido with hir fals luf
Enee' [1.564], a criticism of Aeneas which he had dropped by the
time he began the Eneados).

It seems to me that Chaucer's influence is present in Prologue
IV not just in the verbal echoes, or in the metre (rhyme royal,
like the Troilus), but even more in the general uncertainty of
tone. If this were really a conventional clerical diatribe against
love, surely we would expect the argument about 'the cheyn of luf'
and its power over God to be developed as a formal alternative to
lust, rather than inserted in the middle of a traditional catalogue of victims of earthly love; nor would we expect such sympathy for young girls led astray by pimps and lechers, or for
Dido's 'dowbill wound'; nor the final advice to 'lusty ladeis
quhyte' to beware of strange men. I think that in this Prologue
Douglas is heavily influenced by the narrator of the Troilus, with
his reluctance to commit himself to a single standpoint, his
foreknowledge of the 'blynde lust' of his lovers, and his
optimistic belief in the doomed love affair. Douglas's Prologue
reads like a backwards version of the end of the Troilus. The
enthusiasm of Chaucer's narrator for love and its benefits lasts
more or less intact until the end of Book V; as late as 11.1772ff.
he is still giving advice to the ladies in his audience about

love, and criticising men for betraying them. But then after Troilus's death his optimism disintegrates rapidly amidst harsh condemnation of the world's 'brotelnesse', to be replaced by the dedication to moral Gower and the exhortation to the audience (or readers) to love God alone. Douglas includes all these elements: but whereas Chaucer's narrator moves from fervent belief that love makes the world go round to hysterical rejection of everything to do with earthly love, Douglas seems to move from vitriolic criticism of love and lovers and insistence on the priority of love of God to a much more understanding, if still critical, position, culminating in practical advice to 'lusty ladeis quhyte'.

All the examples of love's casualties in the early part of Prologue IV are men from the legendary and literary past (with the single exception of Hero). But later Douglas shows himself sympathetic to young women betrayed by bawds and to young ladies tempted by courtly appeals for 'grace' and 'rew', situations which sound much more contemporary; and the mention of moral Gower is followed immediately by Augustine weeping for Dido and her 'dowbill wound'. Douglas is never explicitly misogynistic in his denunciation of love in Prologue IV, as a self-proclaimed 'spiritual man' might easily have been; indeed in the last section he seems to be concerned exclusively with women's fortunes and misfortunes. He is of course introducing the story of a queen and her tragic love affair, whereas Chaucer was ending the story of a prince and his tragic love affair. If Douglas was to translate 'the pity and tenderness latent in Virgil's words', as Mrs Bawcutt puts it (Douglas, p 146), he could not be too condemning.[15] Context is crucial to a reading of the Prologue.

But so is Chaucer. From the Troilus Douglas learnt, I think, that it is possible to give ambivalent, even contradictory responses to a love story. The poet is omniscient: he knows the full tragedy, and sees that its cause lies in Augustine's 'imperfyte' love and 'fowle delyte'; but he is also human, and like Augustine and Chaucer's narrator, he weeps for the victim. The first and longer section of Prologue IV suggests that as a 'spirituall man' Douglas wants to disapprove of a story of 'byrning carnaill hait delyte'. But in spite of his praise for moral Gower, his comments towards the end of the Prologue are more sympathetic to Dido than one would have expected from the author of Prologue I, who criticised Chaucer for championing Dido and misrepresenting Aeneas as a treacherous deceiver. Douglas explains 'venerabill' Chaucer's deviation from Virgilian authenticity with the famous remark that 'he was evir (God wait) all womanis frend' (1.449). Douglas himself rejects Cytherea as a muse at the beginning of Prologue IV, but Dido, representing 'lusty ladeis quhyte', seems almost to have become his muse at the end. Can it be that, almost against his own will, Gavin Douglas was also to some extent 'womanis frend'? The evidence of the final stanza of Prologue IV makes me go farther than Priscilla Bawcutt, who sums up Douglas's treatment of Dido throughout the Eneados as follows:[16]

> Although he departs from Chaucer in his interpretation of the characters of Dido and Aeneas, in the translation his attitude to Dido is almost as sympathetic as Chaucer's and is

certainly not one of moral censure. Douglas was far from being what he said of Chaucer – 'all womanis frend' (1 Prol 449) – but he responded to the pathos of Dido's situation.

Prologue IV suggests to me that Douglas also responded to the pathos of the situation of contemporary women – or at least made a gesture in that direction, in accordance with current literary fashion.

Notes

1   See Gavin Douglas, Virgil's Aeneid, D F C Coldwell (ed), 4 vols, STS (Edinburgh, 1964), I, 87; all quotations are taken from this edition. The letter 'yogh' has been replaced by 'y' throughout.

2   Denton Fox, 'The Scottish Chaucerians', in Chaucer and Chaucerians, D S Brewer (ed) (London, 1966), 164-200 (191).

3   Priscilla Bawcutt, Gavin Douglas: A Critical Study (Edinburgh, 1976), pp 164-5.

4   Prologue IV appears as no. 380 in The Bannatyne Manuscript, W Tod Ritchie (ed), 4 vols, STS, (Edinburgh, 1928-34), IV, 108-16; see also the facsimile edition with a introduction by Denton Fox and William A Ringler (London, 1980), ff.291r-294v. Bannatyne omits the last stanza of the Prologue, apparently because several folios are missing at that point, as Fox and Ringler suggest (p.xxxviii). Bannatyne includes many of the marginal notes found in the Copland edition of 1553, apparently copied either from the Copland text or from its source, as Denton Fox notes in 'Manuscripts and Prints of Scots Poetry in the Sixteenth Century', in Bards and Makars, ed A J Aitken and others (Glasgow, 1977), 156-71 (161-2). Both Bannatyne and Copland sum up stanza four as 'the commodeteis of luve'; they detect the 'remeid' in the last line of stanza five, 'Wit/strenth/riches/Nathing bot grace availis' (Bannatyne, 1.35). These marginal notes continue throughout the Copland text, but become very sparse after the first eighteen stanzas in Bannatyne.

5   Vergil, Bucolica et Georgica, T E Page (ed) (London, 1968), III, 244.

6   All references to Chaucer are taken from the Works, F N Robinson (ed), 2nd edn (London, 1966).

7   See John Gower, Confessio Amantis, Book 8, 11.3152ff. in vol 3 of The Complete Works, G C Macaulay (ed), 4 vols (London, 1899-1902); the quotations are taken from 11.3162-4 and 3167. Earlier in this book, the Lover swoons and sees Cupid with his entourage of lovers, including Dido, 'forsake which was with Enee' (1.2550-3).

8   It is not easy to paraphrase 11.266-9; Coldwell's punctuation is not very satisfactory. I take them to mean that ladies

should beware lest strange men work enchantments on them (the ladies) to their (the ladies') damnation; and that women learn from Dido's story only how to attain wanton love. Priscilla Bawcutt has suggested to me (in a letter, 16 August 1987) that in 1.268 the variant reading 'woundis' (Lambeth and Bannatyne) might be preferable to 'woundris'; as she points out, 'it would refer back to 1.215 [dowbill wound], and could be explained by eyeskip from 'strangeris' just above'. I am grateful to Felicity Riddy, Flora Alexander, Jack Aitken, Rod Lyall, and especially to Priscilla Bawcutt for help in construing this passage. I am also grateful to David Parkinson for his helpful comments when this paper was read (in an earlier version) at Aberdeen; and to Mike Patzold for his careful reading and constructive criticism of the final draft.

9   See The Testament of Cresseid, 11.610–13, in Robert Henryson, Poems, Denton Fox (ed) (Oxford, 1981).

10 In the introduction to his anthology Ballatis of Luve (Edinburgh, 1970), John MacQueen remarks that courtly love lyrics were very popular in Scotland by the end of the fifteenth century, and notes that Douglas includes 'two accomplished specimens of the genre' in The Palice of Honour (p.xxvii). Perhaps the address to ladies at the end of a poem was part of the same fashion.

11 The Palice of Honour has been edited by Priscilla Bawcutt in The Shorter Poems of Gavin Douglas (Edinburgh, 1967); all quotations are taken from the London text.

12 Priscilla Bawcutt, 'Gavin Douglas and Chaucer', Review of English Studies, n.s. 21 (1970), 401–21 (405–7).

13 See George Economou, 'The Two Venuses and Courtly Love', in The Pursuit of Perfection: Courtly Love in Medieval Literature, J Ferrante and G Economou (eds) (Port Washington, NY, 1975), 17–50 (20).

14 Ian Ross points out the parallel with the first lines of the Troilus, though he does not comment further on it: see his article '"Proloug" and "Buke" in the Eneados of Gavin Douglas', in Scottish Language and Literature, Medieval and Renaissance, D Strauss and H W Drescher (eds) (Frankfurt, 1986), pp 393–408 (396). Douglas also uses the phrase 'dowbill wound' about Dido in his list of the contents of each book of the Eneados at the end of Prologue 1: 'The ferd rehersis of fair Queyn Dido/The dowbill woundis and the mortale wo'.

15 Bawcutt, Douglas p 146.

16 Ibid.

Chapter 19

'THUS EUERY MAN SAID FOR HYM SELF':
THE VOICES OF SIR DAVID LYNDSAY'S POEMS

Janet H Williams

One of the most interesting phases of Lyndsay's long career begins
in 1528 and covers the fourteen years of James V's personal rule.
The foundations for this phase had been laid twenty-one years
earlier, when Lyndsay had been appointed by King James IV to serve
his sons: first, as attendant to the short-lived James, Prince of
Scotland and the Isles, and a few years later, in 1512, to attend
a second boy, who survived to become the seventh Stewart king.[1] In
eleven years of service to this young prince, Lyndsay had held
the many household offices of the trusted familiar at court.[2]
Lyndsay's loyal commitment, as he himself records it, had had an
almost paternal aspect, that did not lessen with the death of the
boy's father at Flodden in 1513.
    Change came with the rise to power of the boy-king's step-
father, Angus. By 1525 Lyndsay was supplanted at court, and James
introduced to the corrupting pleasures put forward by less responsible attendants than Lyndsay had been. Even so, the bond between
the absent Lyndsay and the adolescent boy remained strong. When,
at the age of sixteen, James had shaken off his guards and begun
his personal reign, Lyndsay was among the few who retained the
king's trust and favour.[3]
    By 1530 Lyndsay was herald as well as 'familiar servitour' to
the king.[4] Soon after, Lyndsay was often acting abroad as chief
herald, even before the position of Lyon King of Arms was officially bestowed.[5] In his administrative, judicial and executive
functions, Lyndsay could, from this time on, correctly be regarded
as standing in place of the king.[6]
    All of this needs to be emphasised, for it distinguishes the
position of Lyndsay, and the basis upon which he wrote, from those
of predecessors, such as the cleric William Dunbar, whose familiarity with his court audience did not prevent him from at times
pointedly standing apart from it. It distinguishes Lyndsay from
contemporaries, such as William Stewart or Alexander Kyde, whose
extant petitionary and advice poems show an undoubted familiarity
with the obligations of any courtier-poet's life, but little
attempt to cater to the circumstances of a particular king.[7]
    Can we trace the effect of Lyndsay's close relationship with
the king - personal as well as deeply ceremonial - on Lyndsay's
writing? One way to do so is to examine Lyndsay's methods of pre-
senting his poems: each one has notable differences. I propose to
do so, selecting those early poems, The Dreme, The Complaynt, The

Testament and Complaynt of the Papyngo, The Complaint and Public
Confessioun of Bagsche, and The Answer to the Kingis Flyting, that
were written for James as he defined and established the reign as
his own. I shall be concentrating, very selectively, on one
aspect: Lyndsay's use of narrative voices, because Lyndsay demonstrates his awareness of the benefits of using voices, both his
own and others, from his earliest known poem.

In this earliest work, The Dreme (1528), Lyndsay's presentation
of the Commonweal of Scotland, through the voice of the ragged and
desperate John, clearly belongs to the vox populi tradition. Yet
Lyndsay, as scholars have recognised, does make his own contribution.[8] Lyndsay's John brings to the discussion of the state of
Scotland the immediacy of an individual victim of the maladministration during the king's minority. He speaks as one of the poor
commons, his plain speech peppered with emphatic alliteration and
proverb. His allusions are vivid because they pertain to actual
circumstances and are directed to a particular king. He refers,
for example, to the regions of Scotland - 'the Mers and Lowmabane'
(955), 'the oute Ylis' and 'Argyle' (964) - known to James for
their unrest and rebellion.[9] This articulate and urgent voice is a
persuasive illustration of the dramatic potential inherent in the
method. Lyndsay develops this, but in later poems he also develops
other aspects of the use of different voices, and I shall be discussing them.

What of Lyndsay's own voice? Lyndsay speaks as 'officer of the
Crown and of the kingdom'.[10] A contemporary Scottish heraldic
treatise tells us what that means:

> first pursewant syn herald & yan king
> Ichone of yis bering gre abone gre
> Be land & see priuilegit in all thing ... [11]

Lyndsay interprets this poetically with great care, using his own
voice, especially when it is mixed with others, as a point of
reference. We can see how Lyndsay begins to create such distinctiveness in his direct address to the king which opens The Dreme.
This address might be classed as a passage of petitionary autobiography, but practical petitionary intentions are clearly not
the central issue. Lyndsay uses the role largely for other purposes, as we shall see.[12]

Lyndsay's first words are courtly; James is a 'Potent Prince,
of hie Imperial blude', Lyndsay a servant to his 'Celsitude' (3)
and Excellence' (6). These words differ markedly from the blunt
address to James IV frequently used by Dunbar to open apparently
similar poems, of 'Schir'. Lyndsay's high style at once makes
obvious that he speaks from a distance, to a monarch no longer a
captive, but at the beginning of a strong personal reign. The
humble petitioner's stance that Lyndsay then adopts enhances this
distance.

By the second stanza, the diction has modulated: it is plainer.
As Lyndsay recalls the loving care with which James was tucked
into bed and entertained in infancy, Lyndsay's voice takes on
again those less distant tones of the nursery companion. Repetitio
lightly underlines the diversity of Lyndsay's employments and the

constancy of his attendance:

> Sumtyme, in dansing, feiralie I flang;
> And, sumtyme, playand fairsis on the flure;
> And, sumtyme, on myne office takkand cure ... (12-14)

Then Lyndsay repeats his theme of royal service in different
words, delivering a catalogue of his household positions. He has
been server, cupbearer, carver, pursemaster, secret treasurer,
usher, chief of the bedchamber. He returns to the present via this
list, ending it with the emphatic words, 'Quhilk, to this houre,
hes keipit my lawtie' (25), and he takes up the punctiliously
correct distance of servant to patron found in the poem's opening
stanza. Lyndsay thanks the 'blyssit Trynitie' (26) that he, 'ane
wracheit worme' (27), could be fit to serve 'sic ane Prince' (28).
    Continuing in courtly style, Lyndsay stresses the king's grow-
ing intellectual ability. 'Bot, now, thov arte, be Influence
naturall,/Hie of Ingyne ...' (29-30). But the ending defines the
limits of the king's maturity: James is 'Hie of Ingyne ... and
'rycht Inquisityue/Off antique storeis and dedis marciall' (30-
31). With this reference to an interest that, though possibly
morally improving, is plainly a youthful pastime, Lyndsay again
returns to the perfect tense and the easier, middle level style:
'More plesandlie the tyme for tyll ouerdryue/I haue, at lenth, the
storeis done discryue/Off Hectour, Arthour, and gentyll Iulyus,
/... of leill Luffaris .../... mony fabyll,/ ... /And Seigis all
...' (32-4, 39, 40, 42). Notably, Lyndsay recalls sometimes
'Confortand' - cheering and strengthening[13] - his then-guarded boy
sovereign, with the ancient Scottish prophecies of 'Rymour, Beid
and Marlyng' (43), and with the nursery, or 'fireside tales' of
'the reid Etin, and the gyir carlyng'(45).[14]
    As a continuation of these varied stories, Lyndsay now offers
his own. He submits it with the expected apology for his 'laik of
Eloquence' (52), concluding with a wry reference to his 'besynes':

> 3it, nocht withstandyng all my besynes,
> With hart and hand my mynd I sall adres,
> As I best can ...   (53-55)

'Besynes' - industry, diligence.[15] The word is not elevated, and
as used here is self-mocking: 'In spite of all my diligence I'll
do my best'. Yet it also encapsulates the attitude of dedication
to the king's service that is behind Lyndsay's recall of past
details, and it implies that his new story will further that same
end.
    What features of Lyndsay's voice emerge from this opening
'Epistil'? With evident warmth, Lyndsay has charted the shifts
and interdependencies of the long-established relationship between
himself and his royal auditor. To do so, Lyndsay has changed the
perspective several times. He has controlled these changes first,
by references to specific details and times in the past, present
and future; secondly, by the juxaposition of two levels of diction
with a dignified middle level ultimately dominant; and thirdly, by
corresponding tonal changes - highly formal to intimate, serious to

lightly teasing. This is a recognisable voice, and its withdrawal in the remainder of The Dreme is thus made noticeable.

In the central section, the dream vision, the dreamer and the allegorical dream-guide Remembrance take over the narrative. There is a lightly-made link between the waking Lyndsay (of the epistle and the prologue) and Remembrance: like Lyndsay-to-the-king, companion and comforter, Dame Remembrance comes to the dreamer for his 'pastyme and plesoure' (155), 'to beir (him) companye; (156), and because she sees him 'so sore perturbit be malancolye' (158).

But the voice-characters of the narrators within the dream are not developed, either in the same way Lyndsay has developed his own voice-character, or in the 'personalising' manner of Chaucer in the House of Fame, or Douglas in the Palice of Honour.[16] The exchanges of Lyndsay's narrators enliven the presentation of the material without individualising, or drawing attention to, the spokesmen. That this pertains to Lyndsay's purpose for his poem – the education not of a poet, but of a particular young monarch – is made obvious by the choice of the mental quality of memory for the allegorised guide-narrator. We know that for Lyndsay and his auditor King James, memory was a part, along with intelligence and foresight or reason, of the virtue of Prudence, one of the four great cardinals traditionally associated with good kingship.[17] Within this accepted scheme of thought, The Dreme's Dame Remembrance thus represented for the king more than a tutor whose very name suggested the schoolroom. She does indeed set out facts and counsel for the king's memorisation, using the entertaining and ordering structure of the cosmographical journey to lighten the king's task, and ultimately, to tailor her words specifically to a Scottish king's outlook. But she also embodies that traditional idea of Prudence in the aspect most vital to a young monarch at the beginning of both his reign and adulthood: the ability to order the future, not only by a consideration of the present, but by the remembrance and evaluation of the past. Her voice is in keeping: that of a caring, yet distant, higher authority:

> So, I conclude that, throw the necligence
> Off our infatuate heidis Insolent,
> Is cause of all this realmes indigence,
> Quhilkis in Iustice hes nocht bene delygent ...(904-7)

At the end of the dream, though Lyndsay now directly addresses the king once again, he does not reassert his familiar voice. Indeed, Lyndsay's withdrawal here of the opening intimacy is palpable. These ten stanzas are singled out and elevated by their nine-line form and stern address. Now Lyndsay uses the 'Schir' of Dunbar to his king and offers to him a model speculum principis,[18] with direct references to the cardinal virtues and carefully chosen historical exempla. This section is clearly intended to balance the opening 'Epistil', with several words and phrases from it here taken up and more gravely directed.[19] Against the personal tone of the opening, the impersonality of Lyndsay's voice, as it sets out these uncompromising precepts, becomes a narrative device in itself, stressing the seriousness of the king's new occupations. No longer are they to be the sharing of 'plesand storeis' and the taking of comfort, but instead, the isolating and more difficult tasks, of wise government of the realm, and the restoration of comfort to his till now 'desolate' (1060) people.

Unlike his method in The Dreme, Lyndsay maintains his recognisable voice and presence throughout the shorter Complaynt, written in the following year. Its unpretentious four-foot couplets have an affinity with the flow of ordinary conversation, and Lyndsay makes the most of this. Its audience is not so tightly defined: Lyndsay begins by addressing the king, but remarks in a later aside, 'to ʒow, my Lordis, that standis by' (109), and this device, too, makes a disarming link with possible real circumstances. The distinctive features of Lyndsay's voice – the specific references, to actual events past and present, and to people by name; the gentle teasing that is usually self-directed but occasionally includes his principal auditor; and above all, the variations on a middle-level style, with a diction sometimes homely, sometimes subtly weighted, but always appropriate to the matter – lend themselves well to the greater degree of informality here.

In an earlier paper I have discussed the Complaynt in detail,[20] but I do want briefly to recall something of the fine control of narrative voice that Lyndsay has in this poem. It is particularly evident in the central section, in which Lyndsay is concerned with the faction-ridden government of James's minority, and I take my example from it.

Within this section (109–372), Lyndsay's own responses to the usurpers' actions, to their effect upon himself and in turn, to their effect upon the king, are present as the ground bass, in a string of forthright, yet not carping comments. He uses, for instance, a simple double rhyme to underline his attitude: 'I wyll nocht say that it was treassoun,/Bot I dar sweir, it was no reassoun' (151-2). Later, he uses alliterative alliances to make pithy points, as in 'I gat the soure, and thay the sweit' (282). Lyndsay also laments, not with a high style planctus, but shortly, with the revealing, almost homely detail of the king as the butt of a children's game: 'Me thocht it was ane pieteous thyng,/To se that fair, ʒoung, tender kyng,/Off quhome thir gallandis stude no awe, /To play with hym, pluke at the crawe' (227-30).

Lyndsay interweaves his direct commentary with a series of overheard speeches between the flattering courtiers. Within these quoted speeches, Lyndsay himself makes only an occasional facilitating comment: 'sum wald say' (161); 'quod he' (186); 'quod ane vther' (241), and in this way Lyndsay gives to the courtier-voices a semi-independent existence. This impression is deepened because, though the courtiers remain unnamed, they are not presented as personified courtier-qualities. They thus appear to belong to the world of Lyndsay and his audience. The vigour of their idiomatic exchanges, stylistically so different from Lyndsay's voice, further contributes to this sense of separate actors. Indeed, the quoted speeches form little dramatic interludes. Here is one example:

> Quod ane: the Deuyll stik me with ane knyfe,
> Bot, schir, I knaw ane maid in fyfe,
> Ane of the lusteast wantoun lassis,
> Quhare to, schir, be gods blude scho passis,

Hald thy toung, brother, quod ane vther,
I knaw ane fairar, be fyftene futher.
Schir, quhen ȝe pleis to Leithgow pas,
Thare sall ȝe se ane lusty las.
Now trittyll, trattyll, trolylow,
Quod the thrid man; thow does bot mow.
Quhen his grace cumis to fair sterlyng,
Thair sall he se ane dayis derlyng
Schir, quod the fourt, tak my counsall,
And go, all,to the hie boirdall.   (237-50)

Diction and style reflect the corrupt matter. Addressing the king, the false flatterers use colloquial phrases, oaths and boasts, mixing them without decorum with the mock-respectful 'Schir' and the more elevated 'his grace'. The broken rhythm suggests the jostling for the king's ear. The couplet rhyme of 'counsall' (advice) and 'boirdall' (brothel) strains in its linking of words with senses that are more naturally opposed. This is 'onlesum' language, which illustrates, strikingly, the results of a deviation from responsible action and appropriate rhetoric. And when Lyndsay takes up the narrative, with a forthright summary that nevertheless contains some wry irony, the point is made again: 'Thus euery man said for hym self,/And did amangis thame part the pelf' (253-4).

Whereas in the Complaynt Lyndsay introduces other semi-independent voices, giving his distinctive commentary a dramatic dimension, in the Answer to the Kingis Flyting (c.1535) dramatic tension has been imposed from without, by the demands of the flyting form. The king's 'ragment' of challenge, described by Lyndsay as 'wennemous' (16), is lost. Even so we must be aware that Lyndsay's reply to some extent depends upon and reacts to the individual voice and person of his opponent. This is a feature of earlier literary flytings. Battle is waged over poetic and metrical skills, but it is also fought with other weapons, including the social position and physical appearance of the various contestants.[21] Kennedy, for instance, reacting to Dunbar's taunts on his family's uncouthness and poverty, puns on the word 'Dunbar', working out a spurious ancestry for his attacker: 'Generit betuix ane scho beir and a deill' (259) - 'Dewlbeir' (260).[22]

King James V possibly chose to attack his chief herald in a similar way, using, aptly, the heraldic aspect of genealogy. To the ancient Lyndsay arms, our Lyndsay had added for his crest, a heart in flames, transfixed with an arrow and surmounted by a scroll with motto: 'Caritas, Caritas, Caritas', alluding to the purity and truth of knightly love. The remaining theological virtues, 'Fides' and 'Spes', were placed, as two maidens proper, for supporters. Lyndsay's motto was 'J'Ayme', again specifically with the Christian significances intended. The king's reported attack on Lyndsay's failures in 'Uenus Court' was perhaps a 'demoralisation' of these heraldic symbols,[23] and certainly made an oblique allusion to Lyndsay's office: as Lyon Depute, Lyndsay was the conductor of the full Scottish Court of Chivalry.[24] For Lyndsay on the other hand, such a method of abuse was laughingly untenable. A Dunbarian attack on the king's ancestry, for example, could amount to treason. To expect it from the keeper of the royal genealogy would have been a flyting ploy of the wickedest. Lyndsay himself refers to this mock-tension: 'Schir, with my Prince pertenit me nocht to pley' (22). He presents himself as cornered, for once, by a special relationship and a position that normally work in his favour. How does Lyndsay use his voice in his response?

Even if an ironic undertone is intended, 'Redoutit Roy' is an unusual beginning for a flyting. Where is the aggressive fieriness of Kennedy's 'Dirtin Dumbar, quhome on blawis thow thy boist' (25)? The enriched alliteration is there - 'Redoutit Roy, ʒour ragment I haue red' - but it works against as much as for Lyndsay's flyting purpose. More curious still for a flyting, Lyndsay follows with equivocal references to his own inadequacies. In line 2 he mentions his 'dull Intendement', in line 4, his lack of a 'Tygerris toung'. Then, perhaps with a shade too much humility, Lyndsay even begs pardon for his impatience at the king's attack, but he begins to gather force as he denounces James's 'prunʒeand pen' (6). This soon dissolves, as Lyndsay reveals James's taunt and its effect: Lyndsay's inadequacies in 'Uenus Court' (7), and his subsequent rejection by its 'Lustie Ladyis' (8). This process, of a gathering force of concentrated alliteration and abusive imagery which reaches a climax only to be undermined, is repeated several times. Comically, it is not, as with Dunbar and Skelton, Lyndsay's opponent who falls on his knees with the penitential cry 'Cor mundum crea in me' (20), but the defending Lyndsay himself.

Having stressed his poetic humility, Lyndsay asserts his social inequality in a similar way. He will produce his flyting reply only because the king 'hes geuin me sic command' (23) and he is an obedient servant. This stance has a hint of ambiguity - is Lyndsay refusing to accept responsiblity for what follows? - and it is also slyly well-timed. As the attack proceeds, his distance from the king begins to be a point in Lyndsay's favour.

The king has attacked Lyndsay's amorous inadequacies. Lyndsay attacks the opposite in James - his over-vigorous and undiscriminating sexual prowess. Lyndsay begins slowly, using the animal imagery common to earlier flytings to stress his case: 'Thocht ʒe be now strang lyke ane Elephand,/And in till Uenus werkis maist vailʒeand,/The day wyll cum .../That ʒe wyll draw at laiser ...' (25-28). (But Lyndsay's image is not without a jocular undertone. In the bestiaries, elephants were highly regarded for their size and intelligence, but were also a symbol of chastity.[25]) Lyndsay concedes his failure in 'Uenus werkis', introducing his other main source of imagery, the appurtenances of warfare, to do so: 'The tyme hes bene, I was better artailʒeit/Nor I am now .../Quharefore tak tent, and ʒour fyne powder spair,/And waist it nocht ...' (31-2, 34-5).

In these and similar lines, Lyndsay is at some distance from the images of tournament combat traditionally used in the literary flyting.[26] In its inelegance, Lyndsay's imagery of actual artillery, powder and crossbows, wounds the king where he is most vulnerable: he has recently received the chivalric order of St Michael; is soon to marry the French princess, and in his own court fosters love-songs and épitres-galantes.[27]

Lyndsay presses his advantage, but there is an ambivalence established here. At one level, James's bachelor preference for amorous adventure is given almost complimentary prominence under the guise of flyting pungency, with the perennial debate between age and youth adding a mock-serious warning chorus. At a second level, the wider implications of such play are revealed, and the flyting becomes an unlikely but arresting context for some pointed advice to the king. The battle imagery equates James's impetuous pleasure-seeking to the misuse of his country's military equipment. At this level, the whole realm is involved in James's misdirection of energy; Lyndsay, as guardian and preserver of the royal pedigree, not least. There might even be a momentary parallel with the downfall of James's grandfather, or with that of his father, James IV. That monarch was known, as is said in the Testament of the Papyngo, for his 'iustyng, and knychtly game' (502), yet finally, 'in his tryumphand glore,/Distroyit ...' (510-11), 'Nocht be the vertew of Inglis ordinance,/Bot be his awin wylfull mysgouernance' (512-13).

This ambivalence is felt in another way. Lyndsay's outbursts, possessing full flyting intensity, pervade the poem, and culminate libellously in the anecdote of the king's encounter with a slut in the royal ale cellar. Yet Lyndsay's energetic abuse is never maintained for more than a few lines at a time. Indeed, some lines do not follow an alliterative pattern. Other couplets promise virulent spite - 'Quharefore be war ...' (39) - but dwindle, this one to end rather hauntingly: 'For mony ane dois haist thair awin saule knellis' (40). Later, Lyndsay curses, not his flyting opponent, but the king's Council, almost dropping the flyter's mask altogether in his gravity: 'I giue ʒour counsale to the feynd of hell,/That wald nocht of ane Princes ʒow prouide:/... /Waistand ʒour corps, lettand the tyme ouerslyde" (43-44, 46). Whereas, in the longer poem-groups of Dunbar and Kennedy, or Skelton, such plain lines are perhaps accepted as a rapid 'drawing of breath', the shortness of Lyndsay's poem, of ten stanzas, draws attention to them.

In the final stanza, Lyndsay jestingly puts all to rights. He lauds the king's 'ornate Meter' (66); puns on the terms of the knightly tournament; proclaims the king a noble 'flour' of chivalry and of rhetoric, and admits his own inability to flyte. If this last seems all too accurate, it is also clearly deliberate. Lyndsay has used the characteristic tendencies of his voice to achieve just this effect. He has not succumbed to the self-sustaining verbal pyrotechnics common to other literary flytings, and by not persisting in his impudent abuse, Lyndsay has slowed the pace and periodically diluted the aggressive tone. His diction has been appropriately low and often heavily alliterated, but he has retained much that is plain, even conversational or gently comic, along with an occasional learned or elevated word. Lyndsay has also used more similes and metaphors than any other flyter (though the Answer is the shortest of the well-known literary flytings[28]), and this has had a softening effect upon his insults. Ultimately, Lyndsay's constant inversion of flyting expectations is so finely controlled that his Answer is a teasing, very accomplished entertainment. Yet it is also something more. Under

the camouflage of poetic insult, Lyndsay and the king are arguing
about codes of kingly behaviour. Lyndsay puts his stylistic
restraint to work here, sagely, to staunch the flow of the king's
venomous voice, and so also to arrest his improper actions.

The two remaining poems of Lyndsay's written early in James's
reign add substantially to the information we have been collect-
ing: in both the Testament and Complaynt of the Papyngo (1530) and
the Complaint and Public Confessioun of Bagsche (c.1535), other
voices besides Lyndsay's own are conspicuous. These poems derive
much of their impact from their appositeness to contemporary
circumstances: a particular interest in both exotic birds and
hunting dogs is amply attested by the records of this time.[29]

For the earlier Papyngo, impact is also derived from its stylistic ingenuity. Lyndsay seeks to use the poem, it is evident, to
establish furth of Scotland the pretensions to literary sophisti-
cation of James and his young court. Thus the Papyngo is a complex
blending of the well-established native styles with those made
recently fashionable abroad, by such poets as Jean Lemaire and
Clément Marot. Its numerical patternings of stanzas and parts are
concomitantly skilfully devised, as Mrs Shire has shown us in her
1978 Strasbourg paper. Lyndsay's use of voices in the Papyngo adds
its own evidence that this court sought to display its literary
precocity.

In the Papyngo, as in the poems previously discussed, Lyndsay's
own voice acts as a point of stylistic and moral reference. Yet
because of the Papyngo's complexity of styles and addition of
several other, allegorical voices, Lyndsay is here able to use his
voice with more subtlety.

In the opening of the poem, the restrained simplicity of
Lyndsay's voice that has become recognisable is replaced by the
elevated diction of the high style. The key to the continuation of
his distinctiveness is here found in Lyndsay's careful control and
of tone and matter. The tributes to the 'Poetis auld' (4) are
elaborately made. Lyndsay establishes the overall high-seriousness
of this set piece, and of the poem as a whole. Yet the equivocal
touches within his tributes to his poetic contemporaries add to
the tonal formality both lightly comic and ironic gradations. And
in his choice of the matter — the fall of the fat and cossetted
court parrot — Lyndsay adds the piquancy of a topical and less-
than-heroic subject.

Lyndsay's voice constantly shapes the ensuing action. He moulds
judgements, and literary expectations, by beginning his bird tale
with the formula opening of the sermon or the tragedy: 'Quho
clymmis to hycht, perforce his feit mon faill' (73). Within the
elaborate setting out of the bird's 'cas', however, Lyndsay introduces other elements. He conflates fiction and reality as he reveals, now in his familiar easy and dignified voice, first the
king's role, and then his own part in his own tale:

> One Papyngo, rycht plesand and perfyte,
> Presentit was tyll our moist nobyll kyng
> Of quhome his grace one lang tyme had delyte:
>   ...

This proper bird he gaue in gouernyng
To me ...   (80-2, 84-5)

and he lightens the mood still further by the entertaining resumé
of his attempts to teach the king's parrot 'language artificiall,/
To play platfute, and quhissill fute before' (87-8). Was this, and
the following description of the bird's ability to 'Bark lyke ane
Dog' (94) and 'buller lyke ane bull' (95) illustrated by appropriately hilarious sounds and actions? Did it remind the king of
his earlier games and activities with Lyndsay? Very skilfully,
Lyndsay has used his voice to draw his audience into the play of
the poem.

Telling of the parrot's downfall and mortal wound, Lyndsay's
voice is now joined by the quoted speeches of the bird. Lyndsay
keeps his own voice prominent, but he draws attention to the
characteristics and details which mark the papyngo as avian. His
warning, for example, appeals to the dangers of her world: 'The
gredie gled, I dreid, scho the assailʒe' (160), and his picture of
her vanity is again, in her terms: 'With wyng displayit, scho sat
full wantounlie' (165). Lyndsay also hints, conversely, at a human
dimension to the bird, as he describes her life at court: 'Thov
art rycht fat, and nocht weill vsit to fle' (159), and is less
equivocal later as he reports: 'scho cryit for a preist' (170).

Human and avian worlds are again mixed in the bird's formal
complaint to Fortune, which follows. The parrot regrets both her
courtier-like overweening ambition, and the change that Fortune
has brought to her 'forme and feddrum fair' (206).

By devices from courtly literature, Lyndsay several times
emphasises his detachment from the words he reports. He hides,
like a chanson d'aventure narrator, 'onder ane hauthorne grene'
(188) to hear the complaint. Later, he speaks of overhearing the
parrot's words 'in myne Fantasie' (222). With these self-distanc-
ing details, however, Lyndsay also indicates his presence as
reporter throughout the bird's epistles to her king and court
brothers. The human point of view is thus kept uppermost aptly, in
a manner reminiscent of Henryson's similarly-placed narrator in
the Preiching of the Swallow.

This is especially important in the parrot's first epistle, her
'cedull' to King James. In it the parrot's words, tone, and style,
with some extra details of the king's adult interests, are very
similar to Lyndsay's own carefully selective speculum principis at
the end of the Dreme. The connection between the bird-made-wise-
by-experience and the poet-Lyndsay is lightly ironic; the parrot
dryly alludes to the numerous poetic documents of counsel that the
king has already received (263). Perhaps there is also a nimble
reference to Jean Lemaire's Ovidian epistles to Margaret of
Austria, written in the voice of her parrot lover. But the recom-
mendations are practical, almost parental, and, in their plea to
study 'bot half one hour' each day 'The Regiment of princelie
gouernyng' (306-7), certainly knowing of the king's attention span.

In the second epistle, to the bird's 'brethir of courte', the
narrating voice moves a little further away from the human point
of view by some telling avian touches. The papyngo warns her
brothers of vainly ambitious courtiers who 'wantit wyngis' (366).

Later, in her northern fall-of-princes catalogue, she tells of
Cochrane and his company, who 'wantit fedderis' (466) to escape
their fate. This very specific treatment of the <u>ubi sunt</u> theme is
much better said to the court by a dying parrot, for she takes her
examples up to the present day before returning to safer classical
figures.

The section ends with a witty and regretful farewell to the
four royal residences. The point of view is avian, in the recall
of the echoing bird sounds at Stirling, but a hint of a human
viewpoint is also there, as the bird alludes to the poor opinion
held by anonymous 'Courte men' of Falkland's (bad) ale (640-6).

In the final section of the poem, the 'Commonyng' between the
papyngo and her executors, the bird allegory is fully developed.
The characteristics of the bird voices predominate. Their actions,
such as their initial gathering at the papyngo's deathbed, are in
keeping with the behaviour of birds of prey. The bird world here
is discrete. It mirrors the human world but there is no equivocal
integration with it. Lyndsay makes it plain that he is again the
overhearing reporter of the action. He has many asides of the type
'Than said the Rauin' (976), and otherwise proffers only an occasional judgemental verb or adjective: 'Thay <u>contrafait</u> gret cair'
(663, my emphasis); 'that <u>fals</u> gled'(1068, my emphasis). Like the
animals in Henryson's <u>Fables,</u> the birds are allowed largely to
reveal their own natures. The pye, for example, says 'I pray ʒow,
mak prouisione for ʒour spreit' (650), and condemns herself by the
next words, 'Dispone ʒour geir' (651), for she clearly equates
spiritual salvation with the bestowal of material possessions.

This section of the poem is richly varied in diction. There is
a tragi-comic simplicity and a graceful formality about the dying
parrot's bequests: '... to the Guse, ʒe geue, quhen I am gone,/My
Eloquence and toung Rethoricall' (1104-5). This contrasts sharply
with the colloquialisms, invective, interjections and pseudo-
elevated language of the clerical triad. Their description of the
papyngo's funeral pomps - 'The reukis sall rair, that men sall on
thame rew,/And cry <u>Conmemoratio Animarum</u> ...' (696ff) - is ironically most reminiscent of apocalyptic passages from the flytings,
and like them, concerned with rhetorical display before meaning.
These contrasts in diction are at once dramatically satisfying - a
development from Lyndsay's quoted speeches in the <u>Complaynt</u> - and
a way, once again, of stressing that proper action and stylistic
decorum are related.

The poem ends with the flight of the rapacious birds - after
the gled who has seized the heart, and away from Lyndsay's observation. The fiction of detachment is preserved. Nevertheless,
Lyndsay has established a subtle and teasing point and counterpoint between his own voice, world, and position, and those of the
parrot. There is the stylistic parallel, seen clearly in the
'Cedull' to the king. There are the verbal allusions: at the
beginning, Lyndsay desires 'Ingyne Angelicall' and at the end, the
papyngo, close to death and divinely inspired, refers to her
possession of a 'voce Angelycall' (1103). There is the comic
undercurrent, that permits a parrot, not a poet, to speak counsel
to the king. And there are the heraldic touches: the papyngo's
wing is 'displayit' (165); she leaves her heart to the king; she

refers to her 'deuyse' (730) and describes the 'heuinly hewis' of the phoenix by the tinctures of heraldry (1111-2). Her 'fair speiche' undoubtedly has a place in the nexus of heraldic ideas about the bird.[30] Against this, the voices of the pye, raven and gled draw more obvious rhetorical and moral contrasts. They also create the vivid dramatic interlude on church corruption, which forms part of the larger tragi-comedy.

Lyndsay's use of voices in the Papyngo brilliantly acknowledges a monarch whose literary and dramatic tastes are demanding greater ingenuity. In the less ostentatious Bagsche, Lyndsay's use of the voice of the irascible royal hound has behind it the same assumption. This shorter animal tale, however, takes Lyndsay's experiments even further. Inspired by Henryson, but extending that poet's techniques of narrative self-effacement to their limits, Lyndsay here becomes a 'silent' narrator, with the nuances of the dog's voice, and the degree to which his mental outlook is thus made vivid, Lyndsay's only means of controlling mood and tone. A seemingly simple poem, mixing petition-complaint, beast fable and fall-of-princes tragedy, Bagsche is made lively, mock-heroic and very artful drama by its strictly first person canine narrator.

In an earlier paper I discussed in detail the methods Lyndsay has used to reveal the character of this over-proud member of the royal kennels.[31] Here, there is only time briefly to note Lyndsay's important use of the dramatic monologue to maintain an ironic cross-patterning of human and animal worlds. Lyndsay has not, as Henryson does in the Fables, used this ultimately to enlarge the meaning of the particular tale, allowing it to bear differing interpretations. On the contrary, at either canine or human level, Bagsche's king is James V, and his fellows are names, be they the courtier George Steill, or the dog Lanceman. In this tightly defined context, the integration of levels is subtly achieved through Bagsche's words: is this a tale of a dog's disgrace? or a courtier's fall? Even Lyndsay, the poem's silent creator, has a jesting part, for in his position as Lord Lyon he punningly spans both worlds. The assured silence of Lyndsay's own voice, together with the retention and even enlargement of the dramatic dimension he has created in other works by the juxta-position of several voices, is a notable achievement.

Earlier, I referred to Lyndsay's forthright words in the Complaynt: 'Thus euery man said for hym self'(253). In that comment, several senses of the word 'said' are implicated. In the immediate circumstances, of the usurping courtiers sharing out the booty, 'said' has the sense 'spoke up', 'demanded', 'claimed for' onself. Perhaps there is also a sense of the verb 'assay' there; 'to attempt', 'to try for' oneself.[32] In the larger context of the poem as a whole, with Lyndsay's voice set against the false idiom of the flatterers, 'said for hym self' admits also the sense 'revealed his character ...', 'showed his style and worth by the manner of his words'. This last usage is apposite to the way in which Lyndsay, during this period, uses narrative voices. Lyndsay himself speaks to the king as his 'familiar daylie servitour',[33] always providing a stylistic and moral fulcrum which is especially obvious when other voices are also involved.

Through these other voices, Lyndsay is able, with some dexterity,

to experiment, both with the degrees of detachment from his matter
and with the varied, usually morally weighted, effects of the juxtaposition or blending of different levels of diction and style.
These other voices, providing several points of view, add dramatic
dimensions to Lyndsay's poems, making of them the domestic, king-
and court-centred equivalents of Lyndsay's public, kingdom-encom-
passing devisings, such as the 'greit preparatiuis' of welcome for
the princess Madeleine, or the 'triumphand frais' and address to
Marie de Guise at St Andrews. Later, after the death of the sovereign whom Lyndsay had counselled, protected and represented since
birth, Lyndsay changes the focus of his work quite consciously,
dispersing his counsel, altering the emphases of theme and method.
Within our period, however, there are voices, direct and oblique,
but always appropriate, for the Scottish King James and his court.

Notes

1   Exchequer Rolls of Scotland, ed J Stuart and others (Edin-
    burgh, 1878-1908), XIII, 127 and Accounts of the Lord High
    Treasurer, T Dickson and J Balfour Paul (eds) (Edinburgh and
    London, 1877-1916, hereafter 'TA'), IV 441.
2   See, for example, TA, V, 37; V, 112; V, 127; V, 160; V, 196.
3   See editor Hamer's discussion in The Works of Sir David
    Lindsay, 4 vols. (Edinburgh, Scottish Text Society, Third
    Series Nos 2, 4, 6 and 8, 1931-36, hereafter 'Hamer'), III,
    57, note to lines 255-62.
4   See Innes of Learney, 'Sir David Lindsay of the Mount: Lord
    Lyon King of Arms, 1538-1555' (Part II), Scottish Notes and
    Queries, 13, Third Series (November 1935), 172-3.
5   See the 'Protocol Book of Mr Meldrum, 1520-33', Scottish
    Record Office B 30 1/1/1, fol. 110^V, where Lyndsay is
    described (4 January 1529) as being 'nomine et ex parte
    Leonis armorum'. See also Hamer's discussion, IV, 288-9. See
    further, R F Green, Poets and Princepleasers (Toronto, 1980),
    p 25.
6   See introduction (unpaginated) to Court of the Lord Lyon:
    List of His Majesty's Officers of Arms and Other Officials,
    ed F J Grant (Edinburgh, Scottish Record Society, 1945) and T
    Innes of Learney, 'Heraldic Law', An Introductory Survey of
    the Sources and Literature of Scots Law, ed H McKechnie
    (Edinburgh, Stair Society, 1936), pp 379-95.
7   See The Bannatyne Manuscript, 4 vols. ed W Tod Ritchie (Edin-
    burgh, STS, New Series, Nos. 22, 23 and 26; Third Series No
    5, 1928-33), II, 242-5 (Kyde), and II, 231-2 (W Stewart) and
    Maitland Folio Manuscript, 2 vols, ed W A Craigie, 2nd edn
    (1919 and 1927; repr Edinburgh, STS, New Series, Nos 7 and
    20, 1972), I, 353-55 (W Stewart). But see the discussion of
    the various 'Stewart' poets in The Bannatyne Manuscript, D
    Fox and W Ringler (eds) (London, 1980), p.xlii.
8   For more detail, see J E H Williams, 'The Poetry of Sir David
    Lyndsay: A Critical Study', Diss. Australian National Univ.,

1978, pp 100-6, and R J Lyall, 'Narrative Technique and Moral Purpose in Middle Scots Poetry', Diss. Glasgow, 1979, pp 420-1.

9   See J Ferguson, 'The Personal Reign of James V, King of Scots 1528-1542', Diss. Princeton, 1961, Ch. I, p 11ff.

10   See Innes of Learney, 'Heraldic Law', p 383.

11   B M Harley MS 6149 (fol 154v), compiled by Adam Loutfut, Kintyre Pursuivant, in 1494. The poem is published, with punctuation added, in Queene Elizabethe's Achademy, ed F J Furnivall (London, Early English Text Society, Extra Series VIII, 1869), pp 93-104. I am most grateful to Professor Jack Aitken for allowing me to consult his transcript of the manuscript held in the DOST archive, from which I quote.

12   See J A Burrow, 'The Poet as Petitioner', Studies in the Age of Chaucer, 3 (1981), 61-75.

13   See DOST, s v 'confort'.

14   See A J Aitken, 'Oral Narrative Style in Middle Scots', Actes du 2e colloque de Langue et du Littérature Ecossaises (Moyen Age et Renaissance), Université de Strasbourg, 5-11 Juillet, 1978, p 109.

15   See DOST, s v 'Besynes'.

16   For a discussion of Douglas's presentation of his narrator, for example, see the introduction to The Shorter Poems of Gavin Douglas, ed P J Bawcutt (Edinburgh, STS, Fourth Series, No. 3 1967), pp.xxciii-xlv.

17   See J A Burrow, 'Henryson: The Preaching of the Swallow', Essays in Criticism, 25 (1975), 25-37 and, for example, Prologue X, 66-70, of Virgil's Aeneid Translated into Scottish Verse by Gavin Douglas, ed D F C Coldwell (Edinburgh, STS, Third Series Nos 25, 26, 28 and 30, 1957-64).

18   See R J Lyall 'Politics and Poetry in Fifteenth and Sixteenth Century Scotland', Scottish Literary Journal, 3, No 2 (December 1976), especially pp 21-23. (It should be noted that Lyndsay was never 'tutor to the young king' (p 21). This was Gavin Dunbar's position.

19   See S Cairns, 'Sir David Lindsay's Dreme: Poetry and Propaganda in the Scottish Court', The Spirit of the Court: Selected Proceedings of the Fourth Congress of the International Courtly Literature Society (Toronto 1983), ed G S Burgess and R A Taylor (Cambridge, 1985), pp 110-11; J E H Williams, 'The Poetry of Lyndsay', pp 106-8.

20   'Although I beir nocht lyke ane baird': Sir David Lyndsay's Complaynt', Scottish Literary Journal, 9, No 2 (December 1982), 5-20.

21   See Priscilla Bawcutt, 'The Art of Flyting', Scottish Literary Journal, 10, No 2 (December 1983), 5-24, and D Gray, 'Rough Music': Some Early Invectives and Flytings', Yearbook of English Studies, 14 (1984), 21-43.

22   The Poems of William Dunbar, ed James Kinsley (Oxford, 1979). All quotations are from this edition.

23   See Lord Lindsay, Lives of the Lindsays, 3 vols (London, 1849), I, 54-58. This is conjecture: neither the date of the poem nor the date at which Lyndsay added to the Lyndsay of the Byres coat of arms is certainly known.

24   See, for example, Grant, Court of the Lord Lyon, unpaginated introduction.

25   See, for instance, The Palice of Honour, 11.330-1, Shorter Poems, ed Bawcutt.

26   See J W Kurtz, 'The Flyting', Diss. Columbia, 1964, pp 58-63.

27   See Ballattis of Luve, ed J MacQueen (Edinburgh, 1970) and its review by H M Shire in Medium Aevum, 41, No. 2 (1972), 180-4.

28   Kurtz, 'The Flyting', p 145.

29   'Bawte', for example, appears in the separate accounts for the king's personal expenses, 'Accounts of the King's Pursemaster 1539-40', ed A L Murray, Miscellany X (Edinburgh, Scottish History Society, 1965) p 40. 'Bagsche', found in TA VII, 96, has, appropriately, been 'mended' by Johne Campbell, the 'leiche'.

30   See, for example, 'Collectanea Domini Dauidis Lindesay de Mounthe, militis Armorum Regis, 1586', National Library of Scotland w.4.13, which has been published selectively in The Complaynt of Scotlande, ed J Leyden (Edinburgh, 1801). The observations of the heraldic significances of the parrot are found on pp 60-1.

31   'The Lyon and the Hound: Sir David Lyndsay's Complaint and Confessioun of Bagsche', Parergon, No 31 (December 1981), pp 3-11.

32   OED, s v 'say', sb^2 sense 8.

33   See Grant, Court of the Lord Lyon, introduction: 'The Lord Lyon, Heralds and Pursuivants formed an important part of the Royal Household of Scotland and as his 'familiar daylie servitors' were in early times in constant attendance on the King...'.

Chapter 20

THE SCOTTISH KIRK IN MEDIEVAL AND RENAISSANCE LITERATURE

J Schwend

John Ker says in his book The Scottish Nationality and other
Papers: 'Wallace made a nation and Knox a people. The one secured
the soil on which the other built up the church polity, and in
which he implanted the religious principles that have since been
associated with the name of Scotland ...'[1] The Kirk of Scotland
has always been of major importance and has influenced everyday
life in Scotland more than its English counterpart did in England.
The reasons for this are certainly numerous and no final conclusive answer will be given. But it will be investigated in what way
certain writers portrayed the church and its representatives in
their works. We will start with Barbour's Bruce, go on to Blind
Harry's Wallace and from there to Lyndsay's Satyre of the Thrie
Estates as the major works of art. Other texts will be touched
upon, but the argument will rest mainly on these three examples.
It must, however, be considered that with The Bruce and The
Wallace we have heroic epic poems, whose authors' intention was
not social criticism but a eulogy of Scottish heroes and the
Scottish Wars of Independence. The approach was for instance
completely different from that used by Chaucer when he wrote at
roughly the same time his Canterbury Tales. This will also make
clear why the Kirk is only of minor importance in the two epics
and is definitely not the subject or the object of criticism.
Nevertheless, bearing this in mind, the poems can be seen as
documents of the times and taken as such.
  We shall begin by considering the medieval church as it existed
in the times of Robert the Bruce and Edward I and II. We have of
course a united Roman Catholic Church; Whitby is more than 600
years past. In his bull of 1192 Pope Celestine III declared the
Ecclesiana Scoticana as embracing the sees of St Andrews, Moray,
Ross and Caithness, directly subject to the Pope or a legate
especially sent from his side. Papal government of the Church was
accepted as an efficient system of law and administration. The
links to the English sees were close, even though frequently
contested, especially when the question of the supremacy of the
Archbishop of York was concerned. Wyclif was not yet born when
Robert the Bruce was victorious at Bannockburn, and Barbour, when
he wrote The Bruce, might well not have heard much of him. It took
another 100 years at least until Tyndale began to make himself
heard. The Roman Catholic Church is the established church with
all the rights which go with this position. Nevertheless there is
already criticism of clerical abuses in contemporary writers.

Geoffrey Chaucer makes fun of friars and pardoners and criticises mismanagement and maladministration in the ecclesiastical hierarchy. But this is England, and we are concerned with Scottish affairs as they are described by Barbour in his poem.

The medieval Church was the centre of learning; those who could read and write were as a rule clerics. Aberdeen became a centre of history-writing in the second half of the fourteenth century. The kings, who as a rule knew better how to handle a sword than a pen, relied on clerics for the everyday administrative functions of running a country. The infrastructure depended on ecclesiastical support. Not much could be done, if the clerics refused to co-operate. Secular clerics and prelates were in all the influential positions as counsellors of the monarch, and the church was the second largest landowner after the crown. Jurisdiction turned out to be a controversial subject as early as the twelfth century; Thomas à Becket lost his life for the cause of ecclesiastical jurisdiction. And it continued to be a controversial subject until the Renaissance and even after that date. 'English common law had always held that ecclesiastical courts, and even the Pope himself, derived their jurisdiction from the Crown.'[2]

Medieval clerics represented the intelligentsia of a nation. They helped their kings to run the country, and profited materially from this function. The enormous wealth that was heaped up in abbeys and monasteries had to be defended, and the ecclesiastics could not always rely on secular help. So the fighting cleric is a common figure in the Middle Ages and down to Flodden, where eminent churchmen lost their lives, such as the Archbishop of St Andrews, the Bishop of the Isles, the Abbots of Kilwinning, Inchaffray, Cambuskenneth, and Glenluce. The tradition of the fighting cleric goes back at least to the times of Columba, when the monks were not exempt from military service, but were called upon by their clan. Scottish bishops and abbots stood by Robert the Bruce and James IV. Fionn MacColla in At the Sign of the Clenched Fist[3] introduces in the fictive trial of a heretic a bishop who is still suffering from his battle wounds. Churchmen fought side by side with the knights, and the bishops sent their troops of men as the land-owning secular nobility did.

Anthony Bek, Bishop of Durham, was Edward I's right-hand man against the Scots, and in The Bruce (XVII, 546f) it is said that the Archbishop of York was made the English captain. The Bishop of St Andrews took an active part in raiding parties against the English after the defeat at Falkirk. William Lamberton served as a diplomat for the case of Scotland in negotiations with the Pope and France: Bishop Lamberton had been the co-ordinator of Scottish resistance against the English for years, and together with Robert the Bruce he signed a bond of mutual help and support for Scotland in the Abbey of Cambuskenneth on 11 June 1304. Lamberton is also mentioned in The Bruce (I, 412). And it was Robert Wishart, Bishop of Glasgow, who gave Robert absolution after his murder of Comyn. When the English marched northwards to avenge this murder, both the Bishops of Glasgow and St Andrews were taken prisoner (see Bruce, IV, 13). The clergy, however, remained loyal to Bruce, which alleviated the blow his cause had received by the imprisonment of these two powerful helpers. The Bishop of Moray took over as ecclesiastical leader and it was he who declared the war against the English to be a holy war.

The idea of the fighting cleric is once again resuscitated by the author of The Complaynt when he calls upon the clergy to defend the rights of the church against the English enemy. The English, being excommunicated infidels, are worse than Saracens and thus it is justified to rise in arms against them.

What was the situation like in the Renaissance, at the turn of the fifteenth and sixteenth centuries and later in the sixteenth century? Chaucer either had better information than Barbour, or the English church in his time was further gone in corruption than the Scottish; or else Barbour, starting from a different approach and aiming at a different sort of literary work of art, simply was not interested in corruption within the ecclesiastical system. In any case, the positive, patriotic image of the Church, as we find it in The Bruce, by the Renaissance period had completely disappeared. The majority of the prelates enjoyed a life of luxury; corruption and moral decay were rife. Eric Linklater in The Lion and the Unicorn puts it as follows: '... the excessive wealth, the widespread incompetence, and the serious corruption of the Roman Church in Scotland ...'[4] However, to be fair, we should state here that both kinds of pre-Reformation bishops existed. There were those who were clearly unworthy of their office, frequently very young illegitimate sons of nobles (for instance James IV's eleven-year-old illegitimate son was appointed to the bishopric of St Andrews), but there were of course also those who distinguished themselves for their piety, learning, and rectitude, those who fulfilled the pastoral office of a bishop and tried to achieve reforms within the traditional church. An example for the latter category would be Bishop Elphinstone of Aberdeen. John M Ross describes the latter type as follows: 'the Scottish Church, even at its worst, could boast of men who may favourably compare in learning, culture and piety with the choicest spirits of the Reformation.'[5]

The wealth of bishops contrasted with the poverty of parish priests. The property and income of the church was misused. Instead of spending the money on the upkeep of buildings, the maintenance of the clergy or for the poor, the resources were squandered on cards, dice, mistresses and all sorts of wordly luxuries, as well as on rich dowries for the illegitimate offspring of the prelates. Church buildings were in a state of dilapidation, church attendance low and irreverence rife. The so-called poverty of the friars was downright prosperity compared with the real pauperism of the common people. The reputation of friars had not improved since Chaucer's times, and what his Summoner had to say about friars seems to be still correct. Neglect of their duties and wordly ambitions were prevalent.

The public function of clerics as counsellors and administrators was no longer of importance. A new type of specialist had arisen, people with no noble name but possessing eloquence, erudition and knowledge, who served the king better. These new men did not rise as a class but as individuals who put their frequently humble origins behind them and rose in society. They were frequently envied their newly-won influence by the old families, and were accused of sycophancy. Skelton, e.g. in Magnificence, gives examples of such parvenus. So does the author of The Complaynt of Scotland, who says that there is nothing more odious than a parvenu who, as a rule, turns into the worst tyrant imaginable: wealth without culture only ends in vice.[6] Literacy, learning, and a new critical attitude were spreading and making people more aware of what was going on around them.

As early as the thirteenth century the church on the continent was troubled by opposition and reforming movements, which, however, did not affect Scotland. In the late fourteenth century Wyclif appeared as the 'Morning Star of the Reformation'[7] and voiced a national political opposition to the Papacy in Avignon. His ideas of the supreme authority of the Scriptures were taken up by reformers. But Scotland was not touched by Wyclifism, even though the evils he attacked were as patent in Scotland as in England. Scott's The Fair Maid of Perth deals cursorily with Wyclifite trends in fifteenth-century Scotland. But when the reforming ideas of Knox reached Scotland they appealed to the common people, and the negative example of the clergy made it difficult for them to preach convincingly on morals, chastity, and rejection of worldly goods. With dispensations for all and sundry, the Papacy was so manifestly an obstacle to good government that there was little to be said for it. Thus papal authority was often simply ignored.

The Renaissance kings, and Henry VIII most of all, became more powerful as the Pope's power dwindled away. A new kind of nationalism appeared and foreign interference, for instance by the Pope of Rome, was rejected. The Papacy as a strange bedfellow with the Turkish empire was regarded as the Antichrist, the institutionalised agency of evil. The king claimed to be the highest authority in his realm and would not tolerate anybody else above him. Both Tyndale and Archbishop Cranmer defended the supreme position of the monarch. According to the Scriptures it is the king who must be obeyed and not the Pope, who is not even mentioned in the Bible. And the Scottish Reformers were among the first to assert the divine right of the monarch against the interference of papal claims. The notorious immunities of the church from temporal jurisdiction were largely abolished; ecclesiastical courts were ousted. This is also made clear by Lyndsay in his play, when he says that only God is above the king. In this respect the Reformers were at one with Luther's claim that the clergy were the subjects of the secular monarch like other people and that it was the duty of the secular magistrate to undertake reform of the church. The Second Book of Discipline strengthens, however, the claim for a theocracy and demands that laymen accept the inspired law, which is of course imposed by the Church and its representatives, who exercise their power according to the Word. The right exegesis of the Word was of course left to the Reformers, 'the sancts of God', as MacColla puts it through his baker.[8] This approach left the gates open for all sorts of troubles and in the end splits within the Reformed Church.

Tyndale also saw in the Pope and the bishops usurpers of power which was by right the king's. The function of the clergy was to preach the word and minister the sacraments. Apart from these questions of doctrine, obedience to the Papacy meant financial loss to the king, because of a continuous flow of money to Rome. Henry VIII was always short of ready cash.

In The Bruce and The Wallace the authors show us a strongly patriotic church. The two texts are characterised by the desire to show the nation's struggle against an outside enemy and only those who took an active part in this struggle are mentioned. Church matters are only of interest for Barbour and Blind Harry in so far as the church played its part in the liberation of Scotland from a foreign yoke. There are only few quotations from the Bible and invocation of God is usually connected with asking for His help before a battle (Bruce, XII, 476ff), or thanking Him for His help after the victory over the enemy. The conception is apparent that freedom and right can only be granted by God.

Both of the heroes represent truly Christian virtues and appear as pious believers who attend service whenever possible. The moral theme of freedom and personal liberties is based on a religious foundation which makes it quite clear right from the beginning where the goodies and the baddies are: 'For we haue the gret avantage./ ... we haf the richt;' (Bruce, XII, 234f). The moral climate is without ambiguity. Especially in The Bruce do we find a Scottish clergy who support the cause of Scottish patriotism against the odds of English occupation and the twofold excommunication of Robert the Bruce. Clerics supported the Scottish king right from the start and stuck to him even in adversity.

The fighting cleric is present on the English and the Scottish sides and is seen as something natural. We have clergymen take an active part in the fighting, not the kind of religious zealots who for the sake of doctrine foiled Scottish hopes, purged Leslie's troops, drove his men to certain death, and helped Cromwell to his victory at Dunbar in 1650. The patriotism which is apparent in Scottish clerics in the Middle Ages gives way to religious zeal in the seventeenth century. The nation was sacrified to the Covenant. Whenever Barbour mentions clerics, which is, however, not too often, he shows them in a very advantageous light, as for instance in the case of the Bishop of Dunkeld who makes the Scots turn back and confront the English landing party and finally repulse them (Bruce, XVI, 574ff, 603ff).

The Pope on the other hand is described as a foreign power who sides with the English against the Scots. The Pope is not the enemy per se, but as he is in the enemy's camp, the author's sympathies are definitely not with the Bishop of Rome but with Scottish clergymen who helped their king. The relationship between king and clerics is without tension, a relationship of mutual trust and help as far as possible. And Robert I was grateful enough to the Kirk to give them a generous recompense for their help. He is the one who acclaims St Andrew as patron saint of Scotland and has the cathedral of St Andrews consecrated and generously endowed in gratitude for the victory of Bannockburn. Similarly David I founded most of the Scottish monasteries and his grandsons Malcolm IV and William the Lion continued his work. Later on foundations of new monasteries and grants to old ones became rarer, 'monasticism ceased to hold its pre-eminent place among the objects of Christian esteem and liberality.'[9] This new

attitude led James I to call David I 'ane sair sanct to the
crown', and he chided abbots and priors for neglect of their
pastoral duties. In 1559 reforming zealots, whom Knox called the
'rascal multitude',[10] pulled down St Andrews Cathedral in the
frenzy of iconoclasm. The generosity of Bruce is not even mentioned in Barbour's epic. Barbour's aim is to show his two heroes,
Robert the Bruce and the Douglas, in the best light: the situation
of the Church is not really of interest for him, even though he
himself was a churchman.

The situation is completely different in Renaissance literature, and here in particular in Lyndsay's Satyre. Even though
Lyndsay did not follow the Reformers, he was very critical and
propagated reforms within the Roman Catholic Church. His aim was
not a heroic poem but social criticism which is above all aimed at
the church. Whereas Barbour and Blind Harry tried to praise the
heroic achievements of Scotsmen, Lyndsay drew the attention of his
audience to the predicament his country was in. The approach of
the authors is different, but their works can be seen as reflecting the prevalent attitude of the people at the time of writing.
Lyndsay's time was not a time for writing heroic poems but for
social criticism. He describes and utilises events in his play
from the Reformer's point of view. Lyndsay seems to despair of the
state of affairs in Scotland and seeks to effect change and to
abolish the maladministration of the country by satirising the
social, political and ecclesiastical situation. His play is
addressed to those who have suffered from the corrupt Kirk but
have not yet joined the ranks of the Reformers. The culprit for
Lyndsay is not the king but his entourage. Similar accusations
were made by John Knox when he spoke of the king being abused by
'... crafty, covetous, wicked and ungodly counsellors.'[11] Whereas
in the Middle Ages the bishops fulfilled this important function
as chief vassals of the king, valued and almost indispensable
because of their learning, they abused this eminent position in
the Renaissance period and cherished their own private interests.
The image of the clergy is almost exclusively negative, and if we
take contemporary reports, this situation is corroborated.

Or let us look at Bale's King John (c.1561), in which all the
villains wear clerical garb: Dissimulation appears in the disguise
of a Cistercian monk, Treason as a priest, Private Wealth wears a
cardinal's garb, and Usurped Power disguises himself as the Pope.
Bale's intention of disparaging the clergy is made obvious in this
kind of visual satire which is also found in Lyndsay's play when
Falsehood, Flattery and Deceit don clerical clothes (720). Lyndsay
describes it with the image of the wolf in a wether's skin (4275).
The clerical garb is not used as camouflage, but to open people's
eyes.

In both texts, Bale's King John and Lyndsay's Satyre, criticism
of the clergy is most striking. The higher clergy in particular
are under attack. Only a few bishops fulfilled their office and
proved worthy of the respect which their station demanded. The
discrepancy between the ecclesiastical office and the incumbent's
practice offended the authors and is exposed in the satires. The
majority were unqualified for their position. We may take for
instance the case of the Bishop of Dunkeld, who professed never to

have read the Bible. 'I thank God that I never knew what the Old and New Testament was.'[12] This did not stop him from being instrumental in the arrest and burning of heretics. Ignorance is seen as the mother of all vices and the council of 1549 attempted to ameliorate this deplorable situation. Lyndsay's Pardoner is certainly not the only one who thought that the New Testament was written by Luther. Many bishops lived in idle luxury and could not be regarded as successors to the Apostles but only as 'dumb dogs' and 'idle bellies'.[13] The antipathy towards idleness is a typically Reformist attitude, as industry and the gain of material values were important features in the Protestant outlook on life.

Widespread corruption, lechery, and general immorality connected with the sin of pride were characteristic of the church at the beginning of the sixteenth century. Lyndsay makes this quite obvious. The Registers between 1510 and 1560 disclose an enormous increase in the legitimation entries of children from clerics. For the church it was a worse crime to be married than to have a concubine. The pauper's point of view on this question is completely different and stated unequivocally by Lyndsay.

As prototypes of the ambitious and immensely rich prelate can be seen Cardinal Wolsey in England and Cardinal Beaton in Scotland. Beaton was 'a prelate whose greed and ambition surpassed even his talents'.[14] He tried to influence politics as far as possible and favoured of course the French faction in Scotland, as the English had him imprisoned in 1542 and authorised the circulation of the Bible in English. Beaton's private life was openly immoral and his public life was more devoted to politics than to the pastoral duties of a bishop. In this respect he stood in the tradition of Forman of Moray, who was an outstanding example of a Scottish diplomat and career politician, and who renewed the Scottish-French alliance which made war with England unavoidable. With all these political functions and with a luxurious private life, the clerics did not find the time for reforms within the church hierachy, which led to the impoverishment of parishes and the resultant anti-clericalism typical of the Reformation period. The place of the outside enemy for the common man was taken up by the Pope and finally by France as a Catholic naton. Lyndsay criticises France as the place where Flattery comes from. And Knox rejoiced in the vengeance which resulted in the murder of Beaton. Personalities such as Beaton can be made responsible for the widespread anti-clericalism which was rife in Lyndsay's time and which led to the elevation of the status of laymen within the reformed church as a sort of controlling body over the ministers.

The anonymous author of The Complaynt of Scotland makes it clear what the prelates have to expect once the English take over in Scotland. Henry VIII's purges were still in everybody's memory, 'the cruel volfis of ingland'[15] who had been used by God as a scourge for Scotland's sins. With this in mind he calls upon the clergy to take up arms and declares the fight against the English a holy war, because they are infidels and excommunicated. The same thing was done in The Bruce with nationalistic reasons for the war against England.

The wealth of bishops led to complaints not only from the poor common people, but also from the burghers in the cities and from

the lesser nobles and the gentry who were unable to get their
daughters married, as they could not provide them with the lavish
dowries the clerics would pay. Illegitimacy was no disadvantage,
as long as the money was good enough. Pecunia non olet. As
Mathieson puts it: 'The wealth of the superior clergy induced even
women of good family to live with them in a species of licensed
concubinage. Their [the clergy's] daughters were considered a good
match for the sons of the nobility.'[16]

The riches of the prelates had to come mainly from the
parishes, which resulted in the impoverishment of parish priests.
The lowly paid office of a parish priest did not attract people of
learning, who could easily find more convenient and above all
better paid work. The parish priest had to find all sorts of
additional sources of income, as his stipend would not keep him
alive. This might explain the exploitation of the parishioners as
described in Ane Satyre by the pauper, a sort of national under-
dog. Pluralities and resulting absenteeism, mortuary dues and
other fees were a means for the parish priest to survive. Looking
after the bare necessities left the priest little time to care for
his parishioners or bother about mass. John M Ross gives the
following picture of a parish priest:

> The parish priests had grown utterly indolent and worldly.
> They almost never preached, contenting themselves with
> mumbling the service, after which they were wont to join
> their rustic congregations in the gross frolics of the
> churchyard or the noisy debauchery of the alehouses.[17]

The parish priest had little time for preaching because he had to
work too hard for his livelihood, and the bishops, who were mainly
men of merely secular and mercenary ambitions, had no time for
preaching or the enforcement of discipline either, because their
time was spent in enjoying the good, i.e. worldly, things in life.
'With bishops made at Court in furtherance of a courtly policy,
with abbots who were not Churchmen, and parsons who could neither
preach nor read, the Church became thoroughly mercenary in
spirit'.[18] No wonder that many were accused of only joining the
ranks of the clergy to avoid having to do a good day's work.
Surprisingly it is in The Complaynt that the question is discussed
whether the ploughman can be considered as worthier than the
aristocrat. The daily work was certainly left to the common folk.
The preaching was done by friars, who professed poverty, but in
fact led a more comfortable life than the ordinary common people.
By means of flattery the friars acquired the confidence of women,
who told them more secrets than their own husbands. Lyndsay sees
in the friar the real source of all the evil in the country. And
Dunbar describes the good life he lived while he wore the cowl of
the friar. One could even detect some envy in Dunbar's descriptions of the wanton and sensual priest, especially when it was a
question of wealthy benefices. What Chaucer had said more than one
hundred years earlier seems still to have been valid in the times
of Lyndsay and Dunbar. But let us be fair: Boece, in his Lives of
the Bishops of Aberdeen (1522), gives examples of studious and
earnest churchmen, the complete contrast to Dunbar's characters:

'both were contemporary, and both were real, though the first were
a mere handful in comparison with the second.'[19] And Major, who
must be seen as a sober and critical historian, rather supports
Dunbar's picture.

Even the author of The Complaynt of Scotland is critical about
the church, although he keeps his criticism rather in general terms
and is obviously biassed in favour of the church. His satire is
mainly directed against the courtiers. He probably was a cleric
himself who nonetheless recognised the need for reforms, though
rejecting Reformation ideas as the Reformation for him was connected with England, and what the clergy had to expect from England he
made quite clear. For him Henry VIII was the Auld Enemy, no doubt
about that. The author of The Complaynt sympathised with a historic
church, in which all three estates would be united in enmity
against England.

For both Lyndsay and Dunbar the situation is not quite as clear
and simple. Dunbar in his 'Orisoun' complains about the internecine
fighting in Scotland, but he does not blame the English for the
predicament of Scotland. As a matter of fact Dunbar is rather
sympathetic towards the English, as we see in his poem 'A Treatise
of London' or of course in 'The Thistle and the Rose'. Dunbar
remained a devout Catholic all his life. He was more of a tradi-
tionalist than an eager reformer, but he also sees the abuses of
power. Lyndsay is more outspoken about the clergy. As courtiers
Dunbar and Lyndsay could not really blame the king for the situation, so they put the blame on counsellors and on the immorality
of clerics whose bad character provided the king with an excuse for
his own vices. As dutiful subjects, Dunbar and Lyndsay simply warn
the king against his weaknesses and remonstrate against the vices,
but they stress the undercurrent of virtue which is quite obvious
in the king's person. There is an alliance between king and
commoner against the ecclesiastical hierarchy.

The Pope in Rome was to be blamed. An end had to be put to the
outflow of money to Rome, to immorality, and the exploitation of
the poor. With his criticism of the church Lyndsay is in the
tradition of literature of the estates of his time. As a rule the
clergy is accused of lust, excessive drinking and eating, covet-
ousness, and extravagant life style at the expense of the common-
alty and the lower clergy. Lyndsay's criticism is anti-papal and
anti-monastic in the Wyclifite tradition. His concern springs from
a nationalist source. He satirises the church and churchmen, but he
wishes for reform of the church, not its destruction. He sees the
extremity of the commonwealth and calls for reasonable reformation.

In this respect Lyndsay is much more democratic or revolutionary
than Dunbar, let alone the author of The Complaynt. With Lyndsay
the voice of the common man is being heard in Scottish literature.
Dunbar complains in his 'Satire on Edinburgh' about the dirt of the
city and the vast numbers of poor, while the burghers get richer
and richer, but it is Lyndsay who turns out to be the advocate of
the commonwealth; he is the one who criticises all three estates
and leaves only the pauper unscathed. He represents a truly
enlightened ideal by taking up the cause of the poor and admonishing the nobles, the clergy in particular, and the merchants and
craftsman to stop exploiting the weak and poor in society.

In Lyndsay's satire the representatives of Spirituality are the ones who try to procrastinate, who are openly defiant and who reject reforms, who will not give up their privileges. The only reason they can name is the right of consuetude. Things have gone in their favour for so long; why should they give up all the good things they have enjoyed for ages?

All three authors in various degrees accept the fact that reforms have to be made in the interest of a national cause. Whereas Lyndsay puts the blame definitely and openly on the clergy, Dunbar expresses his criticism in a slightly veiled manner, and the author of The Complaynt is even more careful and sticks to a list of very general faults, trying to blame rather the temporal estates than the spiritual. But even he says that the clergy has not the excuse of ignorance. Ecclesiastics should know better, and when they sin, they sin against the light. This attitude coincides with the one expressed in Starkey's Dialogue, where it is said that clerical immunities are preposterous and that crime in the clergy should be punished more severely than in others. The faults of the clergy are there in spite of their knowledge, or, to put it differently, they ought to know better than to behave the way they do. But it is a common feature of Renaissance texts, and this applies not only to Scottish but also to English writers, that the need for reforms in the church is a national undertaking. John Knox appears in this context for the common man as the 'grand old soldier-priest',[20] carrying George Wishart's two-handed sword in front of him in defence of the commonwealth which is threatened by foreign powers. Lyndsay can be seen as the poet who prepared for the Reformation and John Knox as the prophet and preacher who brought it into being.

The international appeal of the Papacy is confronted with a claim for national welfare and the common good of the nation. The enemy from outside is the Papacy - with the exception of The Complaynt - and reform is the only way out of the dilemma. The Romish priests are described by Knox as 'the wery troubleris of commonweltheie and the downputaris of all princeis authoritie, be their fallss usurpit jourisdictioun'.[21] The Commonweal is foremost in the minds of enlightened writers and the threat to the commonweal is usually seen to lie in the Catholic Church and their representatives. The 1590s show a 'consistent effort to link a reformed Scottish church with a specifically Scottish nation.'[22]

The decline in papal power began when the King of France openly defied Boniface VIII and with the great schism of the fourteenth century. The Council of Constance led to a further reduction of papal power when the Pope was forced to make concessions to kings in order to save his position. The moral decay in the ecclesiastical hierarchy only speeded up this development. The European upheavals in the sixteenth century were a direct result of the failure of the Roman Catholic church to adapt to new circumstances. Instead of reforms the old hierarchy tried to hold fast to its privileges. There were of course exceptions, if we think for instance of Bishop Elphinstone and his Catechism; but these reforming Catholics were the callers in the desert, unheard by the great majority.

The reformed church responded to the change in society, to the new literacy, the end of scholasticism. It became attractive to this new society because it catered for its needs, and it used the national approach successfully. The nation-state became more important than the international claim of the pope. As early as The Bruce we can detect a new emphasis on a national cause and the end of chivalric ideals of knight errantry. Vernacular Scots was an important part, but only one part in this development.

The national appeal, which was quite obvious in the sixteenth century, disappeared later, and the Scots fell back on internecine warfare over minute details of doctrine. The Covenanters of the seventeenth century gave up the idea of a nation and a national church in the interest of their very narrow exegesis of the Bible and their intolerance of all those who did not share their views. The ideas of predestination created in Scotland a two-class system, the elect and the damned, and the damned were thought to have no chance whatsoever of improving their lot, as good works would be of no consequence. Predestination led to the dominance of the one over the other. Scotland was once again torn by warfare, and this time the enemy was not an external foe. The Kirk of Scotland, even though established by law at the end of the seventeenth century, could hardly be called a national church any more. The schism of the nineteenth century was not solely over questions of theology or church structure, but it strengthened the centrifugal trend.

John Ker, who was quoted at the beginning of this paper, wrote:

> The spirit of Knox is the key to the religious history of Scotland, and his influence is seen in the fact that each section of the Presbyterian community claims to possess the larger part of his mantle.[23]

The religious revival at the turn of the eighteenth and nineteenth centuries brought to Scotland a split in its national church. Because of intolerance and dogmatism party strife developed after the schism.

For Wales the revival resulted in a national, though nonconformist church. Whereas Wales in the nineteenth century had nonconformity as a uniting national ecclesiastical movement in opposition to the Church of England, and whereas Ireland had Catholicism as a bond and a national church, Scotland had nothing of the sort. The Scots once again had their squabbles among themselves, each sectarian body seeing itself as the upholder of the national tradition in the Kirk. They had no foreign church superimposed upon them, as was the case in Wales and Ireland. They did not need that; they had their own home-made splits and schisms as a result of questions of doctrine and of a general intolerance and lack of pragmatism. In an article in the Scotsman in 1853 it is said that the Scots are grateful for living under a British government,

> ... which protects us not only 'from our too bigoted ecclesiasticism and our too narrow nationality', but also 'from one another - church from church, class from class, even district from district, as the comparatively tolerant and moral East from the bigoted and bibulous West'.[24]

Wales and Scotland united, as it were, in their rejection of Irish Roman Catholicism, but apart from that they could not find common ground. The Scottish nation was once again split by party strife and sectarian narrow-mindedness.

Notes

1   John Ker, Scottish Nationality and other Papers (Edinburgh, 1887), p 6.
2   John W Allen, A History of Political Thought in the Sixteenth Century (London, 1928), p 162.
3   Fionn MacColla, At the Sign of the Clenched Fist (Edinburgh, 1967), p 75.
4   Eric Linklater, The Lion and the Unicorn (London, 1935), p 53.
5   John M Ross, Scottish History and Literature to the Period of the Reformation (Glasgow, 1884), p 125.
6   The Complaynt of Scotland, ed James A H Murray, Early English Text Society, Extra Series, XVII, Part I (London, 1872), pp 142f.
7   J H S Burleigh, A Church History of Scotland (London: Oxford U P, 1960), p 117.
8   MacColla, Fist, p 91.
9   Burleigh, Church, pp 56f.
10 Charles Rogers, Scotland, Social and Domestic (London, 1869), p 33.
11 Edwin Muir, John Knox, Portrait of a Calvinist (London, 1929), p 47.
12 Joanne Spencer Kantrowitz, Dramatic Allegory (Lincoln, Nebraska 1975), p 54.
13 Gordon Donaldson, The Scottish Reformation (Cambridge, 1960), p 102.
14 Ross, History, p 315.
15 The Complaynt, p 2
16 W L Mathieson, Politics and Religion in Scotland 1560-1695, 2 vols (Glasgow, 1902), p 27.
17 Ross, History, p 185.
18 Mathieson, Politics, p 31.
19 Ross, History, p 223.
20 Ross, History, p 407.
21 Spalding Club Miscellany, IV (Aberdeen, 1849), pp 88-9.
22 Arthur N Williamson, Scottish National Consciousness in the Age of James VI (Edinburgh, 1979), p 39.
23 Ker, Nationality, p 33.
24 Sir Reginald Coupland, Welsh and Scottish Nationalism (London, 1954), p 287.

John Barbour, 'The Bruce', ed Walter W Skeat (London, 1968).
The Poetical Works of Sir David Lyndsay of the Mount, 2 vols ed D Laing, (Edinburgh, 1871).

Chapter 21

DISMANTLING A STRAW MAN:
THE RELIGIOUS PERSONALITY OF JOHN KNOX

David W Atkinson

Despite the best efforts of historians and theologians alike, John
Knox remains in the voluminous literature dwelling on the Reformation considerably less than the towering figures of Luther or
Calvin; and, despite his peripatetic activities on the continent
and his heroic efforts in the French galleys, he somehow seems
outside the mainstream of Reformation life. One obvious explanation for Knox's 'minor league' status is that the development of
Protestantism in Scotland constituted itself a relatively minor
chapter in the Reformation. But even this comprises only part of
the answer, for there are those who argue that, even within
Scotland, Knox enjoyed no sustained influence on the Church and
had little long range impact on the political life of the nation.[1]
If anything, Knox is remembered as a caricature of the fire-and-
brimstone preacher, and is seen to possess little appeal as one
capable of offering instruction and comfort to the wayward
Christian. Impetuous, religiously radical, and at times politically inastute, Knox is not without justification viewed as a
revolutionary who dared to advocate the overthrow of a monarch.
     It is true that Knox's polemical voice was rarely silent, and
that, given the exaggerated overstatement on which polemic turns,
he appears at times unreflective and insensitive to political and
religious realities; hence the fiasco of his First Blast of the
Trumpet Against the Monstrous Regiment of Women. This is, however,
only one side of Knox, and belies a much more complex religious
personality. While Knox railed against apostasy and the false
teachings of Rome, his ultimate concern always rested with the
devotional life of the Church and with the religious need of the
individual Christian. This devotionalism, which runs throughout
much of Knox's prose, is something we too easily overlook in our
preoccupation with making him an historical figure, as well as one
of literary importance. A number of things figure in understanding
Knox's devotionalism; among these are his concept of the preacher
as prophet, the balance he maintains between a psychology of fear
and a psychology of hope, his use of Reform theology to articulate
the spiritual dynamics of election, and his careful use of argument and rhetoric to communicate how election works within the
individual.
     Any discussion of Knox's religiosity must begin with a consid-
eration of how Knox saw himself as a preacher, which is itself
understandable only within the larger context of his perception of
'calling'.[2] God's call to the one true Church, Knox says, is

manifested in two ways. First, there is a 'generall vocation, by which all the chosen are called to a Christian religion, having one Lorde, one Faith, one Baptisme'.[3] Beyond the general calling of election, however, each member of the elect is called to a 'special vocation', by which one serves the true Church. The Pastour has in this regard the crucial responsibility of preaching 'the true Evangell of Jesus Christ',[4] which serves to bring together God's true Church in the first place. So Knox talks of himself as 'one of that nombre whom God appointed to receave that bread, (as it was broken by Christ Jesus,) to distribute and geve the same to suche as he had called to this banket'.[5] Here he remains within a distinctly Calvinist mould by allowing that nothing he does as a preacher comes from individual initiative; to this end, Knox observes how 'it is not in my knowledge nor judgement to define, nor determine what portion or quantitie every man receaved of this bread'.[6]

Knox's model for the preacher rests with the Old Testament prophets; that he saw himself in this way is unmistakable when he contends how 'God hath revealed unto me secretes unknowne to the worlde; and also that he made my tong a trumpet to forwarne realmes and nations, yea certaine great personages, of translations and chaunges'.[7] Thus Knox speaks of being 'cald of ... God to instruct the ignorant, comfort the sorowfull, confirme the weake, and rebuke the proud, by tong and livelye voyce in these most corrupt dayes'.[8] Consistent with this role, Knox saw what he calls 'the great shipwrack of Godis trew religion' in England[9] as a reenactment of how Israel was originally alienated from God. The prophets of Israel had appeared to remind God's people how Satan had used the vanities of the world to turn them from their special mission in history. As these prophets 'did ... planelie and opinlie proclame the desolatioun of that place',[10] Knox writes with similar prophetic urgency in stressing how England is repeating the mistakes of history, and how, as with ancient Israel, divine wrath is an immediate reality rather than a vague distant possibility. 'Considder, Deir Bretherne', he writes, 'gif all thingis be alyke betuene England and Juda befoir the destructioun thairof: Yea, gif England be worse than Juda was, sall we think that the Lordis vengeance sall sleip, mannis iniquitie being so rype'.[11]

In filling his role of preacher as prophet, Knox draws on a psychology of fear; his intentions are clear when he writes, 'when I have once pronounced threatnings in His name ... I do no more deny them, then I dare deny that god hath made me a messinger to forwarne the inobedient of their assured destruction'.[12] A crucial issue here is how Knox's stress on divine wrath works within the context of justification: if God justifies each individual, why is there need to generate so obtrusively moral and spiritual transformation? The explanation is that, while God possesses a predetermined plan for His Church, the realisation of that plan gives the appearance of conscious response: simply put, fear of damnation motivates God's elect to turn to Him, although it is also the case that such fear finds fertile ground only because one is already possessed of the Holy Spirit. Knox recognises, in other words, that fear is a powerful instrument of persuasion in awakening the conscience to God in the first place.

As well, fear is crucial in maintaining the elect on the gradual path of sanctification, which leads from initial calling to final glorification. To this end, Knox focuses on the spiritual complacency of his time, bringing attention to how one, while initially called and therefore never without sustaining faith, still moves step by step along the path of sanctification continuously subject to the dangers of temptation. The warning is that one should not rest secure in one's election; indeed, healthy insecurity is a necessary sign of the awakened conscience.

No one would deny that the language of Knox's psychology of fear is at times excessive and even abusive. Yet it is not the case that Knox is unaware of this excess; indeed he recognises that what he writes and how he writes are hardly what people wish to hear. As he observes, 'my rude plainnesse displeased some, who did complaine that rashly I did speake of mennes faultes'.[13] For Knox, though, the issue is not to please but to be heard and understood; plain speaking is therefore the only possible way. In fact, he worries that he has not spoken as bluntly as he should. 'But alasse,' Knox says, 'this day my conscience accuseth me, that I spake not so plainly as my dutie was to have done'[14] and 'I was not so fervent in rebuking manifest iniquitie, as it became me to have been.'[15]

Knox may well have seen his role as one of warning and admonishing those who ignore God, but it would be a misrepresentation of Knox not to see him as one concerned with providing consolation and hope in the face of trial and persecution. Knox's many epistles to his 'afflicted brethren' offer comfort to those who persevere in the face of the trials of the Christian life, as he repeatedly stresses how 'God is alwaye[s] nyghe to those that calleth upon hym faithfully'[16] and how 'the majestie of his presence shal conduct, convey, and carye his sore troubled flocke to the lyfe and reste for which they travel.'[17]

Beyond this, Knox specifically looks to provide the comfort that comes from knowing that one is of God's elect. As the Calvinist he is, Knox accepts the notion of irresistible grace manifested through faith, and sees works as the inevitable consequence of faith. Because salvation cannot be earned, then, the crucial issue is assurance that one is predetermined to salvation, as in this regard one must look within for those signs that witness the presence of God.

Here Knox argues that this assurance is found in temptation and tribulation, for it comprises a test whereby one's faith in God is confirmed. While God 'permitteth Sathan to rage, and as it wer to triumph for a time, that ... the delyverance of Godis children may be mair to his glorie', Knox focuses on the extent of divine mercy, on how God's 'hand is so puissant, his mercie and gudwill so prompte, that he delyvereth his litill anis frome thair cruell enemy'.[18] By stressing how God determines the extent of temptation, Knox not only affirms the glory of God, but also implies that God never demands of His elect more than that of which they are capable. Thus temptation is transformed from a test into an act of love; temptation, Knox says, 'is profitable, gud, and necessarie, as a thing proceiding from God, wha is [the] fontane of all gudnes ... to the profit of the sufferer'.[19]

One thing, then, is clear: Knox's reputation as a prophet of doom concerned only with divine justice and the consequences of sin is clearly misinformed; rather his capacity as a preacher, which demands that he at once motivate, instruct, and console, turns on a psychology of fear that is tempered with one of hope and comfort. So it is that he asserts, 'suspect not, Brethrene, that I delyte in your calamiteis, or in the plagues that sall fall upon that unthankfull Natioun. No, God I tak to recorde that my heart mourneth within me, and that I am cruciate with rememberance of your trubillis'.[20] But even though Knox's sympathies lie with God's suffering children, he never forgets that expressions of sympathy by themselves are insufficient and can lead to spiritual complacency. 'Gif I should ceas', Knox writes, 'then suld I do aganis my conscience, as also aganis my knawledge, and so suld I be guiltie of the blude of thame that perischeth for a lack of admonitioun, and the plague not a moment the langer be delayit'.[21]

Knox's devotionalism figures prominently in his several epistles addressed to his Scottish and English brethren, which at once admonish against defection from the true Church and provide comfort and consolation to those remaining constant in God's ways. This dual purpose is clearly the driving force behind both the structural and stylistic development of the letters, of which one of the most carefully crafted is A Faithful Admonition to the Professors of Gods Truth in England, generally known as The Admonition to England. There is no question that contemporary affairs in England had much to do with the writing of the work, for, while warning against apostasy, the Admonition also condemns the planned marriage of Mary and Philip of Spain as threatening to English sovereignty. Despite its polemical overtones, however, the work remains predominantly devotional, and to this end is patterned to conform to the process of Christian regeneration; in this regard, it falls naturally into six sections.

The first section of Knox's epistle establishes a context for the rest of the work. In recounting the miracle of the loaves and fishes, Knox brings attention to how Christ removed himself from the people because 'by him they sought a carnal and worldly libertie' rather than 'the kingdome of God' (III, 265). Knox draws the parallel with an English Church which, having degenerated into a vehicle for worldly advancement, has experienced the same withdrawal of the Holy Spirit. He then refers to the story of Christ's disciples on the sea to assert how one should fear being separated from God, for in such separation there is opportunity for the devil 'to persecute and trouble the true churche of Christe' (III, 280). Knox's point in this first section is that one must constantly be aware of the devil and 'his servauntes' (III, 280), and to this end he stresses the consequences of spiritual lassitude:

> But alasse! we sleped in suche securitie, that the sounde of this trompet coulde of manye never be perfectly understanded, but alwayes we perswaded our selves of a certain tranquil-litie, as though the troubles, wherof mencion is made within the Scriptures of God, appertained nothing at al to this age, but unto suche as of long tyme are passed before us (III, 267).

Simply put, then, Christian transformation begins with new awareness and it is towards generating this awareness that Knox properly begins his work; after all, instruction is of no use unless it falls on fertile ground. For Knox, of course, the devil's forces of which we must be aware are 'the pestilent Papistes' (III. 280), who not only exist to subvert the church, but represent the antithesis of true spirituality. To make his point, Knox alludes to the Catholic doctrine of transubstantiation, which, as a product of human ingenuity, illustrates the human vanity that puts the individual before God and prevents the very awareness that Knox sees as the first step in spiritual rejuvenation.

Despite, however, the spiritually deprived condition of the English Church and the constant dangers the Church must confront, Knox still finds the positive in the negative; he concludes the first section with the affirmation that those who should hear will hear:

> And therefore, beloved Brethren in our Savioure Jesus Christ, holde up to God your handes, that are fainted thorowe feare, and let your hertes, that have in these dolorouse days sleeped in sorow, awake, and heare the voyce of your God, who swearth by him selfe, That he will not suffer hys Churche to be oppressed for ever; neither that he will despyse our sobbes to the ende, yf we will rowe and stryve against this vehement wynde. (III, 286-287).

This affirmation serves as an effective transition into the second section of the epistle, which emphasises God's mercy and in giving new hope balances Knox's earlier stress on the rigour of divine justice. Knox also talks of his own spiritual revewal, which itself marks this shift of emphasis and provides a sense of immediacy and reality:

> Thus shortly have I passed thorowe the outrageous tempest, wherein the disciples of Christ were tempted, after that the great multitude were, by Christ, fedde in the deserte, omittinge many profitable notes which myght well have bene marcked in the texte, because my purpose is, at this present, not to be tediouse, nor yet curiouse, but onlie to note such thinges as be aggreable to these most dolorouse dayes. (III, 289).

Of importance in the second section is the way Knox alerts his readers to how tribulation anticipates the final deliverance of the elect. He exhorts them therefore to have patience a little longer: 'The trouble is come, O deare Brethren! looke for the comforte, and ... abyd in resistinge this vehement storme a little space' (III, 288).

Knox might exhort his brethren to look for comfort in tribulation, but such exhortation still begs the question of why God's elect must suffer tribulation in the first place. Knox clearly knows this, and appropriately turns his attention to the meaning of tribulation in the third section of the epistle. His answer here is the standard Christian one: that the tribulation of Christ's faithful is a sign of election in which there is to be found great comfort, and that this comfort is only possible if one is fortified with the power of the Word, for in such fortitude is found further confidence of one's own spiritual renewal. Commonplace as Knox's answer is, however, the power of his rhetoric transforms it into a celebration of hope:

> This I writte, beloved in the Lorde, that ye, knowynge of the Worde of God not onely to be that whereby were created heaven and earth, but also to be the power of God to salvation to al that beleve; the bryght lantarne to the fete of these that by nature walke in darkenesse; the lyfe to those that by synne are dead; a comforte of such as be in tribulation; the tower of defence to suche as be moste feble; the wysedome and great felicitie of such as delyteth in the same. And to be shorte, you knowe Goddes Worde to be of suche efficacie and strength, that therby is synne purged, death vanquyshed, tyrauntes suppressed, and, finally, the Devel, the author of all myserie, overthrowen and confounded. (III, 301).

In answering the question of why there must be tribulation, Knox concludes with the point that divine intention is ultimately incomprehensible, that, given the immense distance between God and humankind, mere human understanding will never fully grasp the ways of God, and that one must fall back on the acceptance of God's ways gained through faith. Yet, at the same time, God's incomprehensibility is not to be feared; rather one must take comfort in the mystery and overwhelming power of God. In short, one must 'knowe Goddes Worde to be of such efficacie and strength, that thereby is synne purged, death vanquyshed, tyrauntes suppressed, and, finally, the Devel, the author of all myserie, overthrowen and confounded' (III, 301).

This emphasis on divine incomprehensibility is also important in marking an effective transition into the fourth section of the epistle, which provides concrete Biblical examples of what is required from the wayfaring Christian and how the wayfaring Christian responds to the problem of life. Knox's message is that, despite the mystery of divine intention, the religious life is one of tangible action in the world. Also in the fourth section, Knox writes about the working of the Holy Spirit in the elect, and brings attention to how faith for the elect is not a constant thing, but wanes and gives way to doubt. While Knox again admits that humankind cannot ultimately fathom God's purposes, or, as he says, 'albeit that we coulde render no reason of this worke of Christe, yet were the worke it selfe a sufficient reason' (III, 315), he also recognises how this waning of faith has the recognisable purpose of removing the arrogance that separates humankind and God. Knox writes, 'to correct and reforme both presumptuous arrogancy, and fraile imbecillitie and weaknes of faith, Peter was permitted once to sincke, and thryse most shamefully to refuse and denye his Maister; to the intent ... that he myght more largely magnifie Goddes free grace and mighty delyveraunce' (III, 317). The elect must come to understand their own frailty and that whatever worth they possess comes only as a free gift of God's grace. Moreover, only in such an attitude of humility can any action one takes in the world bring religious comfort and consolation.

Always with an eye to maintaining a balance between fear and hope, Knox dwells in the fifth section on the assertion that in the elect faith never truly disappears. That the elect doubt their salvation and are concerned with their spiritual health itself signifies God's presence. Knox notes how Peter's words, 'Lorde, save me', were, despite Peter's doubt, 'a declaration of a lyvely and quick faith, which lay hyd within his afflicted and sore affrayed herte' (III, 318). That Peter called for 'Christes help by prayer' (III 318) is an indication that hope is present, which is itself a gift of grace; as Knox writes, 'in extreame perils, impossible it is that the herte of man can crye for Goddes helpe without some hope of hys mercye' (III, 318). All this discussion merely anticipates, however, Knox's response to the question on everyone's mind, 'how shall it be knowen in whome the sparke and roote of Fayth remayneth, and in whom not' (III, 324), which is itself couched in a series of seven succinct questions which turn one's focus inward to examine the state of one's soul and which thereby comprise the very devotional center of the work:

Fealest thou thy sole fayntynge in fayth as Peter felt his body sincke downe into the waters? Arte thou as sore affrayed that thy soule should drowne in hel, yf thou consentest or obeyest idolatrye? ... Desyrest thou as earnestly the delyveraunce of thy soule, as Peter dyd the delyveraunce of his body? Belevest thou that Christ is able to delyver thy soule, and that he wyl do the same accordynge to his promise? Doest thou call upon him without hypocrisie, nowe in the daye of thy trouble? Doest thou thrist for his presence, and for the lybertie of his worde agayne? Mournest thou for the great abhominations that now overflowes the Realme of England?

(III, 325)

If any of these premises 'remaine yet in thy harte', Knox asserts, 'then arte thou not altogether destitute of fayth; neither shalt thou descend to perdition for ever' (III, 325). Thus Knox provides a mechanism by which one can find assurance of salvation. This inward examination is, moreover, the most crucial dimension of spiritual life, for only in such examination can one affirm one's election.

So it is that the epistle moves from focusing on chastisement and divine wrath to celebrating divine forgiveness. In this context, the concluding section is largely extended prayer which at once acknowledges sin, asks forgiveness, extols the glory of God, and recognises the dependence of the elect on God, even while the prophet's voice demanding divine justice is never fully silenced. Knox's prayer elicits a sense of confidence, as if, in having read through the epistle, his readers have necessarily come to new understanding and faith and thereby renewed hope for the future; in other words, the literary shape of the epistle reflects the internal spiritual transformation of calling, and thereby

serves as a singular example of what Knox means when he talks of
his own special calling as a minister of God.

The psychological balance of Knox's devotionalism evident in a
longer work such as The Admonition to England is also a factor in
his shorter works, where there is even more evident the positive
tone that celebrates divine grace over divine justice. In A
Comfortable Epistell Sente to the Afflicted Church of Chryst, for
example, Knox begins as he does in The Admonition to England:

> When I ponder wyth my selfe, beloved in the Lord, what was
> the state of Christes true churche immediatlie after his
> death and passion, and what were the chaunges and greate
> mutacions in the commonwealth of Judea before the finall
> desolation of the same: As I cannot but feare that like
> plagues, for lyke offences shall strike the Realme of
> Englande ... (III, 239)

But almost immediately Knox sees in exactly the same situation
cause for celebration:

> ... can I not but rejoice, knowing that Godis most mercifull
> providence is no lesse carefull this day, over his weake and
> feeble servantes in the Realme of Englande, than it was that
> day, over his weake and sore oppressed flocke in Jurye. (III,
> 239).

While Knox celebrates divine mercy, however, one does sometimes
see in these shorter works echoes of the condemning voice that
characterises, for example, his famous First Blast. A good example
is how Knox appears in the Comfortable Epistell to gain comfort,
not only from knowing that the trials of God's Church will eventually end, but also in knowing 'that the judgemente of these
tyrantes that now oppresse us shall not slip, but that vengeaunce
shall fal upon them without provision' (III, 244). Such statements
seem to exude a spiritual arrogance conflicting with the entire
notion of Christian humility that Knox so stresses and that is so
central to Calvinist theology. Most certainly they suggest that
Knox gains satisfation in knowing he is one of God's elect, and in
seeing himself possessed of a special voice called to speak God's
word. While one cannot entirely overlook Knox's rather unChristian
attitude here, one must see what he says over against his main
concern: that the Church is under siege, and there is absolutely
no room for compromise. In the case of A Comfortable Epistle,
furthermore, Knox never completely closes the door on the possible
spiritual rebirth of those 'blinde, cruel, and malicyous tiraunts'
(III, 244). He exhorts his followers that 'ye lerne of Chryst to
pray for your persecutors, lamenting and bewayling that the Devyl
shold so prevaile against them' (III, 244). Knox knows full well
that God can call even the greatest sinners at any time in any way.

Not only is Knox capable of restraining his condemning voice;
he can also put it totally aside. This is the case, for example,
in An Epistle to His Afflicted Brethern in England. In contrast to
other letters, Knox, while mentioning the tribulations of God's
Church, does not dwell on them. His sole aim in mentioning the

state of God's Church is to establish a context for the central
theme of the epistle, 'for yit my gud hoip is, that ane day or
uther Chryst Jesus, that now in Ingland is crucifeit, sall ryse
agane in despyt of his enmyis, and sall appeir to his weak and
sair trublit discipillis ... to whome he sall say, Peace be unto
yow (III, 232). Gone, as well, is the heaping condemnation directed at the 'tirantis of Ingland' (III, 234): while Knox cannot deny
'the fyre that never salbe quencheit' (III, 234), he takes no
pleasure in the eventual perdition of the reprobate and goes so
far as to say, 'theis tirantis is mair to be piteit and lamentit
than either feiret or haitit' (III, 234). Thus the epistle exudes
a Christian forebearance far more appealing than the vindictive-
ness Knox sometimes expresses.

Yet another letter, A Letter Addressed to the Commonality of
Scotland, also suggests that Knox's devotionalism is more important than his polemic. Again he expresses the commonplace sentiment
that 'Papistes by their awne sentence condemne themselves and
theyr religion' (IV, 525). But again, he does not entirely close
the door on those who refuse reformation. One of Knox's major
criticisms here is a Catholic Church that refuses 'examination and
trial' (IV, 525), and in this regard he exhorts the Bishops to
entertain such examination as if it would affect real change.
Again, then, he leaves the suggestion that reformation is
possible, even among those furthest from God.

Other devotional implications also exist in this letter. Knox
makes the point that religion is not merely a thing of tradition
but must constantly be evaluated against 'the plaine Worde of God'
(IV, 525). Not to ask questions of what one believes is, for Knox,
a sure sign that one is refused election. This is not to say that
Knox condones human presumptuousness about things that are properly the domain of God; rather he sees a place for a lively faith
that 'is engendred, norished, and mentained in the heartes of
Goddes elect by Christes Evangile truelie preached' (IV, 527).
This, he claims, is 'the Spirit of wisedom' (IV, 537); or, put
another way, to question is to be alive spiritually, although
God's Word remains as an absolute beyond which the elect cannot go.

The lesson to be learned is that the Christian life is not one
of complacency; justification by faith and its implications of
predestination do not presume that the elect are mere puppets in
the working out of the divine plan. It is because one is possessed
of the Holy Spirit that one is capable of actively responding to
'the trubles of this transitorious life' (IV, 537). One hardly
need mention, of course, that Knox runs up against the theological
chestnut of predestination and freewill. But like so many other
Christian writers of his time, Knox turns a blind eye to theological exactitude in the face of devotional need. It is a simple
fact of Christian life that one needs to feel involved in one's
own spiritual growth; it is not enough to leave everything up to
God, whatever the implications of theology might be. So Knox
leaves the clear impression that God warns so that His elect can
respond. 'Be ye assured Brethren', Knox says, 'that as he [God] is
immutable of nature, so will he not pardon in you that which so
severely he hath punished in others' (IV, 537).

A pivotal devotional document demonstrating Knox's concern for the spiritual life of the individual Christian is <u>A Declaration of the True Nature and Object of Prayer</u>; indeed <u>A Declaration</u> is not only a practical 'how to pray' book in the fashion of other 'how to' books of the time, but it is a clear declaration of the God-person relationship. That prayer is a sign of faith and hence of election Knox makes clear at the very beginning of the treatise. 'God', Knox writes, 'steireth up our myndis, giving unto us a desyre or boldnes for to pray' (III, 85). God also gives his elect a true understanding of prayer, which, Knox insists, is necessary for prayer to have meaning. 'Suche as understand not what thai pray', Knox writes, 'profit nothing in prayer' (III, 85). Prayer is not simply rote repetition; behind the words our hearts must 'be inflamit with continewall feir, honour, and love of God' (III, 85).

At the same time that prayer 'springeth forth of trew Faith', it is also seen as an active and conscious petition to God on which salvation is conditional. Prayer requires, in other words, that one freely go to God; Knox writes how through prayer 'we run for support and help whensoever danger or necessitie requyreth' (III, 85). We must, as well, 'boldlie aske of him whatsoever is necessarie for us, as sustentatioun of this bodie; health thairof ... delyverance frome trubille ... [and] prosperous success in oure vocatiounis, labouris, and effairis, whatsoever thai be' (III, 99). Regardless of theology, Knox, while not asserting anything like justification by works, still allows a place for human endeavour, even if, from the perspective of God's inscrutable will, everything is predetermined.

The essence of prayer, for Knox, is that it affirm in the devotee's mind that the individual is nothing without God; prayer, in other words, allows the individual to bridge the gap between God and himself that is created by humankind's ego centeredness. Quoting from the prophets, Knox remarks how there is in their prayers 'no mentioun of thair awn justice, thair awn satisfaction, or thair awn merittis' (II, 87). Rather prayers of the prophets are each a 'humill confessioun, proceiding frome a sorowfull and penitent hart; haveing nothing whairupon it mycht depend, but the frie mercie of God allone' (III, 87). Similarly, our prayers must be measured by their sincerity; one must mean what one says. Knox writes how 'suche as haif callit, or calleth presentlie unto God by any uther name then Jesus Chryst allone, doith nothing regarde Godis will, but obstenatlie prevaricateth and doith aganis his commandementis' (III, 95).

One final work deserving consideration as a work of Christian devotion is Knox's <u>Exposition Upon Matthew IV</u>. Knox looks to answer four questions in this treatise concerning Christ's temptation, the intent being to draw parallels with the temptation experienced by God's elect. The questions are the obvious ones: what does temptation mean, who is tempted and when, why is one tempted, and what are the results of temptation? In answering these questions, Knox ties the entire sermon together with one central theme: everything is done to 'opin and mak manifest the secret motionis of menis hartis' and to reveal 'the puissance and power of Godis Word' (IV, 96). Put another way, Knox looks to assert the glory of God while affirming God's concern with the welfare of His elect. Although accepting the hidden purpose of divine initiative, Knox stresses that God does nothing without purpose. Thus one should not despair but find strength in how Christ Himself struggled through temptation and overcame adversity.

The devotional thrust of An Exposition Upon Matthew IV is one which celebrates the capacity of God's elect, sustained by the power of the Holy Spirit, to withstand the temptations of Satan. Noteworthy, though, is Knox's emphasis on Christ's humanity, which runs counter to the general Protestant tendency to stress Christ's divinity, given that to emphasise the acts of Christ seems to imply the efficacy of good works. This is not to say that Knox ignores the importance of Christ's divinity; indeed, the magnitude of Christ's sacrifice and its significance for humankind are foremost in Knox's mind when he writes, 'Chryst Jesus hath fouchtin oure battell, he him self hath takin us in his cair and protection .... To him be all glorie, for his mercies maist aboundantlie pourit forth upon us' (IV, 104). But he also sees in Christ's teachings and actions a model for human action; as he says, 'with what weapons we ought to fight against enemyis and assaltis, we sall learne in the answer of Chryst Jesus' (IV, 119). More than this, though, it is in Jesus overcoming Satan's assaults that is signalled the capacity of the elect to overcome Satan's temptations; Jesus as a human being supplies the hope of success to others who would follow in his path.

However one might stress the devotional aspect of Knox's writing, and allow that it in large measure mitigates the shrillness of his prophetic and polemical voices, one is still left to deal with the obvious extremes of Knox's First Blast of the Trumpet Against the Monstrous Regiment of Women as inconsistent with a perception of Knox that stresses his concern with Christian patience and understanding. Little needs to be said here about how Knox's First Blast has left him with a reputation for being an outspoken radical as well as an obvious woman-hater. While he certainly had political and religious argument on his side in rejecting the idea of a female ruler, Knox moved onto problematic, if not dangerous ground, when actively advocating the overthrow of the monarch. In an age that placed great stress on divinely determined order, it was unthinkable that the secular arm of that order should be overturned.

Knox's views on women are clear enough: 'Nature, I say, doth paynt them furthe to be weake, fraile, impacient, feble, and foolishe; and experience hath declared them to be unconstant, variable, cruell, and lacking the spirit of counsel and regiment' (IV, 274). Whatever Knox might say about exceptions to the general rule, this is clearly overshadowed by the harshness of The First Blast, which, with broad strokes, places woman in a subservient position to man and paints her as one who in no way possesses the capacity to rule. At the same time, however, it is also the case that much of this diatribe against women is largely a repetition of such standard authorities as Aristotle, Tertullian, Augustine, Chrysostome, and Ambrose. In no way, then, is Knox saying anything that had not been said before by others. As well, Knox's views on women must not be separated from the remainder of the tract, which is aimed at one particular woman, not so much because she is a woman, but because she is a persecutor of God's elect and denies divine order. Mary is condemned because she ignores 'that God hath subjected Womenkinde to man, by the ordre of his creation, and by the curse that he hath pronounced against her' (IV, 390). To suggest the overthrow of the monarch, then, is not to upset divine order but to put right the order that has been corrupted.

The work is not simply an effusive outburst, but proceeds systematically as Knox commits a large section of the work to anticipating and then rejecting the arguments of his opponents. This may not assuage those who reject Knox's basic presupposition that women are subject to men, but it does counter in some measure the common viewpoint that the work is little else than vituperative invective. Thus is Knox's concern about the persecution of his brethren couched in the more convincing terms of reasoned discourse, although one must still accept that the issue of a woman ruling men was one that drove Knox to particular heights of abusive polemic.

The First Blast should, of course, in no way be construed as a work of Christian instruction, and, even if it were, this would be insufficient to excuse fully either its matter or its manner. Yet even in this work that is so directly polemical there is a message that is at once instructive and comforting to the Christian believer. First, the centrality of divine law once more asserts the existence of the plan and intention of which God's elect are a part. Second, there is the call for divine justice, and, insofar as there is also a call to overthrow a cruel monarch, there is implied that God's elect must work as God's agents in the realisation of divine plan. Thus it is suggested that human actions do count, and are by no means inconsequential.

No one questions that the Reformation was a period of extremes, as is the case in anything which is fundamentally a reaction against the status quo. And in this regard Knox stands as a typical spokesman for reform; he is abusive, contemptuous, belligerent, and sublimely confident in the truth about which he speaks. This side of Knox, moreover, can never be explained away, nor indeed ought it to be; Knox was, after all, a man of his age. But the Reformation was more than simply a reaction, and Knox is more than a firebrand radical. The Reformation signalled a new way of seeing the relationship between God and humankind that demands of the preacher and Christian teacher a particular kind of sensitivity to meet the needs of the wayfaring Christian. With the emphasis now being on justification through faith, the immediate need of the Christian was to be assured that one is of the elect; at the same time, there remained the need to be personally involved in one's own salvation, even though the theology of election prevented this from being so. Despite the logical inconsistency that inevitably surfaces, Knox manages to do both. This balance between doctrinal correctness and devotional need runs parallel to how Knox balances criticism with consolation, fear with hope, and rhetoric with argument. Knox recognises, in other words, the multi-faceted nature of the human personality which must be given recognition if the Christian message is to flourish.

Knox's sense of his role as preacher allows him to keep his eye firmly on his goal: the calling and maintaining of God's true Church. Knox's prose works are not those of a writer with a great deal of time on his hands. But even though Knox was writing with a certain degree of urgency, this did not erode his capacity to spread the Christian message. In affirming the glory of God and God's immense mercy, Knox reveals a very human side of his religious personality that runs counter to the stereotype that is too much perpetuated today.

Notes

1   See Jenny Wormald, Court, Kirk and Community: Scotland, 1470–1625 (London, 1981), pp 109–21.
2   Knox is very much in line with Calvin here; see John Calvin, Institutes of the Christian Religion, trans. Ford Lewis Battles, ed John T McNeill (Philadelphia, 1960), II, 1053–64 (IV, 3, 1–12).
3   John Knox, 'A Briefe Sommarie of the Work of Balnaves on Justification', in The Works of John Knox, ed D Laing (Edinburgh, 1846–64), III, 25. References to Laing's edition are inserted parenthetically into the text except in those cases where titles are not identified in the text.
4   Ibid, pp 25–6.
5   Knox, 'A Faithful Admonition to the Professors of God's Truth in England', in Works, III, 268.
6   Ibid.
7   Knox, 'A Sermon on Isaiah XXVI. 13–21', in Works, IV, 229.
8   Ibid.
9   Knox, 'A Godly Letter of Warning or Admonition to the Faithfull in London, Newcastle and Berwick', in Works, III, 166.
10 Ibid, III, 184
11 Ibid.
12 Ibid, 231
13 Knox, 'A Faithful Admonition', III, 269.
14 Ibid.
15 Ibid, 270
16 Ibid, 319
17 Ibid, 322
18 Knox, 'An Exposition Upon Matthew IV Concerning the Temptation of Christ in the Wilderness', in Works, IV, 97.
19 Ibid, 96
20 Knox, 'A Godly Letter', III, 168.
21 Ibid.

Chapter 22

THE RHETORICAL APPLICATION OF SYNTAX IN KNOX'S FAMILIAR EPISTLES TO MRS BOWES

Kenneth D Farrow

Perhaps a sad reflection on the Scottish literary critic is that the prose of John Knox has not yet been seriously and comprehensively dealt with as literature per se.[1] For the most part, Knox has remained the property of historians, biographers and to a lesser extent, of theologians.[2] The reasons for such literary neglect are legion, but probably the most powerful is that Knox the writer has been almost totally obscured by Knox the man; not the man he truly was, but his popular, though inaccurate, conception in the of mind of Scotland, and indeed, in the mind of the world. In his native country, the name of Knox is still known to nearly all, and its invocation usually incurs expressions of distaste.

Those who celebrate the name are few but vehement. In the last century Thomas Carlyle and David Laing stood together as his most distinguished advocates in a literary context, and the early works of Dr Thomas McCrie and Professor P Hume Brown now constitute the first standard biographies. More recently, P Janton, David Murison and Ronald Jack[3] have demolished many of the myths and fallacies surrounding the Reformer's writings, offering penetrative, thought-provoking and important literary articles, which despite their comparative brevity, are infinitely more valuable than the glut of biographies this century has called forth. Hugh MacDiarmid's article 'Knox, Calvinism and the Arts'[4] on the other hand, stands alone as sometimes acute, sometimes unsubstantiated, more often inaccurate. However, it should be clear by now that Knox calls forth both odium and enthusiasm, both penetrative criticism and inexactitude.

This paper attempts to dispense with the ogrish and uninviting image of Knox which has stimulated such contradictory extremes: reactions for and reactions against, assessments, reassessments and Quatercentenary reappraisals, and the best way of doing this, of course, is to return to the evidence (not something which the Scots are very good at). The Works of John Knox as we now have them were first collected and annotated by David Laing in a monumental six volume set, which opens with the famous Historie of the Reformatioun and contains all of Knox's politico-religious texts, together with nearly all of his public and private letters.[5] Ironically, textbook histories of Scottish Literature have reduced Knox studies to such a state of turgidity that it may come as a surprise to general readers when they discover the Reformer wrote more than a witty account of Cardinal Beaton's murder and a notorious political faux pas: The First Blast of the Trumpet against the Monstrous Regiment of Women.[6]

With this in mind, I have chosen for my subject matter the body of material loosely classified by Laing as Knox's Familiar Epistles, which are for the most part written to the Reformer's mother-in-law, Mrs Elizabeth Bowes. This choice reduces the massive Knoxian canon to manageable proportions, and allows us to explore a largely neglected area of sixteenth-century Scottish prose. Again there are grounds for the assertion that the Reformer has been unfairly treated. After all, as the historian Gordon Donaldson points out 'with Knox we have, almost for the first time in Scotland, a quantity of intimate personal letters'.[7]

However, my purpose in probing these texts is not solely to rediscover them, but to establish certain truths about Knox's style. First of all, we must never lose sight of the fact that Knox was unquestionably a powerful preacher and rhetorician. James Melvill, as well as Knox himself, bears witness to that.[8] Such skills are especially evident throughout the Familiar Epistles, in which he performs the role of spiritual counsellor to insecure Mrs Bowes. What I want primarily to explore is how Knox's syntax, his sequencing of words, clauses and sentences, ultimately contributes to the overall persuasive efficacy of his rhetoric. Moreover, I hope to establish that differing syntatic patterns correspond to clearly marked stylistic and topical shifts within the prose.

There are twenty-eight letters in the series. Here are two passages from Letter VIII. The first reveals Knox in a very apocalyptic vein:

> O miserable, unthankfull, and maist mischevous warld! What salbe thy condempnatioun, when He, that has sa oft gentillie provokit ye to obey his treuth, sall cum in his glorie, to punish thy contempt? Wha sall hyd thee frome the presence of that lyoun whom thou did persecut in everie age? What sall excuse thee, that sa tiranfullie hath sched the bluid of sic as faithfullie labourit to bring thee frome blind ignorance and idolatrie, when that stubburne contemperneris sall cry 'Mountanis fall on us, and hyd us fra the presence of the lord!'[9]

Then almost immediately after this, Knox changes his direction altogether. Prose which entails a degree of autobiographical narrative subsequently comes to the fore.

> Urgent necessitie will not suffer that I satisfie my mynd ynto you. My Lord of Westmureland hes written unto me this Wednesday, at sex of the clok at nyght, immediatlie thair-efter to repair unto him, as I will answeir at my perrell. I culd not obteane license to remane the tyme of the sermone upon the morrow. Blissit be God wha dois ratifie and confirme the treuth of his word fra tyme to tyme, as our weakness sall require![10]

Even the most perfunctory of glances is enough for one to conclude that these passages are quite radically different. For instance,

the first is made up of two exclamatory phrases and three rhetorical questions. The second is much more straightforward, and
builds steadily towards a final sentence which combines the
functions of exclamation and a liturgical formula ascribing glory
to God. Indeed, this sentence heralds yet another change of
direction.

Generally speaking, Knox favours complex sentences in both
passages. Only the third sentence in passage two, which begins 'I
culd not obteane license to remane...' is simple. Paradoxically,
however, passage two contains Knox's one use of a binomial verbal
couplet: 'ratifie and confirme'. At the level of lexis, these
items seem to be borrowed not from a religious or devotional
vocabulary, but a legal one. Indeed, it is worth remembering that
during the early part of his life, while still a Catholic priest,
Knox was employed as a notary. By using such items he brings to
his text a powerful aura of certainty, which may reassure his
addressee on a subconscious and subliminal level. If so, he
achieves not only sureness of tone, but subtlety.

The closest Knox comes to using a verbal couplet in the first
passage is with the phrase 'fall on us and hyd us', but he is
quoting directly from the Book of Revelation 6:16, and in any
case, the verbs here are easier to differentiate between. There is
a clear difference in deep structure between 'fall' and 'hyd'.
Knox's aim however is still to create an authoritative voice, and
he compensates by invoking scripture, which, to radical Protestants, is infallible.

Syntactical patterning is more in evidence in the opening
passage than in the second and it also performs a more sophisticated rhetorical function. For instance, Knox relies heavily on
adjectival phrases to modify pronouns and nouns, which refer
sometimes to Christ, sometimes to the reader. The phrases 'that
hes sa oft gentilie provokit ye ...' and 'whom thou did persecut
in everie age' modify 'He' and 'lyoun' while 'that sa tiranfullie
hath sched the bluid' refers to 'thee'. By these means, the individual reader's relationship with Christ is foregrounded, and Knox
ensures that we are aware of the gravity he is seeking to communicate.

Passage two contains only one adjectival, in the fourth sentence, but it performs no definite rhetorical function other than
to ensure effective flowing prose. Knox is more concerned with
conveying information to the reader as quickly and efficiently as
possible. The syntax mirrors this. He uses only one adjective
('urgent') compared to seven ('miserable','unthankfull', 'maist',
'mischevous', 'everie', 'blind' and 'stubborne') in the first
passage, and one adverb ('immediatlie') compared to three ('gen-
tillie', 'tiranfullie' and 'faithfullie') in the second. The
vividness and splendour of passage one thus gives way to the
economy of passage two. Both, however, rely heavily on temporal
phrases such as 'salbe', 'when', 'sall cum', 'sall excuse', 'sall
cry', 'at sex of the clok at nyght', 'the tyme of the sermone',
'on the morrow' and 'fra tyme to tyme' but passage one is set for
the most part in future-time and passage two for the most part in
present-time. Hence, Knox conveys imminence in the first and
immediacy in the second. The reader must surely be stimulated.

The Reformer, after all, makes complacency almost impossible.

A similar, yet more subtle relationship between syntax and content is evident in passages such as this one, from Letter II. Knox warns Mrs Bowes about the dangers of spiritual complacency:

> But, O, Mother! thocht na erthlie creature suld be offendit with yow, yit feir ye the presence and offence of Him, who, present in all places, searcheth the verie hart and reynis; whais indignation, anis kendillit aganis the inobedient (and no syn mair inflameth his wraith than idolatrie doith) na creatur in heavin nor in earth, that onlie is creatur, is abill to appais the same.[11]

Knox opens with an adverbial of concession and adverb of contrast ('thocht na erthlie creature suld be offendit...' and 'yit feir ye the presence of Him...') with which he suggests that although Mrs bowes offends no mortal, her sins do offend God, since He is everywhere present. This theological notion is crucial to Knox's shaping of the passage. By using non-restrictive apposition ('who, present in all places, searcheth ...'), possessives ('whais indignatioun'), participles ('anis kendillit aganis the inobedient') and a qualificatory parenthesis ('and na syn mair inflameth his wrath') Knox invokes the name and presence of the Deity in nearly all of the clauses and vividly realises God's eternal presence in the life of the individual believer. Surely what we have here is a highly sophisticated, perhaps even intuitive rhetoric which relies heavily on syntax to augment its fundamental assertions.

Letter II tells us more about Knox's personal relationship with Mrs Bowes than Letter VIII, however, and in this respect, II is more typical of the Familiar Epistles in general. Among the most compelling texts is Letter IV. Knox has been reading Matthew's Gospel when a messenger delivers to him a letter from Mrs Bowes. This text (now lost) presumably poses spiritual dilemmas, to which the very passage he has been meditating upon offers the solutions. Knox is so impressed by the incident that he evidently considers it a minor miracle and is inspired to turn to his copy of Chrysostom for further clarification. He subsequently tells Mrs Bowes:

> In reiding of this his halie judgement, your battell and dolour was befoir my eis; and as I prayit God that ye myght be assistit to the end, sa wissit I that ye had bene present with me; and evin at the same instant callit your seruand, whairof I praisit my God, and addressit me to wryt efter the reiding of your letter as I myght.[12]

Again, this passage is rather different from the two we have already discussed, but Knox is still wringing rhetorical effect from his choice and structuring of language.

For example, one of the first things we notice about these lines is that they exhibit a differing relationship between the first person pronoun and attendant verbs. Admittedly Knox uses the standard constructions 'I prayit', 'I praisit' and 'I myght', but the order is inverted in the phrase 'sa wissit I'. Even in sixteenth century prose this type of expression has a solemnity and dignity not present in the more orthodox construction. Knox, then, rises to moments of eloquence but by intermingling styles he manages to convey the impression that he is a dignified man who is nonetheless still in touch with day to day matters and with apparently ordinary individuals like Mrs Bowes.

Moreover, Knox twice uses the same verb, first as part of a non-finite prepositional phrase ('in reiding') and then as a gerund ('the reiding'). This may not appear very significant until one reflects that the repetition perhaps illustrates Knox's desire to emphasise the <u>means</u> by which the minor miracle occured. The item 'reiding', which is first used as part of a locative phrase, and then substantivally, apparently makes God's miraculous power <u>seem</u> more tangible. The coded message which Knox conveys to Mrs Bowes is simply that, if she is diligent in Bible study, she too will reach that plane of spiritual knowledge which posits the hand of God in all things, no matter how trivial, and subsequently find consolation. I am not for a moment suggesting that Knox was fully conscious of what he was about, here, only that his Calvinistic world-view is deeply rooted in the sub-structure of his language and syntax. That the text subsequently has greater rhetorical power and persuasive effect is merely a corollary. Indeed, if one is cynical about the depth of penetration in Knox's language which his Calvinism entails, a careful study of these epistles will completely dispel any doubt.

Even so, one must not make the mistake of thinking that Calvinism rigorously and dogmatically excludes artistry from polemical prose. This is a popular misconception, but one which has no basis whatever in fact. Knox himself provides ample proof of this. For example, in Letter XX, he consoles a distraught Mrs Bowes:

> Abyd, Mother, the tyme of harvest, befoir whilk must neidis goe the cald of winter, the temperat and unstabill spring and the fervent heit of summer: to be plane, ye must neidis saw with teiris or ye reap with gladiness; sin must in yow ga befoir justice, deith befoir lyfe, weaknes befoir strenth, unstabillnes befoir stabilitie and bitterness befoir comfort.[13]

This passage is among Knox's most richly poetic and highly wrought. The artistry however is geared solely towards the end of persuasion and the invocation of conviction in Mrs Bowes. Knox employs a whole range of syntactical devices with which to achieve this end. The clauses, for instance, are mixed in length. They are sometimes terse, sometimes long and rather pendulous. This allows Knox to vary his approach. He can be both direct and discursive.

He begins by placing a disjunctive noun immediately after his opening verb, in the phrase 'Abyd, mother'. Knox thus introduces a direct personal appeal into the middle of an otherwise hortatory passage. This has the effect of increasing the fundamental seriousness of his tone and also augments the mood of intimacy surrounding the letter. A warmer response is ensured. The auxiliary modal verbs in the phrase 'must neidis goe ...' which occurs in the second clause, are again, apparently designed to augment Knox's authority. Both are definitive, and imply necessity. Moreover, they seem to be drawn from the Biblical milieu which surrounds Knox's prose. This allows him to create a mood of Scriptural fatalism and devout resignation. After these verbs, Knox leads his reader into a splendid series of images, and the means by which he achieves the images is crucially important to the success of the passage. He relies heavily on antithesis and on the use of antonyms. First the oppositions are of nouns: 'cald/heit', 'winter/summer', 'teiris/glaidnes' 'sin/justice', 'deith/lyfe', 'weaknes/strenth', 'unstabilness/stabilitie', and finally, 'bitterness/comfort', and then of adjectives and verbs ('temperat/fervent', 'saw/reip'). Knox revolves nearly all of his antonyms around the same preposition ('befoir'), creating an almost incantatory as well as inculcatory rhythm. The infinitive phrase 'to be plane' in the third clause enhances the rhetorical effect of the passage, but in a wholly deceptive way since it merely ushers in another related stratum of the same rich imagery. Knox sounds more frank even if the effect is illusory.

Although Knox's Protestantism impinges deeply into his prose, it is obviously none the worse for that, as our earlier extracts show. We have seen that Calvinism and 'poetry' are not mutually exclusive, at least in Knox's case. Nor does his Calvinism undermine Knox's dialectic art. Take the following passage from Letter XIV. He has apparently received a letter from Mrs Bowes, in which she reveals fears that he has been deceiving her. Knox posits Satanic subterfuge, of course, and subsequently writes:

> That fals and leying spreit dois according to his wickit and dissavabill craft, when he wald caus yow belief that I know your rejectioun. Na, fals Devill! he leis: I am evin equallie certified of your electioun in Christ, as that I myself preacheth Chryst to be the onlie Saviour.[14]

In the previous passages, I have shown that Knox is preoccupied with bringing certainty and authority to his text. What makes this letter particularly interesting is that it reveals Knox in a position where his own authority has been undermined. Although he is angry and very much on the defensive, he neither falls short of rhetorical effects nor skilful syntactical manoeuvres. The analogy which Knox builds up to is not unelaborate, and is couched by exclamatory fervour. Moreover, he attempts to restore his damaged credibility by juxtaposing personal and emphasising pronouns in the phrase 'I myself'. He invokes his own powerful personality not once but twice. Just as Knox sets pronouns together, he uses intensifying adverbs in 'even equally certified' to realise his own beliefs as vividly as possible. However, the real quality of Knox's dialectic art is more in evidence when he appears fully at ease with his role as spiritual counsellor. In the following lines, he assures Mrs Bowes that her union with Christ is inviolable.

> To embrace Chryst, to refus idolatrie, to confes the truth, to love the memberis of Chrystis bodie, ar the giftis of God, thairfour he can not repent that he hath maid yow pertaker thairof.[15]

This passage seems very plain, but in fact, Knox is using a two-step categorical syllogism which combines partial asyndeton, hypotaxis and rhythmic synonymous and syntactical parallelism. He couches these within a framework of definito and conclusio favoured by the medieval rhetoricians. Stylistically the most significant feature of the passage is Knox's repeated use of infinitives: 'to embrace', 'to refus', 'to confes' and 'to love'. These allow him to use action verbs without the creation of clauses and to stress his own urgency and insistence. He also enables his first main verb ('ar') to carry a whole range of meanings across to his reader. Knox may have had what R D S Jack calls 'a limited academic and theological training',[16] but obviously it has not been wasted on him.

We have already established at least something of the richness present in these letters and seen what Knox's rhetoric reveals about him. I would like now to turn to Letter I in order to examine a passage which is among the most compelling in the series. Knox outlines to Mrs Bowes an unenviable situation in which his conscience is pricked by his own preaching. It surely makes for engaging reading.

> I am compellit to thounder out the threattnyngis of God
> aganis obstinat rebellaris; in doing whairof (albeit as God
> knaweth I am no malicious nor obstinat synner) I sumtymes am
> woundit, knawing my self criminall and giltie in many, yea,
> in all, (malicious obstinacie laid asyd,) thingis that in
> utheris I reprehend.[17]

This passage illustrates Knox in his most confessional mode. It must also be significant that his syntax here is the most contorted and complex that he ever allows. We have one complex multi-clause sentence. Three of the clauses occur in parenthesis. These parenthetical phrases are deliberately positioned. They post-modify each section in which Knox reveals his sins to Mrs Bowes, and they are all exculpatory in nature. The first is an adverbial of concession ('albeit as God knoweth...'), the remaining two ('I am no malicious nor obstinat synner' and 'malicious obstinacie laid asyd') are clauses of double exclusion and exclusion respectively. Knox, then, goes to some lengths to mitigate the seriousness of the sins which he has just been confessing and he also reveals a deep concern to be properly understood. Thus he can use his own experiences and weaknesses ultimately to fashion a hortatory model for Mrs Bowes, without losing sight of his own belief that he is no ordinary sinner, and indeed, no ordinary man.

Again, it must be significant that Knox's most confessional sections tend to form participal '-ING' phrases ('in doing whairof' and 'knawing my self criminall and giltie'). The active present tenses suggest immediacy and make us aware of Knox's offences 'here and now' but we tend also to read them rather quickly. Content with such admissions and with the catharsis they have afforded him, Knox can hurriedly move on to reassert his divinely inspired status as a minister of the Reformed faith, and the reader moves with him. Not even the intimacy he enjoys with his mother-in-law outweighs the responsibility which accompanies that particular role.

In spite of all that it tells us about Knox's psychology, the passage comes across as rather awkward. This is by no means typical of Knox, however, and it would be wrong to censure him overmuch. The reason why he is forever qualifying things in this inimitable, even paranoid manner, is a complex one. Like many of the founding Fathers of Protestantism such as Luther and Calvin, Knox began his career in what he himself calls 'the puddle of papistrie'.[18] Orthodox sacramental confession was thus a regular part of his early life, and presumably fulfilled the function of spiritual panacea. When his incipient Protestantism deprived him of it, Knox perhaps found himself still with the need to confess but also with a newly found belief in individual faith (and later, of course, in arbitrary grace) as a redemptive power. My contention is that an uneasy balance between two mutually exclusive theological doctrines is captured and enshrined in Knox's language, here, specifically in the syntax. Real, perhaps even bitter experience, and the remnants of a struggle within can surely be traced to the words on the page. This makes Knox's rhetoric very convincing and indeed almost moving. For Mrs Bowes, travelling a path with a guide who knows the way is, after all, much easier than stumbling in the dark by herself.

Again at the level of lexis, Knox is also communicating very subtly with his reader. 'Compellit' for instance, suggests that he sees himself as acted upon rather than acting. He is probably suggesting that the source of his compulsion is divine, in which case he is asserting his special status as an agent of the Deity. This is an excellent example of what R D S Jack means when he suggests that God performs the role of 'energetic second in the Reformer's corner'.[19]

Moreover, Knox uses 'obstinat' in one form or another three times within this passage. First he condemns 'obstinat rebellaris' and then points out that he is neither guilty of 'obstinacie' nor being an 'obstinat synner'. Just as Shakespeare's Edmund in King Lear has a fixation about 'baseness' and 'bastardy', Knox has a fixation about obstinacy. Presumably he regards it as the most noxious of sins, and he is anxious to point out that, wicked as he is, stubbornness has not been one of his faults. Given Knox's undoubted intransigence, this is probably one of the greatest unconscious ironies he ever achieved. My basic point, however, remains. Knox's language is rich with coded messages which we can interpret by detailed analysis of its finer points.

We find precisely the same features of language, lexis and syntax in other confessional passages such as this one, from Letter III. Knox reminds Mrs Bowes 'all too cryptically'[20] of what he did:

> ... standing at the copburd at Anwick; in verie deid I thoght that na creature had been temptit as I wes. And when that I heard proceid fra your mouth the verie same wordis that he trubillis me with, I did wonder, and fra my hart lament your sair trubill, knawing my selfe the dolour thairof.[21]

Here the participles ('standing at the copburd' and 'knawing my selfe the dolour') are not immediately post-modified by parenthesis, but they still form an integral part of the confession. The first outlines time and place, while the second consummates the emotional link between the shared experiences of Knox and Mrs Bowes. The repeated line in this passage is 'trubill' and its use perhaps illustrates Knox's notions about the necessary recurrence of vexation in the life of a Calvinist. After all, without trouble there will be no triumph. To Knox, this is a fundamental Christian tenet.

Until recently it has been commonplace of Knox studies to assert that the Reformer's life was somehow puzzling, mysterious or paradoxical. Indeed, the critic James S McEwen writes that 'no one who studies Knox can fail to be struck by the mystery of the man himself, and the more one studies, the deeper grows the mystery'.[22] Campbell McLean follows suit when he suggests that 'there are no paradoxes like Knoxian paradoxes'.[23] These judgements, I think, are wholly wrong, and I hope I have shown why. We can gleam an immense amount about the man from the words he wrote. The literary critic, and indeed the linguist, should have realised this a long time ago.

Notes

1   The closest any critic has come to a full literary appreciation of Knox may be found in Pierre Janton's John Knox, l'Homme et l'Oeuvre (Paris, 1967), p 407–508.

2   One of the best and most modern studies of Knox in this respect is Theology and Revolution in the Scottish Reformation: Studies in the Thought of John Knox, Richard Greaves. (Grand Rapids, Michigan, 1979).

3   See David D Murison, 'Knox the Writer', in John Knox: A Quatercentenary Re-appraisal Duncan Shaw (ed) (Edinburgh, 1975); R D S Jack, 'The Prose of John Knox: a Reassessment', in Prose Studies IV (1981) pp 239–51; P Janton, 'John Knox and Literature' in Actes du 2e Colloque de Langue Et de Littérature Ecossaises (Moyen Age et Renaissance) Universite De Strasbourg 1978, pp 422–9.

4   See Hugh McDiarmid's 'Knox, Calvinism and the Arts' in MacDiarmid, McLean, Ross John Knox (Edinburgh, 1976).

5   In his massive sixth volume of Knox's Works Laing himself admits that 'it is by no means improbable that a few more letters of the Scottish Reformer are in existence and may still be recovered' (Laing VI: 8).

6   Roderick Watson's modern study The Literature of Scotland (MacMillan, 1984) may be taken as typical. Previous literary historians such as Maurice Lindsay are even worse. Only J H Millar's Literary History of Scotland (London, 1903) presents a satisfactory summary of Knox's works.

7   G Donaldson, 'Knox the Man', p 18, in A Quatercentenary Re-appraisal.

8   When a young student at St Andrews, Melvill witnessed Knox's preaching and suggested 'he wes sa actiue and vigorous that

he was lyke to ding that pulpit in blads and flie   out   of   it'
The Autobiography and Diary of Mr James Melvill, R Pitcairn,
(ed) Edinburgh, for the Wodrow Society 1842) p 27.   Indeed,
Knox   made   Melvill   so apprehensive that 'he culd nocht hald a
pen to wryt'.

9   Laing's Knox III: 357.   See also Job 10:16, Ps.   7:2, Hos.
    13:7, Rev. 4:7, 6:16, 10:3, 13:2.
10 Laing's Knox III: 357.
11 Laing's Knox III: 346. 2 Cor 6:3, Ps. 7:9, Heb. 4:13.
12 Laing's Knox III: 351.
13 Laing's Knox III: 385. Josh 3:15, Jdgs. 15:1, 2, Sam 23:13,
    Ps 126:5, Pr. 25:13, Jer. 50:16, 51:33, Mt. 13:30.
14 Laing's Knox III: 369. 1 Kgs. 22:22-23, 2 Chr. 18:21-22.
15 Laing's Knox III: 350. Rom. 11:29, 1 Cor 6:15, 9:10, 12:27.
16 R D S Jack, 'The Prose of John Knox: A Re-assessment' p 239.
17 Laing's Knox III: 338.
18 Laing's Knox IV : 439.
19 R D S Jack, Scottish Prose 1550-1770 (London, 1971) p 20.
20 G Donaldson, John Knox: A Quatercentenary Re-apparaisal, p 18.
21 Laing's Knox III: 350.
22 James S McEwen, The Faith of John Knox: The Croall Lectures
    (London, 1961), p 101.
23 Campbell McLean, in John Knox (MacDiarmid, McLean, Ross) p 11.

Chapter 23

A MIRROR FOR A DIVINE PRINCE:
JOHN IRELAND AND THE FOUR DAUGHTERS OF GOD

Sally Mapstone

John Ireland's Meroure of Wyssdome was begun in the last decade of
the reign of James III and completed in 1490, shortly after the
installation of the new king, James IV.[1] It is thus a text
produced at a time when what constituted good kingship was a live
issue. Though the magnate rebellion in which James III, to use the
parliamentary phrasing of the time, 'happinnit to be slane',[2] may
have been a self-interested and unrepresentative revolt,[3] the
factionalism in the nobility both before and after his death must
have bred a certain nervousness as to how his son, still officially a minor, but who had himself had a role in the rebellion, would
be able to restore a sense of order. For those composing advisory
literature the circumstance of a reign opening in discord and
minority rule was not, of course, unusual in Scotland, but for
John Ireland there was a particular delicacy in his own circumstances. As one who had been a diplomat for James III, had sat in
parliaments and with the Lords in Council in the early 1480s, and
who had been by his own account confessor to the king, he might
have been identified with the cause of the dead ruler. Whether
this was so or not, Ireland sought in the prefatory material to
the Meroure to emphasise the positive continuity of interest
between James III and Jamses IV. Thus, though he reminds the new
king of the services he performed for his father, he also argues
that what is valuable for one king may be so for another.[4] Tactful
and diplomatic such an approach may have been in the circumstances; but it also well shows up that particular paradox of
medieval kingship, that the personality of a ruler could be
crucial to the prosperity of the realm, but equally crucial was
what he signified as king, epitome of justice and stability. This
was a problem resolved, in theory and in practice, in rather
different forms across Europe, in France, Scotland, and England.
Ireland's Meroure reflects both his acquaintance with contemporary
theorising on the subject and, through his choice of language and
exposition of sources, his awareness of its relevance to the
monarchy of late fifteenth-century Scotland.
    It is possible, then, that Ireland may have written the Meroure
in an attempt to consolidate his position with James IV; and on
the face of it he duly wrote a thoroughly conservative and
academic work.[5] His argument on good kingly government in Book VII
follows six books of essentially, though not exclusively, theological instruction, and its advice is couched in traditional organic

imagery of the body politic and the four cardinal virtues. There
is hardly any specific reference to contemporary events. Yet an
investigation of the sources of Book VII gives certain indications
that this comfortable picture of Ireland's _Meroure_ is not an
entirely accurate one.[6]

The _Meroure_ is the fifteenth-century culmination of a branch of
Scottish advisory writing which is ideologically indebted to
continental, often French, political theorists. Early Scottish
examples, which Ireland may have known, are to be found in the
writings of Sir Gilbert Hay and the poem De Regimine principum.
But with Ireland it is more than a debt to ideas. Large parts of
Book VII are translated from a number of sermons by Jean Gerson
preached in the late fourteenth and early fifteenth century.[7] The
important thing, here, however, is that while Ireland borrowed, he
also cut, rearranged, and added to his material.[8] Some of his
additions reflect an interest in the concept of equity, which is a
subject to which we shall return later; but his cuts show a deliberate intention to exclude Gerson's controversial justification of
tyrannicide. This was an argument that would not, yet, be admitted
into Scottish political thought.

This might seem to confirm the conservative nature of Ireland's
position, but there is other material to be considered. We know
that Ireland also borrowed from a version of the _Melibee_ story for
his chapter on good counsel.[9] More interesting still is that he
chose to include a long chapter in Book VII on the merits of
hereditary or elective kingship. A discussion of this subject at
this length is unparalleled in Middle Scots literature. His source
here was the _Defensor pacis_ of Marsilius of Padua (1324).[10] It was
a source that Ireland employed to refute: his final position is a
strongly pro-hereditary one. Yet at the same time the case for
elective kingship is given a very good airing; and the mere fact
that the matter was raised might suggest that Ireland's position
was more equivocal than might at first sight appear. He was, after
all, a firm conciliarist on the question of restraints on papal
authority.[11] While this was hardly a position to be developed on
kingship by one seeking the approval of the monarchy, there are
places in the _Meroure_ where Ireland argues a careful case for the
balancing of power between king and counsellors. Such balancing
acts were staple fare of contemporary political theory; but as
Marsilius of Padua, Gerson, and Fortescue differed in focus and
resolution according to their perception of specific national
circumstances, so too did Ireland.

I shall attempt here to gain a fuller sense of Ireland's position on kingship by looking at the imaginative processes involved
in his treatment of his sources. But, despite my preamble, I shall
not be looking at Book VII of the _Meroure_, which, like Book VI, is
still unpublished. I want to look instead at a part of the _Meroure_
which has long been in print, but has not received the critical
attention it deserves. The section in question is the debate of
the Four Daughters of God in Book II. We see here Ireland blending
together material from a mixture of sources, in this instance both
English and continental, and shaping and adding to them to construct an extended piece of advice to a divine prince. An exposition of his techniques may shed some light on the process of

composition in Book VII, as well as showing how ideas which are given full doctrinal expression there take dramatic shape earlier in the Meroure. Indeed, kingship is a dominant theme of the six earlier books. The ideas that recur there, all primarily within a theological context – the nature of kingly justice, the role of mercy, the place of reparation and remission – also make the debate a perfect vehicle for ideas that manifestly have a temporal as well as a spiritual bearing.

The debate of the Four Daughters of God, which takes its origin from Ps. 84: 11, Misericordia et veritas obviaverunt sibi, iustitia et pax osculatae sunt, had a well established tradition of narrative representation in various versions, from its early appearances in parables of Hugh of St Victor and St Bernard.[12] Influential renditions included the pseudo-Bonaventuran Meditationes vitae Christi, the sermon Rex et famulus and Grosseteste's Château d'Amour. It features frequently in Middle English writings, notably Piers Plowman, The Castle of Perseverance and The Court of Sapience. Ireland's use of the allegory has more in common, formally, with versions of the debate primarily concerned with the theological issues than with the other important branch that takes the form of a 'feudal narrative', a dispute between a king and his daughters, son, and servant. But, as we shall see, Ireland was certainly acquainted with at least one work of this type.

Ireland's lengthy presentation, almost dramatisation, of the debate takes up two chapters of the second book. It constitutes a significant part of the account of man's original sin and the necessity for his redemption by Christ. It is evident that the debate engaged Ireland's imagination. Its two chapters are longer than the others, and its dramatic nature stands out all the more when set against the characteristically didactic style of much of the rest of the Meroure. This change in stylistic level may in part reflect the dramatic nature of a number of Ireland's sources; it may also, however, represent a conscious desire to attract and interest his audience in the particular focus given to the debate.

The opening of the first chapter sums up how man's first ancestor had caused 'discord and discencioune' between God and mankind by 'the gret syn and offens of hurt maieste', so that for five thousand years no means of reconciliation may be found until the time of grace when the Father sends his Son (pp 106–7). The legalistic context established by the term hurt maieste, the crime of high treason and an established part of the legal canon,[13] is now continued and heightened in Ireland's invitation to his readers to see the question of the Incarnation as discussed in heaven, where 'ware present, foure nobile, excellent wertuis, secretaris and wis counsalouris, Merci, verite, justice, and pece', who after man's fall from grace had been exiled from earth and 'maid of the sacret counsale of the hie and nobile king of paradice and the haly trinite' (pp 107–8).

The court or council setting had often been an element in the tradition,[14] but Ireland is distinctive in establishing the virtues not simply as advocates for their respective arguments, but as members of the king's secret or privy council, a body developing in influence in Scotland during the fifteenth century.[15]

In 1489, for example, the lords of the secret council were appointed to aid the administering of justice and to give the king their counsel 'in all materis concernyng his maieste and his realme'.[16] Yet on another level the four virtues are all aspects of the divine king himself. As in the 'inner council' section of Hay's Buik of King Alexander or the final allegory of The Talis of the Fyve Bestes, allegorical figures signify, paradoxically, both the essential value of counsellors to the monarchy, and the containment of all good governing virtue within that monarchy itself.[17]

The principal debate in the first chapter is conducted between Mercy on the one side and Truth and Justice on the other. Their arguments are framed in such a way that the ethical issues of divine kingship are very much to the fore. For instance, Mercy in her opening remarks asks for clemency for mankind who has laboured under the tyranny of the devil for more than five thousand years, a characteristic argument in the tradition; in this version, however, she goes on to claim that to have pity on mankind would be 'gret honoure to thi maieste' (p.109). The appeal for mercy along with the claim that this will bring honour to the king might remind us of the speech of Henryson's mouse to the lion king, or how kings are instructed by Gilbert Hay to be 'ay mercifull and pitous apon thame that thou has subiectioun apon' for 'a rype discrecioun with gude diliberacioun is a grete glore to the dignitee ryale'.[18]

In arguing against Mercy, Truth raises another ethical question: 'King of angellis and souuerane lord of all wertu, necessare is to al Kinge and lord to kep thi behest and promys'; and she maintains that he should therefore hold to his ordinance that if Adam and his lineage broke his commandment they would incur 'baithe bodely deid and spirituall' (p 109). The law of God must stand, otherwise there would be no perfection in the deity. The idea that a king's word is his bond is a common injunction in advice-to-princes literature, and while the tenor of Truth's arguments here is similar to other versions, Ireland's account has placed especial emphasis upon the demands of good kingship.[19]

It is at this point that we must begin to consider the question of Ireland's sources for the debate. It has not previously been observed that by far the closest rendition to that given in the Meroure is in The Court of Sapience, a poem composed in the mid to late fifteenth century, with a terminus ad quem, of 1480-3 (that is, only a few years before the completion of the Meroure), when it was printed by William Caxton.[20] There are areas of difference between the Meroure and the Court beyond those of prose and verse. The context in which the debate appears in the Court is that of the feudal narrative; and the larger framework is a dream-vision concerned with the exposition of sapience.[21] But this interest in 'wisdom' also links the Court to the Meroure of Wyssdome. Its latest editor writes of the Court's version of the debate of the Four Daughters that 'In the Court the conflict in heaven is realized more vividly, both as a family quarrel and as a legal dilemma, than in the sources'.[22] It is in relation to the second aspect that there are notable correspondences with the Meroure.

Mercy's first speech in the Court bears no strong relation to

the Meroure, but in argument and phrasing the counter-case by
Truth offers the first of many indications that Ireland either
knew the Court or (far less likely) an as yet unidentified source
for it. There are several verbal parallels, particularly 'thyne
eterne deyte/Were vycyate with imperfectyon' (Court, 11.241-2) and
'litile perfeccioune ware in thi diete' (p 109), though were this
to be all the evidence for borrowing the case would hardly be
proven.[23] Comparison also shows how Ireland phrases Truth's
arguments more powerfully in terms of the requirements of kingship, 'necessare is to al Kinge and lord to kep thi behest and
promys' (p 109). In the Court, Truth is concurrently defining her
own position as the king's daughter, and therefore the focus is
different.

Mercy's response begins in the Meroure 'My scistir ... ȝe knaw
that I am sempiterne, and without me may be na duracioune of
ressonabile creature, na reparacioune of humane linage (p 109),
surely modelled on very similar phrasing in the Court:

> Than sayd Mercy, 'Unworthy is that assent,
> For every reasonable creature
> Withoute mercy may not lyve ne endure.
>
> Know ye not wele that I am sempyterne,'
> Quod Mercy tho ...
>   (Court, 11.250-4)

But Ireland is not blindly following one source. A dialogue
between Mercy and Truth in the Court is shaped into a single
speech by Mercy, the fundamental point of which is that her
existence itself would be futile if she were unable to make
restoration for man.

Truth replies 'My scistir ... I am my faderis child als wele as
ȝe' (p 110); exactly the same words as are used in the Court
(1.291).[24] But whereas in the Court her argument is that to
suggest that God is variable would be to deny his foreknowledge,
Truth in the Meroure gives priority to the point that there should
be no imperfection in him, laying stress once more upon the exemplary nature of divine kingship.

Now Justice, or 'dame equitee', is introduced to support Truth
and to 'put all strif to ressoune and gud conclusione' (p 110),
phrasing which recalls the claim of Ryghtwysenes in the Court:

> 'My sustres stryve,' quod she, 'with voyce on hyght;
> I wyl dyscusse, and theyr contencyon,
> As ryght asketh, brynge to conclusyon.
>   (Court, 11.299-301)

It is consistent with Ireland's approach that he paraphrases her
arguments concerning the sin of Adam and the virtues of the
godhead, so that she opens with a categoric statement on the
nature of the divine king's justice:

> 'O fader of treuth and werray richtwisnes, thi ressoune is
> law, thi will is equite; sene thou art god and hiest in

maieste, conserue thi law, and keip thi promys, and brek
nocht verite ... '   (p 110)

There is no comparable passage in the Court.[25] Ireland is very
skilfully evoking both the spirit of advice to princes writing and
one of its most important principles, but at the same time he is
allowing a sense of the incompleteness of this particular argument
to emerge. Justice stresses that it is the king of heaven's responsibility to uphold both the law (his promise) and the higher
principle of equity (his present judgement of the matter). But
what is omitted is the necessary concomitant value of mercy,
arising from love and charity. This is well brought out by another
comparison with Hay's Buke of the Governaunce of Princis. A king,
he claims, should do to his subjects 'as dois God him self, in all
charitee, lautee, justice and equitee. ... For all the governaunce
and ordinaunce of the warld is governyt, manetenyt and uphaldyn be
justice in perfyte ordre of equitee, lufe, and charitee'.[26] The
last two qualities – the conditions from which springs merciful
judgement – are lacking in the appeal of Justice in the Meroure.
     Justice's arguments are further supported by Truth. In the
Court, by contrast, the intervention of Peace occurs at this
stage. Truth reiterates her case, but concludes with what turns
out to be a major debating error, acknowledging as the voice of
Truth that if the Father sends his Son to earth to redeem man he
will be cruelly put to death. She ends by asserting that the
Father must keep to his original promise, for 'Super omnia vincit
veritas' (p 112). Within the traditional confines of the debate
Ireland has highlighted the premises that the heavenly king should
hold to his word and act with equity. It is clear that any counter-
argument will have to deal with these basic tenets of advice to
princes.
     This is acknowledged in Mercy's response, a speech that owes
nothing to the Court, and is one of Ireland's most carefully
constructed pieces of oratory. She makes an eloquent redefinition
of equity, by arguing against excessive rigour in the execution of
Justice, in a manner that recalls Henryson's mouse's claim that
'Quhen rigour sittis in the tribunall/The equitie of law quha may
sustene?/Richt few or nane, but mercie gang betwene'.[27] She
refutes Truth's argument by stating that it was a promise of the
Father and an article of truth that his son would come to redeem
mankind. In countering the case made by Justice, she immediately
takes up the theoretical issue:

     ... my scister knawis that justice suld stand in werray
     richt and ressoune, and in werray equite and nocht in
     wourdis. And oft tymes necessite is, for werray richt to
     lefe the wourdis of the law, and follow the richt and gud
     entencioune of the lord and makare of the law ...
                                        (pp 113–14)

Ireland, in a manner most uncommon in the history of the debate,
is giving exposition to a principle that will receive considerable
attention in Book VII.[28] He chooses here to have Mercy illustrate
her case by an exemplum, attributing it to Aristotle, though he is

not in fact its source. Ireland reveals the eclecticism of his
imaginative working by adapting and greatly extending a well-known
classical rhetorical case, found in Cicero's De oratore, and later
in the rhetorical manuals of Quintilian and others.[29]

A city had a law that no strangers should ascend its walls by
night on pain of death. Some strangers come to the city and have
to spend the night outside the walls, during which time they
defend it from attackers, ascending the walls in so doing. But in
the morning the city's governors insist that they should be put to
death for breaking the law. True equity would not allow this kind
of decision. Similarly, claims Mercy, 'be werray equite' God's
commandment concerning the fate of Adam and his lineage meant that
they 'suld nocht be restorit to thar hie state and dignite, quhil
thai forthocht and knew thar faute and gret trespas, and quhil
satisfaccioune ware maid for thame' (p.114).

The legalistic connotations of this sort of language are manifest, but Ireland then makes them even more explicit. Mercy gives
another example, God's sentence of judgement upon Nineveh, and how
Jonah was sent to warn the people, and to give them the chance to
repent and gain grace for, she says, 'The sentens was nocht put to
execucioune, but it was condicionale and comminiatore' (p 114).

The only other example I have been able to locate of a version
of the debate referring to the Nineveh story and making this legal
point is a French mystery drama, Le mystère de l'incarnation et
nativité de notre sauveur et rédempteur Jésus-Christ, which was
presented in Rouen in 1474, a date when Ireland would have been in
France.[30] This version does not consistently match the Meroure,
though it is in the theological and legalistic branch of the tradition. The context in which the Nineveh example occurs is also a
little different, but in Misericorde's speech comes the claim '...
ce n'est pas diffinitive/Sentence, mais comminative/Seulement'.[31]
Though the term was also current, as one would expect, in medieval
Latin,[32] it is not otherwise recorded before the early sixteenth
century.[33] Thus the shared use of the example and the terminology,
'comminiatore/comminative', might well suggest that Ireland had
encountered the idea in the Rouen Mystère, or another play like
it. There are indeed other elements of narration in this part of
the Meroure, which could suggest a recollection of a dramatic
enactment.[34]

In the Meroure Mercy supports further her argument by citing
the example of the penitence of Hezekiah, after which the Father
'suspendit his sentens, for it was nocht absolute bot condicionale
... all this was equite' (p 115). By the conclusion of her case,
therefore, Mercy has established through example, the language of
law, and the idiom of advice to princes, that ideal divine kingship should be founded in perfect equity and mercifulness. Ireland
has consistently moulded the presentation of the daughters' arguments to make the debate less of a disagreement between them and
more the counselling of advisers to the king. The morals for a
temporal king are obvious.

Ireland's indebtedness to French sources may also be suggested
by his inclusion of two new characters at the end of this chapter;
'divine orison' and Dame Charity. These two came quite late into
the tradition and are frequently found in French versions,

including mystery plays.[35] Ireland's Dame Charity is given a lengthy speech in support of Mercy, stressing the virtues of 'luf and cheritee' that we have earlier seen to be essential requisites of the truly merciful and just king. Another important figure, Sapience, also appears at the end of the chapter, when we are told that Verity and Justice see 'the souuerane lady, dame sapience, be werray ressone and equite inclyne to mercy and mannis redempcioune' (p 117), at which they feel ashamed and greatly desire to have concord with Mercy. Sapience, of course, had a highly significant role in the Court and a lengthy speech in the debate.[36] While Ireland makes no attempt to give her comparable status (indeed, unlike Charity, she has no speech at all), he yet accords her a small pivotal role in the argument.

That Sapience like the other virtues is an aspect of the divine king is fluently evinced in the speech of Peace which opens the next chapter. 'O prince of pes, O wisdome infynit, and reulare of all creature, in thi realme may na way this strif Endure' (p 118). Peace commonly entered the debate at an advanced stage, but her importance in the Meroure is also signalled by the division of chapters at this juncture. The argument that she expounds is placed very much within the advisory genre, with its familiar themes that no realm may prosper under conditions of strife and that it is a king's responsibility to resolve such a state of affairs.[37] At this point Ireland may return to the Court as a source, though the stages in the debate at which the respective speeches occur do not coincide. In the Meroure Peace intercedes when the other virtues are looking for a means of resolution among themselves. In the Court, as was noted, she appears when the angry arguments are still taking place. Again the effect in the Meroure is that her remarks are addressed directly to the heavenly king. The links between the respective speeches are certainly not as close as other instances, but they do both share the same sententiae, which are given thus in the Meroure:

> 'Omne regnum in se diuisum desolabitur, et domus super domum cadet, et, si sathanas in se ipso esset diuisus, non staret regnum eius. Na realme may lang stand na endure with discord and diuisioune – salustius: Concordia praue res crescunt, discordia vero maxime delabuntur.'   (p 118)

In the Court the same quotations, though with slightly different wording, are used at a distance of about forty-five lines from each other.[38]

When Peace's speech has finished this is the time in the Meroure when the four virtues embrace one another; and the three hierarchies and nine orders of angels applaud. Ireland describes the hierarchies as the 'thre nobile staitis of his hevinly realme' (p 120); and they give a series of appeals for God's mercy upon man. Versions of the debate in the tradition influenced by the Meditationes vitae Christi not infrequently included the supplicating angels.[39] But commonly their appeals come earlier in the debate, and if the angels are distinguished it is in their nine orders (as in the Rouen Mystère) rather than the three hierarchies.[40] The only other version in which I have encountered the three hierarchies making separate prayers is in <u>The Court of Sapience</u>.

Here the context is again not quite the same as Ireland's for their appeals take place after Sapience has moved the resolution of the debate through the Son. The hierarchies then go to council:

> To pray for man it was theyr hole entent,
> That he myght come to his old herytage
> Oute from the carybde, and the smoky cage
> Of servytyte, the whiche hym had incluse
> Four thousand yere; he myght it not refuse.
> (<u>Court</u>, 11.612–16

This is how it is put by Ireland:

> ' ... he mycht be deliuerit fra the dyrk place of pluto and the dyrk, gret and hevy seruitute of the auld serpent, and cum agane to his auld heretage.'   (p 120)

We may note not only the verbal parallels of 'seruitute' and 'auld heretage' but also Ireland's interesting rendering of Charbydis or 'the smoky cage' as the 'dyrk place of pluto'.

Ireland calls the first hierarchy, 'counsalouris assistant to the diuinitee'.[41] The <u>Meroure</u>'s borrowings from the <u>Court</u> are at their most obvious here:

> The to byhold is our soverayne solace,
> Our lyf, our lust, and oure ay lastyng blysse;
> The hyghe glory that shyneth in thy face
> The wyt of kynd may not conceyve, ywys,
> And syth that man soo lyke unto the is,
> And fourmed was unto thyne owne lykenesse,
> Oute of thy blysse why lyeth he in derkenesse?
>
> What honour is, or yet what worthynesse
> To thy godhede to suffre thyn ymage
> Devoured be, and drenched in derkenesse,
> For whome thou made lyght to be herytage?
> And syth our blysse is hole in thy vysage,
> O welawey! why shold the shap of it,
> The to dysteyne, alwey in derkenesse sit?
>
> Wherefor we pray, O prynce ful of grace,
> Thou have pyte of man thy creature;
> His bondes strong vouchesauf ones to unlase;
> Lete not thy shap so long derkenes endure;
> Yeve somme reward unto thyn owne honoure –
> For now is tyme of Mercy and of Pees,
> And tyme is come that al vengeaunce shold cees!'
> (<u>Court</u>, 11. 624–44)

O hiest lord and souuerane prince of maieste, our glore, oure blis, all oure delit and plesaunce is, thi natur to knaw, and euir to consider and behold thi bricht face, thi

powere and thi wertu. And sene mankind is maid to thi
similitud, that is sa lik to thi ymage, lord of maieste, oure
prayere is, thou schaw to him thi mercy and thi grace. And,
fader of mercy, of wertu, of all honour and worthines, quhat
honour may be to thi hie deite, to suffer all mankind eter-
naly in sic mischaunce and hevines, that was fyrst ordand for
eternall blis and heretage. Tharfor we all on kne richt
humylly makis supplicacioune for mannis help and deliueraunce
and pes, sene now is tym of mercy and of grace, and that al
wengeauns suld ces; schaw, fader, to us, for thi honour, for
mankind, thi mercy, thi piete and thi grace; lat nocht,
mychtty lord, this hevinly place stand in Ruyne na desolacioune, for lak of mercy to thi humyll seruand and creatur.

(p 120)

But again we should note divergences in emphasis. While both ask
the same question about what honour there would be in allowing
mankind to remain in misery, Ireland characteristically prefaces it
with an assertion of the virtues residing in the heavenly king;
similarly while both conclude with the claim that 'now is tym ...
that all wengeauns suld ces', Ireland runs on a little further to
appeal to the king to put an end to the ruination of the realm.
    Ireland may perhaps have responded so strongly to this section
of the Court because the appeals of the hierarchies are directed
forthrightly to the Father, very much in keeping with his own
presentation of the debate. But that he continually adapts them to
his own particular purposes is well evinced by comparison of the
appeals of the second, knightly, order. Both versions make something of the imperial nature of divine kingship, the Court poet
referring to 'thy lawe imperyal' and 'thyn empyre' (11.647, 649),
Ireland to the king as 'emperoure souuerane' (p 120). Both appeal
for mercy to mankind and ask how long he must suffer under the
oppression of the devil. The terms in which they continue well
illustrate how the Court contrives to evoke a sense of active
kingship, which will be confirmed in its fuller evocation of the
actions of the son, while Ireland presents a more formal appeal for
clemency to a king who is the absolute seat of justice:

> Syth thou art lyf, why hath deth soveraynte?
> If thou be kyng, to thyn honour thou see!
> Soo bynd the fend, and take man by conquest
> Unto thy blysse, and set thy regne in rest.
>
> (Court, 11. 662-5)

And, hie emperoure and lord souuerane, sene thou art werray
lif and prince of piete, hou lang sal thou tholl cruell deid
to haue dominacioune one thi humyll seruand and thi ymage,
nature humane. And sene thou art king of blis, bynd thi
innemy, lous thi seruand, and bring him to rest and pece.

(pp 120-1)

There is, however, considerable disparity between the third
order, Ireland's 'nobile and worthi officiaris of this realme
celestiall and hevinly court' (p 121) and those in the poem. This is

undoubtedly because their speech in the <u>Court</u> deals with details of the debate not relevant to the <u>Meroure</u>. Here the argument is essentially resumptive and is unusually related as reported speech, but Ireland stresses the oppressive power of Satan and the 'princis of myrkness' (p 121), who are depicted as tyrants who have resisted the will of God and usurped his dominance over mankind. This produces a vivid contrast between types of kingship: the perfect justice of God and the tyranny of Satan. Secular distinctions inform the depiction of heavenly kingship in such a way as to reflect back upon the conduct of earthly rulers.

By now Ireland has established a firm impression of the concordance of the holy estates of angels with the privy (secret) counselling virtues. They next beseech the Father together on the two main principles, of his merciful nature and his promise to Mercy that Christ would be born to redeem mankind. There are henceforth no more precise parallels between the <u>Meroure</u> and <u>The Court of Sapience</u>, which moves into dialogue between the Son and the daughters. Ireland, in contrast, is concerned to preserve the focus on the king, who is presented in the style of those who preside over courts and councils as having 'hard' and 'considirit' the evidence,[42] including 'the desolacioune of the hevinly realme, the gret ressonis, contencioune and argumentis maid be the nobile and hevinly wertuis, his luffit dochteris, and secretaris of his consale' (p 122). And his response is the classic one of the merciful monarch: 'He knew his awne propir nature and condicioune, sa gretlie inclinit to mercy' (p 122). Ireland cleverly contrives to suggest both that the Father's response is instigated by the advice and pleas of his subjects <u>and</u> that it arises naturally from his own ideal being.

Ireland deals succinctly with the offer of the Son to take human form in order to redeem mankind,[43] further evidence of his concern to fix attention firmly on the role of the heavenly king. The legal context is still maintained: the Father issues his 'sentens diffinitive' (p 123), to be distinguished from the 'condicionale and comminiatore' sentence issued earlier. The form in which it is delivered is a fitting conclusion to Ireland's treatment of the debate. The Father's sentence is formulated in the style of a royal charter, and though a final statement by the deity was a feature of the tradition, there is no other version which is markedly similar to Ireland's. The whole idea clearly owes much to the genre of the 'charter of Christ', but it is here a charter delivered not by Christ at Calvary as was customary, but by God the Father.[44]

Charters of Christ commonly evoked legal prototypes, and Ireland's can usefully be compared with contemporary Scottish documentaion. His charter opens with an invocation which places its emphasis on the role of the Father: 'I, god, creature and fadere of hevin, makis kend to all my creaturis and to my seruandis sendis salutacioune' (p 123). Though there are vernacular charters of this period, the phrasing is closer to the Latin of royal charters and edicts, such as this of 1491, 'Iacobus dei gratia Rex Scotorum. Omnibus probis hominibus totius terre sue, clericis et laicis, salutem'.[45] The charter in the <u>Meroure</u> continues, 'I will ȝe knaw', formal phrasing more like the 'Sciatis'

of the royal charters than those in the vernacular phrasing, 'anens
the gret discensioune and discord that lang tyme has indurit betuix
me and my seruiture and wassale, humane linage' (p 123), terms
that, however formulaic, it is interesting to compare with those
used in parliamentary records of the time to describe trouble in
the realm: 'anent the deuisioun, debaitis and discordis', or 'al
discenciouns and discordis now standand'.[46] After detailing the
tools which will inscribe the charter, in a manner based on the
charters of Christ, he concludes with the signing and sealing of
the document, 'And this letter of grace be the consent of the hale
trinite is gevin in oure gret counsale of hevin' (pp 123–4). The
king has thus ratified the document on an agreement taken with the
advice of his secret counsel in the presence of an institution, the
'gret council', that was another legislative body, composed of
members of the three estates, though of a slightly less formal
nature than a parliament.[47] The point is clear: the heavenly king's
decision is both his own and one taken constitutionally with his
counsellors.

This is effectively the conclusion of the debate of the four
daughters of God in the _Meroure_. Thereafter the advice elements are
far less prominent, the remainder of the chapter being concerned
with narrating the events of the Incarnation. We have thus seen
Ireland expertly handling a wide range of sources to make the
debate an exemplum of good advice and good government, in which the
principle of equity triumphs. But by focusing upon the divine king
Ireland throws inevitable comparison upon the problems that might
beset a mortal imitator. A paradox of medieval political thought
was that kingship was the best form of government, provided the
king was a good one.[48] As elsewhere in the _Meroure_ Ireland is not
given to explicit discussion of what might happen if the king were
a bad one. But there are perhaps a number of implicit points being
made in his version of the debate, which have a particular
resonance for the 1480s and 1490s.

We have seen the emphasis upon the role of counsellors, the
invocation of Scottish institutions, the contrast between tyranny
and good kingship. And we have noted the legalistic associations of
the language of the debate. Quoted above were some parliamentary
references to 'discord and discencioune', and it is worth dwelling
on the fact that both of those dating from 1483 and 1488 deal with
discord among the nobility. Compare the phrasing of the _Meroure_
'anens the gret discencioune and discord ... for to compleit pes
and concord betuix human linage and me', with the text of the 1488
edict 'Item al discenciouns and discordis now standand or beand
betuex ony Lordis or gret baronis of baith the partis salbe drawing
be the wisdome of the said lordis to vnite concord sa that luf and
fauour may stand ymangis oure souerane lordis liegis and peax to be
had and Justice to proced'.[49] The associative links between
Ireland's phrasing and that of the parliamentary records written at
the very time of the _Meroure's_ composition are striking, and
perhaps indicative of underlying anxieties. Could such discords be
equitably resolved by the new regime and the new king? In 1490
Ireland affirms an optimistic belief in good hereditary kingship,
but the issues he raised, however indirectly, in the _Meroure_ did
not go away. Twenty years later the question of the merits of

hereditary or elective kingship was taken up by John Mair, and continued to be raised with increasing vigour throughout the sixteenth century.[50] It is easy to see Ireland's Meroure as a quintessentially medieval work. But perhaps we should also see it as one that in a number of small but significant ways looks forward to the sixteenth century.

Notes

1   The best account of Ireland's career is J H Burns, 'John Ireland and "The Meroure of Wyssdome"', The Innes Review, 6 (1955), 77-98. On the date of composition, see also The Meroure of Wyssdome by Johannes de Irlandia, vol 1 (Books I-III), C Macpherson (ed), Scottish Text Society, New Series 19 (1926). All quotations below are taken from this edition (hereafter Meroure, I). The distinction between i and j and the long β have not been preserved. In all other quotations the same conventions have been adopted and abbreviations silently expanded.

2   The Acts of the Parliaments of Scotland, vol II, T Thomson (ed) (Edinburgh, 1844), p 211-15.

3   See the discussion in N Macdougall, James III: A Political Study (Edinburgh, 1982), pp 235-68; also J Wormald, Court, Kirk, and Community, Scotland 1470-1625, The New History of Scotland, 4 (1981), pp 16-19.

4   Meroure, I, p 15.

5   Roger Mason, 'Kingship, Tyranny, and the Right to Resist in Fifteenth Century Scotland', Scottish Historical Review, 66 (1987), gives, amongst much else, an excellent appraisal of Ireland's political thought, though it may be argued that neither Ireland nor other Scottish advisory writers were quite such entrenched conservatives as he suggests. Dr Mason's article had not yet appeared in print at the time of the completion of this paper, and I am most grateful to him for letting me consult his typescript. I have, however, been unable to supply page numbers to this article. An extended discussion of the advice in the Meroure is also to be found in S Mapstone, 'The Advice to Princes Tradition in Scottish Literature, 1450-1500'. Unpublished D Phil thesis, University of Oxford, 1986, pp 356-442.

6   Mapstone, pp 435-43; for a different view, Mason.

7   Books VI and VII are being edited for the STS by Dr Craig McDonald and the relation between Gerson's sermons and the Meroure will also be discussed in detail in his edition.

8   Mason; Mapstone, pp 408-45.

9   C McDonald, 'John Ireland's Meroure of Wyssdome and Chaucer's Tale of Melibee', Studies in Scottish Literature, 21 (1986), 23-34, argues for Ireland's indebtedness to Chaucer. It should be noted, however, that Ireland may have had more than one source: he gives the sententiae in Latin, which is not how they are rendered in either Chaucer's version or the

French text of Renaud de Louens. McDonald's view is that, 'Evidently, Ireland relied on his own knowledge of the sources or else he translated from the English back into Latin' (34).

10   Mapstone, pp 433-43.

11   Burns, 82-3.

12   For the debate's complex early history, The Middle English Translations of Robert Grosseteste's 'Château d'Amour', K Sajavaara (ed), Mémoires de la Société Néophilologique de Helsinki, 32 (Helsinki, 1967), pp 62-90; though superseded on transmission, still useful is, H Traver, The Four Daughters of God, a Study of this Allegory with Special Reference to those in Latin, French, and English, Bryn Mawr College Monographs, 6 (Bryn Mawr, 1907).

13   The term had already been used in Meroure, I, pp 90-1. The Regiam Maiestatem had a section 'De Crimine laesae Majestatis', and a 1457 parliament spoke of 'lesyng makaris and tellaris of thame the quhilkis ingeneris discorde betuix the king and his pepill', Regiam Majestatem and Quoniam Attachiamenta, ed. Lord Cooper, Stair Society, 11 (Edinburgh, 1947), pp 249-51; APS, II, p 52/37.

14   On this aspect of the debate see also H Traver, 'The Four Daughters of God: A Mirror of Changing Doctrine', PMLA, 40 (1925), 44-92.

15   Discussed in Alexander Grant, Independence and Nationhood, Scotland 1306-1469, The New History of Scotland, 3 (1984), p 148; on its composition, R K Hannay, 'Early Records of Council and Session, 1466-1649', in An Introductory Survey of the Sources and Literature of Scots Law, Stair Society, 1 (Edinburgh, 1936), pp 16-24 (22).

16   APS, II, p 220/12.

17   Mapstone, pp 12-42; idem, 'The Talis of the Fyve Bestes and the Advice to Princes Tradition', in Scottish Language and Literature, Medieval and Renaissance, D Strauss and H W Drescher (eds), Scottish Studies, 4 (Frankfurt, 1986), pp 239-54.

18   'The Lion and the Mouse', 11.1461-8, The Poems of Robert Henryson, D Fox (ed) (Oxford, 1981); Gilbert of Haye's Prose Manuscript, vol. II, J H Stevenson (ed) , STS, 1st Series 62 (1914), pp 95, 99.

19   Cf., for example, 'Château d'Amour', 11.363-94; A Critical Edition of John Lydgate's Life of Our Lady, J A Lauritis et al. (eds), Duquesne Studies, Philological Series 2 (Pittsburgh, 1961), Book 2, 11.205-21; Ludus Coventriae, K S Block (eds), Early English Text Society, E.Series 120 (1922), 11.56-63, p 99. Only in the first example is the theme of kingship at all prominent.

20   The Court of Sapience, E R Harvey (ed), Toronto Medieval Texts and Translations, 2 (Toronto, 1984), pp.xxi-xxiv; quotations are from this edition.

21   Ibid., pp.xxiv-xlv.

22   Ibid., p.xxx.

23   Compare also 'Fro thy godhede put oute al varyaunce,/Stable thy sentence, and thy just jugement'; (Court, 11.246-7) and

'... bot gret instabilite and wariaunce ... thi sentens and jugisment mone stand ferme' (Meroure, I, p 109); both also refer to the execution of the promise.

24 In the Court, however, the phrase completes her speech.

25 Other versions touch on the concept of equity, but to nothing like this extent; cf. Lydgate's Life of our Lady, Book 2, 11.205-31, Ludus Coventriae, 11.131-2, p.101, Le Pélerinage de Jhésucrist de Guillaume de Deguileville, J J Stürzinger (ed), Roxburghe Club (1897), 11.367-75.

26 Prose MS, II, p 145.

27 'The Lion and the Mouse', 11.1472-3.

28 Mapstone, 'Advice to Princes', pp 417-19. Cf. the interesting comments on the conceptual place of equity in the thought and practice of William Elphinstone in L J Macfarlane, William Elphinstone and the Kingdom of Scotland, 1431-1514 (Aberdeen, 1985), pp 33-4, 89-90.

29 Cicero, De oratore, II, 100: Quintilian, Institutio oratoria 7, 6, 6 gives the example thus in a discussion on the relation between equity and the letter of the law: '"Peregrinus si murum escenderit capite puniatur. Cum hostes murum escend-issent, peregrinus eos depulit: petitur ad supplicium."', M Winterbottom (eds), 2 vols (Oxford, 1970), II, p 407). For pre-1500 copies of Quintilian in Scotland, see J Durkan and A Ross, Early Scottish Libraries (Glasgow, 1961), pp 98, 111, 158.

30 P Le Verdier (ed), Société des Bibliophiles Normands, 3 vols, (Rouen, 1884-6), I, pp 125-6; discussed in Traver, Four Daughters of God, pp 103-9.

31 Ibid., p 125.

32 Revised Medieval Latin Word-List, R E Latham (ed) (1965), commin/-atorius.

33 OED, comminatory, a.

34 Although indebted ultimately to pseudo-Bonaventure, the very vivid description of how 'we may ymagin' the opening of the parliament (p 108) suggests that Ireland may have seen a dramatic representation of the debate, as does the visually dramatic account of the descent of Mercy from her throne (p 112); cf. the mise-en-scène of Mercadé's Mystère de la passion, quoted in Traver, Four Daughters of God, pp 78-9; also E Mâle, L'art religieux de la fin du moyen âge en France (4th edn, Paris, 1969), pp 36-8.

35 Traver, Four Daughters of God, pp 102, 76-9.

36 On the figure of Sapience in the Court, see Harvey's comments on p.xxx of her edition; also C F Bühler, The Sources of the Court of Sapience, Beiträge zur Englischen Philologie, 23 (Leipzig, 1932), pp 25-7.

37 Cf. the different emphases in Lydgate's Life of Our Lady, Book 2, 11. 106-75; Ludus Coventriae, 11. 113-28, p.101; The Castle of Perseverance, 11. 2483-521, in The Macro Plays, M Eccles, (ed), EETS, O Series 262 (1969).

38 These Latin quotations occur in two MSS of the poem, but not in Caxton's printed edition; Harvey (p.xv) considers that 'There seems to be no good reason why the Latin notes ... should not be considered as authorial', but does not include

them within the body of her text (they are included in the notes, pp 50-1); they are given in position in the text in The Court of Sapience, R Spindler (ed), Beiträge zur Englischen Philologie, 6 (Leipzig, 1937), pp 137-9.

39   Comparisons with the Meditationes may be easily made from Meditations on the Life of Christ, I Ragusa and R B Green (eds) (Princeton, 1961), pp 5-6.

40   Cf. Traver, Four Daughters of God, p 104.

41   One of the MSS of the Court has Latin glosses, describing the various orders. Spindler, pp 149-51 includes them with the text; Harvey cites them in the notes, pp 98-100. Ireland's descriptions seem, however, to have more in common with the vernacular verse renditions in the Court.

42   Cf., for example, The Acts of the Lords in Council in Civil Causes, vol I, T Thomson (ed) (Edinburgh, 1839), p 216/28.

43   Cf. the elaborate scene in the Court, 11.719-77.

44   See R R Raymo, 'Works of Religious and Philosophical Instruction', in A Manual of the Writings in Middle English 1050-1500, A E Hartung (ed) (New Haven, Conn., 1986), 7, pp 2343-4, 2548-60.

45   APS, II, P 270/2.

46   Ibid., pp 165/8, 210. The charter here also broadly accords with the models set out in the fourteenth and fifteenth century collections, 'De Composicione Cartarum', J J Robertson (ed), Stair Society, Miscellany, 1 (Edinburgh, 1971) pp 78-93.

47   The term more commonly used was 'general council', but it is interesting that there are also references to great councils in the works of other advice writers, such as Gilbert Hay and the author of De Regimine principum: Mapstone, 'Advice to Princes', pp 127, 138-40.

48   Excellently discussed in P Lewis, 'Jean Juvenal des Ursins and the Common Literary Attitude to Tyranny in Fifteenth Century France', Medium Aevum 32 (1965), 103-21.

49   APS, II, p 210.

50   J H Burns, 'Politia Regalis et Optima: The Political Ideas of John Main', History of Political Thought, 2 (1981), 31-61.

Chapter 24

JOHN IRELAND'S LITERARY SENSIBILITY:
THE MEROURE OF WYSSDOME, BOOK 7 [1]

J C McDonald

Shortly before his death, in a note in the Review of English
Studies, Professor J A W Bennett commented that John Ireland's
admiration for Chaucer 'was heartfelt, not conventional'.[2] Unknown
to Bennett, since only two-thirds of the Meroure of Wyssdome had
been published, Ireland's admiration, I believe, extended to
borrowing a substantial portion of the 'Tale of Melibee' in his
seventh and as yet unpublished book.[3] Growing interest in the
Meroure over the years since the appearance of Bennett's article
has further revealed that Chaucer was not the only author Ireland
copied or at least relied upon heavily.[4] The middle of Book 7 is
nearly a point-by-point refutation of Marsilius of Padua's
argument for royal election in Defensor Pacis. The same book
contains translations (sometimes close, sometimes mere summaries)
of parts of five of Jean Gerson's French sermons (Vivat Rex,
Diligite justiciam, Veniat pax, Rex in sempiternum vive, and
Adorabunt eum). Even when Ireland claims personally to be making a
point, as in f.352v., where he writes 'Zit I will mak a morale
exposicioun ...',[5] he sometimes borrows Gerson's authorial
identity: Gerson in the parallel passage writes 'prenons'. Such an
apparent ring of authenticity is twice more undercut (ff. 332r.,
350v) and should warn us against attributing original passages to
Ireland simply on the basis of the first person.
    For all his unabashed 'plagiarism', however, Ireland does bring
to his task some care and thought. Besides selecting and reorgan-
ising the received material, he adds stories, commentary,
explanation, and admonition of his own. Such additions, modestly
sandwiched as they often are between large slices of Gerson,
Marsilius, and Chaucer, cause us naturally to ask why, when
Ireland has borrowed so extensively, he deviates at such and such
a place? Answers to such a question, especially when asked of
passages of poetic or rhetorical interest, namely, Ireland's
exempla, afford us a glimpse at the literary and critical temper
of the age, not by one who is writing poetry at the moment, but by
an interpreter whose aim is to bring poetry (and, for that matter,
history) to bear on a subject of political moment.
    We might begin our study more generally with a look at two
issues that give us a sense of Ireland's critical temper: the
literature familiar to him and his exegetical method. As to the
first, Brother Bonaventure Miner has argued that Ireland 'shows
himself to be influenced, however unconsciously, by the Renaissance spirit and more particularly by humanist thinking'.[6]

Miner adduces two pieces of evidence from Book 7 to substantiate his claim: Ireland's use of classical sources and his emphasis on the dignity of man (144-5). How much we have to modify the first of Miner's claims, the breadth of Ireland's reading, is apparent by the list of references also found in parallel passages in Gerson's sermons or Chaucer's 'Melibee'. But Ireland's debt to Gerson and Chaucer notwithstanding, the list of authors he is familiar with, both classical and non-classical, is certainly impressive.

The most popular of Ireland's sources, by the sheer weight of numbers, are Virgil, Sallust, Livy, and Ovid, not exclusively the writers of republican Rome who, as Matthew McDiarmid has argued, influence so greatly fourteenth- and fifteenth-century Scottish historians and epic poets, but Roman nonetheless.[7] This tallies with the interest shown by Gavin Douglas, Ireland's contemporary, though younger by two generations, as Priscilla Bawcutt has shown.[8] The interests of the two coincide roughly. For both, Ovid is 'a treasure house of myth and heroic legend' (Bawcutt, p 113) instead of a poet of love. And Aeneas is an idealised prince (cp. Bawcutt p 116).

But for all these similarities, the differences are great. Bawcutt shows Douglas's admiration for the artistry and style of the Roman authors, and notes the considerable influence of such Italian humanists as Boccaccio, Valla, and Landino upon Douglas's thinking. Ireland's appreciation for Virgil and Ovid extends simply to their value as moral teachers. He may have consulted Boccaccio when interpreting the myths he finds in Gerson, or introduces himself. The interpretations are too general to argue this convincingly. And he demonstrates from time to time a literary awareness that informs the telling of his stories. But the issue of style, a principal concern of the Renaissance, never enters into the discussion. The primary reason for this difference between the two men is, of course, the nature of their writing. The subject of Bawcutt's inquiry is Douglas's poetry, ours is Ireland's prose. Bawcutt's hypothetical question asked of Douglas, 'What have Aquinas or Pierre d'Ailly to do in a secular poem like The Palice of Honour?' (109), might be just as easily restated, 'What have Boccaccio or Landino to do in a political treatise like the seventh book of The Meroure of Wyssdome?' But the whole tenor of the two men's attitudes towards the past seems vastly different – for Ireland there is little to distinguish Scipio Africanus from Aeneas; both are exemplary rulers – and we must agree with Professor James Burns, 'Ireland was no humanist, but the world of classical humanism was not totally alien to him'.[9]

Ireland's exegetical method is worth considering since his approach to poetry is fashioned after his approach to Scripture. Ireland follows his mentor Gerson in articulating this method, though in a more abbreviated fashion. Gerson employs the allegorical mode to exegeting Scripture, when he interprets Nebuchadnezzar's statue literally (as the four kingdoms of the world), mystically (as the four ages of the world), and morally (as the four cardinal virtues of the individual, which are also manifest in the realm) (Rex in sempiterunum vive, OC 1012-13). Ireland's interests are simply tropological. In pursuit of economy, he does not even name the first two levels, dismissing them in a single clause, 'and suppos this ymage and visioun haue mony diuers significaciounis of diuers realmes and age of men as doctouris exponis And first daniell the prophet/Zit I will mak a morale exposicioun ...'(f.352v).

Elsewhere, Gerson writes of his exegetical method in interpreting the expression 'hoc erit ius regis' (I Kings 12:1-19), which is critical of the Israelites' desire for a king. Knowing full well the extreme volatility of such a passage for his own king, Gerson carefully argues that one cannot look at a passage of Scripture only from the point of the 'signification grammaticale et vulgaire des moz "the grammatical and common signification of the words"' (Vivat Rex, OC 1157). One must call into play logic and philosophy, as well as divine inspiration and the comparison of one text with the other. Again, Ireland refrains from this sort of prefatory discussion and simply states, 'And gif thou allegis/ that it is writtin in the first buk of kingis hoc erit ius regis/ quhen saul was institut king of israel/I ansuer to that/ quod hoc erat dictum enunciatiue et non preceptiue nec determinatiue' (f.328v). He then does what Gerson has prescribed, following Gerson, in fact, by weighing the circumstances and the true intent.

Ireland is quite capable of exegeting Scripture independently of Gerson, although it is true that a source may lie elsewhere. On f.316r-316v. he ingeniously allegorises the gifts of the three kings of the Orient as three levels of good government: the personal, the temporal, and the spiritual. Myrrh signifies the personal, the man who rules his passions and in whom the kingdom of God dwells. It defends the man from putrefaction and sin. Gold remedies indigence, and as such it represents the well-ruled kingdom, whose prince brings sufficience by ensuring peace. The spiritual realm, Holy Kirk, is symbolised by frankincense, which is used in the service and worship of God.

Since the aim of Book 7 of the Meroure is to exposit the virtues of good kingship, Ireland's allegorical interest in each case is primarily tropological.

Turning to Ireland's interpretation of poetry, we find that he operates in a similar fashion with a similar interest. I must say at this point, though, that were we to look for something in the Meroure as sophisticated as Boccaccio's interpretations in De genealogia deorum gentilium or the moralisings of Ovid, we would be gravely disappointed. We are not surprised, of course, when Ireland decides upon prose as his own medium because of the seriousness of his subject. He argues that 'the hie materis of theologie are teichit jn thire bukis jn my maner of speking', i.e. in prose. Even Chaucer, in the 'Parson's Tale' and, as Ireland implicitly acknowledges by his copying, in the 'Tale of Melibee', had resorted to prose when he 'cummys to sad and gret materis'.[10] Despite this quite normal attitude to prose, however, he commends the poets Chaucer, Gower, and Lydgate for 'jnduceand personis to lefe vicis and folow wertuis' and allows that 'thai suld be gretlie thankit tharof, for jn thar bukis thai teich a tragedy, that schawis in this waurldly plesaunce – jn the begynnyng gret plesaunce and dilectacioune, And in the ende, all manere of sorow and displesaunce'.[11] Poetry, as we learn here and elsewhere in the treatise, is greatly esteemed; and although the <u>Meroure</u> certainly makes no claim to treat the matter of literary interpretation systematically, part of its task as a mirror of wisdom is to consider the mirror-like effects of poesy.

Accounting in large measure for the appeal of poetry to Ireland, is, as the passage just cited illustrates, the capacity of poets to teach lessons of moral significance. In the seventh book of the <u>Meroure</u>, issues of morality are political in scope, and aid of the poets and historians is enlisted accordingly. Dr R J Lyall has indicated the moral concerns of fifteenth-century Scottish political poetry,[12] and Ireland's poetic interests are no exception. Gerson himself lists poets among theologians, jurists, and philosphers as providing the king with good doctrine (in this case, the superiority of kingship to other forms of government) (<u>Vivat Rex</u>, <u>OC</u> 1139). Ireland follows suit.

At times, though, Gerson will simply describe or quote from a passage of poetry and leave the interpretation to his reader. Beginning with some such words as 'This is poesy and it signifies ...' Ireland in schoolmasterly and preacherly fashion makes all plain for his distinguished reader, James IV. Ian Jamieson has argued that many fifteenth-century Scottish poets are concerned with 'the moral purpose of poetry', but that they are also 'aware that such a purpose is not easily achieved – it is dependent on the attitudes of its audience, for instance'.[13] Ireland is loath, it seems, to let this moral significance escape the reader's notice and attempts to bridge the gaps in an understanding eroded perhaps by an indifferent attitude. His interpretations are both tropological and euhemeristic.[14] Ireland follows Gerson (<u>OC</u>, 7.1176) and thus Virgil, Ovid, and the like by embodying tyrants in the likes of Polyphemus, Busirus, and Lichaon, who 'liffit of the substaunce of the pur peple be thar rapyn and oppressioun' (f.333v). But he goes further than Gerson in designating the people's deliverers – Hercules, Ulysses, and Jupiter – specifically as 'wis and noble <u>knychtis</u>' and as a '<u>king</u>'. Moving on, a lustful king is like Ovid's Mars, who with Venus is entrapped in Vulcan's golden net (f.330v). This story, in Ireland's words,

> signifyis/that quhen the gret strenth of the king or prince mellis it w^t wenus that is wolupte than he tholis scham and confusioun befor all the wys pepil of his realme.

The gods who witness the shame of Venus and Mars have been transformed into the wise people of the realm.

A passage interesting because it appears elsewhere in the <u>Meroure</u> and thus out of the political context of the seventh book is to be found in the second published volume of the <u>Meroure</u>.[15] Here, in the midst of a discussion about the will, Ireland interprets the conflict between the gods in the poetry of Ovid, Virgil, and Homer as a battle of wills not only in the individual but also in the realm. The battle is left unresolved because there is no single nature, lord, or prince to provide 'gud reule and gouernaunce':

> And thus thar war gret discord in the waurld as the noble

poetis Omeir virgill and ouid fenzeis that in the battale of
troy the goddis war diuidit/ and a part/ fauorit tha grecis/
and ane vthir part the troianis and thus the gud and euill
operacioun of man/ war nouthir rewardit nor punyst.

Since wisdom (which for Ireland is synonymous with prudence) is
the keynote of the seventh book, the number of literary exempla
illustrating directly its practice or abuse is proportionately
great. These I would like to examine more carefully because it is
through them that we can come closest to discovering Ireland's
ideas on poetry.

Ireland comments freely on a story not to be found in Gerson,
the account of Phaeton's fall (from Ovid's Metamorphoses 2). This
is Ireland's fullest treatment of a literary passage.

And phitone led the cart and chair of the sone hier na his
fader that signifyis that the king or prince at vsis prid and
elacioun distroyis mekle of his realme/ and at the cart
discendit sa fer/ at it brynt the Erd and causit the ethiops
and men of Inde to be blak/ for the ardent heit that signifyis that quhen the prince is full of ire and crabitnes
w^{t}out ressoune he hurtis gretlie his realme and peple/ And
eftir this ȝoung / child and wantoune phitone filius solis
was perist for his inprudence as sais the poetis (ff.319r –
319v).

The political instruction inherent in the story had struck earlier
interpreters, like Boccaccio, Gower, and Pierre Busuire in his
Ovidius Moralizatus. Even Erasmus, writing a quarter of a century
later, includes the story as an example of a prince's imprudence.
And George Sandys does much the same in the time of Elizabeth I.
But unlike these, Ireland attaches moral significance to the spatial dimensions of the story. Phaeton is not simply the imprudent
or negligent prince. Aspiring to take the chariot higher than his
father had done signifies pride; burning the earth, irrational
anger. Ireland also adds that the failure of Phaeton springs from
two causes, the one a fault of knowledge, the other a lack of
virtue. The remedy is such knowledge as the Meroure of Wyssdome
teaches and the wisdom it promises.

Classical representations of such wisdom are the Palladium of
Troy and the Mirror of Virgil. On ff.317v–318r. Ireland follows
Gerson by recounting the story of the Palladium and the protection
it offered to its inhabitants. Again, though, Ireland's commentary
is a departure from the source:

and this is poesye/ and signifyis that als lang as the wis
men be thar wisdome gouernit the tovne of troy it mycht nocht
be wone/ for thar wisdom was the ymag of pallas that is
goddes of wisdome eftir the poetis/ bot quhen thai tynt the
palladium that was wisdome/ and the grekis gat it than thai
tynt thar tovne/ and the grekis war masteris to thame.

He interprets the Mirror of Virgil in like fashion:

that menys als lang as the romanis be thar wisdome gouernit
and saw be thar prudens the thingis to cum as in a merour sa
lang stud in honour and triumphe the gret empyr of rome.

The image of the mirror as a symbol of prudence, the ability to
foresee the consequences of one's actions, naturally calls to mind
the relationship, at times the conflict, between physical sight
and moral or spiritual insight, and Ireland iterates this motif
further on in the same passage when he calls prudence the light of
the four cardinal virtues and argues that the prince sees the
future by his discretion (318r-318v). The unstated but analogous
effect of all this is that poetry is itself a mirror that reflects
the future and a light that illuminates the virtue of prudence.
Phaeton's fall, by its example of 'inprudence', provides in
Ireland's words 'doctrine prudencial/ that nane is wourthi to
gowern the realme w^{t}out the wertu of prudens'. History, we might
add, acts in a similar way for Ireland. Historical exempla, like
Scipio's condemnation of a prince who fails to see the evil
consequences of an action (f.318v), also illustrate prudent
behaviour. Pressing the analogy even further, we might say that
The Meroure of Wyssdome, as its name implies, acts as a mirror,
not only of prudence and right action, but also of those other
mirrors of poetry and history, reflecting upon and interpreting
for the king's benefit the reflections he sees there.

As we have seen, what Ireland's Meroure reflects of its literary inheritance is its strong moral character. The figure of
Aeneas provides an appropriate focal point for this discussion. As
Priscilla Bawcutt has noted, Virgil would have been the steady
diet of any medieval schoolboy, and so it is not unusual that we
would find Ireland plundering him. To be sure, some of his references to the Italian poet are through Gerson. But Ireland shows a
firsthand knowledge of the Aeneid and holds the Trojan hero up as
an exemplary prince, not in the common medieval garb of an
individual soul on a pilgrimage through life. He commends Aeneas
for justice, piety, and martial prowess, twice citing Aen. 1.544-5
(ff 320v, 350r). On f.321r. Ireland enjoins the prince by Aeneas'
example to rule his people in the ways of peace (6.852-4), and
later states that the hero could be found 'in profound pensy and
meditacioun/ Considerand quhow that he suld gowerne be wisdome and
prudence his peple and realme baith in wer and pes' (ff.351r-
351v., referring to Aen. 1.209). Finally, he upholds the twin
virtues of justice and mercy by citing from 6.854 'Parcere
subiectis and debellare superbos' (f.350v). These references to
Virgil, scattered as they are throughout Book 7 and joined to
those borrowed from Gerson, bespeak not only a familiarity with
the Roman epic, but an eye alert to the political nourishment to
be found in the classics.

Ireland's literary endeavours are not simply limited to interpretation, however. Ireland avails himself of the opportunity of
elaborating on stories he receives from Gerson, both fictional and
historical, attending to details of human interest that Gerson
sometimes omits. The changes are slight, but effective.

The first concerns the story of Trajan and the woman whose son
had been killed, a story also told by John of Salisbury in the

Policraticus 5.8. In fact, because of similarities in details it might be argued that Ireland was aware of the story in the Policraticus and used it to supplement his reading of Gerson, though we must add that John emphasises lessons other than those of Gerson and Ireland. We might note the changes that underscore Ireland's admonition to James that a king be responsive to his people's pleas for justice. The disparity between the two actors in the scene is accentuated. Trajan is 'gret and noble', the 'heid of the iustice'; the woman, like John's, is 'pur'. The woman cries 'lamentabli' for the death of her son that has been committed 'wrangwisly'. Both these ideas are expressed in John. Trajan responds 'humely w^t pete to the woman', yet his intention to go into battle first is emphasised by the fact that he 'remanit stil on his hors', a detail not to be found in either Gerson or John. This posture makes his later descent from the horse that much more dramatic (and threatrical) a sign of Trajan's humility. The woman emphasises the wrong done to her, rather than to Trajan, by the murder, a difference arguing perhaps that the king should not limit his administration of justice solely to what touches him only. She also reminds Trajan of his mortality, especially in the light of the impending battle. Finally, Ireland comments, 'And this Empriour traiane was a pagane'. These additions heighten the contrast between the poor woman and the emperor and emphasise the emperor's devotion to duty. If Trajan as a pagan took such pains to satisfy the demands of a poor woman, how much more should a Christian prince be sensitive to the claims of his people. All of these details Gerson implies, but Ireland intensifies the story and sounds more aggressively the note of compassion; and if the result is not quite a lively piece of prose, it is yet an improvement on the original. Such a treatment argues a rhetorical, if not purely literary, sensibility on Ireland's part.

We find this process at work elsewhere. On f.320v Ireland follows Gerson in naming Agamemnon and Augustus Caesar as paternalistic kings. The greatness of the two monarchs was certainly well established, but Ireland briefly enumerates their deeds to enhance their stature. Augustus's reputation is manifested in 1) his being the successor of Julius, 2) the ruling monarch at the birth of Christ, and 3) the lord of the whole earth. Agamemnon achieved greatness by destroying Troy, thereby bringing 'gret honour to all the land and Empyr of grece'. Gerson's moral axiom — that the function of true greatness is directly proportional to fatherly concern for one's subjects — Ireland makes unmistakably clear. Should the Scottish king assume the same humble posture as these two monarchs, one historical, the other poetic, he stands, paradoxically, only to increase in stature.

We might cite several other minor examples of this sort of treatment. I will close with one of my favourites. Into Gerson's account of the wounded man tormented by flies, a story originating in Aristotle's Rhetoric 2.20, Ireland inserts this whimsical, but appropriate exclamation that is, I believe, typical of his narrative sense. When offered help by the well-meaning but blundering good Samaritan, the hurt man cries out, 'in gret dolour/for goddis saik lat thir fleis rest heir for thai ar now fow of my blud/ for and thar cum new fleis thai will aluterly consume me thai ar sa masterfull and hungry' (Ireland's additions underlined).

If the mirror Ireland holds up to poetry distorts for most modern readers the object it is meant to define more sharply, and if it is a borrowed mirror at that, it is nevertheless a mirror wielded by one whose hand is sure and whose literary appreciation is indeed 'heartfelt'. Book 7 of the Meroure is more than large portions of Gerson, Chaucer, and Marsilius swallowed whole and lying undigested in Ireland's imagination. I would argue instead that Ireland ruminates on the moral value and literary possibilities of his sources and to an extent limited (and here, I think, we can be generous) by the professed aims of his treatise defines these values and realises these possibilities. The literary legacy, admittedly, is not great. Its greater value lies elsewhere, as a record of literary taste in an age that produced Henryson, Dunbar, and Douglas.

Notes

1 For financial assistance in preparing this paper and attending the Fifth International Conference of Scottish Language and Literature, I gratefully wish to acknowledge grants from the Andrew Mellon Foundation, administered through King College and the University of Kentucky, and from the National Endowment for the Humanities (USA).

2 Bennet, 'Notes: Those Scotch Copies of Chaucer', RES, NS 32 (1981), 294-6 (296).

3 Quotations from the seventh book of the Meroure are taken from NLS Adv MS 18.2.8 by permission of the Trustees of the National Library of Scotland.

4 I wish to acknowledge here my debt to Mr David Brown, who first suggested the relationship between Ireland and Gerson; to Dr Roger Mason, who made a detailed account of Ireland's indebtedness to Gerson; to Dr Sally Mapstone, who pointed out an additional passage that Ireland borrowed and who also provided convincing evidence that Ireland relied heavily on Marsilius' Defensor Pacis 16 for the framework of his arguments on hereditary succession; and to Professor James Burns, for invaluable advice on matters of political importance.

5 Subsequent quotations from these sermons are from Gerson's Oeuvres Complètes (hereafter OC), 11 vols, P Glorieux (ed), (Paris, 1962).

6 Miner, 'The Popular Theology of John Ireland', Innes Review, 13 (1962), 130-46 (144).

7 McDiarmid, 'The Kingship of the Scots in their Writers', Scottish Literary Journal, 6 (May 1979), 5-18 (10).

8 Bawcutt, 'The 'Library' of Gavin Douglas', in Bards and Makars: Scottish Language and Literature, Medieval and Renaissance, A J Aitken, M P McDiarmid, and D S Thomson (eds) (Glasgow, 1977), pp 107-26 (111-17).

9 From an unpublished paper entitled 'John Ireland: New Light and Fresh Problems', p 14.

10 The Meroure of Wyssdome, vol 1, Charles MacPherson (ed),

Scottish Text Society 2.19 (Edinburgh, 1926), p 74.
11   Meroure, MacPherson (ed), p 164.
12   Lyall, 'Politics and Poetry in Fifteenth and Sixteenth Century Scotland', Scottish Literary Journal, 3 (1986), 5–29 (25).
13   Jamieson, 'Some Attitudes to Poetry in Late Fifteenth-Century Scotland', Studies in Scottish Literature, 15 (1980), 28–42 (40).
14   The euhemeristic mode of interpretation is, of course, not unusual. One has only to look at Boccaccio's De genealogia and even to Gower's Confessio Amantis (one of Ireland's acknowledged 'masters') 5.835 ff to see the process at work. But Ireland employs this mode in places where Gerson, his immediate source, has not.
15   The Meroure of Wyssdome, vol 2, F Quinn (ed), Scottish Text Society 3.2 (Edinburgh, 1965), p 123.23ff.

APPENDIX

Ireland's non-Biblical and non-Scholastic Sources
Quoted or Described

Source	Location in Ireland
Ambrose	
De virginitate 3.14 (d)	2.42.2
criticism of Cicero and Aristotle	1.31.5
Apuleius (called Apollonius by Ireland)	
The Golden Ass (d very generally – firsthand?)	f.255r
Aristotle	
Analytica Posteriora 1.7 (d)	2.16.3–8
general	2.82.17, 91.10
Analytica Priora 1.23 (d)	2.91.27
2 (also 1?) (d)	2.139.5
general	2.82.17, 91.10
De anima 1.1 (d)	(see 2.103.36 n.)
2.4 (d)	f.245r
3.6 (d)	2.91.11
Categoriae (in Ireland, Praedicamenta)	
1.4 (d)	2.91.6–7
general	2.11.7
De celo 2.11 (d)	2.78.17
De interpretatione (in Ireland, Perearminias) 9 (q)	f.243v
11 (d)	2.91.8
9, 12 (d)	2.93.26
Metaphysica 1.1 (q)	f.312v
2.2 (d)	2.96.20
4 (d)	2.93.25

12.10 (cf 317r) (q)	2.97.22
12 (d)	2.90.28
12 (d)	1.31.4
general	2.11.7
De mundo (6-7) (d)	f.278v
Nic Eth. 2.9 (cf Homer, Iliad, 3.158)	1.103.26
4.1 (d)	f.333v
4.6 (d)	(see 2.110.23 n.)
5.1 (q)	f.344r
5.10 (d)	f.313v
Oeconomica 1.3-4 general	f.306r
De partibus animalium 1.1 (d)	(see 2.85.4 n.)
Physica 2.2 (q)	2.70.13
2.8 (d)	f.245r
	2.120.9
3 (d)	(see 2.20.27-9 n.)
4 (d)	2.119.26
8 (d)	2.90.27
Politica 1.1 (q)	f.312v
1.2 (d)	f.241r
1.12 (d)	f.346r
1.7 (d)	f.334v
2.1-6 (d)	f.306r
2.9, 11*; 3.14*, 17*; 5.10* (d)	ff 345v - 346r
3.7-8 (d)	f.310r
3.15 (d)	f.341r
7.2	f.241r
Rhetorica 3.8.2 (q)	1.72.10
1.5, 9* (d)	f.344r
2.15, 16* (d)	f.344r
2.20 (d)	ff 343v - 344r
Topica 3.2 (q)	f.349r
4.5 (q)	2.114.34
9 (Elenchi Sophistici) (d)	2.91.10
general	2.82.19
(*also in Marsilius' Defensor Pacis)	
Augustine	
De civitate dei 2.18 (d)	2.150.18
4.4 (q)	f.347v
18.16-18 (d)	f.255r
18.30 (d)	2.37.20-22
22.20 (q)	2.77.16
De dono preseruantiae 1.23 (q through	
Lombard)	(see 2.145.23 n.)
Enarratio in Psalmum 127 (128) : 6	324v
unacknowledged quotations from :	
Contra epist. Manich 5	(see 2.65.18 n.)
Super Johannem 36	2.21.35
De unitate Ecclesiae contra Donatistis	2.68.16
pseudo-Augustine	
De fide ad Petrum	(see 2.37.22 n.)
Bede	

unnamed (d)   1.79.2

Boethius
De consolatione 2 pr.6 (d)   f.333v
   5 pr.6 (4pr.6 ?) (d)   2.143.7
'De disciplina scholarum'2   f.342r
(on the passions -- an allusion)   f.311r

Chaucer
'Tale of Melibee'   354v-357r
'Parson's Tale'   1.74.15
Troilus   1.74.5
(Praised for understanding, discussion
   of rime and meter, 1.164.19)

Cicero
De officiis 1.20 (q)   ff.323v - 324r
De oratione 1.5,19 (q)   1.9.1
In questionibus Tuscalanis 1 (d)   f.279r
   8 (d)   f.311r
general reference to Rhetorica and Topica   2.82.20

criticised by Ambrose   1.31.5

Demosthenes (quoted by Cicero? --I have
been unable to locate the source)   f.321r
Gower
Confessio Amantis 7.819-47 (d)   ff.354r-v

Horace
Ars Poetica 141-2 (after opening of
   Odyssey -- q)   f.355v
Epistles 1.17 33-34 (q)   f.321r

Jerome
Adversus Jovinianum 2.29 (d)   2.45.17
         generally described   2.59.6
                                                            2.75.11
                                                            2.77.24

Epistles 100 (q)   f.348r

Josephus
Antiquities 16.9.1-6 (cf Macrobius below)   f.322v

Justinus
Historiae Philippicae 7.2.5-12 (d)   ff.349r-v

Juvenal
Satires 2.152-3 or 13 (?) (d)   f.279r

Livy
History 2.32 (d)   f.323r
   23.2-5; 26. 12-16 (d)   f.331r

26.50 (d in detail, though w/ changes)   ff.339v - 340v
Scipio tells solders to put away hind-
rances; not found; from missing leaves?
Valerius Maximus (2.7.1) tells the story
in its general outlines, but does not
assign days to the commands   f.338v

Lucan
Pharsalia 1.8-10 (q)   f.330r
   1.92-93 (quoted in G; Ireland names Lucan
as the author)   f.317r

Macrobius
Somnium Scipionis 1.11.1-2; 2.17.3.13 (d)   f.279r
Saturnalia 1.11.32 (d--the allusion is   f.322v
ambiguous; Gerson quotes from 2.4.11,
but Ireland appears to go directly to
Josephus for his assessment of Herod)
   2.7.12-14 (d)   f.351r

Ovid (perhaps through a moralisation?)
Metamorphoses 1.6 (q)   2.85.32
   1.76 (q)   2.85.35
   1.84 (q)   2.86.3
   1.149-50 (q)   1.108.5
   1.163-243 (d)   f.333v
   2.153-328 (faulty q; d in great detail)   ff 319r-v
   13 (q,d)   f.355v
   (general)   2.123.24
Tristia 2.3   1.115.9
pseudo Ovid
Liber de vetula (d)   2.97.10

Plato
Republic 5.473 (q)   1.5.3.
   10.615a-b (d generally)   f.278v
Timaeus (paraphrase ?)   f.259v

Sallust
Jugurtha 10   1.118.14
Catiline 1.4 (q)   f.335r
   1.6 (q)   f.318v
   51.1 (q what G alludes to)   f.318v
   52 (d of Postumenus)   f.339r
   52.2 (q)   f.278v
   53.3 (q)   f.337v

Seneca
Epistles 9.4 (q)   f.323v
In trigidius (a general reference to
   the tragedies?)   f.311r

Solinus
Collectanea Rerum 65 (q)   f.342v

Strabo
  unnamed (d)   1.79.2
Suetonius
  <u>Lives of the Caesars</u> 1.26,38,67,73–75 (d)   f.322v
      3.49 (conjectured; unnamed in Ireland)   f.333r

Terence
  <u>Andria</u> 266   2.82.3

Valerius Maximus (conjectured; unnamed in Ireland)
  <u>Factorum et Dictorum</u> 7.2.2   318v

Virgil
  <u>Aeneid</u> 1.209 (d)   f.351r–v
    1.544–5 (q)   ff.321r,350v
    3.588–691 (d)   f.333v
    5.344 (q)   1.102.32
    6.625–7 (q)   f.279r
    6.852–4 (q)   ff.321r,350v
    7.19–20 (d)   f.255r
    10.467–9 (q)   f.279r, 335r
    (general)   2.123.24

  <u>Eclogues</u> 1.71–2 (q)   f.335r
    2.65 (q)   1.63.3
                                 2.132.3
    4.1 (q)   1.108.6
    8.70 (d)   f.255r
  <u>Georgics</u> 3.5 (d – not identified in Gerson)   f.333v

General references:
  Cicero and Demosthenes   1.74.11–12
  Gower and Lydgate   1.164.19

Chapter 25

RUTHERFORD AS ENTHUSIAST

David Reid

Samuel Rutherford was a Covenanting divine. Under the bishops he published an anti-Laudian and anti-Arminian treatise and for that was banished in 1636 from his parish of Anwoth in Galloway to Aberdeen, 'this unco town', whose citizens he found 'cold, general and dry in their kindness.'[1] There, nevertheless, he was able to carry on his ministrations in letters addressed, not only to his parishioners, but to a remarkable array of influential people, magnates, lairds, ladies and other prominent figures, chiefly in the South-West. Among them, he could presume on a kindness that was warm, particular and overflowing. All were sympathisers with the anti-episcopal cause; many became Covenanting leaders or worthies. Rutherford complained of persecution, of imprisonment, even of chains.[2] But in fact he was only confined to the city limits and forbidden to preach, and the authorities must have been lenient indeed to allow him to carry on a seditious correspondence in which he maintained and built up an anti-episcopal network.

Under the rule of the Covenant his zeal and his abilities got him important positions. He was made principal of St Mary's at St Andrews and one of the commissioners to the Westminster Assembly. He was a formidable controversialist, but what made him formidable then makes him unreadable now. He speaks disparagingly of 'the Needle-headed Schoolemen.'[3] His own controversial method, however, is protestant scholasticism, a method which educes positions from authorities, codifies them and refines upon them by splitting hairs. Even Rutherford's fellow Covenanters might talk impatiently of 'Mr Samuel' and 'his logick syllogismes',[4] and certainly to a later age his controversial style is unattractive intellectually because its intention is dogmatic rather than inquiring; and as for literary or rhetorical attractions, it shuns them in the pursuit of dry, technical exposition.

On the face of it, Rutherford as controversialist seems an entirely different character from Rutherford as letter writer. The style of the letters is rhapsodic. Instead of aiming at technical plainness there, Rutherford wraps up his sense in a densely figurative texture, often grotesque and visionary in effect and always set apart from the way people normally speak, let alone conduct rational discourse. It is a style which claims to be inspired - not how humans speak, therefore more than human. Replying to one of his correspondents who had found it hard to follow him, Rutherford writes, 'Ye complain to me that ye cannot hold sight of me. But were I a footman, I would go at leisure;

but sometime the King taketh me into his coach and draweth me, and
then I outrun myself. But alas! I am still a forlorn transgressor'
(Letters, CCLXXXV, II, 237). You will notice that even his explanation is fairly hermetic. You have to know that the King in
Rutherford's inward communings is always Christ and you have to
think that outrunning oneself means being rapt beyond one's merely
human faculties, at the same time that it may seem to suggest a
desperate stumbling to keep up with the rush of one's ideas, power
and ineptness going together. In this vein, Rutherford sounds
remarkably like the English Ranters and Seekers, extravagant types
of those Antinomians that he spent so much polemical energy
denouncing in his treatises.[5]

It would be interesting if Rutherford were a self-contradictory
character, a fiercely orthodox presbyterian by conviction but a
Ranter at heart. That antisyzygy, however, will not stand up to
examination. The differences between Rutherford's enthusiastic
style and the Ranters' are more significant than the similarities.
And indeed his enthusiastic extravagances run entirely within the
channels of Presbyterian orthodoxy. One might even say that Presbyterian orthodoxy called for outpourings such as his, though the
remarkable style of his outpourings is his own invention.[6] This
rather disappointing conclusion, that Rutherford's extravagance is
extravagance within Presbyterian bounds and quite in keeping with
his position as a controversialist, is what I shall try to
establish in this paper.

That is the conclusion I want to establish, but on the way I
hope to bring out what an extraordinary writer Rutherford is. He
is an eccentric like Urquhart, but unlike him has received very
little critical attention. He did receive quite a lot of attention
in the nineteenth century from ministers, usually of the Free
Church persuasion.[7] But while we owe editions of the letters and
the sermons to the Rev Andrew Bonar, neither he, nor the Rev
Robert Gilmour, nor the editor of Rubies from Rutherford attempts
more than desultory literary criticism. And they do not offer any
other sort of criticism. For them, Rutherford is a saint of the
Covenant. His fanaticism, his abuse of spiritual authority, his
busying himself in the witch-hunt at St Andrews go unremarked. It
is enough that he should be so staunch an upholder of the
protestant religion. Nor did Rutherford receive much critical
attention from John Hepburn Millar, who was a literary critic of
the Saintsbury school. This was because Millar found Rutherford
what he undoubtedly is, 'a particularly gross offender against
decency and good taste.'[8] He breaks off his discussion in a
chapter entitled 'The Nightmare of the Covenant', with 'I frankly
confess to you that I am unable to face regaling you with this
heavenly Christian's odious ecstasies.'[9] Millar is not a fool and
it may be a fault not to be nauseated, as I am not, but all the
same he is perhaps rather too complacent about his limitations
here. At any rate it is not until Hans H Meier's article, 'Love,
Law, and Lucre: Images in Rutherford's Letters' that anyone looks
closely at Rutherford's style.

Meier concentrates on images for the reciprocal and even con-
tractual relations between the believer and Christ. What I wish to
add to his discussion of Rutherford's style is a consideration of

its extraordinariness and its air of laying claim to an extraordinary experience. And to do this I shall take my material, not
just from Rutherford's letters, but from his tract Christ Dying
and Drawing Sinners to Himself. This tract is a curious hybrid, at
once a commentary on John's account of Christ's dying and redemption of his elect and a polemic against the Antinomians. Stylistically it veers between stretches of scholastic disputatiousness
and passages in Rutherford's high-flying manner at its most
astonishing. More obviously than the letters, Christ Dying brings
out how closely his enthusiasm is tied to his orthodoxy. He
himself glories in how the love of God turns to hatred of those
who depart by the fraction of a hair from the letter of Presbyter-
ianism.

> If then Love, and so deep Gospel-love be despised, broken Men
> slighting Surety-love, and Marriage-love, and then dying in
> such Debt as trampled on Covenant-love, Blood-love must be
> arrested with the saddest Charge of Gospel vengeance. I would
> have saved you, and ye would not be saved, coming from the
> Mouth of Christ, must be a seal to all the Curses of the Law,
> and a vengeance of eternal Fire beyond them. (Christ Dying,
> 'To the Reader', n.p.)

About the politics called for by raptures such as these he is
quite untroubled.
  The most striking feature of Rutherford's enthusiastic style is
its imagery and for that he has a flair. Some of it is immediately
accessible: 'His love-visits are thin sowen, as strawberries in
the rock' (Christ Dying, p 89); 'Oh all that I have done in Anwoth
... is like a bird dying in the shell' (Letters, CLXIII, 1,380);
'Within less than fifty years, when ye look back to it, ye shall
laugh at the evanishing vanities thereof as feathers flying in the
air, and as the houses of sand within the sea-mark, which the
children of men are building' (Letters, CLXXIII, 1,406). The
Letters and Christ Dying are full of felicities such as these
drawn from country life. They are similes, stating both tenor and
vehicle and keeping them apart, not hiding the one in the other as
some of Rutherford's metaphorical flights do. In figures such as
these he seems to play the part of the good minister bringing his
heavenly ideas through analogy down to earth and indeed to local
experience. But the effect is not just of simplification and
making concrete. The context in which these similes occur is
unremittingly figurative and so, cumulatively, the details of
Scottish country experience are involved in a manner of speaking
that presents all experience glinting with spiritual meaning. It
is not that he makes continuous allegory like Bunyan's. His
figures are broken up and heterogeneous. But all the same his
figuration leads us inward into an inner world of spiritual
concern rather than outward into practical and moral actuality.
However concrete, familiar, and even Galwegian, some of Rutherford's imagery, the effect in the end is more of defamiliarising
or spiritualising the everyday than of taking familiar hold of the
spiritual. And there is another way in which Rutherford makes the
familiar otherwordly: he gives his imagery biblical shapes. The

bird dying in the shell is a reminiscence of Job.[10] The children
building sandcastles not only are 'the children of men', but as
the parable has it, build on sand.[11] Like so many of his fellow
divines, Rutherford is immensely skilled in discovering or hinting
at the biblical types of spiritual reality disguised in the world
he lived in. And even the freshest of his imagery may be informed
by the Bible.

Let me give one further, more elaborate, yet surely enchanting,
example of this sort of thing, taken from the 'Epistle Dedicatory'
to The Tryal and Triumph of Faith.

> Christ now interceding for us at the right hand of God, is
> these sixteen hundred years the great Apple Tree, dropping
> down Apples of Life for there hath been harvest ever since
> Christ's Ascension to Heaven ... all that falleth from the
> Tree, leaves, apples, shadows, smell, blosomes, are but
> pieces of Grace fallen down from him who is the fulnesse of
> all and hath filled all things: We shall never be blessed
> perfectly till we all sit in immediate Union under the Apple
> Tree.[12]

Here again is a country image, the apple tree. This is demater-
ialised in an interesting way. It casts solid things, like leaves
and apples. But by a pun, almost, it casts shadows and smell also,
intangible attenuations of itself. There are less refined ways in
which the apple turns from an earthly to a spiritual tree. It is a
metaphor, not a simile, for Christ. It is identified with Christ:
'Christ ... is the great Apple Tree'; it is not just compared to
him as something different from him. And the identification is
forced as Rutherford develops his conceit so that the apple takes
in un-apple-like parts of Christ. The apple tree is sixteen
hundred years old, it drops apples of life and all the elect can
gather under it. The distortion of the vehicle by the tenor makes
the apple tree unnatural, supernatural. It becomes a world tree,
and the mythical effect is helped by the standard Christian
typology of the Tree of Life and Christ on the tree redeeming the
elect from the undoing of the other apple tree, the Tree of
Knowledge.

The incongruity in this image, if not exactly muted, at least
does not violently thrust the discontinuity between the natural
and the spiritual order upon us. I turn now to much more bizarre
images where Rutherford does thrust this discontinuity upon us.

> Now see faith to be faith indeed, if ye can make your grave
> betwixt Christ's feet, and say, 'Though He should slay me, I
> will trust in Him. His believed love shall be my winding-sheet
> and all my grave-clothes; I shall roll and sew my soul, my
> slain soul, in the web, His sweet and free love. And let Him
> write upon my grave, 'Here lieth a believing dead man,
> breathing out and making a hole in death's broadside, and the
> breath of faith cometh forth through the hole'. (Letters,
> CCXCV, II, 283).

The incongruity here takes real imaginative flight. But as inspired discourse, it differs from the Ranters' prophetic flights, which at first sight it resembles. It yields to analysis in terms of conventional ideas. As with the Apple Tree figure, incongruity arises partly because the tenor irrupts into the figure, but it is not as simple as that. Roughly, the tenor is that the Christian can survive Christ's anger by believing in Christ's love. Christ's anger is figured in the metaphor of killing: Christ's anger is to the soul as killing is to the body. This metaphor is overdetermined: there are many compelling reasons in the language of Christianity and of love for selecting the figure of death besides the relation of likeness or proportion between anger and killing. But I'll leave it as a simple metaphor and pass on to the metaphor for Christ's love. Rutherford feels compelled at this point to develop his ideas in a conceit or miniature allegory, and so the metaphor of love will be determined, not just by its likeness to love, but by its fitting in with the figure of death that he began with. He has set up a chain governing his choice of metaphor.[13] This explains the incongruity of representing love as a winding sheet. Somewhere in the background are the biblical reminiscences of the believer dying to himself and putting on Christ through faith.[14] And somewhere in the foreground are suggestions of being tightly embraced and wound about by the love of Christ. And these reminiscences and suggestions help to ease the incongruity into place. But still the metaphor is strained and, typically, Rutherford's expressive power depends on strains such as this. Here, however, it is not that the tenor has intruded on the figure, as with the incongruous Apple Tree. It is the demands of the figure or vehicle that cause the distortion. Death needs a winding sheet, so let the winding sheet stand for love, however far-fetched.

With the second incongruity in the conceit, though, it is the tenor that distorts the figure. The incongruous figure is of the man breathing in the grave, 'making a hole in death's broadside', whatever that may mean.[15] This extraordinary image is brought about because Rutherford wants a figure for surviving Christ's anger through faith in the love of Christ. He has started off by finding a figure for anger in death. Having begun with a figure of extinction, he can only find a figure for continuing by a reversal of his original figure with the paradox of living in the grave. Under the pressure of the tenor, like the Apple Tree, this grave resembles no other grave. Again there are biblical reminiscences easing the incongruity. There was the man who walked among the tombs, taken by Rutherford elsewhere as a type of the believer who had gone down into the deep of what he calls soul-desertion,[16] and there is the psalmist who is counted with them that go down into the pit; 'Thou hast laid me in the lowest pit, in darkness, in the deeps. Thy wrath lieth hard upon me' (Psalm. 88:6-7). But again we are first of all conscious of the strain and reversal of expectation in the image.

One sort of incongruity has particularly distressed Rutherford's readers. Notoriously his otherwordly longings express themselves in erotic imagery: 'That the Gospel-tongue of the Physician Christ should lick the rotten blood of the soules wound, speaketh more than imaginable free-love' (Christ Dying, p 38).

Other passages involve startling anomalies of gender:

> I dare swear, there is a mystery in Christ which I never saw;
> a mystery of love. Oh, if he would lay by the lap of the
> covering that is over it, and let my greening soul see it! I
> would break down the door, and be in upon Him, to get a
> wombful of love. (Letters, CLX,I,369).

This sort of thing would have sounded more conventional in Rutherford's time than it does now. Erotic devotion flourished, not just
among the poets and saints of the Counter-Reformation, but also
among left-wing Protestants. Rous, for example, an English Puritan
with the Song of Solomon very much in mind, wrote a treatise, The
Mysticall Marriage, about the believer as lover and wife of God,
and discussed many of Rutherford's favourite love themes.[17] But
Rutherford's treatment is more indecorous than most. Unlike Rous's
rather measured exposition, Rutherford's exclamations and short
sentences convey the immediacy of his desires. And instead of
writing about women mystics, as Crashaw did, or personifying his
soul as a woman, Rutherford presents himself as a woman possessed
of a womb and of violent love-sickness. He recommends to his women
correspondents, by the way, the same role and the same desires,
adding to one of them that 'each of us hath a whore ... beside our
Husband Christ' (Letters, CXCII, II,12). His spiritualised love is
curiously indifferent to gender. In other places he pictures
Christ as a mother rather than a husband. Talking of the joys
Christ infuses in the redeemed, he asks, 'Who knoweth what the
eternal milkings, the everlasting intellectuall suckings, of the
glorified ones are?' (Christ Dying, p 351). Again talking of how
Christ weans the believer to a more active faith, he remarks, 'We
love always to have the pap put in our mouth' (Letters, CLXXXI,
I,439).[18] Mother imagery, like his sexual imagery, expresses a
desire for a unitive knowledge of God or for his immediate
presence. And probably in a world where women were inferior, the
main point of becoming a woman in relation to Christ was to insist
on one's unworthiness and also on one's duty to accept God's
harshness in the spirit of the patient Griselda: 'faith will teach
you to kiss a striking Lord' (Letters, XXV, I,15). But though
change of gender can go in different ways and is not significant
for itself, Rutherford, nevertheless, exploits its incongruity as
he exploits the incongruity of violent sensuality directed at a
spiritual being, for its expressive effect. To this, a correct
response would go something like, 'Blasphemous, no, not blasphemous', and the exertion of contradicting would thrust us from
the profane into the sacred. The next age would not allow that
separation of levels and the line of Pitcairne's Assembly, The
Scotch Presbyterian Eloquence and 'Holy Willie's Prayer' reduces
the heavenly-mindedness of Rutherford and his followers to
'spiritualised bawdry'. In this there is some shrewdness, but for
the moment I am trying to enter into the spirit of Rutherford's
imagery.

Rutherford delights in incongrous imagery as if in turning the
ordinary world upside down it was a manifestation of the spirit:

> A mortified Saint drawne up to heaven from the earth, is an
> odd person ...; the world and the Towne he lives in may be
> well without him; as Joseph was the odde ladde separated from
> his brethren ... The world is crucified to Paul, for it looks
> like a hanged man, it smells like a dead corps to a Saints
> sences. (Christ Dying, p 497).

Paradox is the stuff of religious symbolism and it is the stuff of
Rutherford's enthusiastic style:

> Dissention smelleth more of Heaven then of any other thing; it
> is the disease that follows the Royall seed. (Christ Dying, p
> 54).

> What heaven can there be liker to hell, than to lust and green
> and dwine and fall a swoon for Christ's love and to want it.
> (Letters, CCXXVI, 11,95).

> A soul bleeding to death, till Christ were sent for, and cried
> for in haste to come and stem the blood, and close up the hole
> in the wound with His own hand and balm, were a good disease,
> when many are dying of a whole heart ... God send me such a
> hell as Christ hath promised to make a heaven of. (Letters,
> CCIII, II, 38).

With paradoxes such as these, we have to do, not just with
incongruity, but with an entire affective reversal: hell is
heaven, disease is health. They don't just mark off the way of the
spirit from the way of the world. They aim to change one's mind,
wretchedness into hope, grief into consolation. Rutherford has an
extensive repertoire of such transformation imagery, for it is
particularly apt to his master theme: soul-desertion is the way to
heaven, God's anger is the mask of his love, the sour cross is the
perfumed cross and so on. But I will say more later about this
Rutherfordian negative way and about how his paradoxes work.
    The transformation of evil into good is a standard operation of
Christian symbolism. Rutherford, however, has a characteristic
trick of his own for transcending experience. He will offer a
figure for a spiritual idea, then say it is inadequate and enlarge
it enormously, only to say that it is still inadequate and so go
on piling up figures with a sort of pious Faustianism striving
beyond himself towards infinity.

> Suppose omnipotencie would inlarge the globe of the world, and
> the heaven of heavens, and cause it to swell to the quantity
> and number of millions of millions of worlds, and make it so
> huge and capacious a vessell, and fill it with so many millions
> of elect Men and Angels, and then fill them, and all this wide
> circle with love; it would no more come neere to take in
> Christs lovely beauty, then a spoon can contain all the Seas.
> (Christ Dying, p 300).[19]

Then, on the other hand, instead of expanding toward infinity he
can shrink toward 'Mother-nothing' - 'God alone goeth between the

mightiest <u>Angel</u> in Heaven and <u>Nothing</u>' (<u>Christ Dying</u>, p 13).

> Imagine that for one Spring and Summer-Season, that [sic] all
> the light, heat, motion, vigour, influence of Life, should
> retire into the body of the Sunne, and remain there, what
> darkness, deadness, whithering should be upon flowres, herbs,
> trees, mountains, valleys, beasts, birds, and all things
> living and moving on the earth? Then what wonder, that
> <u>Christs</u> Soule was extremely troubled, his blessed Sunne was
> now downe, his Spring and Summer gone; his Father a forsaking
> <u>God</u> was a new world to him. (<u>Christ Dying</u>, p 22).[20]

This remarkable passage abolishes the world of outward appearances
to express an intense feeling of privation and nothingness. Oddly
the expansive passage also works by contradicting the outward
shows of things. These are not enough to express the inexpress-
ible. They are annihilated as Rutherford reaches for the infinite.
In either case, expanding or contracting, the ordinary world is
abolished to convey his spiritual apprehensions. So much for the
ideas at work, but Rutherford also has an explanation for his
expanding and contracting that shows some appreciation of the way
that, in the irrational and incongruous life of the psyche, 'the
frontiers of height and depth border on each other':[21]

> Often the Time of some extreme dissertion and soule trouble
> is when <u>Christ</u> hath been in the soule with a high spring-tide
> of divine manifestations of himselfe ... When Paul hath been
> in the <u>third heaven</u>, on an <u>hyperbole</u>, a great excess of
> revelations. God thinketh then good to exercise him <u>with a</u>
> <u>messenger of Satan</u>. (<u>Christ Dying</u>, p 50)

Rutherford's religious explanation cannot quite disguise his
knowing that a high is followed by a downer,

> as it sometimes chanceth from the might
> Of joy in minds that can no further go
> As high as we have mounted in delight
> In our dejections do we sink as low.[22]

I have said enough about the strangeness of Rutherford's
imagery and how the strangeness is the expressive form of his
spirituality. I want now to look at the quality of that spirituality more inquiringly.

Rutherford's enthusiastic style, especially in the letters,
manages an effect of spontaneity. Its short sentences and
unelaborate syntax avoid the appearance of art and the imagery
seems thrown off in inspired confusion by the pressure of what he
has to say. But though spontaneous, Rutherford is not at all
intimate with his correspondents. His experience is all general.
Something important, he tells them, happened to him in Aberdeen.
He had thought that Christian life was easy and delightful but
found that its reality was the experience of desertion. He makes
this theme through repetition and figurative intensity his own,
but he never describes any specific experiences. He never mentions

anything like Bunyan's neurotic fear that the steeple would fall
on top of him.[23]   Instead he writes that 'we' 'can hardly endure
to set our paper face to one of Christ's storms, and to go to
heaven with wet feet, and pain, and sorrow. We love to carry a
heaven to heaven with us, and would have two summers in one year,
and no less than two heavens' (Letters, LXXXI, I,205). Though the
metaphors are struck off with an effect of immediacy, they
generalise his experience and express it as an idea rather than as
the story of himself. His metaphors are frequently visionary, but
if he had any visions or hallucinations, as Bunyan and the Ranters
did, he does not tell us about them. The style of his letters is
like the style of his preaching. The only specific thing he does
tell us about his confinement in Aberdeen is how being forbidden
to preach afflicts him as God's absence; he feels the Word is
imprisoned also.[24]   The letters are a way in which he can write
himself out of this absence. They are rhetorical performances that
produce, or at least reproduce, spiritual experience and give him
an immediate sense of divine presence or inspiration. They do so,
not merely by the immediacy of their imagery, but by the grammatical forms of exclaiming, commanding, undertaking; even his
allowings and lettings of God to be God are a sort of passive
performing on his part.[25]

If his relation to himself is rhetorical, his relation to
others is equally so. He does not speak to his correspondents as a
man speaking to men - or to women. In The Assembly it is assumed
that Scotch Presbyterian erotic eloquence is a disguised language
of seduction. But there is nothing so personal as that in
Rutherford's letters to the women he counselled spiritually. He
usually signs off his letters 'Yours in Christ' and that points to
how he can meet the people he is addressing on the ground only of
inspired soul-concerns. As a consequence his humanity seems rather
undeveloped. His letters of condolence have been much praised. He
lost a wife and eight out of his nine children. The subject must
have touched him nearly. But the letter he wrote his fellow
minister David Dickson on the death of his son is beautiful or
sublime rather than feeling.[26] And he never gets beyond the self-
centred calculations so typical of seventeenth-century Calvinism.
The disasters that befall others are really God's dealing with
oneself. To Mrs Hume, who had lost her husband, he writes 'I know
it is not for nothing ... that ye have lost one in earth. There
hath been too little of your heart in heaven, and therefore the
jealousy of Christ hath done this. ... Your sympathising brother,
S R' (Letters, CCXII, II, 322-3). No doubt poor Mrs Hume, who had
lost her husband, was grateful to be taken so seriously, but it
still seems to me that Rutherford's ideas here are ethically
impoverished.

Rutherford talks of being cut off from other people: 'Our life
is hidden with Christ in God. ... Every Saint is a mystery to
another Saint, and that is the cause that our love to one another
is so cold' (Christ Dying, p 191). He did, however, link up with
others, not just through the exchange of spiritual bulletins, but
through his hopes for the spiritual community. He shared with his
correspondents, not only his private hopes for the consummation of
his desire for God, but his public ones that what the Kirk was

going through would lead up to a grand apocalyptic marriage with
the Lamb. Here strikingly he sees his individual life in the image
of the life of the church. And so the eroticism, which at first
sight looks like an exuberant expression of subjectivity, conforms
rather closely to the designs of high Presbyterian politics. That
again goes with the generalising of individual experience that
Rutherford's rhetoric effects.

The best illustration of how Rutherford's rhetorical spirituality generalises and fits into an orthodox pattern is his treatment
of soul-desertion where he is most extravagantly and intensely
himself:

> Death is death, as clothed with apprehension of terror; no
> man is wretched actu secundo, within and without, but hee
> that beleeveth himselfe to be so: here are terrors, selfe-
> terrors. Jeremiah could prophesie no harder thing against
> Pashur; The Lord hath not called thy name Pashur but Magor
> missabib (Jer.20.3). Thou shalt be a terror to thyselfe.
> Compare this with other paines; Job would rather chuse
> strangling, or the dark grave; and the grave to nature is a
> sad, a black and dreadful house; but a beleever may get
> beyond the grave. What doe the glorified spirits fear a grave
> now; or are they afraid of a coffin, and a winding sheet, or
> of a lodging with the wormes and corruption? or is burning
> quick a terror to them? No, not any of these can run after or
> over-take them; and they know that. But selfe-terrors are a
> hell carried about with the man in his bosome, hee cannot
> runne from them. O! hee lieth down, and hell beddeth with
> him; he sleepeth and hell and he dream together: he riseth
> and hell goeth to the fields with him; he goes to his garden,
> there is hell. ... The man goes to his table, O! hee dare not
> eat, hee hath no right to the creature: to eat is sin, and
> hell; so hell is in every dish: To live is sinne, hee would
> faine chuse strangling; every act of breathing is sin and
> hell. Hee goes to a Church, there is a dog as great as a
> mountaine before his eye. (Christ Dying, p 41)

Put that passage alongside one from Bunyan's Grace Abounding on
the same theme:

> And now was I both a burden and a terror to myself, nor did I
> ever know, as now, what it was to be weary of my life, and
> yet to be afraid to die. Oh, how gladly now would I have been
> anybody but myself! Anything but a man! and in any condition
> but mine own! for there was nothing did pass more frequently
> over my mind, than that it was impossible for me to be
> forgiven my transgression, and to be saved from the wrath to
> come. (Grace Abounding, p 46).

It fairly stands out that Bunyan's account, though also general,
nevertheless seems to say 'I was there', whereas Rutherford's
tries to produce self-terrors in the reader through rhetorical
energy. The brilliance of the performance makes it hard perhaps to
take it quite seriously. It is clear, too, that what is individual

with Rutherford is not the idea but the treatment of it. Indeed the theme of soul-desertion, of which self-terrors are a compartment, belongs to the main line of Reformation divinity. Luther had said that 'Christ suffered damnation and desertion more than all the saints.'[28] And the theme surfaces with English Puritanism, for example, in Rous's treatment of Christ's withdrawal from his lover,[29] and with dreadful intensity in Bunyan.

It seems odd that Rutherford, who believed himself numbered among the elect, should insist so emphatically on soul-desertion as one of the trials of the Christian life. If being saved means believing one is saved, then the elect should be radiantly confident that God was with them and regard self-terrors as a pretty bad sign. Such were the views of the Antinomians, who took the idea of election to what looks like a logical conclusion: because the elect were filled with the immediate presence of God, they could not doubt their election, nor could they do any wrong. But Rutherford wrote against those ideas as blasphemy. He and all the Scottish Reformation divines followed Calvin in thinking that election was one thing and sanctification another.[30] No one could become an absolute saint on earth. Sanctification was a process completed only in heaven, where 'there is a general assembly of immediately illuminated Divines round about the throne, who study, lecture, preach, and praise Christ night and day' (Christ Dying, 'To the Reader', n.p.). On earth even the divines of the General Assembly do not enjoy beatific vision or immediate illuminations, and lecturing and preaching have to stop at night. Against the Antinomians' idea of regeneration now, Rutherford maintained that regeneration was incomplete on earth, and against their conviction of being immediately illuminated he insisted that a Christian life took the way of the cross, that a believer typically imitated Christ in his suffering and being deserted by God. In the letters it is clear that he experienced God's presence chiefly as his absence, but this personal stress in his spiritual life, not only conforms to orthodox Calvinism, but asserts itself against Antinomian nonconformity.

It is striking that seventeenth-century Scottish divines are not deeply troubled whether they are of the elect. They do not write conversion narratives, autobiographies of the crises that forced them to their conviction of grace.[31] If anything, they write sanctification narratives. At any rate their anxieties are all about whether the work of sanctification is going on. The conviction of being saved, so far from putting an end to anxiety is only its beginning. Self-terrors are for Rutherford, not the despair of those who fear themselves lost, but the anguish of those who believe themselves among the elect. He maintains that 'What peeces of hell or broken chips of wrath are set upon the soules of the deserted Saints, are honied and dipped in heaven' (Christ Dying, p 39). It is hard, however, to think what sweetness can be found in the self-terrors he describes. I discussed earlier how paradox in Rutherford's imagery transforms experience from evil to good. But it seems to me equally true that it makes experience ambiguous. If it can make a heaven of hell, it can make a hell of heaven. It is an imagery that goes with a constant state of anxiety. For Rutherford, as for Herbert, a good state of mind is a 'sonlie-commotion', a violent oscillation in which God is constantly 'Killing and quickening, bringing down to Hell/And up to Heaven in an houre'.[32]

The Antinomians' view that the elect were entirely regenerate delivered them from this sort of agitation. In its extreme manifestations, Antinomianism led to libertine and pantheistic beliefs that the elect were filled with God in all their doings. The most shocking doings were the holiest, the basest the highest. Abiezer Coppe, for instance, went around England preaching and acting an orgiastic Christianity:

> And then (behold I shew you a mystery, and put forth a riddle to you) by base things, base things so called have been confounded also and thereby have I been confounded into eternall Majesty, unspeakable glory, my life, my self. ... And then again, by wanton kisses, kissing hath been confounded; and eternall kisses, have been made the fiery chariots, to mount me swiftly to the bosom of him whom my soul loves (his excellent Majesty, the King of glory). Where I have been, where I have been, where I have been, hug'd, imbrac't, and kist with the kisses of his mouth, whose loves are better than wine, and have been utterly overcome therewith, beyond expression, beyond admiration. ... Yea, could you imagine that the quintessence of all visible beauty should be extracted and made up into one huge beauty, it would appear to be meer deformity to that beauty, which through BASE things I have been lifted up into.[33]

At first this sounds very like Rutherford's 'odious ecstacies', except that where his ecstasies were all in the head, Coppe was transported to heaven by bodily intercourse. But Coppe's rhetoric also works differently from Rutherford's. The poles of heaven and hell in Rutherford's paradoxes stay apart. One can turn into the other, but the two never collapse into each other. They exchange places. In Coppe, however, the opposites do coincide. The base is the high, the carnal the spiritual. There is no distressing oscillation between extremes, but a promiscuous oneness of all things.

Coppe had not only liberated himself from the tyranny of polar distinctions. He had liberated himself from social laws. He is an extreme example of how religious and political radicalism went together in the English revolution. In Scotland, by contrast, the Covenant never escaped tight social and political control by landowners and clergy. In England, far less wild men than Coppe drew radical conclusions from the Calvinist doctrine of election. The elect were set free from the law in such a way that they had practical visions of a new heaven and a new earth. But in Scotland, orthodox Calvinism was the rule. The elect were set free from the law, certainly, and good behaviour wouldn't help you. But the doctrine of incomplete sanctification reintroduced the demand for good behaviour in a devious way. Only the elect were in the process of becoming sanctified, so only those who showed signs of saintliness could think of themselves as elect. And with that the condition of debt and anxiety, which the doctrine of election cancelled, was brought back again, with all those spiritual commotions that Rutherford gives such lively expression to. I hesitate to suggest that the doctrine was a means of social control, but it is noticeable that an English revolutionary, even a non-Antinomian one, like Milton, might put forward an idea of individual anarchic energies all working together in an encompassing irregular symmetry, whereas even an extreme Scots Covenanter, like Rutherford, stayed within exacting patterns of Presbyterian conformity.[34]

Among the Scottish writers of the seventeenth century, Rutherford stands out as an original. Even in the wider field of British literature in an age of remarkable eccentrics Rutherford makes his mark. He has a genuinely exotic inner flora and expressive gifts to match. Yet all this exuberance conforms to a rigid orthodoxy. His bizarre hyperboles are ways of making old doctrines intensely present, not of finding expression for new ones. The incongruities he delights in as manifestations of the spirit yield, in spite of their visionary effects, to the sort of analysis I attempted of vehicle and tenor. Like the heterogeneous ideas yoked together by violence of Donne's and Herbert's conceits, which yield to the same sort of analysis, Rutherford's incongruities make received ideas new, whereas the actual visions and prophetic discourse of the Ranters either attempt to convey new ideas or to break the mould of old ones with irrationality. Rutherford's eccentricities are perhaps an odd variant of the kind that arise from extreme conventionality.

Notes

1   The Letters of Samuel Rutherford, Andrew A Bonar (ed) (Edinburgh, 1891), LXVII, 1, 173.
2   Prison: e.g. CLXII, 1,379; chains: e.g. CLXXV, I, 411.
3   'To the Reader', Christ Dying and Drawing Sinners to Himself (London, 1647), A2v.
4   Lord Seaforth in Robert Baillie's Letters and Journals, D Laing (ed) (Edinburgh: Bannatyne Club, 1841–2), 1, 252.
5   In Christ Dying and A Survey of the Spirituall Antichrist (London, 1648).
6   Hans H Meier, 'Love, Law and Lucre: Imagery in Rutherford's Letters', Historical and Editorial Studies in Medieaval and Early Modern English, M-J Arn et al. (eds) (Groningen, 1985), p 93, notes Rutherford's successors. Rutherford's figurative style should be distinguished from the methodical expansion of a biblical figure by heads such as can be found in James Row's 'Red Shankes' Sermon (1638) or Andrew Cant's 'A Sermon Preached after the Renovation of the National Covenant' (1638).
7   In addition to the Letters, Bonar edited Quaint Sermons of Samuel Rutherford (London, 1885). Robert Gilmour wrote a sort of biography, Samuel Rutherford; A Study Biographical and Somewhat Critical in the History of the Scottish Covenant (Edinburgh, 1904). W J Mathams, the florilegist of Rubies

from Rutherford (Edinburgh, 1906), was a minister in the Church of Scotland, unlike Bonar and Gilmour, who were Free Church of Scotland ministers.

8   John Hepburn Millar, Scottish Prose of the Seventeenth and Eighteenth Centuries (Glasgow, 1912), p 51.

9   Millar, p 51.

10 'The ostrich which layeth her eggs in the earth ... And forgetteth that the foot may crush them', Job 39:13f.

11 Matthew, 7:26.

12 The Tryal and Triumph of Faith (London, 1645), n.p.

13 The figuration here could be more elaborately analysed in terms of syntagmatic chains, paradigmatic relations between them and the disruption of syntagmatic chains for expressive reasons. A model here could be found in Claude Levi-Strauss's analysis of Mr Wemmick's castle (Great Expectations) in The Savage Mind (Chicago, 1962), p 150. But I am concerned here to show how Rutherford's incongruity yields to simple tools for decoding: vehicle and tenor easily supply a 'rational' sense. By contrast the figuration of Ranter discourse requires more resourceful, and possibly elaborate structuralist, decoding.

14 E.g. Romans, 13:14; Galatians, 3:27.

15 'In at the broadside' in Letters, LXXXI, 1, 205, means 'suddenly' but that sheds no light on the present instance. The first edition of the letters, Joshua Redividus (Rotterdam, 1664), gives 'broad side', which is equally baffling.

16 Mark, 5:12. See also Christ Dying, p.68, where Jonah is taken as a type of Christ and the believer in the deep.

17 Francis Rous, The Mysticall Marriage, or Experimental Discoveries of the Heavenly Marriage betweene a Soule and her Saviour (London, 1635).

18 Catherine Walker Bynum has studied examples of maternal imagery in medieval devotional writing in Jesus as Mother: Studies in the Spirituality of the High Middle Ages (Berkeley, 1982), see esp. pp 138ff.

19 Cf. John Carey, John Donne (London, 1981), pp 125-30.

20 Cf. Donne, 'Nocturnal on St Lucie's Day' and 'An Anatomy of the World'. Perhaps Rutherford had read Donne. 'The foure angles of this clay-globe' (Christ Dying, p 195), sounds like 'the round earth's imagined corners'. He borrowed Bacon's image of the silkworm spinning webs out of itself for vain learning (Christ Dying, p 181). Though he had a head stuffed with surprising images of his own, he probably appreciated them in others. I suspect the development of his enthusiastic style in Christ Dying was stimulated by reading the English wits while he was in London.

21 Jonathan Swift, A Tale of a Tub (London, 1909), p 101.

22 Wordsworth, 'Resolution and Independence', Poetical Works, Thomas Hutchinson and Rev Ernest de Selincourt (eds) (London 1936), p 155.

23 John Bunyan, Grace Abounding to the Chief of Sinners (London, 1976), p 15.

24 See Letters, CLXIII, 1,379 (cf. XCIC, 1,254) and CLXVII, 1,393.

25 Note for example the passage quoted earlier from Letters, CCXCV, 2, 283, about making one's grave between Christ's feet.

26 Letters, CCXCVIII, II, 292.
27 E.g. Letters, CLXXXII, 1,443; CCXCV, II,283.
28 Luther, Lectures on Romans, trans Jacob O Preuss, Luther's Works, vol 25 (St Louis, 1972), p 382; see also Alister McGrath, Luther's Theology of the Cross (Oxford, 1985), pp 148ff. For Calvin on the way of the cross, see Institutes of the Christian Religion, trans Henry Reynolds (London, 1949) Bk 3, ch 8:1-2, vol II, 16-18.
29 Rous, ch 5, 'The Spouse's Estate in Desertions', pp 95ff; cf. Walter Craddoch, 'An Exposition of Ephesians, 3:20', Divine Drops Distill'd (London, 1650), pp 217-18.
30 There is a good summary of Calvin's views on sanctification in Francois Wendel, Calvin: The Origins and Development of his Religious Thought, trans Philip Mairet (London, 1963), pp 242ff.
31 The stress in English and New English puritanism on the conversion narrative will be connected with adult admission to the gathered churches of the Independents, the Scottish santification narrative with a devout life inside a national church into which one was admitted through infant baptism. See Patricia Caldwell, The Puritan Narrative: The Beginnings of American Expression (Cambridge, 1938) pp 45-58.
32 Christ Dying, p 23; Herbert, 'The Flower'.
33 Abiezer Coppe, A Fiery Flying Roll (London, 1649), in A Collection of Ranter Writings from the Seventeenth Century, ed Nigel Smith (London, 1938), pp 108-9.
34 See Milton on the order of heaven as a pattern for the order of the church in The Reason of Church Government, Yale Prose, 1,725, and also his parable of the house built of irregular stones in Areopagitica, Yale Prose, 2,55.

Chapter 26

MONTGOMERIE'S LANGUAGE

David J Parkinson

It is not yet time for a thorough, authoritative study of the
language of Alexander Montgomerie, foremost Scots poet of the
1580s. The canon of Montgomerie's work is uncertain, and the text
of those poems most securely associated with his name (notably The
Cherrie and the Slae and the Flyting with Hume of Polwart) is
riddled with complex, unresolved problems. Still, using the tools
to hand, one may begin to get some sense of Montgomerie's skill as
a user and maker of Scots.[1]

   As even a cursory view may show, range of diction is one of
Montgomerie's strengths, especially considering the energy and
diversity of his colloquial expressions. Montgomerie really hits
his stride when his topic allows him to draw almost simultaneously
upon his rich resources of colloquial and polite terms. Often, he
is the earliest Scots writer to use a particular colloquial expression; indeed, he would seem to have coined several expressions
which subsequently passed into common speech. His ranging through
various levels of diction is matched on occasion by his extraordinary heaping-up of jargon. When the occasion calls for it,
Montgomerie can utter a profusion of specialised terms: disease-
names, nautical, astronomical, or occult terms, even words and
phrases from French, Dutch or Gaelic - and he tends to do so with
precision. In short, Montgomerie's poetry shows him renovating a
number of closely-related, crucial features of Middle Scots poetic
style: passages of assertive reliance upon the colloquial; local
exploitation of all manner of specialised topics of language; and
rapid, easy transition between sharply contrasted levels of
diction.[2]

   To be sure, Montgomerie's Scots versions of lyrics by Marot and
Ronsard and his familiarity with the work of Elizabethans such as
Watson and Constable show that he worked to make a place for Scots
poetry in the mainstream of contemporary poetic fashion.[3] He did
not, however, abandon the native tradition of making as a consequence. When European fashion and Scots tradition take equal hold
of his attention, Montgomerie achieves an extraordinary range and
flexibility of diction. He is, among other things, the last Scots
poet to have something of the opportunity, the ambition, and the
inventiveness to write Dunbar's kinds of verse.

   That is not to suggest that an easy parallel can be made
between the setting in which Dunbar wrote his poetry, and that in
whch Montgomerie worked. At the court of James VI in the early
1580s, insecurity and poverty had reached quite striking levels,

even for a Scottish court: victimised by the nobility, railed against by the Kirk, chronically short of necessities, let alone luxuries, this would hardly seem on the face of it to have been a court where poetry would flourish. But poetry did flourish there: with his own literary aspirations and with the limits set on his larger ambitions, the young James offered poets a degree of critical interest possibly greater than that of any of his predecessors – certainly greater than the Kirk or most of the Scottish nobility would have bestowed on them at that time.

The pursuit of poetry at the court of James VI may seem a hothouse oddity, too selfconscious and fragile to have lasting value. But that selfconsciousness can be valuable for us now: James's poets often disclosed circumstances and details of their courtly pastime; and from these disclosures we can begin to understand how that pastime had grown out of affinities in earlier Middle Scots verse. It becomes possible to claim that court poetry during the first decade of James's majority sustains a traditionally Scots interest in low styles and subjects.[4]

Montgomerie's many-levelled, often vigorously colloquial diction reflects the perennial Scots interest in common language. Townish and uplandish sorts of talk, continually generating new terms and idioms in the language of courtly poetry, remained fertile ground through the sixteenth century, while the Chaucerian jargon of the higher style in Middle Scots verse became exhausted. Apart from well-polished – perhaps fossilised – polite topics such as the 'pleasant place' opening (as in Hume of Polwart's Promine or Montgomerie's Cherrie and the Slae), the courtly mode has to be imported anew from England and the Continent. And just as the poetic interest in colloquialism has not waned, so the rougher, hardier qualities associated with such terms have kept their vigour: themes of conflict and expulsion, racy narrative, bustling, noisty description, and aggressive, debasing language – all these now thrive in Montgomerie's poetry as much as ever before.[5] In fact, it is in these areas that Montgomerie works with greatest confidence as Dunbar's successor.

In Montgomerie's most variegated work, the conjunction of traditional and fashionable can be traced through various large and small patterns; but the case for his intertwining of tradition and innovation can be made most concisely by looking at particular items in his vocabulary. Strikingly often, Montgomerie is the earliest writer to use a certain word or idiom: items like the borrowing fanfare (for which the earliest English usage is dated 1676; DOST, s.v. Fanphar, and OED, s.v. Fanfare), the learned coinage retrospicien, the abusive participle dridland (cf. SND, s.v. driddle, v., n.2 (2) 'To urinate in small quantities ... Also used of animals: to stop frequently and eject small quantities of dung') and the idiom to get a blind demonstrate Montgomerie's readiness to move into the margins of established Scots vocabulary, his keen ear for the varieties of terms and idioms current in Scots.

Each of my next three items from Montgomerie's lexicon is cited in one or another of the great historical dictionaries as the earliest example of the word being used in Scots; and each of these items goes on to thrive as a colloquial or even dialectal feature of the language:

1   GEES: Ill guyding genders mony gees (Sonet xxv.9)
        DOST, s.v. Gee: fit of pettishness.

2   DORTY: right dortie to come ouir the dur (Sonnet lxv.12)
        DOST, s.v. Dortye [cf. Dorts: sulks, ill humour]:
        unwilling? (cf. Douglas, Eneados III.v.86 for dortynes)

3   HINK: Houbeit mishap be in my harte a hink (Misc. Poem
      xl.47)
        OED, s.v. Hink, sb.1: Faltering, hestitation, misgiving
        [cf Hink, v.: earliest citation is Henryson, 'Reasoning
        of Age and Youth', 62] DOST, s.v. Hink, n. (from 14c
        Icel. and Faer. hinkr) [Montgomerie's line is earliest
        citation].

All three words have to do with stubbornness and hesitation.
Etymology is uncertain in the first two instances, guessed-at in
the last one. This last item, hink, undergoes some change in
meaning in Montgomerie's usage, from concrete to figurative: the
verb form (as used by Henryson) meant literally 'to limp or
stagger'. Figuration is a universal feature of semantic extension,
and Montgomerie uses it recurrently.
    Here, for instance, are some items referring to games of
various kinds; each term has been given some figurative extension
of meaning:

1   PLAYMEAR: A plane playmear for vanitie devysit (Sonnet
      lxx.12)
        OED, s.v. Play, sb. IV.17 (attrib. and Comb.): play-mare
        (Sc.)=HOBBY-HORSE (cites only Scott, The Abbot xiv):
        [the costume and performer in morris dance and mumming].

2   BARLACHEIS: Then Barlacheis or Barlachois advyse (Misc.
      Poem xxxii.64)
        DOST, s.v. Barlacheis, -chois: cf. barlafummill
        [Christis Kirk xvi], barlabreikis, and barley [all
        calls for truce or 'time out' in games]⁶

3 NEVIE NEVIE NAK: ... nevie nevie nak
        A pretty play, whilk children often wse,
        Quhair tentles bairnis may to their tinsall tak
        The neiv with na thing, and the full refuse.
                        (Misc. Poem xxxii. 65-68)
        DOST, s v Nevie-nevie-nak [this passage is earliest
        citation]; cf. Ferguson, Proverbs 1096 ('Nevie nevie
        nak quhilk hand wil you tak').

The second and third of these items occur in a passage concerned
with choice and chance, in the lyric 'The Poet Reasons with his
Maistres'. Montgomerie has used these colloquial Scots terms —
terms which many Scottish children would know, now as then — into
something of a Petrarchan conceit; the passage as a whole may be
an ornament of persuasive rhetoric, but it also involves some
rather homely allusions.

Also in this group of play-terms is the rare item playmear,
used here as an abusive name, much the way Shakespeare uses its
synonym hobby-horse in Love's Labour's Lost (III. i 28-30).
Montgomerie's usage antedates by centuries the next recorded usage
of playmear; but nevertheless, he does seem to be extending the
meaning of a current name for a particular role in folk drama.
Note that the term occurs in a passage redolent of the stage: in
the line cited appears the participle devysyt, applied especially
to the preparation of a performance; and of course vanitie was a
common term in Kirk attacks upon such performances.

Clearly, Montgomerie was an inventive finder of abusive names.
The next four items would all seem to have been strongly colloquial, but none of them is especially common in the richest
source of abusive colloquialisms, the Burgh and Kirk records of
proceedings against flyters:

1 BIRD: Baxters bird (Sonnet xxiv.1)
   DOST, s.v. Bird, n. 1: ... 2. A young animal; a person
   regarded as offspring or progeny [a common abusive
   pattern, as in 'son of a ...'; cf. DOST, s.v. Get, n.
   for similar abusive function] (cf. Sempill, Satirical
   Poems xxv. 29; also 'carlis birdis' in a 1542 entry to
   The Elgin Burgh Records, I.72)

2 BLUITER: bluiter beggar (Sonnet xxiv.1)
   DOST, s.v. Bluter, adj. (cf. 'blutter cairlin', 1583
   entry to Lanark Burgh Records, 89; also sb. usage in
   Montgomerie's Sonnet lxx.10: 'A bluiter buskit lyk a
   belly blind')
   OED, s.v. Bluter, adj.: 'Dirty' [cites Robin Hood play,
   c.1550: 'any bluter base beggar']

3 SKYBELL: skurvie skybell (Sonnet xxiv.11)
   OED, s.v. Skybald, Sc. and north. dial.: low, rascally,
   contemptible, lean, worn-out, worthless (1572 John
   Knox, History of the Reformation in Scotland, II.11;
   1580 entry in Extra Burgh Records of Glasgow, I.77)
   [The -ald suffix is a regular feature in abusive terms]

4 NIRLEND: (Flyting 479 [Tullibardine MS])
   DOST, s.v. Nirlend: dwarf, crumb, shrivelled object
   SND, s.v. Nirl, n.: 3. puny person, dwarf ... v. 1 : To
   shrink, shrivel, contract, to stunt in growth,; ppl.
   adj. n(j)irlin, nurlin[7]

Only the last of these items comes from Montgomerie's parts of his
Flyting with Patrick Hume of Polwart (a poem which, for all its
textual problems, I have found impossible to leave entirely out of
discussion here); the others all appear in a virulent sonnet
against the poet's lawyer. Like Montgomerie's own Flyting, that
sonnet also contains a number of reminiscences of that poetic
monument of abuse The Flyting of Dunbar and Kennedie ('barkit
hyde','poysond vp', 'brybour baird that mekle baill hes breud'),
as well as the learned term retrospicien (mentioned above), which

(according to the OED) seems derived from the Vulgate Latin phrase respiciens retro (Luke ix. 62). Abuse is indeed a many-levelled thing for Montgomerie: together with strongly alliterated colloquial phrases, there appear no less emphatic items drawn from earlier poetry, as well as contemporary religious controversy.

This mixing of kinds of terms conforms to the poetic decorum James VI prescribed for invective in his 'Schort Treatise' on Scots poetry: here are the seeking out and fresh compounding of 'corruptit and vplandis wordis', as well as the 'Running' of 'the maist pairt of your lyne ... vpon a letter'.[8] But one device James recommended for invective, the headlong effect of 'cuttit schort' words, occurs with surprising rareness in the text of Montgomerie's poems; perhaps reduced forms were to be supplied ad lib. during recitation, if the kind of verse being read allowed for it. Montgomerie may use contracted forms on occasion in order to complete rhymes, but rarely outside the Flyting does he admit them:[9]

1 POW ('poll'); HOW ('hole'); STAW (stole); AW ('own' or 'owns'): (Flyting 66, 67, 70)

2 I'SE: 'I'se fell the', 'I'se gar the stink' (Flyting 105, 111)

3 SCROWIS OBSCUIR: (Flyting 106)

In the first of these examples, the apocopes may contribute to the raciness of style, but they also serve to complete patterns of internal and double rhyme in the stanza where they occur. In the second example, however, Montgomerie moves closer to James's notions about 'cuttit schort' forms: these idioms simply enhance the colloquial sound of the passage. That could not be said as confidently of the last reduced form to be considered (3): this item is quite literary, having been used by Kennedie in his Flyting with Dunbar (26), in reference to poetic texts. Montgomerie stresses the literariness of the reduced term by appending a rather formal-sounding adjective.

While reduced forms occur in isolated patches in Montgomerie's text, other idioms of common speech are more pervasive. Although his turns of phrase are by no means without literary precedent in the next examples, here he demonstrates his fine ear for colloquial idiom:

1 GOD NOR: 'in hemp, God nor ȝe hing!' (Sonnet lxv.7)
cf. Lindsay, Testament of the Papyngo 1165 (god nor I rax in ane raipe'); Sempill, Satirical Poems xxii.50 ('God nor the gleddis ȝe get')[10]

2 PLAY A SPRING: 'Experience will play ȝou sik a spring Sonnet xxii.7)
cf. Sempill, Satirical Poems xxxviii.21

3 CLEIK AWAY: 'ȝe come to cleik away my King' (Sonnet xxii.2)
cf Lindsay, Satire of the Three Estates 2733; DOST s.v. Cleik, v.2: To snatch ... away

4 LEN A LIFT: (Sonnet xviii.13)
   DOST, s.v. Len, Lend, v ... 4d: to len(d) a lift (also
   a put) (to) a person or a thing, to lift or push or
   help in lifting, etc.; freq. fig.: to help out of
   difficulties (Montgomerie's line is earliest citation).

In this aspect of verse style, Lindsay and Sempill are Montgomerie's teachers. The first of these items is especially characteristic of the colloquial voice in their poems. The remaining three
items may have less poetic currency, but they do show once more
the figurative use of colloquial expressions: each of these
remarks expresses abstract social behaviours in terms of clear,
simple physical gesture and action. In each case, the idiom
signals a (usually sudden) coarsening of expression, often to
indicate a heightening of feeling, a flash of contempt or impatience. In Sonnet Twenty-two (another sonnet against lawyers),
the pacing of such idioms makes for a crescendo of aggressive
statement.
   By now, the outlines of Montgomerie's particular skill with
colloquial Scots may be emerging. What deserves closer attention
are his apparent innovations in the form and function of colloquial terms, innovations perhaps to be related to the 'corruptit'
words which (according to James VI) were especially characteristic
of invective:

1 COPPING: copping courts (Sonnet xxvi.2)
   DOST, s.v. Copping: [exclusive to Montgomerie?] High,
   exalted (cf. COP, Coppit)
   OED, s.v. Copped, 4a: 'Stuck up" conceited, proud
   (cites Urquhart's Rabelais II.11); 4b: Saucy, peevish,
   crabbed (cites Montgomerie, Misc. Poem x.23; James VI,
   Daemonologie 120)

2 GLORIFLUIKIMS: (Misc. Poem ii.26)
   DOST, s.v. Glorifluikims, n.pl. [Fanciful from glory?]
   unique[11]

3 JUMPE: Jumpe not with justice (Sonnet vii.11); jumpe
   not in a jote (Sonnet xxi.7)
   DOST, s.v. Jump(e), v.1: To trifle or shuffle; to
   practise trickery or dishonesty [exclusively
   Montgomerie's word?]; cf. Gimm and Jimm

4 DE ... FAMES: Deserve not de (before ʒour Lordships) fames
   (Sonnet xx.13)

5 BRYRIE: My tongue is lyk the lyons: vhair it liks,
         It brings the flesh lyk bryrie fra the banes
         (Sonnet lxii.11-12)
   OED, s.v. Briery: a place overgrown with briers (cf.
   DOST, s.v. Brery and MED, s.v. Breri, both of which
   also feature in place-names)
   SND, s.v. Breerie, 2.n: Collectively for briers.

In Montgomerie's lexicon, the epitome of such 'corruption' must be the fanciful compound <u>glorifluikims</u>; and the rhetorical breaking of <u>defames</u> (4) shows the poet's manipulation of language reaching an opposite extreme. The third item in this list is less gaudy but more problematic than these: the poet's use of <u>jump</u> may have originated in a misapprehension of the word <u>jimm</u>, but the misapprehension need not have been due to the poet alone. Here as often elsewhere, Montgomerie may simply have echoed a form current in common speech; and yet his usage turns out to be the first or even the only one extant. Thus he may use words unique in Middle Scots but fairly well attested in later Scots dialects (e.g. <u>kytrell</u> (<u>kite</u> plus the diminutive suffix <u>-rel</u> [<u>Flyting</u> 480]) and <u>bumbie</u> ('bumblebee', i.e. 'drone, idler'[<u>Flyting</u> 99]; cf. the commoner form <u>bombart</u>, as well as Montgomerie's more extravagant <u>bumbill-batie</u> [<u>Flyting</u> (Tullibardine MS) 779]).

Montgomerie's language still has more than its share of blurs, but the evidence grows clear enough to suggest that he pursued Henryson's, Dunbar's, and Douglas's great goal of having 'language at large' – and, consequently, of enlarging the language. Like his predecessors (in the Middle Scots tradition and behind that, in the English alliterative tradition), he gives vent when the context allows it to a profusion of topically specialised terms, often finishing with the sort of comic disavowal of any expertise in the specialty just displayed at which Henryson and Douglas excelled. The relatively early performance-pieces <u>The Navigatioun</u> and <u>The Flyting</u> are especially marked by exuberant displays of this sort. In the Tullibardine MS text of <u>The Flyting</u>, for instance, there occurs a four-stanza catalogue of 100 names of diseases, some afflecting humans, others horses or dogs; a great many of these terms having already appeared in Sir John Rowll's <u>Cursing</u>, Montgomerie simply augments a topic already well-stocked in Middle Scots verse. A more confined (and hence more manageable) list of jargon occurs in <u>The Navigatioun</u>:

1 <u>FRAUGHTIT</u> (90)
   <u>DOST</u>, s.v. <u>Fraucht</u>, v.2 To load (a vessel) with cargo

2 <u>TAUNTIT TO THE HUINS</u> (93)
   <u>DOST</u>, s.v. <u>Hune</u>, <u>Huin</u>, n. [F. <u>hune</u>] A hound: a projection at the mast-head serving as a support for the trestle-trees (<u>OED</u> records English usages as early as c.1000)[12]

3 <u>SHAIK OUT THE BLIND</u> (97)
   <u>DOST</u>, s.v. <u>Blind</u>, <u>Blynd</u>, n.[1] [Du. <u>blind</u>, G. <u>blinde</u>]: A spritsail (used thus by William Stewart and Robert Sempill); apparently unrecorded in English[13]

4 <u>OUR BONNETS</u> (98)
   <u>DOST</u>, s.v. <u>Bonet</u>, <u>Bonat</u>, n.2: An additional piece laced to a sail (1494, 1496 Lord High Treasurer's Accounts; Douglas)

5 <u>OUR MISSENS</u> (98)

DOST, s.v. Missen, a: a mizzen-sail (Complaint of Scotland) 41/17; this line from Montgomerie)

6 TO THE GUEIT FATTIS FOR TO BEDEU THE SAILLS (99)
DOST, s.v. Gueitt fat [Flem. geute, a splash or shower of water]: a cask containing water for wetting the sails [Montgomerie only]

7 OUR TAIKLE DRAUIS AND HAILLIS (100)
DOST, s.v. Hale, Hail(1), v. To draw or pull; to drag or haul (freq. in nautical use)

8 ROUM BETUENE TUA SHEITS (102)

As befits this verbal flourish, Montgomerie ends the passage with the disclaimer that 'We passingers went to the chesse to play; / For in that airt we nothing vnderstude' (106-7). For all his very conventional protestations, though, Montgomerie is striving to outdo his poetic forbears in their own catalogues of jargon: his stock of terms must be seen to be the greatest yet; he must demonstrate unprecedented control over his lexical riches.

Montgomerie demonstrates a strong sense of Scots poetic tradition; he seeks to make a prominent place for his own verse within that tradition. He has not lost an awareness of the importance of alliterative style, for instance. In his comic scenes, he plays in the manner of the Bannatyne MS grotesqueries with conventional tags of alliterative verse: thus in the 'Second Invective' of the Flyting, he describes the 'goode nichtbouris' of his witches' Sabbath all 'hovand on hicht' - remaining stationary while mounted on their peculiar steeds (273). The phrase recurs in Scots epic and history: in Barbour, Wyntoun, Douglas, and William Stewart, however, the ones usually 'hovand on hicht' are knights awaiting the charge into battle.

Montgomerie does not always use alliterative phrases with burlesque effect, nor does he merely transcribe phrases common in the older poets. Alliterative phrases of various kinds permeate his work; indeed, his styles are no less pervasively alliterative than those of Henryson or Dunbar. Nevertheless there are times when he hunts the letter without holding to the traditional diction or syntax of such poetry, and then the result can be as lame and garish as any of the more decadent, over-ornamented lines in Tottel's Miscellany (e.g. 'Come, troup of tuinis, about his temple tuyn / ʒour laurell leivis with palmis perfytly plet' [Sonnet viii 9-10]). The poet had more than one stylistic model; some of his models have worn better than others. A Tudor depth of prosodic incompetence in one poem is readily countered with one masterful passage among many in other poems:[14]

> Quhen with a quhisk sho quhirlis about hir quheill,
> Rude is that rattill running with a reill,
> Quhill top ouer taill goes honest men atains.
> Then spurgald sporters they begin to speill;

> The cadger clims, neu cleikit from the creill;
> And ladds vploips to lordships all thair lains:
> Doun goes the bravest, brecking al their banis.
> Sho works hir will; God wot if it be weill.
> Sho stottis at strais, syn stumbillis not at stanis.
> (Misc. Poem iii 28-36)

This stanza moves from variation and amplification of conventional images, to a pair of aphorisms which appear to be no less conventional. Fortune sets off 'with a whisk' – a phrase Barbour, Henryson, and the writer of King Hart all use to signal a rapid transition, a sudden change in fortune. As she did in the alliterative romance Morte Arthure (3261), Fortune whirls her wheel; and as it does in Robert Sempill's 'Premonitioun', this wheel whirls 'with a reel'. Still, in the second line quoted, as often elsewhere, Montgomerie has been far more interested than his predecessors in making imitative harmony. But to move on: with their prominent verbs, participles, and prepositions of strong motion, the satiric lines on the climbers (4-6) sustain the high momentum of the opening straight on to the forceful Doun of the third-last line. The sententious balance of the last two lines sounds traditional, although I have not found evidence that these sentences are not Montgomerie's invention; certainly the phrase 'all thair lains' is a colloquial feature uniquely prominent in this poet's writings. In sum, Montgomerie has confidently assumed the voice of popular wisdom, and has made statements both original and traditional. Give this Scots poet a topic with a still-vigorous native tradition, and the seam between tradition and invention will be hard to trace in his resulting work.

There is one such topic which recurs throughout Montgomerie's poems, and which never fails to stir the poet's energy and inventiveness. This topic, which remains imperfectly described for Middle Scots verse in general, has to do with a narrative scene referred to as 'the mobbing'.[15] As a complete scene, mobbing has these elements: first, a vainglorious outsider intrudes upon a community and shows disrespect to (or simply disregards) its laws and authorities – or at least is accused of doing so; then, acting on behalf of the community (or just claiming to do so), an assailant literally or figuratively 'plucks' the intruder of 'borrowed feathers', attributes the intruder has often pilfered from or been awarded by the chief personage in the community; the intruder is then befouled with soot, mud, boot-black, or some even more unpleasantly staining substance, and is expelled from the presence of the authority. This pattern (which may perhaps have some relevance to tragic figures such as Henryson's Cresseid, as well as various personages in Dunbar's comic verse or Lindsay's satires) also seems to take particular appositeness when Scots poets apply it to themselves or even to the poems they write. The imagery and language of mobbing is common to flyting, and also to the mock modesty of epilogues and envoys.

To look no further than the plucking part, the reader finds Montgomerie well accustomed to drawing on the mobbing scene for his flyting and invectives. In the sonnet 'To his Aduersars Lauyers' mentioned earlier, he assures his opponents that

Experience 'sall pluk ȝour pennis' (Fortune plucks Troy in Chaucer's Troilus and Criseyde, 5. 1541-47); and elsewhere, without saying that he will do it himself, Montgomerie threatens Polwart that his 'pen salbe plukkit' (Flyting 80). This threatening reference to the other poet's quill draws the notion of 'borrowed feathers' into Montgomerie's larger accusation that Polwart has cooked up left-over portions of Chaucer and Lindsay.

In this rough sort of joking, the befouling part of the mobbing becomes especially prominent. Retorting to Polwart's insults (in the Flyting again), Montgomerie announces that 'I dow not induir to be dobbit with ane duik' ('I'll not put up with being muddied with - or by - a duck' [104]), alluding to the duckpond downfall of an earlier high flier, Dunbar's naughty prelate John Damian. And in turn, Montgomerie envisions Polwart being 'Draiglit throw dirtie dubbis and dykis' (381).

The dirt associated with this befouling process does not always have to come from duckponds, or even barnyards. It is more often, and more suggestively, the outcome of having too close proximity to dirty work in town, especially the work of cooks, colliers, smiths and cobblers. Indeed, the implication is often made (in poems by Dunbar, Lindsay, and James VI as well as Montgomerie himself) that some aspirants to poetry and other high matters merely parody truly noble persons, and come off looking more like menials. The earliest victim of a mobbing in Middle Scots verse, the Rook-Bard of Sir Richard Holland's Buke of the Howlat, emerges 'lyke a smaik smorit in a smedy' (825); the birds of Dunbar's so-called 'Fenȝeit Freir' mistake the soaring abbot (his head sooty from the 'smowking of the smydy' [51,56]) for Mars's blacksmith or Saturn's cook (67-68); and so Montgomerie envisions Polwart 'smeirit our with sute' (Flyting 285).

The topic can be more genially comical than this, however: in The Cherrie and the Slae, for instance, Montgomerie depicts himself (in the person of the dreamer) being plucked of 'borrowit pennis' (184). Having been lent Cupid's wings and bow, the dreamer 'As Icarus with borrowit flycht' (144) becomes over-confident with his lendings, and crashes to earth after accidentally shooting himself. Propriety is restored when Cupid 'spulȝeit me of my geir' (205). Now Cupid does not bring about the befouling of the dreamer, or at least he does not do so in any obvious or concrete way. Watching the god depart, the dizzy dreamer's eyes grow dim and 'ewerie thing appeirit twa / to my barbulȝeit brane' (216-17). The verb barbulȝe has to do with actual staining or smearing, by extension with less substantial kinds of mess and confusion. The Scottish printer Henry Charteris talks about the earliest prints of Lindsay's poems being 'schamefullie blottit and barbulȝeit'.[16]

This business of getting mucked up can be applied more specifically to poetic thoughts and works, however. In a complaining sonnet addressed to musician and fellow court-poet Robert Hudson, Montgomerie complains about the poor ale and bread in the country by calling them 'barme and blaidry' which 'buists up all my bees' (Sonnet xxv.8). 'Blaidry' is garbage, which 'dirties up' his poetic invention, his 'bees' (a term used in various later Scots dialects to refer to fanciful ideas). And in another sonnet, Montgomerie excuses himself from having written a scurrilous invective by declaring that 'I refuse sik filthie these or theam, / Houbeit at hame mair vncouthnes we wse' (lxiv.12; note the occurrence of the rare word these, paired with its synonym theam). Dirty 'themes' are specifically rustic themes: here re-emerges the notion about the rustic corruption of poetic style which interested James VI in his essays on poetry. Poems on ignoble subjects may be called dirty; with their low language, they make a grubby comparison to the pure style of more conventionally courtly poems. Thus Montgomerie uses a suggestive figure of modesty to compliment James on his Uranie: 'thy cunning maks the knoune; / Ours helps not thyn: we stein3e bot our aune [i.e., in praising yours]' (Sonnet xiii.1, 13-14). And by extension, Montgomerie (following Marot) refers to the eloquent expression of mean ideas as 'fairdit' ('painted') language (Misc. Poem xlvii.83).

Montgomerie has good Scots precedent for imagining thoughts and poems to be stained. Finishing the envoy to his Testament of the Papyngo, Lindsay forbids his poems to associate with other books or with nobility or royalty, and passes this judgement on it:

> With coit vnclene, clame kynrent to sum cuke:
> Steil in ane nuke, quhen thay lyste on the luke,
> For smell of smuke men wyll abhor to beir the;
> Heir I mansweir the; quhairfor, to lurke go leir the
> (1181-85)

By Montgomerie's time, however, this jocular notion would seem to have assumed a larger, more complex part in the whole persona of the poet and the game that poet was expected to participate in at the court of James VI. Language of the smithy, already seen as a common element in the befouling phase of the mobbing scene, now becomes central to the notion of making poetry at court. In the country, Montgomerie longs to see the 'sillie smiddy smeik' of poetic activity at court (Sonnet xxv.2); in another sonnet, Christan Lyndsay says on Montgomerie's behalf that the 'smoky smiths' themselves – Robert Hudson and the other court poets, that is – do not care about Montgomerie's plight excluded from court (Sonnet xxx.13); and James himself, in his Admonition of the high-flying Montgomerie (hiding once more in humiliation), remarks that in his absence, 'elfegett Polward helpes the smitthie smuike' (14); and speaking from his rustic exile, Montgomerie refers to a particularly close hit of insult with a suggestive blacksmith's idiom when he wonders whether he has 'shod' his victim 'strait, or on a vane' (Sonnet lxvii.15).

Given the vigour of Montgomerie's language, the smithy game seems the ideal ground for this poet to prove his pre-eminence at James's court (where the place of honour was still the chimney nook); but this vigour would become liable to censure as the court's taste for pastime changed. The language and the game may have had a way of isolating and rebounding upon their most energetic and gifted user. The very range and liberty of Montgomerie's language – what might have been seen as its increasingly dangerous instability – would hardly have proved an advantage for the longer race of flattery and propaganda in which James's poets were ultimately to win or lose.

Notes

1 Following is a select list of materials for the study of
   Montgomerie's language: James Cranstoun (ed), The Poems of
   Alexander Montgomerie, Scottish Text Society, 1st series, 9-11
   (1885-87); Rudolf Brotanek, Untersuchungen (Vienna, 1898);
   George Stevenson (ed), Poems of Alexander Montgomerie:
   Supplementary Volume, STS, 1st series, 59 (1910); [DOST] A
   Dictionary of the Older Scottish Tongue from the Twelfth
   Century to the End of the Seventeenth, William A Craigie, A J
   Aitken et al. (eds) (Chicago and Aberdeen, 1931-); [SND] The
   Scottish National Dictionary, William Grant and David D
   Murison (eds) (Edinburgh, 1931-760; [OED] The Oxford English
   Dictionary [corrected re-issue of A New English Dictionary on
   Historical Principles], J H Murray et al. (eds) (Oxford,
   1933); [MED] Middle English Dictionary, Hans Kurath, Sherman M
   Kuhn et al. (eds) (Ann Arbor, Michigan, 1952-).
2 A J Aitken, 'The Language of Older Scots Poetry', Scotland and
   the Lowland Tongue: Studies in the Language and Literature of
   Lowland Scotland in Honour of David D Murison, J Derrick
   McClure (ed) (Aberdeen, 1983), 46-47.
3 L Borland, 'Montgomerie and the French Poets of the Early
   Sixteenth Century', Modern Philology, 11 (1913-14) 127-34;
   George Stevenson, 'New Sources of Montgomerie's Poetry',
   [Appendix C of Supplementary Volume; R D S Jack, Alexander
   Montgomerie (Edinburgh, 1985), 41-45.
4 Helena Mennie Shire, Song, Dance, and Poetry of the Court of
   Scotland under King James VI (Cambridge, 1969), 88.
5 A J Aitken, 'Variation and Variety in Written Middle Scots',
   Edinburgh Studies in English and Scots, A J Aitken, Angus
   McIntosh, and Hermann Palsson (eds) (London, 1971), 176, 196.
6 Iona and Peter Opie, The Lore and Language of Schoolchildren
   (Oxford, 1959), 146-50.
7 Priscilla Bawcutt and Felicity Riddy, Longer Scottish Poems,
   Volume One: 1375-1650 (Edinburgh, 1987), 411.
8 The Poems of James VI of Scotland, James Craigie (ed), Vol I,
   STS, 3rd series, 22 (1955), p 75.
9 A J Aitken, 'Language', 44.
10 R D S Jack, Montgomerie, 61.
11 A J Aitken, 'Variation and Variety', 175-77.
12 Bertil Sandahl, Middle English Sea Terms II. Masts, Spars, and
   Sails, Essays and Studies on English Language and Literature,
   S B Liljgren (ed), 20 (Upsala, 1958), 46-47.
13 Sandahl, Sea Terms, 116-17.
14 C S Lewis, English Literature in the Sixteenth Century
   Excluding Drama, The Oxford History of English Literature,
   Bonamy Dobree and Norman David (eds), vol 3 (Oxford 1954),
   pp 109-10.
15 David J Parkinson, 'Mobbing Scenes in Middle Scots Verse',
   Journal of English and Germanic Philology, 99 (1986), 494-509.
16 The Works of Sir David Lindsay, Douglas Hamer (ed), vol 1,
   STS, 3rd series, 1 (1931), p 402.

Chapter 27

DUNGEONS AND LARDERS: THE ROMANCES OF PATRICK GORDON

Michael R G Spiller

The most enthusiastic supporters of Scottish literature would be hard put to it to name the great Scots Renaissance epic, or indeed any Scots Renaissance epic: I suppose the credit for achievement, if not for merit, would go to Sir William Alexander, whose epic poem Doomsday, or the Great Day of the Lords Judgment, runs to ten thousand impeccably rhymed and mortally dull lines. It is probably true to say that a successful epic has to be driven, or powered, by some kind of national fervour, as in Spenser and Milton; though not necessarily a progressive nationalism, for it usually combines with nostalgia the desire to celebrate a heroic past of ideal purity just at the point where modern life is making it impossible: this might be said of Virgil, of Spenser, of Milton, of Tasso, even of Dante - though Dante did not regard himself as an epic writer. The Scots seem not to have grasped that nostalgic moment, at the end of the sixteenth and the beginning of the seventeenth centuries: such literary talents as were among them then were rapidly trying to adjust to the poetic voices of the south.

It is probably futile to speculate why literary works of a given kind were not written when they might have been, but in thinking about the non-existent Scots Renaissance epic we do have a straw in the wind from a young Scotsman who at least made an attempt, Patrick Gordon, who in 1615 published two works at Dort. One was a Spenserian fragment called The First Book of the Famous Historye of Penardo and Laissa, otherways callid the Warres of Love and Ambitione; the other was an attempt at a Scots epic, The Famous Historie of the Renouned and Valiant Prince Robert surnamed the Bruce.

I shall be mainly concerned with the second one, but I want to say a little about Penardo and Laissa, which seems to me to deserve a lot more attention than it has received.

Part of the difficulty attending Penardo and Laissa is that it is almost unobtainable, and perhaps has been so since the eighteenth century. It was never reprinted, and there seems to be only one copy in Britain, in the British Library (apart from a fragment in Cambridge). The Huntingdon and Folger Libraries have one copy each, and it is by courtesy of the Huntingdon Library, a microfilm of whose copy is now in the Bodleian Library, that I have myself been able to read it. It seems doubtful whether those previous historians of Scottish literature who mention Penardo and Laissa were able to find a copy. From a nationalistic perspective, the work is less interesting than the _Bruce_, but narratively more competent and imaginatively superior. It is a dungeons-and-dragons fantasy, based on the paradigm or type of the stainless knight and the warrior maid with whom he falls in love, made famous by Tasso's story of Tancred and Clorinda, to which it owes a great deal. The plot - or plotting, since the narrative is multiple - is apparently Gordon's invention, following Sidney's creation of Arcadia, and is set in 'Achaea', the same kind of medieval and classical never-never land, in which all the apparatus of Greek mythology can be used along with the medieval resources of wizardry and chivalry. In this Middle Earth of Renaissance, we encounter the Transylvanian princess Vodina, the wizard Mansay, the treacherous Olinda, the evil Prince Sigismund, various giants and dwarves, Pallas Athena, the Furies, and even the Nine Muses: these last appear in a unique role, for they discover Laissa abandoned by her cruel father on Mount Helicon, and bring her up to be the wonder of womankind; but then they grow jealous of her beauty and resolve to kill her, enlisting the aid of the Furies - does any other romance heroine have nine wicked foster-mothers? - and from this bizarre action the whole tale develops.

Gordon wrote seventeen very Spenserian chapters, each prefaced by summary verses, of what he called the First Book, amounting to 960 six-line stanzas, and plainly intended to write more: he develops a very complicated multiple plot, and breaks off the narrative with a very Spenserian diversion. Penardo and Laissa have just been reunited after elaborate adventures, when they are interrupted by thirty knights and a coach containing the poem's Duessa, the treacherous Olinda. Penardo is compelled by enchantment to leave Laissa and chase after Olinda, at which point the book ends with three stanzas from an anonymous friend encouraging the author to continue with the project. He didn't, which we must regret: for Patrick Gordon has a decided talent for fantastic landscape: in Caput XI, for example, the imprisonment of Laissa in a cave, upon a Bed of Sleep, alternately scorched by fire and boiled in blood, is only part of a mise-en-scène in a subterranean realm with hidden entrances, moving pillars and mysterious inscriptions, the kind of surreal landscape that has its antecedents in Virgil, and extends from the _Hypnerotomachia_ of Poliphilus through to Spenser and David Lindsay. No explanation is given for the apparatus of this phantasmagoria, except that they are obstacles placed in the way of lovers: a psychoanalytic reading would probably suggest that they are displaced symbols of sexual frustration, a kind of architectural and geological concretion of Petrarchan symbolism. We are certainly taken into the darker realms, in all senses, of the sexual adventure, and I should like to be able to claim Patrick Gordon as a forerunner of David Lindsay and Alasdair Gray as an early master of what I think is a kind of macabre fantasy congenial to, if not distinctive of, the Scottish imagination.

Whether _Penardo and Laissa_ was written before the _Bruce_ is not known: whether it was printed before the other, both at Dort in 1615, might be determined by a close study of type and ornaments. My guess is that it is the later work, being much more competent narratively. About Patrick Gordon himself, it is usually conjectured

that he was the same person as Patrick Gordon of Ruthven (1580–
1650), who in 1650 wrote the prose tract A Short Abridgement of
Britain's Distemper (Spalding Club, 1844). Gordon of Ruthven was a
cousin of William Douglas, eleventh earl of Angus, who is one of
the dedicatees of the Bruce; further, Gordon of Ruthven's father,
Thomas Gordon of Cluny, was a supporter of the earls of Huntly,
and one of the dedicatees of Penardo and Laissa is Lord George
Gordon, son of the sixth earl. The evidence is fair, if not
conclusive, for an identification of the earlier Gordon with the
later. What Gordon of Ruthven was doing in Dort is not known, but
it is clear that the Bruce, at least, was written two years
before, in Scotland, because it carries the imprimatur of the
Archbishop of St Andrews, dated December 1613. Gordon also managed
to obtain commendatory verses for both poems from his friends in
Scotland, which suggests that he had been able to circulate manuscript drafts.

One of the commendatory poems in Penardo and Laissa is a sonnet
from Drummond of Hawthornden, addressed to Laissa herself:

> Thy sire no pickpurse is of others witt:
> Those jewels be his owne which thee adorne –

a little waspish of Drummond, thus to praise Gordon's originality
by quoting an author to whom he was much indebted; but he
continues by consigning him to posterity along with not only
Spenser but also Shakespeare:

> And though thou after greater ones be borne,
> Thou mayst be bold even amidst the first to sitt,
>   For while fair Juliet or the farie quene
>   Do liue, with theirs thy beauties shall be sene.

However, Laissa remains unrevived to this day; it was the Bruce
that James Watson edited and reprinted at Edinburgh in 1718, in
his usual meticulous fashion: he modernised the spelling, but
otherwise reproduced exactly the contents of the 1615 edition, and
if anyone reads the Bruce now, it is likely to be in Watson's
edition (or in what was probably a pirated reprint, by John Hall
at Glasgow in 1753). My quotations are from Watson's edition.

The original 1615 edition of the Bruce, dreadfully typeset upon
very flimsy paper, is yet worth a linguist's attention, because,
as Gordon plaintively says in his Errata to the volume, 'the book
was printed in ane uther cuntrey where the setters did not understand the language,' and as a result, 'their is sindrie errours
escaped, both in the Orthographie and want of single letters.' The
printers appear to have set exactly what was in Gordon's ms., and
we have therefore a reasonably accurate record of early seventeenth century Scottish orthography and punctuation, preserved by
the setters of Dort. The punctuation is bad, to the point of
unintelligibility in places.

Like Penardo and Laissa, the Bruce calls itself a First Book,
and is written in seventeen chapters, in the slightly weightier
eight line stanza, rhyming abababcc. This time it is not so
obvious that the First Book is a first book, because the final

chapter ends with Bannockburn, and it is hard to see that   he   could
have   got   much   more   than one other Book out of Bruce's life after
that. His source   is   Barbour,   from   whom   he   takes   most   of   his
material,   but   it is particularly interesting to note his political
stance in 1615. The poem   contains   a   great   deal   of   flattery   of
various   noble   families,   and particularly of King James and Prince
Charles. Like Shakespeare in Macbeth, he goes   out   of   his   way   to
show   a   line   of   kings;   in   his   Preface,   he   says   that he had
originally inserted   a   history   of   the   kings   of   Scotland   before
Bruce, but

> after   I   had   fully accomplished it with the rest of the book,
> fearing it should be too tedious for the reader   I   have   taken
> it   out   and   in   the   place   thereof   insert   those   princes
> descended of the Bruce ...

ending, as I said, with Prince Charles, of whom   he   prophesies   the
most amazing nonsense: but he goes on:

> neither   would   I   be   offensive for adding of these fragments,
> for I know that sume curious heads   will   alege   that   I   wrong
> the union   ...   neither   do   I   therein wrong the English, but
> rather to my power extol their valour and   with   more   mildness
> modifie   that   which   our   writers   most sharplie have written:
> thereby to extinguish, if   possibill,   the   evil   opinion   that
> hath   bin   so   long engraftid in the hearts of manie by reading
> of these old historeis, hoping yet   that   this   may   haply   mak
> thois   that   treteth of the same matter to be forgotten by time
> ...

Gordon is a historical   revisionist: he   sees   the   peacemaking   of
James   VI   as   something that is affronted by the nationalism of the
old chroniclers, and attempts   to   obliterate   their   work.   He   had
certainly   read   Barbour,   and seems also to have used the Chronicle
of Melrose; but it seems hard to   think   that   he   could   have   read
Barbour   with   much   attention   to   his   attitudes,   because   it   is
Barbour,   not   Gordon,   who mentions the most discreditable military
actions of Bruce, the devastation of Carrick   and   the   harrying   of
Buchan;   though   Barbour   is   certainly very severe on the English
garrisons in the   southwest,   he   is   very   willing   to   praise   the
chivalry   of   the   best   English   knights, such as Ingram de Umphraville and Aymer de Valence. Treachery   for   Barbour   as   for   Gordon
tends to be the prerogative of the lower classes.
   It   has   to   be   said   that   history   made   things   difficult for
Patrick Gordon. The campaigns of Bruce,   Douglas   and   Edward   Bruce
in   the   years   before   Bannockburn   provided   him with a very large
number of small incidents, battles,   skirmishes   and   sieges,   which
become   structurally   very   repetitive. Barbour is a chronicler, not
an epic poet: it is his job to relate as faithfully as he   can   how
each   action   happened,   and   though   he   makes good use of military
exploits, such as the daring capture   of   Linlithgow   Tower   by   the
humble   farmer   and   carter   William Binnock, he is quite content to
mark the advance of Bruce's control over Scotland by   itemising   all
the   successes   of   his   lieutenants, as one fortress after another,

'stuffed all with Englishmen' as Barbour repeatedly says, falls to
Bruce. This is only interesting if it can be done in detail, as
Barbour does, because it is the details that create the variety;
Gordon, writing at much shorter length than Barbour, simply loses
control of this mass of events, and produces an extremely confused
narrative. That said, he shows the Renaissance poet's fondness for
the striking exemplum, and can order actions well enough, aided by
antithesis and epigram, inside a single stanza, as in his terse
handling of the 'Douglas Larder':

> Low in a vault, the Captain first he [Douglas] band,
> And all the other Captives him beside;
> The Grain, the Flour, the Beer and Wine he fand,
> Which they before could ne'er enough provide,.
> With this he fil'd the House wherein they stand.
> Thus chockt with Meat, and drown'd with Drink, they dy'd,
>   Whose greedy Gorges ne'er suffic'd with Ill
>   Now in their Death, might gormandize their fill.
>   (Ch. 7, st. 52)

His earlier chapters are more creative, and show him consciously trying to shift from chronicle into romance. One of the
strong elements in Renaissance romantic epic is, as I said,
nostalgia: the writer tries to recover an ideal past which can be
regarded as the legitimate predecessor of the present, as Virgil
had done in selecting Aeneas as the founder of the Roman state.
One of the epic devices this nostalgia generates is the genealogical vision, in which a character in the epic, usually a wizard or
soothsayer, foresees the future achievements of the descendants of
one of the heroes: the poet may elect to do this himself, if
wizards are not readily available. This of course fits very well
into the aristocratic patronage system under which so much high-
level Renaissance poetry was composed: and Gordon quite shame-
lessly inserts two very long lineages tracing the descent of the
two dedicatees of his poem, the earl of Angus and the earl of
Morton, from the followers of Bruce, introducing an English wizard
for the purpose. The flattery is crude, not so much because of the
genealogy itself as because the wizard is not used in any other
way in the plot: yet, of course Spenser manages only slightly
better in Book III of The Faerie Queene, when Merlin traces the
descent of Queen Elizabeth from Britomart and Artegall. Another
extended example is the long account of the line of Scottish kings
in Chapters Four and Five (IV.st.35 -V.st.34), culminating in
Prince Charles; there is a fourth instance in the run-up to the
battle of Bannockburn, when Gordon takes occasion to foretell the
birth of Lord George Gordon - probably related, as has been said,
to the poet (Chap.XV.st.55-61). We are apt, in our reading of epic
as narrative, to forget how very closely related the epic is in
the Renaissance to praise poetry and epideictic eulogy. The habit
survives even in Milton, whose survey of the descendants of Adam
at the end of Paradise Lost is a developed version of the same
device.

The element of foretelling has another effect. Going back into
the past, historical or legendary, to foretell the future creates

an impression of inevitability: it suggests that the hero is
destined to produce successful issue, biologically or politically;
and if some magical figure is brought in to utter the prophecy, a
kind of cosmological approval is given, which obviates more
pedestrian political analysis. Barbour has no sense of this at
all: when he assesses his characters, it is usually in terms of
some general reflection upon human conduct: for example, at the
incident of the defence of the ford in Glen Trool, when Bruce
singlehandedly slew fifteen English opponents, Barbour launches
into a discussion of the peculiar quality of <u>worship</u>: that is, of
the kind of knightly achievement that makes a man the sort of
leader that others love to follow: this is to explain Bruce's
success not in political terms but in moral and psychological
ones. Gordon's admiration for Bruce leads him to suggest that
Bruce succeeds because he is divinely guaranteed - as Aeneas is
under the special protection of Venus, Bruce is favoured by Jove,
who sends an angel to Thomas the Rhymer (a figure combining
wizardry and Scottishness) to bid him bring comfort to Bruce in
the wilderness:

> Great Prince, quod he, I yield to your Desire,
> Rymour I heght, your Slave and Servant old,
> My Love and my last Duty to discharge
> I hither came, as you shall know at large.
>
> For the appointed Time is drawing near,
> When my poor Soul must leave this ruin'd Tow'r:
> Know then an Angel did to me appear,
> And of these Revelations gave me Pow'r,
> Only for thee, because the Lord doth hear
> The woful Plaints and Groanings ev'ry Hour
> Of thy still tortur'd Land, which Heav'n surmounted,
> And Mercy beg'd, where Mercy never wanted.
>
> That only thou selected for Relief
> By the ONE-TRINE eternal Majesty,
> Cross'd with Misfortune, Sorrow, Pain, and Grief,
> For that vile Slaughter sacrilegiously
> In Jove's sole sacred House; but that Mischief
> Hath thy unfeign'd Repentance freed from thee;
> Should here by me Heav'n's endless Bounty know,
> For to remove thy Cares, and Comfort show.
>   (Book I, Cap.5, st.38-40)

This obviates the problem of explaining Bruce's success in
political terms, and by invoking a Deity at once Christian and
epically decorous - a One-Trine Eternal Majesty who is also Jove -
offers political and military success as the outcome of a scheme
of national sin, repentance and forgiveness, personified in Bruce.
Scotland's sin is faction, which allows Edward of England to
succeed for a time: Bruce personifies this faction in his murder
of the Red Comyn, and then as Scotland repents, and unites behind
Bruce, he personally repents his crime, and divine approval is
then granted via Thomas the Rhymer.

The following stanza then turns to genealogical vision, with rather curious results:

> Persist thou still then in thy just Desire,
> For mighty Jove stands arm'd against thy Foes,
> Now all thy bad Misfortunes shall retire,
> Hence shalt thou ever win and never lose:
> Thou freely shalt possess a free Empire,
> And such Renown, such Fame, and Glory goes
> Of thy great Name, that thou shalt have more Praise
> Than ever had a Prince before thy Days.
>
> Now, quod the Prince, old Father, I would know
> If these great Kings shall beautify my Name,
> No, no, quod he, but from thy Loins shall grow
> One Tree, whose Fruit shall flourish still with Fame,
> And on the Banks of Silver Forth shall show
> Two Branches fair for to adorn that Stream,
> Who turns and bows his crooked Shores about,
> To keep such Heav'n-bless'd Treasure ungotout.
>
> (Ibid., st.41-42)

Gordon's own footnote - a device he used frequently to explain historical particularities which epic decorum excluded from the poetic text - adds that 'King Robert had a base son that was Earl of Ross, of whom is descended the Two famous Families of Clackmannan and Airth, both sirnamed Bruce.' Strictly, of course, the House of Bruce did not become the royal house of Scotland, and Gordon is correct to have Thomas say that the Kings of Scotland did not 'beautify his Name'; but the Stewarts were nevertheless lineally descended from Bruce, though on the female side, via Marjorie Bruce. Perhaps, in Gordon's family relations, it was at this point important to flatter the Bruces of Airth and Clackmannan.

Another example of the uneasy interface between history and romance is shown in Gordon's treatment of places. Obviously, to the historian the haeccitas of a place is important, and Barbour plots Bruce's campaign by indicating exactly where he went, writing for an audience who would know where Inverurie or Dunstaffnage was. Gordon tends to be circumlocutory: the decorum of high epic writing makes it difficult to mention humble places like Netherford or Glen Trool, and Gordon tends to substitute generalised romantic topography of mountains, valleys, rivers and so on, very often using footnotes to carry the historical specifics. The problem of how to romanticise historical reality was not properly solved until Sir Walter Scott; but Gordon makes a good shot at it when he comes across an appropriately epic location like Stirling Castle. Poets who used landscape description a good deal, like Drummond of Hawthornden, developed a special device for blurring the everyday reality of their home ground, which we see Gordon using here. The trick was to mention the name of the place, and then immediately to compare it to a mythological or classical place, and as it were conflate the two. So here with Stirling:

In midst of famous Scotland does there ly
A Valley grac'd with Nature, Art, and Care,
As fertil as the Soil of Araby,
As pleasant as Thessalian Tempe fair,
On which from heav'n no blust'ring Tempests fly,
Nor Zephyre blows but sweet and wholesome Air;
Along whose Side the Ochel Mountains rise,
And lifts their swelling Tops above the Skies.

Down thro' the midst of this fair Valley glides
The christal Forth with glancing Silver hue,
Whose roaring Streams on golden Channel slides
With Murmur sweet in Thetis Bosom-blue,
Of Brooks supply'd with lib'ral Store besides,
Which Tops of tow'ring Mountains still renew,
Whose Springs the dry insatiate Meads supplies,
And Moisture lends to Herbs, to Fruits, and Trees,

In midst of this fair Valley doth arise
A mighty mounting Rock of wond'rous height,
On whose ambitious Back, as in the Skies,
A City stands, impregnable to Sight;
A Castle on his lofty Crest espies
The Valleys round about, the Mountains height:
Below the Rock the glancing River glides,
In whose cold Streams he cools his hoary Sides .
(Book I, Cap.V, st.13-15)

The topos of the locus amoenus is combined with a romantic exaggeration of heights not unlike that of the landscape painters of the eighteenth and early nineteenth centuries, who commonly make mountains much more mountainous than they are; but apart from the plain untruthfulness of calling the Forth's waters 'roaring' as they pass below Stirling Castle, the topographical sense is well employed.

The effect of this romanticising of the landscape – something quite alien to Barbour – is, in an odd and possibly unintended way, to help Gordon's stated aim of 'modifying that which our writers most sharplie have written': his Scotland is substantially the Scotland of Walter Scott's Lady of the Lake, a land of pastoral beauty and wild and remote savagery, where, though there are no giants or dwarves, there are ladies to be rescued, wolves to be hunted, impregnable castles, treacherous villains, fugitive princes, stratagems and spoils. When history begins to press hard upon him, as it does in the later stages of his book, in the campaigns up to Bannockburn, he is much less happy, and his narrative is confused and tedious: in the wilds of Galloway or the Borders, his heroes move in an almost dreamlike landscape, not very distant from the imaginary world of Penardo and Laissa.

The effect is to make of Scotland what Drummond, for rather different purposes and in a different mode, made of it: the ideal country of the European Renaissance imagination, with the historical specificities consigned, as they often are by Scott, to footnotes, lest their everyday reality break the decorum of the heroic style. His poems are prentice work, despite Drummond's flattering remarks, and have basic faults of narrative technique – he is inclined to forget, for example, whether he is speaking or one of his characters, and he has very little sense of how fast to tell an incident. But I do cherish the hope that someone will produce an edition of his two poems: Scotland is not so rich in Spenserian romance that we can afford completely to forget Patrick Gordon.

Chapter 28

THE CRATHES CEILING INSCRIPTIONS

Henry Hargreaves

The principal purpose of this paper is to make available a basic
text of some material that falls within the purview of students of
medieval and renaissance Scots but which hitherto has been pretty
inaccessible.

Crathes Castle, which the conference visited on 5 August, is
situated in Grampian, fifteen miles to the west of Aberdeen. On
the ceilings of three of its rooms are certain paintings and on
the sides of the beams that support the ceilings are a series of
inscriptions, dated 1599 and 1602. In two of the rooms - the Nine
Nobles room and the Muses room - there is an obvious relationship
between the pictures and the inscriptions; in the third room, the
so-called 'Green Lady's' room, there is no obvious link. Paintings
and inscriptions have been known since 1876, when they were revealed by the removal of lath and plaster which had been covering
them up. What the inscriptions then looked like is demonstrated by
one fragment in the Nine Nobles room which has been left as it
was, but in the nineteenth century there is some mention of 'restoration' and 'repainting'. The text of the inscriptions as it
appeared then was printed by James Allardyce in an Appendix to his
volume on the family of Burnett of Leys,[1] and this is the only
text generally available. It has not been much used; the Dictionary of the Older Scottish Tongue, it seems to me, has missed from
it galȝardine, hydropolie, insegnarie and palȝardine, all unrecorded elsewhere. The inscription from the Nine Nobles room used
to be printed in the old guide book[2] and from there has been
printed by Horst Schroeder;[3] and some few verses, mostly from the
Green Lady's room, are used as chapter-headings in the new guide
book written by Schomberg Scott in 1971.[4] There are hand-boards
available in the castle in each room giving the text. None of
these sources displays quite as much accuracy over details of
spelling and letter-forms as a scholar demands. And if the printed
sources, such as they are, are unreliable, so too is what now
appears on the beams as the prime authority. Apart from the restoration done when the inscriptions were first uncovered, there
was some 'retouching' in 1921 and a complete 'conservation' programme, which involved the complete dismantling of the ceilings,
in 1961, though fortunately the major fire of 1966 did no more
than minor smoke-damage. The old guide book speaks of some of the
nineteenth-century 'new and rather unsympathetic decoration' as
having been 'photographically recorded' but 'removed' during the
conservation. I tried in 1974 to trace any photographs of the

inscriptions that had been taken, but they were not with the National Trust, and my own suspicion is that the inscriptions were then repainted de novo, with probably less care in reproduction than the pictures. I have therefore, in the text that forms an appendix to this paper, taken the liberty of making, within square brackets, a few emendations that seemed to me to be crying out to be made, but for the rest my text is meant to reproduce what is now on the beams. The textual critic, I am sure, will have great fun reconstructing, through two restorations after the natural fading of 300 years, what the original craftsman wrote. What, for example, does he make of the form I claim to have been missed by DOST, hydropolie (B 8 e); is the l to be found in all the printed versions right, or should it be tall s, to give us a more easily recognised form of hydropsy? And in vincult (A5n) too? And by what route does Thais (B 6 e) derive from Quhais, as it surely must?

The first general point I would make about the text is one so obvious that I am almost ashamed to make it; it is the range of language from English to Scots. Pure English are the Bible quotations in the Green Lady's room (B, all the western side of the beams). With only a few differences, these are exact quotations from the Geneva version of the Bible, including the Apocrypha, not much in favour in Geneva. The differences are mostly trivial, such as to for vnto (B 3 w), The for A (B 6 w) and the deceatful for he (B 4 w), but in one or two instances greater (for B 7 w Geneva has 'The Lord will not famishe the soule of the righteous, but he casteth away the substaunce of the wicked'). And as exact quotations they follow English usage exactly - hath, doeth (B 4 w), maketh (B 6 w), delyuereth (B 8 w), turneth (A 1 s). Not all the verses are long enough or well-composed enough to provide the firm evidence in rhyming forms or scansion for English or Scots sources. I suspect that some of the short verses of moral instruction in the Green Lady's room are more likely to be of English origin than Scots; be (B 10 e) as a plural present indicative is not good Scots, but insegnarie 'education' (B 4 e) looks more so; 'fortune's false inconstancie' (B 9 e) rings English. The introductory verses in the Muses room and those on the seven virtues have English forms in maketh (C 1 w) and doth (C 2 w) and present participles in -ing (C 2 w, 3 e, 3 w, 4 e, 5 e, 5 w), the -o-forms in most (C 2 w, 3 e) and onlie (C 4 w), and the rhyme gloir - more (C 3 w); but the rhyme refrain - one (C 2 w) is good only in Scots. The Muses verses proper have one participle in -ing (C 10 e) to set against plesand (C 8 e), and nothing in rhyme to suggest either English or Scots sources, yet somehow they look more Scots; if there has been any assimilation, it has been done thoroughly. The same is true of the Nine Nobles verses, which twice rhyme ring 'reign' with king (A 6 s, 8 s), good only in Scots. But such a linguistic mixture is entirely characteristic of much of the literature that has survived from the turn of sixteenth-seventeenth century in Scotland. We do not know who the craftsman was who first recorded on the beams the words which, by whatever process of transmission, have given us our present text; nor do we know from what exemplar, printed text, manuscript copy - his own or his master's - or oral dictation, that craftsman was working. All we do know is that the text he produced illustrates

well how, even before the Union of the Crowns, despite the pros-
ecution in the capital of a vigorous cultural life in the vernacular, in a provincial setting the process of anglicisation is well
under way.

Perhaps it would be as well to diverge from the text for a
moment to the family, to indicate some of the routes by which
English linguistic features might well, in the Burnett family,
have been finding their way to Crathes. The Alexander Burnett who
finished Crathes, first inhabited in 1588, was the great-grandson
of the man who had started the building; he had five brothers, and
a letter from one of these, Duncan, suggests that his father's
ambition had been that his sons should be men of learning and
culture. Duncan himself was a physician who practised in Norwich.
The other brothers were Robert 'a divine' (though whether in
England or Scotland is not clear; in a later generation a Gilbert
went south to become Bishop of Salisbury), Thomas, who was an MA
of Cambridge and also a physician of eminence in Braintree in
Essex, Gilbert a professor of philosophy at Basle and later at
Montaubon, and the youngest, John, the only one of the five who
was not a learned man, according to Duncan. When discussing the
education of younger sons he cites the interesting proverb 'the
ould laird's father's brother is the pooreste man about the place'
and makes some observations which are not unlike the moral adages
found in the Green Lady's room. He indicates too that he has
recently come home from Germany – German affinities have been
claimed for some of the paintings, the women in particular being
described as 'robust blondes of Teutonic appearance'. For these
reasons Christopher Hussey makes a half-hearted suggestion, in
Country Life for 18 September 1937, that Duncan may have been
involved in the composition. He adds, honestly enough, that there
were dozens of other young men who were perfectly capable of
composing them. And certainly there are enough links with the
south amongst Alexander's brothers to show how English verses and
books other than the Geneva Bible might have come north.

Let me now deal briefly with each room, taking the Green Lady's
room first, where I have already said there is no obvious relationship between the paintings and the inscriptions. The paintings are
principally pairs of human figures, exceptional in Crathes in that
the first and third sets have to be viewed from the south, the
second from the north; some are in sixteenth century British
dress, one pair in what looks like Flemish dress and two pairs in
oriental dress. The inscriptions are moral reflections, those on
the western side of the beams in prose from the Geneva Bible,[5]
those on the eastern side in verse. Hussey claims to see 'a kind
of antiphony' between gloomy proverbs in prose and more optimistic
reflections in verse, citing as his example B 5 w-e; I suppose B
10 w-e might be called into service to reinforce the suggestion.
But 5 w-e, being on opposite sides of the same beam, cannot be
seen simultaneously – cannot indeed be seen successively without a
good deal of moving and neck-craning. Those facing each other
across the gaps do not seem to bear on the same topics; 9 e urging
one not to despise the unfortunate because of possible reprisals
by 'fortune's false inconstancy', does not impinge upon the warning against quarrelsomeness in 10 w, nor 10 e on the necessity of

keeping good company on 11 e and its promise of destruction for robber and liar alike. And in any case the antithetical pattern characteristic of the Hebrew poetry of the book of Proverbs hardly leaves such texts as those on B 6 w, 7 w, 8 w and 9 w as 'gloomy'. I see in some of the verses warnings against some of the deadly sins - B 8 e against avarice, 9 e against pride, 7 e against lust and greed, 3 e also perhaps against greed, but is this not inherent in comment on morals? I see no overall pattern for the group.

In the Muses room there is the greatest correspondence between the paintings and the inscriptions, especially for the Muses themselves. Perhaps it is significant that the staff at Crathes tend to speak amongst themselves not of the Muses room, but of the Music room, and exhibited in it nowadays are specimens of early musical instruments, though nothing of a date comtemporary with the decoration. The association is forced upon us by the fact that no fewer than seven of the nine figures are shown as playing on a musical instrument named in the verse. If you want to know what a monochord looked like, you can see one being played by Polymnia, and a sistrum by Erato. Despite its etymology in <u>mono-</u> 'single' and <u>chord</u> 'string', the instrument shown surely demonstrates the assimilation of the Greek prefix <u>mono-</u> to the Scots <u>monie</u> 'many', since it shows some sixteen strings and keys well beyond a full octave. Erato's <u>seister</u> is in construction identical to Terpsichore's lute, though smaller in size, and so quite unlike the <u>sistrum</u> described in the New Grove:

> A type of rattle. Its shape was roughly that of a stirrup, consisting of a U-form with a straight knuckle protruding from the bottom. The U is traversed by loose-fitting metal rods which jingle upon being shaken. Frequently small loose discs are fitted to these rods to create additional sound.[6]

This concentration on music is the most important feature in the depiction of the Muses at Crathes. Modern classical scholars, of course, when writing about them, spend a long time discussing their origins in Hesiod, who is the first classical author to give their number and names, but tend to be dismissive about later developments: 'The idea that each of them has some one province (e.g. Urania for astronomy) is a pedantry of later grammarians', says a modern account.[7] But of course these 'later grammarians' were the authorities whose identifications and special details were picked up, elaborated and developed by writers of the medieval and renaissance periods. Let me briefly run through what was generally regarded as normal in the depiction and description of the nine, using the order of the Crathes list since there seems to be no generally recognised other one. Clio, history, is given a scroll and a laurel wreath; Thalia, comedy, a comic mask and an ivy wreath; Melpomene, tragedy, a tragic mask and an ivy wreath; Terpsichore, choral song and dance, a lyre; Euterpe, lyric poetry, a double flute; Calliope, epic poetry, a wax tablet and pencil; Erato, erotic poetry, a small lute; Urania, astronomy, a celestial globe, and Polymnia, sacred hymns, is always shown veiled, in an attitude of thought. The Crathes verses do of course maintain adequately the basic patterns, with Clio's 'ancient historiis', Thalia's 'al mirriness' and Melpomene's tragedies. Terpsichore obviously hints at relaxation, Euterpe with 'melodie and plesand sound' at lyric, and Calliope with 'ballet royall' at epic. Erato strongly dissociates her erotic poetry from harlotry, Urania says she is mistress of astronomy, and Polymnia is the only one whose link with a specific type of literature is less clear; what she concentrates on, memory and intelligence, are needed, to our mind, for all. But it is, as I say, their musical instruments that are specially mentioned, and I am not enough of an art-historian to be familiar with the iconography. Hall's <u>Dictionary of Subjects and Symbols in Art</u> gives a list which leaves only Urania without an instrument; he points out that 'their attributes and particularly their musical instruments are liable to change at different periods, though from the seventeenth century onwards the attributes given by Ripa's <u>Iconologia</u> were generally followed'.[8] It was the third, the illustrated, edition of this standard work, issued in 1603, that was so influential.[9] So Crathes, virtually contemporary, is obviously recording an independent development of tradition. For comparison, here is Hall's list, again in the Crathes order: Clio - trumpet; Thalia - small viol, rarely some other instrument; Melpomene - horn; Terpsichore - viol, lyre or other stringed instrument; Euterpe - flute, often a double flute, or a trumpet; Calliope - trumpet; Erato - tambourine, lyre, or more rarely triangle or viol; Urania - none; Polymnia - portative organ, more rarely lute. Well, the portative organ is clearly enough equated with the 'monicordis' and Thalia's fiddle could well be a small viol, but Melpomene's viol is out of step. The whole list provokes a host of questions, but they are questions for historians of art and of music, and none of them am I competent to answer.

The other half of the same ceiling is less well integrated, with some and only some of the principal virtues identifiable in pictures but not as distinctively linked to the verses; there is nothing in these to enable us to identify Justice, Wisdom, Charity and Hope. The modern guide-book suggests that, the seven virtues being insufficient to fill up the spaces available, Honour and Fame are elevated to the rank of virtues, which thereby equal the muses and the nine nobles in number.[10] It may be so, and for Honour I could agree. The verse is cast into the same third person of description as for the other virtues and in all respects seems to parallel closely the seven; but Fame is quite incongruous (C 2 e), being cast into the first person of address and concentrating on details of a visual presentation which is not in fact pictured, the adjacent space being filled with pattern decoration.

But much the most interesting room for most members of this conference will, I am sure, be the Nine Nobles room, where the inscriptions are linked to the pictures in that there are nine named warrior-like figures painted on the ceiling to correspond. King David is shown in regal rather than warrior dress, though Charlemagne and Arthur are not, but apart from a book grasped by David to show his authorship of the Psalms (not a point mentioned in his verse), the figures would seem to be essentially conventional representations; there is nothing to pick out one from another, unless someone has skill enough to point out significant details of armour shape or of heraldry.[11] Certainly there is nothing to link any one hero with his verse - no Goliath's head for David or pile of nineteen crowns for Hector. Our attention must be concentrated on the verses, and these can therefore be treated just as a literary text. And if they are so treated, there is a mass of material in Latin, French, Middle English, Scots and German with which to make comparisons. Most of it has been printed by Gollancz in his edition of The Parlement of the Thre Ages, the text with the longest English account, and by Loomis in Modern Philology for 1917.[12] Schroeder adds more references and some comment, printing the Crathes verses but omitting The Buik of Alexander.[13]

Let me draw attention first to some of the features that are common to the Crathes verses and the tradition, taking as the tradition that established by Jacques de Longuyon about 1312 in Les Voeux de Paon, what Loomis calls 'the very earliest authoritative treatment of the Nine Worthies in literature', and continued for Scotland in The Buik of Alexander, a fairly close translation of this,[14] and The Ballet of the Nine Nobles, stanzas found in two manuscripts of the chronicle of John of Fordoun.[15] Both these date from the mid fifteenth century and so can be taken to represent the Scottish tradition as it existed a century before the inscriptions were written. In this tradition are Hector's nineteen kings, more numerous subordinates and his death, specifically treacherous, at Achilles' hands, Alexander's conquering of the world in twelve years and complaining in Parliament of having insufficient to rule, Caesar's conquest of Greece, Syria and Africa, Joshua's defeat of thirty-one kings and conquest of their lands and the parting of Jordan, David's slaying of Goliath, Judas's slaying of Antiochus, Arthur's conquest of France and Spain, Charlemagne's fight for Christianity and Godfrey's slaying of Soliman and rule over Jerusalem.

Not so prominent in the tradition are Caesar's German exploits and his death at Brutus's hands, David's shepherd origin and wars against the heathen, Judas's death at Demetrius' hands, Charlemagne's Scottish treaty, Arthur's Round Table and Godfrey's conquest of the Holy Land. Some of this material is not difficult to find: David's origin and wars could well come from a very generalised knowledge of the Bible; Arthur's Round Table is such a commonplace that one is merely surprised not to find it brought out more prominently in the Scots tradition - it is on this that The Parlement of the Thre Ages most concentrates. That it was Brutus who killed Caesar could be derived from a very general knowledge of Roman history, but it is not specified in the tradition (though Caesar's own killing of Pompey is); that Demetrius killed Judas Maccabeus is much less general knowledge than the facts about David, though it derives from the Apocrypha - and, taken in conjunction with the other Crathes attention to causes of death, it shows more concern about how the heroes met their ends than other contemporary accounts. These differences from or additions to the tradition are of minor interest but not, I think, as important as the addition for Charlemagne. This constitutes, it will be seen at once, a whole stanza on its own, giving Charlemagne two full stanzas in contrast to the one each for the other eight. And examination of the overall arrangement of the stanzas on the beams reveals other features of interest.

After an introductory stanza (A 2 n) the three pagans have each one stanza on their exploits, presented in the first person (3 s, 3 n, 4 s). This is followed by a versification of Psalm Vulgate 100.8, AV 101.8 on beam 4 n; the wording in AV is 'I will early destroy all the wicked of the land; that I may cut off all wicked doers from the city of the Lord.' This serves as a sort of interlude, separating the pagans from the Jews. Then come the three Old Testament heroes (5 s, 5 n, 6 s), each with one stanza, but now all presented in the third person. One would expect next on 6 n a second interlude, to separate the Jews from the Christians, but instead one finds the additional Charlemagne stanza, with its emphasis on the Auld Alliance, and then the three Christians, with one stanza each presented in the third person (7 s, 7 n, 8 s). The whole is concluded by a sort of <u>envoi</u> on 9 n and s, a short beam. But the replacement of the expected second interlude by the additional Charlemagne stanza leads to an unusual order for the three - Charlemagne, Arthur, Godfrey. In Latin verse it is not unparalleled for a different order to be found, for metrical reasons, and some other aberrations are known, but when the nine occur together, in English at least, they tend to keep their historical or quasi-historical order - Hector, Alexander, Caesar; Joshua, David, Judas; Arthur, Charlemagne, Godfrey.

Perhaps this is the best point at which to stress another abnormality on which I have already touched, the mixture of first person address and third-person presentation. None of the parallels assembled by Gollancz and Loomis shows such a mixture. Loomis points out what is obvious enough, that first person is appropriate for dramatic presentation, as in a mumming play of the time of Edward IV or the Coventry pageant, and perhaps in imitation of these in French, Low German and High German verses on wood-cuts, and others on wall-paintings not unlike ours;[16] the third person is more appropriate for quasi-historical use, as in <u>Les Voeux de Paon</u>, <u>The Buik of Alexander</u> and <u>The Ballet of the Nine Nobles</u>. The unparalleled mixture here suggests that someone started to present the nine as if in a pageant, but then realised that for at least one of the heroes to come the first person would create a difficulty. Such a difficulty, I suggest, is caused by the contents of our extra stanza, especially the last line with its mention of 'this present day'.

For the different ordering of the stanzas Schroeder has a different explanation.[17] He points out that the painter had only six panels on the ceiling and nine figures to accommodate. So he elevates one of each trio to a special pre-eminence, gives him a full panel for his portrait and leaves his two fellows to share one. He thus needs for each pre-eminent hero enough verses to fill two sides of a beam. Schroeder accepts that the first is an exception, met by the use of a stanza of general introduction. He does not recognise the source of A 4 n in the Psalms, specifically in a 'Psalm of David'. This is not appropriate to Joshua, the 'pre-eminent' Jew alongside whom it stands, but to David, who shares the next panel; and in any case, being spoken in the first person, is out of pattern for the Jewish trio. Two of Schroeder's pre-eminent three thus lose their special status, and we are left with the one whose extra stanza is exceptional in its positioning.

It is also exceptional in its structure. While every other stanza, including the second Charlemagne one, touches on at least three points of its hero's prowess, this is confined to a single point, the establishment and maintenance of the Auld Alliance. Moreover, making due allowance for the difference between Scots verse and Latin prose, its words bear a close resemblance to those of the earliest Scottish historians. Those of John of Fordoun (which were not printed till 1871) run, when he is speaking of Achaius, the brother of Gilmer who was one of Charlemagne's peers:

> Amicitia confoederationis inter reges Scotorum et Gallorum et eorum regna, quae nostris adhuc durat diebus illaesa, laudetur Deus, per magnum regem Carolum et hunc Achaium initium habuit.[18]

His words were taken over without alteration in Bower's reworking, the Scotichronicon of just before 1450. Later historians such as Mair (1521), Hector Boece (1526), Leslie (1578) and Buchanan (1582) elaborate various details in the material but with no wording that comes as close to the Scots of Crathes as Fordoun's.

The prominence thus given to the Auld Alliance may well be regarded as illustrating the conventional and for its period natural emphasis on the fundamental basis of Scottish foreign policy before the Union of the Crowns; but in other ways it could be thought rather strange. The version of the Scottish tradition of the nine nobles that is probably closest to the Crathes verses – though there are differences, some of which have been pointed out above – is that of The Ballet of the Nine Nobles, found associated with Fordoun's Chronicle in manuscripts. After nine stanzas, one for each of the nine nobles in their usual order, this adds a tenth:

> Robert the brois throu hard feich[t]yng,
> Wytht few, venkust the mychtthy kyng
> Off ingland, edward, twyse in fycht,
> At occupit his realme but rycht;
> At sumtyme wes set so hard,
> At hat nocht sax till hym toward.[19]

and a conclusion remarkably similar to that at Crathes which I called an envoi:

> ȝe gude men that thir balletis redis
> Deme quha dochtyast was in dedis.

The addition of a tenth, a local noble, is shown by Schroeder to be fairly common throughout Western Europe;[20] in France, it was particularly Bertrand de Guescelin, in England Guy of Warwick or Henry V. In Scotland Bruce is added not only in the Ballet but also in three lines of Latin in a manuscript prepared for and possibly used in Sweetheart Abbey, Kirkcudbrightshire:

Ector Alexander Julius Josua David Machabeus
Arthurus Carolus et postremus Godofrydus
Robertus rex Scotorum denus est in numero meliorum.[21]

Given the importance of Bruce in this religious site in the
south-west of Scotland, one is not surprised to find him elevated
amongst the nine nobles there; but equally, if there is any house
in the north-east where one would have expected to find him similarly celebrated, it is at Crathes, on the wall of which the
modern visitor still sees carefully preserved the hunting horn
which the new guide book claims is connected with authority over
the royal hunting forest at Drum granted to Alexander Burnard by
Robert the Bruce in 1323. Why did the family of Burnett of Leys,
when decorating the ceiling of a room in their own house, neglect
the chance to extol the patron of their ancestors? In 1595
Shakespeare in Love's Labour's Lost parodied the nine nobles in
the same way as he did Pyramus and Thisbe in A Midsummer Night's
Dream;[22] clearly for the sophisticated audiences of London such
material was old hat, worthy stuff for buffoonery. At the same
time, by Burnett of Leys it was taken seriously, but the lesson
drawn was not to enhance purely family prestige, but to make a
point of national political importance.

Notes

1   The Family of Burnett of Leys, from the papers of the late
George Burnett edited by James Allardyce, New Spalding Club
(Aberdeen, 1901), pp 330-8.

2   A Guide to Crathes Castle and its Gardens published by the
National Trust for Scotland (Edinburgh, 4th edn 1963), p 21.

3   Horst Schroeder, Der Topos der Nine Worthies in Literatur und
bildender Kunst (Gottingen, 1971), p 103.

4   Schomberg Scott, Crathes Castle: an Illustrated Account, The
National Trust for Scotland, 1971.

5   References are for the successive beams: Prov. 9,10; Prov.
3,28 and 33; Prov. 26,25; Prov. 26,16; Prov. 10,4; Prov.
10,3; Prov. 10,2; Prov. 10,1; Ecclesiasticus 22,24;
Ecclesiasticus 20,25; Prov. 13,22; Prov. 16,5.

6   New Grove Dictionary of Music and Musicians, Vol 17, p 354.

7   Chambers' Encyclopedia New and revd edn, 1966, Vol 9 p 599.

8   James Hall, Dictionary of Subjects and Symbols in Art
(London, 1974), p 217.

9   Cesare Ripa, Iconologia, 3rd edn (Rome, 1603) pp 346ff.

10   Crathes Castle p 36.

11   The arms attributed to the nine nobles are of course without
authenticity, since all except Godfrey predated the period in
which conventional heraldry originated, but they are nevertheless widely represented in early blazonry. The fullest
list, extending to some 109 records, is in Schroeder Der
Topos der Nine Worthies (see n3), pp 261-99. Since Schroeder
apparently had access only to the earlier guide-book, he

includes for Crathes only the three whose monochrome photographs appear in that. To complete his list, the arms on the Crathes ceiling are: for Hector, per pale argent and sable, two lions combattant counterchanged; Alexander, gules, a lion (apparently) sejant or, holding a Lochaber axe; Caesar, or, a double-headed eagle displayed sable; Joshua, lozengy gules and argent, a basilisk sable; Judas Maccabeus, argent two ravens sable; David, azure a harp argent; Charlemagne, per pale; dexter, or, half a (doubled-headed?) eagle displayed, sable; sinister, azure, three fleurs-de-lys or; Arthur, azure, three closed crowns or palewise; Godfrey, per pale; dexter a hinge (?) argent; sinister left blank, probably because the restorer found it inaccessible. The arms of each of the nine are surmounted by a closed crown, the three Christians having a cross topping the crown. There are many identities with and only a few differences from the arms assigned to the nine in The Book and Register of Arms (1542) of Sir David Lindsay of the Mount, Lord Lyon King of Arms, reproduced in facsimile by David Laing (Edinburgh, 1878). Thus on the Crathes ceiling the 'chair' on which Alexander's lion is apparently seated looks more like a clothes-maiden (see plate in Allardyce, The Family of Burnett of Leys facing p 333), as it does also in Lindsay, but other sources make its purpose plain. Arthur's crowns are in Lindsay, as always elsewhere, open crowns. The device here described as a 'hinge' in Godfrey's arms is so called only because elsewhere in Britain the hinge or half- hinge of Cleves is a part of his arms alongside the so-called 'cross of Jerusalem', perhaps omitted from the sinister side here. For the nine, Lindsay carefully distinguishes the closed crowns of emperors (Alexander, Caesar, Charlemagne) from the open crowns with fleurs-de-lys of royal personages (Hector, David, Arthur, Godfrey) and the coronets of non-royals (Joshua and Judas); so perhaps the Crathes painter's use of only closed or imperial crowns suggests a provincial's ignorance of the niceties of such matters.

12   The Parlement of the Thre Ages, Israel Gollancz (ed), Select Early English Poems 2, (London, 1915). His volume is unpaginated, but the Appendix at the end contains some eighteen 'texts illustrative of the Nine Worthies'. R S Loomis, 'Verses on the Nine Worthies', Modern Philology 15 (1917-18) pp 211-19, adds another eight parallels to Gollancz.

13   Der Topos der Nine Worthies, pp 103-4.

14   The Buik of Alexander or The Buik of the most Noble and Valiant Conquerour Alexander the Grit, R L Graeme Ritchie (ed), Scottish Text Society 17, 12, 21, 25 (Edinburgh, 1925, 1921, 1927, 1929). This includes the text of Les Voeux de Paon.

15   Printed by W A Craigie, 'The Ballet of the Nine Nobles', Anglia 21 (1899), 359-69, and also by Gollancz, Appendix, X; Ritchie in The Buik of Alexander I (STS 17), pp.cxxxiv-cl; and Schroeder, p 214.

16   See Gollancz, Appendix, XIII; Loomis VII p 217; Gollancz Appendix XIV; Loomis VIII 219.

17   Der Topos der Nine Worthies p 103.
18   Chronica Gentis Scotorum, W F Skene (ed), The Historians of
     Scotland I (Edinburgh, 1871) Book III Chapter 48, retained in
     Scotichronicon: Johannis de Fordun Scoticronicon cum supple-
     mentis et continuatione Walteri Boweri Insulae Sancti
     Columbae Abbatis (Edinburgh, 1759) 1, p 165 Liber III cap.
     lvii.
19   My text is from Craigie; he suggests an alternative reading
     and for at in the penultimate line, and a gloss, that he had
     for at in the last line.
20   Der Topos der Nine Worthies, pp 203-16.
21   Loomis, I, p 211.
22   Love's Labour's Lost, Act V scene ii.

APPENDIX

The inscriptions are given in the order the rooms are usually
entered on a tour of the castle. Within the rooms, the sides of
each beam are indicated n, s, e, w according to their general
orientation, to give a system of reference. Verses are written
continuously, as on the beams; punctuation is omitted. Where I
have made amendments, note that the beams read: B 3 e greinis, B 8
e As and C 3 w Cyid.

A. Nine nobles room

   1s As a dog turneth to his owne vomit so the foole returneth
       to his owne foolishnes
   1n Blesed is the Riche whiche is founde without blemishe And
       hath not gone efter nor hoped in money & tresures
   2s They that rejoyce at the fall of the righteus Salbe taken
       in the snare & anguishe Sall consume them before they die
   2n Lerne gallant ȝouthes to aternise ȝoure name As did thir
       nyn with deids of endles fame Whose martial actes nobil-
       itates for ay Their glourius names but deing or decay
   3s I nyntein kings but help of any slew A thousand Greeks in
       on day I ouerthrew Had not Achilles slayn me tressonablie
       Troy ȝit had stand and lost no libertie
   3n I Alexander conquest in short space The world & joyt this
       monarchie in peace Yet all this wealth fulfilled not my
       desire Sick was my lust by mesure to Impyre
   4s ... was emperiour and wan By armeis Africk egipt france &
       Spain I past the rhyne and dantit Germanie Brutus at hame
       syne slew me crewalie
   4n Betymes I will destroy euen All the wicked of the land
       That I may from Gods citie cut The wicked workers hand
   5s Josuee of Jewes first wass frie Ane & threttie kings
       conquerit he And reft thame of there lands also The
       floode Jordan he parted in tuo

5n This Judaes manheid all Israell maid frie From seruile
30k of heathen tirrany He vincult Licias & Antiochus
After gryt weris slayn by Demetrius

6s For wit & manheid Dauid was maid king From schepirds
ranke ouer Israell to ring He slew the gryt Goliath hand
to hand And did gryt damage to the heathen land

6n A league wit Scottis of mutuall amitie This Charlis maid
to last eternalie Whais successors obseruis the same
alway Inuiolat unto this present day

7s This Charlis was for his Christian faith renownit And
emperiour for deids of armis crounit He be his micht &
worthie cheualrie Was cheif defence of Christianitie

7n King Arthur crounit was Emperiour & wan Gryt bounds in
France and all the lands of Spain The knichts of the
round table he ordained Whais praise sall sound unto the
warldes end

8s From rage of Turks this Godofried maid frie The holie
land to Christian libertie Gryt Soliman he slew & crounit
was king Ouer all the land of Jurie for to ring

9n Sea3e not thy Harte on welth or earthlie gains They
perish suine but honor still remains

9s Gude reder tell me or thou pas Whilk of thir nyn maist
Valliant was   1602

10n ... in earth hes spent there deyes

B. Green Lady's room

1w - blank -

1e A maidin but modestie A clarke but courtesie A howsewyfe
langinge fairleis to see Wants all there seimleist
propertie

2w The begining of wisdome is the feare of the Lord and the
knawledge of holie things is understanding

2e The mouthe of euerie wicht Defames that graceles man Quha
by his sloothe tynes onie richt That his forbears wan

3w Say not to thy nightbour go and cum agayne and tomorrow
will I giue you if thou now haue it The curse of the Lord
is in the house of the wicked but he blessed the habita-
tione of the righteus

3e Praise be to him quhoise verteus deids Through payn and
labor gr[awis] Schame to the belliegod that feids On
sueat of others brawis

4w Thoughe the deceatfull speake fauorable beleue him not
for he hath seuen abominations in his hart Intending hurt
against his nighbour seing he doeth duell without feare
by the

4e At vertues stoole lerne first thy grounds Renounit if
thou walde be Insegnarie conteins all bounds Of true
nobilitie

5w The sluggard is wyser in his awen conceit then seuen men
that can render a reasone Stryue not with a man causlesle
when he hath done the no harm

5e Thryce happy is that man indeed That weids ane vertues wyf Sho is the blessing of his seid And comfort of his lyff

6w The slothful hand makethe poore but the hand of the diligent maketh riche

6e Blessed wil his house for euer be Quha seruis the Lord alway Thais wallis his awin posterite Inherit sal for ay

7w The Lord will not famishe the soule of the righteous but the soule of the wicked sal be consumed

7e Wine wemen taken insatiablie Has brocht gryt kings to miserie Therefor my god I pray to thie Keep me from crymes and harlotrie

8w The tresures of wickednes profite nothing but righteousnes delyuereth from death

8e Ane auarious mans plentie [I]s to him selfe hydropolie For quhy the mair in welth he flows The thirst for riches gryter grows

9w A wise sone makethe a glad father but a foolishe sone is an heauinesse to his mother

9e Contemne no man in miserie Augment with spyt no poore mans sorow For fortunes false inconstancie May cause his case be thine tomorrow

10w As the vapour and smooke of the chimney gooth before the fyre so euil words rebukes and threatnings go before bloodschedding

10e Flie sone al naughtie companie From fools no freindship craue Keep fellowschip with such as be Both wittie sage and graue

11w A theif is better than a man that is accustomed to lie but they both sall have destruction to their heritage

11e —

12w The good man sall giue inheritance unto his childrens children & the riches of the sinner ar layd up for the Just

12e —

13w All that are proude in hart ar an abominatione to the Lord though hand joune hand he sall not go unpunished

C. Muses room

1e —

1w Honour & grace is the dew recompence Of vertueus warkes done in this lyfe Quhilk maketh men to be haid in reuerence And als their praise to be soundit most ryfe

2e I Fame be my eies & wingis wondrous fair Ane trumpet shyle through all the warlde wide Am drawin thus my heid doth perce the air Althocht my feit heir on the earth abyde

2w Temperance of things most doth refrain The frailty of man as with a stong bitt Bridling the affectis of lustis euery one Stryfing with reasone a reuler most fitt 1599

3e Fortitude is most power onto man A vertue recht and stillt in equitie With curage balde doing quhat sho can Wrong to repelle and despyse miserie

3w Wisdome is the ground of all praise & gloir Fe of the lyff contrar to Ignorance Teaching quhat will speake euermore [G]yid of all vertues quhilk men do aduance

4e Justice is a vertue quhilk ane doth frame All thingis in this lyff with ane juste ballance Holding a suorde to execute the same That no wrang bot richt may have affiance

4w Faith is a truth and constancie of things Spoken and promised be god or man The gyft of god quhilk onlie with it brings Lyff for Christis saik to ilk Christian

5e Hop is a vertue of singular grace Groundit on faith quhilk to the conscience Expelling all dout brings joy and peace Awating still with a sure confidence

5w Charitie is a vertue principall The chyld of faith accomplesing the law With pitie bent to seik the weill of all And as a nureis to babes ʒoung & raw

6e I Clio craftelie dois wryte As eldest of thir sisters heir Of ancient historiis I indite And marciall featis of men of weir

6w And I dame Thalia may be sein To loupe and fling with – My fiddile furth shawes my ʒeris grein As maistres of al mirriness

7e Melpomine man be my style With viole to supply my versis Of tragidies I doe compyle As Bochas in his buke rehersis

7w Heir Terpcichor take tent to me To play on lute I haue profest Al troublit myndis to molifie Efter trauel to take sume rest

8e Euterpe I am this arte did found To play on quhissile first deuysit All melodie and plesand sound Be me they be better prysit 1599

8w For cunning Caliope dois excell With harp in hand ʒe may persaue In ballet royall I bear the bell And prasit be poetis by the leaue

9e Erato heir behalde and se With seister set for galʒardine The law of loue come leir at me Bot nocht veneriall palʒardine

9w Urania behalde me heir My globbe may trauel testifie I reule the planetis and the speir As maistres of astronimie

10e Polymnia the last of nyn My monicordis may weill expresse Quick memorie and scharp ingyn Abhoring still forʒetfulnes

10w –

11e Sum tyme be thou mirrie and sum tyme be thou sad As plaice & tyme requiris to be had For in a wise man it is no maner of cryme His maners to cheang ––

11w –

12e Ether with a mirrie hart ouircum all heuines Or with a faithfull freind redd all cairfulnes

Chapter 29

THE SCOTS-GAELIC SCRIBES OF LATE MEDIEVAL PERTHSHIRE:
AN OVERVIEW OF THE ORTHOGRAPHY AND CONTENTS OF
THE BOOK OF THE DEAN OF LISMORE

Donald E Meek

The Book of the Dean of Lismore is one of the best-known manuscripts in Scotland.[1] Like some other key manuscripts, it assumes
great importance because it is a particularly fortunate survivor
from the medieval past. It may be that, because of its special
place as a unique manuscript, it assumes rather too much importance, but its contents and the nature of its orthography would
suggest that it deserves to hold the centre-stage in the field of
medieval Gaelic literature, at least for the immediate future. Over
the last few years, there has been something of a revival of
interest in this manuscript, after a 'closed season' of some forty
years.[2] Such a revival of interest is to be welcomed, since there
is still much to be learned about the Book and its scribes. Indeed,
it is apparent that, as its mysteries are uncovered, the Book of
the Dean of Lismore provides an ever-broadening perspective in
which to view eastern Perthshire in the Middle Ages. This is the
region in which the manuscript was compiled, and it is a part of
Scotland which has received comparatively little attention as an
area of literary activity in the medieval period.

The reference in the title of this paper to the 'Scots-Gaelic'
scribes of late medieval Perthshire has been chosen with care. It
will be noted that the defining phrase is not 'Gaelic' or 'Scottish
Gaelic'. The point is that to define its scribes in strictly Gaelic
terms would be to overlook a most important dimension of the Book
of the Dean of Lismore, namely the Lowland Scots dimension. The
manuscript intermingles Gaelic culture and Scots culture in a
manner which may appear remarkable, if not bizarre, to us today.
When our Scots-Gaelic scribes were active, however, it may have
seemed entirely natural to fuse the cultures in this way. Such
fusion may well have been wholly in keeping with the conventions of
their time and place.

It will be useful if we remind ourselves, at the outset, of the
distinctive features of that time and place. The Book of the Dean
of Lismore was compiled, it would seem, in the first half of the
sixteenth century, and its compilation falls within a period which
was bounded by historical events of considerable significance. In
1493 the Lordship of the Isles was forfeited by the Crown, although
attempts were made thereafter to restore it by force. The forfeiture marked the end of the MacDonalds as the major political family
in the Gaelic west.[3] As the power of the MacDonalds declined, that

of the Campbells grew. The MacGregor scribes who were involved in the compilation of the Book of the Dean were vassals of the Campbells of Glenorchy. Like the MacGregor scribes, the Campbells generally had an interest in Gaelic culture and Scots culture, and they owed much of their prestige to the manner in which they could operate in both Lowlands and Highlands. The Campbells were ready to absorb new impulses from the Lowland south, and this is underlined by the espousal of reforming principles by their leaders some time before the Reformation Parliament of 1560.[4] The Reformation is the second historical event of relevance to the compilation of the Book of the Dean of Lismore. While its scribes do not show any nascent sympathy for Protestantism, certain aspects of the compilation of the manuscript may suggest that the influence of Renaissance humanism could have been percolating through to eastern Perthshire. As I hope to show, the Book of the Dean of Lismore is a manuscript which owes its format to a number of strong impulses, some from within the Highlands, and others from the far side of the Highland line.

In assessing the Book of the Dean of Lismore, it is important to realise that we see 'through a glass darkly'. We have to hazard an intuitive guess where hard evidence seems to fail, and we have to struggle with an orthographic system to which we, in large measure, have lost the key (or are merely in the process of rediscovering it). The struggle to interpret the manuscript, in its broader and narrower aspects, can be frustrating, and we cannot but sympathise with those who have given vent to their feelings by condemning the Book and its scribes. The Gaelic scholar, faced with its peculiar orthography and appearance, may regard it as deviant and grotesque in terms of the native Gaelic scribal tradition; the Scots scholar will appreciate the format more readily, but will soon find that, while the application of Middle Scots orthography to Gaelic may facilitate his pronunciation of the language, it will provide no easy bridge to the contents of the manuscript. There are, in fact, some very basic questions about the manuscript which are not likely to be resolved easily. We do not know how many other manuscripts of this kind were compiled, and we do not know whether the Book of the Dean is complete as it stands. Wherever we look, there are puzzles and problems, but these add to the fascination of the manuscript as a whole.

Scribes and Period of Compilation

The Book of the Dean of Lismore would appear to be the work of a group of scribes, although it is extremely difficult to define the size of the group or the contributions of its individual members. The manuscript itself takes its name from one of the three scribes who identify themselves clearly in its pages. This is sir James MacGregor, titular Dean of Lismore, who records his name and refers to the manuscript as his 'liber'. At his death in 1551, James MacGregor held the benefice of Fortingall in Perthshire, his native district, as well as the office of Dean of Lismore, of which he had possession from at least 1514.[5] If the Dean received a university education, he evidently did not progress beyond the

level of bachelor, since he uses the title <u>dominus</u> ('sir') rather
than <u>maister</u> ('master'), the latter signifying, in this period and
later, a graduate who had gone through the full Arts curriculum of
a Scottish university.[6] His brother Duncan was also involved in
the compilation of the manuscript, which contains a number of his
poems.[7] The manuscript may attest the signature of the father of
the MacGregor brothers, Dubhghall mac Eoin Riabhaich, but his
contribution to the manuscript is difficult to determine. In one
poem in the manuscript, Dubhghall is portrayed as a man of literary taste, capable of compiling a <u>duanaire</u> ('poem-book'). The poet
asks him to compile a poem-book without delay, and informs him
that MacCailein, the Campbell chief, knows a good poem when it is
taken to him to be read. It has been suggested that the poem-book
in question was, in fact, the Book of the Dean, and that Dubhghall
may have delegated the work to his sons.[8] This identification is
arguable, since the poem does not occupy a prominent place in the
manuscript itself, but it does show that the compilation of poem-
books was by no means unknown in Perthshire. In addition to his
apparent literary interests, Dubhghall acted as a notary public,
and both he and his son James are on record in this capacity in
1511.[9]

The evidence thus indicates that the Book of the Dean had a
fairly specific connection with the family of James MacGregor,
Dean of Lismore. That it may occasionally have gone beyond the
family circle is suggested by the signature of a certain William
Drummond, curate in Fortingall, who writes a brief note in Latin
at the top of a page containing the opening of a well-known Gaelic
ballad, <u>Laoidh Fhraoich</u> ('The Lay of Fraoch').[10] Drummond's note
and signature need not imply that he had any significant part in
the compilation of the manuscript, if indeed he added anything
other than his signature. Presumably such manuscripts could have
travelled among different scribes and readers who would have
enjoyed their contents and would have been wholly familiar with
the Scots-based orthography which now seems so strange to us.

The Book of the Dean contains a number of dates by which its
period of compilation can be determined fairly accurately. The
earliest of these is 1512, and the latest 1542.[11] The dates
recorded between those years suggest that the scribes worked on
the manuscript fairly consistently throughout this period of
thirty years. The compilation of the manuscript was obviously not
a hasty business; it reflects the gradual accumulation and recording of relevant material over a generation.

Script and Appearance of the Manuscript

In writing their material, the scribes of the Book of the Dean of
Lismore employed what is known as secretary hand. This form of
handwriting was employed by literati in England and Scotland from
the late fifteenth century, and by the mid sixteenth century it
functioned as the normal business hand of both countries. In
Lowland Scotland, its range of uses – legal, ecclesiastical,
personal and literary – is attested by a wealth of material, much
of it written in Scots and Latin.[12]

The use of this hand connects the Book of the Dean of Lismore

with the wider literary world of Lowland Scotland and England, and
sets it apart from Gaelic convention, both in Scotland and
Ireland. In the Gaelic west, scribes generally used the script
known as corr-litir (literally 'peaked-letter'), a development of
medieval insular book-hand. The Gaelic hand was highly ornate, and
could be richly elaborated by means of decorated initials and such
devices as rubrication.[13] Compared with medieval Gaelic manuscripts in conventional Gaelic script, the Book of the Dean looks
dull and even amateurish; but it is similar in style to Lowland
Scots compilations, such as the Asloan Manuscript.[14] Only
occasionally do its scribes attempt to provide a decorated
initial, and such decoration is decidedly plain. It corresponds to
the type of decoration sometimes found on contemporary notarial
instruments.[15] This is what one would expect, since the scribes
were schooled in the tradition of the Lowland Scots notary public.
It is difficult to know whether they had any practice in the
writing of Gaelic script, although it is highly probable that they
could read manuscripts written in that script.

The scribes of the Book of the Dean were capable of using
different forms of secretary hand. For their poems, they employed
a 'set' form of the hand, in which letters stand unconnected. For
occasional jottings they often use a 'free' form of the hand with
a more prominent cursive element.[16]

Orthography: the social and cultural background

The greatest difference between the Book of the Dean and most
other manuscripts containing Gaelic material lies in its orthography. Not only have the scribes used a form of hand quite different
from Gaelic script, they have also employed a spelling system
largely unrelated to the standard orthography of classical Common
Gaelic, which was taught in the bardic schools, and which can be
seen in John Carswell's translation of The Book of Common Order of
1567.[17] The scribes were evidently not ignorant of normal Gaelic
orthography, since characteristics of that orthography are fossilised in certain of their spellings, and entire words occasionally
appear in Gaelic form, where it would have been possible for the
scribes to produce alternative spellings more in line with the
basic patterns of their own method. This might suggest that their
decision to reject conventional Gaelic orthography was deliberate,
but that this orthography continued to exert some influence,
particularly when non-Gaelic orthography was incapable of
conveying the desired sounds, or could do so only clumsily.[18]

The basis of the orthography in the Book of the Dean has long
been recognised to be that of Middle Scots, the term usually
applied to the stage in the development of Scots - the vernacular
language of the Scottish Lowlands - which had been attained by
c.1400, and which persisted until c.1560.[19] The extension of
Middle Scots orthography to Gaelic is a step of much greater
significance than the adoption of an alien script, especially when
it is maintained consistently throughout the Gaelic items in the
manuscript, with only occasional evidence of conventional Gaelic
orthography. The degree of scribal commitment to the Scots-based
system is all the more striking when one considers that the

manuscript is probably the work of more than one scribe, that it was compiled over a long period, and that James MacGregor, whose name it bears, must have encountered practitioners of 'tradition-al' Gaelic orthography. The question of why the scribes utilised this orthography must be asked, since it is integral to our under-standing of the manuscript.

Hitherto, it has been customary to relate the nature of the orthography to the type of verse contained in the manuscript, and in particular to the widely-held view that the verse was recorded from oral transmission.[20] Such an opinion implies that the or-thography constitutes some form of shorthand, better suited to rapid writing than conventional Gaelic orthography. Quite apart from the fact that it is by no means certain that the verse in the Book of the Dean was transcribed from oral transmission, it is apparent that words written in the orthography of the manuscript make markedly less use of scribal abbreviations than material in normal Gaelic orthography. While the orthography of the Book of the Dean does indeed allow for the removal of certain syllables which were evidently not pronounced in the scribes' dialect, it also insists on writing in full certain other syllables which would have been abbreviated in standard Gaelic scribal practice. In the Middle Ages, speed in writing was more a matter of script than orthography, and it was this which led in large measure to the emergence of secretary hand, which the scribes use. Oral transmission of the material might be a partial explanation of the use of secretary hand in the manuscript, were such an explanation needed, but it does not account for a radical orthographic change, such as is found in the Book of the Dean. Equally unsatisfactory is the view that the scribes may have been trying to bridge the seeming gulf between the literary language of the time and the vernacular by adopting an orthography which would give greater prominence to Scottish Gaelic and to its dialects. The orthography of the manuscript preserves a great deal of the classical language alongside the vernacular; and, in any event, conventional Gaelic orthography could have been modifed to incorporate vernacular features where desired, as the appearance of modernisms in con-temporary (and earlier) Gaelic manuscripts amply demonstrates. At the other end of the scale, it seems unwise to attribute obscur-antist motives to the scribes, since this violates the principles of manuscript compilation in the Middle Ages.[21]

More cogent reasons for employing the type of orthography found in the Book of the Dean are suggested by a consideration of the linguistic situation in Scotland and the relative status of the country's two main languages in the period in which the manuscript was compiled. While Scottish Gaelic was still spoken by the bulk of the population in Galloway and Carrick until at least the time of the Reformation,[22] the language had begun its regression from the Lowlands by the second half of the fourteenth century.[23] By c.1400, the southern boundary of Gaelic speech probably coincided with the geographical line distinguishing Highlands from Lowlands, with the exception of the areas already defined. Yet even by 1500 it would be the language of much of the Lennox, Menteith and Strathearn.[24] In the east and north-east, few Gaelic speakers would be found on the coastal plain. Here, as in the Lowlands, the inhabitants spoke 'Inglis', that form of the Northern dialect of Anglo–Saxon which, by 1494, had come to be known by the more familiar name of 'Scottis'.[25] This change of nomenclature acknowledged the status of Scots as the national language of Scotland. At the same time, Scottish Gaelic, which had once been known in official documents as 'lingua Scotica', had come to be called 'lingua Hibernica', or 'Erse' in Scots.[26] From a Lowland viewpoint, therefore, Scottish Gaelic was to be identified with Ireland rather than with Scotland in the fifteenth century. It is probably significant that the first comic Highlander who appears in Lowland Scots verse, and who is described in The Buke of the Howlat of c.1450, is said to be 'a bard owt of Irland'.[27] Indeed, Lowland commentators who included 'Erse' in their descriptions of Scotland did so only to emphasise the deep cultural gulf separating the so-called Wild Scots from the 'domesticated' or 'house-holding' Scots. Thus, in 1521, John Major could write:

> One-half of Scotland speaks Irish, and all these as well as Islanders we reckon to belong to the Wild Scots. In dress, in the manner of their outward life, and in good morals, for example, these come behind the householding Scots.

Major made it clear that the language of the latter was English.[28] In developing his theme of contrasting cultures, Major has nothing to say about the possibility of Scots/Gaelic bilingualism of the kind so obviously attested by the Book of the Dean of Lismore.

The importance of Scots, at least in the Lowlands, had not come about overnight. As far back as 1398, the Scottish parliament had endorsed the status of 'Inglis' by authorising its use as an alternative to Latin when recording Parliamentary business.[29] Such innovation served to increase the prestige of Scots in the higher domains of commerce and law. During the fifteenth century, also, the literary range of the language was being extended considerably by the Makars, whose works have come to represent the high-water mark of the Middle Scots period.[30] By the beginning of the sixteenth century, therefore, Scots had become a powerful, all-purpose language. There is evidence that it had already begun to cross the Highland Line, probably well before 1500.

In promoting the use of Scots within the Gaelic-speaking Highland area, no influence was more potent than that of Lowland central government. During the last quarter of the fifteenth century, the Scottish Crown continued its attempts to bring the Wild Scots of the north and west under its direct control.[31] This policy struck most noticeably at the Lordship of the Isles, which was finally forfeited in 1493. It also furthered the interests of clans known to be sympathetic towards central government.[32] The increasing prestige of such clans was underpinned by documentation, principally charters and bonds of manrent. The Campbells, in particular, were careful to consolidate their position in this way, and their expansion eastwards into Perthshire is witnessed by a substantial body of bonds, dating back to 1488 and continuing well into the sixteenth century. These bonds were drawn up in Scots, and they are now preserved in the Black Book of Taymouth.[33]

It is of great importance that these bonds contain evidence of

the application to Gaelic of a system of spelling which is similar
to that in the Book of the Dean. This system is applied primarily
to place-names, personal names and surnames, but it also includes
Gaelic epithets. The practice is maintained throughout this corpus,
and it would appear to represent a deliberate policy by the
notaries who drew up the documents. In some respects the system
found in the Black Book bonds resembles the orthographic treatment
given to the effusions of the 'bard owt of Irland' in The Buke of
the Howlat. In the case of the latter, however, the composer
desires a comic effect, and he was not himself a Gaelic speaker.
The Black Book bonds, on the other hand, show the application of
Scots orthography to Gaelic in official documents, and the notaries
may have included men who were themselves Gaelic-speaking.[34]
     Equally impressive evidence for the pervasiveness of Scots
orthography in a Gaelic context in this period is furnished by West
Highland monumental sculpture.[35] Here too, Gaelic personal names
and surnames have often been 'Scotticised', with the occasional
appearance of epithets in similar form.[36] Chronologically, the
monuments suggest that the method was much in vogue after 1500, but
that its beginnings may be traced well into the fifteenth century,
if not the fourteenth.[37] While the Black Book bonds are pre-
eminently concerned with Perthshire, stone monuments bearing
'Scotticised' forms of Gaelic names occur in the Hebrides and
mainland Argyll.[38] Indeed, the inscriptions most heavily influenced by the conventions of Scots orthography are found at Kil-
michael Glassary in Mid Argyll.[39] It is suggested that this may
reflect the fact that

> of all the districts lying within the area in which late
> medieval West Highland carving is found, Glassary had been
> most open to Lowland influences for the longest period of
> time. Thus, since c.1374 the leading family in Glassary was
> that of Scrymgeour, whose main centre of activities was
> Dundee, of which they were constables.[40]

The settlement of families of Lowland origins in the Gaelic-
speaking area may well have been another important factor in
encouraging the extension of Scots orthography to Gaelic. In
mainland Argyll, such settlement is not surprising, given the
strong Lowland affiliations of the dominant clan, the Campbells.[41]
     The use of 'Scotticised' forms of Gaelic names on monumental
sculpture is a significant indication of the status of this orthographic trend. Clearly, such a convention was acceptable to the
nobility who commissioned the monuments. Equally clearly, there
existed men of letters who could supply inscriptions of this kind,
and who were familiar with the basic principles of the type of
orthography found in the Book of the Dean. This, together with the
evidence of the Black Book bonds, is sufficient to suggest that the
orthography of the Book of the Dean was not devised by its scribes.
While they may have helped to develop this orthographic style, it
is hard to believe that they invented it.[42]
     While the orthography of the Book of the Dean is closely related
in form to the examples found in the Black Book bonds and on monu-

mental sculpture, the scale on which it is employed in the manuscript is obviously much greater. Apart from the Book of the Dean
itself, we lack evidence which might indicate at what precise time
such orthography began to be used extensively in Gaelic writing, or
what stimulated such a departure. The apparent fluency of the
scribes of the Book of the Dean, and the small number of blunders
which can be ascribed to orthographic uncertainty on their part,
would suggest that they were working within what was already a
relatively stable tradition. Indeed, it has been argued recently
that certain errors in the manuscript text are to be explained in
terms of miscopying from an exemplar written in the same orthography.[43]   Given the misfortunes which have so severely reduced the
number of Gaelic manuscripts surviving from the Middle Ages, it
would be foolish to emphasise the uniqueness of the Book of the
Dean since other compilations of a similar nature may once have
existed.

In stimulating the emergence of a developed orthography based on
Scots, such as one finds in the Book of the Dean, it seems likely
that the question of linguistic status would have been important,
the more so in the unsettled period which preceded, and followed
from, the forfeiture of the Lordship of the Isles.[44] It may have
been envisaged by certain bilingual Scots/Gaelic scribes that the
advance of Lowland bureaucracy into the Highlands, at the hands of
a Scots civil service, would alter the existing orthographic base
of Gaelic. Indeed, scribes like James MacGregor, who operated as
notaries public on the frontier of Scots and Gaelic, would have
been particularly prone to think in these terms. Whatever the
precise reason for the development of its orthography, the Book of
the Dean certainly bears witness to a strong Lowland consciousness
on the part of its scribes, and the evidence of monumental sculpture in particular suggests that they were not alone.

With hindsight, it is possible to conclude that the Book of the
Dean of Lismore coterie had over-estimated the potential effect of
Scots linguistic dominance on Gaelic orthography. Clearly, native
Gaelic scribal tradition employing conventional orthography
continued well beyond 1500, and the orthography of present-day
Scottish Gaelic is based ultimately on that of Classical Common
Gaelic. In guaranteeing the survival of the tradition, we may owe
more than has hitherto been conceded to John Carswell's translation of Knox's Book of Common Order. Appearing as Foirm na
nUrrnuidheadh in 1567, Carswell's translation employed the
orthography of Classical Common Gaelic, and it had the vital
distinction of being the first printed book to be published in
Irish or Scottish Gaelic.[45] As a work of major liturgical significance, it would have exerted an influence over the writing
habits of literate Gaelic ministers even if it had remained in
manuscript.

The importance of such liturgical documents in directing the
orthographic development of a language is paralleled, though not
precisely, in the instance of Manx. Bishop Phillips' translation of
the English Prayer Book into Manx, which was completed c.1610,
adopted an orthography based on that of English. Although this
translation was not, in fact, available in print until the nine-

teenth century, it evidently set a trend, since the first Manx printed book, a bilingual version of Bishop Wilson's Principles and Duties of Christianity, published in 1707, also adopted an orthography based on English. While the orthography employed in the translation of Wilson's Principles differed from that of Phillips, and from that of subsequent Manx works, the distinctive nature of Manx orthography was thereby confirmed.[46] If the first specimen of printed Scottish Gaelic had employed a spelling system similar to that of the Book of the Dean, the orthography of the language might well have assumed a form very different from what we know today.

Principal Contents

The Book of the Dean of Lismore bears eloquent testimony to the cultural ferment of the southern Highlands (and particularly of Perthshire) in the late Middle Ages. The manuscript intertwines no less than three different cultures: Gaelic culture, in both its Irish and Scottish dimensions, which supplies the bulk of its material; Scots culture, which provides its orthography and script; and the medieval Latin culture of the pre-Reformation church.

Although the Book of the Dean is devoted primarily to verse, it does contain some prose items, mainly in Latin and Scots. The longest of these would appear to be a Latin canonical text, written on the former vellum covers of the manuscript (and therefore indicating that the Book of the Dean as we now know it consists of at least two different manuscripts). There is a substantial amount of historical material, consisting chiefly of king lists, chronicles and pedigrees;[47] and there is a wide variety of notes and jottings, relating to domestic, personal, scientific and business matters, some of these being in Gaelic.[48] The relative scarcity of Gaelic prose material in the manuscript is interesting, and suggests that the scribes were aware of a distinction between the roles of the languages at their disposal. The manuscript clearly indicates language-switching (Gaelic/Scots /Latin) and probable diglossia (Gaelic/Scots).[49]

If Gaelic prose items do not figure prominently in the Book of the Dean, Gaelic verse accounts for the largest part of its contents. Extracts from the Scots poets Dunbar and Henryson, and the English poet Lydgate, do of course appear, and these are an important indication of the compilers' contact with the literary world of the Lowlands and beyond;[50] but they are overshadowed by the large collection of Gaelic poetry found in the manuscript. This collection consists wholly of dán or syllabic verse, in varying degrees of strictness. Such verse was the primary literary product of the classical Gaelic world.[51]

Apart from individual quatrains, which are often very difficult to classify in broad terms, the Book of the Dean contains three main types of dán. These intermingle throughout the manuscript, although sequences of related items occur from time to time. The most conspicuous category is bardic verse, which includes elegy, eulogy, satire and religious poetry. Irish and Scottish authors are represented, the latter outnumbering the former by about 44 to

21.[52] Much, but not all, of this type of verse has been edited.[53] Heroic verse or 'ballads' forms the second largest category of poetry in the manuscript.[54] The third category of _dán_ in the Book of the Dean is courtly and satiric verse, ascribed to Irish and Scottish authors. This has received much less attention than the other two types, but it is currently being studied in considerable detail, notably by Professor William Gillies, who has produced very important editions of the poetry of Sir Duncan Campbell of Glenorchy.[55]

Provenance of bardic verse in the Book of the Dean of Lismore

Although the compilers of the Book of the Dean operated in the Perthshire area, the contents of the manuscript indicate that they were drawing on the resources of the classical Gaelic world, embracing Ireland and Gaelic Scotland. The bardic verse in the manuscript is of particular value in demonstrating the specific parts of Ireland and Scotland in which they were interested, and to which they had ready access.

The Irish material in the Book of the Dean represents the following areas and families:

Tyrone	Ó Néill (1 poem), MacGillmurray of Clandeboy (1 poem) 56
Brefny	Ó Ruairc (2 poems) 57
Connacht	Ó Conchobhair (? 6 poems), MacDiarmaid (3 poems), de Burca (2 poems), Ó Ceallaigh (1 poem) 58
Fermanagh	Mág Uidhir (2 poems) 59
Westmeath	Mág Eochagáin (1 poem) 60
Thomond	Ó Briain (2 poems) 61
Munster	Ó Caoimh (1 poem) 62

Such evidence would seem to show that the scribes of the Book of the Dean were interested in the north and west of Ireland, but that they were pre-eminently concerned with Connacht (and specifically the district to the east and south of Sligo).

The territorial bias of Scottish bardic verse in the Book of the Dean has been recognised for some time. The following Scottish families are represented: MacGregor, MacDonald, Campbell of Arygll, MacDougall of Dunollie, MacLeod of Lewis, MacLeod of Harris and Dunvegan, Stewart of Rannoch, MacNeill of Gigha and MacSween of Knapdale.[63] Dr John Bannerman has recently argued that this distribution pattern, beginning at Fortingall and proceeding westwards to the islands of Lewis and Gigha, 'would be an extraordinary one seen in any light other than that of the Lordship of the Isles'.[64] The manuscript seems indeed to confirm on other evidence that the scribes were in touch with poets who had enjoyed the patronage of the Lordship in the concluding years of its _de iure_ existence. Giolla Coluim mac an Ollaimh, for example, is represented by four poems in the Book of the Dean, two of which deal with matters relating to the Lordship - the one a lament on the death of Angus, son of John of the Isles, and the other lamenting the demise of the Lordship itself.[65] It seems possible that Giolla Coluim was a member of the most prominent bardic family within the Lordship, the MacMhuirichs.[66]

The territorial and cultural interests of the Lordship of the Isles were not restricted to Gaelic Scotland. Ireland came firmly within its orbit, and the links between the Lordship and the north of Ireland were especially strong from the late fourteenth century, when John Mór acquired possession of the Glens of Antrim through his marriage to the Bisset heiress.[67] Such marriages served to strengthen the wider political framework, within which there existed a web of interconnections, linking Scottish professional families - clerics, poets, craftsmen, doctors, musicians - with their Irish blood relations.[68] The MacMhuirichs provide a fine example of a Scottish family of poets descended from an Irish ancestor, Muireadhach Ó Dálaigh. At the time of his flight to Scotland in 1213, Muireadhach resided at Lissadil, near Sligo - a geographical point of interest which may bear on the regional pattern of Irish bardic verse in the Book of the Dean.[69] It is certainly evident that the scribes of the Book of the Dean afford considerable prominence to Ó Dálaigh poets.[70]

It would be incorrect to suggest, however, that the Irish material in the Book of the Dean was acquired solely through the MacMhuirichs, or that kin connections were indispensable. Professional men moved between Ireland and Scotland in pursuit of patronage from willing employers. Two Scottish poets represented in the Book of the Dean - Fionnlagh Ruadh and Giolla Críost Brúilingeach (the latter possibly a Galbraith from Gigha) - evidently attended the court of the MacDiarmaids of Loch Cé in Connacht in the mid fifteenth century. Giolla Críost was also familiar with the court of Mág Uidhir of Fermanagh.[71] Both courts lie in the part of Ireland of greatest interest to the scribes of the Book of the Dean.

While the Lordship of the Isles provided outstanding opportunities for cultural links between Scotland and Ireland, these links did not cease with the collapse of the Lordship. The Campbells, it must be remembered, had strong Gaelic interests, with Irish dimensions. Their own poets, the MacEwans, were probably a branch of the Irish bardic family of Ó hEóghusa (O'Hosey).[72] Irish poets also came to the Campbell court, as when Mac Cailein received, sometime around 1555, a chief-poet on an errand from an O'Donnell chief.[73] A consciousness of Ireland is evident too in the work of John Carswell, himself a protégé of the Argyll house with a classical bardic training.[74]

While the Book of the Dean may be retrospective in its choice of material, and much indebted to the heritage of the Lordship of the Isles, it must equally be emphasised that it has close connections with the Campbells. Its scribes were vassals of the Campbells of Glenorchy, it contains verse dedicated to or even composed by members of the Campbell aristocracy, and the whole manuscript was compiled in territory under Campbell sway.[75] Such circumstances suggest continuity of traditional Gaelic values among a clan usually portrayed as enemies of the old Gaelic world. The question

The nature of the scribes' sources: oral or literary?

of whether the scribes of the Book of the Dean used oral or literary sources, particularly in the compilation of their Gaelic verse
material, has not yet been investigated with reference to the
entire manuscript. Opinions expressed hitherto have applied to
specific genres within the manuscript, or even to individual items
of verse. The dangers of generalisation, or mere assumption, must
therefore be emphasised in view of our knowledge to date and the
intrinsic complexity of the manuscript. However, we may review the
conclusions reached by scholars since 1803.

Early investigators do not appear to have been troubled by this
matter. The Highland Society's Inquiry into the Authenticity of the
Poems of Ossian – more concerned with the existence of Ossianic
verse than with its transmission – did not pronounce on the
possible sources of the Book of the Dean's ballad texts. Their
Report draws attention to the correspondence between the items in
the Book of the Dean and versions in later collections from oral
tradition.[76] This could indicate that the Book of the Dean was
regarded as drawing on what was available orally. Nevertheless, the
Report also notes that the pedigree on p 144 of the manuscript was
derived from 'the books of the history of the kings'.[77]

One suspects that the heroic ballad material in the Book of the
Dean was of considerable importance in determining scholarly
attitudes to the compilation of the manuscript, especially since
numerous collections of heroic verse had indeed been made from oral
transmission in the Highlands in the eighteenth and nineteenth
centuries. This, in part, may well have influenced Professor Donald
MacKinnon to conclude that 'the greater part, if not the whole, of
the Gaelic verse must have been written to dictation or from
memory'.[78] This general conclusion was inscribed in a preface to
the manuscript which was added (presumably by Professor MacKinnon)
when it was rebound in 1911. MacKinnon was, however, prepared to
admit that 'the writers may have sometimes transcribed from manuscripts', and he too noted the significance of the scribal note on
the source of the pedigree on p 144 of the manuscript.[79] It would
seem, therefore, that he made a distinction between Gaelic verse
items in the manuscript and other material.

Support for the view that the Book of the Dean drew on oral
sources was also derived from certain features of the manuscript
itself. Neil Ross argued in 1939 that 'the reproduction of the
spoken dialect, and the nature of the corrections, tend to show
that the ballads were not transcribed from a written source'.[80]
More recently, the unusual orthography of the manuscript has been
adduced as evidence of transcription from dictation or recitation.[81]

This approach to the compilation of the Book of the Dean has not
received unqualified acceptance, nonetheless. In 1931, Professor
Christiansen noted the close correspondence between certain of the
ballad texts of the Book of the Dean and versions in Irish manuscripts. He concluded from a detailed scrutiny of one particular
text that it was 'legitimate' to think that 'the Dean copied this
from some songbook, and did not write it down from what he heard
recited'.[82] In 1937, Professor Watson, with specific reference to
the bardic verse in the manuscript, wrote: 'Whether the writers

consulted manuscripts or depended mainly on oral sources is a difficult question'.[83] This non-committal statement is at least interesting in that it does not endorse fully the prevalent oral theory.

The latest textual research on sections of the Book of the Dean, undertaken by Professor William Gillies, has similarly raised the possibility that the scribes had access to manuscripts, at least in certain cases. Gillies has also suggested that, on occasion, they may have used exemplars in an orthography similar to that of the Book of the Dean itself. Yet, in the case of one poem, the same editor concludes that

> there seems at least a possibility that ... [it] was at some stage written down from recitation or dictation by someone who did not recognise or comprehend all he heard.[84]

The evidence of the body of heroic ballads in the manuscript suggests that most of these items were probably transcribed from manuscripts, and not recorded from oral transmission as has generally been maintained. Such a conclusion is by no means inconsistent with the methods of transmitting ballad verse, or with the nature of the medieval Gaelic world, which supported a vigorous scribal tradition alongside a flourishing oral culture. At the same time, it does not deny the possibility that such verse could have been transmitted orally before it was placed in the exemplars which may have been used by the scribes of the Book of the Dean.

Scribal Alteration of Texts

The question of whether the scribes of the Book of the Dean of Lismore had access to oral or written sources is raised by the manner in which they present some of their texts. In a number of texts, especially among the ballad items, the scribes have obviously been at work emending their first drafts, and their emendations are generally represented by the cancellation of words, phrases and occasionally whole lines. When the scribes cancel their first readings, they write their 'new' readings in superscript, immediately above their cancellations. When the superscript readings are checked, it can be seen that they derive from alternative versions of the texts. In some instances further quatrains are added to the text, usually in the bottom margins of pages. Such emendation is to be distinguished carefully from scribal attempts to correct spelling or to rewrite 'difficult' words employing a more satisfactory 'set' of letters from the options available within their orthographic system. Elsewhere I have given a fairly detailed account of these emendations as they affect the ballad texts in the manuscript, and I have discussed their significance for the likely development of the texts themselves.[85] On this occasion I wish merely to draw attention to the wider implications of these emendations for the compilation of the manuscript; and I wish to conclude the paper with a speculative touch, since the Book of the Dean of Lismore sometimes invites speculation.

It needs to be noted that the Perthshire scribes' practice of visible emendation within the manuscript is, as far as I am aware, unique within the Gaelic and Scots tradition in the Middle Ages. Gaelic manuscripts, compiled in the traditional manner in Ireland or in Scotland, do not show emendation of this kind. The same family of scribes could record different versions of the same poem, but this is normally done in separate manuscripts. I know of no other Gaelic manuscript before 1600 which shows signs that a scribe was comparing one version of a poem with another, and making alterations as he went along. Evidence for this sort of 'editing' is, however, found after 1600, chiefly in the manuscript collection of the Rev James McLagan, which includes many ballad texts collected in the Highlands after 1750.[86] On the Scots side, I am informed that there is no equivalent to the practice of the scribes of the Book of the Dean.

We may be permitted to draw one or two conclusions from the evidence of the Book of the Dean of Lismore with regard to the attitudes of the scribes to the texts available to them. The first conclusion is that they were poring over different versions of their texts, and looking out for textual divergence. When they found divergences, they attempted to produce a single text of an eclectic type, perhaps believing that there ought somehow to be a single, reliable text of a poem. The second conclusion which, I think, is warranted, is that the scribes were probably using manuscript versions of at least some of their poems. It is very difficult for me to conceive of their 'editing' in terms of memorisation and subsequent comparison of orally-derived versions, especially in instances where the poems are extremely long.[87]

The real difficulty, however, is to find a suitable context for such activity, and to know why the scribes should have operated in this matter. It is at this point, therefore, that I propose to become speculative, and to use the conference as a sounding-board for what can be no more than a theory. My guess is that we are seeing here some degree of humanist influence, and I suspect that our scribes, although tucked away in their corner of eastern Perthshire, are responding to a characteristic urge of the European scholars of the Renaissance, namely the desire to gather, compare and 'edit' manuscripts.[88] The humanists were primarily concerned with classical texts, and sought to edit influential Greek and Latin works; but it is not impossible that some turned to the vernacular tradition, since an interest in vernacular languages was developing in this period.[89] We are, of course, entirely in the dark as to how the Perthshire scribes may have absorbed such principles. It would be intriguing to know who taught them to write, and whether they even paid the occasional visit to that centre of humanism in the north, namely the University of Aberdeen.[90]

Conclusion

The Book of the Dean of Lismore can be viewed in many different ways, depending on which strand of its complex make-up one is prepared to emphasise. It owes much to the cultural riches of the defunct Lordship of the Isles; its catchment area extends as far north as Lewis and as far south as Co. Clare in Ireland, through a network of family loyalties and cultural relationships; it was compiled in an area under the jurisdiction of the Campbells of Glenorchy; and its scribes employ an orthography which is unashamedly derived from that of Middle Scots. Yet, if we persist in seeing the manuscript in terms of individual strands, we do it less than justice. It is more satisfying, if at times more perplexing, to take the broadest possible view, and to see this 'fortunate survivor' as part of a larger European cultural tapestry which was being woven in the first half of the sixteenth century.[91]

Notes

1   The manuscript is owned by the National Library of Scotland, Edinburgh, shelf-mark 72.1.37.

2   Three important works on the manuscript were published in the late 1930s: Scottish Verse from the Book of the Dean of Lismore, W J Watson (ed), Scottish Gaelic Texts Society (Edinburgh, 1937); Poems from the Book of the Dean of Lismore, E C Quiggin (ed) (Cambridge, 1937); and Heroic Poetry from the Book of the Dean of Lismore, N Ross (ed), Scottish Gaelic Texts Society (Edinburgh, 1939). A new wave of editing began in the 1970s.

3   K Steer and J W M Bannerman, Late Medieval Monumental Sculpture in the West Highlands, HMSO (Edinburgh, 1977), pp 211-2.

4   D E Meek and J Kirk, 'John Carswell, Superintendent of Argyll: A Reassessment', Records of the Scottish Church History Society, 19 (1975), 1-22 (4-5).

5   Watson, Scottish Verse, pp. xiv-xv.

6   It is not unusual to find references in this period to clerics who apparently did not obtain the level of Master in the Arts curriculum.

7   Watson, Scottish Verse, pp 212-7.

8   Ibid, pp 2-5.

9   Ibid, pp xiv-xv.

10 MS, p 301. I am grateful to Mr Ronald Black for allowing me to consult a draft of his forthcoming catalogue of the Book of the Dean, in which this identification is made.

11 MS, pp 35, 82, 144.

12 L C Hector, The Handwriting of English Documents (London, 1958), pp 60-1; G G Simpson, Scottish Handwriting 1150-1650 (Edinburgh, 1973, repr Aberdeen, 1986), pp 14-16, and plates 11-20.

13 For an introduction to the early form of this script, see W M Lindsay, Early Irish Minuscule Script (Oxford, 1910).

14 The Asloan Manuscript, W A Craigie (ed), Scottish Texts Society, 2 vols (Edinburgh, 1923-5), II, plates facing pp xii and 141.

15 An example occurs on MS, p 301; cf. Simpson, Handwriting, p 25.

16 Ibid, pp 5, 15, and plates 11-14.

17   K   Jackson,   'Common Gaelic', Proceedings of the British
      Academy, 38 (1951), 71–97; B O Cúiv, 'The Linguistic Training
      of the Medieval Irish Poet', Celtica, 10 (1973), 114–40;
      Foirm na n-Urrnuidheadh, R L Thomson (ed), Scottish Gaelic
      Texts   Society (Edinburgh, 1970). See also J Bannerman's
      important discussion of 'Literacy in the Highlands' in The
      Renaissance and Reformation in Scotland: Essays in Honour of
      Gordon Donaldson, I B Cowan and D Shaw (eds) (Edinburgh,
      1983), pp 214–35.
18   On the orthography, see further D E Meek, 'Gàidhlig is
      Gaylick anns na Meadhon Aoisean', in Alba agus a' Ghàidhlig:
      Gaelic and Scotland, W Gillies (ed) (forthcoming).
19   Bannerman, 'Literacy', 220–1; D Murison, The Guid Scots
      Tongue (Edinburgh, 1977), pp 4–5.
20   Cf. B O Cúiv, The Irish Bardic Duanaire or 'Poem-Book', The R
      I Best Memorial Lecture (Dublin, 1973), pp 14–15.
21   Most of the views considered in this paragraph have been
      encountered in discussion.
22   J   MacQueen, 'Gaelic Speakers of Galloway and Carrick',
      Scottish Studies, 17 (1973), 17–33.
23   W F H Nicolaisen, Scottish Place Names (London, 1979), pp
      121f.
24   R Nicholson, Scotland: The Later Middle Ages (Edinburgh,
      1978), Map A.
25   J Templeton, 'Scots: An Outline History', in Lowland Scots, A
      J Aitken (ed), Association for Scottish Literary Studies
      Occasional Papers, 2 (Edinburgh, 1978), 4–19 (6).
26   Murison, Scots Tongue, p 5; D Murison, 'The Historical
      Background', in Languages of Scotland, A J Aitken and T
      MacArthur (eds), (Edinburgh, 1979) 2–13 (8).
27   M A Mackay, 'The Scots of the Makars', in Aitken, Lowland
      Scots, 20–37 (27).
28   Scottish Historical Documents, G Donaldson (ed) (Edinburgh,
      1974), p 101. The reference is presumably to Inglis, the
      earlier name for Scots.
29   Murison, Scots Tongue, p 4.
30   Mackay, 'Scots of the Makars'.
31   R   Nicholson,   'Domesticated   Scots   and Wild Scots: The
      Relationship between Lowlanders and Highlanders in Medieval
      Scotland', Scottish Colloquium Proceedings (Guelph), I.
32   Steer and Bannerman, Monumental Sculpture, pp 207, 210–1.
33   The Black Book of Taymouth, The Bannatyne Club (Edinburgh,
      1855), pp 177f.
34   See further Meek, 'Gàidhlig is Gaylick'.
35   Steer and Bannerman, Monumental Sculpture, pp 91–2.
36   Ibid, p 142, no 71.
37   Ibid, p 146, no 76.
38   Ibid, pp 97, no 2 and 99, no 5.
39   Ibid, p 143, no 71.
40   Ibid.
41   Ibid, pp 210–1; cf W D H Sellar, 'The Earliest Campbells –
      Norman, Briton, or Gael?,' Scottish Studies, 17 (1973),
      108–25.
42   For the view that the Dean of Lismore may have been regarded

by his Argyllshire contemporaries 'with disfavour as a Scotticised Perthshire innovator', see D S Thomson, 'Gaelic Learned Orders and Literati in Medieval Scotland', in _Proceedings of the Third International Congress of Celtic Studies_, W F H Nicolaisen (ed) (Edinburgh, 1968), pp 57-78 (68).

43   W Gillies, 'The Gaelic Poems of Sir Duncan Campbell of Glenorchy (I)', _Scottish Gaelic Studies_, 13, part I (1978), 18-45 (24). Parts II-III of this series are to be found ibid, part II (1981), 263-88, and 14, part I (1983), 59-82.

44   Steer and Bannerman, _Monumental Sculpture_, pp 209-10.

45   Meek and Kirk, 'John Carswell'.

46   R L Thomson, 'The Study of Manx Gaelic', _Proceedings of the British Academy_, 55 (1969), 177-210 (178-84).

47   MS, pp 27, 44, 78, 83, 141, 144, 171, 186, 242, 243.

48   MS, pp 48, 59b, 74, 92d, 250.

49   Items such as shopping-lists tend to be in Scots rather than Gaelic.

50   MS pp 48, 77, 92b, 144, 184.

51   For a general introduction with numerous references to the Book of the Dean, see E C Quiggin, _Prolegomena to the Study of the Later Irish Bards 1200-1500_, American Committee for Irish Studies (reprinted from _Proceedings of the British Academy_, 5).

52   T F O'Rahilly, 'Indexes to the Book of the Dean of Lismore', _Scottish Gaelic Studies_, 4 (1934), 31-56.

53   Watson, _Scottish Verse_, contains only a selection.

54   D E Meek, 'The Corpus of Heroic Verse in the Book of the Dean of Lismore'. Unpublished PhD dissertation, University of Glasgow, 1982.

55   W Gillies, 'Courtly and Satiric Poetry from the Book of the Dean of Lismore', _Scottish Studies_, 21 (1977), 35-53; see also note 43 above.

56   MS, pp 75, 122.

57   MS, pp 8, 54.

58   MS, pp 16, 20, 41, 97, 101?, 106, 153, 244, 246, 269?, 286, 287.

59   MS, pp 177, 244.

60   MS, p 177.

61   MS, pp 124, 310.

62   MS, p 226.

63   Watson, _Scottish Verse_, pp xvii-xviii.

64   Steer and Bannerman, _Monumental Sculpture_, p 206.

65   Watson, _Scottish Verse_, 66-95.

66   D S Thomson, 'The MacMhuirich Bardic Family', _Transactions of the Gaelic Society of Inverness_, 43 (1960-63), 276-304.

67   Steer and Bannerman, _Monumental Sculpture_, pp 162-3.

68   See, in general, J Bannerman 'The Lordship of the Isles', in _Scottish Society in the Fifteenth Century_, J Brown (ed), (London, 1977), pp 209-40, and Thomson, 'Gaelic Learned Orders'.

69   Thomson, 'MacMhuirich Bardic Family', 277-8.

70   Thomson, 'Gaelic Learned Orders', 74.

71   Ibid, p 69; Watson, _Scottish Verse_, pp 32-59, 148-57.

72 Bannerman, 'Lordship', 234.
73 W Gillies, 'Some Aspects of Campbell History', Transactions of the Gaelic Society of Inverness, 50 (1976-8), 256-95 (260).
74 Thomson, Foirm na n-Urrnuidheadh, p 10.
75 Gillies, 'Campbell History', 258-9.
76 H MacKenzie, Report of the Committee of the Highland Society of Scotland appointed to Inquire into the Nature and Authenticity of the Poems of Ossian (Edinburgh, 1805), p 301.
77 Ibid, p 300.
78 D MacKinnon, A Descriptive Catalogue of Gaelic Manuscripts (Edinburgh, 1912), p 229.
79 Ibid.
80 Ross, Heroic Poetry, p xiv; cf. MacKinnon, Catalogue, p 229.
81 Ó Cuív, Irish Bardic Duanaire, p 14.
82 R Th Christiansen, The Vikings and the Vikings Wars in Irish and Gaelic Tradition (Oslo, 1931), pp 40-6, and esp p 42, note 7.
83 Watson, Scottish Verse, p xviii.
84 Gillies, 'Duncan Campbell (I)', 24, 31, 35, 41,; W Gillies, 'A Religious Poem Ascribed to Muireadhach Ó Dálaigh', Studia Celtica, 14-15 (1979-80), 81-6 (83-4).
85 D E Meek, 'Development and Degeneration in Gaelic Ballad Texts', in The Heroic Process: Form, Function and Fantasy in Folk Epic, Bo Almqvist et al. (eds) (Dublin, 1987), pp 131-60.
86 See, for example, the text of the 'Lay of Fraoch' in McLagan MS 245. (The McLagan MSS are housed in Glasgow University Library).
87 The poem which shows the greatest amount of emendation is 72 quatrains in length; see Meek, 'Development and Degeneration', 141-3, 147-51.
88 Studies in this field include J R Hale, Renaissance Europe (London, 1980), especially Chapter 8; and R H Bainton, Erasmus of Christendom (London, 1972), especially Chapter 6. For Scotland, see the succinct discussion of 'Humanism' by A Ross, in A Companion to Scottish Culture, D Daiches (ed) (London, 1981), pp 173-4.
89 It is important to bear in mind that the Book of the Dean contains an extensive selection of the 'classical' Gaelic verse of the Middle Ages.
90 Ross, 'Humanism'.
91 I am very grateful to Mrs L Niven and Mrs A Kelly for their help with the production of this article.

Chapter 30

FROM SAGA TO FOLKTALE: 'THE DEIRDRE STORY' IN GAELIC TRADITION

Caoimhín Mac Giolla Léith

> Nathos is on the deep, and Althos, that beam of youth,
> Ardan is near his brothers; they move in the gloom of
> their course. The sons of Usnoth move in darkness from
> the wrath of car-borne Cairbar. Who is that dim, by
> their side? The night has covered her beauty. Her hair
> sighs on ocean's wind; her robe streams in dusky
> wreaths. She is, like the fair ghost of heaven, in the
> midst of the shadowy mist. Who is it but Dar-thula, the
> first of Erin's maids?

With these words James Macpherson introduced readers of his
'Ossianic' poem Dar-thula, first published in 1762, to the tragic
heroine he describes as 'the most famous woman of antiquity'.[1]
This is the kind of language, as the late Professor E G Quin
remarked, 'in which the story of Deirdre and the sons of Uisneach
(whose names are originally Naoise, Ainnle and Ardán in Gaelic
tradition) impinged for the first time on the outside world and
made its contribution to the beginnings of the Romantic movement
in European literature'.[2]
     Unlike that other celebrated figure of Gaelic literature, Fionn
mac Cumhaill, to whom we find tantalising references in medieval
Scots literature in the works of Barbour, Dunbar, Douglas and
others,[3] Deirdre's first appearance outside Gaelic literature is
relatively late.[4] Apart from a disputed reference in The Welsh
Embassador, an anonymous play written about 1623,[5] the first brief
mention outwith Gaelic literature of what has become popularly
known as 'the Deirdre story' appears to be that in Hugh MacCurtin's
1717 treatise A brief discourse in Vindication of the Antiquity of
Ireland (Dublin). The earliest full-length treatment is in Dermod
O'Connor's General History of Ireland, first published in Dublin
in 1723. This is a very free 'translation' of the seventeenth-
century Irish historian Geoffrey Keating's History of Ireland or
Foras Feasa ar Éirinn, a work we shall return to later.[6] O'Connor's
is the only English language adaptation that predates Macpherson's.
     The Deirdre story, then, does not appear in English or Scots
literature within the historical period that is the proper concern
of this conference. Its history within Gaelic tradition, however,
has been long and august. Its roots go back at least to the ninth
century and it blossoms still today in the oral lore of Gaelic
Ireland and, to a lesser extent, Scotland. The purpose of this
paper is, in the first instance, to sketch the history of the

Deirdre story in Gaelic tradition and, secondly, to touch upon
some issues and problems of Gaelic literary history raised by
previous treatments of this material.

The oldest surviving version of the Deirdre story is the early
Irish saga Longes mac nUislenn, 'The Exile of the Sons of Uislio',
which is preserved in the twelfth-century Book of Leinster, the
fourteenth-century Yellow Book of Lecan and the early sixteenth-
century British Museum MS Egerton 1782.[7] Like the bulk of early
Gaelic saga-material the tale itself is much older than the earliest manuscript in which it occurs and has been dated to the late
eighth or ninth century. It is the version of the Deirdre story
most familiar to Celtic scholars and might be summarised as
follows: Conchobhar, king of Ulster, is feasting at the house of
his storyteller, Feidhlimidh mac Daill, when Feidhlimidh's wife
gives birth to a daughter.[8] Cathbhadh the druid prophesies that
the child will grow up to be a woman of surpassing beauty but that
she will bring destruction and ruin to Ulster. The men of Ulster
wish to kill her at once but the king intervenes and orders that
she be reared in isolation and in due course become his consort.
Upon reaching maturity, however, Deirdre meets and elopes with
Naoise mac Uisleann, one of the king's warriors.[9]

Accompanied by Naoise's two brothers and a retinue of one
hundred and fifty warriors, women, servants and dogs, the lovers
are pursued throughout Ireland by the king. They are eventually
forced to flee to Scotland, where they are initially welcomed, and
the three enter the service of the king of Scotland. The king,
however, is told of Deirdre's great beauty and desires her for
himself. The exiles are once more forced to flee, this time to an
unspecified island. On hearing of their plight the men of Ulster
prevail upon Conchobhar to invite them back to Ireland. The exiles
return with guarantees of their safety from a number of Ulster
warriors, chief among whom is Fearghus mac Róigh. On reaching the
king's residence at Eamhain Mhacha the sons of Uisliu are slain by
Eoghan mac Durthacht of Farney at Conchobhar's behest. Fearghus
and the other guarantors, enraged by what they perceive as the
king's treachery, join battle with the Ulstermen killing three
hundred of them including one of Conchobhar's sons. They then go
into exile in Connaught along with three thousand men. Deirdre
spends a year with Conchobhar in constant mourning for her dead
lover. The king eventually decides to give her to the hated Eoghan
for a further year. The following day Conchobhar and Eoghan are
bringing the unfortunate Deirdre to the assembly at Macha when
Conchobhar gibes her cruelly. She promptly commits suicide by
jumping from the chariot in which they are riding and dashing her
head against a rock.

Longes mac nUislenn (LMU) is written in the spare, concise and
relatively unadorned prose characteristic of early Irish saga,
interspersed with three verse passages in syllabic metre and three
passages in the alliterative, archaic (or perhaps archaising)
style known as rosc(ad). It has been deemed by many the crowning
glory of early Gaelic narrative. According to Myles Dillon 'it is
the noblest saga, and probably the finest in all Irish literature'.[10] Mac Cana has commented on 'the extraordinary quality of
the story of Deirdre as written in the eighth or ninth century'

and describes Deirdre as 'one of the great tragic heroines of literature'.[11] The great Swiss scholar Rudolf Thurneysen called LMU 'ein wahres Juwel unter der vielen bunten Steinen der irische Sage',[12] and while this may seem an unduly harsh judgement on early Irish saga as a whole it is some indication of the high esteem in which LMU has long been held.

I have said that the composition of LMU has been dated to the eighth or ninth century and it has generally been assumed that, in common with other early Irish sagas, the material drawn upon in its composition had previously had a long life in oral tradition. But this view of the antiquity and ultimate oral provenance of these tales has been radically undermined in recent years by a number of scholars building on the pioneering work of Professor James Carney, who was the first seriously to call into question what he termed the 'nativist' view of early Gaelic literature.[13] In the case of LMU it is worth noting that there are few references to this material which can be dated to the Old or early Middle Irish period (i.e. pre-AD 1000). The earliest is a reference to the death of the sons of Uisliu in a poem attributed to Flannacán mac Cellaich úa Carmen, king of Bregia, who was killed in AD 896.[14] Their death is also noted in the poem Aidheda Forni do hUaislib Érenn, 'The Violent Deaths of a number of Nobles of Ireland', which is attributed to Cinaed úa hArtacáin, who died in AD 975.[15] Carney drew attention some time ago to the lack of chance references to Deirdre in other early tales and suggested that LMU's is 'a fiction composed in the Old Irish period [which] ... has no ancient roots in Irish tradition'.[16] Carney points out that LMU is not an independent story but has a definite purpose in the so-called 'Ulster Cycle' of tales. The centrepiece of this cycle is the famous Táin Bó Cuailnge, 'The Cattle Raid of Cooley', which has been called the Irish Iliad and indeed occupies a place in Gaelic tradition analogous to that of the Iliad in Greek. As Carney remarks:

> in TBC Fergus mac Róig and a band of Ulster exiles were on the Connaught side against their native province, and the function of LMU ... within the Ulster Cycle is to give an explanation of this peculiar circumstance. But this story is not apparently the 'traditional' story which explained the reason for the exile of Fergus. It replaced another story [Fochunn Loingse Fergusa meic Róig (FLF), 'The Cause of the exile of Fergus mac Róig'] of which a mere fragment is preserved. It is then hardly 'traditional' but a literary addition to a pre-existing saga cycle.[17]

Thurneysen had previously suggested that the usurping of FLF's position in the Ulster Cycle by LMU was due to the superior literary qualities of the latter.[18] Carney, however, has recently put forward the view that this replacement of an early tale by a later composition is not an isolated phenomenon but 'part of a constant policy in early monastic schools of revising early traditions for either religious or political reasons' and has cited instances of several other tales similarly treated.[19] This is in keeping with a recent tendency in early Irish history which stresses the need to

reconsider various Irish prose narratives as sophisticated political propoganda consciously designed to support the aspirations of
a particular dynasty or monastery at a given point in time. In the
case of our text, however, it is not entirely clear what political
or religio-political purpose the replacement of FLF by LMU might
have served. Carney has attempted to reconstruct the lost FLF
using material from the genealogical tradition. His primary source
is the poem beginning Conailla Medb michuru attributed to the poet
Luccreth moccu Chíara (Chérai) and preserved in the Laud genealogies[20] (the prose of the genealogies, it is claimed, used the poem
as a source but supplied some additional information). It should
be pointed out that much of this poem is obscure and has so far
resisted translation. Carney, nevertheless, makes the (considerable) assumption that 'in the genealogical tradition we have, no
doubt, the essential elements of the lost saga'.[21] Genealogical
tradition and saga alike, it is argued, reflect a belief held by a
number of Munster septs that they were not originally from Munster
but had come from the neighbourhood of Tara and were ultimately
descended from Fearghus and his band of followers, Fearghus having
left Ulster under a cloud, probably on account of his dishonourable desire for Meadhbh of Cruachan. The genealogical tradition,
then, and by extention FLF, 'shows Fergus in a bad light' and by
providing an honourable reason for Fearghus's exile 'the fiction-
writer who created the Deirdre story has done a first-rate job of
white-washing'.[22] Despite the ingenuity of Carney's argument,
however, the precise reason for the eighth- or ninth-century composer of LMU's attempt to redeem Fearghus's tarnished reputation
remains obscure. It might be added that Carney's assertion elsewhere in this article that 'these "revisions" could go as far as
fictional creation and this, once embarked upon, could become a
habit'[23] is less than convincing.
     Be that as it may, it is clear that the Deirdre story, once it
had gained a foothold in Gaelic tradition, was, as it were, there
to stay. The title Aithed Derdrinne re maccaib Uislenn (ADMU),
'The Elopement of Deirdre with the sons of Uisliu', is included in
one of the two Middle Irish tale-lists which purport to register
the complete repertoire of the ollam filidechta, the highest grade
of professional poet.[24] It has been assumed that, despite the
difference in title, ADMU refers to LMU. The tale-lists use a
system of classification which groups titles under common subject-
headings such as comperta 'births', tána 'cattle raids', aitheda
'elopements' and so on. Now while many of our extant sagas appear
in the lists under the appropriate and expected headings a problem
must have arisen, as Mac Cana has pointed out, with titles which
did not fit easily into any of the recognised categories.[25] In
such cases one of the options seems to have been simply to change
the title of a given text so as to accommodate it more readily in
the lists. Thus, for example, our putative precursor of the
Deirdre story, FLF, appears in both lists as Tochomlad Loingsi
Fergusa a hUlltaib, 'The Setting forth of Fergus's Band of Exiles
from Ulster', under the rubric tochomlada 'setting forth'. There
is no separate category of loingsi 'exiles, banishments' in the
lists although five titles containing the term longes appear in
one of them (Thurneysen's List A) subsumed under the rubic immrama

'sea-voyages'. Mac Cana's suggestion, however, that this somewhat
heterogeneous category is a late innovation lends some support to
the idea that at an earlier stage in the evolution of the tale-
lists the anomalous title of LMU was changed to accommodate it
under the heading aitheda.[26]

The evidence of the tale-lists is important (if somewhat confusing) as is the identification of ADMU with LMU. For LMU is by no
means the only version of the Deirdre story in Gaelic literature;
it is merely the earliest. Now one of the categories of tale which
appear in both lists is that of aideda/aitte 'violent deaths'. One
of the most popular tales in the modern Irish manuscript tradition
of the seventeenth to the nineteenth century belongs to this
category. It is Oidheadh Chloinne hUisneach (OCU), 'The Violent
Death of the Children of Uisneach'.[27] The composition of this
romance has generally been dated to the fourteenth or fifteenth
century. The earliest surviving manuscript in which it appears,
albeit in incomplete form, is the so-called 'Glenmasan MS'. This
was probably written in Ireland around the beginning of the
sixteenth century and is preserved in the National Library of
Scotland. OCU is also found in almost one hundred Irish MSS dating
from the seventeenth to the nineteenth century.

I have referred to OCU as a romance. This is common practice in
the literature despite the fact that the application of the
conventional distinction between saga and romance or epic and
romance to Gaelic narrative is by no means straightforward. In
Gaelic literary history the distinction is based largely on considerations of style and structure. The study of the form of Gaelic
literature is, to an even greater degree than that of its content,
as yet in its infancy and it may be that we shall ultimately prefer
to view the change from the prose style of Early Irish to that of
the Modern period as a gradual development punctuated, perhaps, by
several periods of relatively rapid change. The possibility of the
co-existence at any one time of widely differing styles, in prose
and in verse, must also be countenanced. Nevertheless, the most
commonly held view of the development of Gaelic prose is one which
draws a sharp distinction between pre-Norman and post-Norman
styles. Unfortunately this distinction on the descriptive level is
all too often accompanied by a corresponding distinction on the
evaluative level. The most extreme example of this is Frank
O'Connor's assertion that 'after the year 1200 there is no [Irish]
prose worth discussing' and that by the thirteenth century 'Irish
prose was dead'.[28] Even so circumspect a commentator as Mac Cana,
however, feels justified in referring to 'the palpable disparity in
kind and quality between the written prose of the pre- and post-
Norman periods' (my emphasis) as an established and observed
fact'.[29] The pervasiveness of this view, which like all such views
sheds more light on the aesthetic values of the present day than on
those of the period in which these texts were composed and transmitted, has resulted in the unfortunate neglect of the later tales,
including OCU. As Dillon commented, OCU 'has been the victim of
rather fastidious censure by scholars who had acquired a taste for
the Cistercian bareness of the early sagas and could not appreciate
the baroque in literature'.[30] The following quotation from Gerard
Murphy is a case in point:

The kingly grandeur, the genuine picture of ancient barbar-
ism, and the unity of structure which mark so many Old Irish
tales disappear [in the period between 1200 and 1600] ... and
are replaced by the piling of incident upon incident. The
unrealistic beauty of the Early Modern <u>Oidheadh Chloinne
hUisneach</u>... is, for instance, in marked contrast with the
warrior realism which delights us in so much of its eighth or
ninth century forerunner.[31]

It is ironic that Murphy, who was the foremost proponent of the
theory that much of early Gaelic saga consisted of mere plot-
summaries to be fleshed out in oral performance, should find the
more elaborate style of Early Modern romance, which is so much
closer to the style of modern oral narrative, so unpalatable. This
is surely a case of a scholar wanting to have his cake and eat it.
    Murphy was not alone in his low regard for OCU. Thurneysen had
previously stated that 'es ist fast schmerzlich zu berichten, wie
diese ergreifende alte Erzählung (LMU) einen späteren Bearbeiter
gefunden hat, der dem einstigen Verfasser in keiner Weise eben-
bürtig war'.[32] Vernam Hull, in the introduction to his edition of
LMU, opined that 'whereas the earlier version [LMU] is characterised by its economy of words and by its emotional restraint, the
later version [OCU] exhibits neither of these qualities, nor indeed
are these qualities to be found in almost all other Early Modern
Irish versions of older tales'.[33] The wording here is significant.
OCU lacks certain of the qualities of LMU, of which it is an
inferior <u>later version</u>. The prejudice against the style and form of
Early Modern romance in general, and OCU in particular, is com-
pounded by the notion that the later text is merely a revision or a
modification of the earlier. That this is Hull's view is made
explicit by his use of verbs such as 'omits', 'expands', 'magni-
fies' and 'substitutes' to describe the composition of OCU. The
fact is, however, that OCU is not an elaborately revised version of
LMU but simply a different tale concerning the same characters and
events but with significant, and in some instances irreconcilable,
differences in detail. Thus, while we may refer to LMU and OCU as
different versions of what we have, in deference to popular usage, been
calling 'the Deirdre story', we should not refer to OCU as a
'version' of the earlier LMU.
    The differences between LMU and OCU are not merely stylistic.
The events treated at length in the two tales are, to borrow a term
from linguistics, almost in complementary distribution. The
earliest version of OCU, preserved in the Glenmasan MS, begins with
a feast given by Conchobhar, king of Ulster, at a time when the
sons of Uisneach have already been in exile for some years. This
means that what one might be tempted to describe as the first half
of Deirdre's 'heroic biography', as outlined above, does not
appear.[34]
    OCU begins with a scene in which Conchobhar sets in motion the
chain of events that will ultimately lead to the deaths of Deirdre
and the sons of Uisneach and his own downfall. This he does by
persuading the Ulstermen publicly to admit their hitherto un-
voiced belief that the exile of the sons of Uisneach constitutes a
blemish (the words <u>ainimh</u>, <u>locht</u> and <u>uireasbhaidh</u> are used in

various MSS) on the king's household (teaghlach). Having been made
manifest by public utterance this blemish must be set to rights.
Conchobhar interviews the warriors Conall Cearnach, Cú Chulainn
and Fearghus mac Roigh in turn and chooses Fearghus as his messenger to the exiles and guarantor of their safety upon their return.
Fearghus and his sons depart for Scotland where they persuade the
sons of Uisneach to return – against the better judgement of
Deirdre who continually warns them of Conchobhar's treachery and
counsels prudence. Upon arriving in Ulster Fearghus is separated
from the party by the king's intrigues. The returned exiles are
then lured to the House of the Red Branch. There they are surrounded by the men of Ulster who set about firing the house. There
follows a great battle during which one of Fearghus's sons, Buinne
Borbruadh, betrays the company and defects. (At this point the
Glenmasan MS breaks off but the ending of the tale can be recon-
structed with the aid of later MSS.) Fearghus's other son, Iollann
Fionn, is slain in battle by Conall Cearnach. It is only when
Cathbhadh, the druid, intervenes, at Conchobhar's behest, and
ensnares the sons of Uisneach in a magic sea that they are finally
rendered powerless. As none of the Ulstermen is willing to execute
them the task falls to Maine Lámhgharbh, son of the king of
Lochlann, who beheads them simultaneously with Naoise's sword as
none of the three wishes to witness his brothers' execution.
Deirdre laments their death bitterly, drinks her dead lover's
blood, kisses him and dies forthwith. Cathbhadh curses Eamhain
Mhacha and swears that none of Conchobhar's descendants will ever
rule there again on account of the king's treachery.

Now a comparison of the précis of LMU given earlier with this
summary of OCU up to the point where the Glemasan MS breaks off
shows no outright inconsistencies between the two texts. A closer
reading of OCU, however, quickly puts paid to any notion that it
is a modified version of the earlier saga. The section of LMU
which deals with the events from Conchobhar's initial decision to
invite the sons of Uisneach to return to Ulster down to their
death takes up just 28 of the 320 lines in Hull's edition. But
these same events account for about 85 per cent of OCU, the bulk
of which comprises a series of scenes unique to this text.

By comparison with LMU the characters of Conchobhar and Deirdre
are not merely fleshed out but substantially different. In LMU
Conchobhar is the wronged king exacting a terrible but not explicitly unjust vengeance. In OCU, on the other hand, we are
presented with one of the most Machiavellian characters in Gaelic
literature. Conchobhar cunningly manipulates the complex system of
duty and obligation to overcome the universal high regard in which
the sons of Uisneach are held and bring about their downfall.

Deirdre's character is similarly more fully developed in OCU
than in LMU, though this development has not been to everyone's
taste (Eleanor Hull, for instance, speaks of the transformation
of the 'wild woman' of LMU 'into the Lydia Languish of a later
age').[35] The proud tragic heroine of LMU is, in OCU, both shrewd
counsellor and gifted prophetess. Deirdre and Leabharcham, the
female satirist, alone are free to match Conchobhar's machinations
with deception, prophesy, delaying tactics and prudent advice,
though their efforts are ultimately in vain. They alone have

recourse to the heightened language of poetry to this end.

The characters of the male warriors, Naoise and his brothers, Fearghus and his sons, and the sundry smaller roles filled by the warriors of Ulster are, by comparison, prosaic and one dimensional. These characters are not appreciably more developed in OCU than they are in LMU. They are mere pawns in the struggle between Conchobhar's desire for revenge and Deirdre's attempts to prevent him from exacting it. Their actions are constrained and predetermined by their duties, obligations and geasa, or tabus, and the author of OCU makes full use of this in weaving the complex tapestry of this underrated romance.

It will have been obvious from a comparison of the two plot summaries that LMU and OCU differ most profoundly in their respective accounts of the death of the sons of Uisneach and, subsequently, that of Deirdre. In the earlier LMU the brothers are slain by Eoghan mac Durthacht of Farney immediately on reaching Eamhain Mhacha and Deirdre lives on for a year before her eventual suicide. OCU ends quite differently. Deirdre and the sons of Uisneach are lured to the House of the Red Branch. There they are surrounded and the house is set alight. The heroes escape from the house but are then ensnared in a magic sea by Cathbhadh and almost drowned. Finally they are beheaded by Maine Lámhgharbh. This elaborate end, which is yet another example of the well known 'Motif of the Threefold Death' in Gaelic literature, is in marked contrast to their expeditious despatch in LMU.

The fact that the earlier LMU states that Eoghan mac Durthacht of Farney killed the sons of Uisneach might initially lead us to suspect that Maine Lámhgharbh is the late invention of the Early Modern Gaelic compiler of OCU. That this is not the case is clear from a passage in Tochmarc Luaine ocus Aided Athairne (TL), 'The Wooing of Luaine and the Violent Death of Athairne', which, according to its most recent editor, was probably put together in the second half of the twelfth century from previously existing material. One section of this text treats of a personage called Manannán mac Athgno, who is portrayed as the friend and mentor of the sons of Uisneach in Scotland. In the opening passage of this section it is explicitly stated that Naoise and his brothers killed the father of Maine Lámhgharbh during their time in Scotland, that Maine and his two brothers subsequently came in exile to Ulster and that it was they who killed the sons of Uisneach as deputies of Eoghan mac Durthacht (conid iad ro marb trí meic Uisnig fri láim Eogain meic Durrthacht).[36] It may be that here the twelfth-century compiler of TL was attempting a harmonisation of two independent accounts of the death of the sons of Uisneach, what we might call the LMU account and the OCU account.

The evidence of this section of TL concerning Manannán mac Athgno, along with a few other stray references in roughly contemporary non-narrative materials, suggests that already by the twelfth century there was in existence a certain amount of material concerning Deirdre and Naoise's sojourn in Scotland.[37] While there is no evidence that this material was available to the compiler of LMU, in which the Scottish episode is treated in a fairly general manner (i.e. no specific place- or personal names are given and it might just as well have taken place almost anywhere outside Ireland), it seems almost certain that it was drawn upon by the compiler of OCU. Apart from the extensive use of Argyllshire place-names in OCU, indicating an intimate knowledge of the area, one notes, first of all, the agreement of all complete MS versions of the romance in designating Maine Lámhgharbh as the executioner of the sons of Uisneach. Second, there is the fact that a number of MSS agree with TL in giving the names of Maine's brothers as Iathach and Triathach though they play no part in the narrative of OCU (in fact it is stated that they were killed by Naoise along with their father). Third, OCU refers on two occasions to Deirdre and Naoise's receiving gifts from a Manannán. It seems more than likely that this was originally the Manannán mac Athgno of TL. That eighteenth-century MSS should convert him into his infinitely better known namesake, Manannán mac Lir, is hardly surprising.

I have so far treated OCU as if it were a monolithic fixed text faithfully copied over and over throughout the three and a half centuries spanned by its MS history (roughly from the beginning of the sixteenth century to the middle of the nineteenth). This is far from being the case. OCU underwent the usual range of alter- ations, modifications, additions and omissions common to other Gaelic romances which survive in the modern MS tradition. These changes might be classified roughly under two headings: (a) the mistakes, inaccuracies and failure of comprehension of individual copyists and (b) the elaborations and modifications introduced by scribes consciously adding detail or comment. (The former is a factor in the transmission of Gaelic MS literature which has, perhaps, been hitherto overemphasised, the latter one which has been unduly neglected.) The extent to which scribes felt free to modify saga and romance texts has led some scholars, most notably Melia, Slotkin and Ó Coileáin, to advocate the abandonment of the notion of the fixed text in favour of a view of these texts as, in Melia's words, 'inherently multiform'.[38] Before we abandon the traditional Lachmannian principles entirely, however, we need to learn much more about the precise extent to which Gaelic scribes felt free to alter this material if we are to guard against the danger of throwing the baby out with the bathwater, as it were. When Slotkin suggests, for example, that scribes most probably 'treated saga-texts as the multiform oral products they ultimately were'[39] this begs the important question of the original proven- ance of these texts. It also runs the risk of assuming that the processes of change at work on a given text during the course of its MS transmission are similar to, if not the same as, those at work in the oral transmission of prose narrative. This is, to my mind, a wholly unwarranted assumption.

In the case of OCU I have recently shown that the single most important factor in the development of variants of this text was the co-existence in the MS tradition, from the mid seventeenth century on, of Geoffrey Keating's History of Ireland, or Foras Feasa ar Éirinn, which I had cause to mention briefly at the beginning of this paper.[40]

Little enough is known of the life of Geoffrey Keating. He was born sometime around 1580 in Burges in County Tipperary, and was educated at Bordeaux where he gained a doctorate in divinity. He returned to Ireland and to his native parish about 1610. There he spent most of his remaining years preaching and attending to his priestly duties. He died sometime during the mid to late 1640s and is interred in the little church of Tubrid, just a few miles from his place of birth. Keating wrote a certain amount of verse and a number of devotional treatises, but it is for his History of Ireland that he is best known. This work was completed sometime before 1640 and was destined to become the most popular prose work in the Modern Irish MS tradition.

While Keating's status as a superb prose stylist has never been seriously disputed, his reputation as a historian has not withstood the test of time or the scrutiny of his contemporaries in the field and their modern counterparts.[41] What is important for our purpose, however, is the unique authority accorded to him by eighteenth- and nineteenth-century Irish scribes.

Keating's History includes a version of the Deirdre story clearly based on LMU though considerably attenuated and with some additional material from another source or other sources.[42] The style is elegant if brisk by comparison with the romance. Unlike the romance or the earlier saga there are no intercalated verse passages. That the existence of this version should confuse and disconcert eighteenth- and nineteenth-century scribes was inevitable. We have seen that the most significant divergences between LMU and OCU occur at the beginning and at the end of these tales. Keating follows LMU in including an account of Deirdre's birth, youth and elopement with Naoise. He also follows LMU in his account of Naoise's death at the hand of Eoghan mac Durthacht and Deirdre's suicide a year later.

Almost all of the surviving MS versions of OCU written during the eighteenth and nineteenth centuries, which number almost one hundred, show some attempt to reconcile these conflicting accounts. The vast majority of these MSS preface OCU proper with an account of the earlier part of Deirdre's life taken from Keating, and the varying degrees of success with which this introductory matter was incorporated into the tale in different MSS sheds valuable light on scribal practice during this period. The ending of the tale presented even greater difficulties than the beginning. Some scribes retain the original OCU ending and simply ignore Keating. Others retain the original ending but openly admit that according to other sources (Keating is specifically mentioned in some instances) it was Eoghan mac Durthacht and not Maine Lámhgharbh who killed the three brothers. Some scribes try to smuggle Eoghan in the back door, as it were, by stating that Conchobhar intially asked Clann Durthacht to act as executioners and when they refused the task devolved upon Maine. Finally, a small number of MSS defer to Keating's authority and abandon the original OCU account of the deaths of the sons of Uisneach and of Deirdre, replacing it with Keating's.

Two other developments in the MS transmission of OCU in the course of the eighteenth century deserve to be mentioned. First, a poem explaining the interrelationship of a number of the main characters of the Ulster Cycle entitled <u>Cathbhadh mac Maolchró na ccath</u>, 'Cathbhadh son of Maolchro of the battles', is regularly appended. Secondly, OCU is linked in a number of MSS with two other tales of a similar nature and structure, Oidheadh Chloinne Lir, 'The Violent Death of the Children of Lir', and Oidheadh Chloinne Tuireann, 'The Violent Death of the Children of Tuireann'. This triad of tales is known as Trí Truaighe na Sgéaluigheachta, 'The Three Sorrows of Storytelling'.

We have so far in this survey of the Deirdre story in Gaelic tradition spanned roughly one thousand years. We have discussed three versions of the story, the eighth- or ninth-century saga LMU, the Early Modern romance OCU and Keating's seventeenth-century account. We have seen that these latter two versions were very much alive in the eighteenth and nineteenth centuries and interacting vigorously in the Irish MS tradition. We have almost come to the end of the journey from saga to folktale alluded to in the title of this paper. Almost, but not quite. For during the late eighteenth and early nineteenth century two developments arise, one in Scotland and one in Ireland, which I shall discuss just briefly.

In the early 1760s, as is well known, James MacPherson published a number of volumes purporting to contain English translations of the epic poetry of a third-century Scottish Gaelic poet named Ossian. One of the happier effects of the ensuing controversy concerning the validity of Macpherson's claim to have discovered an ancient Gaelic epic was the awakening of an interest in the heroic ballads preserved in the oral tradition, and to a lesser extent the MS tradition, of the Gaelic-speaking Highlands. The bulk of the material collected during this period was eventually published by J F Campbell in his Leabhar na Féinne (London, 1872). This book contains a number of ballads or laoidhean concerning Deirdre and the sons of Uisneach. Much of this verse appears to be genuinely traditional and clear echoes of the verse passages in OCU may be discerned. Some of it, however, shows traces of the influence of Macpherson's Dar-thula from which I quoted at the beginning of this paper. The careful sifting of this 'unruly material', as Professor Thomson has described the Leabhar na Féinne texts,[43] is a daunting task but one which must be faced up to before we can begin to understand the later development of the Deirdre story in Gaelic tradition. We are fortunate that the foundation for this work has been laid in Thomson's pioneering book The Gaelic Sources of Macpherson's Ossian (Aberdeen, 1951). Reidar Christiansen has also made an important contribution with his The Vikings and the Vikings Wars in Gaelic Tradition (Oslo, 1931) but much remains to be done.

The second noteworthy development during this period took place in Belfast sometime between 1805 and 1809 when a local scribe, Samuel Bryson, produced a version of the Deirdre story entitled Imthiacht Dheirdre la Naoise agus Oidhe Chloinne Uisneach, 'The Elopment of Deirdre with Naoise and the Violent Death of the Sons of Uisneach'.[44] This is clearly based on a MS version of OCU which included the preface from Keating but has been substantially altered and embellished. Whether this embellishment is the work of Bryson or not is unclear. It is tempting to view this text, which differs considerably from all other MS versions of OCU, as a re-casting of the tale by an accomplished man of letters unimpeded by the constraints of the Irish MS tradition of his day, freely adding material either of his own creation or from oral versions of the tale current at the time, or both.

The interaction of the co-existing oral and MS modes of transmission in Gaelic, as in other traditions, is a thorny problem
indeed and one which has been keenly debated in Celtic studies. In
the case of the Deirdre story a third element intrudes which has
less frequently been discussed, for the simple reason that it is
largely irrelevant to the history of Gaelic literature until
relatively recent times, i.e. print culture. For in 1808 Theophilus
O'Flanagan published the first edition of both LMU and OCU along
with English translations of both texts.[45] Henceforth readers of
English had access to all three pre-eighteenth-century versions of
the Deirdre story (O'Connor's 'translation' of Keating, we have
noted, had already been published in 1723). That O'Flanagan's
edition of OCU had some effect on the MS transmission of the
romance can be demonstrated.[46] That it also had an effect on oral
tellings of the tale is not improbable.[47]

The late nineteenth and the present century have seen the
collection of a number of these oral versions, mostly in Ireland,
though Alexander Carmichael's Deirdre, collected from John MacNeil
in Barra in 1867 and subsequently published in the Transactions of
the Gaelic Society of Inverness and in book form deserves special
mention.[48] These tales were possibly circulating in oral tradition
for a number of centuries prior to their being collected in modern
times.

This period also saw the widespread adaptation of the Deirdre
story into English by writers such as Samuel Ferguson, W B Yeats, J
M Synge, James Stephens and many others. Indeed this story has
accurately been described as 'the single most widely adapted Irish
narrative into English'. It is an indication of the enduring
quality of the Deirdre story that MacPherson's 'most famous woman
of antiquity' should have retained her fame down to the present
day.[49]

Notes

1   Fingal, an Ancient Epic Poem ... composed by Ossian the son
    of Fingal (Dublin, 1762), 169. (First published in London,
    [December 1761] 1762).

2   'Longas Macc n-Uisnig', in Irish Sagas, Myles Dillon (ed),
    (Dublin, 1968), 53.

3   See James MacKillop, Fionn mac Cumhaill: Celtic Myth and
    English Literature (Syracuse, 1986), 72-4, for a presentation
    and discussion of these references.

4   In this paper the term 'Gaelic' is used to refer to the
    literary tradition shared by the learned classes of Gaelic
    Scotland and Ireland down to the seventeenth century. In
    deference to common usage the more chauvinistic term 'Irish'
    is occasionally used when referring to the earlier period.

5   The Welsh Embassador (Malone Society Reprints, 1920), 37.
    This is discussed by Marcia Kelley in 'The Deirdre Legend in
    English Literature', (unpublished PhD dissertation,
    University of Pennsylvania, 1950), 69-70.

6   Published, with an English translation, by the Irish Texts
     Society (ITS vols IV, VIII, IX and XV) under the title The
     History of Ireland - Foras Feasa ar Éirinn (London, 1902-
     1914), Vol I, D Comyn (ed); Vols II-IV, P S Dinneen (ed).
7   Vernam Hull, Longes mac n-Uislenn (New York, 1949).
8   Gaelic orthography has changed considerably throughout the
     centuries from our earliest records down to the present day.
     The names of the principal personages in the Deirdre story are
     here spelt in accordance with the norms of the modern language.
9   The name of Naoise's father *Uisliu (genitive Uislenn
     Uisleann) becomes Uisneach (genitive Uisnighd, later Uisneach)
     in the late Middle Irish and Early Modern period. This change
     has yet to be satisfactorily explained.
10   Early Irish Literature (Chicago, 1948), 16-17.
11   Literature in Irish (Dublin, 1980), 31.
12   Die irische Helden- und Königsage bis zum siebenzehnten
     Jahrhundert (Halle, 1921), 322.
13   See his Studies in Irish Literature and History (Dublin,
     1955), passim.
14   Kathleen Mulchrone, 'Flannacán mac Celaich rí Breg hoc
     carmen', The Journal of Celtic Studies 1 (1950), 80-93.
15   W Stokes, 'On the Deaths of some Irish Heroes,' Revue Celtique
     43 (1902), 308, 320, 326.
16   Carney, Studies, 235. The quotation is from a more recent
     article: idem, 'Early Irish Literature: the State of
     Research', in Proceedings of the Sixth International Congress
     of Celtic Studies, Gearóid Mac Eoin (ed) with the collabor-
     ation of Anders Alqvist and Donncha Ó hAodha (Dublin, 1983),
     113-130.
17   Carney, Studies, 234.
18   Heldensage, 322
19   Carney, 'Early Irish Literature', 127.
20   K Meyer, 'The Laud Genealogies and Tribal Histories', Zeit-
     schrift für Celtische Philologie 8 (1912), 291-338.
21   Carney, 'Early Irish Literature', 125.
22   Ibid, 125
23   Ibid, 127
24   Thurneysen's suggestion that both lists are based on an older
     list, the composition of which he dated to the tenth century,
     has been accepted by Mac Cana in his edition of the lists in
     The Learned Tales of Medieval Ireland (Dublin, 1980).
25   Learned Tales, 67
26   Ibid, 76. The existence in List A of the title Feis Emna,
     which Mac Cana suggests may refer to FLF, and, in the
     miscellaneous section of List B, of the title Longus nUlad,
     which he suggests may refer either to FLF or to the Deirdre
     story, does not help to clarify matters. It must also be
     pointed out that the whole question as to what status, if any,
     many of these titles enjoyed outside the immediate context of
     the tale-lists, and to what extent we are justified in posit-
     ing the existence of 'lost tales' on the basis of their
     occurrence in this context, has yet to receive the attention
     it deserves.

27 W Stokes, 'The Death of the Sons of Uisneach', Irische Texte
    2/2 (Leipzig, 1887), 109-18. The writer is at present prepar-
    ing a new edition of this text.
28 Quoted in Mac Cana, Learned Tales, 9.
29 Ibid, 9
30 Early Irish Literature, 16
31 The Ossianic Lore and Romantic Tales of Medieval Ireland
    (Cork, 1955), 31.
32 Heldensage, 327
33 Longes, 1
34 Deirdre's is, of course, the biography of a non-martial
    heroine and, it must be admitted, one conspicuously lacking a
    compert or 'conception tale/episode', but in general it con-
    forms to the pattern of the heroic biography. For a demonstra-
    tion of the usefulness of this pattern in the explicaton of
    early Irish narrative see Tomas Ó Cathasaigh, The Heroic
    Biography of Cormac mac Airt (Dublin, 1977).
35 'The Story of Deirdre in its Bearing on the Social Develop-
    ment of the Folk Tale', Folk-Lore 15 (1904), 25. The history
    of the Deirdre story is here seen as a gradual degeneration
    which reaches its nadir in Samuel Bryson's version of the tale
    which appears in a MS of the early nineteenth century. R A S
    MacAlister was similarly unimpressed with this transformation.
    In a somewhat eccentric article in which, inter alia, he
    argues the case for the relative superiority of Oidheadh
    Chloinne Tuireann (OCT), 'The Violent Death of the Children of
    Tuireann', which is associated with OCU in the later MS tradi-
    tion, he states that OCT is fortunate in that, unlike OCU,

        it possesses no suffering heroine to be rhapsodized over
        ... There is no Deirdre to be taken in hand by sundry
        ecstatics and literary persons to be rouged and raddled,
        enamelled and Eton-cropped, until Noísi himself would
        neither recognize nor acknowledge her; and till from being
        quite an interesting specimen for the dissecting room
        table of the scientific ethnologist she has become one of
        the most tedious puppets in all literature (Béaloideas 1
        (1928), 13).

36 Liam Breatnach, 'Tochmarc Luaine ocus Aided Athairne', Celtica
    (1980), 11. Maine Lámhgharbh is also mentioned en passant in
    the (twelfth century?) tale Aided Guill meic Carbada ocus
    Aided Gairb Glinne Rige (Whitley Stokes, 'The Violent Deaths
    of Goll and Garb', Revue Celtique 14 (1893), 396-449.
37 T Ó Raithbheartaigh, Genealogical Tracts 1, 166; Margaret C
    Dobbs, 'The Banshenchus', Revue Celtique 48 (1931), 173;
    Trinity College Dublin MS H.3.17, col.865 10-20.
38 Daniel F Melia's review of Táin Bó Cuailnge: Recension 1 in
    Speculum 53 (1978), 607-09; Edgar M Slotkin, 'Medieval Scribes
    and Fixed Texts', Eigse 17 (1977-79), 437-50; Seán Ó Coileáin,
    'The Structure of a Literary Cycle', Eriu 25 (1974), 88-125.
39 Slotkin, 'Medieval Scribes', 449.
40 'Oidheadh Chloinne hUisneach: Innovation and Modification in
    the Transmission of a Gaelic Romance', (paper delivered at the

Eighth International Congress of Celtic Studies in Swansea, July 1987).

41 For a contentious but persuasive re-appraisal of Keating as a historian see Breandán Ó Buachalla, 'Annála Ríoghachta Éireann is Foras Feasa ar Éirinn: an comhthéacs comhaimseartha', Studia Hibernica 22-23 (1982-3), 50-105.

42 Keating, History of Ireland Vol II, 190-6.

43 Introduction to the 1972 Irish University Press facsimile of Leabhar na Féinne, v.

44 Breandán Ó Buachalla (ed), in Zeitschrift fur Celtische Philologie 29 (1962), 114-154

45 Transactions of the Gaelic Society of Dublin (1908), 178pp.

46 A number of nineteenth-century MS Versions of OCU are in fact direct copies of O'Flanagan's text. One eighteenth-century version, that in British Museum MS Egerton 662 written in 1770 by the northern Irish scribe Muiris Ó Gormáin, was later emended by one James MacQuigge to conform to O'Flanagan's edition.

47 Standish Hayes O'Grady's assertion in 1857 that he had

> heard a man who never possessed a manuscript nor heard of O'Flanagan's publication relate at the fireside the death of the sons of Uisneach without omitting one adventure, and in great part retaining the very words of the written versions (Tóruigheacht Dhiarmada agus Ghráinne (Dublin, 1857), 29)

is worth noting in this context despite its author's assumption of independent oral transmission.

48 TGSI 13 (1886-7), 241-57; Alexander Carmichael, Deirdre and the Lay of the Children of Uisne (Edinburgh, 1905).

49 I should like to thank Professor Breandán Ó Buachalla who read a draft of this paper and made many valuable suggestions for its improvement. I alone, of course, am responsible for any errors which remain.

Chapter 31

THE OTHER SCOTTISH LANGUAGE – ORKNEYINGA SAGA

O D Macrae-Gibson

There were numerous papers at this conference, naturally, on the
Scots language and its literature, and some on Gaelic. In this
paper I draw attention to the fact that over many centuries, and
over extensive parts of what is now Scotland, the language spoken
was neither of these, but the 'other Scottish language' of my
title, one which in the form of the 'Norn' finally became extinct
less than a century ago.[1] The areas it used to cover are regularly
known as the Earldom of Orkney, or 'Jarldom' if one prefers the
form of the Earls' own language. But this 'Earldom' is not to be
thought of as a tidy, unitary nation-state whose Head bore the
title of Earl, like the Grand Duchy of Luxembourg or the Princi-
pality of Monaco. The areas over which the writ of particular
Earls ran varied with their individual power, based always in the
Northern Isles but extending to parts at least of what they called
the Southern and we the Western Isles, and at times to quite
extensive parts of mainland Scotland, centring on what we agree
with them in calling the Souther Land. There was not always a
single Earl; quite often two or more divided the territories
between them, or ruled in collaboration, or were at war with each
other. Sometimes they owed their title to a grant by the King of
Norway, or less often the King of Scots, who thus claimed an over-
lordship; sometimes to inheritance from their fathers, sometimes
it seems simply to their own might and main. But in any case they
presided over an extensive land-occupancy in the northern parts of
our country by a people speaking a Scandinavian language, which
would have been a minor dialectal variant of the Norwegian or
Icelandic of the time. Linguistically, as a Scottish language, it
would clearly fall within the ambit of the conference title.
Nothing is directly known, of course, about its medieval or
Renaissance state, but something might be inferred from its
residual forms. Thus if the first word of the refrain from the
Shetland ballad of King Orfeo, scowan, is in fact the Norse skógr
plus suffixed definite article, then a vocalising of velar g
parallel and presumably contemporaneous with the Middle English
change must in some circumstances have occurred. I admit ignorance
of whether any such work has been done; it is certainly not what I
am attempting in this paper, and in trying instead to include this
language on the literary side of the conference I may be thought
to be straining facts unduly, for Scottish Norse is not reckoned
to have left any literary remains except for a few scraps of verse
which barely survived, much corrupted, long enough to be collected

in the nineteenth century, of which the Orfeo refrain is one.

Now it has been held, on the contrary, that in Orkneyinga Saga (or as it should perhaps be more accurately titled Orkneyinga Jarla Saga, the Story of the Orkney Earls) we do have an Orkney Norse document, and a specific Orkney author has been found for it, one Bishop Bjarni. The case was argued by Jón Stéfansson in 1907,[2] but it is now agreed to be quite ill-founded, and the saga, from its use of and in turn use for undoubtedly Icelandic texts, is now universally accepted as an Icelandic document. The authors of the most recently published version, Pálsson and Edwards, are quite categorical:

> It was written not by an Orkneyman but by an Icelander, probably around 1200. The name of the author is unknown, but there seems little doubt that he must have been associated with the intellectual centre at Oddi in Southern Iceland.[3]

I do not want to challenge the location in Iceland or the more exact suggestion of Oddi, but I do want to take issue with the view of composition implied by the phrases 'an Icelander', 'the author'. The work as we have it was doubtless compiled by an Icelander, very probably at Oddi, but in basing himself, as he plainly did, on a variety of sources we are not to suppose that he digested them all and then wrote the whole work in his own style; that was simply not how an 'author' worked at the time. If material reached him in a form that could be directly incorporated he would quite naturally do so, though he would of course normalise the linguistic forms to Icelandic as he went.

Here I am rather with A B Taylor than with Pálsson and Edwards. In the analysis prefaced to his translation of the saga[4] Taylor distinguishes several portions stylistically, and treats them as incorporations of different written sources. It is not practicable to create by inference from the saga as we have it a full catalogue of its distinct sources, though Taylor has tried to, coming up with no less than thirty-four separate ones. What is certain, however, is that among them, whether directly communicated to the compiler by Orkneymen who certainly visited Iceland, or as underlying written sources that he used, was eyewitness evidence from the islands themselves. In one case the authority of a local informant is explicitly acknowledged, for the exchanges between Earl Hakon and his supporters which preceded the killing of Earl Magnus: 'Svá segir Holdboði, réttorðr bóndi í Suðreyjum'. So says Holdbothi, a veracious witness ('rettorðr', 'rightworded'), a farmer from the Southern Isles, the Hebrides, who was with Magnus as one of his two immediate supporters when he was captured. Now if when the saga turns to matter for which such detailed local authority was clearly needed we find also a change of style, it is at least to be considered whether this might be because in form as well as substance the material came from Scotland (though of course it could also be that the Icelandic author was moved to a different style by the greater amplitude and interest of his information).

The first point at which such a change of style suggests itself to me is in connection with the first Earl Rognvald. Before that,

the saga relates the squabbles and battles of a series of Scandinavian kings, of whom the earlier ones are mythological (thus Nor,
the founder of Norway); then following a stated subjugation of the
Northern and Western Isles by the undoutedly historical king
Harald 'hárfagri' ('fine-hair') it follows the fortunes of the
earl Sigurth whom Harald created as his viceroy in the island, and
his successors. There is little individuality about any of these
men, and little literary interest in the saga. But with Rognvald
it improves. He is, as so often happened, at war with his uncle
Earl Thorfin about their shares of power; Thorfin has won a hard-
fought naval engagement and Rognvald has fled to his patron King
Magnus 'the good' in Norway, but (ch. 28) he returns secretly,
surprises Thorfin in the house where he is in residence, and - as
he supposes - burns him and all his men inside it, though in fact
Thorfin succeeds in breaking out and escaping in the smoke and
darkness. Rognvald now makes himself master of all Thorfin's
territories, but is in turn surprised by Thorfin, in turn escapes
from his burning house, but this time is identified as he flees,
pursued, and killed, betrayed by the barking of his pet dog which
he has taken with him (where Thorfin fled carrying his wife).
Except for that last touch this is all standard, impersonal stuff.
So is the fact that Rognvald becomes supernaturally aware of
impending doom before Thorfin's attack declares itself. But the
way in which this awareness manifests itself is not standard. In
an Icelandic saga we would expect something like the vision Njal
has of the tables covered in blood before the famous burning of
Njáls Saga (ch. 127). What we get is this: they have sat for a
long time 'við bakelda', literally 'beside (the) bake-fire' but it
is themselves they are 'baking', until the man looking after the
fire reports that wood is running low. The earl says that they
will have 'baked' quite enough by the time the fire is burned out:
'þá eru vér fullbakaðir ...' (we'll be fully baked'). At least,
that is what he meant to say, but it came out as 'þa eru vér
fullgamlir' ('we'll be fully aged', i.e. the fire will outlast
their lives). The tradition which created this would not seem to
be an Icelandic one.[5]

When the news of the death of his protégé reaches King Magnus
he swears vengeance, but cannot undertake it at once because he is
at war with King Svein of Denmark. As he lies with a fleet in
pursuit of this war two longships enter the harbour; one comes
alongside the king's ship and a man wearing a white hooded-cloak
comes aboard, walks aft to where the king is sitting at his meal,
and then 'tók til brauðsins ok braut ok át af' ('reached out to
the bread and broke a piece off and ate it'); then he asks the
king for peace: 'Grið viljum vér, motunauðr' ('companion at
food'). As he has now 'taken the king's meat' the king is morally
barred from killing him even when he reveals himself as Thorfin
(there are more turns to the story, but he establishes his rule in
the islands). This motif of the covert creation of a situation of
hospitality is not a characteristic Icelandic one, though such a
situation can in Iceland be openly imposed on and accepted by an
acknowledged adversary; it is, I think, well known in Celtic
tradition.

In these cases I have been able to offer at best only motif-

evidence suggesting a possible Scottish source for the tale. I can
go, perhaps, a little further with my next passage (chs. 47-49),
concerning that same Earl Magnus whom I have already mentioned,
Saint Magnus as he was to be reckoned to be. He and his cousin
Hakon have been ruling jointly; then troublemakers cause dissen-
sion; then there are moves to arrange a settlement, which appear
to succeed, but 'þa eindagaði Hákon jarl með falsi ok fagrmæ lum
stefnudag'. 'With falsehood and fair-speaking'; such a phrase has
not appeared in the saga before, and this use of ok, which usually
implies close associaton, for an ironic linkage of opposites is
not as far as I am aware a usual Icelandic rhetorical trick. At
all events, Hakon thus deceitfully appoints the meeting; Magnus on
the other hand accepts 'án allra grunsemða, svika ok ágirnðar'
('without all suspicion, deceit and ambition'), again a phrase not
characteristic of Icelandic. Each leader is to come with two ships
only, and an agreed number of men. As Magnus is making his way to
the rendezvous an extraordinary event occurs: a breaker rears
itself out of deep sea and falls over where he sits, thus predict-
ing his imminent death. Hakon is indeed treacherous and comes with
a large warfleet; Magnus is captured, and our author opposes the
warrior-behaviour of the one earl to the saintly bearing of the
other. On the one side 'þa hljópu þeir þangat með ópi ok vápna-
braki' ('they rushed thither with shouting and clashing of
weapons'); on the other 'þá signdi hann sik ok mælti til Hákonar
jarls með staðfostum hug' ('he crossed himself and spoke to Earl
Hakon with steadfast heart'). This neatly opposed contrast between
warrior and Christian behaviour is once more not a characteristic
Icelandic saga feature. When the themes are conjoined at all,
which is rarely, it is in a more commingled way, as with Flosi's
reluctant resolution to go ahead with the burning of Njal's hall
although it is a terrible thing for a Christian to do.[6] Magnus, to
save Hakon's oath rather than to save his own life, offers first
that he will undertake a pilgrimage to Jerusalem and swear never
to return to Orkney, then that he be sent to guarded exile in
Scotland, finally that he be blinded or mutilated and imprisoned.
The first two are rejected out of hand with the formula 'þessu var
skjótt neitat': 'this was quickly rejected', but þessu is dative
and the verb impersonal, so more closely 'was quickly rejected as
to this'. I have not traced this formula anywhere else; in Icelandic usage neita with dative is standard, but it regularly has a
personal subject. Hakon is minded to accept the third alternative,
but his supporters declare that they do not intend to leave both
of them alive and contending for power: 'drepa munu ver annanhvarn
ykkarn' ('we're going to kill one or other of you'). Oath or no
oath Hakon has no doubt which: 'drepið hann heldr, því at fyrr vil
ek rá ð a ríki ok londum en deyja sva bratt' ('kill him for preference, for I'd rather control realm and lands than die so quickly')
- these are the exchanges vouched for by the Hebridean farmer
Holdbothi. Magnus then gets a properly resolute and saintly death,
and the usual post-mortem signs of divine favour quickly mark him
as a saint, in much less interesting passages. I suggest that the
whole lively episode leading up to his death can fairly be seen as
a literary artifact of Scottish Norse, incorporated in Orkneyinga
Saga.

Another portion of the saga for which I put forward a similar claim, on evidence perhaps rather stronger, concerns a later earl with some claim to Christian excellence, although he never became established as a saint, the second great Earl Rognvald (so named after the earlier one; his original name was Kali). Here I draw attention particularly to an episode in chapter 81 in which the Icelander Hall Thorarinsson is refused a place in Rognvald's household, despite the support of his Orkney host Thorstein Rognuson of 'Rinansey' (North Ronaldsay). His hostess, Thorstein's mother Ragna, now intervenes on his behalf. She is a woman of standing and influence, a woman of much perception. Her intervention is oblique. She calls on Rognvald about some other business, and evidently slides in the matter of Hall. When she comes 'hon var svá buinn, at hon hafði gaddan rautt á hofði, gort af hrossahári' ('she was thus arrayed: she had on her head a red gaddan, made of horse-hair'). The word gaddan is hapax legomenon; all scholars agree in proposing a Gaelic etymology, a diminutive in -an of gad ('withy, as used for binding'). Ragna's array is clearly unusual; when the earl sees it he improvises a verse in which he declares that in his experience noble ladies wear a dúk, a kerchief, on their heads, but she has got herself up with a mare's tail at her neck. She would seem to have bound her own hair with this dyed horse-hair to produce something like the modern 'pony-tail'. It is evidently a forward thing to do, what you might expect from a woman to whom Rognvald's rival, Earl Pal, has earlier found himself saying sharply that she might be a wise woman but 'eigi hefir þu hlotit jarlsnafn í Orkneyjum' ('you haven't got yourself the title of earl in the Orkneys'). Rognvald takes occasion in his verse to use for her two 'kennings' (poetic epithets) which would ordinarily belong to a distinguished man. One of them moreover is unique in its detailed form: menja myrðir. Menja is the genitive plural of men, which is a necklace, but not simply as adornment; it can be a convenient way of stringing together portable bullion. One who 'reduces the number' of such necklaces, menja fættir, is a man who generously gives them away, and similarly one who 'does harm to' them (presumably by breaking the string to give away the 'beads'), menja lestir. But Rognvald's menja myrðir makes it one who commits upon them morð ('dishonourable killing' - honest killing is víg), using a word which no other skaldic poet has used in any such phrase. It gives the same fundamental sense as menja lestir, but with clear pejorative overtones, and he couples it with the observation that Ragna is not being modest with her words either. She replies drily that he hasn't got it quite right,'því at þetta er af hesti, en eigi af meri' ('that comes from a stallion, and not from a mare'), and with that she takes out a silk kerchief which she has evidently had ready, puts it on, and goes on with her business. I take her implication to be that if she is being forward it is not on her own behalf but on a man's, on Hall's. Her persistence in due course wins the day, and Hall becomes an honoured member of Rognvald's household. If this episode had been written by our 'Icelandic author' on the basis of information from Orkney, he would hardly have put in, unexplained, the word gaddan, which would be unfamiliar to himself and unknown to many of his expected

readers; but if he were transcribing material which already stood
in form, written in a place where a <u>gaddan</u> was known, it would be
quite natural for him to let it stand.

Another episode related to Rognvald, too, in chapter 85 of the
saga, is I suggest worth attention. Taylor[7] regards it as a 'folk
tale' which has become attached to the earl, and perhaps it is,
but if so it has certainly been localised in the islands, and the
way the story ends suggests that it must have become attached to
an actual incident of Rognvald, not just to his name. There was in
Shetland 'einn bóndi ok félítill'. A bóndi is an independent
farmer, but since 'félítill' ('poor') we could translate as 'a
crofter'. The structure of 'einn bóndi ok félítill' ('a crofter
and poor') is one I have not encountered in Icelandic practice.
Our crofter is waiting to go fishing off Sumburgh Head, but his
companion has not joined him, though the other boats have all gone
out. There comes to him a man wearing a white hooded-cloak (we
remember that such a garment has once before been used by someone
wanting to conceal his identity), and offers to row for him, so
they put out, the crofter fishing in one of the tide-races around
'Hundholma' (now Horse Island) while his volunteer crew holds the
boat in the eddies beside it. This requires care, lest the boat be
swept into the race, but the man in the cloak is not careful and
the boat is swept away. The crofter despairs of his life, but the
man in the cloak assures him that 'sá mun okkr ór draga rostinni
er okkr lét í koma' ('he will pull us out of the race who let us
get into it'). It is left obscure whether he means 'himself' or
'God', but at all events he does pull the boat out of the race,
they land their catch, and the hooded man accepts his one-third
share (presumably on the accepted basis of one share per person
and one for the boat) but then gives it all away to the poor
people who are about. So far this is a fairly standard Christian
tale, though its details demand knowledge of local fishing conditions. What makes it unusual is that it is given a comic twist
at the end. The cloaked man walks away up a steep bank, but this
is muddy after rain, and he slips, and slithers back down again,
and everybody laughs, led by the woman who first sees it. He
responds with a verse. She is unduly mocking his umbúð, he says –
'the state I've got myself into', but the word can also imply
'covering', or here 'dress', and that is the sense that he plays
on, using for the crofter woman the honorific kenning 'Sif silkis'
as if she were a silk-clad noble dame, and coining of himself what
became a proverb, 'fár kann jarl í fiskivoðum'. 'Few know an earl
in ...' – and the next word could imply either 'fishing nets' or
'fishing clothes', so '... when they catch him in their nets' or
'... when they meet him in work-clothes'. He was, of course,
Rognvald. A stock moral tale perhaps, and the verse and the
incident perhaps imperfectly joined since the one suggests mockery
of his appearance and the other of his accident, but the junction
itself suggests use of an actual incident, and the whole emerges
as a rather individual piece of racontage which I would want to
add to my claim for this corner of the early Scottish literary
tradition.

Even if such claims are rejected, however, both this and my
previous episode bring me to an area in which I think they must

stand, for both have included verses ascribed to Rognvald. Nobody
has suggested otherwise than that they were composed by him. As a
general principle it is dangerous to assume that the verses in a
saga were in fact the work of the characters to whom they are
ascribed. In some cases the traditional view that they are authentic, and indeed preserve the basis round which the saga was
constructed, is probably sound, but in others dialectal tests show
that they could not have been; they have been composed for incorporation in the saga because such verses form a traditional part
of the genre. Often one cannot tell. In our case, though, a number
of the verses ascribed to Rognvald show a quite distinct quality
of gentle humour which is not at all characteristic of skaldic
verse, and which much more points to an individual poet than to a
saga-writer wishing to adorn his tale. There has been some of this
in the verses I have already mentioned, but an earlier one in the
same chapter 85 makes the point more clearly. The earl has been on
a visit to King Ingi of Norway, but on his return he has to make
an emergency beaching of his ships in Shetland when a storm blows
up. After salvaging as much of their gear as they can he and his
party go to seek out lodgings, and the earl's hosts make up a big
fire for them to dry out by. A serving-wench, Asa, who has been
out to get water, stands by, shivering so much that nobody can
make out what she is saying. Rognvald offers to interpret, and his
verse makes her say: 'You're sitting comfortably by the fire, but
I'm huddled in the wet. Where am I going to sit? I'm cold!' It is
puffed out into the formalities of a <u>dróttkvætt</u> ('court metre')
half-stanza by using onomatapoeic representations of the girl's
teeth-chattering to create two of the half-lines, bearing alliteration and rhyme in the proper formal arrangement. First 'atatata':
it continues the vowel alliteration from the opening line 'Dúsið
_ér_ en _Ása_' ('you are - dozing perhaps - but Asa ...'), and provides the required full internal rhyme on the last word of its own
line, 'vatni' ('water', giving 'in the wet'). Then 'hutututu',
giving the correct half-rhyme on the last word of its line,
'sitja' ('sit'), and introducing an <u>h</u>-alliteration which is then
carried forward. Good Germanic alliter<u>a</u>tive verse uses important
words to carry stress and alliteration; by using the teeth-
chattering Rognvald is making a joke of it. I know of no other
skaldic poet who ever did such a thing.

Then, later in the same chapter but in a different tone, there
is an episode (in itself of a quite usual type) of a competition
to make verses on a scene from one of the hall wall-hangings, with
the embroidered figure of a warrior. Rognvald improvises a stanza,
and challenges a visiting Icelandic skald, Oddi, to reply with
another. Oddi's verse takes a heroic line. The swordsman is waiting to strike from his stance in the tapestry: 'stendr ok hyggr at
hǫggva' ('stands and thinks to hew') - high time to make peace
before we get an injury! Rognvald's is different. He sees the
warrior as trapped and ageing in the tapestry, his sword flopping
down from his shoulder (one supposes the cloth hanging somewhat in
folds) - poor old man, his legs won't carry him to battle any
more. Again, an individual approach, not from the skald's regular
stock-in-trade; and one could cite others of Rognvald's verses.
The one I should like finally to examine, though, I bring in with

hesitation because it is not ascribed to Rognvald but to the Hall mentioned above, the Icelander who had been refused a place in his household. He is said to have made it in indignant comment on the refusal, and it puts into Rognvald's mouth a 'kenning' applied to Hall as a man of Iceland, 'grúpans granni', formed from grúpan ('sausage') and granni ('neighbour'). Icelanders were known for their taste for fat-rich sausages, and the kenning imagines the land as peopled by sausages, so that any human inhabitant is their neighbour. The insulting kenning is a well-recognised feature of skaldic verse. Snorri Sturluson, the great medieval scholar of the genre, gives a whole category of them, formed just like those whose base is a god-name but with an attribute attached which converts it to an honorific for a man, except that these make their base a giant-name instead[8] – a straight, full-blooded insult. Egil Skalla-grimsson, the acknowledged master-skald, hurls at an enemy the abusive appellation 'kumbla brjǫtr' ('destroyer of cairns', i.e. 'grave-desecrator'),[9] with no more precision intended than in a modern obscene abuse-term like 'mother-fucker'. The wry accuracy of aim of 'grúpans granni' is unlike these, much more in line with Rognvald's inventive poetic taste than with anything one would have expected Hall to coin against himself or an Icelandic saga-author to devise for him, though it is obviously hard to know to what tradition to ascribe the complete poem which contains the phrase (the rest of it is much less memorable).

That problem crystallises the difficulty I have in putting any exact limits on the case I am trying to advance. There are other pieces of racontage in Orkneyinga Saga that I would gladly claim for my Scottish Norse storyteller or tellers, but none for which I could support with any positive evidence a clear impression that they are Scottish-written rather than Icelandic. Therefore I rest at this point a case which I must state in perhaps rather unsatis-factory terms: although the limits are uncertain one can very plausibly argue from this saga the existence, in this special corner of the medieval Scottish literary tradition, of one or more admirable prose story-tellers, and certainly one poet with a quite individual voice, to add to those authors in Scots and in Gaelic who are discussed in the other conference papers.

Notes

1   Jacob Jacobsen reports that in 1894 there were still people in Foula who could speak sentences in Norn: An Etymological Dictionary of the Norn Language in Shetland (London and Copehangen, 1928), p. xviii.
2   Orkney and Shetland Old Lore Series (Viking Club, January and April, 1907).
3   Hermann Pálsson and Paul Edwards (tr and intro), Orkneyinga Saga: The History of the Earls of Orkney (London, 1978), p 13.
4   Alexander Burt Taylor, The Orkneyinga Saga (Edinburgh and London, 1938).
5   In the paper as delivered I suggested that it might rather be

Gaelic. However, although the notion of the slip of the tongue (Gaelic _tapag)_ is familiar in Celtic, and so is that of fate tied to imprudences in words, the motif of a fatally pregnant slip does not apparently appear. See an extensive discussion of the present and other slips of the tongue in Bo Almqvist, 'The Death Forebodings of Saint Óláfr, King of Norway, and Rognvaldr Brusason, Earl of Orkney', _Bealoideas_, 42–44 (1974–6), pp 1–40; on the present point particularly p 15. Almqvist calls attention to the rather dissimilar nature of the words supposed to have been confused, and is able in this and other cases to construct linguistically plausible and much more confusable originals, which may suggest that whatever the original source of the motif the Icelanders who wrote the preserved forms did not really grasp the point. I am grateful to Professor Almqvist and Professor William Gillies for help on this point subsequent to delivery of the paper.

6   _Njáls Saga_ ch. 128.
7   Translation, p 87.
8   _Skáldskaparmál_, ch. 39 as divided in Mágnus Finnbogason's edition of Snorri's _Edda_ (Reykjavik, 1953).
9   _Egils Saga_ ch. 44.

Chapter 32

MIDDLE SCOTS DIALECTS - EXTRAPOLATING BACKWARDS

C I Macafee

In this paper I would like to re-open some of the minor footpaths
of Scots philology, from the point of view of the modern dialects.
The occasion for taking up this topic is the recent publication of
the third volume of The Linguistic Atlas of Scotland (LAS), containing the phonological data of the Linguistic Survey of Scotland
and also the publication this year of The Linguistic Atlas of Late
Mediaeval English (LALME), whose completion frees its authors to
extend their methods to Middle Scots dialectology.[1] This paper
will air some of the questions which may now turn out to be
answerable in the future.

In general, there is a strong sense of discontinuity between
Older Scots and Modern Scots. Although A J Aitken has drawn
attention to the variability of Middle Scots and pointed out
specific regional dialect forms that occasionally find their way
into written Middle Scots,[2] most people who encounter the language
will probably share the impression of G Gregory Smith that 'the
uniformity in the practice of Middle Scots is one of its most
striking features'.[3] What we are seeing here, of course - and Dick
Leith has described the process clearly in A Social History of
English[4] - is an emergent standard Scots. As this is corrupted by
and absorbed into London English, the writing of broad Scots
becomes an extraordinary rather than a natural choice for the
anglicised urban bourgeoisie, and the writing of Scots again in
any quantity awaits the great political and cultural flowering of
the Scots-speaking working-classes in the nineteenth century - not
that they had, or have, a monopoly on the language, but that they
provided a mass market, as William Donaldson has shown.[5]

Some of the spoken dialects north and south of the Central Belt
are rather exotic, and the result is an impression of Modern Scots
quite the opposite of Smith's:

> As the national language fades out, a series of dialects
> supersedes it all over Scotland ... disintegrating as they
> are, they have come to colour more and more such literary
> Scots as is still written. Whether a Scots literature, as
> opposed to a Scots dialect literature, exists any more, is a
> fine point ...[6]

But this discontinuity, however real it may be as a literary fact,
is exaggerated by the selectivity of what survives and of what we
encounter as the Scots language. We do know that Middle Scots
already had dialects.

Map 1. Agricultural areas of the Lowlands. Based on Snodgrass.

 cattle rearing 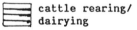 cattle rearing/ dairying 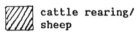 cattle rearing/ sheep

 dairying   mixed arable   sheep

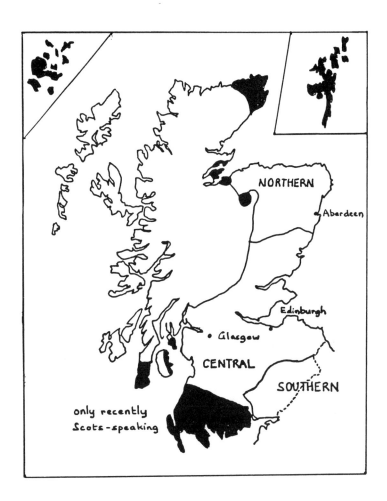

Map 2. Scots dialect areas. Based on Speitel
and Mather.

Continuity in regional dialects can take two forms, which can be illustrated from the dialects of England. In the first type, there is a dialect (and culture) boundary which persists over a long period of time, because it is determined by underlying geographical factors. For instance, the boundary between Northern and North Midland dialects in England[7] corresponds roughly to the southern boundary of the Scandinavian belt, the area in which Old Norse persisted longest as a spoken language. This is also roughly the dividing line in the Old English period between Anglian and Mercian. The influence of geography on communications is brought out very clearly by Kristensson, who shows that the /a: $\sim$ ɔ :/ line (one of the components of this boundary) moved northwards after the fourteenth century, following the draining of river marshes, particularly in Lincolnshire.[8] Because it is basically a geographical fact, such a boundary repeats itself in different periods of the language. Some linguistic features relate to the boundary as an ethnographic division (for instance, Old Norse loan words in the Scandinavian Belt); others simply 'pile-up' onto the existing boundary.

The second type of case is where the geographical distribution of a single linguistic feature persists over long periods. A striking case is the rounding of /a/ before /n/ in the West Midlands of England.[9]

Turning now to Scotland, where the geographical divisions of the country are very marked, we expect — and find — that the dialect divisions bear a visible relationship to them. Map 1 shows the main agricultural divisions of the Lowlands,[10] while Map 2 shows the broad dialect areas. Since these divisions are so obviously geographically determined, they are likely to be significant also in Middle Scots. I have referred here to the mapping of Hans Speitel and James Mather,[11] which has the additional advantage of identifying those areas which became Scots-speaking only recently (towards the end of the Older Scots period or later).[12]

Taking the three broad divisions of Modern Scots in turn, Southern Scots is basically a transition zone to the dialects of the north of England. The peculiarities of the modern dialect are chiefly archaisms — such as the retention of /ø/ — or features shared with northern England — such as diphthongal (latterly glide + vowel) realisations of /e/ and /o/ initially, and vocalisation of /x/. Local innovations, such as diphthongal realisations of /i/ and /u/ finally, need not be of any great antiquity.

Central Scots (or Mid Scots) has two urban foci, Glasgow and Edinburgh. It is probably their influence that has squeezed the Southern dialect area. North of the Forth-Clyde line, Fife is in a similar geographical position to East Anglia, and similarly tends to be a relic zone for various linguistic items, for instance retention of /ø/ and a separate reflex of $\bar{e}$.

Angus is a transition zone between Central and Northern areas — Grant actually counts it as a sub-division of Northern Scots.[13] It is in Northern Scots, in this rather autonomous culture area focused on Aberdeen, that we find a dialect which must already have diverged significantly from Central Scots even in the Middle Scots period.

A J Aitken has assembled Middle Scots written dialect forms that are still characteristic of the modern dialects, including several North-eastern forms, such as ⟨f⟩ for ⟨quh⟩.[2] Here I will discuss four features of modern North-eastern Scots, for whose antiquity I will adduce philogical and lexicographical evidence.

(i)   The first item to be considered is /i/ in words such as ane, bane, stane. Using Aitken's numerical notation,[14] Vowel 4 has the reflex normally associated with Vowel 2 and in some dialects with Vowel 3. Heinrich Mutschmann implies that the merger is of Vowel 4 with Vowel 3.[15] If this is correct, then Vowel 4 cannot reach /i/ except in those dialects where Vowel 3 also does. This is confirmed by LAS vol III, Maps W144 ONE and W142 LEAN, combined here as Map 3. (Excluding the derivative dialects of Caithness, Orkney and Shetland - see footnote 12 - there are only two aberrant localities, i.e. where LEAN has /e/ but ONE nevertheless has /i/. Other Vowel 3 words in LAS vol III show similar patterns within the North-east, except for three items where the /e/ reflex is very widespread, but the fit is not so perfect as with LEAN). It is attractive to speculate that this might be a very early merger.

Traditional symbols	Aitken numbers	Early Scots	Great Vowel Shift	Modern Scots
$\bar{\varepsilon}$	3	ɛ: ___ ɛ: _____	e: _____	i
$\bar{a}$	4	a: ⟋ a: _____ (before /n/)	ɛ: _____	e

Raising of $\bar{a}$ before /n/ would lead to capture by $\bar{\varepsilon}$, whereas later raisings do not lead to such a merger, since the whole system is moving in the same direction in the context of the Great Vowel Shift. Unfortunately the spelling evidence does not support such an early sound change. A Dictionary of the Older Scottish Tongue (DOST) shows that spellings in ⟨ein(e), eyne(e), ene⟩ are quite frequent but only from the mid sixteenth century, most of them clearly North-eastern (see for intance BANE, GA, MANE n2, NANE).

However, there is other internal evidence for an early merger of Vowel 4 with Vowel 3 in certain environments. A number of words, with both Vowel 3 and Vowel 4 originally, have /əi/ in modern North-eastern Scots. The environment is not consistent, but there is usually a labial element, e.g. wame, weaver, quine. /əi/ arises from various Middle Scots sources, but the merger is most probably with Vowel 1.[16] In Aitken's reconstruction, Vowels 1 and 3 pass phonetically close to each other, Vowel 3 having reached /e/. That the merger with Vowel 1 should be at this point, before Vowel 3 moves (in some dialects) to /i/, is confirmed by the modern distribution as shown by LAS vol III, Maps W2 SWEAT, W25 WADE and W95 WAME, combined here as Map 4. The distribution of /əi/ forms is regardless of the outcome of Vowel 3 (cf. Map 3). This merger is surely of some antiquity, since those words originally with Vowel 4 have a considerable phonetic distance to cover. The spelling evidence is less readily available in this case, since DOST has not reached ⟨w⟩, but one very common word in this group is great, and here we find that the spellings ⟨gryit, gryte⟩ are found from 1450 and are common from around 1540 (s.v. GRYT(E)).

...... /i/ in ONE

-|-|- /e/ in LEAN

Map 3. /i/ in ONE, /e/ in LEAN. Based on LAS vol.III,
Maps W142, W144.

Map 4. /əi/ reflexes of ā, ę̄. Based on LAS vol.III,
Maps W2, W25, W95.

Traditional symbols	Aitken numbers	Early Scots	Great Vowel Shift	Modern Scots
ɪ̄	1	i: _____	ëi _____	ai, aɪ (after labials)
ē̜	3 ɛ:	ɛ: _____	e:	i
		(before /n/ and after labials)		
ā̜	4 a:	a: _____	ɛ: _____	e

   (ii) Another North-eastern sound change affects the words <u>coal</u>
and <u>coat</u>. These are /kwəil/ and /kwait/ in conservative modern
dialect. According to <u>The Scottish National Dictionary</u> (s.v. QUILE,
QUITE, CWITE) these forms are found in Banffshire and Aberdeenshire.[17] LAS vol III does not map these items, but there are a few
occurences in the lists, mapped below (Map 5).[18] The single
instance of /kwol/ shows that the intrusion of /w/ is prior to the
change in the vowel.[19] An intermediate stage with a rounded first
element of the diphthong would seem necessary, and this is neatly
supplied by Aitken's reconstruction of Early Scots <u>ui</u>, Vowel 10,
with which these Vowels 5 words can merge.[20]

Traditional symbols	Aitken numbers	Early Scots	Great Vowel Shift	Modern Scots
ø̜̄ 21	5	ɔ: _____	o: _____	o
			(after /kw/)	
ui	10	ui _____	ui ___ öi _____	əi

   (iii) In North-eastern Scots, there has been a change of /w/ to
/v/ in two specific environments where /w/ has been lost in other
varieties of English (in the latter case by about 1400), namely:

       wr > vr e.g. <u>wrocht</u>

       aw > av e.g. <u>gnaw</u>, <u>chaave</u> (Old English ă ɣ and ăw).[22]

The existence of these forms may be relevant to the question of the
orthographic alteration of ⟨w,v,u⟩ in Older Scots, since they would
tend to suggest a phonological basis for confusion of ⟨w⟩ and ⟨v⟩.
As a further point <u>for</u> a phonological basis, it might be worthwhile
to revive Mutschmann's v > w hypothesis:

       I am inclined to assume that in MSc., French (and Latin)
       initial <u>v</u> was represented by <u>w</u> at least in the pronunciation
       of the uneducated classes. There was no initial <u>v</u> sound in the
       Northern dialect as there was in the South.[23]

If the source of the ⟨v,w⟩ alternation is indeed to be sought in
multilingualism, we might add that Scots speakers would encounter
initial /v/ also in Gaelic and Low German. An indirect piece of
evidence for Mutschmann's hypothesis comes from Orkney Norn. There
was a Scandinavian sound change w > v about 1200. That this change
is established in Norn is shown by place-names such as Vinquoy.
Place-names are generally more conservative in pronunciation, yet
other Orkney Norn words have /w/, e.g. <u>waffle</u> < <u>vafla</u> 'entangle'.[24]

Map 5. Intrusive /w/, merger with /əi/ in COAL or COAT.
Based on LAS vol.III lists.

The suggestion is that the tendency of uneducated Scots speakers to substitute /w/ has swamped the Norn pronunciation.

The main argument _against_ a phonological basis is the lack of any necessity for one. Since the 'double u' (actually a 'double v' in many hands, including the Scottish secretary hand) is a relatively new letter, its value is not fixed by use in Latin or French, and it enters into variation in Scots not only with ⟨v⟩ but also with ⟨u⟩, for which there is certainly no phonological warrant.[25]

(iv) The final case is a similar one. In a few words – _micht_, _nocht_, _dochter_ – north-eastern Scots evidences /θ/ instead of /xt/, although there is no recent sign of this in LAS vol III (where it would have been recorded in the endnotes to the lists).[26] This may be relevant to the Middle Scots habit of alternating ⟨t, th, cht, tht⟩. The usual argument that this set arose through the confusion in handwriting of ⟨c,t⟩ is unconvincing, since there is no superscript ⟨c⟩, whereas the other forms are confirmed by their occurrence in print as well as in manuscript.

It may be that the received view of these variations as merely orthographic is quite adequate, but when relevant modern dialect reflexes exist, the possibility must certainly be considered that they provided the basis for the orthographic confusion (bearing in mind that the modern geographical distribution could be the remnant of a formerly wider distribution). That _the_ major non-standard dialect of Middle Scots should turn out to have implications for the written form of Middle Scots is doubly intriguing.

Notes

1   James Mather and Hans Speitel (eds), The Linguistic Atlas of Scotland, Vol III (London, 1986). Angus Mcintosh et al., A Linguistic Atlas of Late Mediaeval English, 4 vols, (Aberdeen, 1987).
    I am grateful to various colleagues and conference participants who discussed this paper with me, and particularly to A J Aitken and Hans Speitel for their comments on the final draft.
2   A J Aitken, 'Variation and variety in written Middle Scots', in Edinburgh Studies in English and Scots, A J Aitken et al. (eds) (London, 1971), pp 177-209.
3   G Gregory Smith, Specimens of Middle Scots (Edinburgh and London, 1902), p. xii.
4   Dick Leith, A Social History of English (London, 1983).
5   William Donaldson, Popular Literature in Victorian Scotland (Aberdeen, 1986).
6   David Murison, The Guid Scots Tongue (Edinburgh, 1977), p 7.
7   Martyn Wakelin, English Dialects. An Introduction (London 1972, 1977), Map 7.

8   Gillis Kristensson, 'On Middle English dialectology', in <u>So Meny People Longages</u> and <u>Tonges</u>. <u>Philological Essays in Scots and Mediaeval English</u> Presented to Angus McIntosh, Michael Benskin and Michael Samuels (eds) (Edinburgh, 1981), pp 3-13.

9   LALME vol I, Map 95 MAN (<u>mon</u> type). Harold Orton <u>et al</u>., <u>The Linguistic Atlas of England</u> (London, 1978), Map PH5 MAN.

10 Catherine Snodgrass, 'Map of economic regions of Scotland', <u>The Scottish Geographical Magazine</u>, 59 (1943), 15-18.

11 Hans Speitel and James Mather, 'Schottische Dialektologie', <u>Zeitschrift für Mundartforschung</u>, Neue Folge 6 (1968), 520-41.

12 The detailed history of these peripheral dialects will be difficult to retrace, especially where there is a significant element of dialect mixture (in addition to any influence of the substratum languages). Peter Trudgill's new book, <u>Dialects in Contact</u> (Oxford, 1986) introduces some anarchic new principles to philology - in particular, in the right demographic situation, any change is as likely as not to produce sporadic, hypercorrect cases of the opposite change; and dialect contact gives rise to forms strictly derivable from <u>neither</u> source variety.

13 Most readily accessible in <u>The Concise Scots Dictionary</u>, ed-in-chief Mairi Robinson (Aberdeen, 1985), p. xxxi.

14 A J Aitken, 'How to pronounce Older Scots', in <u>Bards and Makars</u>. <u>Scottish Language and Literature, Medieval and Renaissance</u> (Glasgow, 1977), pp 1-21. Aitken numbers the vowels as follows:

1. ɪ̄	8. ai	15. ɪ̆
2. ē	9. oi	16. ɛ̆
3. ę̄	10. ui	17. ă
4. ā	11. ei	18. ɔ̆
5. ǭ	12. au	19. ŭ
6. ū	13. ou	
7. ǖ	14. iu	

15 Heinrich Mutschmann, <u>A Phonology of the North-Eastern Scotch Dialect</u> (Bonn, 1909). Mutschmann is agreed to be unreliable, but there may nevertheless be merit in some of his suggestions.

16 If the merger is with Vowel 1, the modern reflexes should be subject to the Scottish Vowel Length Rule, i.e. the reflex should be, not /əi/, but /aɪ/ before voiced fricatives, /r/ and finally. (See A J Aitken, 'The Scottish Vowel Length Rule', in <u>So Meny People Longages and Tonges</u>, op.cit., pp 131-57). But in practice, /əi/ is found in a number of words before voiced fricatives, e.g. <u>weave</u>, <u>clathes</u> (Eugen Dieth, <u>A Grammar of the Buchan Dialect</u>, vol I (Cambridge, 1932), p 69). Conversely, /aɪ / forms sometimes appear for /əi/ from other sources (namely Early Scots <u>ai</u>, Vowel 8, and cf. Map 5 below). The picture of / ə i/ and /aɪ/ alternation is rather confused in the North-east in any case. Dieth (p 7 fn.1) is inclined to doubt the earlier evidence of Ellis and Mutschmann that /aɪ/ was once more general, but if so it would suggest that the North-east previously manifested some

tendency to carry through the development of /əi/ to /aɪ/ with less regard to the constraints of the Scottish Vowel Length Rule. The local peculiarities, with /əi/ in Vowel 3 and Vowel 4 words, would tend to escape correction towards the Scottish Standard English distribution of /əi, aɪ/.

17   The Scottish National Dictionary also records /kwit/ in Moray. For /i/ where /əi/ is expected, cf. Dieth, op.cit., p 22, p 24.

18   The Shetland localities are included because they have [œ] for both coal and boil, but this is actually a realisation of /o/, not /əi/.

19   DOST has ⟨quote⟩ from Fife, 1516 (s.v. COTE), but A J Aitken points out to me that this may be a reverse spelling, as many ⟨quo-⟩ words show variants in ⟨co-⟩. See e.g. QUORUM, QUOTIDIAN(E, QUOY. Spellings like ⟨quote⟩ are found for other ⟨co-⟩ words, e.g. QUOD(D)OCH(E, QUOMON, QUONCIENS.

20   It is interesting to compare this sound change with a similar diphthongisation in the West Midlands of England (The Linguistic Atlas of England, Ph134a COAL, Ph135a FOAL, Ph136 (OVER)COAT), where the modern outcome is /ɔi/.

21   ǭ arises from ǒ by Open Syllable Lengthening. Aitken represents this as [oː] throughout, but I have followed the convention that Open Syllable Lengthening also lowers the vowel.

22   In the case of aw > av, the consonantal status of /w/ has perhaps been strengthened by the wider glide movement from the open /a/ to a close vowel in following inflections.

23   Mutschmann, p 202. An authority sometimes cited in favour of a phonological confusion of /w/ and /v/ in Middle Scots is Moritz Trautmann, 'Der Dichter Huchown und seine Werke', Anglia, 1 (1878), 109-49. Trautmann finds ⟨v,w⟩ alliteration in the Morte Arthure and Golagros and Gawayne, but in the light of Mutschmann's remarks, initial /v/ in words like vertuous (Trautmann's example) and other Romance loans, was perhaps /w/. On the other hand, Trautmann also finds that the Morte Arthure (unlike for instance the Troy Book) also alliterates /ʃ, s/ and /ʍ, w/, so the alliteration of /v,w/ may be merely an indication of the looseness of the poet's practice.

Gaelic speakers might be imagined as complicating the situation by substituting /v/ for /w/ in their Scots (since Gaelic has no /w/). This substitution was known in the speech of the elderly in Islay in the 1930s (Nils Holmer, Studies in Argyllshire Gaelic, Uppsalla, 1938, p 92). I am indebted to Ian Quick for this reference.

24   Hugh Marwick, The Orkney Norn (Oxford, 1929), p. xlvii.

25   Bertil Sundby, 'Middle English overlapping of v and w and its significance', Anglia, 74 (1956), 438-44, appears to allow Old Norse influence on the change w > v in the North, but not in Devon and Somerset, where it also occurs (although medievalists do now recognise Old Norse influence in the South-west of England). But he is inclined to see ⟨w,v⟩ alternation as purely orthographic, certainly when ⟨w⟩ appears for /f/. This occurs in the overlap between 'the land of zed' and 'the land of wee', i.e. where voicing of initial fricatives overlaps with /w,v/ alternation. The area of ⟨w⟩ for /f/ can be clearly

seen in LALME vol II, Map 125 FIRST. There   are   no   indications
in modern dialect of a combined sound change f > v > w.

26   ⟨th⟩ forms also   occur   in   Middle   English,   mainly   in   East
Anglia.   A   route   xt >   x θ > θ is suggested by a wide Midland
and Southern distribution of ⟨ȝth⟩ type forms   (see   LALME   vol
I, Maps 329, 330, 334 MIGHT, and vol II, Map 53 MIGHT).

Chapter 33

THE SOURCES OF THE ⟨I⟩-DIGRAPHS: THE PLACE-NAME EVIDENCE

Veronika Kniezsa

I

The history of a language can be studied only through a careful analysis of written texts. A description of the characteristics at a given date in time sums up the synchronic stage of the language, as a series of descriptions of succeeding points in time provides the basis for study of the changes affecting the language in its written and its spoken forms. The only means of reconstructing the possible acoustic characteristics of an early stage is spelling; the working theory being that languages which adopted the Latin alphabet for their writing system would strive for a phonetic orthography, adjusting the symbols originally marking Latin sounds to represent native pronunciation. It is also accepted that the spoken language is in constant change and that these changes will eventually surface in the written medium, i.e. changes in pronunciation will appear as changes in spelling.

Since the material available for historical phonetic research is the texts, the above argument can be reversed to state that if there is a considerable change in the spelling at one period of the language compared to an earlier one, it can be deduced that important sound changes had occurred during the interval. Thus if at Stage A there are two graphs marking two etymologically distinct sounds, and at a later Stage B these graphs appear as free variants to mark both sounds, it can be concluded that the sounds merged, i.e. that at Stage B there is now one sound with two alternative spellings.

Accepting that changes in medieval orthography signal underlying phonetic-phonological changes, the analysis of the evidence must be carried out with the utmost care. Too rash conclusions can be and have been misleading, and whole branches of scholarship can be led astray.

II

The digraphs ⟨ai, ei, oi, ui⟩ started appearing in Scottish manuscripts at the end of the fourteenth century as a spelling form to mark Middle English long vowels. James Murray took these forms as a proof of sound changes and ascribed the appearance of the digraphs to the monophthongisation of the diphthongs such spellings usually stand for, e.g. /ai, ei, oi, ui/, which thus should have merged with 'a, e, o, u', (Murray 1873). It seems that Murray automatically applied the rule that changes of spelling indicate changes of pronunciation without checking first the actual phonological processes. Because of Murray's authority, especially since he was a native Scottish speaker, that remark on the early Scottish mono-phthongisation has been quoted in every history of Middle English phonology (e.g. Luick 1964, Jordan-Crook 1974, etc).

III

An analysis of the ME and present-day dialects proved that there was no phonetic development in the early ME period which could have resulted in the digraph ⟨ei⟩ marking ME /e:/. Not only ME /ei/ of native origin, but also the same dipthong in Scandinavian and later French loan-words, followed the same pattern and developed into ME /ai/ written ⟨ai⟩ since the thirteenth century (Heuser 1890).

Scandinavian /ei/ ⟨ Germ. ai, however, became a monophthong around the ninth and tenth centuries in Scandinavia; and thus the diphthong was lacking in the vowel system of the Scandinavian speech of those groups which settled in Normandy and changed their language to French. Due to the Scandinavian substratum, they simplified the Old French diphthongal system and monophthongised OF /ei/ and /ie/, preserving the orthographic notations ⟨ei⟩ and ⟨ie⟩ as free spelling variants to mark long front mid vowels: piece, deis (Fouché 1959). This Norman French scribal tradition was then introduced into the notation of English words as early as the last decade of the eleventh century: the Domesday Book frequently shows ⟨ei⟩ for OE e: and æ: in pre-Conquest personal and place-names: leiuegar ⟨ OE Leofgar, etc (Feilitzen 1937:64). Thus it is true that ⟨ei⟩ became a marker of vowel length through the merger of /ei/ and /e:/. The change occurred, however, not in English but in Norman French.

IV

The early merger of Northern ME /ai/ and /a:/ has been accepted as a characteristic feature of Northern texts. Present day dialect studies have proved that ME /ai/ and /a:/ have been preserved not only in Southern Scots, the native dialect of Murray, but also in all the Northern English dialects. In Scottish dialects, however, there are monophthongisations; but much later and due to combin-atory sound changes. Mergers also occur in Northern English, but again not as a general tendency, only as a special combinatory sound change which may vary from region to region (Linguistic Atlas of England, 1978, Linguistic Survey of Scotland, 1987, Kniezsa 1982, 1983). In this case Anglo-Norman does not offer any basis for the rise of ⟨ai⟩ because if AN /ai/ was monophthongised, however early, it developed into ME /ɛ:/, as is proved by early spellings, e.g. pais in the 'Peterborough Chronicle' 1137, pes in the 'Owl and the Nightingale' - 'peace'.

V

The largest number of ⟨ai⟩ for ME /a:/ has been found to occur in Yorkshire texts, the earliest ones in words where in cognates

Northern English had a long monophthong /a:/ but Scandinavian a
diphthong /ei/ > ME /ai/. The place-name material of the counties
which belonged to the Danelaw supplies a great number of such
words. Early OE monophthongised Germanic ai into a: (e.g. stan), in
ON it was preserved as a diphthong, though fronted and raised to
/ei/ (e.g. steinn). In England ON /ei/ > ME /ai/ written ⟨ai, ay⟩.
Thus in the Northern counties there was a phonetic as well as a
social context which would give rise to an /a:/ ∼ /ai/ alternation.
Moreover, Scandinavian settlers frequently moved into earlier
English settlements and re-named them, though this often meant only
a slight phonetic-phonemic change in the original name: a replace-
ment of Scandinavian ei for OE a: being one of the most frequent.
Ever since the Domesday Book there were alternations between ⟨a⟩
and ⟨ai⟩ forms in place-name elements which can be traced back to
Germanic ai: e.g. STAINBURN (YW): Stanburn 1086 ∼ Stainburne 1086
(Kniezsa 1988).

From the middle of the twelfth century on ⟨ai⟩ appears in words
which had ME /a:/, whether English, Scandinavian or French in
origin: CADEBY (YW): Catebi 1086 - Caitebi 1190 < ON Kati, GREAT
AYTON (YW): Atun 1086 - Haiton 1202 < OE ea, a: 'water'. The new
type of ⟨ai⟩ spelling seems to be connected to the fact that
Scandinavian ceased to be a spoken language in England around the
first half of the twelfth century, as can be judged from the
evidence of runic inscriptions (Ekwall 1930, Page 1971). English
prevailed with the monophthongal /a:/ pronunciation, thus there was
no longer an /a:/ ∼ /ai/ alternation in phonetic reality: ⟨ ai ⟩
became a mere orthographic symbol, an alternative to mark northern
ME /a:/. From the fourteenth century on ⟨ai⟩ (and of course its
variant ⟨ay⟩) became more and more frequent and its use gradually
moved northward. It is clear, then, that the rise of ⟨ai⟩ as a
spelling for ME /a:/ is not due to any sound change that occurred
in English or any other language spoken in medieval England; rather
it was the result of a real phonetic alternation in cognate words
in two living and closely related languages used side by side for
centuries both as a spoken and - to a certain extent - as a written
medium.

VI

/oi/ is a newcomer in the English vowel system. It usually occurs
in loan-words of French and to a lesser extent Dutch or Flemish
origin. It is usually understood as being introduced together with
the early French borrowings and thus represents a foreign element
which could not have developed naturally in English. Diphthongs
with an i-glide developed through the vocalisation of the palatal
fricative /j/ < /g/ which in turn was the result of the palatalising influence of neighbouring front vowels /i, e, æ /. In late
OE, pre-consonatal and final /j/ were vocalised to /i/ and formed a
diphthong together with the preceding vowel: /e/ > /ei/ ⟨ei, ey⟩
and /æ/ > /æi/ ⟨ai, ay⟩. According to these sound-rules, /o/ did
not have such a palatalising influence. Thus no i-diphthong could
have regularly developed.

K Dietz has studied the early forms of English place-names and
discovered that there were instances - though rare enough - when

/oi/ developed spontaneously in native words: through an early loss of intervocalic /v/: BOYNTON Bovinton 1086; or a rare palatal vocalisation of /h/: HULLAND Hoyland 1086 < hoh; etc. There is only one example of such a native /oi/ in standard words: the past participle broiden; in the dialects there are variants: oither, noither. It is interesting to note that the most numerous examples of early /oi/ developments coming from one area are from Yorkshire in the Dietz material. Another noteworthy fact is that in Yorkshire this velar palatalisation seems to be a tendency affecting non-high back vowels: RENALTHORP HALL (YW): Raynaldesthorp thirteenth century < ON Ragnald, though the examples for /a/ are much later.

In the thirteenth century new /oi/ spellings appear in the place-names of the West Riding of Yorkshire and in Lancashire in a well-defined context: in words where ME /o/ underwent lengthening in an open syllable: Goyt (Db) 1162 < OE gota 'water channel', Herteleroyd (YW) 1326 < OE rod 'clearing', etc. The digraph in these cases meant the accurate phonetic notation of an actual diphthongal pronunciation. According to the LAE, the present-day regional pronunciation of words 'coal, foal, coat' still is [oi] in the southern part of the West Riding and the adjacent areas of Lancashire, in contrast to [u] in the other northern areas. Thus when the scribe of the 'Wakefield Pageants' spelled hoil 'hole', he marked an actual diphthong by his digraph. In another dialect, however, this spelling would have referred to a long monophthong, ME /ɔ:/ and thus represented a mere orthographic element, e.g. in the 'York Plays' and other documents written in York. Even in the West Riding place-names ⟨oi⟩ started appearing also as a variant to represent ME /o:/: Royston 1411 < ON personal name Hróar. The digraph ⟨oi, oy⟩ for ME /o:/ and /ɔ:/ became freely used in Yorkshire in the fifteenth century.

VII

Another special West Riding development can be observed in the changes of spelling forms. In the Northern dialects ME /o:/ was not only raised but also fronted at an early period. Since the fourteenth century this change was represented by ⟨u⟩: gud, tuk, etc. In the present-day Northern English dialects this sound developed into [iᵒ] (in East Riding, Cumberland, Westmoreland), [iɤ] (Durham, Northumberland), [iu] (North Riding). In the West Riding we find a unique development into [ui], probably a cross between the North Eastern [iᵒ] and South Western [u:].

In words with ME /o:/ ⟨ui⟩ appears considerably later: FEWSTON (YW): Fuiston 1454, TOOTHILL (YW): Twythill 1534, ROYSTON (YW): Ruyston 1539. These examples are not very numerous. No examples were found in Northern texts for ⟨ui⟩ spellings. In Scottish texts ⟨ui⟩ started appearing at the end of the fifteenth century and became more numerous in the sixteenth. The restricted spread of West Riding ⟨ui⟩ compared to ⟨oi⟩ of the same origin could indicate that it was too local a development which in addition occurred at too late a time to reach York, the cultural centre of the area, and thus had no chance to find its place in the Northern orthographic system. Standard (London) spelling became influential in the North too, especially when it became reinforced - with the introduction of the printing press - by the spellings used in printed books.

VIII

It seems that we can state that Yorkshire is an area where phonetic-phonological developments can be observed which could result in the introduction of the digraphs ⟨ai, oi, ui⟩. These in this area represented the actual pronunciation, but for the scribes speaking any other dialect, they would have meant only an ortho-graphic alternative to mark a long monophthong. Yorkshire is a convenient area from the cultural point of view as well, for in spite of the Danish supremacy, York managed to preserve its role as an ecclesiastical centre and the Yorkshire schools too maintained their centuries-old scholarly traditions. York therefore could also become the centre of the development of a special northern scribal tradition and also the starting point from which these traditions could travel further north, e.g. to Scotland, where the ⟨i⟩ digraphs represented an entirely notational device and became a characteristic feature of Scottish orthography.

Scholars usually make light of the digraph spellings occurring in Northern English manuscripts, and have completely overlooked their frequency in Northern place-names. Oakden remarks that ⟨ei, ai, oi⟩

> 'occur occasionally in the 'York-' and 'Towneley Plays', but not in Rolle, ⟨ey⟩ occurs rarely for e in Manning ... but there are no examples for ⟨ay, oy⟩. The spellings are very common in 'The Bruce', for the feature is Scottish and ex-treme north'. (1937.I.65).

Indeed Oakden's remark served as a model to evaluate northern orthographic characteristics in text editions. If we consider only those texts and authors Oakden mentions in his short but dismis-sive paragraph, his misconception concerning the origin of the digraphs becomes evident. It is also evident that scholars do not seem to be entirely certain how to treat spelling as a linguistic feature.

In a rough count, the 'Towneley Plays' contain 38 words and forms with ⟨oi, oy⟩: 27 reflecting ME /o:/, 11 ME /ɔ:/ < ME /o/ lengthened in an open syllable; in contrast the Edinburgh MS of the Bruce contains 15 words with ⟨oi⟩. The MSS of Rolle are too early for ⟨oi⟩ to be used in them, and the MSS of Manning's writings are too southern in their spelling: for northern ME /a:/ < OE /a:/ they consequently have ⟨o⟩, thus the primary context for the appearance of ⟨ai⟩ is entirely missing.

Another problem is that the usual references to the Bruce are too vague to be of any relevance. It is not clear whether it is meant as a late-fourteenth-century text or as two late-fifteenth-century MSS. If the former, it is quite mistaken to quote it as an example for the digraph spellings: Scottish texts contemporary with the Bruce do not show digraph spellings with the exception of ⟨ei, ey⟩, and these also occur in Mannyng, being a common, dialectally unmarked spelling in ME introduced by Anglo-Norman scribal tradi-tion, but one which later became more frequent in the north - and incidentally went out of use in the south. If, however, the extant MSS of the _Bruce_ are meant, then those would represent a later stage in Scottish orthographic development than the texts mentioned by Oakden. From the point of view of orthographic analysis, the _Bruce_ should be treated as representing the last decades of the fifteenth century; and as two independent MSS at that, since the Cambridge MS shows a considerable southern influence in its spelling, and the Edinburgh MS represents a more typical example of a Scottish text. It is interesting that ⟨i⟩-digraphs are unfailingly reported where Scottish texts are mentioned, probably because notice has been repeatedly drawn to them; the same kind of spellings remain overlooked or dismissed in MSS written in northern England because, it seems, the forms are simply not expected to occur.

IX

The results of the present analysis are the establishment of the origins of the various ⟨i⟩-digraphs:

⟨ei, ey⟩ from AN scribal tradition based on the monophthong-isation of OF /ei/;
⟨ai⟩ through an alternation of ME /a:/ and Scandinavian /ei/>/ai/ in the pronunciation which appeared as an ⟨a⟩ ~⟨ai, ay⟩ alternation in writing;
⟨oi, oy⟩ and ⟨ui, uy⟩ as a local, West Riding diphthongis-ation, which in the case of ⟨oi⟩ found wider, though still regional (Yorkshire) employment, though this failed to happen in the case of ⟨ui⟩. These northern orthographic developments gradually found their way into Scottish texts in the fifteenth century.

In addition to the above results, there are a number of other considerations which might be of use in the future analyses and interpretations of medieval writings:

a) In connection with ME the importance of Scandinavian and French influence is usually stressed, but in descriptions it is not always included. The usual treatment is to analyse the phonology of Scandinavian and French loan-words separately from the native developments. Frequently spelling changes in French words are described as the result of sound change occurring in English and not as reflexes of special French changes which would appear on the orthographic level in English;
b) Accepting that changes in spelling signal phonetic-phonological changes, all the possible speech areas must be checked to discover which is the centre of the change in question and what exactly is the character of the change. Thus e.g. the rise of ⟨oi⟩ was due to regional diphthongisation rather than a mono-phthongisation and merger as explained by Murray. Another important conclusion is that if an orthographic feature becomes characteristic in an area, it does not necessarily follow that the underlying phonological change also occurred in the same area; it could just as easily have been adopted on the level of scribal influence;

c) The most important lesson, however, seems to be that texts
should be examined thoroughly for every kind of linguistic
evidence they can offer and data checked against the traditional
textbook descriptions, even if this should mean the modification
of classical textbook statements. Unfortunately the usual pro-
cedure is to collect material which corroborates the statements
in secondary literature, which could result in the restatement
and reinforcement of mistakes. What is even more serious,
valuable new information about phenomena might be entirely
overlooked this way, which makes a more exact description of the
history of the language difficult, and most importantly, makes
it impossible to discover how inner and outer influences truly
work on the linguistic process.

BIBLIOGRAPHY

Sources

The Place-Names of Northumberland and Durham, Sir Alan Mawer (ed)
 Cambridge Archeological and Ethnological Series (Cambridge, 1920)
The Place-Names of Lancashire, Eilert Ekwall (ed)(Manchester, 1922)
The Place-Names of the North Riding of Yorkshire, A H Smith (ed)
 English Place-Name Society (EPNS) vol 5 (Cambridge, 1928)
The Place-Names of Northamptonshire, J E B Gover (ed), EPNS vol 10
 (Cambridge, 1933)
The Place-Names of the East Riding of Yorkshire, A H Smith (ed),
 EPNS vol 14 (Cambridge, 1933)
The Place-Names of the West Riding of Yorkshire, A H Smith (ed),
 EPNS vol 32 (Parts i-viii) (Cambridge, 1957)
The Place-Names of Derbyshire, Kenneth Cameron (ed), EPNS Vol 28
 (Cambridge, 1959)
The Place-Names of Lincolnshire, Kenneth Cameron (ed), EPNS vol 58
 (Part i) (Nottingham, 1985)

Books

Agutter, Alex, 'A taxonomy of Older Scots orthography', in The
 Nuttis Shell, C Macafee, I MacLeod (eds) (Aberdeen, 1988)
Brunner, Karl, Altenglische Grammatik (Tübingen, 1965)
Cameron, Kenneth, Place-Name Evidence for the Anglo-Saxon Invasion
 and Scandinavian Settlements, EPNS (Nottingham, 1975a)
Cameron, Kenneth, 'Scandinavian Settlement in the territory of the
 Five Boroughs: the place-name evidence', in Cameron 1975a,
 pp 115-38.
Cameron, Kenneth, 'Scandinavian settlement in the territory of the
 Five Boroughs. Part II. Place-names in thorp', in Cameron 1975a,
 pp 139-56.
Cameron, Kenneth 'Scandinavian settlement in the territory of the
 Five Boroughs. Part III. Grimston hybrids', in Cameron 1975a,
 pp 157-71.

Campbell, Alistair, Old English Grammar (Oxford, 1959)

Dietz, Klaus, 'Mittelenglisch oi in heimischen Ortsnamen und Personennamen: der Typus Croydon', Beitrage zur Namenforschung (1981a) NF 16:269-340.

Dietz, Klaus, 'Mittelenglisch oi in heimischen Ortsnamen und Personennamen: II Das Namenelement Boi(e) und Etymologie von boy', Beiträge zur Namenforschung (1981b) NF 16:361-405.

Dietz, Klaus, 'Mittelenglisch oi heimischer Provenienz', in Weltsprache Englisch in Forschung und Lehre, P Kunsmann, O Kuhn (eds) (Berlin, 1981c), pp 81-109.

Ekwall, Eilert, 'The Scandinavian element', Chapter iv, in Introduction to the Survey of English Place-Names, A H Smith (ed), EPNS vol 1 Part i: 55-92 (Cambridge, 1924)

Ekwall, Eilert, 'How long did the Scandinavian language survive in England?', in A Grammatical Miscellany Offered to Otto Jespersen, N Bøgholm et al. (eds) (Copenhagen, 1930)

Ekwall, Eilert, 'The Scandinavian settlement' Chapter iv, in Historical Geography of England before 1800, H C Darby (ed) (Cambridge, 1936) pp 133-64.

Feilitzen, Olof von, Pre-Conquest Personal Names in the Domesday Book (Uppsala, 1937)

Fellows Jensen, Gillian, Scandinavian Settlement Names in Yorkshire (Copenhagen, 1972)

Fellows Jensen, Gillian, Scandinavian Settlement Names in the East Midlands (Copenhagen, 1978)

Fellows Jensen, Gillian, Scandinavian Settlement Names in the North West (Copenhagen, 1985)

Jordan, Richard, and E J Crook, Handbook of Middle English Grammar: Phonology (The Hague, 1974)

Kniezsa, Veronika, 'The Problem of the Middle English /a:/ - /ai/ Merger in Northern England', in Current Topics in English Historical Linguistics, M Davenport et al. (eds) (Odense, 1983a) pp 95-102

Kniezsa, Veronika, '⟨ai⟩ and ⟨a⟩ in Mediaeval Northern English Manuscripts', Folia Linguistica Historica (1983b) iv/I :45-54.

Kniezsa, Veronika, 'What happened to Old French ai in Britain'?, in Scottish Language and Literature, Mediaeval and Renaissance, D Strauss, H W Drescher (eds) (Frankfurt, Scottish Studies Centre, 1986)

Kniezsa, Veronika, 'Stancliff∼Staincliff: The Scandinavian influence upon English orthography' (forthcoming)

Kohler, K J, 'Aspects of Middle Scots phonemics and graphemics: the phonological implications of the sign ⟨i⟩', Transactions of the Philological Society, pp 32-61.

Mather, J Y, and H H Speitel, The Linguistic Atlas of Scotland, vol iii: Phonological Atlas (London, 1987)

Orton, H et al., The Linguistic Atlas of England (London, 1978)

Murray, James, The Dialect of the Southern Counties of Scotland (London, 1873)

Oakden, J P, Alliterative Poetry in Middle English (Hamden, Conn., 1936, 1968[2])

Page, R I, 'How long did the Scandinavian language survive in England? The epigraphical evidence', in England before the Conquest, P Clemoes, K Hughes (eds) (Cambridge, 1971) pp 165–81
Sawyer, P H, The Age of the Vikings (London, 1971^2)

Chapter 34

THE HELSINKI CORPUS OF OLDER SCOTS

Anneli Meurman-Solin

The Scottish language of the fifteenth, sixteenth and seventeenth centuries is an interesting case for scholars using the new methods suggested by socio-historical linguistics. The complex history of Older Scots can be studied to illustrate not only processes from a state of uniformity and interdependence towards differentiation and independence, but also processes from an independent use of a non-standard variant towards gradual standardisation.

The method of variation analysis has not been used, as far as I know, in diachronic studies of lexical intake. My study is an attempt to apply this method to the characterisation of French and Latin loanwords, their forms, functions and uses in varying text types and styles in Middle Scots. I have analysed intra- and extra-linguistically conditioned variation and then organised the distributions of variants into meaningful categories in order to be able to trace the acclimatisation process of loanwords.

The material analysed for the study was selected during the process of preparing a supplement of Scottish English texts for the Helsinki Corpus of OE, ME, and EModE texts, which will come out in a computer-readable form. The main aim was to find representative samples for various prototypical text types for the purposes of diachronic studies of Scottish English, and to add to these other text types, which were important, but not necessarily well-established, genres throughout the time periods chosen.

An abundant use of loanwords has traditionally been considered to be a stylistically marked feature. In studies based on a corpus of various text types dating from different time periods, it is possible to make a clear distinction between borrowings which are extralinguistically motivated and those which reflect intrasystemic developments in the language. Consequently, the study of lexis becomes as disciplined a process as the study of grammar is expected to be. When words are studied as units in collocations of various kinds, in wider or in more restricted linguistic contexts, then the influence of subject matter, stylistic preferences or models, the social status or education of the writer, and other extralinguistic factors of a similar kind, play an inferior role in the final analysis of linguistic features.

Before discussing the Scottish corpus in detail, it is necessary to characterise the basic corpus, the so-called Helsinki Corpus of English Texts, compiled by a group of scholars in the

Department of English at the University of Helsinki. In their
paper presented at the Seventh International Conference on
English Language Research on Computerized Corpora held in
Amsterdam in 1987,[1] Matti Rissanen, Ossi Inhalainen and Merja
Kytö[2] sum up the aims of the basic corpus in the following way:

> The purpose of our diachronic corpus is to provide a tool
> for conducting empirical research and analysing variation
> at the past stages of the English language. This corpus
> will consist of a collection of texts and text extracts in
> a machine-readable form, on magnetic tape and, possibly, on
> hard disks as well. The earliest texts date from the eighth
> century (Caedmon's Hymn), and the latest from the early
> eighteenth century. The corpus is intended mainly for
> syntactic and lexical studies, but we hope that students of
> phonology, morphology and even style may find it useful. We
> have endeavoured to copy our texts from the most reliable
> editions available.

The compilers of the corpus sum up the theoretical basis of the
project as follows:[3]

> We assume that change in language is best approached
> through synchronic variation. The variant expressions of
> the same meaning can be described in the form of variant
> fields, the structure and complexity of which is regulated
> by linguistic and extralinguistic factors. The study of
> syntactic and lexical change does not primarily concentrate
> on the description of the loss of forms and the emergence
> of new ones, but, rather, on the analysis of the changes in
> the structure of variant fields in successive periods of
> time.
>   In order to form a coherent picture of the influence of
> linguistic and extralinguistic factors on the changing
> variant fields, we need a structured corpus of texts, coded
> according to chronology and textual parameters.
>   Another theoretical assumption is related to the import-
> ance of spoken language in linguistic change. A comparison
> of the variable features in speech-based and non-speech-
> based texts in successive periods of time will provide us
> with insights into the actual process of change.

The size of the basic corpus will be close to two million
words. Samples (mostly 5,000 - 10,000 words each) are mainly
selected from prose texts, but the corpus will also contain
extracts from Old English poetry and Middle English verse,
'mainly because the early Middle English centuries would otherwise be very meagrely and one-sidedly represented, and because
the total avoidance of verse would mean that certain highly
relevant texts should be omitted.'[4] Fifteenth- and sixteenth-
century verse drama has also been included.
    At present, there are eighteen textual parameters in the
coding scheme. The most important among them are date, geographical dialect, and text type. Other reference categories tell the

user of the corpus, for example, about the possible difference between the date of composition of the original and the date of the writing of the extant copy, about the degree of formality, the author-audience relationship, the communication situation, the author's age, sex and rank. Scots is one of the alternatives in the parameter coding dialect or regional variety, but the Scottish English texts form a perfectly coherent whole and can be used separately.

There are thirty-five values in the reference category defining the text type. In an ideal case, a text type is represented in all time periods covered by the corpus (e.g. history, law, instruction). On the other hand, there are text types which are typical of the OE and ME periods (e.g. saints' lives and homilies). There are extracts from romances only in the ME period, diaries and trials only from Early Modern English, British and American. The text type categories will be discussed in detail in the context of the corpus of Older Scots.

Now to the main theme of this paper. The Helsinki Corpus of Older Scots is structured according to the same principles as the main corpus, and its computer format and parameter coding are identical. It consists mainly of texts dating from the fifteenth, sixteenth and seventeenth centuries. The material is divided into four periods: the first (1450-1500) corresponds to the last fifty years of the Middle English period in the basic corpus, the second (1500-1570), the third (1570-1640) and the fourth (1640-1700) to the periods of the Early Modern English corpus.

The principal chronological periods of the corpus do not correspond to the established time periods in the history of Scots.[5] It was considered important to keep to the periods chosen for the main corpus, because this would enable the users to broaden the textual basis of their study to Scottish material, for example for purposes of comparison. As the earliest prose texts date from the 1450s, it is easy to establish the time limit of the first period. We can safely use the label Early Middle Scots for the texts of the second period 1500-1570. Very few texts have been included from the 1550s and 1560s. Besides, as far as I can judge, Quintin Kennedy's Two Eucharistic Tracts (c.1561) are fine representatives of Early Middle Scots, if we compare them, for example, with William Fowler's Answer to Hamiltoun, dated 1581, or James Durham's The Dying Man's Testament to the Church of Scotland, or a Treatise concerning Scandal, dated c.1658.[6]

It has, of course, not been possible to find samples of each text type from all the four periods. The two earlier periods in particular remain incomplete. Translations have been accepted when no original texts could be found. In Scottish prose some text types which are well-established in English prose are not found until the seventeenth century.

I have classified the material into four main categories, each of them comprising from two to five different text types:[7]

    (i) instructive or directive,
    (ii) expository or informing,
    (iii) narrative or documentary, and
    (iv) interactive or argumentative.

The subcategories of instructive and directive texts are laws, statutes and charters, translations of the Bible, sermons, and secular and religious instruction. Early books on science and handbooks are expository, the former more theoretical, the latter more practical. Chronicles and histories, biographies (including autobiographies), diaries, travel books and letters are the text types referred to by the label 'narrative', whereas pamphlets , apologies, disputes, political treatises, trials and plays share the characteristic of being interactive or argumentative.

The norm for the language of law is suggested by extracts from the Acts of the Parliaments of Scotland; variants are illustrated by means of text samples from the records of the burghs of Edinburgh and Peebles, possibly also from the records of Lanark, Prestwick and Stirling. The language of official records, legal contracts, deeds, testaments, indentures, lawyers' treatises, etc is distinguished from the language of court trials. The latter provide valuable material for the study of 'oral narrative style'. Samples are selected from the Criminal Trials of Scotland (1488-1624), The Sheriff Court Book of Fife (1515-1522), and some isolated texts, such as the Trial of Isobel Inch (1618) and the Trial of David Roy (1601), the last period being represented by The Tryal of Philip Standsfield ... for the murder of his father (1688). A very important source for material of this kind is The Register of the Minister Elders and Deacons of the Christian Congregation of St Andrews comprising proceedings of the Kirk Sessions, and available in two volumes in the Scottish History Society publications.

It is rather difficult to follow up the development of the language of secular instruction because of the heterogeneity of the texts dating from different periods. If not direct translations, the Middle Scots texts derive more or less clearly from the common European heritage. Gilbert of the Haye's Prose Manuscript (1456) and Porteous Nobleness (c.1490) could be mentioned as examples. The Basilicon Doron (1598) is a valuable representative of the genre in the third period, but I have not been able to find a non-religious text with a didactic purpose which would fit the time limits of the second period. From the minor prose texts of James VI I have included the treatise against tobacco. Satan's Invisible World Discovered (1685) by George Sinclair is of great interest, as it contains lively stories of witches with direct speech interspersed.

Handbooks form an important subcategory among texts labelled as prose of secular instruction. Gilbert Skeyne's medical tracts are the earliest of the kind found in Scots: Ane breve Descriptioun of the Pest (1568) and Ane breif Descriptioun of the Qualiteis and Effectis of the Well of the Woman hill besyde Abirdene (1580). The period 1570-1640 gives us Alexander Huntar's Weights and Measures. George Sinclair's contributions in the field of astronomy and science date from the latter half of the seventeenth century: The Hydrostaticks (1672), Natural Philosophy Improven by New Experiments (1683), and The Principles of Astronomy and Navigation (1688). Extracts have also been selected from The Scots Arithmetician (1685) by James Paterson. In addition to these, the Scottish corpus includes samples from agricultural treatises dating from the third and the fourth period: Archibald Napier's Gooding and Manuring (c.1600), John Skene's Of Husbandrie (c.1669), John Reid's Scots Gard'ner (1683), and James Donaldson's Husbandry (1696). Unfortunately, what is true of many other text types is also true of scholarly treatises: the fifteenth-century specimens of this text type are rare. At present, the transcript of the Loutfut MS, which has been used by the Dictionary of the Older Scottish Tongue, will have to do, but I have been told that a new edition of this text is being prepared. Art of Music (c.1550-c.1580) is perhaps too derivative and too technical to be included in the corpus.

Texts labelled as religious instruction are rather conventional. The corpus contains Craft of Deyng (c.1450), Wisdom of Solomon (c.1460), extracts from John of Irland's Meroure of Wyssdome (1490), and, possibly, from John Gau's Richt Vay to the Kingdom of Heuine (1533). Polemic writings with a religious aim are categorised under pamphlets.

The subcategory of sermons is incomplete: there are specimens only from the third period: D Fergusson, Ane Sermon preichit in the Kirk of Leith (1571) and one of Robert Bruce's sermons (1590-1591). John Welsh's sermons are available only in a modernised version, so they have been omitted. Instead, J Row's Red-Shankes Sermon (1638) and one or two of James Durham's sermons (c.1658) have been selected. In addition, sermons by J Spalding (1696) and by John Welch of Irongray (1679) are included to provide material for the study of this text type at the end of the seventeenth century. The Corpus of English Texts has a special section for translations of the Bible. Purvey's scotticised New Testament (c.1520), which would otherwise be of less interest in this context, has been included in the Scottish corpus only to provide material for comparison.

Non-fictive narration is illustrated by samples from Bellenden's translation into Scots of The History and Chronicles of Scotland, written in Latin by Hector Boece (1531), John Knox's History of the Reformation in Scotland (1558-1566), John Leslie's History of Scotland 1436-1561 (1570), and Robert Lindsay of Pitscottie's chronicle The Historie and Chronicles of Scotland (c.1578). For the third period I have chosen an extract from David Moysie's Memoirs of the Affairs of Scotland, 1577-1603, and, for the fourth, from John Spalding's Memorialls of the Trubles in Scotland and in England, 1624-1645 (c.1650).[8]

Subcategories of non-fictive narrative, i.e. autobiographies, diaries and travel books, can be found only from the seventeenth century. The passages chosen from the existing Scottish travel books are intentionally not accounts of experiences in the Holy Land. I have preferred to include less conventional passages from William Lithgow's Totall discourse of the rare adventures ... of long nineteene yeares trauayles from 1632. The corpus includes the whole text titled Prince of Tartaria (his) Voyage (to) Cowper in Fife from 1661. Interesting samples of travel accounts were also found from Journals of Sir John Lauder, Lord of Fountainhall (1665-1676).

As to autobiographies and diaries, samples have been selected from the following works. The Autobiography and Diary of Mr James

Melvill, Minister of Kilrenny, in Fife (1600, 1610) and Memoirs
of his own Life, 1549-1593 by Sir James Melville of Hallhill
(c.1610) serve to illustrate the characteristics of the text type
in 1570-1640. The period 1640-1700 offers numerous other sources:
The Diary of Mr John Lamont of Newton, 1649-1671; The Diary of
Alexander Brodie of Brodie, 1652-80, and his son, James Brodie of
Brodie, 1680-85; The Diary of Andrew Hay of Craignethan, 1659-60;
The Diary of Sir Archibald Johnston of Warriston, 1632-60; The
Diary and General Expenditure Book of William Cunningham of
Craigends, 1673-80. It is rather difficult to make a distinction
betwen diaries and autobiographies, and it remains to be seen
whether it is a useful one. I have assumed that detailed linguistic analyses might reveal significant differences in the features
of the two text types. This has been considered probable mainly
because of the more or less obvious difference in the author-
audience relationship: diaries need not have been written for the
general public, whereas writers of autobiographies might have had
political, ecclesiastical or social aims in mind. Among autobiographies I have included The Memoirs of Henry Guthry, late Bishop
of Dunkeld (c.1676), Memoirs of the Somervilles (1679) by James
Somerville, Memoirs of his own Life and Times, 1632-70 (c.1686)
by Sir James Turner, and Life of Alexander Reid, a Scottish
Covenanter (c.1706).
    The text type consisting of correspondence is subdivided into
royal letters, official letters, letters written by citizens to
public authorities on private affairs, and family letters (the
last-mentioned including correspondence between friends). They
have been selected from the following collections: the Douglas
Correspondence, the Correspondence of Mary of Lorraine, the
Cromarty Correspondence, the Waus Correspondence, the Ruthven
Correspondence, the Rutherford Correspondence, the Melrose Correspondence, the Wemyss Correspondence, the Grant Correspondence,
the Colville Correspondence, and The Red Book of Grandtully.
    The first and the third period contain material for the study
of the language of drama. Sir David Lindsay's play Ane Satyre of
the Thrie Estaitis dates from 1540, and The Assembly or Scotch
Reformation: a comedy by Archibald Pitcairne from 1692. Scottish
English fictive narration is of a relatively late date. Only the
fourth period can be covered: the samples are from Sir Thomas
Urquhart's Jewel (1651) and Sir George MacKenzie's Aretina (1660).
It is possible that this text type will be omitted from the final
version of the corpus, because of the scarcity of material.
    A text type of special interest in Scottish prose literature
is the category of texts which includes polemic writings of
various kinds, some of them highly literary, others more
straightforward and unsophisticated. In the corpus there are
samples from Robert Wedderburn's Complaynt of Scotland (1549-
1550), works of Ninian Winzet (1562-1563), Chamaeleon from George
Buchanan's vernacular writings (1570), William Fowler's Answer to
Hamiltoun (1581), James Durham's treatise The Dying Man's Testament to the Church of Scotland; or, a Treatise concerning Scandal
(c.1658), The Scotch Presbyterian Eloquence (1692), and An
Apology for the Clergy of Scotland (1693), attributed to A Monro.
William Birnie's Blame of Kirk-buriall (1606) was also considered
interesting, and so was William Lamb's Ane Resonyng of ane Scottis

and Inglis Merchand Betuix Rowand and Lionis (1549), of which a new edition by Roderick J Lyall is available.

As the parameter coding is based on extralinguistic data, no preconceptions as to what linguistic features will be prevalent in the various text types influence the analysis. A structured corpus of this kind makes it possible to identify processes of linguistic change which can be shown to be general tendencies in the development of the English language. On the other hand, it is possible to indicate which features are conditioned by extralinguistic factors, such as style, register, or audience. For example, the corpus provides information about the morphosyntactic features of verbs borrowed from French or Latin during the Middle Scots period. If these verbs mainly occur in the passive in all text types, it is apparent that there is a tendency in all the language to introduce these verbs in a fixed linguistic structure. However, if they are used in passive verb phrases only in text types of a specific kind, it is necessary to take into account the possibility of interpreting the feature as diagnostic of style or register.

The Helsinki Corpus of Scots lends itself ideally to studies of standardisation, both as to the development of the Scottish standard and the gradual anglicisation process after the Scottish Reformation of 1560. It is quite evident that the consideration of other than primarily literary text types changes the established views on when and how these processes took place. We know that prose texts are more useful, as anglicised forms occurred much earlier in verse than in prose. It is, of course, the text types reflecting features of informal language usage that interest us most in this respect. When only literary texts are studied, the loss of typically Scottish features is seen as a rapidly expanding process which was completed before the eighteenth century. When text types such as diaries, travelogues, trials and private letters are included in the material studied, changes can be shown to have happened gradually and in different ways in different idiolects, styles and text types.

The revival of Scots as a literary language took place soon after the standardisation process was completed. Suzanne Romaine sees it as deplorable that it was confined to a popular tradition and speaks about 'the severe functional restrictions of Scots.'[9] A detailed mapping of linguistic features will show which text types developed, in the Middle Scots period, into sophisticated media with established characteristics of their own, and which remained less successful attempts to imitate southern English or European standards. My assumption is that the study of the corpus material will make it possible to draw conclusions about the functionality and self-sufficiency of the Scottish variant when used for other than literary purposes.

In earlier studies of the Scottish variant of the English language, it has been claimed that the language was highly imitative and derivative in most contexts in which it was used: that it drew upon the European tradition of literary models and was also strongly influenced by southern English literary styles. With its emphasis on other than literary texts, the Helsinki corpus gives a more reliable picture of what the language was really like.

At least a concise version of the Helsinki Corpus of Older Scots will, hopefully, be available for scholars by the end of 1990, after a short test study period.[10] At present, we are busy writing the texts into a machine-readable form, but there are still problems to solve. However, I have been able to use part of the texts in my study on the use of loanwords in various text types. This study shows that recent borrowings tend to favour a closely definable set of linguistic contexts at the early stage of their use in the new system, and that certain syntactic structures are more receptive to loans than others. As long as this individual study is in process, the Helsinki corpus of Older Scots cannot be used by other scholars for research on French or Latin loanwords, complex noun phrase structures or verb complementation structures.

Notes

1   Ossi Ihalainen, Merja Kytö and Matti Rissanen, 'The Helsinki Corpus of English Texts, Diachronic and Dialectal: Report on Work in Progress', Corpus Linguistics and Beyond, ed Willem Meijs, Costerus, New Series 59 (Amsterdam, 1987), p 21.

2   Matti Rissanen and Ossi Ihalainen are the leaders of the corpus project, Merja Kytö a research assistant responsible for the practical aspects in the compiling of the corpus. In addition to the corpus of OE, ME and EModE texts, a corpus of present-day British English dialects will be produced. It is planned to be about half a million words.

3   Ibid., p 21.

4   Ibid., p 22.

5   A J Aitken, introduction to The Concise Scots Dictionary (Aberdeen, 1986), p. xiii.

6   Bibliographical references to the texts mentioned in this paper can be found in the combined register of titles of works quoted in The Dictionary of the Older Scottish Tongue.

7   Werlich's categories have been adapted for the use of historical corpora by the members of the EModE work group of the project.

8   At present, a transcript of Adam Abell's work The Roit or Quheill of Tyme, available at the Dictionary of the Older Scottish Tongue in Edinburgh, is the only other text we could choose to illustrate non-fictive narrative in the early sixteenth century, if we want to avoid using Bellenden's translation.

9   In R W Bailey and M Görlach (eds), English as a World Language, Ann Arbor (University of Michigan Press), 1982, p 63.

10   Because of the lack of sufficient funds, we will have to concentrate on prose texts for the time being, but we hope that at some later date we can also cover verse. Whatever the date when the verse corpus will be ready for international use, the categorisation of texts will no doubt be based on Professor A J Aitken's classification of Older Scots poetry, in J D McClure (ed), Scotland and the Lowland Tongue, Aberdeen 1983, pp 18-49.

Chapter 35

'THE WEASEL SCOT': SOME CHARACTERISTICS OF
SHAKESPEARIAN DEPICTION IN HENRY V AND I HENRY IV

A C Calder

In Henry V, I.ii. the Bishop of Ely utters a famous warning. To
Canterbury's dismissal of the Scottish threat, he replies (166):

> But there's a saying very old and true
>   'If that you will France win,
>   Then with Scotland first begin.'
> For once the eagle England being in prey,
> To her unguarded nest the weasel Scot
> Comes sneaking, and so sucks her princely eggs,
> Playing the mouse in absence of the cat,
> To 'tame and havoc more than she can eat.[1]

Eagle versus weasel: the military warning is succintly and memorably conveyed. This immediacy of depiction is one of the features
that strike us when we think of Shakespearian treatments of
nationality (since it is Shakespearian delineation which is in
question, I stress that I am not myself presuming to characterise
the English as aquiline, or - still less - designate my fellow-
Scots as musteline). Although Ely is uttering a piece of conventional wisdom, articulating a council-chamber commonplace, his
description is far from inert; the doggerel verse gives way to an
enticing picture of craft and 'sneaking' depredation ('tame =
attame, to break into). One can see, even within the partial and
restricted scope of Ely's speech, evidence of a Shakespearian
fascination with identity and nationality. In The Truth of Masks
(1891), Oscar Wilde remarked of Shakespeare that:

> He is even true to the characteristics of race ... the
> Princess Katharine is as entirely French as the heroine of
> Divorçons. Harry the Fifth is a pure Englishman, and Othello
> a true Moor.[2]

In the context of Scottishness, there is a distinct interest to be
found in pursuing Wilde's dictum.
    The singular nominative Scot appears in three of Shakespeare's
plays: 1 and 2 Henry IV and Henry V. Of these sixteen occurrences,
'the weasel Scot' is perhaps the most striking: the others read as
follows:[3]

That ever valiant and approved Scot   (1 Henry IV, I.i.54)

By God, he shall not have a Scot of them;
No, if a Scot should save his soul, he shall not
                                        (Ibid., I.iii.214-5)

that sprightly Scot of Scots, Douglas   (Ibid, II.iv.343)

Well said, my noble Scot   (Ibid, IV.i.1)

I hold as little counsel with cold fear
As you, my lord, or any Scot that this day lives
                                        (Ibid, IV.iii.11-12)

I was not born a yielder, thou proud Scot
                                        (Ibid, V.iii.11)

O Douglas, hadst thou fought at Holmedon thus
I never had triumph'd upon a Scot   (Ibid, V.iii.14-15)

Hold up thy head, vile Scot   (Ibid, V.iv.39)

'Sblood, 'twas time to counterfeit, or that hot termagant Scot
has paid me scot and lot too   (Ibid, V.iv.114-5)

The noble Scot, Lord Douglas   (Ibid, V.v.17)

....that furious Scot,
The bloody Douglas   (2 Henry IV, I.i.126-7)

But lay down our proportions to defend
Against the Scot   (Henry V, I.ii.137-8)

But fear the main intendment of the Scot,
Who hath been still a giddy neighbour to us
                                        (Ibid, I.ii.144-5)

But that the Scot on his unfurnished kingdom
Came pouring like the tide   (Ibid, I.ii.148-9)

Occurrences of the plural noun are met within 1 and 2 Henry IV and
in Henry V - they include of course the handsome sobriquet of the
Douglas shown above (Scot of Scots);[4] and there is one instance in
1 Henry VI, IV.i.157 ('Because, forsooth, the King of Scots is
crowned'). Scottish occurs in 1 Henry IV, I.iii.259 and III.i.84.
The Quarto text of The Merchant of Venice preserves Nerissa's
original inquiry at I.ii.77 ('What think you of the Scottish lord,
his neighbour?'); Portia's unflattering reply loses its sting in
the Folio, where an innocuous other replaces Scottish - a natural
enough substitution to make in 1623.[5]
    Portia's suitor may have 'borrowed a box of the ear of the
Englishman' and promised to 'pay him again when he was able'; but
such neighbourly charity is untypical of the Scot as depicted by
Shakespeare, as the martial and threatening allusions from the
history plays indicate. The Scottish element in Henry V, much less
pronounced than in 1 Henry IV, is nevertheless not to be neglected,

however great one's reluctance to deal by parcels (rather than intentively) with this great work. In <u>Henry V</u> the Scottish ingredients comprise the series of allusions in I.ii. and the characterisation of Captain Jamy. The debate on the Scottish danger in I.ii. presents three views: the King's forceful and respectful warning about the enemy which can make England 'shake and tremble' (143-154); Canterbury's soothing and flattering portrayal of a chivalric England which can cope happily with the Scottish threat (155-165); and Ely's picture, which shows the Scots as a very serious danger, but a sneaking and unchivalrous one. The vitality of Ely's contribution is already well attested; it will not come amiss if I quote part of King Henry's warning (from 146):

> ... my great-grandfather
> Never unmasked his power unto France
> But that the Scot on his unfurnished kingdom
> Came pouring like the tide into a breach
> With ample and brim fulness of his force
> Galling the gleaned land with hot assays,
> Girding with grievous siege castles and towns,
> That England, being empty of defence,
> Hath shook and trembled at the bruit thereof.

This is a magnificent and stirring depiction; and it is materially enhanced by the incorporation of Quarto readings in 147 and 154. For Q's 'unmasked by his power', F has the tame 'went with his forces'; for Q's 'the bruit [t]hereof', F has the anti-climactic 'th'ill neighbourhood'.[6] Canterbury's comments embody a very different recollection of Anglo-Scottish hostilities: David II was captured and 'impounded as a stray' (160) to swell the fame of Edward III. Canterbury decks out the conclusion of his speech with flowers of eloquence in celebration of Henry's glory, prompting Ely to bring the discussion back to stubborn existence of the Scottish problem – a problem that cannot be covered up by the Archbishop's obsequious rhetoric. In the event, Exeter truncates the debate with his assertion that the 'petty thieves' will be caught by the 'pretty' (i.e. ingenious) English traps; England will be safe, since, while the 'armed hand' fights abroad, the prudent head defends itself at home.[7]

Of Captain Jamy there is little to say. Gary Taylor remarks that 'no actor has been able to make much of Captain Jamy, whose individuality consists solely of a Scots accent (itself not so well conveyed as by earlier, lesser dramatists)'.[8] There is indeed not very much in the way of individuality to adduce. Jamy is taciturn, hardy, dry in delivery. He conforms to a standard notion of the Scot; indeed, he appears in speech-headings as <u>Scot</u> in F (there is no equivalent character in Q). Similarly, Macmorris is <u>Irish</u>, and Fluellen (in this scene – III.ii. or (Taylor) III.iii.) is predominantly <u>Welsh</u>. But the obvious reproduction of broad national types is exactly what is required: there is an enhancement of Henry's enterprise when it is presented as a venture involving the four nations, one of them the dangerous neighbour of I.ii. 'This fair action' becomes not merely an English but a

British enterprise. Jamy's place in the swelling scene is a
subordinate but not ignoble one. He attracts the praise of
Fluellen; Macmorris, says Fluellen, 'is an ass'; but Captain Jamy
is described as a 'marvellous falorous gentleman ... and of great
expedition and knowledge in th'anciant wars' (III.iii.21). There
are one or two interesting examples of Scots colloquial usage in
this scene; at line 60, for instance, it is common to find the
emendation hear instead of F heard, but F in fact preserves a
characteristic usage which elides have after a modal verb in the
past tense. There is no doubt that the contrasts between the
speech characteristics of the captains provide entertainment in
the theatre and contribute to the texture of the play. An aspect
of the greatness of Henry V is its inclusiveness, its encompassing
of loyalty and treachery, valour and 'cold fear', high endeavour
and farcical incident. The texture is rich; and the richness is
created in part by the presence of those 'characteristics of race'
upon which Wilde commented. Separateness, distinctness, diversity
are, as it were, insisted upon: nevertheless, these competing and
contrasting strands of nationality combine in the common enterprise.

In writing his English Histories, Shakespeare had before him a
mass of chronicle detail:

> ... pure crude fact
> secreted from man's life when hearts beat hard,
> And brains, high-blooded, ticked two centuries since.9

Before treating of 1 Henry IV it is as well to remind ourselves of
the 'pure crude fact' preserved in chronicle treatments of the
reign. On 14 September, 1402, there took place the Battle of
Holmedon (Hambledon), in which the invading Scots, commanded by
Archibald 'Tyneman', fourth Earl of Douglas, were defeated by the
army of Henry Percy ('Hotspur'). This event, early in the reign of
the usurping Henry IV, occurred three months after the defeat and
capture of Sir Edmund Mortimer near Radnor, by his Welsh adversary
Owen Glendower, self-styled Prince of Wales and one of the most
formidable opponents of the Lancastrian regime. For his own purposes, Shakespeare juxtaposes the two battles. He begins 1 Henry
IV by showing us the King postponing his intention of taking the
Cross under the press of events at home: the Welsh are in arms,
and the Percies, victors of Holmedon, are refusing to hand over
noble Scottish prisoners - all except Mordake, Earl of Fife, who
as a Prince of the Blood must be entrusted to the King himself. I
quote from the account of the victory given in I.i.67-74:

> The Earl of Douglas is discomfited;
> Ten thousand bold Scots, two and twenty knights,
> Balk'd in their own blood, did Sir Walter see
> On Holmedon's plains; of prisoners Hotspur took
> Mordake, Earl of Fife and eldest son
> To beaten Douglas, and the Earl of Athol,
> Of Murray, Angus, and Menteith.

It is indeed, as Westmoreland admits, a conquest for a prince to boast of. Shakespeare, as the editors remind us, has erred in a couple of points. Mordake (Murdoch Stewart, Earl of Fife) was actually son to the Regent Albany; a printer's error in Holinshed has resulted in his Shakespearian translation into a son of Douglas.[10] Again, Menteith is given in King Henry's list as a separate personage; in fact, the earldom of Menteith was a secondary dignity of Mordake's. But these are not significant matters; what one wants to stress is that this is indeed a great victory and an honourable spoil (cf. line 74) — honourable because of Hotspur's prowess (in the King's words he is 'the theme of honour's tongue') and also by reason of the illustrious quality of the defeated. The list recalls the roll-call in Henry V (IV.viii. 90-99) which concludes:

> ... of lusty earls,
> Grandpré and Roussi, Fauconbridge and Foix,
> Beaumont and Marle, Vaudemont and Lestrelles.

A 'royal fellowship' indeed.

It is noteworthy that in Westmoreland's preliminary account of the battle, Hotspur and his adversary Douglas are presented as being on the same level of distinction: 'the gallant Hotspur' versus 'the brave Archibald,/ That ever valiant and approved Scot' (53-54). Douglas is a potent figure in the play, even though his appearances are few. He is the embodiment of the Scot: Mordake and the other earls are simply mentioned.

The 'Lord Mortimer of Scotland' referred to in III.ii. has an even more shadowy existence; in fact he derives from a misreading of a phrase in Holinshed, the nobleman in question, George Dunbar, Earl of the March of Scotland, having no connection with the English Earls of March, the Mortimers. For all practical purposes, then, Douglas is the Scot. His potency derives to a large extent from the preparation which lays the ground for his appearances late in the play. The words and reports of others establish a sombre and weighty figure. This is in conformity with what Shakespeare found in his source-material. Holinshed gives us a picture of a hardy captain; I quote from his description of the Battle of Shewsbury, in which Hotspur and Douglas are joined in league against the King:

> Here the Lord Henry Percy, and the Earl Douglas, a right stout and hardy captain, not regarding the shot of the King's battle nor the close order of the ranks, pressing forward together bent their whole forces towards the King's person ... [and] ... gave such a violent onset upon them that about the King's standard that, slaying his standard-bearer, Sir Walter Blunt, and overthrowing the standard, they made slaughter of all those that stood about it, as the Earl of Stafford ... and diverse other.[11]

Holinshed also narrates that Douglas struck down the King himself, an incident amplified by Samuel Daniel in his First Four Books of the Civil Wars (1595):

> Hadst thou [Prince Henry] not there lent present speedy aid
> To thy endangered father nearly tired,
> Whom fierce encount'ring Douglas overlaid,
> That day had there his troublous life expired ... [12]

This is what Shakespeare found in his sources; and he reproduces the attributes of fierceness, valour, and hardihood which they ascribe to the character.

But Shakespeare does more that this. He goes beyond the limits of chronicle and creates an altogether more ample figure, possessing a high chivalric lustre that renders the Douglas a noble and puissant (rather than merely baleful) embodiment of the warrior. The House of Douglas, we recall, was no ordinary family of feuding barons but one of the most illustrious houses in Scottish history. Everyone knows of at least one member of the Douglas clan – the Good Sir James, companion-in-arms of King Robert the Bruce. Sir James Douglas was slain while on his way to the Holy Land bearing the heart of the Bruce: hence the bloody heart that figures in the armorial achievement of the House: <u>Argent, a heart gules on a chief azure three silver molets</u>. The Douglas standard also commemorates the association with the Bruce, for it depicts the white cross of St Andrew near the staff, two red hearts, and a white lion passant; the motto is 'Jamais arriere'.[13] The connection between Shakespeare's Douglas and the Good Sir James is that, on the extinction of the legitimate line in 1388, the earldom was granted to Sir James's illegitimate son, Archibald the Grim, who was succeeded by his son Archibald, the fourth Earl – the Douglas who figures in <u>1 Henry IV</u>. He advanced the fortunes of his house by marrying Princess Margaret, daughter of King Robert III. The fourth Earl's career was illustrious; but as his nickmane 'Tyneman' (the Loser) indicates, he failed to achieve success in battle. At Holmedon he was wounded five times and lost an eye; at the Battle of Shrewsbury, in the following year, he was again wounded and taken prisoner. He was eventually released in 1408. He made his first journey to France in 1412 and concluded a treaty with John the Fearless. For the next ten years he pursued what the <u>Dictionary of National Biography</u> calls an 'ambiguous policy', at one time carrying on the Border war with England, at another negotiating with England for the release of James I.[14] In 1419 Charles VI of France requested the aid of Scotland against the English; the result was the sending of 7,000 men under the command of Douglas's son-in-law, the Earl of Buchan. In 1423 a fresh appeal was made for Scottish help; this time Douglas was commander. He was made lieutenant-general of the French army and granted the duchy of Touraine, being greeted by the citizens of Tours as their Duke on 7 May 1423. His new honours were not enjoyed for long. In the following year occurred the Battle of Verneuil (17 August) – a disaster for the Franco-Scottish army. Among the 6,000 who fell were Buchan and Douglas. Verneuil marked the end of the Scots adventure in France; as R L Mackie wrote:

> it was no profit to Scotland that the flower of its manhood should rot on the field of Normandy. Yet few pages in the history of Scotland move one more than the record of that splendid and quixotic sacrifice.[15]

Douglas himself, having proved the truth of his motto - 'Jamais arriere' - was buried in state in the city of Tours. His duchy and earldom passed to his son Archibald.

That is a sketch of a remarkable career - not perhaps quixotic, but undeniably splendid. The record of Douglas's later life is not directly relevant to the actions and personalities portrayed in 1 Henry IV; but it is nevertheless of interest to survey the career of 'fierce encount'ring Douglas' and realise that it was 'all of a piece throughout'. One can apply the same comment to the dramatic Douglas. In a play so saturated in the martial and masculine virtues as 1 Henry IV, where Hotspur is consistently held up (by the King, among others) as the admirable foil to the underrated Hal, Douglas is regarded as the heroic equal to Hotspur himself. The linking of the two warriors extends to 2 Henry IV. In the Induction Rumour asserts that his office is to spread the false news that at Shrewsbury (29-32):

> ... Harry Monmouth fell
> Under the wrath of noble Hotspur's sword,
> And that the King before the Douglas' rage
> Stoop'd his anointed head as low as death.

But Northumberland, in spite of the assurances of Lord Bardolph that victory has favoured the rebels, understands from the demeanour of Morton that the day has brought disaster to their party (I.i.76-81):

> This thou wouldst say, 'Your son did thus and thus;
> Your brother thus; so fought the noble Douglas' -
> Stopping my greedy ear with their bold deeds:
> But in the end, to stop my ear indeed,
> Thou hast a sigh to blow away this praise,
> Ending with 'Brother, son, and all are dead'.

The wrath of Hotspur and the rage of Douglas have not prevailed; Hotspur is dead, and the 'furious Scot / The bloody Douglas' has been defeated. This is a matter for high lament and Homeric allusion; in Northumberland's words to Morton (68-75, abbreviated):

> Thou tremblest ...
> Even such a man, so faint, so spiritless,
> So dull, so dead in look, so woe-begone,
> Drew Priam's curtain in the dead of night,
> And would have told him half his Troy was burnt:
> But Priam found the fire ere he his tongue,
> And I my Percy's death ere thou report'st it.

There are, I think, three ingredients in these speeches that deserve mention: the linking of Hotspur and Douglas; the poetic exalting of their heroic fury (in the case of Douglas his prowess can excuse even flight - cf. Morton's report, lines 129-130); and the solemnity which informs the references to the downfall of Troy.

The part played by Douglas in the narrative of 1 Henry IV is

such that the epic scale of these allusions is felt to be in
conformity with his actions. Douglas, after all, did make the King
stoop before his rage; only the timely rescue by Prince Hal
prevents his father from stooping 'as low as death' (V.iv). Three
times Douglas slays 'the appearance of the King' (decoys dressed
in the King's armour). His exploits at Shrewsbury represent the
climax to his dramatic progress. In I.i. we hear accounts of the
matching prowess of Hotspur and Douglas at Holmedon. In I.iii. he
is suggested as an ally of the Percies. In III.ii. he is lauded by
King Henry in terms which deserve further attention. In IV.i. he
makes his first appearance in the play, offering stout-hearted
counsel to his party. In IV.iii. he advises a night attack on the
royal forces. In V.ii. he makes his (second) entrance after having
thrown 'a brave defiance in King Henry's teeth'. In V.iii. he
kills Sir Walter Blunt, thinking him to be the King. In V.iv. he
fights with the King and has his encounter with the fat rogue
himself. In the final scene he is freed, without ransom, for his
valour. Prince Hal having begged his father for custody of 'the
noble Scot, Lord Douglas', the King grants his wish ('with all my
heart'); upon which Hal instructs Lord John of Lancaster (27-31):

> Go to the Douglas and deliver him
> Up to his pleasure, ransomless and free:
> His valours shown upon our crests today
> Have taught us how to cherish such high deeds,
> Even in the bosom of our adversaries.

We note the gracious chivalry of the Prince's language, a quality
which is maintained in the surrounding references to 'honourable
bounty' (26) and 'high courtesy' (32). Douglas (again, like
Hotspur) is 'noble' (cf. line 19); and the nobility of the
defeated warriors promotes a corresponding gentilesse in the
victors. The Prince's speech also directs attention to the
locution the Douglas. Earlier, he had used the phrase at line 23;
and Hotspur in IV.i. had expressed his tribute to 'the Douglas'
(1-9). In Scotland we are not unfamiliar with the juxtaposing of
definite article and single name; there is, nevertheless, a
peculiar appropriateness to the style in this play. For Douglas —
the Douglas - is not a character amenable to 'interpretation'; he
is not supplied with any tincture or trace of 'individuality'. He
is a stern and stout-hearted embodiment of martial virtue and
northern ruggedness. His power lies in his lack of analysable
'character'. It is perhaps a tribute to the success of Shakespeare's depiction that the Douglas has obstinately resisted
modish critical 'readings'. He is there: bleak, independent,
obdurately non-interpretable.
   That is, in its way, one form of tribute. But there are, in the
play, explicit (as well as implied) tributes to the Douglas. We
think of the King's heartfelt words to Hal in III.ii.; we think of
Hotspur's regard for his 'friend' - regard which is shown not only
in words but also in manner or manners, since Douglas fails to
attract any of the ribaldry, satire, or scepticism which the 'mad
fellow of the North' commonly applies to his dealings with others.
In addition to all this, and in very different register, we have
the Falstaffian allusions in II.iv.

The great Tavern Scene in I Henry IV gives us a remarkable blending of ingredients. Gesture, action, stage-pictures, movement and arrest all enhance the verbal language and help to create the dramatic language which is the compound of verbal and non-verbal features. We all relish the word-play in the mock-interviews staged by Falstaff; but the relish is increased by the magical contrast between the world of the tavern and the world of political affairs. To quote from a later scene: 'The land is burning; Percy stands on high;/And either we or they must lower lie'. In II.iv. the off-stage arrival of Sir John Bracy, bearing his villainous news of the threat posed by the rebels, does present an interruption to the merriment of the Boar's Head. The fiend Douglas, the spirit Percy, the devil Glendower are on the march, and the Prince must to the court in the morning. But for the moment the play extempore, postponed by the appearance of Mistress Quickly announcing Bracy's arrival, can proceed. The stream of time does run; but for this moment in the dead of night, it can seem to have stopped. Contrast is a governing principle – of life, and consequently of drama. In II.iv. contrast is overwhelmingly potent: there is the life of political necessity, of clamours and demands; and there is the immediate warm and localised life of the tavern. The intrusions of the Hostess at 280 and 480, the excited entry of Bardolph (running) at 475, and the imperious knocking which precedes Bardolph's appearance: all these interruptions provide a reminder of the political world with its claims of duty and necessity. That much is obvious; for my present purpose, I shall simply note how well Shakespeare preserves a balance. The threat posed by the rebels is real; the thousand 'Bluecaps' are genuine enough. The news brought by Bracy is at once real and urgent and at the same time, in the glorious present, immaterial – the source of fantasy and invention:

There's villainous news abroad ... that same mad fellow of the north, Percy, and he of Wales that gave Amamon the bastinado, and made Lucifer cuckold, and swore the devil his true liegeman upon the cross of a Welsh hook ... Owen, Owen, the same; and his son-in-law Mortimer, and old Northumberland, and that sprightly Scot of Scots, Douglas, that runs a-horseback up a hill perpendicular...well, he is there too, and one Mordake, and a thousand blue-caps more. Worcester is stolen away tonight; thy father's beard is turned white with the news; you may buy land now as cheap as stinking mackerel...But tell me, Hal, art not thou horrible afeard? Thou being heir apparent, could the world pick thee out three such enemies again, as that fiend Douglas, that spirit Percy, and that devil Glendower? Art thou not horribly afraid? Doth not thy blood thrill at it?

(329-366, condensed)

Not a whit, replies the Prince – 'I lack some of thy instinct'; and with the word 'instinct' he returns us to the comic inventiveness of Falstaff's apologia (263-271). But, of course, the inventiveness has been sustained throughout, as the (somewhat abbreviated) passage of Falstaffian commentary on the 'villainous news' indicates. The Prince gave an energetic parody of a domestic interlude for Hotspur and wife in lines 99-106; now Falstaff gives his own series of glosses on the 'necessity and state of times'. Earnest exegesis would be supererogatory.

I will, however, permit myself one comment. As the piece of bravura elaboration quoted above displays, conventional critical terminology - undermining, undercutting, diminution - is not really adequate if one is attempting to do justice to the dramatic texture. The prowess of these enemies of the Lancastrian régime is not in question, nor is the reality of the threat they pose to 'the peace and safety of our throne' (King Henry's words). Rather, it is a matter of revaluation. Falstaff's glosses present a re-valuing of what the political scenes depict; his myth-making is ample enough to accomodate 'that fiend Douglas', 'that spirit Percy', and 'that devil Glendower'. In the sweetest time of the night, when the doors are clapped to and the gallants in their cups, the insistent demands of the world of action can be trans-lated or transmuted into the stuff of Falstaffian invention.

III.ii. shows us what happens when Hal does go to court; he is, as Falstaff predicts, horribly chid. The terms of the chiding are of great interest. This interview between King and Prince marks the turning-point in their relations.[16] King Henry goes further than ever before in contrasting his son with Hotspur (whom he lauded so strongly in I.i.). He had previously wished that it could be proved that 'some night-tripping fairy' had exchanged the children at birth. Now he even declares that Percy has more right to the succession than Hal; Percy's claim is based on merit, Hal's on mere hereditary custom. And the high point of Percy's renown is that he has vanquished the Douglas (107-111):

> What never-dying honour hath he got
> Against renowned Douglas! whose high deeds,
> Whose hot incursions and great name in arms,
> Holds from all soldiers chief majority
> And military title capital
> Through all the kingdoms that acknowledge Christ.

These are very high claims; the encomium could hardly be more exalted. The King continues:

> Thrice hath this Hotspur, Mars in swathling clothes,
> This infant warrior, in his enterprises
> Discomfited great Douglas, ta'en him once,
> Enlarged him, and made a friend of him,
> To fill the mouth of deep defiance up,
> And shake the peace and safety of our throne.

It is hardly necessary to expatiate on the tremendous gathering of power in this speech. The verse communicates the sense of danger felt by Bolingbroke as he recounts the reconciling of these mighty foes. The phrase I wish to select is the eloquent 'made a friend of him'. Friend (OE freond) has a significance beyond that denoted by the modern (and somewhat indeterminate) usage ('I had some friends round last night' etc). The King's use has an altogether stronger resonance: he is referring to a powerful bond between heroic allies. And this is precisely what is shown to us in the actual depiction of Hotspur and the Douglas in their relation to each other. Hotspur is no respecter of persons; we recall the briskness and bluntness he shows to Glendower in III.i. Yet Glendower is not merely vapouring: he is as Mortimer reminds us, valiant, learned, generous – and out of respect for Hotspur, he checks his own indignation at the northerner's 'crossings'. Worcester rebukes his nephew for being too wilful and for showing 'defect of manners, want of government'. Very well, Hotspur rejoins impatiently, 'I am school'd' (184); let us hope, he continues ironically, that good manners will win you the day. It is all the more interesting, therefore, to observe the opening of IV.i.:

> Well said, my noble Scot! If speaking truth
> In this fine age were not thought flattery,
> Such attribution should the Douglas have
> As not a soldier of this season's stamp
> Should go so general current through the world.
> By God, I cannot flatter, I do defy
> The tongues of soothers, but a braver place
> In my heart's love hath no man than yourself:
> Nay, task me to my word, approve me, lord.
> DOUGLAS: Thou art the king of honour:
> No man so potent breathes upon the ground
> But I will beard him.

This represents a new note in Hotspur's delivery; as for the Douglas, his brief reply exhibits that brand of eloquent taciturnity which Shakespeare confers on him. One is reminded of the speech of Homer's warriors as rendered by Chapman – 'so ordered, so material'. There is a true warrior's courtesy in these short exchanges; the genuine courtesy which consists in speaking truth and abjuring the fopperies of this 'fine' (i.e. over-refined, over-subtilised) age. We do not know what has occasioned the conversation, which begins abruptly, in the middle, with Percy's 'Well said, my noble Scot!'; presumably we are to think that the Douglas has uttered some threat against the King, whom it is his intention to challenge in person. In any event, the abruptness of the opening, the indefiniteness of line 12 ('Do so, and 'tis well'), the delayed thanks in line 13 – all these testify to the press of events and the urgency of action. As a result, the exchange of courtesies is no leisurely affair but very much pared-down or abbreviated: the effect is one of compactness and concentration.

The tone of agreement persists, Hotspur and Douglas responding as one to the news of Northumberland's absence. Hotspur's reaction is given in lines 75-83; the speech is grammatically complete, yet Douglas makes a smooth continuation with his simile:

HOTSPUR: Yet all goes well, yet all our joints are whole.
DOUGLAS: As heart can think: there is not such a word
Spoke of in Scotland as this term of fear.

The courage and optimism of Percy are echoed by Douglas; and the endorsement is strengthened by the syntax. The heroes speak (as Marco and Giuseppe sing) 'as one individual'. In IV.iii. Hotspur and Douglas favour a night attack; Vernon and Worcester favour delay (one notes, incidentally, the succinctness of the Douglas replique at 14).

There is a sober and moving embrace as the rebels prepare to take the field at the end of V.ii. (this contrasts with the high spirits of the conclusion to IV.i); as the battle is upon them, Percy and his allies make their farewell courtesy. Now, at last, in V.iii, the hostilities begin – so long announced and prepared for. It is Douglas's purpose to kill the King in combat; Blunt becomes the second decoy to fall to Douglas, Lord Stafford being the first. On learning Blunt's identity, Douglas utters the chilling threat (26-28):

> Now, by my sword, I will kill all his coats;
> I'll murder all his wardrobe, piece by piece,
> Until I meet the King.

V.iv. (it is necessary to speak editorially for the sake of convenience) is a packed scene that gives us four contests: King versus Douglas; Prince versus Douglas; Prince versus Hotspur; Falstaff versus Douglas. Douglas announces himself in the baleful lines (25-26):

> I am the Douglas, fatal to all those
> That wear those colours on them.

In the ensuing fight, he almost despatches the King; subsequently, the Prince puts Douglas to flight. It is noteworthy that even here we are reminded of the substance behind the Douglas's boast at line 25, for Prince Hal invokes the names of the king's doubles ('valiant Shirley, Stafford, Blunt'). While Hal and Hotspur fight, Falstaff enters and in inimitable fashion encourages his 'sweet wag' – at which point the stage-direction reads (75): Re-enter Douglas; he fighteth with Falstaff, who falls down as if he were dead. Douglas and Falstaff exchange no words; it is impossible to conceive a conversation between, say, Falstaff and Cordelia, and equally impossible to imagine a verbal platform on which the fat rogue and the heroic warrior could meet. So Shakespeare gives us their contest in dumb show. Falstaff, coming to life when the excitement is over and Hotspur safely accounted for, rises up and congratulates himself on his counterfeiting ('Sblood, 'twas time to counterfeit, or that hot termagant Scot had paid me, scot and lot too'). Termagant strikes the required note of ferocity, wildness, and exoticism. Originally, Termagant was the name of a fierce deity whom the Saracens supposedly worshipped (vide the Sultan's prayer in the romance Guy of Warwick).[18] Dunbar's tarmegantis are wild Highlanders[19] whose yells deafen the Devil; Henryson prays to the Virgin to preserve him from Termigant (here, the Devil himself) – 'And fra his cluke that kene is'.[20] Well may Falstaff commend himself for escaping such a relentless foe. It is a pleasantly symmetrical touch that Falstaff, farcically vanquished

by Douglas, now claims to be the conqueror of Percy. The parallelism that has subsisted between the heroes is maintained, in some
bizarre manner, through the agency of the fat knight.

A R Humphreys wrote that 1 Henry IV:

> is about adventure - the adventure of conflict, the adventure
> of Bohemianism. It is consequently also about danger - the
> danger of defeat, the danger of retribution. And it is
> consequently also about courage ...[21]

Its poetry is the poetry of men in action. It is only just to
salute Shakespeare's portrayal of the Douglas as one ingredient in
his presentation of a time when 'hearts beat hard'.

Having alluded to Browning twice, let me invoke his name a
third time. The chronicles of Hall and Holinshed have great
qualities in themselve; but for the student of the English history
cycle, their chief claim to honour is that they supplied Shakespeare with his source-material. One can imagine the chronicles as
the Shakespearian equivalents of that square old yellow book which
Browning found one day in Florence and bought for eight-pence
English just. Browning's small-quarto contained the documents of
the Franceschini murder trial of 1698: 'pure crude fact'. To the
gold of truth the poet added the alloy of fancy, effecting a
'manageable mass'. In a magnificent reflection in Book I, Browning
muses:

> Well, now; there's nothing in nor out o' the world
> Good except truth: yet this, the something else,
> What's this then, which proves good yet seems untrue?
> This that I mixed with truth, motions of mine
> That quickened, made the inertness malleable
> O' the gold was not mine, - what's your name for this?
> Are means to the end, themselves in part the end?
> Is fiction which makes fact alive, fact too?
> The somehow may be thishow.[22]

It is Shakespeare's sovereign ability to quicken inertness. In his
handling - or, better, galvanising - of the old story of the
Douglas in 1 Henry IV, as in his treatment of other and greater
ingredients, our pre-eminent English poet persuades us that the
'somehow may be thishow'.

Notes

1   Henry V, Gary Taylor (ed), The Oxford Shakespeare (1982).
    Following the Quarto text (Q), Taylor gives this speech to A
    Lord. Incidentally, Q garbles the speech, as it does in the
    case of so many others. See the facsimile in Shakespeare's
    Plays in Quarto, Michael J B Allen and Kenneth Muir (eds)
    (Berkeley and London, 1981,) pp 524-50. There is a superb
    facsimile of the Folio text of Henry V (F) in The First Folio

of Shakespeare, prepared by Charlton Hinman (New York, 1968). For convenient comparison of the texts, see Brinsley Nicholson's parallel-text edition for the New Shakespeare Society (1877). Quotations from Henry IV are taken from the Arden editions by A R Humphreys: Part 1 (London, 1960); Part 2 (London, 1966).

2   Oscar Wilde, The Truth of Masks, in Complete Works of Oscar Wilde, introduced by Vyvyan Holland (London, 1966), pp 1060–78 (1070).

3   Marvin Spevack, Harvard Concordance to Shakespeare (Cambridge, Mass., 1973). Spevack uses the text of The Riverside Shakespeare. In addition to the uses of the term Scot in its normal significance, there is also, of course, the punning scot and lot at 1 Henry IV, V.iv.115 (in Humphreys' lineation, 113).

4   The others, as given in Spevack, Concordance, are: 1 Henry IV, I.i.68; I.iii.212; II.iv.103; 2 Henry IV, IV.iv.98; Henry V, I.ii.161; III.ii.74.

5   'The F reads "other" in deference to the susceptibilities of James I, who saw the play on 10 February 1605, and liked it so well that it was acted again before him two days later' – John Dover Wilson, The Merchant of Venice, The New Shakespeare (Cambridge, 1926), p 127.

6   Q actually reads (88–89): 'For you shall read, never my great grandfather / Unmasked his power for France'. Line 93 ends '... hereof'.

7   The main purpose of Exeter's speech is to provide a bridge, by way of the head/hand opposition, to the Archbishop's discourse on the state of man.

8   Taylor, Henry V, p 67.

9   Robert Browning, The Ring and the Book, Richard D Altick (ed) (Harmondsworth, 1971), Book I, 86–88.

10 See W G Boswell-Stone, Shakespeare's Holinshed: the Chronicle and the Plays Compared (2nd edn, London, 1907), p 132.

11 Ibid, p 146 (modernised).

12 Daniel, Civil wars, Book III, st 111 (modernised).

13 C W Scott-Giles, Shakespeare's Heraldry (London, 1950)

14 Dictionary of National Biography, Sir Leslie Stephen and Sir Sydney Lee (eds) (Oxford, 1888), vol 5, p 1170.

15 R L Mackie, Scotland (London, 1916), p 229.

16 The scene also, of course, gives the Prince his first opportunity to speak in his own defence.

17 I quote only part of the S.D.

18 'So help me Mahoun of might,/And Termagant, my God so bright' – cited from H H Furness, Hamlet vol I p 226. This constitutes the third volume of A New Variorum Edition of Shakespeare (2nd edn, Philadelphia, 1879).

19 William Dunbar, The Dance of the Seven Deadly Sins, 1.115, in Poems of William Dunbar, W M Mackenzie (ed) (Edinburgh, 1932).

20 Robert Henryson, The Annunciation, st 7, in Robert Henryson: the Poems, Denton Fox (ed) (Oxford, 1987).

21 Humphreys, 1 Henry IV, p lvii.

22 The Ring and the Book, I, 698–706.

Chapter 36

THE SCOTCHING OF SHAKESPEARE

David Angus

The notion that someone else wrote Shakespeare's plays is now
completely out of fashion - for what that is worth. There was at
one time a craze for finding alternative authors to replace the
Bard. It led nowhere, proved nothing, went to extreme and absurd
lengths, and was finally banished from the realm of respectable
scholarship forever. Or so it seemed. As one wit summed up: 'The
plays of Shakespeare were almost certainly written by another man
altogether - called William Shakespeare.' Being unconcerned with
fashions in scholarship, I recently ventured upon an examination of
some of the odder language in Shakespeare (or whomever), ranging
over the whole corpus of his work. The rest of this paper records
certain findings, and guesses, and tentative conclusions which I
made.

Let me preface the body of the text with one remark. Around the
Shakespearean period (c.1590-1616) there was a great deal held in
common by the languages (the Anglo-Saxon-based languages, that is
to say) of England and Scotland. But there was a great deal that
was not held in common. In other words, there were many differences. The exciting discovery I have made is that, where certain
Shakespearean words and usages baffle English editors, there is
often a purely Scottish interpretation that works well - sometimes
drawn from Lallans or Braid Scots; sometimes even from Scottish
Gaelic. Others besides myself have observed this phenomenon.

Let us examine some of the linguistic evidence, turning to
particular instances. For example, when Proteus, in The Two Gentle-
men of Verona, Act IV, is exasperated with his clownish servant
Launce, he exclaims : 'A slave, that still an end turns me to
shame.' Editors, of course, when they do not know the answer to a
puzzle, are liable to guess; they guess that still an end means
'constantly.' In fact, surely it appears to be a corruption of the
familiar, and still current, Scots phrase still and on, meaning
'nevertheless'. Similarly, when in Act IV of The Merry Wives of
Windsor, the Host of the Garter Inn shouts out to Falstaff, who is
in another room: 'Art thou there? It is thine Host, thine Ephesian
calls,' editors assume that Ephesian is a cant term for 'toper'
(though it is news to me that hosts get drunk with their custom-
ers). But the Host has just referred to Falstaff's speaking 'like
an Anthropophaginian' (i.e. like a cannibal), presumably because of
his enormous eating capacity, and Sir John, in a moment, will
himself address Simple as 'mussel-shell'. Now the Scots jocularly
used Ephesian to mean 'pheasant' (cf. Scots pheesant), and it

strikes me that Ephesian here is merely a link in the chain of the Falstaff-will-eat-anything-and-everything joke running through this passage.

At times editorial ignorance of what I perhaps may be allowed to call the Scottish dimension can lead to Shakespeare's being given credit for linguistic originality he may not deserve. Here is one possible example. When Bottom, newly given an 'ass-head' in Act III of A Midsummer Night's Dream, scores an unexpected point at Titania's expense, he adds complacently: 'Nay, I can gleek upon occasion' (I can jest or scoff at times). Gleek was a noun only in English at this time, and Shakespeare is credited with having introduced the verbal usage. Yet in J Sinclair's 'Observations on the Scottish Dialect' (1780) the habitual Scots verbal use of gleek is duly recorded. Perhaps that is what we get in A Midsummer Night's Dream.

Here is another instance of Shakespeare being given credit which he may not deserve. Before his use of gouts meaning 'drops' (drops of blood, in fact, on the visionary dagger in Macbeth Act II) we find that the Oxford English Dictionary records only two early and obscure uses of the word with that meaning, both dating from the early fifteenth century, and spelt 'gowtyth' and 'gutto'. But gout or gutt (meaning 'drop' and evidently pronounced 'goot') was familiar in Scotland as late as 1708. The Scottish National Dictionary quotes the Atholl MSS for 6 October of that year: 'You may take in the morning, amongst a little wine or ale, from 30 to 40, or 50 gutts'. So Scotland may well offer the likelier source for the 'gouts' in Macbeth.

Editors go to ingenious (and unlikely) lengths to explain what seem to be totally obscure (or corrupt) expressions. Of these last, one of the most celebrated, or notorious, is Hamlet's 'I am but mad north-north-west: when the wind is southerly I know a hawk from a handsaw' (Act II). Now, all are agreed that handsaw must be wrong. But perhaps, some editors say, Shakespeare meant, and wrote, 'hernshaw' (=heron). Well, if he did, he was dropping far below Hamlet's usual high standard of pointed wit, for it is a very flat comparison, or contrast. On the other hand the Scots word handshoe (or haundshae) makes perfect sense here. Surely Hamlet means to say to Rosencrantz and Guildenstern 'I know how to protect myself at need'. A glove or gauntlet was – and is – the falconer's normal protection against the hawk's claws as it sits hooded on his hand. 'Aye, he can tell a hawk frae a haunshae' may well have been a proverbial Scots expression, now lost. In England, where the word was (and is) unknown, such an expression would have been quite unfamiliar and easily corrupted by any transcriber.

(Throughout all this, you are to understand, I am making a fairly large assumption – viz, that an anonymous Scot wrote the plays first, and that later an Englishman (perhaps named Shakespeare) had to make sense of them for London. For some private reason, Shakespeare was allowed to take all the credit.)

Going back to handshoe, this appears first in print only in 1837, in Wilson's Tales of the Borders. But Wilson does suggest a long-established and localised Highland usage, and I quote from him: 'soft handshoes', as they call gloves in the Pictish counties of Scotland.' You should recall at this point that not only handshoe but <u>gutt</u> also first comes to us in Scotland from north of the Highland line. In a moment we shall find what appear to be echoes of Scottish Gaelic in the plays. For instance, in <u>The Winter's Tale</u> Act II, when Antigonus speaks bitterly of someone having lied to Leontes to cause him to suspect Hermione's fidelity, he tells the King:

> You are abused, and by some putter-on,
> That will be damned for't; would I knew the villain,
> I would <u>land-damn</u> him.

'Land-damn', though the general meaning is clear enough, has defeated all attempts to find a source for it. An obscure English dialect word <u>landan</u> (=to abuse) has been resorted to as a feeble and unlikely possibility. In fact, neither English nor Scots seems to offer anything here. But there is a Gaelic hyphenated word <u>lan-damh</u>, meaning 'a "royal" stag with 12 tines to its antlers.' Now, there are several incidental deer-hunting expressions in this play, e.g. 'the mort of the deer' in Act I, and Antigonus's own 'I'll go in couples with her' in this very scene (Act II, Sc.i). <u>Mort</u>, incidentally, is Gaelic for 'slaughter'. So – using a noun as a verb (which this author often did), Antigonus may mean to say, of the 'putter-on', 'I would treat him as a "royal"' – i.e. hunt him down and slay him with particular keenness and pleasure. The multiplicity of tines may suggest another layer of meaning, i.e. 'cuckold him many times over'. There is, of course, a punning echo of 'damn'd' in the previous line.

Still in pursuit of Gaelic – let us consider Hamlet's <u>miching mallecho</u> in Act III of that play. This is taken by some editors as an odd mixture of English and Spanish (Sp. <u>mallecho</u> = evil action), and it is said to mean something like 'a skulking evil deed.' Now, quite apart from the gross clumsiness of this, it is a most unlikely interpretation. Hamlet, you will remember, uses the phrase to Ophelia immediately after the Dumb Show introducing <u>The Murder of Gonzago</u>, the play he has altered and commanded to be produced before the Danish court to note Claudius's reactions to certain scenes and speeches. I suggest it is most unlikely that Hamlet would wax abusive about this play, or any part of it, for he intends the piece to be used as an instrument of good, to hunt out evil and expose it. At this point I would remind you that Hamlet's full reply, when Ophelia asks what the Dumb Show imports, is :- 'Marry, this is miching mallecho, it means mischief'.

Now it so happens there are two closely-related Scots words that this brings to mind. They are both, indeed, Scots versions of Gaelic. The words are <u>michen</u> and <u>muilchioun</u>, and they both mean the common spignel, a plant well-known in the Highlands of Scotland, where its root was chewed like tobacco. It grows in high places, and the proper Gaelic name is <u>muilceann</u>; it seems to mean 'bare hill-head'. So – <u>michen</u> and <u>muilchioun</u> (both = spignel). Spignel, although it does not appear in the play, may remind us of the French word <u>espiègle</u> (= mischievous), which is sometimes used in Scots with the same meaning. <u>Espiègle,</u> in turn, may owe its origin to the German <u>eulenspiegel</u> (= owl-glass or owl-mirror), and of course it is the surname of a legendary practical joker, Till Eulenspiegel.

In employing the michen/muilchioun tautology (if he did, that is), the playwright may have meant to suggest that the Dumb Show was simply another way of saying what the main body of the play said. These were two ways of saying the same thing (again, there may be a lost idiom in the background, like the modern 'same difference') - and they both meant 'mischief' as far as Claudius was concerned. Alert Scots speakers in the audience would get the rather jokey, punning message.

There are at least three other instances of Scots and Gaelic being combined by the playwright in a similar way, in my opinion. One of the witches in Macbeth, you will remember, refers in Act I, Scene iii to a greedy sailor's wife who would not give her roasted chestnuts as - 'a rump-fed ronyon'. The last word, ronyon, also appears in The Merry Wives of Windsor, Act IV where it is applied, again abusively, to Falstaff disguised as a woman. Ronyon defeats all modern editors, but Gaelic offers us rongean (= a bulky, idle person), and Scots the related ronyal (= a large, ungainly person). These seem to fit the bill perfectly. (Interesting that the Gaelic word is closer to ronyon).

I am indebted to one of the organisers of this conference for my next instance. When Derrick McClure read this paper, or an earlier version of it, he wrote to me: 'I'm surprised you don't note one absolutely certain piece of Gaelic in Shakespeare: Pistol's "Calen o custure me!" (Henry V, Act IV, Sc. iv, 1.4), which certainly makes no more sense in French than in English, but is unmistakably a distortion of an actual line from an extant song 'A chailin, an cur stuir thu mi' - or something like it. I haven't got the actual Gaelic text to hand, but it is extant; when I was taking first- or second-year Celtic here (Aberdeen) I came across it and immediately thought "Pistol!"'

Pistol, in this scene, you may remember, had just been addressed by a terrified captured French soldier: 'Je pense que vous êtes le gentilhomme de bonne qualité.' Pistol, who has little French, repeats 'qualité' and tries to make sense of it by association. Then it dawns on him what 'qualité' really means, and 'gentil-homme', and he asks the Frenchman if he is a gentleman. For the rest of the passage poor Pistol wrestles to translate French into his idea of English. Yes - but where did he get the Gaelic?

To return to the Merry Wives: near the commencement of that play, Bardolph, one of Falstaff's gang of petty crooks, finds himself being accused of thieving by Slender. Bardolph, he of the glowing and carbuncular countenance, is much given to malapropisms, as we hear in the following passage, (Act I, Sc.i), where Falstaff confronts Bardolph with Slender's accusation.

> Falstaff: What say you, Scarlet and John?
> Bardolph: Why, sir, for my part I say the gentleman (Slender) had drunk himself out of his five sentences.
> Evans: It is his five senses: fie, what the ignorance is.
> Bardolph: And being fap, sir, was as they say, cashiered; and so conclusions passed the careires.

Now, this is nonsense, of course, but Bardolph does have a serious point to make. He is arguing that because Slender was intoxicated at the time of the alleged robbery, he doesn't really know what happened. Slender's accusation, therefore, is baseless; he has imagined it all.

Fap is a baffling word etymologically, but it is usually understood to mean 'drunk'. Shakespeare seems to have invented it, or at least he introduced it into printed English. At any rate, his is the first recorded usage of fap; the Oxford English Dictionary mentions only one later appearance; in J Brown's Psyche, published in 1818. But Brown may well have borrowed it from Shakespeare.

Cashiered is presumed to be Bardolph's slangy way of saying 'eased of his cash' — an unlikely admission, it seems to me. And careires is taken to mean 'the curvettings of a horse'. It is difficult to see the point of this. Editors may dismiss this snatch of dialogue as being nonsensical or corrupt, or both, and in any case, of small importance. But in the present context, it is worth noting that 'fap' may be 'f'ap', Gaelic for over-ripe; that 'cashiered' may really be 'cashie'd', Scots for made juicy or succulent (an adjective used verbally). In other words Bardolph may be claiming that poor Slender's wits were sodden, stewed in alcohol!

The third questionable word (careires) is perhaps a roughly anglicised and malapropistic form of the Latin quaereres, a plural form of the infinitive meaning 'to ask'. Certainly Slender's immediate comment on this is 'Aye, you spoke in Latin then too ...' Bardolph's meaning may be that Slender's unjustified 'conclusions' go far beyond the evidence, (i.e. answers given by witnesses or what emerges from these). So much for Gaelic meantime, though we shall return to it shortly.

Even non-Gaelic words seem to point us (as we have heard in the cases of gutt and handshoe) in a northerly or Highland direction. When, in Richard III, Act iii, the Duke of Buckingham pleads with Richard (at this time Duke of Gloucester) to take over the throne of England, he refers eloquently to the sad state of the country at that time:

> This noble isle doth want her proper limbs;
> Her face defaced with scars of infamy,
> Her royal stock graft with ignoble plants,
> And almost shouldered in the swallowing gulf
> Of blind forgetfulness and dark oblivion.

There is no meaning or usage of the word 'shouldered' in English that fits here, though we can make one up. But in the Scottish National Dictionary we find that the Scots form shouther was, along the Banffshire coast of the Moray Firth, used to mean 'the swelling part of a wave rising to the crest'. Here the playwright surely uses a noun verbally, as he often does. ('Gulf' in this passage evidently had its archaic meaning: 'what swallows up anything'.)

To return to the editors: there is, I feel, no real excuse for their failure hitherto to detect the Scottishness of Shakespeare. They may be pardoned for their unfamiliarity with Gaelic, with Scots (although OED takes in a good deal of Scots) and with Scots words borrowed by Highland Gaelic. But such a word as stelled is used quite clearly by the playwright in an exclusively Scottish way (to mean 'fixed'), and that is fully established in OED. Stelled

appears, thus used, in the poem The Rape of Lucrece (1.1444), and
in the first line of Sonnet XXIV. In Much Ado about Nothing, (Act
II, Sc. iii) someone should have observed Don Pedro's Scottish
pronunciation of 'doffed' in the line 'I would have daffed all
other respects'. And untented, as used in King Lear (Act I, Sc. iv)
when the King rages at his daughter Goneril:

> The untented woundings of a father's curse
> Pierce every sense about thee...

is clearly intended to bear one of its purely Scottish meanings
(untented meaning 'heedless' or 'uncontrolled'). One team of
English editors desperately suggests 'unsearchable' as a possible
meaning. Now it is true that stelled, daff and untented were all
familiar in English in Shakespeare's day, but they had different
meanings. It seems likely that the man I call the English transcriber simply left them as they were because he did not observe
(or, more probably, did not think London audiences would observe)
their altered meanings.

Of course, not all editors of Shakespeare were, or are, English,
and it is good to be able to report that one Scottish editor did
manage to observe one Scotticism. Any word uniquely Shakespearean
is liable to arouse special interest, of course, and one such word
is pajock which appears in Hamlet as the Prince exults over the
discomfiture of Claudius, after The Murder of Gonzago has sent the
false King flying to his private chambers screaming for lights. You
will recall lines in Act III, Sc. ii, where Hamlet shouts out:

> For thou dost know, O Damon dear
> This realm dismantled was
> Of Jove himself, and now reigns here
> A very, very - pajock.

The Scottishness (indeed the Highland-ness) of this was pointed out
by the Scottish editor, A Dyce, in his nineteenth century edition
of Shakespeare's Works: 'I have often heard the lower classes of
the North of Scotland call the peacock the peajock'.[1] SND notes
Dyce's comment without comment of its own, and indeed, taken in
isolation, it must have appeared eccentric. Not so, however.

Finally, let us look at two Hamlet puzzles in the light of both
Braid Scots and Scottish Gaelic possibilities. First of all, our
old friend 'the mobled queen'. In Act II, Sc. ii, the First Player
shows off his histrionic skills before Hamlet and Polonius by
acting out a lengthy excerpt from a nameless play about Dido and
Aeneas. At one point, in his account of the Trojan War, given for
the benefit of Queen Dido, Aeneas describes Queen Hecuba's distress
as Troy is burned about her by the Greeks. I quote:

> First Player: But who, O who, had seen the mobled Queen ...
> Hamlet (interrupting): The mobled Queen?
> Polonius: That's good: 'mobled Queen' is good.
> First Player: Run barefoot up and down, threatening the
> flames
> With bissom rheum: a clout about that head
> Where late the diadem stood ...

'Mobled' is taken to mean 'muffled' and it is true that such a word does appear in OED with that meaning. But personally I cannot help wondering if the audience, or the Scots in the audience, were not intended to hear the word as mobile'd, from the Scots abbreviation of the Latin phrase mobile vulgus (= excitable crowd): the phrase that in English has been shortened to 'mob'. The Scots use of 'mobile' as a noun is recorded in Chambers's Scots Dictionary, so here we have another instance of the verbal noun, perhaps. 'The Queen rabbled, the Queen "mobled" or excited by suffering' may be intended layers of meaning, in addition to 'muffled'. There is a suggestion of the Queen being degraded among the crowd affected by its excitement.

It is also important to note the word bissom (she 'threatened the flames with bissom rheum', you will remember), which seems to be related to the Scots verb 'bisse' (= hiss). The suggestion is that Hecuba was threatening the flames by spitting or spraying saliva on them in a most unqueenly fashion. Not surprisingly, the playwright seems to have taken a hint here from Gavin Douglas's description of the identical scene in his version of Virgil's Aeneid. 'Sum apon the sparkand gledis the byssand watir strynklys'. (Some upon the sparkling flames the hissing water sprinkle).[2] Typically, the playwright alters the words slightly to echo 'besom', the uncomplementary Scots term for a common woman. Again, there is the suggestion of Hecuba's degradation. The English word 'bisson' (= blind) is meaningless here, unless 'rheum' is taken to mean 'tears', as it sometimes does.

'The dram of eale' presents us with a knottier problem, but one which Gaelic may help us to disentangle. You will readily recall Hamlet's speech in Act I, Scene v, on the notorious drunkenness of the Danes, and of the Danish Court in particular, under Claudius. Hamlet's claim is that this fault is what is noised abroad about the Danes, while their virtues and achievements are ignored. He generalises then about all men. One defect, when it is well known, serves to cancel out all the good that might be said of them. The speech ends thus:

> '...The dram of eale
> Doth all the noble substance of a doubt
> To his own scandal'.

Understandably, this has confused everyone, though once again the general import is plain. Eale is usually taken as a form of 'eisil' (= vinegar). Influenced by the first theme of the speech, editors assume it must refer to a drop of vinegar – in wine perhaps – and the effect it has on spoiling the taste. But it is difficult to see how the context bears this out. So let me present you with an alternative reading.

Now, a 'noble' had, as one of its common meanings in Shakespeare's day, that of 'a kind of gold coin'. It was worth 6/8; a third of a pound. Nobles had been minted as recently as 1590 in Scotland. My own feeling is that the imagery of the three lines in question refers, not to drink, but to counterfeiting, a recurrent topos in Shakespeare.

Let us look at the rest of the passage in the light of that. A dram (or drachm) had as one of its meanings '1/8 of an ounce'. The Dictionary of the Older Scottish Tongue finds it in Scotland with that meaning in 1575. Eale, according to this interpretation, must stand for 'aloy'. There is no such word known in English or Scots of that period. The nearest equivalent is in Scottish Gaelic – eile (= other, used as a pronoun). The writer may have assumed, wrongly, that 'alloy' was derived from the Latin alius (as was eile), instead of from the Latin alligare. Or possibly eile (= the other thing) may have been a cant term borrowed from Gaelic for the inferior metal in alloy. The Gaelic for alloy is truailleadh. 'All the noble' I suggest, means 'all the gold coin', and is in the accusative case. 'Substance' or 'doth substance' I feel is verbal and transitive, and means 'reduces to something merely the worth of'. In Scots doubt has a double meaning. It means doubt, but 'dout' (pronounced doot) is a Scots spelling of doit (from the Dutch duit), a copper coin of very low value. A doit (or duit) was worth half a bodle, or 1/12 of an English penny. 'To his own scandal' probably read originally 'to its own scandal', and referred back to the noble.

Let me repeat the passage:

> 'The dram of eale
> Doth all the noble substance of a doubt
> To his own scandal'.

I see it as meaning: 'The tiny proportion of inferior metal in a counterfeit coin reduces what was hitherto taken for pure gold to the value of a doit, once it is generally understood to be there'. In other words, once people realise that a person is not 100 per cent virtuous, even though he has only one fault that they know about, that person is condemned utterly, however unjustly.

But perhaps enough has been said to lay the grounds of a case against Shakespeare – to commence the process of 'scotching' Shakespeare in more senses than one. Let me sum up. There seems to be linguistic grounds for believing that the plays and poems were not originally written by William Shakespeare but by A N Other. A Scottish A N Other with a Highland, probably N E Highland, background. I belive the earlier plays were originally produced in Edinburgh (and elsewhere in Scotland, on tour), by Laurence Fletcher's company of actors, who went south (presumably), as Fletcher himself did, when King James VI went south to ascend the British throne. Fletcher, you will recall, headed the list of the newly founded King's Men in London with Shakespeare's name immediately after his own. But A N Other had London production very much in mind, just as I believe he had King James's forthcoming accession to the British throne very much in mind. Hence the stress on classical and popular plots of the day and on English history. He was intent on laying the foundation of a national (i.e. British) theatre, and that is what he achieved.

Why the hidden identity? The use of Shakespeare as a stalking horse? I have no idea. I suspect he was an unacknowledged Royal, an embarrassment to James, and someone who could not let himself be famous, lest it cost him his life. I hasten to add that there are other than linguistic grounds for believing all this, but my

space here is limited, and I should leave some of my readers to
find out some things for themselves.

Notes

1   William Shakespeare: <u>Works</u>, Alexander Dyce (ed) (London,
    1857), V, 590.
2   Virgil: <u>The Aeneid</u>, translated into Scottish verse by Gavin
    Douglas, David F C Coldwell (ed) (Edinburgh 1951–64), VIII,
    vii, 178.